167
229
332 !!
380
462

THE
UNBROKEN
CHAIN

THE UNBROKEN CHAIN

Biographical Sketches and the Genealogy of Illustrious
Jewish Families from the 15th–20th Century

by

NEIL ROSENSTEIN

SHENGOLD PUBLISHERS, INC.
New York City

ISBN 0-88400-043-5

Library of Congress Catalog Card Number: 75-2648

Copyright © 1976 by Neil Rosenstein

Published by Shengold Publishers, Inc.
45 West 45th St., New York, N.Y. 10036

Printed in the United States of America

CONTENTS

PART 1: KATZENELLENBOGEN

PART IV: THE CHACHAM ZVI — CHIEF RABBI OF LONDON

CHAPTER XIII:

PART V: CHASSIDIC DYNASTIES

CHAPTER XIV:

CHAPTER XV:

xi

INTRODUCTION

What do Karl Marx, Helena Rubinstein and the Bostoner Rebbe have in common?

The answer: All are descendants of the prominent 16th century rabbi, Meir Katzenellenbogen, known as the MaHaRaM of Padua.

In this biographical genealogy, I have attempted to tell the fascinating story of a great rabbinic dynasty and its descendants, from the 16th century up to modern times. We are introduced to colorful characters from all walks of life . . . princes, and professors, barons and bankers, soldiers and philosophers, rabbis and socialists. Among them is Rabbi Meir's grandson, Saul Wahl Katzenellenbogen, who was chosen "King for a Night" in Poland and who took advantage of his short reign to enact decrees in favor of the Jews.

The tracing of this unusual lineage to the roots of its diversity shows how some branches of the family sought the freedom of the world of enlightenment through intermarriage, while others remained within the narrow confines of the ghetto. This study, possibly the first on the family in English, brings its diverse groups together in an awareness of their proud background and ancestry—which might otherwise be lost in the next few generations.

Who, for instance, would believe that Helena Rubinstein, the cosmetics queen, and her cousin, philosopher Martin Buber, were descendants of the same rabbi? Yet this is precisely the case. The family boasts citizens of note throughout the world, including Karl Marx. His uncle was the Chief Rabbi of Algiers; his nephew, Sir Harry Juta, Attorney General to South African Prime Minister Cecil John Rhodes. Among Marx's descendants were the well-known French socialists of the Longuet family. And all of them trace their ancestry to the same source.

The Anglo-Jewish branch of the family includes such names as Mocatta, Montefiore, Pirbright, Phillips, Salomons and Samuel. Sir George Faudel-Phillips was Lord Mayor of London at the time of Queen Victoria's Golden Jubilee. Baron Denis de Samuel was a banking negotiator for Brazil. Lord Pirbright was a Privy Counselor. From the German branch of the family came Moses Mendelssohn, 18th century philosopher, translator of the Bible, and foremost proponent of cultural assimilation; and his grandson, the composer Felix Mendelssohn-Bartholdy.

Chassidic dynasties which descended from the MaHaRaM of Padua include the Ger, the Bobov and the Horowitz (Grand Rabbi Levi Horowitz, the Bostoner Rebbe), among many, many others. The Rokeach family, the Horowitz-Margareten family of matzoh fame, the Hirshhorn family (creators of the teabag)—the list goes on and on.

But this book is only a beginning, an introduction, unfinished by its very nature, since its recorded families are all part of the never-ending chain of the

1

generations. In addition to collecting primary source materiel from books, manuscripts and correspondence, I have spent much time interviewing different family members, often obtaining confirmation of facts by cross-reference. It is my hope that the facts as related in this book remain as accurate in every detail as they were in the telling. In any case, I apologize at the outset for any errors made unintentionally and for any facts omitted inadvertently.

The book is set up in modified outline form under five general headings. Genealogical charts and lists of well-known family members are also included to assist the reader.

❄   ❄   ❄   ❄   ❄

I should like to express my thanks to all those who took the time and interest, through correspondence and interviews, to give me most vital information.

Also my sincerest appreciation to Moshe Sheinbaum, President of Shengold Publishers, and to his staff, for their effort and patience with this most difficult manuscript.

With deepest affection to my wife, Mavis, for her invaluable help, patience and understanding.

October, 1976   Neil Rosenstein

My abiding gratitude to
ROY V. TITUS
son of Helena Rubinstein Gourielli
whose generosity made the
publication of this book possible.

FOR EXPLANATION OF G3.1 etc.

See P. 683 - "G"

GRAPHIC REPRESENTATION
OF THE UNBROKEN CHAIN

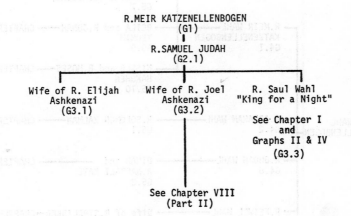

R.MEIR KATZENELLENBOGEN
(G1)

R.SAMUEL JUDAH
(G2.1)

Wife of R. Elijah
Ashkenazi
(G3.1)

Wife of R. Joel
Ashkenazi
(G3.2)

R. Saul Wahl
"King for a Night"

See Chapter I
and
Graphs II & IV
(G3.3)

See Chapter VIII
(Part II)

5

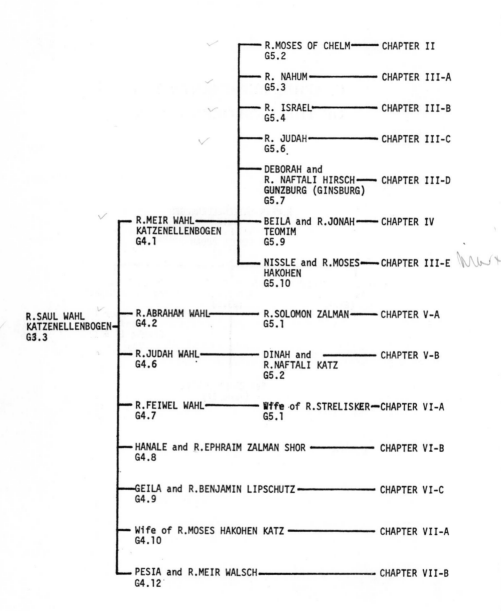

```
                                      ┌─ R.MOSES OF CHELM ──── CHAPTER II
                                      │  G5.2
                                      │
                                      ├─ R. NAHUM ─────────── CHAPTER III-A
                                      │  G5.3
                                      │
                                      ├─ R. ISRAEL ────────── CHAPTER III-B
                                      │  G5.4
                                      │
                                      ├─ R. JUDAH ─────────── CHAPTER III-C
                                      │  G5.6
                                      │
                                      ├─ DEBORAH and
                                      │  R. NAFTALI HIRSCH ── CHAPTER III-D
                                      │  GUNZBURG (GINSBURG)
                                      │  G5.7
                                      │
        ┌─ R.MEIR WAHL ───────────────┤  BEILA and R.JONAH ── CHAPTER IV
        │  KATZENELLENBOGEN           ├─ TEOMIM
        │  G4.1                       │  G5.9
        │                            │
        │                            └─ NISSLE and R.MOSES ── CHAPTER III-E
        │                               HAKOHEN
        │                               G5.10
        │
        │
        ├─ R.ABRAHAM WAHL ──────────── R.SOLOMON ZALMAN ───── CHAPTER V-A
        │  G4.2                        G5.1
        │
R.SAUL WAHL
KATZENELLENBOGEN ─┤
G3.3    │
        ├─ R.JUDAH WAHL ────────────── DINAH and ─────────── CHAPTER V-B
        │  G4.6                        R.NAFTALI KATZ
        │                              G5.2
        │
        ├─ R.FEIWEL WAHL ───────────── Wffe of R.STRELISKER ─ CHAPTER VI-A
        │  G4.7                        G5.1
        │
        ├─ HANALE and R.EPHRAIM ZALMAN SHOR ───────────────── CHAPTER VI-B
        │  G4.8
        │
        ├─ GEILA and R.BENJAMIN LIPSCHUTZ ─────────────────── CHAPTER VI-C
        │  G4.9
        │
        ├─ Wife of R.MOSES HAKOHEN KATZ ──────────────────── CHAPTER VII-A
        │  G4.10
        │
        └─ PESIA and R.MEIR WALSCH ───────────────────────── CHAPTER VII-B
           G4.12
```

6

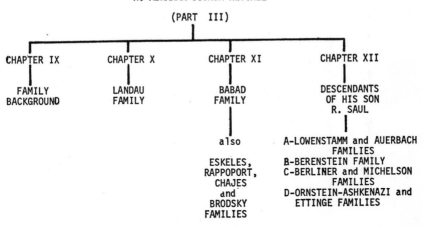

DESCENDANTS OF
R. ABRAHAM JOSHUA HESCHEL

(PART III)

CHAPTER IX	CHAPTER X	CHAPTER XI	CHAPTER XII
FAMILY BACKGROUND	LANDAU FAMILY	BABAD FAMILY	DESCENDANTS OF HIS SON R. SAUL

also

ESKELES, RAPPOPORT, CHAJES and BRODSKY FAMILIES

A-LOWENSTAMM and AUERBACH FAMILIES
B-BERENSTEIN FAMILY
C-BERLINER and MICHELSON FAMILIES
D-ORNSTEIN-ASHKENAZI and ETTINGE FAMILIES

❀   ❀   ❀

DESCENDANTS OF
R. ZVI HIRSCH ASHKENAZI
THE CHACHAM ZVI
CHAPTER XIII
(PART IV)

❀   ❀   ❀

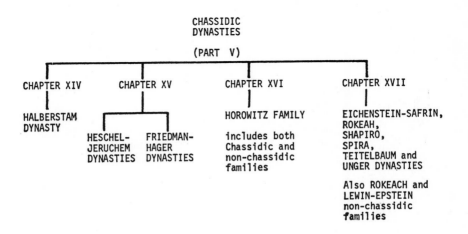

CHASSIDIC DYNASTIES

(PART V)

CHAPTER XIV	CHAPTER XV	CHAPTER XVI	CHAPTER XVII
HALBERSTAM DYNASTY		HOROWITZ FAMILY	EICHENSTEIN-SAFRIN, ROKEAH, SHAPIRO, SPIRA, TEITELBAUM and UNGER DYNASTIES

HESCHEL-JERUCHEM DYNASTIES   FRIEDMAN-HAGER DYNASTIES

includes both Chassidic and non-chassidic families

Also ROKEACH and LEWIN-EPSTEIN non-chassidic families

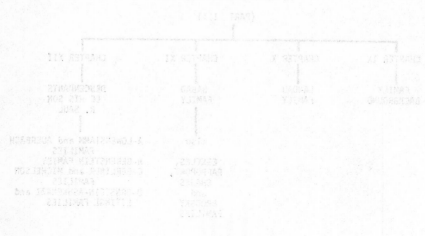

DESCENDANTS OF
R. ABRAHAM JOSHUA HESCHEL
(PART III)

DESCENDANTS OF
R. ZVI HIRSCH ASHKENAZI
DER CHACHAM ZVI
CHAPTER XIII
(PART IV)

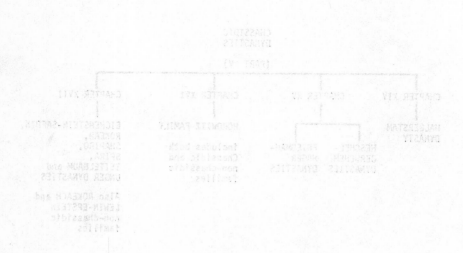

CHASSIDIC DYNASTIES
(PART V)

THE
UNBROKEN
CHAIN

CHAPTER I

THE KATZENELLBOGEN FAMILY

THE BEGINNING—ITS FIRST THREE GENERATIONS

First Generation

THERE can be no doubt that since 1312 Jews settled in Katzeneln-bogen and took their surname from the name of their new home town.

A certain Rabbi Isaac was amongst those Jews of this new community. He later became known as Rabbi Isaac of Katzenelnbogen. In the beginning of the fifteenth century, in the Province of Alsace (Elsace of Elsass) of France to where he had travelled, he married one of the daughters of Rabbi Jehiel Luria.[1] However, the family Luria and Rabbi Isaac did not remain long in Alsace due to the continual persecutions of the Jews there, and undertook the long and perilous journey to Poland.

Rabbi Luria settled in Brest-Litovsk and became Chief Rabbi of that town, while Rabbi Isaac and his wife returned to his tome town of Katze-nelnbogen where in 1482 his wife bore him a son, named Meir. In his youth, Meir and his parents moved to Prague, where they settled. Here Meir studied under the well-known Rabbi and Talmudist Jacob Polak (1460-1530). In his twenties Meir moved to Padua to further his studies, seemingly because Polak moved to Cracow in 1506. Padua, an Italian city, became the seat of a famous academy of Jewish learning as early as the fourteenth century, and its Jews were of high social standing, renowned for their learning and wealth.

On his arrival, Meir entered the Yeshiva of the most prominent Rabbi of his day, Rabbi Judah Mintz (Minz) Halevi. While studying under his learned master, he entered the Rabbinate, and received his Rabbinical title.

11

He soon became known as "Meir Padua," and is acknowledged as the founder of the Katzenellenbogen Family. In the Rabbinical world he was known as "MaHaRaM miPadua." He married Hannah, the daughter of R. Abraham son of R. Judah Minz, granddaughter of his teacher. When his father-in-law died in 1530, Meir succeeded him as Chief Rabbi of Padua when he was about forty-three. He was President of the First Synod held at Ferrara in 1554 to protect Hebrew books from the Inquisition.[2] He held his post until his death in 1565, having been Chief Rabbi about forty years. He was also nominal Rabbi of Venice, and although he visited Venice several times a year, he lived in Padua. His wife died in 1564.

R. Meir was the author of ninety Responsa published under the title *She'eilot U'teshuvot* (Venice 1553).

His epitaph reads:
The heavens are clothed in darkness
And we don sackcloth
Because of the departure of a saint
The foundation of the world, a prince pure
Who submitted with complete faith
To God and his religion.
Better was his name than the choicest oil
Head of the Diaspora, Meir, a righteous man
Who departed on the 10th of Shvat
In the year 1565 this saint departed.

His wife Hannah's epitaph reads:

The Lord took Hannah for himself   unto her resting place
Unto her soul was he gracious   which lies to the right of her father
A learned sage was he, mighty   an example unto his generation
Rabbi Abraham her father.
Her husband was Meir, a   Prince of Padua
Who gave light to all the world   who was watched from the heavens
                                          above
At the end of Adar she was buried   May the Lord guard her while she
                                          rests
As companion to the right of   her father.

Over the centuries, the tombstone of the MaHaRaM began to crumble being made of soft stone, and its inscription was becoming illegible, so that in 1966, four hundred and one years after his death, the community of Padua replaced the tombstone with a new one in the original site. The old stone now stands in the new cemetery of Padua.[3]

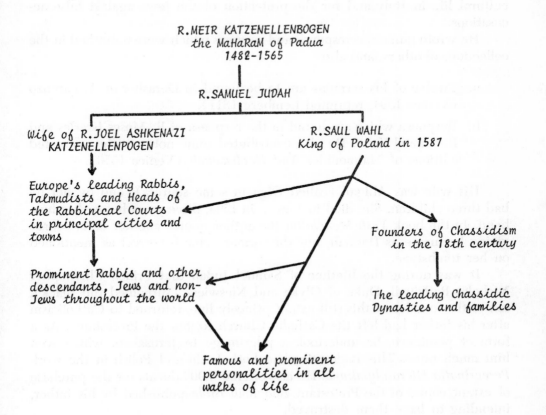

R.MEIR KATZENELLENBOGEN
the MaHaRaM of Padua
1482-1565

R.SAMUEL JUDAH

Wife of R.JOEL ASHKENAZI
KATZENELLENPOGEN

R.SAUL WAHL
King of Poland in 1587

Europe's leading Rabbis,
Talmudists and Heads of
the Rabbinical Courts
in principal cities and
towns

Founders of Chassidism
in the 18th century

Prominent Rabbis and other
descendants, Jews and non-
Jews throughout the world

The leading Chassidic
Dynasties and families

Famous and prominent
personalities in all
walks of life

Second Generation

The children of Meir and Hannah Katzenellenbogen:

G2.1. R. Samuel Judah, born in Padua in 1521. In his youth he was a
distinguished scholar and orator. He studied under his father. In
1565, on the death of his father, Samuel Judah was elected Rabbi
of Venice, at the age of forty-five. He had many pupils including
Elijah Capsali, Jacob Heilpron, Avtalyion Consiglio, Asher Parenzo
and Jacob and Yekutiel, sons of Menachem Hakohen Rappaport. It
is related that Avtalyion had a bust of his teacher made so as to
have him constantly before his eyes.

Samuel was highly respected among the Jews, honored by R. Joseph
Caro, R. Solomon Luria and R. Moses Isserles. He was highly esteemed by
non-Jews and Paul Weidner, a convert to Judaism, dedicated his works to
him (Vienna 1562). His wealth was used for the betterment of the Jewish

cultural life in Italy and for the protection of the Jews against false accusations.

He wrote numerous responsa and sermons which were published in the collections of others, and also

a. Twelve of his sermons are to be found in Derashot of A. Parenzo (Venice 1594, reprinted Lemberg 1811).

b. Responsa which are found in the responsa of R. Moses Isserles and R. Samuel Kalai. He also contributed some notes to the annotated editions of Maimonides' *Yad Hachazakah* (Venice 1550).

His wife was Abigail (called Olga in some sources), and by her he had three children. She died in Venice in 1594, three years before her husband. In the book *Yesh Manchilim* the author quotes another older source giving her name as Hannah, but the former name is correct as mentioned on her tombstone.

It was during the lifetime of Samuel Judah that Prince Christopher Nicholas Radziwill, Duke of Olyka and Nieswiesz (surnamed the Black), son of the founder of this still extant princely line, returned to Catholicism after his father had left the Catholic Church to join the Protestants. As a form of penitence, he undertook a pilgrimage to Jerusalem, which won him much fame. This is described in both Latin and Polish in the work *Peregrinatio Hierosolymitana.* He also offered 5,000 ducats for the purchase of extant copies of the Protestant *Radziwill Bible* published by his father, intending to have them destroyed.

On his homeward journey from the Holy Land, he was attacked by a band of robbers at Pescara. He reached Ancona on a Palm Sunday, finding himself destitute. He then appealed to a Jewish merchant, said to be R. Samuel Judah, for money, first pawning a gold box made of the holy cross obtained in Palestine for which he was advanced 100 crowns. On a second occasion, he received another 100 crowns, this time without any pledge. In this way the prince was able to continue his journey, and in return for the kindness received, dealt leniently with the Jews of his land and also located and protected the Rabbi's son Saul who had settled in Poland where he studied.

The story of Radziwill has an alternative version. The pilgrimage he undertook being, rather, for penance for sins committed as a young man. In this version of the story he went to Rome to enquire of the Pope as to the best way of repentance. On the Pontiff's advice, he abandoned his princely ways and became a beggar for some years. When the time was up, he found himself destitute at Padua, where only Rabbi Samuel Judah believed his story, and restored him to his original position. In return, Radziwill visited numerous Yeshivot in Poland to find Saul, who was finally found at Brest-Litovsk.

On the basis of historical facts and extant material, it would seem that the former is the more accurate historical record.

R. Samuel died in Venice, March 1597, and was buried in Padua. His funeral oration was delivered by R. Leo (Judah Ari) Modena.

His epitaph reads:

What do you see o passer-by—it isn't a grave
    But only a cloak of fine cotton cloth and blue wool
It is a chest which was placed there
    And thus long I for it as attracted to a magnet
A mantle of glory he wore, a prince over a nation
    And their leader under the domain of his kindness
His good in glory, crown of the Torah
    Wise and saviour his wisdom knew no bounds
A genius (gaon) unto Israel a Rabbi like Samuel
    Judah Katzenellenbogen, a descendant of
A Rabbi as renowned as Kalkal and Dardar
    Meir (who gave light) in the heavens above, like a glowing ember
A testimony unto the tribes of God and Venice
    And throughout the world was his wisdom and belief worldwide
                      (or as pure merchandise)
He departed (was taken into captivity) in 1597 on the sixth of Nisan
    His soul commandeth respect in the Garden of Eden
The eternal children (Israel) weep over this prince their protector
    Because now they are like a withering oak
But his mortal remains will rise and emit a fragrance of perfume
    Though the portion of field wherein he rests cannot be taken away
On that special day when the redeemer will come.

G2.2. Bonah, married R. Jacob son of R. Moses Halevi.

G2.3. The wife of R. Zalman Ronkel, author of *Chatan Damim* (Bridegroom of Blood), died in Cracow.

Third Generation

Children of R. Samuel Judah and Abigail Katzenellenbogen (G2.1):

G3.1. Elder daughter, wife of R. Elijah (Eli) son of Eliezer Ashkenazi, Rabbi of Posen, who settled later in Cracow, where he died.

G3.2. Younger daughter, wife of Rabbi Joel Ashkenazi Katzenellenpogen

(with a "p") of Neustadt, son of R. Moses. It is from R. Joel that
the "Katzenelenpogens" are descended. (See Part Two.)

In the seventeenth century a true male descendant of the Katzenellenbogen family filed a complaint before the Jewish Synod of
the Four Lands that many strange Jews who married into the family were assuming the name of their fathers-in-law. Thus it was decided that all such "usurpers" were to change the letter "b" to "p,"
in order to distinguish them from the rightful bearers. In the case
of Joel this did not last many generations, so that many of his distinguished descendants were all known by the name Katzenellenbogen. If others who intermarried ever carried out this change is uncertain, and today there are none of the name Katzenellenpogen.

G3.3. R. Saul, born at Padua in 1545. He left Italy to study in Poland when
he was still young. He died at Brest-Litovsk about 1617. He married
Deborah, daughter of David Drucker.

Two centuries later, in 1842, when the Brest Synagogue was destroyed by a decree of the Czar to make room for a fort, a plaque
was discovered with the following inscription:

*Sir Saul, son of Chief Rabbi Judah of Padua built this synagogue
for women in honor of his pious and virtuous wife Deborah, daughter of . . . . Drucker, in the month of Tevet in the year . . . . . .
her home and house . . . .*

The gaps indicate that parts were destroyed. The plaque was placed
in the new synagogue built afterwards in another part of the city.

KING FOR A NIGHT

The story of the life of Saul is a most interesting one, its tradition being both an oral one passed on from generation to generation, and a written one as recorded in the works of Rabbi Phineas son of Moses Katzenellenbogen, a descendant of Saul (1734).[4]

"My grandfather, Rabbi Samuel Judah of Padua, had a son who was
the illustrious Saul Wahl of blessed memory. The surname Wahl, according
to those versed in history, was conferred upon him because he was chosen
(Wahl means "Choice" in the vernacular) King of Poland by the unanimous
vote of the nobles of the country. I heard from my father and teacher of
blessed memory that this extraordinary event happened in the following
manner.

"Saul was beloved by the great princes of Poland and esteemed for his
remarkable ability. While he was at the peak of his influence, the king of
Poland died. It was the custom of the great nobles to assemble for the election of a new ruler on a specific day on which it was prescribed that a de-

cision must be reached. When that day came, the nobles, disagreeing among themselves, were unable to decide who should be king. They debated until evening when it appeared that it would be impossible to elect a new king on the day prescribed by law. In order not to permit the day to pass without appointing a ruler and thus transgress their own enactments, all the nobles agreed to make the illustrious Saul Wahl king for the remainder of the day and the following night, thereby conforming to the letter of the law. Immediately they crowned Saul, shouting in their own tongue 'Long live our Lord, the King.' They loaded him with royal honors, and he reigned all that night.

"My father told me that they placed at his disposal all the documents of the royal archives, for it is the custom of every ruler to add enactments according to his wisdom. The eminent Saul Wahl inscribed on the rolls many enactments and decrees for the welfare of the Jews. I have forgotten those that my father told me of, excepting one: a decree ordering that any one who murders a Jew should suffer the death penalty just like the murderer of a prince. No ransom was to be allowed—a life for a life. This law had applied up to that time only to Christians of noble rank.

"The following day the nobles agreed upon a candidate and elected a king.

"Now in order that these events may be remembered by future generations, I shall record how it came about that Saul won the esteem of the nobles of Poland, particularly as his father, Samuel Judah, was Rabbi in Padua and Venice in Italy. This is the account my father gave me. In his youth while his father was still alive, Saul was seized by an irresistible urge to travel to foreign countries. He left his paternal home in Padua and journeyed from country to country, and from city to city, until he came to Brisk in Lithuania. There he married the daughter of Rabbi David Drucker and lived in straitened circumstances.

"About that time it happened that Prince Radziwill, who was second in rank to the King and one of the richest nobles of the realm, desired intensely to travel abroad. It was the custom of princes to travel far and wide in order to observe the character and customs of foreign peoples. So Prince Radziwill journeyed from country to country until his purse was empty. As he did not wish to reveal his plight to the princes of the land, he was in a quandry. He was in Padua at that time, and decided at length to reveal his identity to the Rabbi and make a substantial loan so that he might continue on his way. (That is the way of the Polish nobles. They befriend wise Jews, especially Rabbis, in order that they may borrow from them; as a consequence, influential Jews in those days were held in high esteem by the princes.) So Prince Radziwill visited Rabbi Samuel Judah and told him his story. The Rabbi gladly provided him with money and equipment. Whereupon the Prince said to him, 'Quite apart from my financial obligation to you, how can I recompense you? How can I return good for good?'

The Rabbi replied, 'First, I request that you act kindly toward the Jews who dwell in your power. I have another request. A son of mine named Saul lives in Brisk. The good which you desire to grant me, I beg that you grant my son.' The Prince immediately took the name and address of the son so that he might carry out the Rabbi's wishes.

"After he had returned safely and settled himself in his home, he immediately made inquiries about Saul and summoned him. It did not take him long to discover that Saul was man of uncommon ability. Whereupon he granted him many favors, showering him with gifts and appointments and praising him to the skies to the other nobles. They took a great fancy to him and he prospered in their circle. It was then that the incident I have related above occurred. He was chosen king for that night, and consequently they called him—Saul Wahl. I heard this whole story from the lips of my pious and learned father.

"I will digress now to give an account that came to me from another source. When Prince Radziwill left his native land to see the world, he followed the custom of taking with him a large retinue of servants. As his means diminished in the course of his travels, he gradually disposed of the servants so that when he reached Padua, not only did he lack money, but only one servant remained with him. The Prince sent him to Rabbi Judah to arrange an interview. The Rabbi inquired about the Prince's background, and the servant told him the whole story of how he had lost both servants and money. Immediately the Rabbi ordered his household to prepare a banquet in honor of the Prince, and invited him to attend as the honored guest.

"He came and feasted at the table of the Rabbi. Then, in the midst of the festivities, the Rabbi said to his servant, 'Go to the marketplace and fetch me one of the captive slaves.' (It was the custom then, as it still is in Turkey, for every citizen to take one slave from the market, and the owner had the right to do with him as he pleased, even to kill him if he so fancied.) The servant followed his instructions and brought a slave to the Rabbi in the presence of the guests. The Rabbi, pretending to be serious, said to the servant, 'Take the slave away to the proper chamber and kill him." Taking the slave away, the servant waited a while in order to give the impression that he had carried out the order. Then he returned and said, 'I have done as you commanded, my lord.' Thereupon the Rabbi said to him, 'Return to the market and fetch another slave, bigger and comelier than the first.' Again the servant appeared with a slave. 'Well done,' said the Rabbi, 'take him and do with him as you did with the first slave.' The servant put the slave in the same chamber with the first and gave them food and drink. Then he returned and told the Rabbi that he had carried out his command. Then the Rabbi repeated the performance a third, a fourth, and a fifth time, the servant in each instance placing the slave with his fellows and providing him with victuals.

"The prince was bewildered by the performance. He could not restrain himself. He asked, finally, 'What is the meaning of this? Why in the world do you spend your money purchasing five slaves and then killing them off for no reason?' Rabbi Judah responded enigmatically, 'Aren't we Jews required to spill blood? Is not my lord aware of this?' The Prince was amazed at the explanation. He scrutinized the Rabbi's face closely. At length the Rabbi broke his silence, explaining his mystifying conduct. 'I have done what you have seen,' he said, 'in order that you may know that the accusation against us regarding the use of blood is utterly evil and false. Our religion forbids us to spill blood. Yet, as a result of this false charge, many innocent souls have suffered and many have been martyred. Now I know, my lord, that you are a great prince and second only to the King in Poland. Why have I done all this? To show you that even though it was in my power to slay five souls without hurt or murmur or responsibility, I had no such intention. Isn't this proof that the blood accusation is false? Even if we assume that the charge were true—Heaven forbid—why should the Jews of Poland endanger their lives by killing a Christian when it would be possible for us to send them casks filled with the blood of slaves? You can see that this accusation is contrary to fact and reason, and I solemnly hope that in the future you will do all in your power to serve the glory of God by correcting the injustice. Verily, we are innocent just as I am today. For I bought those five slaves, not to slay them, but to provide your excellency with the servants your station requires; and I wish to provide for your other needs.'

"The Prince recognized the truth of the Rabbi's acts and the wisdom of his words, and assured him that he would guard the welfare of the Jews and protect them from this sinful slander. He would like, he continued, to reward the Rabbi's generosity. 'Is there anything else I can do,' he asked, 'to repay you for rescuing me from my plight?' Thereupon, the Rabbi told him that he had a son named Saul who lived in Brisk, as I have related above. The Prince assured him that he would interest himself in his son upon his return. The rest of the story you already know.

"To return to my narrative, I heard more of Saul's history from my learned and pious father in 1773. He lay mortally ill in Furth, a city where many physicians reside. I went there from Markbreit, and I stayed with him for three weeks. When I was alone with him, he dictated his will, which I wrote down word for word. Then, speaking almost inaudibly, he told me the following in order that I might know, he said, what happened to our noted ancestor, Saul Wahl:

"'The King who was elected by the nobles the day following Saul's brief reign placed him in a high position, and he was revered as a leader among the Jews. His success went to his head, however, and he became very haughty. This brought him great misfortune. He had a daughter by the name, I believe, of Handele, a girl of rare beauty and intellect who

was famous throughout Poland. Many suitors sought her hand. Among them
was a brilliant young scholar, the son of a noted Rabbi. (My father did not
reveal his name, either because he did not know it, or preferred not to mention it.) To make a long story short, the Rabbi brought his celebrated son to
Brisk, and, staying as a guest at the home of one of the community's elders,
broached the match. But our ancestor, puffed up with pride, considered
himself high and mighty and thought that his beautiful daughter was
worthy of a more distinguished suitor. This match he would not even consider, thus humiliating both father and son. The whole community was out-
raged. They murmured against Saul Wahl. They sought to assuage the
wounded feelings of the distinguished guests, and one of the most prominent citizens gave his daughter in marriage to the young scholar. But from
that time our ancestor suffered the hatred of the whole community. They
sought eagerly to bring about his downfall.

"'An opportunity came. It happened at that time that the Queen died.
Some of the men of Brisk, intent upon revenging Saul's insult, went to the
nobles with whom they were in favor and spoke to them of Handele. They
described her exquisite beauty and remarkable intellect, as excellences
worthy of a queen. As a matter of fact, was she not a queen? Had not her
father sat upon the throne? They filled the ears of the nobles with such
talk, suggesting that they in turn repeat it to the King and inflame his pas-
sion. Of course, they perpetrated their evil plot most subtly, lest Saul get
wind of it and frustrate them. They cautioned the nobles to act quietly so
that the King might seize the girl before her father became aware of it. The
nobles followed the counsel of these slanderers, secretly winning the ear of
the King. He had the girl brought to the palace secretly by the royal guard.

"'But God, who secretly watches over Israel and dispenses His ever-
lasting mercies, willed otherwise. He had mercy upon Handele and granted
Saul the wisdom and power to prevent the consummation of the plot. With
the help of the Almighty, he acted speedily and wisely. And whoever knew
what had happened and saw the outcome wondered greatly.'"

For many generations this story was passed on more as a legend than
a true historical fact. Other versions of there being a Polish King among
the Jews have also been preserved. One is connected with a certain Abraham Prochovnik, who is alleged to have reigned for one night. In every
legend there is a kernel of historical truth, and although it was definitely
known that Saul Wahl was connected with the Polish Courts, as many
documents still extant in the Warsaw Archives show, it was only during
the nineteenth century that research work by Professor Bershadzky confirmed his reign, however short it may have been.

When Stephen Bathori (Istvan Bathory) died on the twelfth of December 1586, numerous pretenders for the throne of Poland, including

Archduke Maximilian of Austria, and the Duke of Ferrara, and the people of Poland were divided into two factions, the Azmoiski and Zborowski, the two dominant Polish families.

The date for election was set for the 18th August, 1587. Nevertheless, by nightfall it seemed as if they would not arrive at any definite decisions. Prince Radziwill tried to settle the differences, but no compromise was reached, and he therefore suggested that Saul Wahl Katzenellenbogen act as "Rex Pro Tempore," a compromise-king until a definite decision was reached. The following day, the 19th August, Sigismund III, son of John, King of Sweden, was elected, and crowned later during that same year.

Whether there really was a fixed date for the election is uncertain, as is the importance that the Radziwill held by the Polish nobility, but in the third year of his reign, in 1578, Stephen Bathori awarded the salt monopoly for the whole of Poland to "Saul the Jew," as is firmly attested by extant documents. Later Saul became the farmer of imposts. In documents dated 1580, his name is mentioned, along with others of the Brest-Litovsk community, in a lawsuit. During the reign of Sigismund, the king issued the following notice on February 11, 1588:

> Some of our counsellors have recommended to our attention the punctillous business management of Saul Juditsch ("the Jew"), of the town of Brest-Litovsk, who, on many occasions during the reigns of our predecessors, served by his wide experience in matters pertaining to duties, taxes, and diverse revenues, and advances in financial prosperity of the realm by his conscientious efforts.

For ten years he was entrusted with the collection of taxes on bridges, flour, and brandies, paying 150,000 florins for the privilege. The following year he was created a "Royal official" with the following decree:

> We, King of Poland, having convinced ourself of the rare zeal and distinguished ability of Saul Juditsch do herewith grant him a place amongst our royal officials, and that he may be assured of our favor for him, we exempt him and his lands for the rest of his life from subordination to the jurisdiction of any Castellan of Municipal Court, or any court in our land, of whatever kind or rank it may be; so that if he is summoned before the court of any judge or district, in any matter whatsoever, be it great or small, criminal or civil, he is not obliged to appear and defend himself. His goods may not be distrained, his estate not used as security, and he himself can neither be arrested nor kept a prisoner.
>
> His refusal to appear before a judge or to give bail shall in no way be punishable; he is amenable to no law covering such cases. If a charge is brought against him, his accusers, be they our subjects or aliens, of

*any rank or calling whatever, must appeal to ourself the King, and
Saul Juditsch shall be in honor bound to appear before us and defend
himself.*

This decree was distributed throughout the land to the nobility, officials, governors and courts. His name appears in other documents of State,
the latest being 1596. In the chronicles of Brest-Litovsk, he is alleged to
have built a synagogue, a house of learning and a public bath. He also built
a slaughterhouse and nine stores in the market square. He is also said to
be the only Jew to be adorned with a gold chain and medals of distinction
which he willed to be sold after his death and the proceeds distributed
among the poor. In his will, he stipulates that 50 pieces of silver be given
to every boy and 100 pieces to every girl of the family at the time of marriage.

Whether or not Saul actually reigned will always have its doubts, but
that he existed and was closely connected with the Royalty of Poland is
sure. Rabbi Phineas, his descendant, closes his narrative with the following:

*He who has not seen the whole generation, Saul Wahl and his sons,
sons-in-law, and grandsons, has failed to see the union of the Law with
mundane glory, of wealth and honor and princely rectitude.*

*May the Lord bless us by permitting us to rejoice in our children
and children's children!*

FOURTH AND FIFTH GENERATIONS
THE CHILDREN AND GRANDCHILDREN OF SAUL WAHL

Fourth Generation

G4.1. Meir Wahl, A.B.D. of Brest, was known as Meir Shauls or
MaHaRaSH. At the beginning of his career, he was elected A.B.D.[5]
of Tiktin where he was mentioned in the Memorial Book of the Departed. He was one of the Rabbis who helped establish the Council
of the Land of Lithuania which was similar to the Council of the
Four Lands as the controlling body for the Jews of Lithuania, in
1623. At this time there was a court composed of the heads of the
three communities of Brest, Grodno and Pinsk. The leadership of
this council was for a long time occupied by the A.B.D. of Brest and
thus Rabbi Meir Katzenellenbogen became its head when he became
Rabbi of Brest. Because of his highly esteemed position among his
people, the first and subsequent meetings were held at Brest. The
records of this council from its beginning in 1623 until 1764 are extant and were published in 1925 in Berlin by S. Dubnow. In 1627

it is recorded that Meir had an ailment of his hand so that a certain Issachar Ber signed for him, and in 1628 Meir could only manage to sign "Meir" himself.

In the records of his time he is mentioned by the Tosfot Yomtov in his *Megillat Eiva,* published Breslau 1837, and the "BaCH," (R. Joel Sirkes), wrote him a Responsum in his book *Bayit Chadash.*

He was married twice. His first wife was Hinde, daughter of R. Phineas halevi Horowitz, who was the brother-in-law of R. Moses Isserles, known as the ReMa. R. Phineas was the builder of the synagogue known as Pinkas Shul in Prague, where he settled after marrying. His second wife was Beila, who died in Lublin.

G4.2. Abraham Abrashky, was Head of the Yeshiva of the Klaus established by his father in Brest. Thereafter he became A.B.D. of Varnik in Galicia and later at Lemberg (Lvov). His wife was the daughter of R. Abraham Alpersh of Posen. R. Abraham is also mentioned in *Megillat Eiva.*

G4.3. David Wahl, married Tilla, from the family of Isserlin of Cracow.

G4.4. Jacob, A.B.D. of Linkove, married the daughter of R. Jehiel son of Solomon of Lublin. R. Jacob is mentioned in the Responsa of the MaHaRaM of Lublin.

G4.5. Isaac Harif, A.B.D. of Constantin and Lodmir, is mentioned in the Responsa of R. Joel Sirkes. Although he is not mentioned in the history of the Jews of Posen by Pereles,[6] he was apparently Rabbi there. He married the daughter of Jacob Deltsch of Lodmir.

G4.6 (Samuel) Judah, was known as Judah Saul Wahls of Brest and was born after his father's death, to his second wife.

G4.7. Feiwel Wahl is mentioned in the Pedigree in the Responsa *Be'er Yitschak* (Vienna 1894) by Isaac of Posen.

G4.8. Hanale, married Ephraim Zalman Shor son of Naftali Hirsch, A.B.D. of Lublin and Brest, son of Moses Ephraim Shor, author of *Tevu'ot Shor,* first published at Lublin in 1615-6. According to the family tradition, the Polish king sought to marry the daughter of Saul Wahl who was in his capacity a high ranking official. He however went to the elderly sage Shor and asked him to marry his daughter immediately so as to avoid the intermarriage. This R. Ephraim apparently did. He was A.B.D. of Shvershin and after the death of Saul Wahl, became A.B.D. of Brest and later of Lublin. A question of his addressed to R. Joel Sirkes appears in *Bayit Chadash* and also in *Pnei Yehoshua.* His approbation of 1617 appears in *Etz Shatul,* published in Venice 1618, a commentary by R. Gedaliah son of Solomon Lipshutz, to Albo's *Ikkarim.* (See Shor Family Pedigree.)

G4.9. Geila, married Benjamin Beinish (Benas) Lipshutz A.B.D. of Brest, Posen. He is mentioned in the following works:

1. Responsa of the *BaCH*.
2. Introduction of the Responsa of *Heishiv R. Eliezer* and *Siach HaSadeh*, by Eliezer son of Solomon Zalman Lipshutz and his son Israel, published Neuwied 1749.
3. Responsa of the MaHaRaM of Lublin, *Manhir Einei Chachamim*, by Meir son of Gedaliah, published Venice 1618.
4. *Magen Avraham. O.Ch.*

G4.10. Wife of Moses (Hakohen) Katz, A.B.D. Lutsk (son of Judah Katz of Cracow), author of a work of Responsa and Novellae. His approbation appears in *Mekor Chochmah,* published Prague 1611.

G4.11. Wife of Joseph Casas (Cozak), A.B.D. Lvov and Posen, mentioned in the Responsa *Masat Benyamin* by R. Benjamin Aaron Slonik and of the MaHaRaM of Lublin. It is questionable whether he married the widow Hanele, wife of E. Z. Shor as is recorded in the *Gedullat Shaul*. He was buried in Posen.

G4.12. Hesia (Pesia) wife of Meir Wahl (Walsch).

G4.13. Ogla married Zvi Hirsch Alpersh of Posen (Son of Abraham).

Fifth Generation

G4.1. Meir Wahl.

G5.1. Judah, married his cousin, daughter of E. Z. Shor. He died sometime before 1614, and his wife before him. He was a son from the first marriage.

G5.2. Moses, A.B.D. of Lubjeme and Chelm, was also from the first marriage. He married Sarah, daughter of R. Benjamin Benas of Posen, known as Benas Reb Mendels. R. Moses' approbations appeared in *Damesek Eliezer* (Lublin 1646) by R. Eliezer son of Samuel, A.B.D. Apt, and *Ahavat Tzion* (Lublin 1639) by R. Abraham son of Moses Ashkenazi Heilperin, who married his first cousin, the daughter of Judah Katzenellenbogen.

G5.3. Nahum, A.B.D. Slutzk, was from the second marriage, having been named after his maternal grandfather, R. Nahum of Lodmir. Various sources seem to be uncertain of the fact whether or not he was the son or the son-in-law of Meir.

G5.4. Israel of Neshov, married the daughter of R. Samuel Kalisher, was from the second marriage.

G5.5. Benjamin Benas, married the daughter of R. Jacob Deltsch of Lod-

mir.[7] Benjamin signed in the Pinkas (Minutes) of the Council of
the Land of Lithuania a number of times between the years 1639
and 1655.

G5.6. Judah, known as the younger, was the son from the second wife.
He married the daughter of R. Zeev Wolf son of Isaac Bonems of
Vilna. R. Zeev's mother was the daughter of R. Simcha Bonem
Meisels of Cracow, son-in-law of R. Moses Isserles.

G5.7. Deborah, married R. Naftali Hirsch Ginsburg as his second wife.
He was A.B.D. of Pinsk and Slutzk, and died in 1687. Deborah was
from the second marriage.

G5.8. Saul, named after his grandfather Saul Wahl, married the daughter of Elijah A.B.D. of Vengrau, author of *Brit HaLevi* (Lublin
1645), son of Abraham Ittinger.

G5.9. Beila, from the first wife (having the same name as the second
wife of Meir). She married R. Jonah son of Isaiah Teomim, A.B.D.
of Grodno, and thereafter of Metz. He was the first member of
the Teomim family to adopt the name Teomim-Frankel. He was
the author of a Talmudic work *Kikayon D'Yonah,* published first
in Amsterdam in 1699-70. A commentary by his son on the Torah
appears in *Leket Shmuel.* He signed in the Pinkas (Minutes) of
the Council of the Land of Lithuania in 1644, 1647, 1650, and
1655. He wrote approbations to:

1. *Magid Meisharim* by R. Joseph Caro, while he was in Grodno,
   published in Lublin 1646.
2. *Yoreh Deah,* also written in Grodno, published Cracow 1646.
3. *Choshen Mishpat,* also written in Grodno, published Lublin
   1654.
4. *Beit HaLevi* by R. Isaiah Halevi Horowitz, written in 1666
   when he was A.B.D. of Metz and Posen, published Venice
   1666. (He died on the first day of Passover at Metz in 1669.)[8]

G5.10. Nissle, married R. Moses Ha Kohen Katz, A.B.D. Brest, Slutzk, and
later of Lutzk, son of R. Pesach son of Tanchum son of Joseph
(*She'eirit Yosef*). Joseph was the brother-in-law of Moses Isserles,
and son of R. Mordecai Gershom HaKohen of Cracow. In 1664
he wrote his approbation to *Amudeha Shivah* by Bezalel son of
Solomon Darshan of Slutzk and Korbin, published Lublin 1666,
where he signed himself Moses Kahane.

G5.11. Esther, married R. Abraham Ashweig son of MaHaRaSH, A.B.D.
Brody.

G5.12. Chaya, from the first marriage, married R. Leib Ittinger. She died at Zolkiev in 1633.

G4.2. Abraham Wahl.

G5.1. Solomon Zalman, A.B.D. Luvke and Lukov, near Brest in Poland. He married Rebecca, daughter of his uncle Jacob Katzenellenbogen. His approbations to the following works appeared:

1. In 1647 to *Ketoret Hasamim* by Mordecai son of Naftali Hirsch of Kremsir, published Amsterdam 1671-7.
2. In 1652 to *Nachlat Yaakov* by R. Jacob Naftali, published Amsterdam 1652.

G5.2. Isaac of Cracow, who is mentioned in the introduction of *Leshon Limudim* by R. Eliakim Melamed son of Jacob Shatz, published Amsterdam 1686.

G5.3. Esther, married R. Lipman son of Isaac son of Phineas Horowitz. His Novellae appear at the end of *Derech Chayim* by R. Chayim son of Moses Lipshutz, published Sultzbach 1703.

G5.4. Deborah, married R. Samuel son of YomTov Lipman Halevi Heller, as is recorded in *Megillat Eiva*. His name appears in the records of 1679.

G4.3. David Wahl.

G5.1. Eliezer.

G5.2. Judah.

G5.3. Joseph, *Parnas* of Ostrow. His approbation appears in the Atias Edition of the Bible published in Amsterdam in 1678, where he signed his name "Joseph ben David KLB."

G5.4. Naftali Hirsch, *Shtadlan* or Jewish Representative to the Lithuanian Government. He lived in Frankfurt-on-Main and came to Vienna in 1707, in an attempt to improve the Jewish situation there. He died in Vienna on the 4th of Iyar.

G5.5. Feige, married Samuel David Shauls.

G5.6. Deborah, married Moses Lipman Zamels.

G5.7. Gitel, married David Ashkenazi of Hildesheim.

G5.8. Dishna, married R. Zvi Hirsch, brother of R. Moses Mendel Avigdor of Posen.

G5.9. Blume, married R. Abraham son of Simeon Wolf Oppenheim of Frankfurt-on-Main. He died in 1693 and she in 1683.

G4.4. Jacob.

G5.1. Rebecca, married her first cousin Solomon Zalman (See above.)

G4.5. Isaac Harif.

G5.1. Nahum of Slutzk. (See above under Meir Wahl.)

G5.2. Meir, A.B.D. Brest and Lodmir, married the daughter of Nachum, A.B.D. Lodmir.

G5.3. Simcha, scribe of Prague.

G4.6. Samuel Judah.

G5.1. Wife of R. Abraham Heilperin, author of *Ahavat Tzion,* published Lublin 1639, son of R. Moses Ashkenazi Heilperin, author of *Zichron Moshe,* published Lublin 1611, son of Zevulun Eliezer.

G5.2. Dinah, known for her Jewish knowledge as an educated woman who became known as "de Gedole" (the Great Woman). She was first married to Naftali Hirsch Katz, A.B.D. of Prusstiz, Nikolsburg, (Merrin), Pinsk, and Lublin. He was the progenitor of a very prominent Rabbinical family, Katz. His ancestry is said to have dated back to the time of Eli the Priest and is recorded in the book *VeTzivah HaKohen,* published at White Field 1823, by his descendant Aaron Samuel son of Naftali Hirsch Katz. He was the author of *Peirot Genosar,* published Amsterdam 1742. At the time he was A.B.D. of Lublin, Rabbi Abraham Joshua Heschel of Cracow was Head of the city's Yeshiva. Heschel had been one of the distinguished pupils of the MaHaRaM of Lublin, Meir ben Gedaliah (died 1616). Both these two sages gave their approbation to *Damesek Eliezer* by Rabbi Eliezer Samuel of Apt, published Lublin 1646, in 1645, and of the first appearance of the *Yoreh Deah* of 1646.

At the time of Naftali's death in 1649, Rabbi Abraham Joshua had lost his first wife, the daughter of Rabbi Moses Lazers of Brest. Dinah now cherished the hope of marrying this sage who had been accustomed to visit her home and having proposed to him, he married her and they had issue, besides those from their first marriages.

She was buried at Brody and lies between the two daughters of R. Jacob Shor, her second cousins.

G4.7. Feiwel Wahl.

G5.1. Daughter, married Strelisker.

G4.8. Ephraim Z. Shor.

G5.1. Miriam Mirl, married R. Jacob Koppel, A.B.D. Neumark.

G5.2. Jacob Shor, A.B.D. Lutzk, Brest and Brody. He was the author of *Beit Yaakov* published Venice 1693. He is mentioned in the following works:

1. *Beit Hillel* by Hillel son of Naftali Hirsch, published Dyhernfurth 1691.
2. *Beit Yaakov* by Jacob Zausmer, published Dyhernfurth 1696.
3. Responsa *Geonim Batrai*.
4. *Chelkat Mechokek*.

Jacob was a pupil of R. Abraham son of Benjamin (of Slonik, author of *Masaot Benyamin*), A.B.D. Brest. His signature appears in years 1647 and 1649 in the Pinkas (Minutes) of Lithuania following that of Jonah Teomim, A.B.D. of Grodno. His signatures while at Brest appeared in 1650, 1651, and 1655. He also was the author of unpublished responsa and was married to Hannah, daughter of Isaiah son of Moses Lazers of Vilna.

G5.3. Wife of Judah son of Meir Katzenellenbogen (first cousins).

G4.9. Benjamin Lipshutz.

G5.1. Simeon, Head of the Yeshivah and Dayan of Lvov, died there on Chanukah 1668.

G5.2. Meir, signed in the Pinkas (Minutes) of Lithuania in 1655.

G5.3. Wife of R. Solomon Zalman Ravardo, who travelled to Israel where he became Nasi of Jerusalem. He is mentioned in the Responsa *Heishiv R. Eliezer* and in the introduction of *Tiferet Yisrael*.

G4.10. Moses Katz.

G5.1. Ari Lieb HaKohen.

G4.11. Joseph Kazi.

G5.1. Solomon Zalman, died in 1612.

G4.12. Meir Walsch.

G5.1. Judah, married the daughter of Moses Lazer of Brest.

G5.2. Eizik, married the daughter of Jacob Deltsch of Lodmir.

G5.3. Moses Reb Solomons.

G5.4. Miriam, married Simeon, A.B.D. Yazlivitz, son of Abraham Katz of Lvov.

G5.5. Deborah, married Samuel Meir Walsch.

G5.6. Wife of Feiwish Meir Walsch.

CHAPTER II

A.

R. MOSES KATZENELLENBOGEN OF CHELM
(G3.3/4.1/5.2)

G6.1. R. Benjamin Beinish Katzenellenbogen, named after his maternal grandfather.

   G7.1. Issachar Ber, 2. Israel, 3. Reuben

G6.2. R. Meir, A.B.D. Chelm, named after his paternal grandfather.

   G7. R. Benjamin Wolf, mentioned in the Responsa *Chinuch Beit Yehuda*, written by R. Hanoch A.B.D. Shneitach, published Frankfurt-on-Main in 1708.

G6.3. Hanale, married in 1643 to R. Nathan Halevi son of R. Zeev Wolf (son-in-law of R. YomTov Lipman Halevi Heller).

G6.4. Wife of R. Feiwish son of R. Moses Margolioth.

   G7. Rachel, married R. Samson of Tarnograd, son of Haim Reb Maneses.

   G8. R. Ari Lieb, died in 1734, A.B.D. Neustadt.

   G9. R. Samuel, A.B.D. Neustadt and Zmigrad.

   G10.1. R. Abraham Joshua Heschel, Founder of the Chassidic Dynasty of Apt (Opatow). (See Heschel Family Dynasty —Chapter XV.)

   G10.2. R. Meir, Founder of the Jeruchem Family. (See Jeruchem Family Pedigree—Chapter XV.)

G6.5. R. Phineas Katzenellenbogen "The Holy," named after his great-grandfather, R. Phineas Halevi Horowitz.

In the town of Tomashov, a robber, who had stolen from the local synagogue, claimed that he had sold the stolen goods to a Jew whose name he did not know, but whom he could recognize if he saw him again. So the Judge ordered the people connected with the synagogue to line up. Amongst them was the saintly R. Phineas, who studied the ancient laws of Torah, day and night, wrapped in his prayer-shawl (Tallit).

And from Heaven it was decreed that the robber would accuse R. Phineas, so that he was arrested and brought in chains to the city of Lublin for trial. On the way he escaped and fled from his captors. After several hours, he collapsed, exhausted. By then he thought he had covered a goodly distance, but in his panicked flight, had gone around in circles in the darkness of the night.

By prophetic power, his deceased father appeared in a dream, saying that of his four sons, Phineas had been chosen to suffer martyrdom, and he had come to prepare him for this.

And so it was, that Phineas was often seen putting his fingers to a burning candle flame, and on the 19th of the month Iyar 1676, on the Sabbath of the weekly Sedrah "Emor," he was burned to death in Lublin.[1]

On the same day, it is recorded in the records of the Council of the Four Lands, that his widow should be looked after and not left alone. Accordingly, she was remarried to R. Lieb A.B.D. of Glogau.

G7.1. Hanale, wife of Nathan Halevi. See G6.3. above.[2]

G7.2. R. Moses Katzenellenbogen, A.B.D. Olkucz.

G8. Rebecca, wife of R. Judah Maggid.

G9. R. Phineas Maggid of Plotsk, known as the "Plotsker Maggid," where he preached for some ten years. Later he settled in Vilna, and authored *Maggid Tzedek,* a prayer-book commentary, published Sokolov, 1788; *Keter Torah,* published Sokolov, 1788; *Even Bochan,* a short version of the work by Rabbi Kalonymus, published Vilna, 1899; *Shevet MiYehudah,* published Vilna 1803; *Derech Hamelech; Derech Hachayim,* published Grodno, 1804; *Givat Pinchas,* published Vilna, 1808; *Midrash Chachamin,* published Minsk, 1809; and *Rosh Hagivah,* published Vilna, 1823. He was born in 1747 and died in Vilna in 1823.

G10. R. Shalom Israel Maggid, 1804-1847. He married Teivel, daughter of R. Issachar Ber son of R. Hillel son of R. Naftali Hirsch. She died in 1881.

G11. Hillel Noah Maggid-Steinschneider, 1829-1903. A prominent scholar, writer and book dealer. He was also a stonemasoner, hence the second name. He often composed tombstone inscriptions which led to his interest in and research about the lives of well-known Vilna families and personalities. His history of the Gunzburg Family was completed by his son in 1899. He was the author of *Ir Vilna,* published Vilna, 1900, and also wrote additions to *Kiryah Neemanah* by Samuel Joseph Fuenn, published Vilna, 1915.

G12. David Maggid 1862-1942(?), perished in the Holocaust. In 1919 he became Librarian of the Jewish Oriental Department of the National Library at Petrograd. In 1921 he became Professor of Art History at the Russian Institute in Petrograd and in 1925, Professor of Hebrew at the Petrograd University.

G6.6. R. Saul Katzenellenbogen was born in 1617. His first Rabbinical position was A.B.D. of Brody, and later succeeded his father at Chelm about 1672. His last post was A.B.D. of Pinczow. He died 1691/2. He was named after his grandfather who died the year he was born. He wrote approbations to:

1. *Lev Aryeh* by Judah son of Joshua, written at Brody in 1671, published Wilhermsdorf, 1674.
2. *Leket Shmuel* by Samuel Feiwish son of Joseph Katz, written in 1673 at Chelm, published Venice, 1694.
3. *Mayim Chayim* by Chayim son of Joshua Horowitz, written in 1687 when he attended the Council meeting at Jaroslav, published Dyhernfurth, 1690.
4. *Beit Hillel* by Hillel son of Naftali Hirsch, published Dyhernfurth, 1691, where he signed his name "Saul K. of Cracow."
5. *Tzintzenet Menachem* by Menachem Mendel son of Zvi Hirsch, written in 1689, published Berlin, 1719/20.
6. *Shabta DeRigla* by Zvi Hirsch son of Jerachmiel Chatch, written in 1690 at Pinczow, published Furth, 1693. He died before its publication, as he is mentioned "Z.L.—of Blessed Memory," i.e. 1691/2. He is buried next to Aaron Teomim who died two years earlier. He also approved, as one of the Rabbis of the Council of the Four Lands, the publication of the German Bible and *Aderet Eliyahu* by Elijah Kalonymus of Lublin, published Frankfurt-on-Oder, 1694, written in 1677 and 1678 respectively. He was married twice, and had issue from both.

From his first wife:

G7.1. Moses, died young.

G7.2. R. Saadiah Isaiah, initially A.B.D. Essela and later of Meseritz (Poland). His last post was A.B.D. Helishau (Merrin), where he died in 1726. He wrote approbations to:

1. *Berit Mateh Moshe* by Isaiah Katz, written in 1701, published Berlin, 1701.
2. *Yalkut Shimoni*, written in 1708.
3. *Rosh Yosef* by Joseph son of Saul of Przemysl, written in 1709, published Frankfurt-On-Oder, 1709.
4. *Perach Levanon* by Judah son of Joseph Peretz, written in 1713, published Berlin, 1713.
5. *Pnei Moshe* by Moses son of Isaiah Katz of Przemysl, written in 1716 at Meseritz, published Wilhermsdorf, 1716.
6. *Orach Mishor* by Jonathan son of Meir Kremnitzer, written in 1723, published Berlin, 1723.

On his death (according to "Nir LeDavid" in *Gedullat Shaul*), R. Hillel son of Samuel of Helishau wrote a lamentation about him which remained in manuscript. In 1760, some thirty-four years after his death, his nephew, Phineas Katzenellenbogen of Leipnik visited his grave and also obtained a copy of the lamentation from its composer. Saadiah was married to Eidel, daughter of R. Naftali Katz, A.B.D. Ostrow (see Katz Family Pedigree). She died in Lissa. In 1708 Saadiah and his father-in-law wrote a joint approbation to *Yalkut Shimoni*. He was the progenitor of the Padua and Rubinrot Families (see this chapter).

From his second wife, Yente, daughter of R. Jacob Shor, his relative:

G7.3. R. Jacob Katzenellenbogen, suffered martyrdom about 1697, and was the author of novellae which remained in manuscript entitled *Nachalat Yaakov*.

G8.1. R. Phineas Katzenellenbogen, A.B.D. Lvov, died 1750. He wrote approbations to: 1) *Birkat Yosef* and *Eliyahu Rabba* by his pupil Meir son of Joseph Teomim, written in 1741, published Zolkiev, 1747, and 2) *Beit Shmuel* by Samuel son of Israel, published Zolkiev, 1739. He left no known descendants in standard references.

G8.2. R. Zvi Hirsch (Hirschel) Apter, Parnas (President) of the Kalisz community, died about 1704.

G9.1. Elijah (Eliezer Hirschel) Apter, died 1737, married his first
        causin, daughter of Samuel (see below). He was the progen-
        itor of the Samuel Family which settled in London and Phila-
        delphia (U.S.A.). (See this chapter.)

G8.3. R. Samuel Katzenellenbogen, Parnas (President) of the Posen
        community, died in Krotoschin in 1708, and lies buried next to
        the famous R. Menachem Mendel son of Meshullam Zalman
        Auerbach, who died in 1701. He married Reina, who died in
        1701.

G9.1. Jacob died 1703.
G9.2. Joseph died 1759, married the daughter of Aaron (a son-in-
        law of Shabtai Kohen, the *SHaCH*).
G9.3. Wife of Elijah Apter, her first cousin.
G9.4. Wife of Zvi son of Mordecai, A.B.D. Krotoschin.
G9.5. Wife of Moses son of Zalman (a descendant of the *She'erit
        Yosef*).
G9.6. R. Isaac, president of the Krotoschin and Posen communities,
        died at Krotoschin in 1733. His son-in-law R. Auerbach eulo-
        gized him at his funeral. Charles XII (1682-1718), King of
        Sweden, was fighting in 1712 against the Russians, when he
        was forced to withdraw and escaped alone to Poland. Dis-
        guised as a minor official, he came to Posen where, at an inn,
        he sought out a Jewish money changer. The inn-keeper intro-
        duced him to Isaac and when they were alone, he said: "If you
        kill me you'll become very rich," to which the pious Isaac re-
        plied, his hair standing on end: "How can I do such an evil
        thing for money? May the Heavens forbid this. How much
        dearer is human life than all the riches of the world!" Upon
        hearing this, the King made himself known and requested fi-
        nancial help in exchange for his royal goblet, which was all he
        had left. Helping him in every way, the King was able to reach
        Sweden safely. Thereafter, Isaac was visited twice a year by
        a royal emissary who gave favors and gifts to Isaac and his
        family. Isaac himself became known throughout the land and
        was able to appeal on behalf of the Frankfurt-on-Main com-
        munity during their times of trouble. He and his descendants
        were also permitted to live in Frankfurt. (Story from *Gedullat
        Shaul*, 1854.) In true life Charles XII was known to have been
        an honorable person, who was against doubledealship and
        against easy pledges.

G10.1. Wife of R. Menachem Mendel son of Moses Auerbach, A.B.D. of Krotoschin and a descendant of Abraham Joshua Heschel of Cracow. (See Part Three.)

G10.2. Saul, named after his great-great-grandfather. Progenitor of the Krotoschin-Berlin Katzenellenbogen Family. (See Katzenellenbogen Branch B(c)—this chapter.)

G7.4. R. Moses Katzenellenbogen, born at Pinczow in 1670, when his fa-father was fifty-three years old, and died at Furth in 1733. At the age of twenty-four, in 1694, he became A.B.D. Podhajce. In 1699 he was arrested by the town's citizens on false charges and accusations, but managed to escape and became A.B.D. of Schwabach that same year. He became known as the "Schwabacher Rabbiner," and in 1707 wrote an approbation there to *Ir Binyamin Sheni* by Benjamin Ze'ev son of Samuel Darshan, published Furth 1712. Other approbations were to:

1. *Torat Yosef* by Joseph son of Moses Ginsburg of Frankfurt, written in 1715, published Wilmersdorf 1715.
2. Wilherdorf *Mishnayot* Edition, written 1715.
3. *Ohalei Yehudah* by Judah Aryeh son of Zvi Hirsch, written in 1718, published Jessnitz 1719.
4. *Olat Aharon* by Aaron Zelig son of Joel Feiwel of Ostrow, written in 1731, published Offenbach 1733.
5. *Torat Adam* by the RaMBaN, written in 1732.

He was the author of:

1. *Chidushei Halachot*, unpublished.
2. Responsa in manuscript housed in the Bodlein Library at Oxford.

He married Jached (Leah), daughter of Eliezer (Leser Charif) Heilprin (Heilbronn) of Meseritz and Furth. He was progenitor of a large family through three of his sons. (See below, this chapter.)

G7.5. R. Ephraim Zalman Katzenellenbogen.

G8. Matil, second wife of Meir son of Samuel Horowitz, A.B.D. of Tiktin. They were the ancestors of one line of the Friedman Chassidic Family. (See Friedman (Ruzhin) Dynasty — Chapter XV.)

G7.6. Hinde (possibly from first wife), married Jacob, A.B.D. of Lodmir.

B.

DESCENDANTS OF

R. SAUL SON OF R. MOSES KATZENELLENBOGEN
(G3.3/4.1/5.2/6.6)

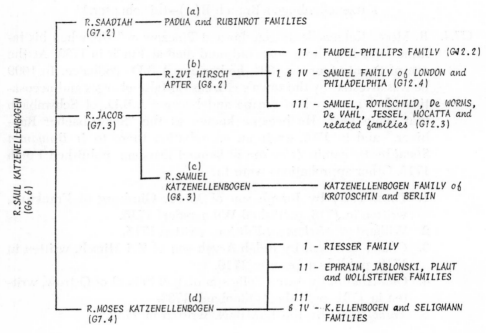

a.

DESCENDANTS OF

R. SAADIAH ISAIAH KATZENELLENBOGEN (G7.2)
PADUA and RUBINROT FAMILIES

ANCESTRY

G8.   R. Haim, married the daughter of R. Gershon son of Moses Pulitz, A.B.D. Nikolsburg. (See Chapter III—Branch E—G6.5/7.2/8.3/9.1.)

  G9.   R. Meir of Brest, recorded in *Anshei Shem*, a history of Brest. He married Yente, daughter of R. Reuben.

    G10.1.   R. Abraham.

      G11.   R. Meir Katzenellenbogen of Brest.

        G12.   R. Samson Israel Rubinrot of Brest.[3]

          G13.   R. Samuel Rubinrot.

            G14.   R. Meir Mendel Rubinrot.

G10.2. R. Aaron Katzenellenbogen of Brest.[4] He was the author of
        Minchat Aharon, dealing with the Talmudic tractate Sanhe-
        drin, published in 1772. He also wrote an approbation to
        Shlamei Simcha. Aaron was married twice. His first wife was
        Sheine, the daughter of R. Jacob son of Abraham HaLevi,
        A.B.D. Brezi, Barki, and Oppenheim. His second wife was
        Achsa, the daughter of R. Moses, A.B.D. Helusk. He died in
        1777.

G11. R. Haim Padua of Brest. He died there in 1837.

G12. R. Jacob Meir Padua, was born in Brest and died in 1855
      (the 21st of Kislev in 1855). He became Rabbi of Pinsk-Kar-
      lin, and was elected A.B.D. of Brest on the death of his rela-
      tive, R. Aryey Katzenellenbogen[5] in 1837. It was not until
      1840 that he accepted this post. He was the author of: *Mekor
      Mayim Chayim,* Sedilkov 1836; *Ketonet Pasim,* 1840; *Teshu-
      vot MaHaRIM,* Warsaw 1854; *Ein Hamayim; Chitzei Yeho-
      nattan;* Commentary on Hagaddah, *Nitfei Mayim,* Warsaw
      1885; *Nachlei Mayim,* Warsaw 1863. His wife was Achsa,
      daughter of R. Saul Levine of Karlin. (See Chapter V—
      Branch A—G9.2/10.2/11.2.) His approbation appears in *Ge-
      dullat Shaul,* by Z. H. Edelman, published in London in
      1854. It was written in Brest and dated *Saul Benir David,*
      numerically equalling 1853.

G13.1. R. Aaron Moses Padua of Karlin, married the daughter
        of R. Haim Nahman Parnas of Vilna (see Margolioth and
        Naftali Katz Family Pedigrees).[6] He died in 1883. He
        was the author of *Beiur HaRam; Chut HaMeshulash;
        Midrash Socher Tov,* published in Warsaw in 1865, and
        a commentary on *Midrash Tehilim,* published in Warsaw
        in 1865. He also edited *Midrash Lekach Tov,* by R. To-
        viah son of Eliezer, Vilna 1884.

G14. Wife of R. Jehiel Michael Benzion, son of R. Meir Kris-
      tianpoller, the A.B.D. of Brody. (See reference below
      under G15. Achsa.)

G15. Achsa, named after her paternal grandmother, mar-
      ried R. Zvi Hirsch Ornstein. (See Part III—Chapter
      XII—Ornstein and Ashkenazi Families—G9.2/10.1/
      11/12.)

G13.2. R. Ze'ev Wolf Padua, married the daughter of R. Joseph son of R. Baruch Frankel-Teomim. (See Chapter IV.)

G13.3. R. Samson Padua, published his father's Responsa work in Warsaw 1854.

G13.4. R. Zvi Hirsch Padua.

G13.5. Karindel Padua, married R. Lieb Rutenberg.

G13.6. Chaya Rachel Padua, married R. Simha Nahum Ginsburg.

G13.7. Esther Padua, married R. Moses Hakohen Zelikin of Smolensk.

   G14. Achsa, married R. Ari Lieb Luntz (engineer). Their sons were Moses, Zvi Hirsch and Jacob.

G13.8. Vita Padua, married R. Ari Lieb Pines of Razinai, son of Mirl Pines, daughter of Rachel Leah Pines. She died in 1877.

   G14.1. R. Meir Pines of Pinsk, married the daughter of R. Saul Ezekiel Sheinfinkel.

      G15.1. R. Haim.

      G15.2. R. Saul Ezekiel.

      G15.3. R. Ari Lieb.

      G15.4. Achsa, married R. Jekutiel son of R. Avigdor Abraham Cohen.

      G15.5. Yente, married R. Isaac Eizik Parnas, the grandson of R. Haim Nahman Parnas. (See Chapter V —Branch B.)

   G14.2. R. Aaron Pines of Vilna, married Feige, the daughter of R. Joseph Heizener.

      G15.1. Ari Lieb Pines of Odessa.

      G15.2. Engineer Ze'ev Wolf Pines.

   G14.3. Sheindel Pines, married R. Joseph Charne. She died in Moscow in 1894.

      G15.1. Engineer Meir Charne of London.

      G15.2. Miriam Charne.

   G14.4. Eidel Pines, married R. Meir Rutenburg of Zhitomir in 1912. Their sons were Joseph and Ari Lieb Rutenburg.

   G14.5. Maasha Pines, died in 1892 in Razinai.

G14.6. Achsa Pines, married R. Joseph Hellas Hakohen of Vilna. Their children were Vita and Rasha.

b.

Descendants of

R. ELIJAH SON OF R. ZVI HIRSCH (APTER) KATZENELLENBOGEN
The Samuel Family of London and Philadelphia

Ancestry

G1.   R. Meir of Padua.
G2.1. R. Samuel Judah Katzenellenbogen.
G3.3. R. Saul Wahl.
G4.1. R. Meir Wahl.
G5.2. R. Moses Katzenellenbogen.
G6.6. R. Saul.
G7.3. R. Jacob Katzenellenbogen, the Martyr.
G8.2. R. Zvi Hirsch (Hirschel) Apter, died 1704.
G9.1. R. Elijah (Eliezer Hirschel) Apter, died 1736/7.[7]

G10.1. Lieb.
G10.2. Michla, married Sander, A.B.D. Lesla, later head of the Jewish Council (Parnas) at Krotoschin. She died in 1737.
G10.3. Joseph (called Ducist or Ducit) of Posen, died in 1759.

G11.1. Eliezer.
G11.2. Samuel, dropped the name Katzenellenbogen, and was called Samuel Samuel. He died in 1758 at Krotoschin.

G12.1. Daughter.
G12.2. Esther, married Phineas Halevi Phillips,[8] who settled in England from Germany in 1775. He was the son of Jonas Phillips, who died in London in 1794. Esther died at Krotoschin in 1822.

Phineas regularly attended the great fairs in Germany, periodically travelling to England before settling there. He carried on an extensive business in gums and indigo. He was held in high esteem by the reigning prince. Phineas was always provided with a special *Schutzbrief* (Letter of Protection) on his journeys throughout Germany. On one occasion, favoring the horticultural tastes of the prince, the Jewish

merchant brought him a collection of Dutch bulbs, which the
latter appreciated throughout his life.

Phineas held the post of Chief of the Jewish community
of Krotoschin. He was the progenitor of the Phillips Family
in London. (See below, Branch II.)

G12.3. Moses Samuel, born in 1740, died in England in 1839.[9] He
married Rachel, daughter of Jonas Phillips, as did his sister
Esther marry a child of the same Jonas Phillips. Together
with his brother David, he settled in England. He became
a prominent merchant in London during the reign of King
George II. He was known as Moses Samuel of Bath and Park
Crescent, and also as Moses Legeorge (Hebraized to Li-
gurik). His children and grandchildren married into the most
prominent Jewish families of England which include Barent
Cohen, DeWorms, Salomons, Rothschild, Jessel, and Goldsmid. (See Samuel Family of England—below III.)

I—DAVID SAMUEL FAMILY OF LONDON

G12.4. David, settled in London. He married Sarah Prager.

G13.1. Isaac Samuel, married his niece Henrietta, daughter of
Samuel Samuel.

G14.1. Augusta, married McLeod.
G14.2. David Samuel.
G14.3. Isaac Bunford Samuel, married Grace Heene.

G15.1. Henrietta.
G15.2. Emily.

G14.4. Maria.
G14.5. Anna, married Levine.
G14.6. Emily.
G14.7. Sarah.

G13.2. Ann (Nancy).
G13.3. Samuel Samuel, married Brindella Benjamin.

G14.1. Henrietta, married her uncle (see above).
G14.2. Frederick Samuel, married Sarah Mocatta.

G15.1. Francis, married Beatrice Julia Henriques.

G16.1. Edgar Samuel, married Hilda Muriel Myer.

   G17.1. Brenda.

  G16.2. Julian, married Margaret Priscilla Mendel.

   G17.1. William.

  G16.3. Wilfred.
  G16.4. Albert.
  G16.5. Gladys E.
  G16.6. Frank.

 G15.2. Lionel Jacob Samuel.
 G15.3. Rebecca.

G14.3. Lewis Samuel, married Catherine Jacobs.

 G15.1. Moses.
 G15.2. Bridget.
 G15.3. Samuel.
 G15.4. Eleanor.

G14.4. Matilda.
G14.5. Emma.
G14.6. David Samuel, born in London 1804, died in Philadelphia 1881. He married Hetty the daughter of John Moss (1771-1847) in Philadelphia in 1827. He was the progenitor of the Samuel Family of Philadelphia (U.S.A.) (See below IV).
G14.7. Bunford.
G14.8. Albert.
G14.9. Morris.
G14.10. Sarah.
G14.11. Caroline.
G14.12. Mary Anne.
G14.13. Eleanor, married her first cousin, David, son of Lyon Samuel.

G13.4. Israel Samuel.
G13.5. Moses Samuel.
G13.6. Hannah (Susannah).
G13.7. Lyon Samuel, married Kate Solomon.

 G14.1. David, married his first cousin Eleanor Samuel.
 G14.2. Maria, married in 1818 to Samuel son of Barnet son of Jonas Phillips (see G12.2 above). Samuel died in 1865/6.

G15.1. Madeline, married Baron Emanuel Todros.

G16.1. Marie Esmeralda, married Baron Giacomo Lumbroso.

G17.1. Alberto Lumbroso.

G16.2. Lionel Todros, died young.

G15.2. Barnet Samuel Phillips, married Phillipa daughter of Phillip Moses son of Moses Samuel. Moses was his great grandfather's brother.

G16.1. Herbert Phillips.
G16.2. Helen, married H. Solomon.
G16.3. Alice.
G16.4. Dr. Sydney Phillips.
G16.5. Walter B. Phillips.
G16.6. Arthur Barnet Phillips.
G16.7. Frederick Solomon Phillips.

G15.3. Robert Lionel Phillips.

G16.1. Anges Phillips.

G14.3. Alfred Samuel.
G14.4. Sarah Samuel, married David Haes.

G15.1. Frank Haes, 1833-1916, prominent photographer, antiquary and vice-president of the Jewish Historical Society, married Adele Valentine.

G16.1. Phoebe.   G16.2. Hubert.
G16.3. Alice Rosa.   G16.4. Zillah.
G16.5. Oswald, married Dinah Rebecca Lary.

G17.1. Lilla Mary, married Baron Charles Cowper.
G17.2. Adele Louisa.
G17.3. Kalvin Oswald, died young.
G17.4. Edgar Oswald, married Beryl Thornton Parkinson.

G18.1. Derek David.
G18.2. Peter Thornton.
G18.3. Jill Muriel.

G16.6. David Haes, married Annie Isabel Robinson.
G16.7. Ada, married Henry Ernest Abraham Bartlett.

G16.8. Dulcie Ethel.
G16.9. Arthur, married Dorothy Bella Levi.

  G17.1. David Felix Haes, married Doris Margurite Ridout.

    G18.1. Michael John.
    G18.2. John David.
    G18.3. Sonia Margurita.
    G18.4. Davida Ann.

  G17.2. Eric Frank Haes.

G15.2. Adeline Haes, married Michael Mayer.

  G16.1. Alfred.
  G16.2. Silvian.
  G16.3. Child.
  G16.4. Frederick.

G13.8. Esther Samuel (?), married Phineas Halevy (?).
G13.9. Simon Davis Samuel, married his first cousin Esther Moses Samuel.

  G14.1. Elizabeth, married Egruist Depre.
  G14.2. Anthony.
  G14.3. George Lionel, died young.
  G14.4. Christopher.
  G14.5. Sarah, died young.
  G14.6. Three children, died as infants.
  G14.7. Horatio Simon, married Henrietta Montefiore.[9a]

    G15.1. Sir Harry Simon Samuel, married Rose Beddington, daughter of Edward Beddington. He was born in London in 1853, the eldest son. He had a partnership in the firm of Montefiore Company until 1884 when he entered politics and in 1895 he won a seat as a Conservative which he held until 1906. From 1910-1922 he was a Unionist candidate and in 1916 he was elected to the Privy Council. He was knighted in 1903, and died in Monte Carlo, Monaco in 1934.

    G16.1 Cecil Harry Samuel, 1892-1966.[9a]
    G16.2. Geoffery.
    G16.3. Edward John, born 1880, married 1) Julia Yates.

G17.1. Rose.
G17.2. Winifred.
G17.3. Harry.
G17.4. Olive.

G16.4. Nora, married Baron Percy George de Worms son
of Baron George, son of Baron Solomon Benedict de
Worms. (Solomon's wife, Henrietta, was the daughter of Samuel Moses son of Moses Samuel.) See
DeWorms Family Pedigree.[10]

II—PHILLIPS FAMILY OF LONDON

ANCESTRY

G3.3.   R. Saul Wahl Katzenellenbogen.
G4.1.   R. Meir.
G5.2.   R. Moses.
G6.6.   R. Saul.
G7.3.   R. Jacob Katzenellenbogen, the Martyr.
G8.2.   R. Zvi Hirsch Apter.
G9.1.   R. Elijah Apter.
G10.3. Joseph Ducit.
G11.2. Samuel Samuel (died 1758).
G12.2. Esther, married Phineas Phillips, settled in England in 1775.

G13.1. Other children.
G13.2. Samuel Phillips, married Hannah Jonas. Samuel was a tailor in
London.

G14.1. Austen Cooper, an English actor.
G14.2. Maurice Phillips, publisher of a fine edition of the Festival
Prayers in Hebrew and English.
G14.3. Others.
G14.4. Sir Benjamin Samuel Phillips, born on January 4, 1811, and
died October 9, 1889.

He had been in failing health for some time and a few months ago his
condition was regarded as extremely critical, but he rallied and some faint
hopes were entertained that his splendid constitution would overcome
the weakness which the attack had left him. The recovery, however, was
only partial and a recurrence of the malady from the severest forms of which
he had suffered for about a year, resulted in his death on Wednesday week,
somewhat more suddenly than was anticipated.[11]

He was educated at Highgate and Kew. In 1833, he married Rachel the only daughter of Samuel Henry Faudel. He soon entered into partnership with his brother-in-law, Henry, thus laying the foundation of the firm of city merchants known as Faudel, Phillips and Sons.

In 1857 he became an Alderman of London, was Sheriff in 1859-60, and Lord Mayor of London in 1865-6. He was the second Jew to be elected to these offices, the first being Sir David Salomons. During his difficult Mayoralty, he collected relief funds for those at home and for India. He also entertained the King and Queen of Belgium. At their invitation, he visited Brussels, where he was made Commander of the Order of Leopold. He was an active member in the Jewish community, and was President of the Hebrew Literary Society. In 1880 he was elected a life member of the United Synagogue, and was a member of the Board of Deputies as representative of the Great and Central Synagogues for thirty years.

During his Mayoralty, Sir Benjamin would arrive at the Great Synagogue on both days of Rosh Hashanah at the early hour of 6:00 A.M. He showed his respect for the Chief Rabbi by presenting him the honor of opening the Ark to the reading of *Shir HaYichud* (Song of Unity).

He was knighted by Queen Victoria. He retired in 1888 from the court of Aldermen, and was succeeded by his second son who was unanimously elected.

G15.1. Sarah, second wife of Lord Pirbright, Baron Henry DeWorms. See DeWorms Family Pedigree.[12]

G15.2. Samuel Henry Faudel-Phillips, the elder son, one of the Lieutenants for the city of London, J. P. for Kent, and in 1898 was elected the High Sheriff for London.

He married Sarah Georgina White.

G16.1. Rachel Faudel Phillips, 1876-1962.

G16.2. Ceril Katharine Phillips, born in 1880.

G16.3. Henry Faudel Phillips, 1884-1970, married 1) Nell D. Tanner and 2) Olive E. Pratt.

G16.4. Henrietta Norah, 1877-1936, married Percy Raworth Heycock.

G17.1. Ceril Mary Georgina, born in 1916, married Prince Birabongse Bhanudej Bhanubhandha, born in 1914, son of

H.R.H. Chao Fa Krom Phya Bhanurangsi, grandson of King Rama IV (Mongkut, who ruled from 1851-68) of the Royal House of Chakri of Thailand.

G17.2. Raworth Henry Faudel Heycock, born in 1914, married Y. Harris.

G18.1. Elaine, born in 1944, married Brian Boden.
G18.2. Philip Henry Faudel Heycock, born in 1941, married Thomasine Trefusis, and have issue, Thomas Henry (born in 1972) and Eleanor Rachel (born in 1974).

G15.3. Sir George Faudel-Phillips, second son, born in 1840 and died in London in 1922. He was educated at University College School, and also in Berlin and Paris. He then entered his father's business. In 1867 he married Helen, daughter of Joseph Moses Levy, who was for many years proprietor of the *Daily Telegraph*. They lived at Balls Park, Hertfordshire, where they were distinguished by their bountiful hospitality. He was appointed Sheriff of London and Middlesex (1884-85), succeeded his father as Alderman of the ward Farrington Within (1888) and became a Governor of the Honorable Irish Society in 1894. The following year he was created High Sheriff of the county of London, and in 1896 he became Lord Mayor of London. As the first citizen of London, and as a Jew, he received Queen Victoria at Temple Bar on the occasion of her Diamond Jubilee thanksgiving service.

He received numerous honors which included the Baronetcy (1897), Order from the King of the Belgians and the King of Siam, and the Grand Cross of the Indian Empire. He was High Sheriff of Hertford in 1900-1, President of the Jew's Orphan Asylum, and Vice-President of the Anglo-Jewish Association. As a lover of books, he owned a valuable library.

G16.1. Benjamin Samuel Faudel-Phillips, born 1871.
G16.2. Sir Lawson Faudel Faudel-Phillips, third and last Baronet, born 1877.

He married in 1908 to Armyne Evelyne, daughter of Lord Granville, Marquis of Huntley.

G17.1. Jean Armyne Eulalia, born 1909.
G17.2. Helen Bridget, born 1918, married in 1941 to the 5th Earl of Kilmorey, Francis Jack Richard Patrick Need-

ham (born in 1915), who succeeded his father in 1961. He was wounded while serving in World War II. They currently live in Italy.

G18.1. Richard Francis, born in 1942 and married in 1965 to Sigrid Juliana Thiessen-Gairdner, only daughter of the late Lernst Thiessen. Their sons are Robert Francis John, born in 1966 and Andrew Francis, born in 1969.

G18.2. Christopher David, born in 1948.

G18.3. Patrick Jonathan, born in 1951.

G17.3. George Lionel Lawson, born and died in 1910.

G17.4. Ann Margaret Faudel, born in 1913.

G16.3. Nellie Cyril Faudel, born in 1869.

G16.4. Beatrice Rachel Faudel, married in 1892 to Sir Philip Joseph Gutteres (1867-1950), son of Alfred G. Henriques (1829-1908). Sir Philip was called to the English Bar of the Inner Temple in 1892. He became the J.P. for Surrey and was one of H.M. Lieutenants for the City of London. From 1934-7, he was Alderman and Vice-chairman and from 1937-40, Chairman of the Surrey County Council. He also held a number of other important posts and received the title of Officer of the Legion of Honour and of the Crown of Italy.

Their children, Alma and Philip, died young.

G16.5. Stella Josephine Faudel, O.B.E. (died in 1958) married in 1903 to Late Honorable Charles Henry Tufton, third son of first Baron and Lord Hothfield (1879-1923).

G17.1. George William Anthony, born in 1904, B. A. Oxford in 1927, retired Lieutenant Colonel. He married in 1936 to Evelyn Margarette eldest daughter of the late Eustace Charles Mordaunt.

G18.1. Anthony Charles Sackville, born in 1939, B. A. Cambridge.

G18.2. Nicholas William Sackville, born in 1946.

G18.3. Jennifer Margaret, born in 1937, married in 1965 to Edward Robert Raikes. Their children are Jason Alexander born in 1966, Benedict Arthur born in 1969, and Stella Mary Evelyn born in 1972.

G17.2. Francis Charles Sackville, born in 1913, M.A. Oxford, retired Lieutenant Commodore, Knight of the Order of Dannebrog of Denmark. He married Eileen Joyce Clara, daughter of Sir Edward Henry Goschen, in 1942.

G18. Edward Philip Sackville, born in 1948, married Mary Josephine.

G17.3. Susan Stella, born in 1908, married Colonel Thomas Alexander Hamilton Cottman, O.B.E. in 1936.

G18.1. Timothy Charles, born in 1939, married in 1964 to Joanne Mary, only daughter of John Richard Bergne-Coupland. Their daughters are Sarah Elizabeth, born in 1966, and Mary Jane, born in 1968.

G18.2. David Alexander, born in 1942, married in 1972 to Mary Cecilie, third daughter of Rt. Honorable William Stephen Whitelow.

G14.5. Rebecca Phillips, married R. Issachar Lichtenstadt, A.B.D. of Krotoschin.

G15.1. Others.

G15.2. Rose Phillips, married her cousin, Louis, son of Benjamin Benas. The Benas Family also claims descent from Benjamin Benas, fourth son of R. Saul Wahl Katzenellenbogen. Louis was originally from London, but transferred his business to Liverpool, where he settled.

G16.1. Baron Louis Benas, J.P. was born in Liverpool in 1844 and died in 1914. The *Jewish Chronicle* of February 6, 1914, reported, "The deceased gentleman had been in ailing health for some twelve months past, but had from time to time rallied! Only a few weeks ago, he celebrated his seventieth birthday."

On the occasion of his seventieth birthday, a few weeks before his death, he had been interviewed by the *Jewish Chronicle*—"An ancestor of mine was one of the Sephardim who may be regarded as having inaugurated Jewish communal existence in Liverpool. My grandmother, Isabel Hoff, was a direct descendant of Don Isaac Abarbanel. Through my mother, on the other hand, I am related to several prominent personages in the earlier communal life of the metropolis."

Louis Benas was instrumental in securing the candidature of Baron Henry DeWorms. He married Amalia, daughter of Louis Schloss of Manchester. Thoughout his life he was a leading figure in the Liverpool Old Hebrew Congregation. He helped found the Liverpool branch of the Russo-Jewish Committee for Refugees of the 1882 emigration. "Persecuted refugees have often had cause to bless his name. Of Jewish education of all over the world, he was the constant and enthusiastic benefactor."[13]

He was also a linguist and an assiduous traveller. He knew much of Jewish religious learning. Outside the community he was President of the Liverpool Literary and Philosophical Society.

G17. Bertram B. Benas, B.A., LL.B., 1880-1968. He died a bachelor.

III—MOSES SAMUEL FAMILY OF LONDON
INCLUDING
DeWorms, Salomons, Rothschild, Primrose, Barent Cohen, Goldsmid, Jessel, Lucas, and Mocatta Families

ANCESTRY

G3.3.   R. Saul Wahl Katzenellenbogen.
G4.1.   R. Meir.
G5.2.   R. Moses.
G6.6.   R. Saul.
G7.3.   R. Jacob Katzenellenbogen.
G8.2.   R. Zvi Hirsch Apter.
G9.1.   R. Elijah Apter.
G10.3. Joseph Ducit.
G11.2. Samuel Samuel, died 1758.
G12.3. Moses Samuel, 1740-1839.

G13.1. Samuel Moses Samuel, married in 1803 to Esther (1782-1859), daughter of the leading Jew of England, Levi Barent Cohen of Angel Court, Presiding Warden of the Great Synagogue. Samuel died in 1873.

G14.1. Behrend, died young.
G14.2. George.
G14.3. Henrietta (died 1845), wife of Baron Solomon Benedict de

Worms, first Baron de Worms of the Austrian Empire. He was born in 1801, and died October 20, 1882. He was the son of Benedict Worms (died 1824) and Jeanette (1771-1859), the eldest daughter of Mayer Amschel Rothschild, father of the five famous Rothschild sons. Baron Solomon was born in Frankfurt-on-Main, came to England at an early age, but eventually settled in Ceylon. He died at Brighton, England. He was a prominent English financier, and a life-member of the Council of the United Synagogue. In 1871 he was created Baron and three years later was granted the Royal Right by Queen Victoria to use his title in England. He was head of the DeWorms Family—see following generations hereafter.

G15.1. Baron George DeWorms, born February 16, 1829. He married his second cousin Louisa, daughter of Denis Moses Samuel (Baron DeVahl). He died in 1912.

G16.1. Anthony Denis Maurice George DeWorms, born January 4, 1869. He was the third Baron DeWorms, and married in 1901 to Lulu (Louisa Matilda) Goldschmidt. He succeeded his father in 1912, and died January 11, 1938.

G17.1. Baron Charles George Maurice DeWorms, born 1903. He is a professor of Zoology.

G16.2. Percy George DeWorms, born November 3, 1873, married in 1900 to Nora, daughter of Sir Harry Simon, son of Horatio Simon Samuel (descendant of David Samuel, G12.4). He was a Barrister-at-Law, and died April 2, 1941. He had a son and daughter.

G17.1. Kathleen Louise, married Farrall Wright. They have two married daughters.

G16.3. Henrietta Amelia, married George Landauer of Vienna. They had a son and daughter. She died in 1966.

G15.2. Baron Anthony Meyer DeWorms, October 12, 1830—November 2, 1864. He married Emma Augusta von Schey.

G16.1. Nina, married Baron Georgo Levi (died in 1936).[13a]

G15.3. Ellen Henrietta (1836-1894), married Adolf Landauer and had issue. His only son George, married his first cousin, Henrietta Amelia, daughter of Baron George De Worms. A daughter, Laura, married her relative, Alfred Joseph Waley (page 53); another, Evelina, married Paul Schey.

G15.4. Baron Henry DeWorms (Lord Pirbright),[14] born October 20, 1840, died January 9, 1903. The youngest son, he was educated at Kings College. In 1863 he became a barrister, and sat in the House of Commons 1880-85 as a conservative member for Greenwich, and 1885-95 for the East Toxteth division of Liverpool. In 1888 he became a Privy Counsellor. He was also an excellent linguist, and travelled extensively. He was also a Royal Commissioner of the Patriotic Fund. His works include *England's Policy in the East* (London 1876); *Handbook to the Eastern Question* (London 1877, 5th Edition); *The Austro-Hungarian Empire* (London 1877, 2nd Edition); and *Memoirs of Count Beust* (London 1887).

Henry was married twice. His first wife was Fanny, eldest daughter of Baron Eduard von Todesco, son of Herman Todesco the Austrian financier and philanthropist (1792-1844). He married Fanny in 1864. He remarried in 1887 to Sarah, daughter of Sir Benjamin Samuel Phillips (see Phillips Family Pedigree).

G16.1. Alice Henrietta Antoinette Evelina married twice. Her first husband was John Henry Warner. Her second husband was David Morrison.

G17.1. Esther Agnes Sophie Morrison.
G17.2. Theodora Antionette Maude Morrison.

G16.2. Dora Sophie Emmy, born 1869.
G16.3. Constance Valerie Sophie, died in 1963 in London. Married in 1895 to Prince Maximillian Lowenstein-Wertheim—Freudenberg—Scharffeneck, Chamberlain at the Bavarian Court. They separated in 1910 and both remarried. Her second husband was Volrath von Alvensleben by whom she had a son.

G17.1. Count Johannes, heir, born 1901.
G17.2. Prince Leopold, 1903-1974.[15]
He was married twice, his second wife being Diana, daughter of the publisher Sir Victor Gollancz. He wrote *A Time to Love—A Time to Die* (1970), dealing with the death of his second wife from cancer. He was raised

in Austria and left Germany for England before the
War, becoming a British citizen in 1936. During the War
he worked on Government documentary films and afterwards was a consultant in psychology. He had two
daughters.

G17.3. Prince Hubertus of Lowenstein-Wertheim-Freuden-
berg,[16] born October 14, 1906 and married in 1929 to
Helga Schuylenberg. He studied at the University of
Munich and under Professor Albrecht Mendelssohn Bartholdy in the University of Hamburg where he obtained
his degree in 1931. In 1937 he was the Visiting Professor
of Carnegie Endowment for International Peace (New
York) having settled in New York in 1934. In 1941 he
was General-Secretary of the Guild for German Cultural
Freedom, Inc. He has contributed much to the English
and German literature, being the author of many books
and articles. His works include his autobiography *Towards the Further Shore,* published in English in 1973.
He is currently the President of the German Free
Authors Union. He has three daughters, Elisabeth,
Konstanzs and Margarete.

G17.4. Sophie Maria Scharffeneck.

G17.5. Fanny Ludowicke.

G17.6. Werner von Alvensleben.

G14.4. Cecilia Samuel (died in 1892), was married twice. Her first
husband was Philip[17] Joseph Salomons (son of Philip Salomons died 1797), and had issue. He was born in 1797, and
was one of the first members of the family to settle in West
London. He was known for his outstanding collection of li-
turgical silver which he used in private Synagogue at Brighton.
He became a very influential member of the Western Synagogue, was among the founders of Jews' College, The Anglo-
Jewish Theological Seminary and a Vice-President of the
Bread, Meat and Coal Charity, and of the Jews' Hospital. He
died in 1866. His wife remarried in 1872 to his first cousin, Sir
David Salomons (1797-1873, son of Solomon Selig Salomon
and Sephrea—the sister of Philip Joseph's father).

G15.1. Bertha (1841-1917) the second wife of Lionel Benjamin, son
of Benjamin (1789-1867) son of Levi Barent Cohen. They
married in 1860. His first wife was Henriette Rachel, daugh-

ter of Joseph Salomons (brother of Sir David Salomons). Lionel Benjamin was born in 1826 and died in 1890. From this union there were no children.

G15.2. Joseph Philip Salomons (1838-1905). He retired to Edinburgh about 1885, having been a Major in the 2nd Tower Hamlets Engineers. Here he was the President of the Hebrew Benevolent Society. He was an amateur artist, and died suddenly on October 20th while visiting London. He had two sons and three daughters.

G16.1. Philip Arthur Salomons, born 1877 and predeceased his father.

G17. Joseph Arthur Salomons, Major in the 7th Rajput Regiment, born 1900.

G16.2. Joseph Lionel Salomons, born 1870.

G15.3. Amelia Judith Salomons, born 1843, married Ernst de Saisset.

G15.4. Hannah (Anna Handeleh), 1839-1906, married Simon Waley (Whalley), 1827-1875. He was the youngest son of Solomon Jacob Levy (died 1864). He became a prominent stockbroker and was elected a member of the London Stock Exchange Committee. He was honorary secretary of the Jews' Free School for nearly a quarter of a century and from 1843 was the official correspondent for England of the Chamber of Commerce of Boulogne. As a talented musician he composed a number of piano pieces and several hymns for the Sabbath and Festival Services, several of which were chanted at the West London Synagogue for many years. His name appears in the *Dictionary of National Biography* and the *Dictionary of Music and Musicians*.

G16.1. Alfred Joseph Waley, 1861-1953. He served as a young man in the ranks of the Victorian Rifles and as an officer in the Tower Hamlets Royal Engineers. He retired as a captain in 1888, and became associated with the firm of Joseph Sebag and Co. in 1881 and became a partner in 1887. He retired in 1935. He was also a leading member of the London Stock Exchange and Treasurer of the Royal Academy of Music from 1924-1946. He married in 1887 to Laura Landauer and had issue, three sons and one daughter. He was the second eldest son, and his mother and his wife's mother were first cousins. (See above—G13.1/14.3/15.3/16.1.)

G17.1. Harry Adolf Simon Waley, 1887-1927, unmarried.
G17.2. Eric George Simon Waley, 1891-1953, married in 1920 to Aida Ades. He served in both World Wars.

> G18.1. Anthony Cecil Simon Waley, born in 1922. His son, Eric Waley born in 1953.
> G18.2. Joan Laura, born in 1925, unmarried.
> G18.3. Susan, born in 1930, married Peter Moser, and have two daughters.

G17.3. Reginald Philip Simon Waley, 1897-1951, married in 1926 to Beryl Gertrude Morrison.

> G18. Simon Francis Norman Morrison, born in 1934, married Ann Pettit. They have a daughter Hendelah (born in 1961) and two sons.

G17.4. Nancy (Hendelah), born in 1900, married in 1928 to an Austrian barrister, Joseph Rudolf Bruell, who died in 1972.

> G18.1. Eric Alfred Albert Bruell, born in 1929, married in 1960 to Audrey Janet Wilson Lindsay. They live in Brazil and have two sons, Jonathan David (born in 1962) and Nicholas James (born in 1964).
> G18.2. Julia Laura Cecilia, born in 1934, married in 1969 to Dr. Francis Percy Moss. Their children, Ruth Nancy (born in 1972) and Joseph Arthur (born in 1974).

G16.2. Sir Frederick George Waley, born in 1860, C.B.E. (1920) and knighted in 1923. He was a J.P. and Honorary Captain of the Royal Australian Naval Reserve. He married Ethel Kate, daughter of A.R. O'Connor of Sydney, and settled in Sydney, Australia. He was the eldest son, and was married three times. His first wife died after a short marriage and his two other wives were from Australia.

> G17. Eileen, married her first cousin, Ronald, son of John Waley, later divorced.

G16.3. Philip Simon Waley, married in 1892 to Mary Charlotte, 1871-1935, daughter of George Gershon Charles Raphael, 1838-1906. Mary's brother, William George Raphael, married a daughter of Sir Julian Goldsmid (see below G13.10 /14.2/15.1/16.7). George Gershon's sister, Alice Gertrude Raphael, married Henry Merton (see below G13.7/14.8 /15.1).

G17.1.   Frank Raphael Waley, born in 1893, married Olga Eleanore, daughter of Gregory Wilenkin (1864-1930, a Russian financial agent).

G18.   Rosemary, born in 1931, married John Philip Sassoon. Born in 1925, John was the son of Major Frederick, son of Joseph Sassoon, 1855-1918, of Ashley Park, Surrey, son of Sassoon David Sassoon (one of the sons of David Sassoon, founder of the family). Their children, Caroline Lucy (born in 1959), Joanna Margaret (born in 1960) and Kathryn Louise (born in 1965).

G17.2.   Gertrude Mary, born in 1910, married in 1937 to Matthew Lewis, oldest son of Colonel Sir Frederick Nathan.

G17.3.   Margaret Hendella, married Shubert David Waley.

G16.4.   John Waley, married 1) the daughter of Alfred H. Beddington (see page 65) and had two sons, and 2) Miss Yearsley.

G17.1.   Aubrey, killed in World War I.

G17.2.   Ronald Waley, married and later divorced his first cousin, Eileen Waley. Their son, Brian.

G16.5.   Alec Waley, married 1) Miss Dreyfus, and had two daughters and 2) Elaine Dickens, granddaughter of Charles Dickens.

G17.1.   Gladys, married three times, and had issue.

G17.2.   May, married twice, and had issue.

G16.6.   Celia (Cecelia), married Oliver Philip Behrens of Manchester, having no issue.

G16.7.   Ada Rachel, married in 1885 to Cecil Quixano, youngest son of David Henriques.

G17.1.   Gerald, died young.

G17.2.   Philip Henriques, settled in Australia, where he died.

G18.1.   Gillian, married Hubert son of Sir E. H. L. Beddington.

G18.2.   Eleanor, married in 1949 to Leonard Harold Lionel Cohen (born in 1922), son of Sir Lionel Leonard,

Lord Cohen of Walmer (born in 1888, and was one
of the most eminent of English jurists). Their children,
Jonathan (born in 1951), Catherine (born in 1953)
and Andrew (born in 1957).

G16.8. Bertha, 1872-1930, married in 1896 to Frank Lionel, 1865-
1955, son of Lionel Louis Cohen, 1832-1887, who was a
prominent member of the Anglo-Jewish community and
succeeded his father Louis Cohen as head of the firm Louis
Cohen and Co., which he founded, and as a member of
the London Stock Exchange.

Frank Lionel was also the great-uncle of Leonard
Cohen mentioned above (G18.2). His schooling was at
the Jewish House established at Harrow. One of his sons
met the author C. P. Snow at Cambridge, and inspired
Snow's novel *The Conscience of the Rich* in which the
central figure was based on the personality of Frank
Lionel Cohen.

G17.1. Constance, 1898-1969, unmarried.
G17.2. Beatrice Hendelah, born in 1899, married in 1922 to Albert Isaac Polack, son of the Rev. Joseph Polack, who
was master of the Jewish House at Clifton.

G18.1. Benjamin Harold Polack, born in 1924, married in
1954 to Elsie Margaret Harrison. Their children, Robin William, born in 1956, Ian Michael, born in 1958
and Ruth Alison, born in 1964.

G18.2. Irene Bertha, born in 1925, married Gabriel Aitman
in 1954. Their children, David Charles, born in 1956,
Timothy John, born in 1958 and Jane Patricia, born
in 1960.

G18.3. Patricia Violet, born in 1928.
G18.4. Ernest Frank, born in 1930.

G17.3. Harold Cohen, born in 1901, unmarried.
G17.4. Dr. Richard Henry Lionel Cohen, born in 1907, married
Margaret Deas. Their son, James, born in 1942, mar-
ried. His sons, Henry Lionel and Richard Lionel.
G17.5. Mary Irene, born in 1911, married Donald William
Lucas, born in 1905, son of Frank William Lucas. He
was a Fellow of Kings' College, Cambridge in 1929, and

Director of the Department of Studies in Classics from 1935-65. He was also University lecturer in Classics in 1933 and the P.M. Laurence Reader in Classics in 1952. He was the author of *The Greek Tragic Poets,* 1950 and *Aristotle Poetics,* 1968; the translator from Euripides of: *Bacchae,* 1930, *Medea* and *Ion,* 1949, and *Alcestis* and *Electra,* 1961; and the contributor to various classical journals and the *Encyclopaedia Britannica.*

G18.1. Susan Elizabeth, married Morley Cooper, and have issue, Ivan S. and Lisa Simone.

G18.2. Peter David Lucas.

G15.5. Henriette Esther Salomons (1845-1900), married her second cousin, Arthur Denis Samuel (De Vahl), son of Denis Moses Samuel (see below).

G14.5. Amelia Samuel, married firstly her uncle, Denis Moses Samuel, and had issue. After his death she remarried in 1872 to George William Hamilton Fitz-Maurice, the Sixth Earl of Orkney 1827-1889), but they had no issue. He was the son of the fifth Earl, Edmond Water, and was succeeded by his nephew.

G13.2. Denis Moses Samuel, Baron de Samuel,[18] married his niece Amelia Samuel, emigrated to South America, and settled in Rio de Janeiro. Here he negotiated several important banking transactions for the Brazilian Government, and was created Baron by Don Pedro I, King of Portugal. He died in England in 1890, having spent seventeen years in Brazil. His biography appeared in the second edition of *Gedullat Shaul,* (Warsaw 1925) under the title *Nir LeDavid Ulezaro,* by Zvi H. Edelman.

G14.1. Louisa, married her second cousin, Baron George DeWorms (see above—DeWorms Family Pedigree).

G14.2. Arthur Denis Samuel (de Vahl), married Henrietta Esther, daughter of Cecilia Samuel, a cousin, and Philip Joseph Salomons. They had four daughters.

G15. Maud (died 1920), married Rear Admiral Bernard Currey.

G16. Henrietta, married Commander Lee Metters. They have three sons and a daughter.

G14.3. Frank Denis, succeeded his father as Baron de Vahl.

G13.3. Joshua Samuel.

G13.4. Phineas Moses (Benjamin) Samuel, married Katherine Jacobs.

    G14.1. Rebecca.

    G14.2. John Phineas.

    G14.3. Rachel, died young.

    G14.4. Horatio.

    G14.5. Sarah, married Isaac (Josias, 1791-1846), son of Levi Barent Cohen, as his second wife in 1827, and had issue.

        G15.1. John, 1828-1836.

        G15.2. Anna Louisa, 1835-1902, unmarried.

        G15.3. Lucy, 1839-1906, unmarried.

        G15.4. Julianna, (1831-1877), married in 1850 to her first cousin, Baron Mayer Nathan Mayer Rothschild (1818-1874), fourth son of Nathan Mayer Rothschild (1777-1836) and his wife Hannah Cohen (1783-1850), a sister to Isaac (Josias) Cohen.

           Baron Mayer was educated at Trinity College in Cambridge, and became a member of the firm of N. M. Rothschild & Sons, founded by his father. He also held a seat in Parliament and in 1857, after acquiring land in Buckinghamshire, he began building his mansion of Mentmore which was later acclaimed for its hospitality and works of art. He was also a stud farmer, raising many famous horses. In 1871 he won the Derby and four other big races, and that year became later known as "The Baron's Year."

        G16.1. Hannah, born July 27, 1851, and died November 19, 1890. She married in 1878 to Archibald Phillip Primrose, 5th Earl of Rosebery (1847-1929).

           He was the son of Lord Dalmeny and received his education at Brighton, Eaton and Christ Church, Oxford. On his mother's side he succeeded his grandfather in 1868 as Earl of Stanhope. He was famous for his horse stable and won the Derby in 1894, 1895 and 1905. In 1878 he was elected Lord Rector of Aberdeen and in 1880 of Edinburg University, in 1881, Under-secretary at the Home Office, in 1884 as First Commissioner of Works, in 1886 Foreign Secretary (under Gladstone), and in 1889 Chairman of the First County Council of London. The following year he visited Germany and on his return found his wife gravely ill suffering from typhoid. Sometime after she died at the age of thirty-nine. Throughout her life she remained true to her religion and was accustomed to light the Sabbath candles on Friday nights. At the time of her death, the funeral service was held at the Jewish Cemetery of Willesden, and attended by the Lord and Barons Rothschild, representatives of Queen Victoria and the family members. For a period of time Lord Rosebery withdrew from public life. In 1894 he became Prime Minister, but the following year the Government was defeated and he resigned. In 1898 he paid a tribute to Gladstone in the House of Lords on the latter's death. Although he withdrew from his public career he rallied in 1901 in support of the Liberal Imperialists. He was also the author of *Pitt* (1891), *Appreciations and Addresses* (1899), *Peel* (1899), *Napoleon: The Last Phase* (1900) and *Cromwell* (1900). In 1908 he was Chancellor of Glasgow University and in 1911 he was elected Lord Rector of St. Andrew's University.

G17.1. Albert Edward Harry Mayer Archibald Primrose, born January 1882, and succeeded his father as the 6th Earl of Rosebery in 1929. He served in W.W.I. as a Lieut. Colonel and later became an honorary Colonel, having received the Legion of Honour, D.S.O. and in 1914 a star and two medals. He was a J.P. of Edinburgh and of Midlothian (he retired in 1910 as Liberal Member for Midlothian) and served as Secretary of State for Scotland from May-July 1945, and held a number of other positions.

In 1909 he married Lady Dorothy Alice Margaret Augusta, daughter of the late Lord Henry George Grosvenor. They were divorced in 1919. He then married Dane Eva Isabel Marian Struitt, the daughter of Henry Campbell Bruce (Lord Aberdare). He was her second husband. He had issue from both wives.

G18.1. Lord Neil Archibald Primrose, born in 1929 from the second wife. He married in 1955 to Alison Mary Deidre, daughter of Ronald W. Reid, M.S., F.R.C.S. They have four daughters and a son: Honorable Harry Ronald Neil, born November 20, 1967, Lucy Catherine Mary, born 1955, Jane Margaret Helen, born 1960, Emma Elizabeth Anne, born 1962 and Caroline Sara Frances, born 1964.

G18.2. Alexander Ronald George Primrose.

G18.3. Michael Primrose.

G18.4. Lady Helen Dorothy, born in 1913 from his first wife, married Honorable Hugh Adeane Vivian Smith in 1933.

G17.2. Neil James Archibald, 1882-1917, served as Undersecretary for the British Foreign Office in 1915 and Parliamentary Secretary for Munitions in 1916. He died of wounds received in action in Palestine. In 1915 he married Lady Victoria Alice Louise, Countess of Halifax, Garrowby and York. She later remarried in 1936 to the 2nd Earl of Halifax.

G17.3. Sybil Myra Caroline Primrose (died in 1955), married Sir Charles John Cecil Grant in 1903. They had issue.

G17.4. Margaret Etrenne Hannah Primrose, second wife of Robert Offley Ashburton Crewe-Milnes. From his father's side he became the 2nd Baron of Houghton and from his mother's the Earl of Crewe and the First Marquess of Crewe. He lived from 1858 to 1945. He succeeded to the title of Baron of Houghton in 1885 and the following year was the Lord in Waiting to Queen Victoria. He was Lord Lieutenant of Ireland from 1892 to 1895 and became the Earl of Crewe in 1895. From 1905 to 1908, and 1915-1916 he was Lord President of the Council, and Lord Privy Seal in 1908 and from 1912 to 1915. From 1908 to 1910 he was Secretary of State for the Colonies and created Marquess in 1911. He became Secretary of State for India in 1910 and served until 1915, President of the Board of Education in 1916, Chairman of the London County Council in 1917, Ambassador to France from 1922 to 1928, Secretary of State for War in 1931 and from 1936 to 1944 he was the Leader of the Liberal Party in the House of Lords. He was the author of *Stray Verses* (1889-1890) and *Lord Rosebery* (1931, his father-in-law). He married in 1899. One son died young, another, Richard George Hungerford lived from 1911 to 1922 and their daughter, Mary Evelyn, married.

G18. Mary Evelyn, born 1915, married in 1935 to Sir George Victor Robert Innes-Ker, 9th Duke of Roxburghe and

the Marquess of Bowmont and Cessford (born in 1913).
She held the Queen's canopy at the Coronation in 1937
of King George VI and Lady Elizabeth (the present
Queen Mother). They divorced in 1953. They had no
issue.

G13.5. James Samuel.

G13.6. Abraham Samuel.

G13.7. Hannah Moses Samuel (1776-1871) married in 1802 to Solomon
(1776-1864), son of Levi Barent Cohen. They had four sons:
Barent (1806-8), Abraham (1808-1879) unmarried, Levi (Lewis
Barent 1812-26) and Joshua (1818-18), G14.1-G14.4 and daughters.

G14.5. Jeanette Cohen, 1803-1867, married in 1825 as the first wife of
Sir David Salomons. They died without issue.

Sir David was born November 22, 1797 in London, and
died there July 18, 1873. He was one of the founders of the
London and Westminster Bank in 1832. In 1835 he became
the first Jewish Sheriff of London and Middlesex. He was also
the first Jew to be appointed Magistrate for Kent (1838) and
High Sheriff of Kent County (1839-40). In 1835 he was elected
Alderman of Aldgate ward, and later of other wards. In due
course, he became the first Jewish Lord Mayor of London in
1855. He was elected a Member of Parliament in 1851. At the
time of "swearing in" he declined to take the oath "on the true
faith of a Christian" which caused much attention and discus-
sion throughout the country. He was then dismissed, and re-
elected only in 1859, after alteration of the Parliamentary oath
in 1858, one year after Baron Lionel Rothschild had taken his
oath and seat as M.P. for the city of London. In 1869 he was
made a Baronet of the United Kingdom. He was the author of:

1. *A Defense of Joint-Stocks Banks* (1837).
2. *The Monetary Difficulties of America* (1837).
3. *An Account of the Persecution of the Jews of Damascus*
   (1840).
4. *Reflection on the Recent Pressure on the Money Market*
   (1840).
5. *The Case of David Salomons* (1844).
6. *Parliamentary Oaths* (1850).
7. *Alteration of Oaths* (1853).

Sir David died without issue from either wife.[19]

G14.6. Harriet Cohen (1804-1879), married in 1836 to John Wagg. Together with John Helbert Israel, they founded the merchant banking firm of Helbert, Wagg and Company, which became defunct in 1964.

G15.1. Emily (Emmy), married Henry E., son of Eleazar Merton (the brother of Ralph and Benjamin mentioned under G15.3 and G14.8 below). The three were the sons of Abraham Lyon Moses, 1775-1854, whose descendants adopted the surname of Merton. Ralph and his descendants are mentioned in Burke's Landed Gentry.

G15.2. Mimmy, married Dr. Henry Behrend (1828-93). No issue.

G15.3. Arthur, married Mathilda, daughter of Ralph Merton (1817-83) son of Abraham Lyon. Her brother Emile R. Merton was the father of Sir Thomas Ralph of Stubbings House. Her other brother, Henry R. Merton, was the father of Eva who married Sir Charles David Seligman (mentioned under G14.8 /15.1/16.4).

G16.1. Alfred Ralph Wagg, born in 1877 and died in 1969, was for many years the director and chairman of Helbert, Wagg and Company until his retirement in 1959. He received the C.B.E. in 1957.

G16.2. Henry John Wagg, O.B.E., died in 1949. He left Eton in 1889 and departed from the family tradition of the city and became a consulting engineer. After World War I, he devoted his life to serving various charities, especially for the blind, and founded the Barclay Workshops for the Blind.

His sons, Kenneth A. and Richard Edward[19a]

His daughter, Marjorie Helen, married 1) Lt.-Col. Joseph Henry Nettlefold (and had issue, Michael) and 2) in 1945 to the 11th Marquess of Tweeddale, William George Montagu Hay (1884-1967). She settled in Tangier.

G16.3. Elsie Margaret, died in 1949, unmarried, secretary of the Sussex County Nursing Federation.

G15.4. Edward.

G14.7. Emily (1809-1841), married in 1835 to Solomon Isaac Joseph of New York (died 1866). They had a son and daughter.

G15.1. Lucy Hannah, 1839-1887, New York, unmarried.

G15.2. Laurens Joseph (1837-1886) of New York, married in New York in 1873 to Florence Grace (1848-1927), daughter of Benjamin Seixas Hart (and his wife Hannah, daughter of Harmon Hendricks).

G16.1. Rupert L. Joseph, born in 1880, unmarried.

G16.2. Twins, died in infancy.

G16.3. Wilfred, born in 1883, of Long Branch, New Jersey.

G16.4. Theodore Harold Joseph (1875-1950) of New York, who was the chief founder of the E-J Electrical Installation Company of New York in 1899, and of which he was president from 1911. This firm of electrical construction engineering designed and installed the equipment for the New York Metropolitan Opera House.

He graduated from Columbia University in 1896, and later became the president a member of the executive committee of the New York Electrical Contractors Association. He did much to shape safety rules devised by the National Fire Protection Association and New York's Department of Water Supply, Gas and Electricity. He was also president and vice-president of other affiliated groups within his field, was a member of the Sons of the American Revolution, United Spanish War Veterans and others.

He was a cousin of Justice Benjamin N. Cardozo, and married 1) Sylvia (1874-1939) daughter of Florian Hart Florance (and his wife, Sarah, daughter of Montague Hendricks, brother of Hannah mentioned above). Florian was the son of Jacob Levy. He remarried 2) Ruth Graff. They lived in Mamaroneck, New York. His obituary appeared in the N.Y. Times, February 2, 1951.

G17.1. Dorothy, unmarried, born in 1902.

G17.2. Barbara, married Caples (New York). They had two daughters (married) and settled in California.

G17.3. Marjorie, born in 1904, married Thorkil Aschehoug of Mamaroneck, and later settled in Boca Raton, Florida. They had one daughter (married, Syracuse, New York).

G14.8. Hannah (1816-1898), married in 1845 to Benjamin Moses Merton (died 1881).

G15.1. Henry Merton, married in 1875 to Alice Gertrude, sister of George Gershon Raphael (see above G13.1/14.4/15.4/16.3), the children of Henry Lewis Raphael (1832-99, a wealthy banker in the firm of R. Raphael & Sons, founded in 1787 by his grandfather, Raphael Raphael).

Henry Benjamin was born in 1848 and died in 1929.

G16.1. Hugh Raphael Merton, 1887-1905.

G16.2. Cyril Benjamin Raphael Merton.

G16.3. Gerald Raphael Merton, 1877-1951, married Lilly Marie Louise, daughter of Bertrand Boy-de-la-Tour.

G17.1. Renée, born in 1902, married I. W. G. Barry, and has two married sons.

G17.2. Air Chief Marshal Sir Walter (Hugh) Merton, born August 29, 1905, G.B.E. 1963 (O.B.E. 1941), K.C.B. 1959, Inspector General of Civil Defence, 1964-68.

After training at the R.A.F. Cadet College, he was commissioned in 1925, became a Wing Commander in 1940 and served in World War II. He later became Director of Organization of the Air Ministry, 1944-45, and, after several other posts, served as Chief of the Air Staff, Royal N.Z. Air Forces from 1954-56 and as Chief of Staff of Allied Air Forces, Central Europe from 1959-60. He retired in 1963, having been made an Air Chief Marshal two years before.

He married 1) in 1930 to B. H. B. Kirby, and had a son, and 2) in 1938 to Margaret Ethel, daughter of J. C. Marco Wilson.

G18. Robin Merton, born in 1931, married Jill Keith Jones. Their children, Simon, born in 1961 and Louisa, born in 1967.

G17.3. Cecil, 1908-71, was awarded the Military Cross with bar, married and had three daughters.

G16.4. Eva Henriette Merton, born in 1879, married in 1899 to Sir Charles David 1869-1954, son of Isaac Seligman, one of the famous Seligman brothers, sons of David Seligman, founder of the family. He was a senior partner of the banking firm of Seligman Brothers in London, Hon. Consul-General for Austria in London from 1931-38 and created a Sir in 1933. He was also a member of a mission that the Federation of British Industries sent to Japan and Manchuria in 1934. Among his relatives was a cousin, Lt.-Col. Leonard Charles Rudolph Messel, maternal grandfather of the present Earl of Snowdon, Anthony Armstrong–Jones, (husband of Princess Margaret).

G17.1. Kathleen, born in 1900, married H. Levy.
G17.2. Douglas, born in 1902.
G17.3. Hugh L., born in 1905.
G17.4. Geoffrey C., born in 1913.

G16.5. Reginald, married Norah McCann, daughter of the Master of University College, Oxford.

G16.6. Margaret, born in 1880, married Philip Lazarus, and had issue.

G15.2. Louisa Emily (1850-1931), married in 1870 to Sir Benjamin Louis Cohen, first Baronet Cohen (born November 18, 1844, died November 8, 1909), son of Louis of Gloucester Place, London (1799-1882), son of Joseph eldest son of Levi Barent Cohen. Sir Benjamin was M.P. for East Islington (1892-1906), and President of the London Orphan Asylum. He was created a Baronet in 1905.

G16.1. Sir Herbert Benjamin Cohen, 2nd Baronet, was born April 26, 1874, and succeeded his father on his death in 1909. He was Barrister-at-Law and received the Order of the British Empire in 1919. He married in 1907 to Hannah Mildred (Nina) daughter of Henry Behrens of Gloucester Square. The Family Crest reads *All for the Best.*

Henry Behrens was the son-in-law of Maurice Moses Beddington (1821-98), who was the brother of Edward Henry Beddington mentioned above (I — G12.4/13.9/14.7/15.1). The two with a third brother, Alfred H., were active lifelong workers and leaders in many of London's communal institutions. They were also the founders of the Central Synagogue in London in 1870.

G17.1. Nigel Benjamin, B.A., born January 18, 1908, died 1931, unmarried.

G17.2. Stephen Behrens, M.A., Barrister-at-Law, born February 27, 1911. He served in World War II, and died unmarried on active service in India, February 10, 1943.

G16.2. Hannah Floretta Cohen, authoress of a collection of memoirs of the Cohen, Merton and related families entitled *Changing Faces*, published London, 1937. The book includes a picture of her great-grandfather, Moses Samuel, whom, she recalls was a descendant of Saul Wahl, their ancestral "Royalty."

G16.3. Arthur Cohen, 1876-1966 and 4. Ernest Cohen, 1877-1955.

G13.8. Rebecca Moses Samuel, married her first cousin Alfred, son of Alexander Phillips (brother to her mother).

G14.1. Clara married Baron Nordeck Ravenna of Italy.

G15.1. Louisa.
G15.2. Adolph.
G15.3. Alice.

G14.2. Charles.
G14.3. Adolphus.
G14.4. Margaret, married Pantese.

G13.9. Frances Moses Samuel, married her first cousin, Michael, son of Alexander Phillips, and settled in the United States.
G13.10. Phillip Moses Samuel of Bedford Place (1787-1871). He married twice, and had issue from both.
From the second wife Phoebe Israel:

G14.1. Phillipa, married Barnet Samuel Phillips, son of Samuel son of Barnet son of Jonas Phillips. They had issue.
From the first wife Julia Goldsmid:
G14.2. Caroline (died 1885) married on July 23, 1834 to Frederick David Goldsmid, M.P. (born January 31, 1812 and died March 18, 1866), son of Sir Isaac Lyon Goldsmid (1778-1859), son of Asher, of the family of prominent English financiers and bankers. He was educated at University College, London. After his marriage, he spent a year in Italy, and upon his return to England became a member of the firm of Mocatta & Goldsmid. He was an active Jewish communal worker, and was President of the Jew's Hospital. He was a Member of Parliament for Honiton from July 1865 until his death in 1866.[20]

G15.1. Sir Julian Goldsmid, the 3rd and last Baronet (his grandfather Isaac was the first, and his uncle Sir Francis Henry who died without issue was the second Baronet). He was born October 2, 1838, and died at Brighton January 7, 1896. He was the eldest son and was educated privately until the age of seventeen. He then entered University College, the Alma Mater of his father. He received his B.A. at University of London in 1859, and his M.A. in 1861. He was made a fellow of University College in 1864, and in the same year was called to the bar which he left when elected M.P. for Honiton in March 1866 on the death of his father who had held that position. During 1894, when he belonged to the Liberal Party, he often had the honor of presiding over the deliberations of the House of Commons. In Jewish affairs he was prominent with the Anglo-Jewish Association, and the Russo-Jewish Committee, of which he was chairman from its foundation in 1882 until 1894. He was elected vice-president of the Anglo Jewish Association at its foundation in 1871, and succeeded his relative Baron DeWorms as President in 1886. He resigned in 1895 due to ailing health. He was also a warden and occasionally lay preacher at the West London Synagogue. He succeeded to his uncle's titles, honors and estates, upon his death in May 1878. He was married in 1868 to Virginia (died 1892), daughter of A. Philipson of Florence. They had eight daughters.

G16.1. Maud, born in 1874, the fifth daughter, married December 1894 to Herbert Merton Jessel, First Baron Jessel born October 27, 1866, died November 1, 1950. He was the son of Sir George Jessel, (1824-1883), son of Zadok Aaron Jessel. His brother Sir Charles James married his wife's sister (see below).

Herbert was educated in Rugby and New College Oxford. He was Alderman for the city of Westminster and Mayor in 1902-3. He was also a J.P. and a M.P. from 1896-1906 and 1910-1918. He was a Colonel in the Army in 1919, and had served as a Captain in India 1887-1890. Among other positions he held, he was created an officer of the Legion of Honor of France and of the Order of Leopold, King of the Belgians. He was created Baron Jessel of Westminster in 1924, having been a Baronet since 1917.[21]

G17.1. Sir Edward Herbert Jessel of Westminster, the 2nd Baron, born March 25, 1904. He was educated at Eton and Oxford, where he received his B.A. in 1925. In addition to being a Barrister-at-Law, he was Director of Textile Machinery Makers Ltd., and also of Dodson &

Barlow. He married February 14, 1935 to Lady Helen
Maglona Vane-Tempest-Stewart, 3rd daughter of the 7th
Marquess of Londonderry. They divorced in 1960 and
he remarried Jessica, daughter of William de Wet and
Mrs. H. W. Taylor of Cape Town.

G18.1. Timothy Edward Jessel, 1935-69, married and had a
daughter, Annabel, born 1968.

G18.2. Camilla Edith Mairi Elizabeth Jessel, born 1940, married in 1960 to the Marques de Caicedo. Their sons
are Miguel, born 1961, and Alfonso, born 1966.

G18.3. Joanna Margaret, born 1945, married in 1967 to Simon
Butler. They have two sons, Ashky, born in 1969, and
Dermot, born in 1971.

G17.2. Gladys Mary Jessel, born May 13, 1896, unmarried.

G17.3. Vera Pearl Jessel, died in 1928. She was married in 1925
to Captain Clive Harrison, son of Charles Harrison
Martyn. Their only child was accidentally drowned in
1927.

G17.4. Doreen Maud Jessel B.A., born February 7, 1909. Married in 1934 to Geofrey William Gerald Agnew, elder son
of Charles Gerald Agnew. He is Chairman of the Fine
Art Dealers of Thomas Agnew and Sons since 1965. He
was born in 1908.

G18.1. Jennifer, born in 1937, married in 1962 to Paul Lazell.
They have three children: Sebastian, born in 1963;
Natasha, born in 1967; and Dominie, born in 1971.

G18.2. Jonathan Agnew, born in 1941, B.A. Cambridge 1963,
banker, married in 1966 to Joanna, younger daughter
of Lord Campbell of Eskan. They have three children: Caspar, born in 1967; Lauren, born in 1969; and
Kate, born in 1971.

G18.3. Morland Herbert Julian Agnew, born 1943, B.A. Cambridge 1965, married Margaret Mitchell in 1972. He
is a director of Thomas Agnew and Sons, Fine Art
Dealers.

G16.2. Edith Goldsmid, born in 1870, married Sir Charles James
(Zadok Aaron) Jessel in 1890. He was first Baronet of
Ladham House, Kent, 1860-1928.

G17.1. Sir George Jessel, 2nd Baronet, succeeding his father in

1928. He was born May 28, 1891, and was married twice. His first wife whom he married in 1923 was Muriel Gladys (died 1948), widow of Major Foster Swetenhorn, and they had issue. His second wife, whom he married in 1948, was Elizabeth, former wife of 2nd Baron Russell of Liverpool. Sir George was educated at Eton and Balliol College, Oxford, where he received his B.A. and M.A. in 1917. He was J.P. for Kent, and served in World War I, during which time he was wounded.

G18.1. Charles John Jessel, born 1924. He served during World War II, and was educated at his father's Alma Mater.

G18.2. Gloria Joan Jessel, born 1925.

G17.2. Sir Richard Hugh Jessel, born 1896.

G18.1. David.
G18.2. Robin.

G17.3. Mina Dorothy.
G17.4. Margery Constance.

G16.3. Grace Catherine Goldsmid (1874-1950), had no issue.
G16.4. Nora Octavia Goldsmid (died 1931), had no issue.
G16.5. Violet Baroness de Goldsmid e da Palmeira (1869-1949), married Sidney Francis Goldsmid Hoffnung in 1889.

G17.1. Vivien, born in 1903, married in 1928 to Vera Levy.

G18. Priscilla, born in 1933.

G17.2. Cyril Julian Goldsmid Hoffnung, born in 1890, married in 1920 to Nancy Macgillicuddy.

G18.1. Michael Lyon, born in 1921.
G18.2. John, born in 1922.
G18.3. David, born in 1925.

G17.3. Ronald Goldsmid Hoffnung, born in 1893, married in 1926 to Dorothy Lawndes.

G16.6. Maria Goldsmid (1877-1944), married in 1914 to Brig. General Hugh Headlam. They had no issue.

G16.7. Margherita Goldsmid (1871-1925), married in 1894 to William George (1865-1912), son of George Gershon

Charles Raphael (mentioned above under G13.7/14.8/ 15.1).

G17.1. Dorothy, born in 1897, married Henry Custon.
G17.2. Elsie Violet, born in 1899, married Humphrey Tolle-mache.
G17.3. Charlotte, born in 1903.

G16.8. Beatrice Goldsmid (1873-1937), married in 1897 to William Louis Lucas (1866-1929) of Oakash[21a]

G17.1. Robert Hugh Arthur.   G17.2. Archibald Julian.
G17.3. Elizabeth V., married in 1934 to John Noble.

G15.2. Helen Goldsmid married Lionel Lucas.

G16.1. Frederick Louis.
G16.2. Ethel Rebecca, married William Elias Hozley.

G15.3. Mary Ada Goldsmid, married in 1857 to Frederick David Mocatta (born London 1828 and died there 1905). He was the son of Abraham (1797-1880), son of Jacob (1770-1825) Mocatta, a prominent family of Bullion Brokers and Bankers of England.

After being privately educated, Frederick entered in 1843 into his father's firm Mocatta & Goldsmid, of which he became Director. He retired from the firm in 1874, and devoted himself to Jewish studies. He was also a philanthropist, communal worker and historian. He was Vice-President of the Anglo Jewish Association, and played a part in the amelioration of the plight of persecuted East European Jewry. He was also a leader in many other organizations, and was particularly interested in promoting Jewish learning. In 1888 he delivered a lecture on *The Jews at the Present Age in their Various Habitations,* which was printed and translated into several languages. He was President of the Jewish Historical Society of England from its inception in 1900 until 1902, which he was mainly instrumental in founding.

On the occasion of his seventieth birthday, 8,000 people, including members of the Royal Family, the Chief Rabbi and the Archbishops of Canterbury, Westminster and Armagh, signed a testimonial of gratitude for his social services, including those of over 200 philanthropic, literary and other institutions of which he was a member.

He founded a great Jewish art collection and library which were bequeathed to the University College of London as the Mocatta Library, founded in 1905. University College was founded in 1826 by his wife's grandfather Sir Isaac Lyon Goldsmid. Some of the many books and art treasures were lost when the library was destroyed in an air raid in 1940. It was rebuilt in 1954. The library is also the home of the Jewish Historical Society. He was the author of:

1. *The Jews of Spain and Portugal and the Inquisition* (1877 and 1928), translated into many languages.
2. *The Jews at the Present Age* (see above).

He subventioned:

1. *Zur Geschichte und Literatur* by Zunz.
2. *Literaturgeschichte der Synagogalen Poesie* by Zunz.
3. *Juden in Rome* by A. Berliner.
4. *Sources of Spanish Jewish History* by Jacobs.
5. *History of the Jews by Graetz* (English translation).

IV—SAMUEL FAMILY OF PHILADELPHIA

ANCESTRY

G3.3.   R. Saul Wahl Katzenellenbogen.
G4.1.   R. Meir.
G5.2.   R. Moses.
G6.6.   R. Saul.
G7.3.   R. Jacob Katzenellenbogen.
G8.2.   R. Zvi Hirsch Apter.
G9.1.   R. Elijah Apter.
G10.3. Joseph Ducit.
G11.2. Samuel Samuel, died 1758.
G12.4. David Samuel.
G13.3. Samuel Samuel.

G14. David Samuel, born in London 1804, died in Philadelphia 1881.[22] He was buried in a family plot in Mt. Sinai Cemetery of Philadelphia. His wife Esther (Hetty) was born in Philadelphia in 1808, and they were married in Philadelphia on October 17, 1827. She died at Bath, England, while visiting there, on May 26, 1857. Her remains were then transported to Philadelphia, and she now is buried beside her husband.

David was elected Secretary of the Congregation Mikveh Israel of Philadelphia, the oldest synagogue of that city, in 1841. They had seven children.

G15.1.　Henry, born 1828 at Philadelphia, and died in 1893 in New York. He did not marry. He was buried in Philadelphia in the family plot.

G15.2.　John, born 1829 at Philadelphia, and died in that city 1913. He was married in Philadelphia on November 5, 1856 to Rebecca Hendricks-Levy (1832-1915), daughter of Hayman son of Solomon Levy of Hanover and later of South Carolina. John was for many years a noted lawyer of the city of Philadelphia, also a member of the Library Committee of the Law Association. Both he and his wife lie buried in the Samuel Family Plot in Mt. Sinai Cemetery.

G16.1.　Bunford Samuel born 1857 at Philadelphia and died 1949 in that city, and buried in the family plot. He was a librarian of the Ridgway Branch of the Philadelphia Library. He was married twice.

On February 2, 1882 he was married in New York to Ella (1853-1920), daughter of David (1820-1875) son of Haym Salomon (1740-1785, Philadelphia). Haym Salomon was known as "The Financier of the American Revolution." They had three children. He remarried in Philadelphia on February 24, 1925, to Edith Lamberton.

G17.1.　Alma Rebecca (1882-1920), unmarried.

G17.2.　Emma Louise (1885-1965), member of the Animal Rescue Society, S.P.C.A., Emergency Aid and English Speaking Union.

G17.3.　Dorothea, born 1898, married in 1924 to Clifford Livingston Pelton.

G18.1.　Bunford Samuel Pelton, born 1927.

G18.2.　Clifford Livingston Pelton, born 1929.

G16.2.　John David Samuel, born 1869, married in 1899 to M. Amilla Robb.

G17.1.　John (1900-1912).

G17.2.　Louis, born 1902, unmarried.

G17.3.　Maria Burnett (1903-1950).

G16.3. Frank Samuel, (1859-1934), manufacturer, pioneer iron exporter. He was educated at a private school in Philadelphia, and spent one year in New York studying the banking business. He returned to Philadelphia to work for a prominent glass manufacturer who later made Frank Vice-President of the Malaga and Milville Glass Company in New Jersey. In 1888 he resigned to accept the Vice-Presidency of the North Branch Steel Company, which was the first to produce the modern street-car rail, making a revolution in this field. In 1894 he resigned and entered commerce to become a general iron merchant, and one of the first to export iron and steel to all parts of the world. He was a member of various social clubs and associations, was both an athlete and sportsman. He was married on December 7, 1887 to Mary Buchanan, daughter of Colonel A. Louden and Elizabeth R. Snowden of Philadelphia.

G17.1. Elizabeth, born 1889, married George Poulyeff.
G17.2. Rebecca born 1890 in Philadelphia, married April 11, 1912, to Francis Robinson.[23]

G18.1. Samuel Snowden Robinson, born 1913 in New Jersey. Married in 1950 to Carol Fotterall.

G19.1. Samuel S. Robinson, Jr., born 1952.
G19.2. Louisa Law, born 1953.
G19.3. Edward Chaplin, born 1954.

G18.2. Francis Robinson, Jr., born 1918, married Shirley Coffey (Villa Nova, Pa.).

G19.1. Francis III.
G19.2. Elizabeth.
G19.3. William Chaplin.
G19.4. Christopher.
G19.5. Anne.

G17.3. Snowden Samuel, born 1893 in Philadelphia. He was educated in the Episcopal Academy, and married in October 1919 to Elisabeth C. Adams. He became Secretary and Treasurer in 1919 of the American Swedo Iron Company, and was admitted to the company in 1926. He was also a member of the firm of Frank Samuel & Company (his father). He served during World War I in France, and thereafter was a member of various social clubs of his home town. He died in 1939. His wife currently resides in Paris.[24]

G18.1. Mary Buchanan, married three times, most recently to Earl B. Ford of New York, in 1972.

G15.3. Charles Samuel, born 1831, died in infancy.
G15.4. Eleanor (1833-1907), unmarried, buried in family plot.
G15.5. Clara (1836-1860), married in 1858 in Philadelphia to Frederick Myers (his first wife), son of Mordecai Myers (1794-1865).

G16. Frances Maria, (1859-194?), married in 1891 in Philadelphia to Dr. William Alexander Thom, Jr. (1853-1894) as his third wife.

G17. William Alexander Thom (1893-1911), Norfolk, Va.

G15.6. Edward (1845-1896), Philadelphia. Married Anne Russell Evans in 1872, and Mary Campbell Evans in 1894.

G16. Edward Jr., born 1895. Married Ethel Butler Cockburn in 1823.

G17. Joan Patricia, born 1924 and died young (Paris).

G15.7. Joseph Bunford (1854-1929), Philadelphia. He married Ellen (1849-1913) on May 28, 1902 in Philadelphia. They had no issue. She was the daughter of Jonas Altamont Phillips (1806-1862). They were both buried in the Phillips family plot of Mt. Sinai Cemetery in Philadelphia. Joseph was widely known for his interest in art. He was especially interested in a series of twenty sculptures dedicated to American Pioneers, which were to be arranged along the bank of the Schuylkill River. His wife had left $500,000 in her will for these statues. He received the Order of the Falax from King Christian of Denmark.

Joseph was the author of a booklet printed for private circulation (100 copies) in 1912 entitled *Records of the Samuel Family*. Within the text are pictures of his parents and paternal grandparents, as well as a wax impression of the seal of Samuel Samuel (his grandfather) with an inscription dated 1798 (London).

c.

THE KATZENELLENBOGEN FAMILY
OF KROTOSCHIN AND BERLIN

ANCESTRY

G3.3. R. Saul Wahl Katzenellenbogen.

G4.1. R. Meir.

G5.2. R. Moses.

G6.6. R. Saul.

G7.3. R. Jacob the Martyr.

G8.3. R. Samuel.

G9.6. R. Isaac Katzenellenbogen, died in 1733 in Krotoschin.

G10.1. Wife of R. Menachem Mendel son of R. Moses Auerbach, A.B.D.
Krotoschin. R. Moses was a grandson of R. Saul son of R. Heschel
of Cracow. (See Chapter IX.)

G10.2. R. Saul Katzenellenbogen, carrying on the name of his royal ancestor, Saul Wahl.

G11. R. Benjamin, a prominent author of the 18th century. He was a
pupil of Samuel Helman (of the Heilprin Family) of Metz, (died
1766). He became A.B.D. of Samter (Prussia) and then of Krotoschin, Krojanke and Gelnhausen.

He was the author of *Or Chachamim*, published 1752 Frankfurt-On-Oder; *Lev Chachamim*, published 1773 Dyhernfurth; and
Menorot Zahav, including *Or Olam*, *Or Chadash* and *Or Torah*,
published 1775 Dyhernfurth.

He wrote approbations to *Pa-amonei Zahav* by R. David Katz
son of R. Joseph Weiner, published Furth 1769; *Chagorat Shmuel*
by R. Samuel son of R. Azriel, published Frankfurt-on-Oder 1772;
Or Lisharim by R. Rafael son of Jacob Jaffe, written in 1776, published Dyhernfurth 1778; and *Torat Moshe* by Moses Kaner, written in 1786, published in 1786.

G12.1. Meir Katzenellenbogen.

G13.1. Hermann (Berlin).

G13.2. Max, married Kato, and lived on Schiffbauerdamm in
Berlin. He was president of the Schlesische Mühlenwerke
Aktiengesellschaft, Breslau, and also a member of the
Ostwerke Aktiengesellschaft in Berlin, as well as other
banks and companies in Breslau, Berlin and Gorlitz.

G13.3. Bertha, unmarried, Berlin.

G13.4. Karl, unmarried, Berlin.

G13.5. Dr. Albert Katzenellenbogen, J.P., born January 15, 1863 in Krotoschin,[25] and was deported on August 18, 1942 to Theresienstadt, and perished soon thereafter.

He moved from Krotoschin, whose Jewish population at that time was approximately 2,300, which comprised thirty percent of the town's population, and settled in Frankfurt-on-Main where he lived on New Mainz Street and lastly on Bockenheimerhand Street.

He married Cornelia Josephine (1870-1940), daughter of Dr. Adolph Heinrich of Frankfurt-on-Main. Adolph was the son of Jacob and Franciska, daughter of Beer Eskeles. She and her children, although originally of the Jewish faith, were baptized as Lutherans. Albert was a jurist and a bank director. He was president and vice-president of concerns in Berlin and Frankfurt, the chief one being the Mitteldeutschen Creditbank (Commerz-und-Privat-Bank in Frankfurt). He was also a member of the board of other banks, textile companies and chemical concerns in various towns in Germany.

G14.1 Professor Adolf Katzenellenbogen,[26] born in Frankfurt-on-Main 1901 and died in Baltimore 1964. He obtained his Ph.D. in Law in 1924, and in Philosophy (Arts) in 1933. In 1935 he married Elizabeth Martha Holzhen in Zurich, Switzerland. They lived in Kostanz, a town in Germany near the Swiss border. Following the incident of the shooting of the German Embassy in Paris in 1938, Adolf was taken to Dachau in December 1938, where he remained for three weeks. Due to a chest infection, he was transferred by ambulance to Switzerland, where he was hospitalized for six months.

In 1939 he was invited to visit the U.S.A. by Professor Erwin Panofsky of Princeton University to speak at the Institute for Advanced Studies. He arrived in 1939, and on the very next day (September 1st), World War II broke out. He remained in the U.S.A. and in 1941 went to Cuba to obtain an immigrant visa. By July, his wife and daughter had also obtained a visa, and the family was reunited in September 1941.

He was Professor of Medieval Art at Johns Hopkins University until his death in 1964.

G15.1. Ruth Pauline Cornelia, born April 8, 1937.
G15.2. John Albert Katzenellenbogen, born May 10, 1944. Married in 1967 to Benita Schulman. They currently live in Urbana, Illinois.

G16.1. Deborah Joyce, born March 29, 1971.
G16.2. Rachel Adria, born December 9, 1972.

G14.2. Gretel Katzenellenbogen, died in World War II.
Her first husband was Reichert, died in World War II.

G15.1. Rolf, born 1918.
Her second husband was Erich Berndt, J.P.
G15.2. Diether, born 1922 in Frankfurt-on-Main.

G16.1. Francisca.
G16.2. Cornelia.

G14.3. Martha Katzenellenbogen, married Fred Mauer.

G15.1. Peter, born 1922 in Hamburg, Ph.D. Economics.

G16.1. Stefan.
G16.2. Sybille.

G13.6. Daughter, married Sussman.

G14.1. Charlotte, married and divorced Hartwigh, living in Palos Verdes.

G12.2. Adolf Katzenellenbogen (1834-1903), born in Krotoschin, and moved to Berlin early in the twentieth century, having retired from his spirit manufacturing business. He married a distant relative, Eva Katzenellenbogen.

G13.1. Martha (1875-1967), married Alfred Bum, and had issue.
G13.2. Ludwig Katzenellenbogen, born 1874 in Krotoschin, perished in World War II, about 1943. He was married twice. His first wife was Estelle Marcuse. His second wife (married in 1930) was Tilla Durieux[27] (her third husband). He had one son and two daughters who settled in the U.S.A. Ludwig was the General Director of Schultheiss Patzenhofer in Berlin, President of the Ostwerke in Berlin and a

vice-president and committee member of various other companies.

His wife, Tilla, was a prominent German actress, who died in 1971 at the age of ninety-one. In 1933 they both fled to Switzerland and then to Yugoslavia to escape the Gestapo. She mentions much about her husband in her memoirs. His financial successes are discussed in an article in *Konzernkrach* (Combined Power) by Erich W. Abraham, Berlin 1933.

G14.1. Estelle Ruth, born in 1921, married in 1953 in Yucca Valley, California to Karol Joseph Mysels of Los Angeles.

G13.3. Fritz Katzenellenbogen, 1880-1937(?), married Ruth Tieniann.

G14. Klaus (West Berlin).

G13.4. Manfred (Fredi) Katzenellenbogen, married Gertrude Friedlander. They had four children. Two were killed in World War II with their parents; one died, and a daughter Ursel, survived in England.

d.

DESCENDANTS OF

R. MOSES KATZENELLENBOGEN OF PINCZOW AND SCHWABACH

I—RIESSER FAMILY

ANCESTRY

G3.3. R. Saul Katzenellenbogen.
G4.1. R. Meir Wahl.
G5.2. R. Moses.
G6.6. R. Saul.
G7.4. R. Moses Katzenellenbogen, died in 1733.

G8.1. R. Phineas Katzenellenbogen was born in 1691 and died about 1760. He was A.B.D. Leipnik, Boskowitz (in Moravia), Wallerstein, Markbreit (in Bavaria), and Schwartzenberg. He was the author of several essays and *Yesh Manchilim*, the manuscript relating how his ancestor Saul Wahl (G3.3) became king, and on which *Gedullat Shaul* published in 1854 is based. This story he received and heard from his ailing father at Furth in 1733.

Responsa by him, his father, and his brother R. Eleazer were published in Frankfurt-on-Main in 1857. It was Phineas who visited his uncle Saadiah's grave in 1760, and obtained a copy of his eulogy. His manuscripts are housed in the Bodlein Library at Oxford.

He married a daughter of R. Gabriel Eskeles, A.B.D. Olkusz, Prague, Metz, and Nikolsburg. (See Eskeles Family under Descendants of R. Abraham Joshua Heschel of Cracow.) At that time, Nikolsburg in Southern Moravia had a Jewish population of approximately 3,000, which was half the total population. Many had settled there following the Jewish Expulsion from Vienna in 1670.

G9.1. R. Gabriel Katzenellenbogen, born sometime after 1718, A.B.D. Mecklenberg and Nikolsburg. He was named after his maternal grandfather R. Gabriel Eskeles. He was surnamed Markbreit where his father was Rabbi and where he was most likely born.

  G10. Sarel (died in 1799), married R. Phineas Lackenbach (died in 1840).[28]

G9.2. R. Jacob Lazarus Katzenellenbogen, A.B.D. of Ettingen, where he wrote an approbation in 1793 to *Ketzot HaChoshen* by R. Aryey Lieb son of Joseph Heller, published in Lvov. He also wrote an approbation to *Yefei Einayim* by R. David son of Mordecai of Brody, published in 1799. He left novellae and ritual decisions, now housed in the Bodlein Library, Oxford. He died in 1796. His wife Leah, wrote a letter to her son in 1794 while he was in Hamburg. This letter, as well as other family documents can be found in Oxford.

  G10.1. R. Lazarus Eliezer Jacob, born in the Riess Valley, Bavaria, in 1763, and became known as Jacob Riesser. He succeeded his father as A.B.D. Ettingen, and died in Hamburg in 1828. He married the daughter of Rafael Hakohen, A.B.D. of Altona-Hamburg-Wandsbeck from 1766-98. Rabbi Rafael (1722-1803) was the son of R. Jekutiel Susskind Hakohen. Jacob succeeded his father in Ettingen and later as Rabbi of Wallerstein. While his father-in-law was A.B.D. in Hamburg, he was secretary to the Beth Din there. In 1799 his fa-

ther-in-law resigned due to disagreements with the Danish
Government. Jacob then went into business, and later published *Zecher Tzadik*, published Altona 1805 and Vilna 1879,
containing *Ma'alalei Ish*, his father-in-law's biography and
two of his sermons. Riesser returned to Hamburg in 1816,
where he remained until his death. His correspondence with
his son Gabriel, some twenty letters, were published by Isler,
entitled *Gabriel Riesser's Leben*. His manuscripts are extant
in Oxford. He had two daughters and three sons.

G11.1.   Gabriel Riesser, the youngest son, born at Hamburg in
1806 and died there in 1863. He studied law at the Universities of Kiel and Heidelberg, and received his degree
in 1826. As a result of his being refused admittance to the
bar at Hamburg, he became a leading advocate of German Jewish Emancipation. He devoted himself to the
publishing of periodicals and books dealing with this subject. His dream was realized when, in 1848, he was elected
to the Preliminary Parliament of Frankfurt. He was subsequently elected deputy of the dukedom of Laurenburg
to the German National Assembly. He distinguished himself as a brilliant orator. He was also a member of the
delegation which offered King Frederick William IV of
Prussia the crown. In 1849 he became a citizen of Hamburg, a privilege he had been previously denied, and in
1850 he was elected to the Hamburg Parliament. Due to
ill health, he resigned in 1857. In 1859 he was elected to
the Hamburg Magistracy, and eventually became its Vice-
President. In 1860 he became the first Jewish Judge in Germany when he was elected a member of the Hamburg
Highcourt.

Many books were written about Gabriel and his life.
The Rathaus (City Hall) in Hamburg has in its main foyer
an honor gallery, and amongst its famous citizens is included Gabriel Riesser. He had no children.

G11.2.   Rafael Riesser.

G12.   Dr. Jacob Riesser, born in 1853. He was baptized in his
youth, and later became a lawyer. From 1885 until 1905
he was director of the Darmstadter bank. In 1905 he was
appointed Professor of Law at the University of Berlin.

From 1816 until 1928 he was a member of the Reichstag. He died in 1932.

G10.2. R. Phineas Katzenellenbogen, succeeded his father as A.B.D. of Ettingen. Many of his letters of correspondence to his father in Ettingen, written while in Schwabach, are found in manuscript at Oxford.

G11. Blumle,[29] married R. Gabriel son of R. Mordecai Marcus Adler, and brother of the Chief Rabbi of the British Empire. (See the Adler Family Pedigree—Chapter VI — Branch B.)

II—EPHRAIM, JABLONSKI, PLAUT and WOLLSTEINER FAMILIES

ANCESTRY

G6.6. R. Saul.

G7.4. R. Moses.

G8.2. R. Eliezer Katzenellenbogen (Eleazar Lazarus) of Alsace, born in 1700. He became A.B.D. in Bamberg in Bavaria, and then A.B.D. in Hagenau in Alsace from 1755-1771. His wife was Jached, daughter of R. Samuel Helman, A.B.D. of Metz (died 1766), of the Heilprin Family and a distant relative of his mother (Leah, daughter of R. Eliezer Heilprin). He was one of those consulted about the Cleves divorce case, which involved his brother and his relative Rabbi Israel Lipschutz (see Lipschutz Family Pedigree—Chapter VI).

He wrote approbations to *Chamesh Shitot LaRaMBaN* by Nachmanides, published Sultzbach 1762 and *Chochmat Shlomo* by R. Solomon Luria, published Sultzbach 1782.

He left novellae on the Talmud in manuscript. His responsa appear with those of his father and his brother, R. Phineas, published Frankfurt-on-Main 1857. In *Or Hayashar* there is a responsum of his to his brother R. Naftali, written in Hagenau in 1766.

G9.1. Naftali Hirsch Katzenellenbogen, born in 1745. He studied under his grandfather R. Samuel Helman of Metz (who was also the teacher of his distant relative R. Benjamin son of Saul Katzenellenbogen of Samter and Krotoschin). On qualifying as a Rabbi, his first invitation to the Rabbinate was from Frankfurt-on-Oder. In 1793, in his letter of acceptance to the leaders of the congregation,[30] he wrote:

To the honorable leaders of the generations and chiefs of the congregation, the Lord hath drawn me close to you and it will be a joy in your midst. Behold, I am prepared to carry out my sacred job whensoever you may desire. May the Almighty grant me wisdom and understanding in the management of my holy flock, as my fathers and forefathers before me. Moreover, that I shall remain with you for six years and not accept a position elsewhere.

> The following year, 1794, Naftali became their Rabbi. He later became Rabbi of Winzenheim, Alsace, at the same time serving as president of the consistory of the Upper Rhine. He had a reputation of being an excellent preacher.
>
> In 1806, Emperor Napoleon convened the first Jewish Sanhedrin in almost two thousand years, in Paris. It consisted of seventy-one members, two thirds Rabbis and one third laymen, with Rabbi David Sinzheim of Strassbourg as President. R. Naftali was one of those Rabbis invited, and on that occasion was called Hirsch Lazare (i.e. Hirsch son of [Eliezer] Lazarus).[31] His published work was *Sha'ar Naftali*, published Frankfurt-on-Oder 1797. The title page lists his genealogy back some eight generations to the "MaHaRaM of Padua."
>
> He also wrote *Sha'arei Binah*, several commentaries, as well as his sermons and ritual decisions which are in manuscript extant in the Strasburg Library (France).
>
> He was married to Rachel, daughter of Feiwell of Glogau. He died in Winzenheim in 1828.

G9.2. Saul Katzenellenbogen (1740-1810), lived in Graetz and Posen.[32] He was married in 1770 to Hannah (died 1826), daughter of Ber Mezeritzer. They had a number of daughters, Frida being the eldest.

G10. Frida, 1781-1870, married David Lieb Ephraim of Graetz (1777-1855).

G11.1. Elieser (Leyser) Wertheim (1806-1863).

G12.1. Max, married and had issue.

G11.2. Sarah (1806-1866), married Kassriel Jablonski (1804-1884).

G12.1. Markus (1834-1870).
G12.2. Johanna (1839-1916), married David Foerder (1839-1912).

G13.1. Bertha, married Abraham Cohn, and had issue.

G13.2. Leo Foerder (1866-1923), married Paula Stern.

> G14.1. Betty, born 1898, married Harry Offenberg (born 1895). They lived in New York until 1971, when they settled in Jerusalem, Israel.
>
> > G15.1. Wolf (Abraham), born 1921 in New York, married and divorced. He has three children.
> >
> > G15.2. Miriam, born 1922, married Jacob Leisten (Tel Aviv), and they have issue.
>
> G14.2. Alice.
>
> G14.3. Margaret.
>
> G14.4. Kurt.
>
> G14.5. Rudolf.

G13.3. Michael Foerder, married and had issue.

G13.4. Henrietta Foerder, married Sigmund Cohn, and had issue.

G13.5. Herman Foerder, married and had issue.

G12.3. Pinchen Jablonski (1841-1903), married Salomon Badt (1841-1914) and they had issue.

G12.4. Sophie Jablonski (1845-1919), married Victor Simon (1833-1898).

> G13.1. Dagobert Simon, 1873-1931, married in 1910 to Hedwig, daughter of Dr. Rudolf Plaut (1885-1949).
>
> > G14.1. Eva, born in Berlin 1911. She studied veterinary medicine in Zurich, Switzerland. Married 1939 in New York to Thomas J. Reynolds, Ph.D., a college professor.
> >
> > G14.2. Susanne, born in Berlin 1913, married in New York 1940 to Frank L. Herz, a businessman.
> >
> > > G15.1. David Stanley Herz, born in New York 1946. He served in the U.S. Army for fourteen months in Vietnam.
> >
> > G14.3. Gabrielle Sophie Simon, born in Berlin 1920, educated at the University of Chicago. She was married in 1939 to Bert Schoenberg (born 1912), physicist, lawyer and pianist. They were divorced in 1944.

Gabrielle remarried in Chicago 1949 to John H. Edgcomb, M.D. (pathologist). He was born in Ottowa, Illinois 1922. They were divorced in 1967.

G15.1. Steven Jonathan Schoenberg, born in Chicago 1941. He was married in 1969 to Naita (Nikki) McMillan (born in Salt Lake City, Utah 1936).

G16.1. Anthony Paul Schoenberg, born in Los Angeles, California 1970.

G15.2. Julia Claire Edgcomb, born in Chicago 1951.
G15.3. John Simon Edgcomb, born in Washington, D.C. 1953.

G13.2. Frida Simon.
G13.3. Hugo Simon, born in Berlin 1880, married Gertrude Oswald (born 1883).

G14.1. Ursula Barbara, born 1911, married Wolf Demeter (born 1906). They live in Sao Paulo.

G15.1. Mark Roger, M.D., born 1931.

G14.2. Marie Sophie Anette, born in Brazil 1917, unmarried.

G12.5. Manasse Jablonski (1852-1882).
G12.6. Jenny Jablonski, married Julius Beer, and they had issue.

G11.3. Saul Ephraim (1810-1838).
G11.4. Karoline (1813-1842), married David Jablonski (1808-1888), and they had issue.
G11.5. Johanna (1815-1891), married David Jablonski, his second wife, and they had issue (including the Wollsteiner Family).
G11.6. Roschen (1815-1890), married Julius Glans (1817-1888).

G12.1. Regina, married Marcus Jablonski, son of David Jablonski (see above G11.4).
G12.2. Rosa (1851-1901), married Dr. Rudolf Plaut,[33] born in Mackenzell in 1843 and died in Frankfurt-on-Main in 1914. He was the son of Heinemann Plaut (1801-1889), son of Jacob Plaut. He became Rabbi in Schwersenz and Karlsbad and later in Frankfurt-on-Main. He was a friend of Baron Mayer Carl Rothschild (1820-1886) of Frankfurt who arranged his appointment in Frankfurt. Alfred Plaut said of his father Rudolf:

My father was born as one of many children of a cattle dealer and cattle farmer in Mackenzell near Fulda. (Mackenzell means some monk had his cell there. It is a Catholic country.) The other brothers and sisters stayed in the small town and became little merchants and bakers and butchers. This boy—his name was Ruben—which he Germanized later to Rudolf—appeared intelligent so they sent him to become a Rabbi. He studied in the Rabbinical schools in Hamburg and Mainz, and taught in high school while a student. He graduated as doctor of philosophy from the University of Berlin, writing a doctor's thesis on the Jewish Roman historian Flavius-Josephus. He studied Oriental languages. He was a very muscular, strong man.

>Rosa Glans Plaut did not lead a happy life. She was married in her teens, was more often pregnant than not, and saw four of her fourteen children die. At the age of 43 she had a stroke and was an invalid from then till her death at age 49.

>Rudolf Plaut was blind in his declining years and because of this he was pensioned off in 1904. Rudolf ruled his household with an iron hand. As they grew up, the children began to rebel. George and Hedwig went to the opera, which was forbidden, and took part in the teenage Wagner worship which was current then. George studied chemistry to please his father, but made his career in opera. He married a Gentile girl. Alice eloped with a "penniless Gentile fiddler" who came to play chamber music in their home. Martha succeeded in breaking out of the woman's role: her school principal pleaded with her father to send her to the University, but she did not continue her career in medicine. Some of the children retained their Judaism, but others, like Alfred, forsook religion altogether.

G13.1.   Frida Plaut, born in Karlsbad 1873, died in Theresienstadt November 8, 1942. She was married in Frankfurt 1895 to Max Mechanik, born Chweidan, Lithuania 1863-4, died Mainz 1930. He was educated at the University of Munich, and was a Doctor of Medicine.

>G14.1.   Alice, born Mainz 1896, died Hamburg 1941, married to Max Levin.

>G14.2.   Anton, born in Mainz 1905. He changed his name to Anthony Menk. He was educated at Hoch's Conservatory, Frankfurt, and the State Academy of Music

in Berlin. He is Assistant Professor of Music at University of Northern Colorado. Two of his compositions were published. He was married in New York 1955 to Mimi Loewin, born in Vienna 1905.

G13.2. Dr. Theodor Plaut, born in Karlsbad 1874, died in Wuppertal 1938. Married in Frankfurt 1904 to Meta Plaut, daughter of Nathan Plaut, R. Rudolf Plaut's brother. She was born in Mackenzell (Fulda) 1875, and died in Frankfurt 1934.

Theodor's second wife was Elli Katzenstein, born 1884, died 1938. Theodor and his wife Elli committed suicide together after the "Kristallnacht," on November 15, 1938, having married the previous month on the 19th of October.

G14.1. Elisabeth, born in Frankfurt 1906. She was educated at Schule Hellirau, Luxemburg, and at the Musieklyceum, Amsterdam. She was married in Bruxelles, Belgium 1936 to Leopold A. L. Meter, born in Koln (Rhein) 1909, and died in Poland 1944. He was a painter.

G15.1. Barbara Phillippine, born in Amsterdam 1939. Married to Mattyn Seip, born Rotterdam 1940. They are both film-makers. Their son, Alan Iskandar, born in Amsterdam 1972.

G14.2. Richard R., born in Frankfurt 1910. He changed his name to Richard R. Plant. He received a Ph.D. in German Literature at Basel, 1935. He wrote five books, among them a novel *Dragon in the Forest*, which gives a picture of old Frankfurt. He also wrote an opera, *Lizzie Borden*, 1965.

G13.3. Ella Plaut, born in Karlsbad 1880, died in New York 1964. Educated at Philanthropin, Frankfurt. Married in 1900 in Frankfurt to Bernhard Baer (1874-1912). He was a Doctor of Medicine.

Ella was remarried in Frankfurt 1915 to Moritz Werner (born Frankfurt 1873, died New York 1939). He earned a Ph.D., was a philologist, teacher at Lessing Gymnasium, Frankfurt. He was the author of *Kleine Beitrage zur Wurdigung Alfred de Mussets,* and numerous articles and contributions to scientific journals.

G14.1. Franz Alfred Baer, born Frankfurt 1901, died Leicester, England 1971. He changed his name to Frank Alfred Barr. He was a college lecturer in classical and modern languages, and a Fellow of the Institute of Linguists (England). He was married in 1933 to Martha Emma Stephanie Henrich, born in Karlsruhe 1898. She was a Froebel-trained teacher.

G15. Claus Bernard Louis Barr, born Offenbach-on-Main 1934. M.A. (Cambridge) in Classics; Postgrad. Diploma in Librarianship (London); Associate of the Library Association (U.K.); Librarian (University of York Library and York Minster Library). Married in Bishopthorpe, York to Evelyn Mary Storey in 1963.

G16. Carolyn Mary Barr, born in York 1965.

G14.2. Adolf Josef Werner, born in Frankfurt, 1917, educated at Goethe Gymnasium, Frankfurt, and at University of Illinois. He emigrated to the U.S. in 1936, and served in the U.S. Army 1943-46. He held several high positions in the U.S. government. He is an economist, and Vice-President of Smith, Barney & Co., Inc., N.Y. He is the author of *Gold is Dead.* He changed his name to Adolphe Joseph Warner. He was married in Oradell, New Jersey 1953 to Ursula Wolfer, born Berlin 1922, educated at Schiller Lyzeum, Berlin.

G15.1. Joan Warner, born in New York, 1955.
G15.2. Theodore Morris Warner, born in New York, 1957.

G13.4. Flora Plaut, born Karlsbad 1881, died Stocksund, Sweden 1964. Married in Frankfurt 1900 to Elias Gut (born Hufingen, Baden 1872 and died Stockholm, Sweden 1942). He was a teacher.

G14.1. Marie Rosalie (Mariechen), born Frankfurt 1901, educated at German Abitur. Married in Frankfurt 1925 to Hans Marcus (born Frankfurt 1901, died Berlin 1967).

G15.1. Rudolph Julius Marcus, born Frankfurt 1926. He

earned his Ph.D. in chemistry in 1954 from the University of Utah.

G14.2. Heinrich (Henry) Gut, born Frankfurt 1906, died Stockholm 1969. He was a businessman. He was married in Frankfurt 1934 to Johanna (Henny) Goldschmidt (born Frankfurt 1908, died Stockholm 1959). She was educated at the Music Conservatory in Frankfurt.

Heinrich remarried in New York 1963 to Emmy (Elisabeth Marta) Hellin nee Stross, born Liebauthal, Czechoslovakia 1911.

G15.1. Allan, born Stockholm 1944. Teacher at Uppsala University. Married in Stockholm 1967 to Anna Karin Hedberg, born Uppsala 1943.

G15.2. Thomas, born Upsala 1946, M.A. (Russian, mathematics, philosophy, education).

G13.5. Paula Plaut, born 1882 and died 1903.

G13.6. Georg, born Frankfurt 1883, died Buenos Aires, Argentina in 1950. He changed his name to Georg Pauly. He received his Ph.D. in chemistry. He was the author of *Aschenbrodel Ohr*. He was married in Berlin 1913 to Hermine C. H. Correns, born Stargard (Pomerania) 1887, and divorced in 1939. She graduated Stern'sches Conservatorium, Berlin. Georg was remarried in Buenos Aires, Argentine, 1950 to Dora Heyman (born 1898).

G14.1. Herta Hildegard Pauly, born Berlin 1913, Ph.D. Columbia University, New York, in philosophy. She was a professor of philosophy, and contributed many articles to professional journals.

G14.2. Irene Marie Pauly, born Breslau 1919. She was married to Pfarrer Siegfried Diemer, born 1915.

G15.1. Cordula, born 1946. She married Gert Rimner, M.D.

G16.1. Timo, born 1971.

G15.2. Heidi (Adelheid), born 1947.

G15.3. Siegfried Andreas, born 1951.

G14.3. Reinhard Georg Pauly, born Breslau 1920. Columbia University, B.A., M.A.; Yale University, M.Mus.,

Ph.D. He is a professor and musician. He is the author of *Music in the Classic Period* (1965) and *Music and the Theater* (1970). He married in South Carolina 1942 to Constance Hare, born Michigan 1920.

G15.1. Deborah, born New York 1948, student at Stanford University, Calif.
G15.2. Rebecca, born Portland, Oregon in 1950.
G15.3. Michael Hale Pauly, born New Haven, Conn. in 1953.

G13.7. Alice Plaut, born Frankfurt 1884, died Honolulu 1972. She was a German teacher, and a volunteer worker with the Honolulu Symphony. She was married in London, England 1907 to Hugo Kortschak, (born Graz 1884, died Honolulu 1957). He graduated Prague Conservatory, was a violinist, head of the Orchestral Instr. Dept., Yale University and Manhattan School of Music. He founded the Hugo Kortschak Quartet.

G14.1. Alice Kortschak, born Chicago, Illinois 1909. She is a pianist and teacher. She was married in New York 1961 to Werner Koenigsberger (born Vienna 1887, died 1972). He was administrator of Gisella Verein Insurance Co.
G14.2. Hugo Peter Kortschak, born Chicago, Illinois 1911, B.S. Yale University, 1933; Ph.D. Zurich, 1936. He is a biochemist, and discovered "C-4 Pathway of Photosynthesis." He has been a violinist with the Honolulu Symphony since 1937. He was married in Honolulu 1937 to Kate Leilani Van Heemskerck Duker (born Kilauea, Kauai, Hawaii 1911), B.S. University of Hawaii. She was principal of Honolulu Junior Academy 1962-66.

G15.1. Nonnie Winifred Van Heemskerck Kortschak, born 1937, died 1969.
G15.2. Alice Margaret Van Heemskerck Kortschak, born Honolulu 1939, B.A. Brown University. Married in Honolulu 1961 to Robert Broderick (born Honolulu 1938), B.A. Washington University.

G16.1. Nancy Rochelle, born LaRochelle, France, 1963.

G16.2. Catherine Edith, born Wailuku, Maui, Hawaii, 1965.

G16.3. Sarah Elizabeth, born Honolulu 1970.

G16.4. Richard Arthur, born in Honolulu in 1972.

G15.3. Beppie Judith Van Heemskerck Kortschak, born 1942, M.A. mathematics. Married in Hawaii 1963 to Michael Joseph Shapiro, born 1940 Hartford, Conn., Ph.D.

G16.1. Jonathan Kamehameha, born in Hawaii in 1968.

G16.2. Miranda Kate, born in Honolulu in 1972.

G15.4. Willa Elizabeth Van Heemskerck Kortschak, born Honolulu, 1945, B.A. University of Hawaii. Married in Honolulu 1966 to Francis W. Souza, Jr. (born Honolulu 1944), B.A. University of Hawaii. Divorced Jan. 17, 1973.

G16.1. Diane Lehualani, born Honolulu 1967.

G16.2. William Hugo, born Honolulu 1969.

G13.8. Hedwig Plaut, married Dagobert Simon. (See G11.2/ G12.4/G13.1. above.)

G13.9. Martha Plaut, born Frankfurt 1887, Doctor of Medicine. She was married in Kiel (Holstein) 1914 to Fritz H. Schulz (born Bunzlau, Silesia 1879, died Oxford, England 1957). He was a professor of Civil and Roman Law, and held chairs in Innsbruck, Kiel, Gottingen, Bonn, Berlin.

G14.1. Renate Helen, born Gottingen, 1917.

G14.2. Thomas F. Schulz, born Gottingen 1918, educated in German schools, London University, University of Chicago. Married in Washington, D.C. 1969 to Susan A. (born Steubenville, Ohio 1943), B.A. Music.

G14.3. Johann Christoph Friedrich Schulz, born Gottingen 1920, B.S. Mount Union College 1942; Ph.D. Syracuse University 1959, Professor of Chemistry. He was married in Brooklyn, N.Y. 1958 to Loretta Emma Salzmann (born in Brooklyn, N.Y. 1936), B.S. in biology Wagner College 1958; M.S. in special education New York University 1969.

G15.1. Kathy Lynn, born Staten Island 1961.

G15.2. Paul Frederick, born Staten Island, N.Y. 1964.

G14.4. Dorothea Luise (Dorli) Schulz, born Bonn 1926, B.A.
(Oxford) in Russian and French. She married in Glas-
gow, Scotland 1951 to Ronald Meek (born Welling-
ton, New Zealand, 1917), B.A., LLM (New Zealand);
Ph.D. (Cambridge). He is a professor of Economics
at the University of Leicester, U.K. They have two
adopted children.

G13.10. Alfred Plaut, born Frankfurt 1888 and died Washington,
D.C. 1962. M.D. Freiburg 1912, and also studied in
Paris and Hamburg. He came to America in 1922, and
worked as a pathologist at Barnart Memorial Hospital,
New Jersey, and at Women's Hospital, New York. He
was Director of Laboratories at Beth Israel Hospital,
New York 1929-49, and also held that position at Winter
V.A. Hospital, Topeka, Kansas. He was a professor at
New York University School of Medicine. He was involved in cancer research, and was the author of over
90 scientific publications. He was married in New York
1924 to Margaret Blumenfeld (born Hamburg 1894,
died Washington, D.C. 1963), Ph.D. in Political Econ-
omy, Heidelberg, 1921. His wife was the daughter of
Martin Blumenfeld and Anna, daughter of Siegmund
(died 1889) son of Aby Samuel Warburg (died 1856),
a member of the well-known family of that name. Siegmund's wife, Theophile, was the granddaughter of Gabriel Jacob (died 1853) son of Naftali Hirsch Gunzburg.
Gabriel was made "honorary and hereditary citizen" by
Czar Nicholas I of Russia in 1848 and his son was the
philanthropist Baron Horace Gunzburg.

G14.1. Thomas Franz Alfred Plaut, born New York 1925,
B.A. Swarthmore College, Pennsylvania, 1949; Ph.D.
(psychology) Harvard University 1956; M.P.H., Harvard School of Public Health 1957. He is a psychol-
ogist-sociologist, and has held various positions in
clinical psychology and psychological research. He
has taught at Harvard University and at Stanford
University, California. He is the author of *Alcohol
Problems* (Oxford University Press, N.Y. 1967), and

over 30 scientific publications. He was married in New York 1950 to Evelyn Zena McPuroff (born Windsor, Ontario, Canada 1927), B.A. University of Western Ontario, London, Canada 1947; Graduate studies in sociology at Wayne University, Detroit, Michigan.

G15.1. Melanie Margaret, born Boston, Mass. 1954. She is a member of the Janosik Dancers (Polish folk-dance company).
G15.2. Anthony Alexander, born Boston, Mass. 1955.
G15.3. Jeffrey Jonathan, born Boston, Mass. 1957.
G15.4. Daphine Ann, born Boston, Mass. 1960.
G15.5. Iris Louise, born Palo Alto, Calif. 1965.
G15.6. Roger David, born Palo Alto, Calif. 1966.

G14.2. Erich (Eric) Alfred Plaut, born New York 1927, B.S. Columbia University, N.Y. 1949; M.D. Columbia College of Physicians and Surgeons 1953. His professional interests include psychiatry and the law; community mental health.
G14.3. Peter Alfred, born New York April 18, 1933, and died New York May 4, 1933.

G12.3. Henrietta Glans, married twice, and had issue.

G11.7. Berhard Ephraim, 1819-1900, married Johanna Bergas (1819-1900) and they had issue.

Note: Full genealogical details can be obtained from "Genealogical Ubersicht" by Max Wollsteiner (Berlin, 1930).

III and IV—K. ELLENBOGEN and SELIGMANN FAMILIES

ANCESTRY

G6.6. R. Saul.
G7.4. R. Moses.
G8.3. R. Naftali Hirsch Katzenellenbogen of Schwabach, died 1800. He was also called Hirsch Moyses. He was born in Schwabach, where his father was the Rabbi. He studied in his youth under Jacob Cohen Popers of Frankfurt-on-Main, and later married his daughter, Frumet, as his first wife. At this time he published his *Toldot Adam* on the Talmud, from an old manuscript written by Moses ben Nachman,

published in Homburg 1740. From 1741-63 he was A.B.D. of Mergentheim, where he wrote approbations to:

1. *Zvi Kodesh* by Zvi ben David, published Sulzbach 1748.
2. *Daled Shitot LaRaSHBA* by Samuel Auerbach, published Furth 1751.
3. *Ma'amar Avraham* by Abraham Wallenstein, published Furth 1757.
4. *Chamesh Shitot* by Nachmanides, published Sulzbach 1762, eleventh edition.
5. *Reishit Chochma* by Elia diVidas, published Furth 1763.
6. Maimonides' *Yad Hachazakah*, published Furth 1767.

After his first wife died in 1733, he married Merle, daughter of Ellen Oppenheim of Hamburg (died Brody 1743) and Lieb Mochiah (father of Isaiah Berlin). She died in 1804. After Mergentheim, he was elected Chief Rabbi of the Palatinate (Pfalz or Kurpfalz) with his seat at Leimen, which he transferred to Manheim in 1768. There, despite ill health, he was surrounded by many pupils. In 1766 he was consulted by Rabbi David Hess of Manheim, who had been involved in the Cleves Case, declaring the "get" (divorce decree) invalid. Naftali, together with his brother, were, however, supporters of Rabbi Lipschutz in validating the "get." Naftali also reprimanded Rabbi Hess for corresponding with the Rabbinical Court of Frankfurt before contacting Rabbi Lipschutz. The case also involved his brother-in-law, Rabbi Joseph Steinhardt of Furth.

Naftali died in Manheim on September 21, 1800, and left behind manuscripts housed in Oxford.

G9.1. Meir Katzenellenbogen, of Lublin, born approximately 1725. He was known as Meir Charif and married Hanale, daughter of R. Haim Jonah son of R. Joseph, son of R. Aryeh Lieb, son of R. Joshua (Ezekiel Feiwel), son of Jonah Teomim.

G10. Nathan, born about 1765, brother-in-law of R. Baruch Teomim.

G11. Akiva, born about 1790, died about 1858, married Hannah who died about 1874.

G12.1. Judah Lieb, died at Pinczow 1934.

G13. Chana, married Abraham Vradlovsky.

G12.2. Etil, married Joseph Rosenberg, died 1914, and had issue.
G12.3. Nathan Mordecai Katzenellenbogen, born about 1824, and

died in Jerusalem 1896, and was buried on the Mount of Olives. He married Sheba, daughter of Jacob Weisenfeld. She died in Lublin 1911.

G13. Hyman Solomon, born about 1848 and died in Lublin 1920. He married Matil (died 1934), daughter of Avigdor Gromb. Their nine children and descendants make up the K. Ellenbogen Family. (See below K. Ellenbogen Family Pedigree—III.)

G9.2. Abraham Hirsch Katzenellenbogen of Vienna.

G9.3. Isaac Baer adopted the name Mannheimer, married in Furth to Frumet Neuberg.

G10. Lea (Luise), married Joseph Oberndorfer.

G11. Nanette, married Abraham Merzbacher, in Munich.

G9.4. Marx, married Fradel.

G9.5. Rachel, married Wolf Sulzbach.

G9.6. Lea, married Lazarus Nathan Halevi Boelling. Their children: Jeanette; Judith; Samuel; Rebecca; Hanchen; Hirsch; Frederika; Malta; Minchen; and Carl Nathan.

G9.7. R. Moses Aryeh Mannheimer,[34] born about 1750 in Mannheim. He married Malka, daughter of Haim Phineas Seligmann, the financial adviser and official agent of the Court of Hanau-Lichtenberg, and settled in Buchsweiler, the capital of the Court's municipality. He became administrator of the Yeshiva established by his father-in-law.

G10. R. Moses (Haim Phineas), born 1778. Under the temporary French rule, he was obliged to change his name in 1808, and adopted that of his maternal grandfather, calling himself Moyse Seligmann. He lived in Landau, and married Blumele Lipman (1784-1827). He died in 1836. They had nine children, six of whom died in early childhood.

G11.1. Malka, 1806-1876.

G11.2. Lena (Magdalene), 1813-1893, married Benedict Kohlmann.

G12. Emil (1852-1918), married twice.

G11.3. Professor Moses Seligmann. (See below IV—Seligmann Family Pedigree.)

III–K. ELLENBOGEN FAMILY PEDIGREE

ANCESTRY

G3.3. R. Saul Wahl Katzenellenbogen.
G4.1. R. Meir.
G5.2. R. Moses.
G6.6. R. Saul.
G7.4. R. Moses, died 1733.
G8.3. R. Naftali Hirsch, died 1800.
G9.1. Meir, born about 1725.
G10. R. Nathan.
G11. Akiva, died about 1858.
G12.3. Nathan Mordecai, died 1896.
G13. Hyman Solomon, died 1920.[35]

G14.1. Jonah Katzenellenbogen (1876-1941/2), married Miriam Greenberg.

G15.1. Nathan Kacen, born 1904, married Rachel (Kfar Saba, Israel).

G16.1. Miriam, born 1943, married Dov Segev (Kibutz Magal). They have two children.
G16.2. Bracha, born 1950, married Moshe Alpert (Kibutz Aphekim). They have two children.
G16.3. Eli, born 1946, married Leah in 1968, and have issue.

G15.2. Abraham, the eldest, born 1901, perished in the Holocaust with family.
G15.3. Reuben, born 1913, married Guta (Tel Aviv).

G16. Miriam, born 1952, married in 1973 Ilan Schechter.

G14.2. Israel Katzenellenbogen, c. 1888-1942.

G15.1. Menachem, born 1916, married Shoshana Halevy (Petach Tikva).

G16.1. Orit, born 1952.
G16.2. Bracha, born 1946.

G15.2. Avigdor Victor, born 1920, married Pnina Duvdevanim (Apheka). They have five children: Israel, Raya, Dorit, Gilead and Eran.
G15.3. Chana, born 1912, married Joseph Roshgold (Herzlia).

G16.1. Eli, born 1935, married Ilana Rabi. Their children: Barak, born 1961; Shelly, born 1963; and Allon, born 1965.

G16.2. Ita, born 1938, married in 1961 Dan Rees. Their children: Galit, Sharon and Liat.

G15.4. Zahavah (Kate) 1909-1960, married in 1939 to Zeev Elbinger.

G16.1. Dan Almagor, born 1935, married in 1960. He is a popular Israeli songwriter and producer of plays. Their children: Orna and Elinora.

G16.2. Bracha, born 1941, married Joseph Lev. Their children: Gali, born 1969 and Tali, born 1967.

G15.5. Raja Katzenellenbogen M.D., perished in the Holocaust.

G14.3. Chanah, married Isaac Goldstein.

G15. Edward Bartol, one-time Polish Ambassador to Washington.

G14.4. Sarah, married Solomon Eisner.

G14.5. Isaac Meyer K. Ellenbogen, born 1865 and died in New York in 1947. By profession he was a real estate broker and the author of a family genealogy entitled *Chevel HaKesef*, printed in New York. His obituary appeared in the New York Times (August 13, 1947).

He arrived in the U.S.A. in 1898 and in 1884 married Malka (Molly) Greenberg, a distant relative of the family. (See Chapter III, G11.3/G12./G13.4/G14.9.) His poetical capabilities find expression in his *Hegyon Libi* "Meditations of my heart" found in his *Chevel HaKesef*, and also in *Divrei Reb Meir*, a book of his sayings printed in New York by one of his sons which includes a short biography (1947).

G15.1. Kate, born 1891, married June 1924 to William Goldstein (died 1969).

G16. Marcella, born 1926, unmarried.

G15.2. Louis, born 1892, married 1924 to Dorothy Menkes. Both teachers by profession (Florida).

G15.3. Anita (1894-1942), married 1924 to Irving Hoffman (he later remarried).

G16.1. Marilyn, born 1925, married 1952 to Robert Aledort (Market Researcher, Little Neck, N.Y.). They have two children: Andrew and Amy.

G16.2 Elinor, born 1930, married in June 1958 to Harold Schapiro (Westport, Conn.). Their children: Anita, Martha and Sarah.

G15.4. Rose (1890-1972), married 1921 to Irving Eiten.

G16.1. George Ph.D., born 1925 (Brazil), married Liene Laine.
G16.2. Miles born 1928, married 1950 to Joy Peyser (Great Neck N.Y.). Their children: Jonathan, Emily, David and Danny.

G15.5. Nathaniel (1898-1969), married 1929 to Evelyn Jackter (N.Y.).

G16.1. Marion, born 1931, married 1956 to Lee Isenberg (West Hartford, Conn.). Their children: Neil and Allison.
G16.2. Ruth, born 1936, married 1958 to Andrew Flaxman (Fort Lee N.J.). Their children: Caroline, Garu and Laura.

G15.6. Mabel, born 1900, married 1922 to Harvey Brightman (Miami).

G16.1. Alfred, born 1929, married 1954 to Barbara Ehrlich (Westchester). Their children: David and Amie.
G16.2. Margery, born 1932, married 1951 to Roy Wallach (Westchester). Their children: Margot, Evan, Wendy and Bobby (died young).
G16.3. Richard, born 1935, married 1957 to Cassandra Sturman (N.Y.). Their son: Seth (adopted).

G15.7. Harry adopted the name Kent, born 1902. Divorced his first wife, and remarried in 1960 to Annuncia Lenze (Eze, France).
G15.8. Alice K. Ellenbogen, born 1904, married 1927 to Herman Meister (Florida) D.D.S.

G16.1. Malcolm, born 1931, Orthodontist, married 1955 to Margaret Shacter. Their children: Steven, Karen and Nancy.
G16.2. Daniel, born 1932, Orthodontist, married 1952 to Glenda Gabe. Their children: Michael, Julie and Susan.
G16.3. Judith, born 1938, married 1959 to Dr. Jerome Reich M.D. Their children: Gary, Jonathan, Andrew and James.

G14.6. Joseph Avigdor K. Ellenbogen (1867-1947). Arrived in the U.S.A. in December 1901. He married twice, his first wife died young, leaving three children. He remarried in 1898 to Mary Weitzenblut (died in 1953) and had issue as well.

G15.1. Louis, born 1888, married 1908 to Rae Shapiro (Nassau).

G16.1. Hilde, born 1910, married 1934 to Louis Sulkes (Manhattan).

G17.1. Ruby, born 1937, married 1957 to Fred Heiman (N.Y.). Their children: Vicky, Nancy and Michele.
G17.2. Paul, born 1941, married 1968 to Elaine Plawner. Their son: Joel.

G16.2. Bernard, born 1915, unmarried (Manhattan).
G16.3. Muriel, born 1923, married 1943 to Jules Dember (Long Island). Their children: Stuart, John (married 1971 to Janet Beck), Larry and Peggy.

G15.2. Jacob (Jack) (1889-1970). Married 1917 to Rose Schreiber. Buried in West Palm Beach.

G16.1. Helen, born 1918, married secondly to Theodore Berin (West Palm Beach).

G17.1. Barbara, married Rotman (D.D.S.).
G17.2. Jeff.

G16.2. Stanley, born 1923, married Doris Blicher. Their children: Paul, Mark and Marcia.

G15.3. Rose, born in 1897, married 1924/5 to Joseph Weiss (died 1954).

G16.1. Malcolm, born 1926, Ph.D. Chem. Eng., married 1948 to Carol Hershorn (Union, N.J.). Their children: Janet, Judy and Daniel.

G15.4. Nathan, born 1899, lawyer, married 1932 to Marion Bleiman. They have no issue.
G15.5. Saul, born 1901, lawyer, married 1928 to Sonni Zamsky. They have no issue.
G15.6. Morton (Morris), born 1903, married 1927 to Julia Weisenberger.

G16.1. Nina, M.D., born 1929 married to Jerome Raim M.D. (Miami). Their children: Ellen and Zina.
G16.2. Richard Ellenbogen, M.D. born 1943, married Rita (also M.D.).

G15.7. Ephraim (Franklyn), born 1904, lawyer, married 1928 to Mollie Berman.

G16.1. Franklyn Junior (1932-1953).

G16.2. Margery, born 1937, unmarried.

G15.8. Aaron (Archie), 1906-71, (West Va.).

G16.1. Peter, born 1942, married Rosanne. Their children: Paul, Charles and Sheila.

G16.2. James, married Celia.

G15.9. Sidney, born 1910, married 1937 to Florence Gleitsman (Manhattan).

G16.1. Linda, born 1939, married 1966 to Sidney Gurkin.

G16.2. Ann, born 1945, married 1967 to Jay Fegelhut (Los Angeles).

G16.3. Ira, born 1948.

G15.10. Abraham, born 1914, married 1941 to Sylvia Slobin. He retired as Assistant Administrator of Commercial Subjects of the New York City Schools.

G16.1. Jay, born 1947, married 1971 to Jane Shapiro and have issue (Montreal).

G16.2. Jon, born 1941, Ph.D. (Puerto Rico), married 1965 to Lou Ann Platnik.

G14.7. Akiva Samuel K. Ellenbogen (1870-1948). Arrived in New York about 1895. He was a United States Marshall of New York and a member of the Seventh Assembly Democratic Organization. He was also manager of the Hudson Terminal buildings, and a member of the Calanthe-Harvard Lodge No. 3, Knights of Pythias and of Tammany Hall. His obituary appeared in the New York Times (October 30, 1948).

G15.1. Rose, born 1899, married Mr. Elliot.

G16. Joseph (California).

G15.2. Nathan (Thomas) Foley Ellenbogen (1901-58), married 1932 to Harriet Hecht. He was an official of the New York City Real Estate Bureau, and an active Democrat in the borough of Queens. His obituary appeared in the New York Times (December 6, 1958).

G16.1. Leonore, born 1937, married 1965 to Stuart Goodman, and have issue.

G16.2. Joan L. Ellenbogen, Lawyer (N.Y.), born 1942.

G15.3. Victor, born 1904, married Beatrice. They had no issue. She has two children from a previous marriage.

G15.4. Ruth born 1906, married 1) Mr. Rosevear and 2) Mr. Mackay. They have no issue.

G15.5. Wilbur, born 1912, unmarried.

G14.8. Malka (Mollie), married 1) Mr. Zucker and 2) Morris Blumen-stock.

G15. Nathaniel Ellenbogen.

G14.9. Elias K. Ellenbogen, 1887-1956, Civil Eng., married Rae Bern-stein.

G15. Shirley, married Paul Rothkrug (Danbury, Conn.).

IV—SELIGMANN FAMILY PEDIGREE

ANCESTRY

G3.3. R. Saul Wahl Katzenellenbogen.
G4.1. R. Meir.
G5.2. R. Moses.
G6.6. R. Saul.
G7.4. R. Moses, died 1733.
G8.3. R. Naftali Hirsch, died 1800.
G9.7. R. Moses Aryeh Mannheimer.[36]
G10. Moyse (Haim Phineas) Seligmann, died 1836.
G11.3. Professor Moses Seligmann, born 1809 and died 1887 in Landau. He was Rabbi in Landau and Kaiserslautern. He studied under Rabbi Solomon Trier in Frankfurt-on-Main, and at the University of Heidelberg and Munich. He married Leonore (1831-1867), daughter of David Neugass (1793-1866) who took part in the Battle of Waterloo.

G12.1. Pauline (1859-1919), married Max Wasserman of Mannheim.

G13.1. Siegfried, born 1885.

G14. Bruno, born 1924.

G13.2. Ernst, born 1889.
G13.3. Paul, born 1891.

G14. Ellen, born 1932.

G12.2. Haim Phineas (Dr. Caesar) Seligmann, was born in Landau in 1860, and became the founder of Liberal Judaism in Germany. In 1889 he became Rabbi of the "Temple" in Hamburg. From 1902-39 he was the Chief Rabbi of the main Jewish congregation in Frankfurt. After the pogroms of November 1938, he emigrated to London, where he died in 1950. Caesar attained international repute in 1910 through his radically reformist *Israelitesches Gebetbuch,* and he also composed a German *Haggada fur der Sederabend* (1913). He was editor of the *Liberales Judentrun,* the official organ of the Liberal Judaism movement. He wrote numerous sermons and short essays under the title *Judentum und Moderne Weldanschauung* (1905) and also other articles on Mendelssohn's philosophies, and a Prayerbook with original poetic renditions.

On the occasion of his seventieth birthday the Hebrew Union College of Cincinnati[37] honored him with the title of "Doctor of Hebrew Law," an honor granted for the first time to a German. The accompanying letter read:

Able and Devoted Rabbi, Spiritual guide of two generations, scholarly interpreter of historic Judaism, fearless and creative Champion of Liberal Judaism, authoritative chronicler of its growth and achievements and pioneer of its renaissance in Germany, zealous participant in the organization of Progressive Judaism and wise and responsible counsellor in the shaping of its purpose and program.

Among his close friends were Rabbi Leo Baeck, Stephen Wise, Claude Montefiore and Lily Montague. "He was of small stature but of immense physical stamina," are the words of his son.

G13.1. Dr. Erwin Seligmann, born 1893, married 1920 to Lydia Mayer-Alapin.[38] He was a judge and attorney in Frankfurt-on-Main and fled Germany in 1938 together with his parents and sisters. They settled in London.

G14.1. Ruth, born 1921, married and divorced. Their son: Michael, born 1958.

G14.2. Margrit, born 1923, married Rudolf Bollheimer. Their children: David, born 1958; Judy, born 1961; and Richard John, born 1964.

G14.3. Erika (Chana), born 1928, married Dan Cohn. They settled in Kibbutz Lahavot HaBashan. Their children: Gilah, Naomi and Deborah.

G13.2. Dr. Leo James Selwyn, born 1896, married 1923 to Lily Birn-
baum. He received his surgical training in the Jewish Hospital
of Frankfurt, and emigrated to the U.S.A. in 1923, settling
in Beverly Hills, Calif., with a practice in Internal Medicine.

G14. Herbert Selwyn, born 1925, Ph.D. Law. His first marriage
ended in divorce. He married a second time to Sheila Aronson
and they were divorced in 1972. His son from his first wife:
Christopher, born 1950. His children from his second wife:
Pamela, born 1958; Brian Keith, born 1960; and Jennifer, born
1962.

G13.3. Ilse Seglow, born 1900, married secondly to Ziegellaub. She
has a Ph.D. in Psychoanalysis.

G14. Peter, born 1934, Sociologist and Economist, married Jean,
daughter of Sir Alan (Aird) Moncrieff, C.B.E., M.D., F.R.C.P.,
F.R.C.O.G. (The Royal Paediatrician). Their son: Jonathan
Paul, born 1968.

G13.4. Lore (Leonore, Evelyn), Ph.D. in Philosophy and Economics,
born 1907, married 1937 to Paul Anderson, later divorced. They
have no issue.

CHAPTER III

BRANCH A

Descendants of

R. NAHUM KATZENELLENBOGEN OF SLUTZK

G9.1. Minz and Greenberg Families
G9.2. Follman and Shereshovsky Families

Ancestry

G3.3. R. Saul Wahl.

G4.1. R. Meir Wahl.

G5.3. R. Nahum of Slutzk.

G6. R. Nathan Katzenellenbogen, A.B.D. Meseritz (near Warsaw). Died in 1689 and was buried in Jerusalem.

G7. R. David, A.B.D. Kotsk, died in 1711.

G8. R. Menachem Nahum Katzenellenbogen.

G9.1. R. Isaac Mintz (Minz), head of Minz and Greenberg Families.

G10. R. Ze'ev Wolf Pastecher Minz of Meseritz.[1]

G11.1. R. Aaron (Arosh), died in Meseritz in 1831. His eulogy appears in *Eivel Yachid* by R. Dov Berish son of David Ploheim of Meseritz. He married Rebecca Lidda.

G12.1. R. Alexander Susskind Minz of Brody.

G13.1. Meir, 1814-1866. He was the author of *Ein Wort Zur Zeit* (1848), *Lelewels Kampf um Recht* and *Die Judenfeinde*.

G14.1. Abraham, married Miriam Gitel, daughter of Israel Bornstein.

104

G14.2. Jerachmeel; G14.3. Israel (Isidore); G14.4. Fischel (Felix).

G13.2. First wife of R. Uri Ber Gunzberg son of R. Aryey Lieb. (See below G12.7.)

G14. R. Aryey Lieb Gunzberg of Vilna.

G12.2. Mattithiah Minz.
G12.3. Avigdor, adopted the name Greenberg.
G12.4. Hirsch, adopted the name Klatzko, married the daughter of R. Samuel Judah Klatzes of Vilna. (See below G12.9.)
G12.5. Judah Lieb Minz of Meseritz, died 1862.
G12.6. Menachem Nahum Minz, married three times:
  1) Zlota, daughter of Haim Rokeah of Dubno.
  2) Chaya Frume, daughter of Isaac Zablodovsky of Bialystok.
  3) Jochebed, daughter of Zalman Bornstein.
  From the first wife:

G13.1. Joshua, married daughter of R. Heschel, A.B.D. Stry.
  From the second wife:
G13.2. Malka, married Jehiel Michael, son of Meshullam Feiwel Friedland (of Slutzk, 1804-1854), son of Samuel Zangwill. Meshullam's son, Moses Aryey Lieb, was the noted bibliophile (1826-1899) whose collection in St. Petersburg (Russia) is known as *Bibliotheca Friedlandiana*. (See Chapter XVII — Rokeach and Lewin-Epstein Families — G12/13.2/14.2/15/16.)

G14. Feiwel Friedland of Warsaw.

G13.3. Pesha, married Shalom Haronstein.
G13.4. Aaron.
G13.5. Alexander Ziskind.
G13.6. Rivke, married Akiva Cohen.
G13.7. Jehiel Michael, born in Bialystok 1838, and died in Berlin 1893. He married Olga, daughter of Meshullam Feiwel Friedland. (A brother and sister of the Minz Family married a sister and brother of the Friedland Family.)

G14.1. Nahum.
G14.2. Samuel Feiwel of Riga who wrote his family pedigree which appears at the end of *Da'at Kedoshim* by Eisenstadt (1897-8).
G14.3. Aaron.
G14.4. Ze'ev Wolf.

G14.5. Mordecai.
From the third wife:

G13.8. Isaac.

G12.7. Channah (died in 1842), married 1) R. Joshua Heschel Marshalkovitch son of R. Samuel Marshalkovitch son of R. Mordecai Zeev Ashkenazi, son-in-law of R. Mordecai Zadok Marshalkovitch of Dubno (see Landau Family Pedigree—G9.2/10.2
/11.2), and 2) R. Uri Ber Gunzberg of Vilna as his second wife
(see above G12.1/13.2).

G13. R. Tuvia Gunzberg, married Channah daughter of R. Mordecai Zeev Ettinge.[1a] (See Part III, Chapter XII; Branch E
G9.2/10.5/11.1/12.3.)

G12.8. Golda, married Eliezer Landau.
G12.9. Toyba Leah, second wife of Samuel (Judes) Klatzkes, son of
Israel Haim ("Wolper"). His first wife was Rivke, daughter of
Judah Klatzkes. Samuel was one of the leaders of the commu-
nity in Vilna, and died there in 1837.

G13.1 David, married the daughter of Isaac Reb Zalman Uries.
G13.2. Zisel (Ziskind), married the daughter of Jacob Friedes of
Sokolov.
G13.3. Heschel.
G13.4. Haim, married the daughter of Ezekiel son of Isaac son of
Abraham Landau.
G13.5. Uri Lieb, married three times:
1) daughter of Isaac Reb Zalman Uries.
2) daughter of Gedalliah.
3) daughter of Heschel Sirkin.

G11.2. Zvi Hirsch Minz.

G12. Daughter, married Isaac Lowenstein, A.B.D. Amsterdam.

G11.3. Meyer Greenberg.

G12. Zvi Ezekiel of Wladova, died 1888.

G13.1. Wolf Greenberg.
G13.2. Sarah Zelda, married Apeldman.
G13.3. Reizel, married Naftali Pernik.
G13.4. Meyer Greenberg, died 1894. He was married twice, and
had eight daughters and a son (from both wives).

G14.1.   Rebecca 1880-1965, married Hyman (Herman) Friedman.
         They arrived in the U.S.A. in 1905.

G15.1.   Meyer, 1901-1964, married Rose Greenberg (daughter
         of Henry son of Nahum; they were third cousins).

G16.1.   Howard Charles, born 1936, married Jessamyn Hiatt.
         They have no offspring. He is an attorney in Man-
         hattan.

G16.2.   Roberta Marilyn, born 1926, married in 1949 to Irving
         Silverfarb, an attorney for CARE. Their daughter,
         Hilary, born 1950.

G16.3.   Elaine Lita, born 1929, married in 1950 to Edward
         Goldberg, a patent attorney. They live in New Jersey.
         Their children, Todd Harley, born 1959, and Melanie
         Sue, born 1963.

G15.2.   Louis,[4] born 1906 in New York, where he attended pub-
         lic schools and Commercial High School in Brooklyn. He
         graduated from New York Law School in 1927, and
         was admitted to the New York State Bar in 1928. In
         1933 he formed a partnership with his brother Malcolm
         under the name of Friedman & Friedman.
         He had been active in many charitable and religious
         drives in his district (16th and 19th Assembly Districts
         of Kings County) when he was a Democratic Senator.
         He was a trustee of the Brooklyn Law School and chair-
         man of the Speakers Bureau of the 16th Assembly Dis-
         trict Democratic Club. He was also a member of vari-
         ous New York bar associations, clubs and charitable or-
         ganizations.
         In 1938 and 1942 he was a delegate to the Democratic
         State Convention. From 1941-44 he was representative
         of the 16th Assembly District of Kings County in the
         State Assembly, and was elected to the State Sen-
         ate in the 1944 general election and re-elected there-
         after. During the Second World War, he was active in
         many war activities, including vice-chairman of the Of-
         fice of Civilian Defense.
         He was married in 1953 to Beth Hollander. Their daugh-
         ters, Ellen Lynne, born 1954, and Cathy Jayne, born
         1956.

G15.3. M. Malcolm, born 1908, attorney in partnership with brother Louis above. He was married in 1953 to Ethel Scheintop. Their children. Lloyd Selby, born 1954, and Hope Bonnie, born 1960.

G15.4. Sarah, born 1911, married Anshel Fishman, living in New Jersey.

G16.1. Fern Barbara, born 1939, married in 1964 to Donald Segal.
Their sons, Richard Mark, born 1966, and Robin, born 1969.

G16.2. Robert Stephen, M.D., born 1945, was Internist Resident at Mt. Sinai Hospital in New York.

G15.5. Edna (Anne), born 1915, married twice. Her second marriage was in 1945 to Henry A. Schillinger (died 1971).

G16.1. Susan Lynn, born 1947, married Ermilo Novelo (Mexico). Their son, Ermilo, born 1971.

G14.2. Beila Greenberg, (from the first wife), died circa 1930, buried in Beth David Cemetery, Elmont, Long Island, N.Y. She married Abraham Rubin who died in Europe circa 1901.

G15.1. Joseph, 1906-1944, married in 1927 to Ida Galchinsky.

G16.1. Fay, born 1931, married in 1953 to Melvin Kwartler. Their children, Jodi born 1961. Robin born 1959 and Jeffrey born 1956.

G16.2. Barbara born 1938, married in 1961 to Jack Catalano (Florida). Their son, Jack born 1963.

G16.3. Philip born 1928, married in 1971 to Eleanore (Florida).

G15.2. Meyer (Murray) born 1896 in Florida, married in 1918 to Sadie (Sarah) Silberlicht.

G16.1. Herbert Robbins born 1919, married in 1947 to Harriet Arbeit. Their children, David, born 1949 and Andrea born 1951.

G15.3. Katie, 1899-1955, married Jack Pattinger (died 1959).

G16.1. Howard born 1920, married in 1948 to Vivian Gewirtz. Their children, Beverly, born 1948, and Jay born 1952.

G16.2. Arthur born 1918, married in 1939 to Ethel Nemeroff.

  G17.1. Edward born 1942, married in 1966 to Judith. Their children, Marcy born 1968, and David born 1971.

  G17.2. Barbara born 1947, married in 1968 to Allan Rogers. Their son Jason born 1969.

G14.3. Isaac Greenberg, married.

  G15.1. Mary, born 1897, married Jack Weinstein.

    G16.1. Eugene born 1927, married in 1968 to Gloria Goodman. Their son, Matthew born 1971.

  G15.2. Meyer died in Haifa, Israel.

G14.4. Bracha (Bertha), 1888-1965, she was the youngest daughter from the second wife. She was married in 1912 to Hyman Goldman.

  G15.1. Meyer born 1913, married in 1948 to Rita Weber. No offspring.

  G15.2. Benjamin (Bernard), born 1915, married in 1941 to Evelyn Dunaisky.

    G16.1. Neisa, born 1948, married in 1970 to Arthur Solop.
    G16.2. Gary, born 1956.

  G15.3. Mattie (Madeline), born 1921, married in 1944 to Arthur Weisenfeld, D.D.S. Their children, Linda, born 1956, and Robert, born 1951.

G14.5. Martha (Matil) 1883-1959, married in 1910 to Sol Anker.

  G15.1. Mary, died in childhood, 1908-1915.
  G15.2. Evelyn, born 1915, married in 1936 to Martin Elkind, an architect.

    G16.1. Elizabeth, born 1940.
    G16.2. Jessica born 1943, married in 1969 to William Brezina. Their son, Eric, born 1971.

  G15.3. Dr. Frank Anker, Oakland, California, born 1913, married in 1942 to Miriam Amster. Their children, Daniel, born 1944, Susan, born 1950, and Elizabeth, born 1954.

G15.4. Marcelle, born 1918, married in 1941 to Norman Dolid. Their children, Margaret, born 1945, and Peter, born 1951.

G15.5. Charlotte, born 1920, married in 1943 to Dick Nelson. Their children, Eric, born 1948, and Lisa, born 1950. She remarried in 1969 to Ernst Von Glaserfeld.

G14.6. Sima Greenberg (from the first wife), married. She visited the U.S.A. in 1930. They had two daughters.

G15.1. Motil, married twice. Her second husband was Mr. Nirenberg of Netanya, Israel.

G16.1. Israel (from first marriage), Canada.
G16.2. Joseph (from second marriage).

G14.7. Reizel Greenberg.
G14.8. Nechama Greenberg.
G14.9. Malka Greenberg, married Meyer, son of Hyman Solomon K. Ellenbogen. (See K. Ellenbogen Family Pedigree—Chapter II, G14.5.)

G13.5. Nahum Greenberg, married Bosha.

G14.1. Hanoch (Henry) 1873-1938, buried Mt. Lebanon, N.Y. He married Toyva Katz.

G15.1. Rose, married Meyer Friedman. (See Meyer Greenberg Family.)
G15.2. Gitel, 1896-1963, married Isidore Kantor.

G16.1. Marion, born 1915, married Charles Cohen.

G17.1. Arlene, married Dean Brandes. Their son, Charles.
G17.2. Ira.
G17.3. Mildred, married Joel Lipkin. Their daughter, Gena, born 1972.

G16.2. Nathan, born 1916, married in 1944 to Eleanor Keller. Their children, Irwin, Mark and Rhona.
G16.3. Leonore, married Clement Tetkowski (Art Director of the University of Buffalo). Their children, Diane, married Miller, Myra, and Neil.

G14.2. Fred Greenberg, 1876-1962, married in 1904 to Rachel Kaplan. He remarried in 1931 to Jeanette Hoffman.

G15.1. Larry Greenberg, born 1911. He changed his name to Lawrence J. Greene. He was married in 1942 to Ruth Hershkovitz, and later divorced.

G15.2. Pearl, born 1905, married in 1929 to Milton Grand, M.D.

G16.1. Richard Grand, M.D., born in 1937, married in 1965 to Myra Mandel. Their children, Peter Frederick, born 1969, and Julia Helen, born 1971.

G16.2. Ellen, born 1940, is an art historian.

G14.3. Samuel (Sam), Greenberg. Had two children.

G14.4. Son, married. After being widowed, she migrated with his daughter to Phoenix, Arizona.

G15.1. Rachel Greenberg married Arnold Smith, and had issue.

Follman and Shereshovsky Families

G9.2. R. Benjamin Benas Katzenellenbogen—Head of Follman and Shereshovsky Families.[5]

G10. R. Judah Lieb Katzenellenbogen, A.B.D. of Viyaski (Lithuania), married Liebe, daughter of R. Isaac son of Liebus Korbel.

G11.1. Nathan Rabinowitz of Semiaticz, died in Jerusalem.

G11.2. Phineas Rosenblum of Tiktin.

G12. Liebel of Warsaw.

G13. Daughter, married Jehiel Michael Isaac Follman of Warsaw (see below G11.4/12.2/13.1).

G11.3. Ze'ev Wolf Follman of Warsaw.

G11.4. Jacob Follman of Danzig, married daughter of R. Nachman A.B.D. Meseritz.

G12.1. Mordecai Isaac of Warsaw.

G13.1. Jehiel Michael of Plotzk.

G13.2. Azriel Judah Lieb of Radomsk.

G13.3. Solomon Nathan of Warsaw.

G13.4. Isaiah Ze'ev Wolf of Pietrokov, married the daughter of R. Michael Michelson (Klausner). (See Michelson Family Pedigree.)

G14.1. Hanoch.

G14.2. Wife of Shabtai Mordecai Halevi Sheinfeld.

G13.5. Israel Aaron of Warsaw.

G13.6. Blume, married Jacob son of Aaron HaKohen Chavit of Warsaw.

G12.2. Judah Lieb of Warsaw.

G13.1. Jehiel Michael Isaac, married daughter of Liebel Rosenblum
(see above).

G14.1. Phineas Menachem of Danzig.

G14.2. Jacob Kalonymus of Brooklyn, N.Y.

G14.3. Solomon of Warsaw.

G14.4. Moses of Jerusalem.

G14.5. Eli, engineer in Jerusalem.

G14.6. Joseph Dov of Warsaw.

G14.7. Judah Lieb, engineer in Danzig.

G14.8. Itel, married Joshua Heschel Epstein of Warsaw.

G14.9. Sarah, married Joseph Fliegelman of Warsaw.

G14.10. Rachel.

G13.2. Gershon of Warsaw.

G13.3. Abraham Benjamin, of Brooklyn, N.Y.

G12.3. Miriam, married Eleazar son of Jehiel Michael Joseph Margolioth of Warsaw.

G12.4. Liebe, married Isaac Appelbaum of Basel, Switzerland.

G13.1. Jacob (Hans), of Berlin.

G13.2. Baruch (Berthold), of Basel.

G13.3. Leah (Lettie), married Blushstein, Ph.D. Philosophy, Tel
Aviv.

G13.4. Channah (Anna), married Dr. Segal of Frankfurt-on-Oder.

G11.5. Menachem Mendel Follman, Parnas of Warsaw, died 1875.

G12.1. Liebus, of Warsaw, died 1886.

G13.1. Chaya Reize Brest, married David Moses son of Israel Asher
(of Brest) Shereshovsky (of Warsaw), died 1915.

G14.1. Raphael Nahum Shereshovsky, Polish political figure.

G14.2. Michael Shereshovsky.

G13.2. Liebe Pearl, married Aaron Zalman Landau, son of R. Alex-
ander (died 1884), son of R. Jehiel Shalom Shakna, son of
R. Joseph of Brody (descendants of R. Ezekiel Landau
Noda BiYehuda). (See Landau Family Pedigree.)

G12.2. Michael Jehiel David.
G12.3. Aaron.

G13.1. Saul Noah of Warsaw.
G13.2. Mirl married Israel Halpern of Warsaw.
G13.3. Hinde, married Kalman Rosen.

G12.4. Nahum of Warsaw, died 1911, married Hinde (died 1921), daughter of R. Joseph son of Saul son of Lieb (A.B.D. Lisk) Popirna. Joseph married the daughter of Mordecai Ze'ev Ettinge (see Ornstein-Ettinge Family Pedigree G9.2/10.5/11.1 /12.2).

G13.1. Mirl, married Abba Tzemach of Warsaw.
G13.2. Mordecai Ze'ev of Moscow.
G13.3. Hinde, married Itamar Goldlust of Warsaw.
G13.4. Liebus of Berdichev.
G13.5. Esther, married Naftali Hirsch Markoshevitz of Warsaw.
G13.6. Deborah, married Nahum Zuker son of Abraham Simcha Zuker.

G14.1. Mirl, married Joseph Rosenowitz of Warsaw.

G15. Abraham Moses (Alexander).

G14.2. Joseph of Warsaw.
G14.3. Sheine Yente, died unmarried in 1926.
G14.4. Abraham Simcha of Warsaw.
G14.5. Menachem Mendel of Warsaw.

G12.5. Feige, married R. Israel Krossotsky, author of *Mitzvot Yisrael* and *Torat Yisrael*. He died in Cracow in 1903.

G13.1. Judah Lieb married daughter of Ze'ev Wolf Mendelssohn, author of *Trumat Zahav*.
G13.2. Nehemiah Gershon of Warsaw.
G13.3. Nahum of Warsaw.

G12.6. Liebe, married Raphael Shapiro.
G12.7. Reizel, married Israel Michael Zetil of Vilna.

G13. Judah Lieb of Warsaw, died 1918.

G14.1. Moses of Zurich, engineer.
G14.2. Malka, married Shlomo Kottlier of Paris.
G14.3. Menachem Mendel of Warsaw.
G14.4. Aaron of Warsaw.
G14.5. Ze'ev Wolf of Warsaw.

BRANCH B

DESCENDANTS OF
ISRAEL SON OF MEIR SON OF SAUL WAHL

ANCESTRY

G5.4.   R. Israel.

G6.   R. Solomon Zalman Katzenellenbogen.

G7.   Wife of R. Moses (born Vilna circa 1661) son of R. Hillel (author
        of *Beit Hillel*). In his youth he studied at Kalicz under R. Abraham
        Abbale (author of *Magen Avraham*), and afterwards went with his
        father to Poland and Germany. At his father's request he arranged
        all his father's manuscripts which were published shortly after the
        latter's death under the title *Beit Hillel* (1691). He became A.B.D.
        Kempen about this time. He later settled in Vilna as A.B.D. where
        he wrote an approbation in 1721 on *Ateret Zvi* by R. Zvi Azriel of
        Vilna, published Jassnitz in 1722.

        He died in Vilna in 1726, the same year that R. Abraham son of
        David Katzenellenbogen met the wonder child Elijah, who later be-
        came a famous Talmudic scholar known as the Gaon (Genius) of
        Vilna.

G8.   R. Solomon Zalman of Vilna.

G9.   Wife of R. Isaac son of Eliezer (A.B.D. Kossov), succeeding his
        father-in-law as A.B.D. of Vilna. He wrote a number of manu-
        scripts as well as annotations to the works of his father-in-law.

BRANCH C

DESCENDANTS OF
R. JUDAH WAHL (KATZENELLENBOGEN)

THE MENDELSSOHN FAMILY

G3.3.   R. Saul Wahl.

G4.1.   R. Meir Wahl.

G5.6.   Judah Wahl, called the "younger," as he was named after his de-
        ceased brother. He married Dreizel, daughter of R. Simeon Wulff of
        Vilna, who settled in Hamburg and died in 1682. Judah and Dreizel
        were distantly related by virtue of the fact that his maternal grand-
        mother Miriam was a sister to Simeon Wulff's ancestor, the prom-

inent Talmudist from Cracow, where the family originated, R. Moses Isserles (known in the Rabbinical world as the "ReMa" 1520-72). [Dreizel the elder, was the wife of R. Simha Bonem Meisel of Cracow.—See chart.]

G6. Saul Wahl, named after his great-grandfather, and thus born sometime after 1620. He went to Dessau in his latter years, in 1682, and died there on July 5, 1717, about a hundred years after his namesake. Dessau was the chief town of the German Duchy of Anhalt. About the time of Saul's arrival there were only twenty-six Jewish families. Among them was R. Moses (Berend) Benjamin Wulff (called the "Tall Jew"), his first cousin, and a Court Jew in Dessau where he had settled in 1672.[6] It seems most likely that Saul went there because of his cousins, who had found life more satisfactory in the Germany Duchy. R. Moses established a Beth HaMidrash there which was headed by R. Benjamin Wolf.

Saul Wahl married Sisa (Susanna, died in 1730) daughter of R. Menachem Man of Kalicz. Through the intercession of the Wulffs, Saul received permission from the Duke Johann Georg of Dessau to open the first brandy factory in 1696. Records also mention Saul and Sisa Wahl as visitors to the popular annual event in the nearby city—the Leipsic Fair. About seven hundred and fifty Jews used to attend the fair in its early years, and were involved in buying and selling the many goods on display. They were even permitted to have their own rooms for prayer *Judenschulen*, so that by the year of Saul's death, there were separate rooms for each of the Jewish groups from Berlin, Dessau, Halberstadt, Hamburg and Prague.

G7. Bela Rachel Sarah, died in 1756, married Menachem Mendel Heymann, a poor Torah Scribe, born in 1683, and died in Dessau in 1766 in the month of Sivan. They had a daughter and two sons.

G8.1. Saul Mendelssohn.

G8.2. Jente Mendelssohn.

G8.3. Moses (Dessau) Mendelssohn, who was born in Dessau on September 6, 1729. In later years he often signed himself as "Moses Dessau." In the Jewish World he was considered to be the "third Moses" with whom a new era of Judaism began. His first teacher was R. Hirsch who instructed him in Talmud and then he studied under the Rabbi of Dessau, David Frankel (also called R. David Mirels). R. Frankel later became the Chief Rabbi of Berlin in 1742 and the following year after he had his Bar-Mitzvah, young Moses followed his mentor to the

Prussian capital. Frankel exerted a profound influence upon his pupil and introduced him to the *Moreh Nevuchim* (Guide to the Perplexed) by the sage Moses Maimonides. He also found him free lodging and a few days board weekly in the house of Haim Bamberger.

In his early childhood, Moses developed a curvature of the spine which left him hunchbacked. Moses also learned mathematics and logic from Israel Zamocz, and Latin from Abraham Kisch. Another friend only six years his senior was Aaron Solomon Gomperz who introduced him to philosophy and inspired him with a love of literature. Through him Moses also learned French and English.

In 1750, as a young man, Moses Mendelssohn became the tutor to the children of the rich silk manufacturer in Berlin, Bermann Zilz, and four years later he became his bookkeeper and finally his partner. At the same time he befriended Gotthold Ephraim Lessing (to whom he was originally introduced by Gomperz), a prominent German liberal writer. Between them a number of books were published between 1755 and 1756. These works revealed his profound understanding of Philosophy.

Through Lessing, Mendelssohn met and became a close friend of the book dealer Friedrich Nicolai. By 1761 he was well established and acclaimed with a large circle of good friends and a small fortune. In April that year he went to Hamburg and was welcomed by both Christian admirers and Jews. The Jewish Community was then headed by the Chief Rabbi of Altona-Hamburg-Wandsbeck, R. Jonathan Eybeschutz. The following year in June, Moses married Fromet (1737-1812) the daughter of Abraham Guggenheim (died 1766), and a great-granddaughter of the Court Jew Samuel Oppenheimer (1635-1703). He was close to thirty-one years of age at the time. His great-grandson, Sebastian Hensel, wrote about him:

Mendelssohn was short and much misshapen; he had a hump upon his back, and he stammered. When Fromet heard that he had proposed to marry her. . . . "She said she was frightened on seeing you." "Because I have a hump?" Guggenheim (her father) nodded. "I thought so; but I will still go and take leave of your daughter."

He (Mendelssohn) went upstairs and sat down by the young lady, who was sewing. They conversed in the most friendly manner, but the girl never

raised her eyes from her work, and avoided looking at him. At last, when he
had cleverly turned the conversation in that direction, she asked him:

"Do you then believe that marriages are made in heaven?"

"Yes, indeed," said he, "and something especially wonderful happened to
me. At the birth of a child proclaiming marriage is made in heaven, He or
she shall marry such and such a one. When I was born, my future wife was
also named, but at the same time it was said, Alas! she will have a dreadful
humpback. O God, I said, a deformed girl will become embittered and unhappy, whereas she should be beautiful. Dear Lord, give me the humpback,
and let the maiden be well made and agreeable!"

Scarcely had Moses Mendelssohn finished speaking when the girl threw
herself upon his neck: she afterwards became his wife, they lived happily
together, and had good and handsome children, whose descendants are still
living.[7]

In June 1763 he won the Prize of the Berlin Academy
of Science, and in October, received the privilege of a protected Jew, thus being exempt from paying Jewish taxes. Another important philosophical work *Phadon* appeared in
1767 which earned him the title of the "German Plato," and
also the "German Socrates." He became highly respected and
was honored by royalty as well. He also corresponded with a
number of prominent people of his generation. He actively defended his belief and his religion whenever he was attacked
by Gentiles or his Orthodox coreligionists alike.

Wishing to teach the people German, he translated the
Bible into German. The work which appeared in 1780 was
welcomed by prominent rabbis, among then R. Hirschel Levin
and his son R. Saul (both also descendants of R. Saul Wahl
Katzenellenbogen). Yet others placed the work under a ban.
His next efforts were directed at emancipation of the Jews.
During this period of his efforts he had the *Vindicae Judaeo-
rum* of Manesseh ben Israel translated from English into Ger-
man, and also wrote his famous *Jerusalem* as a defense against
Christian attacks.

"Mendelssohn's health was always naturally weak, and
had been undermined in early youth by overwork and insuf-
ficient food," writes Hensel. . . . ". . . he caught a cold, which
seemed at first unimportant, but quickly became worse; and
on January 4, 1786 he died (he was fifty-six years old). His
end, like that of nearly all his progeny, was sudden and almost
painless."[8]

His centenary of birth and death were commemorative events, and the city of Dessau erected a monument to him. He did not live to see the birth of any of his grandchildren who became famous in their own right. He had five sons and five daughters.

1. Sarah 1763-64.
2. Breindel (Veronika) Dorothea 1764-1839.
3. Haim 1766-66.
4. Rechel (Reikl) 1767-1831.
5. Mendel Abraham 1769-1775.
6. Joseph 1770-1848.
7. Henrietta (Jette) 1775-1831.
8. Abraham 1776-1835.
9. Susgen, born 1778, died young.
10. Nathan 1782-1852.

Moses Mendelssohn was a descendant of the Wulff Family (see above). One of the daughters of Simha Bonem Wulff (died in 1756), Marianne (died in 1788), was married to Daniel Itzig (1722-1799),[9] the prominent German Court Banker, and financial helper of Emperor Frederick the Great in his wars. He was also the head of the Jewish Communities of Prussia. This couple had five sons and some ten daughters. Through their children and grandchildren, there were inter-marriages into other members of the Wulff Family and with the children and grandchildren of Moses Mendelssohn. One Itzig daughter, Cecelia, married a Simha Benjamin Wulff, and two grandsons, Benjamin and his brother Jacob Israel Itzig, (sons of Isaac Itzig) married Wulff daughters. Another Itzig daughter, Henrietta, married Moses' son, Nathan. Two Itzig granddaughters, Leah and Mariamme, married Moses' son, Abraham, and grandson, Alexander, respectively. There were many other Mendelssohn marriages within the family itself in the later generations.[10]

G9.1. Dorothea Mendelssohn, born in 1764 and died in Frankfurt in 1839. Married 1) the banker Simon Veit in 1783, and had issue. And 2) Friederich Schlegel in 1804, after she had converted to Christianity.

   Dorothea was the eldest daughter and of the children, the most brilliant and adventurous. She received formal

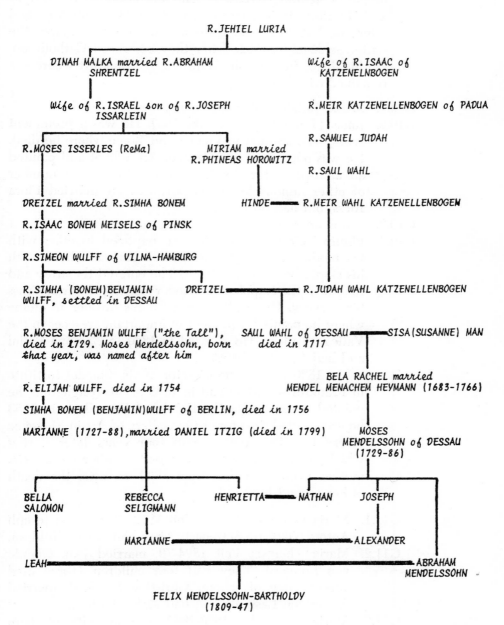

MENDELSSOHN-WULFF-ITZIG FAMILY PEDIGREE

education at home and later took part in theatrical performances in the homes of wealthy Berlin Jews. She also organized reading circles which were attended by Marcus and Henriette Heinz. Her first marriage was unhappy, and after she left Veit, she converted in order to marry the writer Schlegel in 1802. Later they embraced Catholicism. On his death in 1829 she returned to Frankfurt where she remained with her son.

G10.1. Moses Judah Veit, died young.

G10.2. Jonas (Johannes) Veit 1790-1857. He was a prominent artist, who studied in Vienna and Rome where he died. He was one of the neo-German Art School and painted an altar-piece for the Liege Cathedral and a number of other famous Madonna portraits. He married Flora Riess, but had no issue.

G10.3. Abraham Veit 1791-2.

G10.4. Phillip Veit 1793-1877. He was baptized together with his mother at Cologne to Catholicism, and lived with his stepfather in Paris. In 1813 he entered the army and fought in the Napoleonic Wars, receiving the Iron Cross for bravery. He studied art with his brother in Rome where he painted a number of important frescoes in the Vatican Gallery. He married in 1820 to Caroline Pulini and had five daughters.

In 1830 he became director of the Staedel Institute in Frankfurt-on-Main and in 1843 on his resignation, he painted a canvas for the Frankfurt Cathedral. In 1853 he was elected director of the Gallery of Art in Mayence where he died some twenty-four years later during which time he painted a number of other works. His mother lived with him from 1829 on, after the death of her second husband.

G11.1. Maria Dorothea Aloisia Veit 1822-97, married Joseph Anton Nikolaus Settegast. They had seven children.

G11.2. Maria Theresia Veit 1824-70, married Jean Claude von Longard. They had four children (three died young), one of whom, Christine Longard, married Anton von Lassaulx and had eight children.

G11.3. Marie Franziska 1826-1912, second wife of Jean Claude von Longard (G11.2).

G11.4. Maria Benedicta 1828-38.

G11.5. Friederich Anastasia Maria 1830-78, married Walburga Lieber. They had five children.

G9.2. Rechel Mendelssohn, born in Berlin in 1767, died in 1831. She married in 1785 to Mendel Meyer, son of the Court Banker Nathan Meyer, with whom her father had been a close friend. The unhappy marriage was later dissolved.

G10. Rebecca (Becky) 1793-1850, married in 1818 to Heinrich son of Jacob Herz Beer. Their son, Anton Ludwig Beer 1821-1831.

G9.3. Joseph Mendelssohn, born in Berlin in 1770 and died there in 1848. He studied Talmud under Herz Homberg from the age of nine till twelve. During this period Homberg himself became a pupil of the father in the field of philosophy. Under other teachers he was trained in languages and science. Together with his brother Abraham they founded the Berlin Banking Firm of Mendelssohn and Co. He continued his interests in literature and science and also published a number of works. His niece wrote:

Joseph Mendelssohn died early yesterday morning. His end was of unexampled happiness, like his whole life. He was ill only a few days, never confined to bed; only the day before he had busied himself with algebra, read, and slept well through the night. The cough from which he had suffered for several days gave way and he let himself be dressed, then walked alone to his chair, in which after a few minutes he fell asleep.[11]

He married in 1793 to Henriette (daughter of Nathan Meyer), a sister of Mendel (G9.2).

G10.1. Georg Benjamin Mendelssohn 1794-1874, Professor of Geography at the University of Bonn. He married about 1827 to Rosamunde E. Pauline Richter. They had no issue.

G10.2. Alexander Mendelssohn 1798-1871. He succeeded his father as Director of the Berlin Banking firm, and was the last Jewish Mendelssohn of the grandfather Moses. All his children were converts to Christianity. He married in 1821 to Marianne (died in 1888), daughter of Bernhard Seligman (whose wife Rebecca was the daughter of Daniel Itzig).

G11.1. Marie Josephine 1822-1891, married in 1840 to Robert Wilhelm Adolf Warshauer.

G12.1. Marie Anna 1841-1866, married in 1864 to Ludwig Passini.

G13. Marie Clara Louis, born 1865, married in 1888 to Dr. of Law Paul Siegfried von Hermann, and had issue, seven children.

G12.2. Son and daughter died young.

G12.3. Margarethe Marianne Clara, born in 1855, married in 1875 to Ernst Mendelssohn-Bartholdy son of Paul Herman son of Abraham. (See below G9.4/10.4/11.4.)

G12.4. Marcus Robert Alexander Warshauer 1860-1918, married 1) Katharina Eckert, and 2) Adele Louise Thévoz.

G13.1. Marie Katharina, born in 1891, married in 1914 to Edgar Fuld. They had four children.

G13.2. Alice Marie, born 1906, married Dr. Bill Woods of Harvard University.

G13.3. Marguerite Adle Louise, born in 1906, married Kurt Arthur Solmssen (New York). They had two sons, Arthur and Peter.

G13.4. Ernst Robert Emile Thévoz, born 1911, Ph.D. History.

G11.2. Margarette Anna Henriette 1823-1890, married in 1843 to Otto Georg Oppenheim.

G12.1. Rosa Marianna (Else) 1844-1868. She married in 1867 to Dr. Paul Mendelssohn-Bartholdy son of the composer Felix Mendelssohn. (See below G9.4.) Paul founded the chemical concern of AGFA. She died a year after their marriage and Paul remarried her sister Enole. (See below G9.3/10.2/11.2/12.6.)

G12.2. Marie, died young.

G12.3. Hugo Otto Joseph Oppenheim 1847-1921, married in 1871 to his cousin, Anna, daughter of the Consul Rudolph Oppenheim. He was a banker. They had six children.

G12.4. Rosa Marie 1849-1933, married in 1871 to Paul Steffen. They had seven children.

G12.5. Franz Otto Oppenheim 1853-1929, died in Cairo, married 1) in 1881 to Elizabeth Wollheim and 2) to Margarete Eisner. He was the Director of the AGFA Corporation.

G13.1. Rose.

G13.2. Martha, born 1882, married in 1901 to Ernst Berherd von Simson.

G14.1. Anna Elizabeth, born 1902, married in 1929 to Hans Reifenberg Ph.D. They have issue.

G14.2. Else Dorothea, born in 1907, married in 1931 to Friederich Achim von Arnim, and have issue.

G14.3. Martin Franz von Simson 1909-28.

G14.4. Encle Dorothea, born in 1910, married in 1937 to Friederich Karl Erckhinger von Schwerin. (A descendant of Ernst von Mendelssohn—Bartholdy — See below G9.4/10.4/11.4/12.4/13.4.)

G14.5. Professor Otto Von Simson born in 1912, married in 1937 to Princess Schonburg. Doctor of Philosophy and Professor of Art History at the Free University in Berlin. He was formerly Professor of Art History at the University of Chicago from 1945-57. He also taught at the University of Hamburg. Von Simson has been active in diplomacy and is a permanent delegate of the German Federal Republic to UNESCO and was on the Executive Board of UNESCO from 1960-65. In 1959 he was made Counsellor to the Embassy of the German Republic in Paris, and he is also an officer in the Legion d'Honneur. He is considered one of the most important living art historians in the world, especially in the field of relating the development of art history to history and theology. His Doctoral dissertation was on Peter Paul Rubens, and he is the author of *Sacred Fortress, Byzantine Art and Statecraft in Ravenna* (1948), and *The Gothic Cathedral* 1956.

G14.6. Luise Victoria, born in 1915.

G13.3. Franz Caesar Oppenheim 1884-7.
G13.4. Kurt Oppenheim, Ph.D., 1886, Director of the I.G. Farben Chemical Concern, which was united with the AGFA Chemical Company in 1920. AGFA was originally established by his uncle Paul Felix Mendelssohn, son of the composer. (See G9.4 below.) He married in 1914 to Margarethe Seidel, and had three children.

G12.6. Enole Oppenheim 1855-1873, second wife of Dr. Paul Felix Mendelssohn. (See G9.4 below.)
G12.7. Clara Elizabeth, born in 1861, married in 1880 to Adolf Ludwig Sigismund Gusserow, M.D. (Gynecology). They had three daughters.

G11.3. Herman Joseph Ernst Mendelssohn 1824-1891, publisher in Leipzig, married in 1856 to Laura Gramich.

G12.1. Marianne 1857-1905, married Carl Gramich.

G13.1. Hermann 1885-1939.
G13.2. Laura, born 1886, married Anton Kraus. They had three sons: Rudolph, Albrecht and Helmuth.
G13.3. Rudolph 1887-1917.
G13.4. Marianne born 1892, married Dr. Bruno Friedrich (law).
G13.5. Bertha, born 1895.

G12.2. Victor Alexander Mendelssohn 1858-1902, married Martha Troeger. No issue.
G12.3. Walter Rudolph Paul Mendelssohn 1860-1922, worked as a publisher with his father in Leipzig. He married Adele Schiessl. Their daughter, Maria, born 1896.
G12.4. Joseph Johannes Mendelssohn 1863-1928 of Leipzig, married Emmy Niemann.

G13. Hermann Victor Curt Mendelssohn, M.D., born 1893, married Elly Erler. Their children, Hans, Marie and Klaus Dieter.

G11.4. Adolf George Mendelssohn 1826-1851, banker. He married in 1850 to Marie Antoinette Enole Biarnez.

She later remarried his brother Paul Alexander. Their son, Pierre Stephan 1851-2.

G11.5. Paul Alexander Franz Mendelssohn 1829-1889, married in 1856 to his brother's widow, Marie Biarnez. He was elevated to the hereditary nobility.

G12.1. Robert George Mendelssohn 1857-1917, married in 1898 to Guilietta Gordigliani. He was an amateur cellist, and his wife an Italian singer and pianist.

G13.1. Eleonora Mendelssohn 1900-1951. She was named for Eleonora Duse, the celebrated actress who was a close friend of her parents. She was determined to become an actress as well, and made her debut in 1921 as Jessica in *The Merchant of Venice*. Her first husband was the Swiss pianist Edwin Fischer and her second was the Austrian daredevil horseman and aviator, Jedre Jessenski. She was the first member of the family to leave Germany at the rise of Hitler and settled in New York with her brother. She was not very successful on Broadway and lived in a small apartment on Manhattan's East side. She made a success in the 1940 Broadway play entitled *Flight to the West*. She was married a third time to the actor Martin Kosleck, and on the latter's accidental death in 1951, she died from an overdose of sleeping pills.

G13.2. Francesco Otto Mendelssohn, born 1901, cellist.

G13.3. Angelica 1902-20.

G12.2. Franz Pierre von Mendelssohn, 1865-1935. He was the head of the Mendelssohn Banking House, married his cousin Marie Westphal. (See below G9.3/10.2/11.8/12.4.)

G13.1. Emma, born 1890, married 1) Felix Witt and 2) Bernhard Waurik.

G14.1. Margarete Witt, born 1914, married in New York to Heinz Schneider. Their daughters, Eleonore and Nina, born in New York.

G14.2. Enole Witt born 1914, married Just Boedeker.

(See below G9.3/10.2/11.8/12.7/13.2.) Their children, Peter and Detley.

G13.2. Enole born 1891, married Theodore, Baron von Haimberger.

G14.1. Marie, born 1913, married Max Arthur Salemoonsohn. Their children, Johanna, Franz and Hans.

G14.2. Johanna, born 1915.

G14.3. Eleanora, born 1918.

G14.4. Franz, born 1919.

G14.5. Enole, born 1925.

G13.3. Margarete, married Paul Kempner.

G13.4. Lilli, married Emil Bohnke.

G13.5. Robert Franz Carl Mendelssohn. His daughter, Angelica Marie, born 1939.

G11.6. Wilhelm Bernhard Otto Mendelssohn 1831-92. Married 1) Klara Jonas 2) Julie Beseler (no issue).

G12.1. Wilhelm Oscar 1858-9.

G12.2. Alexander Mendelssohn 1856-1935, lawyer, married Jenny von Leyden.

G13.1. Alexander Mendelssohn, Doctor of Medicine, born 1886. His sons, Alexander and Rudolf.

G13.2. Franz Mendelssohn, born 1885, married Elly Wingendorf. Their daughters, Evalrene and Ellionore.

G13.3. Eva, born 1888, married Max von Tenspolde. Their son, Gerhard.

G13.4. Ernst Mendelssohn, born 1891, married Ursula Wiedenfeld. Their children, Ernst and Marianne.

G11.7. Alexandrine Beate Marianne 1833-1900 (died in England), married Joe Horsfall.

G12.1. Joseph John Mendelssohn-Horsfall, born 1853, married Sophy Shinner.

G13.1. John Mendelssohn-Horsfall, born 1883, lived in Ceylon, married Letitia Neville-Griffith. Their daughter, Letitia.

G13.2. Arthur Mendelssohn-Horsfall 1884—World War I, unmarried.

G13.3. Margerete born 1886, married Dr. Guy Douglas-Barton (medicine). Their children, Margaret and Michael.

G13.4. William Mark Horsfall, born 1887, married Frances Carrie Naysmith. Their children, June and Meava.

G13.5. Joseph James Horsfall, born 1888, married Roma Valentini. Their son, Jack.

G13.6. Charles Michael Horsfall, born 1889 (London), married Margaret Norton. Their children, Noel, Mary and Bernard.

G13.7. Dorothy, born 1892, married Rupert Keenlyside (London). Their children, Jane, Pamela, Bridget and Ann.

G13.8. Josephine, born 1897, unmarried.

G13.9. Thomas Mendelssohn-Horsfall, born 1900, no issue.

G12.2. Margaret Anne, died young.

G12.3. Thomas Mendelssohn-Horsfall 1855-1933 (India), married Magdelene King. Their daughters Katheleen and Magdelene, both born in Madras.

G12.4. Alexander John Mendelssohn-Horsfall 1856-1934 (Sussex). He married twice but had no issue.

G12.5. Robert, died young.

G12.6. James Mendelssohn-Horsfall, died in 1897 in New York.

G12.7. Mary Horsfall 1863-1923, married Dr. Herman Kossel (Medicine), Professor at Heidelberg University. Their children, Hans (died young), Marianne (married Hans Koehler) and Dorothea (unmarried).

G12.8. Charles Horsfall, born London 1865, married Helen Leins. No issue.

G11.8. Clara Mendelssohn 1840-1927, married in 1862 Dr. Carl F. Otto Westphal. (He was the son of Dr. Otto Carl Westphal and his wife Caroline, sister of Albertine Heine, the later wife of Paul Mendelssohn-Bartholdy (brother of the composer Felix).

G12.1. Alexander Westphal 1863-1941, Professor of Psychiatry of the University of Bonn.
G12.2. Anna 1864-1943, married Dr. Eduard Sonnenburg (medicine).

    G13.1. Dr. Udo Hans Sonnenburg (law) born 1886.
    G13.2. Louise, born 1887, married Waldemar Schultze. Their children, Ursula, Barbara Veit and Irene Solmssen.
    G13.3. Anna, born 1888, married Wilhelm Kircher. No issue.
    G13.4. Hedwig, born 1889, married Fritz Weiss. Their children, Jutta, Alice and Dietrich.

G12.3. Elisabeth, born 1865, unmarried.
G12.4. Marie Clara, born 1867 married Franz Pierre Walther von Mendelssohn. They were first cousins. (See above G11.5/12.2.)
G12.5. Ernst Carl Westphal, born 1871, married Helene Simon.

    G13.1. Dorothea, born 1902.
    G13.2. Barbara, born 1903.
    G13.3. Cacilie, born 1905, married Kleinmann.
    G13.4. Hans Carl Westphal, born 1907 (South Africa).
    G13.5. Helene, born 1912 (Palestine).

G12.6. Carl Franz Westphal 1875-1937. No issue.
G12.7. Therese, born 1877, married Professor Justus Boedeker (medicine) of Berlin University.

    G13.1. Wolf Boedeker, born 1902.
    G13.2. Just Robert Boedeker, born 1906. Married Enole, daughter of his cousin Felix Witt (G11.5/12.2/ 13.1/14.2).
    G13.3. Hildegard, born 1908.
    G13.4. Margarete, born 1912.

G9.4. Abraham Mendelssohn-Bartholdy, born in 1776 and died in Berlin in 1835. By profession he was a banker starting in 1803 as a cashier in a banking firm in Paris. The following year he married Lea daughter of Louis (Jacob) Salomon and his wife Babette, daughter of Daniel Itzig (see chart). He then went to Hamburg where he and his brother Joseph became partners in the banking firm that Joseph had established in Berlin but moved to Hamburg in 1804. Under the French Army occupation of the city the brothers were forced to flee secretly to Berlin. In 1813 he was named city councillor of Berlin for his patriotic efforts. A year before, his mother, Fromet, died, having outlived her husband by twenty-six years. About this time he became troubled about his religion and was eventually persuaded to convert to Christianity by his brother-in-law Jacob Levin Salomon, who in 1805 had converted and adopted the name Bartholdy and dropped the Salomon. Finally in 1816, Abraham had his children baptized in Berlin. The four, Fanny, Felix, Rebecca and Paul were ten, seven, four and two respectively. Although never completely comfortable with his conversion, he and his wife were baptized in 1822 while visiting Frankfurt. As the generation between a famous father and celebrated son, Abraham wrote of himself: "Before I was known as the son of my father, and now I am the father of my son," referring to his son, the composer Felix.

The fact that the family was descended from the King for a Night of Poland, Saul Wahl, was a known story within the Mendelssohn family circle, and on various occasions Abraham would mention the event as he did in 1829 while touring with Felix when he took ill: ". . . more direct descendants of some Scottish king of yore than I am of Saul Wahl, the one night's king of Poland."[12] Again in 1833 at the Dusseldorf Festival when his son Felix was overwhelmed by the concert audience, he was reminded of the family's royal ancestor. Many trips were made with his son, including one to London in 1833, at which time Abraham had failing vision and health. At that time he witnessed the British Parliamentary debates giving Jews there greater freedom, an event about which his son was greatly exalted. Two years later he died, almost completely blind and in a similar way to his father, from a slight cold, passing away unexpectedly in his sleep. And as his father had been involved in a dispute shortly before his death (with defending Lessing), so had Abraham a bitter quarrel with his former friend Varnhagen whom he felt had offended Lessing by stating that he preferred his own personal writer friends.

G10.1. Fanny 1805-1847, married in 1829 Professor Wilhelm
Hensel. At the age of six she escaped with her family
from Hamburg. She was baptized at the age of ten. She
and her brother were taught music as children and
would also put on Shakespearean plays at home in which
all Abraham's children would take part. Throughout her
life she was very close to her younger brother. As a true
Mendelssohn she inherited an inquiring mind and a deformity of her one shoulder being higher than the other.

Although a brilliant pianist, she was dissuaded by her
father from playing in public and for many years obeyed
his wishes. During this period she would compose music.
Although she married in 1829, she had originally met
her husband as a young artist some seven years earlier
at which time he had proposed. As her mother was
against their corresponding while he lived in Rome, he
used to write to her instead. Eventually they were married and Abraham provided his son-in-law with a studio
in their estate home for his painting and teaching of
pupils. At last in 1838, Fanny made a public appearance
in Berlin and two books of her songs were published.
More followed in 1846. The following year she died, and
today many of her musical compositions are still in
manuscript in the Mendelssohn Archives in Berlin.

G11. Ludwig Felix Sebastian Hensel 1830-1898. As a child of
sixteen when his mother was dying from a cerebral hem-
orrhage, he was sent to find a doctor for her. His father,
as a result of her death became unable to cope with the
situation so that Sebastian went to live with his aunt
Rebecca Dirichlet until his marriage in 1856 to Julie von
Adelson. He was the author of *The Mendelssohn Family*
(from 1729-1847), which appeared in German in 1879.
It was later translated into English. Two of his father's
drawings, of his mother and her brother Felix, can be
found in the book. Sebastian had five children and eighteen grandchildren.

G12.1. Fanny Hensel 1857-1891, married Bernhard Römer.

G13.1. Ilse, born 1887, married Professor Fritz Weege
(archaeology) in Breslau. They had no issue.

G13.2. Eva, born 1889.

G12.2. Cecile Hensel 1858-1928, married Dr. Friedrich Leo.

G13.1. Erika Julie, born 1887, married Dr. Walther Brecht (his mother was a sister of Dr. Adolf Gusserow mentioned by G9.3/10.2/11.2/12.7). Their son, Friederich Brecht, born in 1914 (Vienna).

G13.2. Ulrich, born 1890, Ph.D. Philosophy, married Helen Vagelen. Their children, Thomas and Gerhard.

G13.3. Paul Leo, born 1893, married Anna Siegert. Their daughter, Anna.

G12.3. Hugo Wilhelm Hensel 1860-1930, Ph.D. Philosophy at Strassburg. He married 1) Kaethe Rosenhayn and 2) Elisabeth Nelson, nee Schemman (her first husband was Leonard Nelson). (See below G9.4/10.3/11.1/12.2/13.1.)
From his first wife: Bruno, born 1899. From second: Fanny born, 1918 and Cecile, born 1923.

G12.4. Kurt Hensel, born 1861, Professor of Mathematics, University of Marburg, married Gertrud Hahn.

G13.1. Ruth, born 1888, married Dr. Franz Hayman (law). Their children, Roland, Ilse and Walter.

G13.2. Lili, born 1889, unmarried.

G13.3. Marie, born 1890, married 1) Gerhard Gunther and 2) Hans Schenck.
From Gunther: Wolfram, Hans and Michael.
From Schenck: Konrad, Nikolaus and Elisabeth.

G13.4. Albert Hensel 1895-1933, Professor of Law, married Marie Luise Flothmann. Their children, Kurt and Martin.

G13.5. Charlotte, born 1896, married Werner Bergengruen. Their children, Olaf, Luise, Maria and Alexander.

G12.5. Lili Hensel, born 1864, married Alard du Bois Reymond.

G13.1. Dr. Felix du Bois-Reymond (Orthopedics, Berlin), married Olga Holtappel. Their children, Tycho, Prosper and Lona.

G13.2. Fanny.

G13.3. Lola (Enole).

G13.4. Roland 1896-1922.

G13.5. Leah, born 1899, married Erwin Horwitz. Their children, Viola, Else, Gertrud, Ruth, Angelica and Christoph.

G10.2. Felix Jacob Ludwig Mendelssohn Bartholdy 1809-1847, married in 1837 to Cecile Sophie Charlotte Jeanrenaud. He was the second child and first son of his father Abraham and was baptized at the age of seven. In his younger years his mother taught him to play the piano and later he was taught by Carl Zelter, the director of the Berlin *Singakadamie*. He was a brilliant pupil and through Zelter he met Goethe, the famous German poet. He entered the University of Berlin at sixteen. During his childhood years he was busy in writing, the theatre and painting. But best of all was his interest in music so that by the time he was eleven he had composed some sixty different works. A year later the collection included symphonies, concertos and an opera. In 1825 he went with his father to Paris, his first of many successful travels. Here he met Cherubini, the Italian-born composer, and after a number of compositions, his great *Midsummer Night's Dream* was written in 1826, and performed in Stettin the following year. Yet he was not readily accepted in Berlin and it took him on further travels to England in 1829, the year he spent in the revival of Bach music. In London he had a wonderful time, so that he returned nine times during which he performed for and became the personal friend of Queen Victoria and the Prince Consort. His other symphonies composed about this time were the *Scotch* and *Italian,* and overtures *Hebrides* and *Meerestille.* After his first English visit he paid a visit to his grandfather's home town of Dessau with his father, where they saw the old house and synagogue where he had lived and studied. During 1830-31 he was in Italy, later in Paris and in 1840, after other travels, he was summoned by the new king, Frederick William IV, and offered the position of Head of the Music Division of the Royal Academy of the Arts. He

spent five miserable years in Berlin, during which time
his mother died. Once more he began to travel, including
to England. He declined an invitation to visit the U.S.A.
in 1845. His *Elijah* was performed first in England in
1846. The following year, towards winter, he suffered
a number of strokes and eventually died in his sleep at
the age of only thirty-eight.

It had been his father's hope that his son would
drop the Mendelssohn part of the family name, a point
that Felix never accepted and kept the name Mendelssohn Bartholdy maintaining that he was equally
proud of both, and of his Jewish background. (The use
of a hyphen between the two names was used by his
brother Paul and his descendants).

G11.1. Carl Wolfgang Paul Mendelssohn Bartholdy 1838-
1897, Professor of History at the Universities of Heidelberg and Freiburg. He was the author of a History
of Modern Greece, edited some memoirs about his father's association with Goethe and was a close friend
of Nietzsche. He married I) Bertha Eissenhardt and
2) Mathilde von Merkl.

G12.1. Cecile (from first wife), born 1870, married Otto
Felix Paul von Mendelssohn- Bartholdy, her second
cousin. (See G11.3/12.1 below.)

G12.2. Stillbirth.

G12.3. Professor Albrecht (from second wife) Mendelssohn Bartholdy 1874-1936. After studying Law, he
became Professor of Law at the University of Würz-
burg in 1905, and in 1920 Professor of the Political
Institute in Hamburg. He received an honorary
LL.D. from Harvard and on being dismissed by the
Nazis from his post as Professor of International Law
at Hamburg University, he settled in Oxford where
he was given a Lectureship. He wrote a number of
books on law but being a historian as well, he also
wrote as his last *The War and German Society: The
Testament of a Liberal,* which was published in
1937. He married his first cousin Dorothea daughter of Adolph Wach. (See G10.2/11.5 below.) They
adopted two children.

G11.2. Marie Pauline Helene Mendelssohn Bartholdy 1839-
1897, married in 1860 to Viktor Benecke.

G12.1. Paul Benecke, born 1868, a Professor of Philology
at Oxford.

G12.2. Eduard 1870-95, London. Killed climbing the Jung-
frau.

G12.3. Else 1873-1917, London.

G12.4. Daisy, born 1876.

G11.3. Dr. Paul Felix Mendelssohn-Bartholdy 1841-1880,
married 1) in 1867 Else Rose Marainne Oppenheim
and 2) in 1873, her sister Enole, daughters of Otto
Georg (see G9.3/10.2/11.2). He received a Ph.D. in
Chemistry and as a pioneer in the development in
aniline dyes, he founded in 1867 the famous Company
AGFA (Aktien Gesellschaft für Anilinfabrikation).
Today the company is most noted for its production of
photographic equipment, cameras and film. In 1920 it
joined the I.G. Farben Chemical Corporation.
From his first wife:

G12.1. Otto Felix, born 1867, was raised to the nobility in
1905 as von Mendelssohn-Bartholdy. He was a
banker and during the Nazi era lived in seclusion
in a farm in Potsdam. He married his cousin Cecile
daughter of Carl Wolfgang Mendelssohn-Bartholdy
(see above).

G13.1. Hugo Paul Mendelssohn-Bartholdy, born in 1894,
London, unmarried. He was a banker and collected family manuscripts which were placed in
the International Mendelssohn Bartholdy Society
which he established in Switzerland.

G13.2. Cecile Mendelssohn-Bartholdy born 1898, married 1) Benoit son of Alexander son of the banker
Rudolph Oppenheim (brother of Otto Georg Oppenheim mentioned under G9.3/10.2/11.2), and
2) Gilla Grafstrom. Their daughters, Louise and
Vera.

From second wife:

G12.2. Lili Sophie Mendelssohn-Bartholdy 1876-1927, married Fritz Passini.

G13.1. Paul Otto Passini, born 1897 (Vienna), a banker, married Alma Howell. Their daughter, Lili.

G13.2. Peter, born 1898, author, no issue.

G13.3. Maria, born 1903.

G12.3. Cecile Mendelssohn-Bartholdy 1874-1923, married Dr. William Henry Gilbert (Medicine).

G13.1. Mary Enole, born 1903 (London).

G13.2. Professor Felix Paul Gilbert, born 1905. He emigrated to the U.S.A. in 1936 and during World War II (1943-46) he served as research analyst in the Office of Strategic Services and the U.S. Department of State. After joining Bryn Mawr, he became Professor in 1948, and from 1962, Professor at the School of Historic Studies (Institute for Advance Study) in Princeton, New Jersey. He was the author of *Hitler Directs His War* (1951), *To the Farewell Address: Ideas of Early American Foreign Policy* (1961), two works on Machiavelli (1964 and 1965), co-editor of *The Diplomats* (2 Volumes 1953-63) and *Bankiers, Künstler und Gelehrte* (to appear 1974/5).

G12.4. Ludwig Mendelssohn-Bartholdy 1878-1918, banker, married Edith Speyer. No issue.

G12.5. Hugo Paul Mendelssohn-Bartholdy, born 1879, Ph.D. in Chemistry, and Director of the AGFA-I. G. Farben AG, as successor to his father. He married Johanna Nauheim.

G13. Cecile Mendelssohn-Bartholdy, born 1933.

G11.4. Felix August Eduard Mendelssohn-Bartholdy 1843-51.

G11.5. Lili Fanny Henriette Elisabeth 1845-1910, married in 1870 Adolph Gustav Eduard Louis Wach, Professor of Law and Jurist.

G12.1. Felix Gustav Wach, born 1871, married his cousin Kathe Marie von Mendelssohn-Bartholdy (daughter of Ernst Moses Felix—see below G10.4/11.4).

G13.1. Professor Joachim Wach. He was born in Chemnitz in 1898 and studied at the University of Munich and Berlin. He received his Ph.D. in Philosophy at the University of Leipzig in 1922 and Th.D. at the University of Heidelberg in 1929. He came to the U.S.A. in 1935. From 1924-35 he was Professor of the History of Religions at the University of Leipzig and from 1935-7 was Visiting Professor of Brown University, Providence. From 1935-46 he was an Associate Professor and from 1946 until his death was Professor of History of Religions at the University of Chicago. He was buried in Switzerland where he lived. He never married, and was the author of *Das Verstelen* (1926-32), *Sociology of Religion* (1944) and *Types of Religious Experience* (1951).

G13.2. Hugo Wach, born 1899, married Elisabeth Thomschke.

G13.3. Susanne, born 1902, married Heinz Heigel.

G12.2. Hugo Carl Wach, born 1872, professor and architect, unmarried.

G12.3. Elisabeth Wach, born 1874, married Fritz von Steiger, no issue.

G12.4. Dora Wach, born 1875, married her relative Professor Albrecht Mendelssohn-Bartholdy. (See above G10.2/11.1/12.3.)

G12.5. Mirzl Helene, born 1877, unmarried.

G12.6. Adolph Heinrich Wach, born 1889, Ph.D. Law, married Margita Edelmann. They had two daughters who died young, and a son Thomas, born 1930.

G10.3. Henriette (Rebecca) Mendelssohn-Bartholdy 1811-58, married in 1832 to Peter Gustav Lejeune-Dirichlet, Professor of Mathematics. The younger sister of the famous brother Felix, she was baptized at the age of four. She met and married her husband when she was twenty-one and he a young professor at the Berlin University. In 1843 the couple went to Italy where she contracted an illness while at Naples. At this time she was pregnant and after seven months gave birth to her only daughter in Florence. After the death of her brother Felix, she left Berlin with her husband who accepted the Professorship of Mathematics at the University of Göttingen. She died from an unexpected stroke, and her husband died the following year.

G11.1. Abraham Walter Dirichlet 1833-87, married in 1857 to Anna Caroline Louise Sachs.

    G12.1. George Dirichlet 1858-1920, married Anna Elise Jacobsohn.

        G13.1. Gustav 1890-1915.
        G13.2. Ernst 1891-1914.
        G13.3. Gertrud, born 1899, married Hans Braun. Their children, Lore, Renate and Einhart.

    G12.2. Elisabeth Dirichlet 1860-1920, married Heinrich Nelson Ph.D. Law.

        G13.1. Professor Leonard Nelson (1882-1927), received his Ph.D. in Philosophy at the University of Göttingen and was made a professor in 1919. He was a proponent of the Philosopher J. F. Fries, and founded the "New Fries School." He wrote many articles including a collection of them in English under the title *Socrastic Method and Critical Philosophy* (1949). His greatest interest was in Ethics and some of his unpublished lectures were issued by his students. He was baptized as a child. He married Elisabeth Schemann and had issue, Gerhard David Nelson (born in 1909). She later remarried Hugo Hensel (see above—G10.1/11/12.3).
        G13.2. Lotte Nelson, born 1884, photographer.

    G12.3. Katharina 1861-1918, unmarried.
    G12.4. Gustav Moses Dirichlet 1863-1920, married Julie Flora Toni de Terra.

        G13.1. Walter, born 1890, married Rose Wagner. Their children, Anna, Barbara, Felix and Lili.
        G13.2. Charlotte 1891-1926, married Erich Patschke, no issue.
        G13.3. Lili Dirichlet, born 1894, unmarried.
        G13.4. Felix Georg Dirichlet, born 1896, married Margarete Laupichler, no issue.

G11.2. Felix Arnold Constantin Dirichlet 1837-8.
G11.3. Ernst Gustav Paul Dirichlet 1845-1912.
G11.4. Florentina (Flora) Fanny Auguste 1845-1912, married Dr. Wilhelm Georg Baum (medicine) son of Dr. William Baum, the friend and teacher of the famous surgeon Theodore Billroth.

G12.1. Rebecca Baum, unmarried.
G12.2. Anna, born 1873, married Karl von Schaulin-Egersberg.

G13. Marietta, born 1898, married Hermann von Raumer, no issue.

G12.3. Marie, Ph.D. Philosophy, unmarried.
G12.4. Dr. Ernst Baum (medicine) 1876-1934, married Aenne Weber. Their children, Dr. Wilhelm Baum, Eva Clasen, Gerhard and Harald.
G12.5. Wilhelm 1878-1916, married Irmgard Steffens. Their children, Hans and Margarete.
G12.6. Lotte, born 1880, married Filiberto Vesci.

G13.1. Helga, born 1903, married Omero Munih. No issue.
G13.2. Guglielmo, born 1906 (Rome). His daughter, Marina.
G13.3. Emanuela, born 1911, married Giacomo Ercolami. Their son, Enrico.

G10.4. Paul Hermann Mendelssohn-Bartholdy 1812-1874, married in 1835 to Pauline Lousie Heine. He was baptized at the age of two and as a child used to perform at home with his brother and sisters by playing the cello. His wife was a cousin of the poet Heinrich Heine. He entered the Mendelssohn Banking House and became the Family Head, despite being the youngest, managing the financial affairs of his brother Felix. He elevated the banking firm to a level of great affluence, together with his cousin Alexander Mendelssohn. He also was the financial trustee to Felix's children and helped to arrange the musical manuscripts left on his brother's death in 1847. He himself died some twenty-seven years later after a prolonged illness. He had six children and some of his descendants settled in Sweden where they occupied important positions.

G11.1. Child, died.

G11.2. Felicia Henriette 1844-63.

G11.3. Henriette Cecilie 1846-1906, married Dr. Rudolf Schelske, no issue.

G11.4. Ernst Moses Felix Mendelssohn-Bartholdy 1846-1909, married his cousin Alexandrine Marie Warschauer in 1875. (See above G9.3/10.2/11.1/12.3.) He was a banker, and was elevated to the hereditary nobility.

G12.1. Paul Robert von Mendelssohn-Bartholdy 1875-1935, banker, married 1) Charlotte Reichenheim, 2) Elsa Lucy von Lavergne-Peguilhen and 3) in 1939, but had no issue.

G12.2. Kathe Marie von Mendelssohn-Bartholdy born 1876, married Felix Gustav Wach (son of Lili Fanny Henriette Mendelssohn-Bartholdy—see above G10.2/11.5).

G12.3. Charlotte, born 1878, married Eric Hallin, Government Chamberlain to the King of Sweden.

G13.1. Marie Hallin, born 1900, married Oscar Dyrssen. Their children, Elisabeth, Luise and Marie.

G13.2. Karin 1901-7.

G13.3. Hans Eric, born 1903, unmarried.

G13.4. Nina, born 1905, married Johan August Enhörning. Their children, Britte and Barbro.

G13.5. Louise Hallin, born 1906, married Claes von Peyron. Their children, Marianne, Eric and Knut.

G13.6. Fritz Hallin, born 1907, unmarried.

G12.4. Enole von Mendelssohn-Bartholdy, born 1879, married Albert von Schwerin.

G13.1. Hans-Bone von Schwerin, born 1898, married Hertha von Elbe. (See below G9.4/10.4/11.6/12.3/13.2.) They had four children.

G13.2. Wolfgang 1899-1918.

G13.3. Dorothea von Schwerin, born 1905, married Wilhelm Eckardt.

G13.4. Friedrich Erckhinger von Schwerin, born 1906,

Ph.D. Law, married Dorothea von Simson, daughter of Martha and Ernst. (See G9.3/10.2/11.2/12.5/13.2.) Their daughter, Sibylle, born 1938.

G13.5. Rolf von Schwerin, born 1907, married Elisabeth Gass. They have two daughters.

G13.6. Cordula Johanna, born 1917.

G13.7. Jürgen Wolfgang von Schwerin born 1919.

G12.5. Marie von Mendelssohn-Bartholdy, born 1881, married Felix Johann Busch (formerly Friedlaender, son of Justus son of Daniel Friedlaender (1800-68) son of Benoni son of David and his wife Blumchen, daughter of Daniel Itzig). Their daughters, Barbara, Marie and Dorothea.

G12.6. Alexander Joachim von Mendelssohn-Bartholdy 1889-1917, married Frieda Paech, no issue.

G11.5. Paul Abraham Gotthold Mendelssohn-Bartholdy 1848-1903, married 1874 Pauline Henriette Auguste Else Wentz.

G12.1. Ernst 1875-1915.

G12.2. Edith born 1876 married Wilhelm Neigel. Their children, Anna and Fortunatus Karl.

G12.3. Gustav born 1877, married Elisa Hafenreffer (Buenos Aires).

G12.4. Fanny, born 1879, married Ernst Raithel. Their children, Else married Fritz Schloss and had three sons, and Walther married Margarethe Giesecke.

G12.5. Herbert Mendelssohn-Bartholdy, born 1880, Ph.D. in Music and Philosophy, married Leoni Langer. Their children, Dorothea and Sebastian.

G12.6. Rudolph born 1881, married Georgine Scholl.

G12.7. Emma 1883-1914.

G12.8. Else, died 1885.

G12.9. Beatus, died 1888.

G12.10. Martha, born 1889, unmarried.

G12.11. Paula, born 1892, married Allard de Ridder. They have two daughters.

G11.6. Fanny Elisabeth Mendelssohn-Bartholdy 1851-1924, married in 1872 to Eugen Diprand Anton Samuel Paul, Baron von Richthofen.

G12.1. Paula, born 1873, married Ernst Siemerling.

G13.1. Fanny, born 1894, married Fritz Reuter. They had two daughters.

G13.2. Kathe, born 1898, married Heinz Schafgen. They had two children.

G13.3. Ernst 1899-1918.

G12.2. Anna, born 1875, married Hans von Albert.

G13.1. Hans Eugen, born 1898.

G13.2. Wilhelm, born 1901, married Dorle Seelig.

G13.3. Gisela, born 1907, married Dr. Sato.

G12.3. Kathe, born 1876, married Kurt von Elbe.

G13.1. Hermann, born 1900, married Charlotte von Stumpfeld. They had three children.

G13.2. Hertha, born 1901, married Hans-Bone von Schwerin. (See above G9.4/10.4/11.4/12.4/13.1.)

G13.3. Joachim von Elbe, born 1902, Ph.D. Law.

G13.4. Gunther von Elbe, born 1903, Ph.D. Chemistry. Settled in Pittsburgh, Pa. (U.S.A.).

G13.5. Friederich, born 1906.

G9.5. Nathan Mendelssohn, the youngest son of Moses, born in 1782 and died in Berlin in 1852. He married Henriette, youngest daughter of Daniel Itzig. (See Family Chart.) He was devoted to mechanics, being the first German to pursue the subject in English and French cities. He was the manufacturer of a number of instruments and also produced a journal of mechanics. In later life he was a lecturer at the Polytechnic Society in Berlin which he had helped to establish. Here he taught photography, galvanoplastics, electromagnetism, telegraphy and other related subjects. At one time during his life he was an officer in militia, a tax-collector, inspector of the Chief Mint in Berlin and an inventor. He also impressed Alexander von Humboldt who helped him obtain state subsidy for the construction of a dividing machine. He converted to Christianity in 1823 at the age of forty, and had three children from whom stem a number of prominent family musicians.

G10.1. Dr. Arnold Maximillian Albrecht Mendelssohn (medicine) 1817-1850, supporter and confident of Ferdinand LaSalle.

G10.2. Ottilie Ernestine Mendelssohn 1819-48, married in 1840 to Eduard Ernst Kummer, Professor of Mathematics at the University of Berlin. She was his second wife, the first being Bertha, daughter of Ludwig Cauer, and a descendant of Daniel Itzig.

G11.1. Wilhelm Kummer 1841-7.
G11.2. Marie Elisabeth Kummer 1842-1921, married Dr. Herman Amandus Schwarz.

G12.1. Ottilie, born 1869, married Dr. Charles Sprague, Ph.D. Chemistry.

G13. Charles Mendl Thomas Sprague. He had two children, Roland and Daisy.

G12.2. Wilhelm Schwarz 1872-1911, unmarried.
G12.3. Helene, born 1876, married Karl Federn, a historian. Their sons, Karl and Roland.
G12.4. Dr. Leopold Schwarz (medicine), born 1877, married Gertrude Schmidt and had issue.
G12.5. Heinrich Schwarz, born 1882, married Franziska Koch and had four children.
G12.6. Theodor Schwarz, born 1883, married Elsa Lindemann and had three children.

G11.3. Otto Kummer, born 1844.
G11.4. Ernst Nathaniel Kummer 1847-1923, professor, married Johanna Caroline Reinnold.

G12.1. Ottilie, born 1876, married Dr. Leopold Kummer (medicine). He was the son of Eduard Kummer. They had no issue.
G12.2. Gertrud, born 1877, unmarried.
G12.3. Margarete, born 1879, married Richard Hoffman and had three children.
G12.4. Hedwig Kummer, born 1880 and died about 1930, married Harry Trüller and had two children.
G12.5. Johanna, born 1881, married Kurt Pfeffer. Their sons, Herbert, born 1911 (lived in South West Africa) and Gunther, born 1914.

G12.6. Elisabeth 1882-1914.

G12.7. Reinold Kummer, born 1885, married Anna Stengel
and had two daughters.

G12.8. Ernst Kummer, born 1886, married Amemerie
Schultz-Gebhard and had four children.

G12.9. Frieda, born 1890, married Dr. Felix Bauer (medicine, Vienna). They had a daughter.

G12.10. Ludwig Kummer, born 1892, married Margarethe
Zeite. They had a son.

G10.3. Joseph Elias August Wilhelm Mendelssohn 1821-1866,
married in 1854 to Louise Aimee Cauer (sister to Bertha
Cauer mentioned above—G9.5/10.2).

G11.1. Ludwig Arnold Mendelssohn 1855-1933, married in
1885 Maria Cauer, daughter of Carl Cauer, brother to
Ludwig Cauer (mentioned above—G9.5/10.2). He was
both a composer and teacher and wrote three operas,
three symphonies and a number of other works. From
1880-3 he served as organist and instructor at the University of Bonn, later he was the Professor of the Cologne Conservatory and in 1912 the Professor of the
Hoch Conservatory in Frankfurt. In 1919 he was made
a member of the Berlin Academy and in 1927 received
an honorary doctorate from Tübingen University. He
had four children who left no descendants, Wilhelm,
Helene, Karl and Dorothea.

G11.2. Bertha Ottilie Mendelssohn 1857-1901, unmarried.

G11.3. Ottilie Klara 1858-1929, unmarried.

G11.4. Cornelie Maria 1860-1937, unmarried.

G11.5. Louise Marianne 1863-1923 unmarried.

G9.6. Henriette (Jente) Mendelssohn 1775-1831.) From an early
age she renounced marriage and at the age of twenty-
four went to work as a tutor to a Viennese Jewish Family.
Later she established a boarding house for young women
in Paris which she ran until overcome by ill health in 1811.
In Paris she also became friendly within the literary and
political circles and became an ardent correspondent. Although she first resented the idea of conversion, she nevertheless did so in 1814, eventually becoming a Catholic and
also bigoted in her religious beliefs.

BRANCH D

Descendants of

NAFTALI HIRSCH GINSBURG (GUNZBURG)
Including LIPSCHUTZ Family

Ancestry

G3.3. Saul Wahl.

G4.1. Meir.

G5.7 Deborah, married R. Naftali Hirsch[13] son of R. Isaac Gunzburg of Worms, originally A.B.D. Posen, where he wrote an approbation in 1647 to *Emek HaMelech*. He later became A.B.D. Pinsk and then Slutzk when he signed the Minutes of the Council which convened at Zulz in 1670 and at Chamsk in 1679. He wrote approbations on *Divrei Chahamim* and *Keneh Chochmah* by R. Judah Lieb of Pinsk, published in Hamburg 1692/3 Frankfurt-on-Oder 1681/2 respectively. He died Tammuz 1697, and was buried next to R. Nahum Katzenellenbogen. His first wife was the daughter of R. Moses Lazer of Brest.

G6.1. R. Isaac of Slutzk, died in 1678.

G6.2. R. Saul, A.B.D. Vizin and Pinsk, died 1727. He wrote several approbations.

G7.1. R. Isaac, A.B.D. Mohilev and Dubno, married the daughter of R. Meshullam Zalman Mirls, A.B.D. Hamburg-Altona-Wandsbeck. He wrote several approbations and his novellae are found in *Tekanta DeMoshe* by R. Shemariah son of R. Moses son of R. Elchanan Berlin (Elchanan also married a daughter of R. Meshullam Zalman Mirls), published Alexnitz 1768.

G8.1. R. Meir, A.B.D. Vizin and Dubno. He married the daughter of R. Simcha HaKohen Rapoport, A.B.D. Grodno and Lublin.

G9.1. R. David, A.B.D. Vitebsk.

G9.2. R. Ari Lieb, A.B.D. Vizin.

G9.3. R. Asher, A.B.D. Krislow.

G9.4. R. Naftali Hirsch of Zolkiev, married the daughter of R. Israel Fraenkel of Brody. His novellae appear in *Tekanta DeMoshe* by Shemariah son of Moses, published Alexnitz 1768.

G9.5. R. Jacob, A.B.D. Zamocz.

G10. R. Eliezer, married the daughter of David son of Moses.

G9.6. R. Benjamin, A.B.D. Vizin. His novellae also appear in *Tekanta DeMoshe.*

G10. R. Jonah Gunzburg, mentioned in *Kiryah Ne'emanah* as a Dayan (Judge) in Vilna.

G9.7. R. Joseph, A.B.D. Osat and Petrovicz.

G10. R. Benzion of Pinsk.

G11.1. R. Dov Ber of Grodno, died 1834.

G12.1. R. David.
G12.2. R. Aaron Meir Jacob, born in Grodno in 1820 and died in Vilna in 1860. Although he was a prominent Talmudic scholar, he did not accept any Rabbinical position. In 1858 he published Biurim from a manuscript written by Elijah, the Gaon of Vilna at Königsberg, together with his own commentaries. These, which established his scholarship, were necessary as the manuscript was in poor repair. He also left other works in manuscript. He married Leah Mina, daughter of Zvi Hirsch Lapidot of Vilna. His biography was written in *Tziyun Lametzuyan* as an appendix to *Toldot Mishpachat Gunzburg* by Maggid.

G13.1. Dov Ber, an engineer.
G13.2. Benzion.
G13.3. Lapidot, Ph.D. Philosophy.
G13.4. Akiva.
G13.5. Elijah, a sculptor.

G11.2. Chaya, wife of R. Aryeh Judah Lieb Lipschutz, Parnas and Manhig of Karlin (son of Moses of Karlin, a descendant of Samuel Edels). He died in 1840 at the age of thirty-four.

G12.1. R. Benjamin Jacob Lipschutz, who wrote his genealogy in *Sefer Yochasin* by R. Aaron Rosenkrantz, published Warsaw 1885. He was born in Karlin about 1833 and was orphaned at about the age of seven. He died in Warsaw in 1911. He was the author of *Chelkat Binyamin*. He married Sarah (died 1913), daughter of R. Moses Aaron Tochsk.

G13.1. R. Abraham Abba of Bialystok, born in Karlin in 1866.

G14. R. Aryeh Judah Lieb Lipschutz of Warsaw, born in 1887. Author of *Avot Atarah LeBonim* (Warsaw 1927), dealing with the Saul Wahl *Royal Saga*.[14]

G13.2. Esther Gitel, married Solomon Bergman of Pinsk.

G14.1. Daughter, married.
G14.2. Wife of Judah Lieb Yolles of Warsaw.
G14.3. Joel Judah Lieb of Warsaw.
G14.4. Avigdor Haim of Karlin.

G13.3. Mordecai Eli of Zamir, killed in 1920.

G14.1. Zirl Leah, married Moses Gerstein.
G14.2. Judah Lieb.
G14.3. Esther, married Beryl Katzenelson.
G14.4. Feigel, married Hirsch Levine.
G14.5. Haim.
G14.6. Reize, married Mordkowitz.
G14.7. Naomi, married Saul Schlossman.
G14.8. Abraham Joseph, died 1920.

G12.2. Benzion Lipschutz of Karlin, died 1887.

G13.1. Batsheva, married Solomon Denenberg of New York.
G13.2. Abraham Abba.

G12.3. Dov Ber.

G9.8. Wife of Abraham HaLevi Shor, A.B.D. Emden (son of Jacob Shor son-in-law of Ezekiel son of Abraham Katzenellenbogen—see Descendants of Joel Ashkenazi Katzenellenpogen—Chapter VIII, G7.2/8.4).

G8.2. R. David Gunzburg, A.B.D. Mohilev.
G8.3. R. Meshullam Zalman Gunzburg, A.B.D. Mohilev and Vitebsk. He wrote a number of approbations. He married the daughter of R. Israel, A.B.D. Pinsk and Brest, son of R. Abraham (Abba Mori).

G9.1. R. Gershon, A.B.D. Harky, married Malka, daughter of R. Haim HaKohen Rappoport, A.B.D. Lvov. He wrote several approbations.

G10.1. R. Simcha Asher of Vitebsk, married Stirka Schlossburg.

G11.1. Haim of Vitebsk, married Yota, daughter of Menachem Nathan Halpern of Berdichev.

G11.2. Ita Deborah, married Zvi Hirsch son of Haim Mordecai Margolioth of Dubno. (Haim's brother was the famous Ephraim Zalman of Brody—see Margolioth Family Pedigree — Chapter VII, G7.4/8.4/9.2/10.2 /11.4).

G11.3. Miriam, married Isaac Minkin (Oheler) of Vitebsk.

G10.2. Rachel, married Shabtai son of Eliezer.

G11.1. Haim.

G12.1. Gershon Haim Lister of Vitebsk.
G12.2. Uri Lieb Gunzburg, married Keila, daughter of Joseph Zakheim of Vilna.

G9.2. Malka, married Jacob Uri son of Abraham Pogos of Vilna. She died in Vilna in 1785, and he in 1795.

G10.1. Israel of Vilna, died 1784.
G10.2. Meshullam Zalman of Vilna (Reb Zalman Uris), died 1836. He married the daughter of R. Mordecai Zvi son of R. Isaac (Hamburger) Horowitz (See Horowitz Family Pedigree—Chapter XVI, G10.9/11.3).

G11. Isaac Israel (Eizik Zalmans of Vilna), died 1858.

G10.3. Wife of R. Michael son of Moses, A.B.D. Kletsk.

G7.2. R. Asher Gunzburg, A.B.D. Vizin and Pinsk. His novellae appear in *Naftali Seva Ratzon* by R. Naftali Hirsch son of Simeon Gunzburg, published Hamburg 1708. He married the daughter of R. Abraham Katzenellenpogen (father of Ezekiel—see Chapter VIII, *Knesset Yechezkiel,* who mentioned him a number of times in that work). He wrote a number of approbations.

G8.1. R. Aryeh Lieb Gunzburg, born in 1695 and died in 1785. He was initially A.B.D. of Minsk until 1742, and in 1750 became A.B.D. of Volozhin. He lived in poverty and after a number of disputes with community leaders, wandered from city to city until in 1765 he was elected A.B.D. Metz, where he remained until his death. He was the author of: *Sha'agat Aryeh,* Responsa published Frankfurt-on-Oder 1756; *Sha'agat Aryeh Hachadashot,* Responsa with *Hagahot* by his son Asher, published Vilna 1874; *Turei Even,* published Metz 1781; and *Gevurot Ari,* published Vilna 1862.

G9. Asher of Karlslov, 1755-1837.

G10. Aryeh Lieb.

G8.2. Sarah, married Nathan Nata of Sokolov.

G9. Nathan Nata.

G7.3. R. David, A.B.D. Alik. He later settled in Pinsk in 1745. He wrote several approbations.

G8. R. Meir.

G9. R. Joseph, A.B.D. Pitrovitz.

G10. Wife of Jacob Koppel Berlin (of the Mirls Family).

G7.4. Wife of R. Zvi Hirsch HaKohen Rappoport, A.B.D. Mir, son of Solomon HaKohen, A.B.D. Chelm.

G8.1. Joseph Moses Simha Rappoport, A.B.D. Lubetch, Zmigrad, Onsdorf, and Lentchov. He married the daughter of R. Jacob Halevi Shor (See Chapter VI, Branch B, G6.4/7.2/8./9.1.) He was the author of *Bigdei MiShai* published in Lvov, 1806.

G9.1. R. Jacob Jokel, A.B.D. Yanow (Zamocz District).
G9.2. R. Abraham Zvi Hirsch, who wrote the introduction of the *Bigdei HaKodesh* (which includes *Bigdei MiShai*) by his father.
G9.3. Shprintze, married R. Meshullam Zalman Zak, A.B.D. of Pokroy, later settled in Vilna. He died in Vilna in 1800 and his wife in 1802.

G10.1. R. Asher Zak of Vilna where he died in 1796 at the age of sixty-six years.

G11. R. Jacob Zak of Vilna.

G10.2. R. Israel Zakheim, married the daughter of R. Abraham Abba Soloveitchik (of Kovno).

G11. R. Benzion Zak of Kovno.

G9.4. Grune, married R. Israel Menachem Mendel, A.B.D. Tre-
velo (son of R. Haim of Brody) author of *Bigdei Kavod*
printed as part of *Bigdei HaKodesh* by his father-in-law.

G7.5. Wife of R. Judah son of Lieb.

G8. R. Jacob of Sokolov, author of *Moreh Tzedek,* died in 1775.

G9.1. Aaron.
G9.2. Baruch Sokolover.

G10. Aaron.

G11.1. Jacob, author of *Mishkenot Yaakov.*

G12.1. Alexander Sender.

G11.2. Isaac, author of *Keren Orah.*

G12.1. Abraham.

G13. Aaron.

G12.2. Jacob Baruch.
G12.3. Moses Shalom.

G13.1. Zalman.
G13.2. Isaac Minkowsky.

G12.4. David Judah.

G6.3. Eidel Gunzburg, died 1721, married R. Aryeh Lieb (died 1722)
son of Judah, A.B.D. Kletsk, (author of *Kol Yehudah*).

G7. Naftali Hirsch of Slutzk.

G6.4. Jacob of Posen.
G6.5. David, A.B.D. Alik.
G6.6. Shprintze, married R. Joseph son of Simcha, A.B.D. Mohilev and
later Dayan (Judge) of Posen. She died in Slutzk in 1691.

G7. Daughter, married R. Solomon Zalman son of Simcha Bonems
Meisels, a descendant of Saul Wahl. (See Descendants of Abraham, son of Saul Wahl Katzenellenbogen—Chapter V—Branch A.)

BRANCH E

DESCENDANTS OF
R. MOSES HAKOHEN KATZ[14a]

GINZBURG, FUENN, LWOW AND MARX FAMILIES

ANCESTRY

G3.3. R. Saul Wahl.

G4.1. R. Meir.

G5.10. Nissle, wife of R. Moses HaKohen.

G6.1. R. Joseph, studied under his father in Brest, and became A.B.D. Friedberg. He wrote an approbation to *Beit HaLevi* by his father's pupil, Isaiah Horowitz.

G6.2. R. Judah Lieb of Slutzk, whose novellae appear in *Mareh HaKohen* by his grandson David HaKohen.

G7.1. R. Moses HaKohen, A.B.D. Belz. A Responsa of his is to be found in *Pnai Yehoshua,* dated 1723.

G8. R. David, author of *Mareh HaKohen,* published Zolkiev 1808 and Responsa *Nefesh David,* published Lvov 1796.

G9. R. Ze'ev Wolf HaKohen Buchner of Brody. He was born at Brody and earned his living by writing letters for illiterate people. He also earned a livelihood from his many published works. He travelled through the European countries of Germany, Galicia, Poland and Lithuania, and corresponded with many prominent Jewish personalities of his time. During his travels, he lost the sight of his right eye, due to an injury in Berlin. He was regarded as one of the modern representatives of the medieval school of artificial poetry. Although his works were well received in his day, they lost their popularity during later generations. He was the author of:

1) *Shirei Tehilah,* Berlin 1797.
2) *Tzachut Hamelitzah,* Prague 1805.
3) *Zeved Hamelitzah,* Prague 1794.
4) *Zeved Tov,* Prague 1794.
5) A song in *Chakirat Hagmul* by Moses Margolioth, published Offen 1829.

    6) *Keter Malchut,* Lvov 1794.

    7) *Shir Yedidut,* Frankfurt-on-Oder 1810.

    8) *Shir Niflah,* Frankfurt-on-Oder 1802.

G7.2. Ze'ev Wolf, A.B.D. Lomaz and Brest.

G8. Maradell, married R. Jacob Halpern, A.B.D. Zovnitz, author of *Beit Yaakov.*

    G9.1. R. Ze'ev Wolf, A.B.D. Zovnitz.

    G9.2. R. Solomon Isaac, A.B.D. Borstein, Tarnopol, Choristkov. He was the author of *Yeriot Shlomo* and *Mirkevet Hamishneh.* His Responsa are found in *Beit Yaakov* by his father and in the Responsa works of his contemporaries. He died in 1791.

        G10.1. R. David Weingarten-Halpern, A.B.D. Lyzhansk, wrote an approbation to *Or Pnei Moshe* (published Lvov 1851).

        G10.2. R. Jehiel Michael, A.B.D. Morochov.

        G10.3. R. Jacob.

G6.3. Wife of R. Judah Lieb, A.B.D. Luntchitz.

G6.4. Wife of R. Abraham of Luntchitz, son of Judah Lieb Harif.

G7. R. Elisha, author of *Kav Venaki,* and publisher of *Pi Shnayim* published Altona 1735. He was A.B.D. Grodno. In the introduction to *Pi Shnayim* is his complete ancestry, mentioning his lineage to Saul Wahl Katzenellenbogen.

    G8. Daughter, married R. Mordecai, A.B.D. Pokroy.

    G. Daughter, married R. Ari Ginzburg of Walkavisk.

        G10. R. Judah Lieb Ginszburg of Janau, author of *Avak Mugmar.*

        G11. Daughter, married R. Shabtai Fuenn.

        G12. R. Judah Lieb Fuenn, A.B.D. Slonim.

            G13.1. R. Shabtai, A.B.D. Belitza.

            G13.2. Daughter, married R. Benjamin Ze'ev Wolf Kahn, A.B.D. Malitsch.

G6.5. Daughter (possibly granddaughter), married to R. Joseph Samuel (Haim Isaiah) son of R. Zvi of Cracow. R. Joseph was the A.B.D. of Frankfurt-on-Main from 1690. His valuable cross-references in the Talmud which first appeared in the Frankfurt Edition (1721) and subsequently are entitled *Masoret HaShas.* He died in 1703.

G7.1.   R. Aryey Lieb was associate Rabbi with his father in Frankfurt. He
        married the daughter of R. Samuel Schotten the A.B.D. of Darm-
        stadt, but who lived in Frankfurt and was the "Klaus Rabbi." R.
        Samuel became the A.B.D. of Frankfurt on the death of R. Joseph.

G7.2.   Daughter, the first wife of R. Aaron Moses Ezekiel[15] surnamed
        Lwow or Lemberger. As a young man he was first Rabbi of
        Treves and in 1693 was elected the A.B.D. of Westhofen. He served
        for twenty years until his death November 26, 1712 (27 Cheshvan
        5473). His wife died in 1700 and left two sons, Joseph and Joshua
        Heschel. He remarried Bela, the daughter of R. Gabriel Eskeles.
        (See Eskeles Family Pedigree—Part III, Chapter XI—Branch A.)
        They had a son Moses.

G8.1.   R. Joshua Heschel Lwow, born in 1692 (according to a docu-
        ment which states that he was seventy-five years old in 1767).
        He married Merle the daughter of R. Isaac Aaron Worms
        (Wormser) the A.B.D. of Metz, in which town he held the title
        of *Rabbinatsassessor,* from 1722 becoming the A.B.D. of Treves,
        when his father-in-law, the A.B.D. of Treves, died on July 25
        the same year.
            "Also in the Edition of the Talmud of my Uncle Lieb, my
        mother's brother, son of my grandfather Samuel Haim Isaiah,"
        relates R. Joshua in the Metz Edition of the Talmud which ap-
        peared in 1770 (Tractate Niddah). In *Or HaYashar* (pgs. 72b,
        73b, 75b and 77b), he mentions that he was both descended
        from R. Joseph HaKohen and R. Meir Katzenellenbogen. Hav-
        ing lost his mother when he was about seven, he was raised by
        his father's second wife, Bela, together with his brother Joseph.
            R. Heschel was involved in three important events during his
        lifetime, which had caused considerable conflict within the Ger-
        man Jewish Community and the Jewish world at large. The first
        of these was the accusation made against R. Jonathan Eybe-
        schutz, who was elected the A.B.D. of Altona-Hamburg-Wands-
        beck in 1750. He was suspected by R. Jacob Emden (son of R.
        Zvi Hirsch Ashkenazi—see Chapter XIII), of being a follower
        of the Pseudo-Messiah Shabbatai Zvi. Known for his Cabbalistic
        activities and miracle works, his community rushed to his sup-
        port against R. Emden. Soon the community was split into war-
        ring factions. The most prominent Rabbis of Germany and Po-
        land were involved and consulted about the amulets which R.
        Jonathan had written and led up to pronouncement of a curse

on his amulet text by his former adherent R. Nehemiah Reischer, then Rabbi of Lorraine, and also R. Moses Mai, leader of the Metz community, the Rabbis of Metz, Amsterdam and Frankfurt, and R. Joshua Heschel the Rabbi of Treves. However, the Polish Rabbi Jacob Haim the A.B.D. of Lublin (a pupil of Eybeschutz), did not uphold the ban against him. Thus R. Joshua Heschel was prompted into writing to his younger brother, R. Moses Lwow, the Rabbi of Nikolsburg, to ask his then brother-in-law, R. Jacob Haim, to change his decision and to uphold the ban.

The King of Denmark, Frederick V, who originally supported Emden, was persuaded to the favor of Eybeschutz. Later at the Council of the Four Lands which met at Jaroslav in 1753, the Rabbinical court also decided in his favor, and the matter finally ended with the burning of the literature which had been brought against him.

In 1752 the Amsterdam publisher Proops began printing a new edition of the Talmud with many commentaries which received the approbations of the prominent Rabbis of the period. They decreed that no further edition could be printed for the next ten years, after the Amsterdam Edition was finished (which was eventually in 1765). However at this time the publisher Solomon of Sulzbach also began to print the Talmud similar in all respects to the Amsterdam volumes, which was vehemently opposed by R. Saul HaLevi (son of R. Aryey Lieb Lowenstam—see Chapter XII) whose father was the brother-in-law of R. Jacob Emden mentioned above. With the support of his brother-in-law, R. Isaac Halevi, the A.B.D. of Cracow, in a letter dated 1764, the local Polish Communities were prohibited from using the Sulzbach Edition because its publisher had opposed the Rabbinical Edict. R. Saul also went to R. Isaac Joseph Teomim, a leading German Rabbi, (see Chapter IV) to gain his aid as well in his battle against Solomon of Sulzbach. When Solomon the publisher saw he could not prevail against the Polish Rabbis and R. Lowenstam, he appealed to R. Joshua Heschel Lwow to help him out.

Lwow, already in his seventh decade, gave his legal decision in favor of the Sulzbach Talmud, although R. Lowenstam requested he retract his decision which was contrary to the Rabbinical Majority, and to the ban, which could only be settled by a Rabbinical Council. But R. Lwow maintained his decision and pointed out the Talmudic basis for his reason in a letter to R. Lowenstam dated 1764 and written in Schwabach where he was A.B.D. at that time. This struggle, despite his age, bears witness to R. Joshua Heschel's love of truth and justice.

LWOW-MARX FAMILY

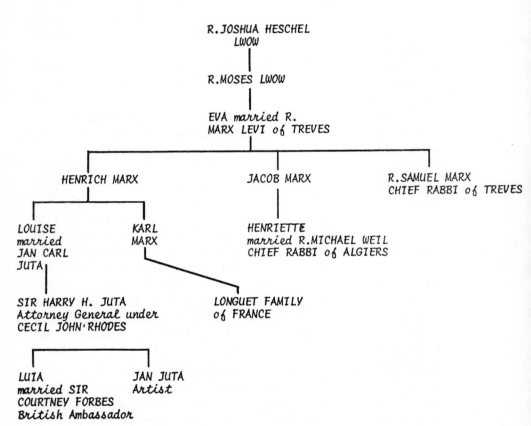

R.JOSHUA HESCHEL
LWOW

R.MOSES LWOW

EVA married R.
MARX LEVI of TREVES

HENRICH MARX   JACOB MARX   R.SAMUEL MARX
                                                CHIEF RABBI of TREVES

LOUISE   KARL   HENRIETTE
married   MARX   married R.MICHAEL WEIL
JAN CARL   CHIEF RABBI of ALGIERS
JUTA

SIR HARRY H. JUTA   LONGUET FAMILY
Attorney General under   of FRANCE
CECIL JOHN·RHODES

LUIA   JAN JUTA
married SIR   Artist
COURTNEY FORBES
British Ambassador

Five years later, when he was now seventy-six years old (1768) he took sides with R. Israel Lipschutz who had originally signed the Cleves Divorce Bill (*Get*) in 1766 (See Chapter VI—Branch C). R. Lwow sided with the other Rabbis who supported R. Israel against the Rabbis of Frankfurt, and he wrote a detailed responsum on this matter showing the validity of the divorce. His collected responsa entitled *Pnei Levonah* were never published, and were kept in the Bodlein Library in Oxford. One of his responsa was printed in the *Or HaYashar* mentioned above, which was a collection of the views of the Rabbis concerning the Cleves *Get* written by R. Aaron Simeon son of R. Jacob Abraham of Copenhagen (published in Amsterdam in 1769). Another responsum appeared in *Shav Yaakov* by R. Jacob Poppers (published in Frankfurt-on-Main in 1741/2), written while he was in Treves.

R. Lwow died in 1771 in Schwabach where he was the A.B.D. for some forty years, and his wife Merle a year later in 1772. His funeral oration was delivered by R. Joseph Steinhard.

G9. R. Moses Lwow, Rabbi of Treves, who wrote an approbation to *Aspaklaria HaMe-ira* a commentary on the Zohar by R. Zvi son of R. Joshua Moses Aaron Horowitz, (published Furth 1776), dated 25 October 1767, and to *Tifateh Aruch* (published in Metz in 1777), dated 13 September 1776. He was also known as Moses Levouf, and succeeded R. Isaac Sinzheim as A.B.D. of Treves. He married the daughter of R. Meir Eger of Furth.

G10. Eva (Chaya), married Meir Levi (later surnamed Marx), Rabbi of Treves, succeeding his father-in-law on the latter's death. Marx died in 1802, following which his wife remarried R. Moses Jacob son of R. Saul Lowenstamm. (See Descendants of R. Abraham Joshua Heschel of Cracow—Lowenstamm Family Pedigree—G6.4/7.2/8.1/9.1.)

G11.1. Rabbi Samuel Marx, A.B.D. of Treves succeeding his father there, and died about 1830.

G12.1. Moses Marx, a teacher in the Congregation of Gleiwitz.

G12.2. Sarah, married Israel Lazarus of Treves.

G12.3. Betty, married Jacob Bahr of Tholey (near Treves).

G12.4. Caroline, married Max Guggenheimer of Tholey.

G12.5. Amalia, first wife of Jacob Bahr of Tholey.

G11.2. Cerf (Hirsch) Marx, born in 1787 in Saarlois, lived in Aachen.

G11.3. Esther (died in 1865), married Gabriel Kosel of Zweibrucken in the Pfalz. They had no issue.

G11.4. Jacob Marx, died in Schlettstadt.

G12.1. Henriette (Eva), married R. Michael Aaron Weill. He was born in Strasburg in 1814, and having received his early education at Metz he received his Rabbinical

Diploma at the Sorbonne at Paris. In 1845 he was appointed instructor at Algiers, where he became the first French Chief Rabbi from 1846-1864. From 1864 to 1876 he held no further position but then accepted the Rabbinate of Toul until 1885. He settled in Paris where he devoted his time to literature, and was the author of a number of French works. He died in Paris in 1889.

G13.   Georges Weill, born in 1865 in Algiers. He was Professor of History at the Lycee-Louis-le-Grand of Paris. Like his father, he wrote a number of works in French.

G12.2.   Rachel, married the banker Isaac Guggenheimer of Marseilles.

G11.5.   Babette married Alexander Blum of Strassburg. She settled in Frankfurt on the death of her husband in Algiers.

   "My dear aunt," writes her niece Emilie (see below) to her on the death of Babette's sister Esther (mentioned above). "Even though the Power of Attorney of our good Sophie is not yet in effect (the Conradis want to wait), and Karl sent it himself, having no more patience, I'll follow as soon as I receive it. It bothers me very much that you my dear aunt are so nervous; I can imagine your depressed state, and I have often experienced the same when we have lost some one dear or valuable."

   This letter was written at the time of the death of Esther Kosel, her aunt, when the will left was found to be legally unacceptable, so that the closest family members are mentioned thus tying the genealogy of the Karl Marx family to that of R. Moses Lwow or Levouf as it is mentioned in the will. The case was successfully handled by the family lawyer Dr. S. Fuld.

G11.6.   Heinrich (Hirschel) Marx 1782-1838. He was a lawyer and judge in Treves. He married Henriette Pressburg, daughter of the Rabbi of Nijmegan, Holland. He converted to Christianity in 1824.

G12.1.   Emilie (author of the letter quoted above) married the engineer Jacob Conradi of Treves.

G12.2. Sophie married the lawyer Robert Schmalhausen of Mastricht.

G12.3. Louise, born in Treves in 1821, and died in Rondebosch, Cape, in 1893. She married in Treves in 1853 to Jan Carel (born in 1824), son of Hubertus Johannes Juta[16] of Zalt Bommel, Holland. A year or two thereafter, the couple went to South Africa. Here Carel Juta opened a "lending library" in Cape Town, having brought a large collection of books with him to the Cape. This later developed into a large publishing firm which still exits today under the name of Juta. He was also interested in law, and became a friend of the Cape judges and his firm brought him into contact with Sir George Grey and other public officials. His latter years were spent in Chiswick, England, where he died in 1886.

G13.1. Two sons died young.

G13.2. Jan Carel Juta, 1855-1883, married in 1873 to Kate Lacey, and had two sons.

G13.3. Louise Amelia married Mr. Hosmer.

G13.4. Wilhelmina Gertruida Albertina Helena, married George Frazer, and had issue, Gertrude (M.D., also married with issue in England).

G13.5. Sir Harry Herbert Juta (born Henricus Hubertus in Cape Town in 1857), the second son, who died in Battle, Sussex in 1930. He became a partner in the firm established by his father, but also studied law, and received his LL.B. with first-class honors from London University, and was called to the Bar by the Inner Temple in 1880. However, he returned to the Cape to practice law, and became prominent as an advocate, and was an examiner in law at the University of Cape Town. In 1890, he was Judicial Commissioner to Swaziland Concession Claims, and in 1892, made temporary Judge of the High Court in Kimberley. The following year he was made Q.C., entered politics, and was Attorney General to Prime Minister Cecil J. Rhodes, succeeding W. P. Schreiner in 1894. Despite his friendship with Rhodes, he was not involved in the Jameson Raid which resulted in the fall of the Cabinet in 1886. Therefore, the same year, he was elected Speaker of the House of Assembly. During this period, he was painted in 1896 by Tennyson Cole. This portrait now hangs in the Cape Town Houses of Parliament. In 1897 he was knighted by Queen Victoria, and in 1914, appointed Judge President of the Cape Division of the Supreme Court. He retired in 1923 from a career which had led him to be considered one of the ablest of South African judges. His latter years were spent in England.

He married in 1883 to Helena Lena (Lady Juta), daughter of Mr. M. Tait of Rondebosch, Cape. She was, on her mother's side, a descendant of Elizabeth Gunning (1734-90), who married the Sixth Duke of Hamilton and Brandon, and then remarried John Campbell, Duke of Argyll. Lady Juta received the O.B.E., and was president of at least twenty-four charitable organizations. The couple had one son and four daughters. Sir Juta was the author of several works on Cape law, of law reports and transactions and others. He published *Reminiscences of Circuit, Tales for Children, Improvisasation for Piano* and *Off the Track*. He was featured in the Who's Who of 1929.

G14.1.   Réné Juta, schooled in England and Paris where she studied painting and writing. She was the author of *The Cape Peninsula* (1910), with illustrations by her brother Jan (1927), *Concerning Corsica* (1926), together with her brother, *Cannes and the Hills* (1928), together with her brother and several novels. She married Luke Hansard of London and had a daughter, Jillian, a member of a Christian religious order in France.

G14.2.   Helen Juta, studied piano and violin in Berlin, and later in London. She was also engaged by the Quinlan Opera Company of London. Here she married J. D. Davis, an English musician and composer. They had no issue.

G14.3.   Brenda (died about 1967), studied the cello in

Germany and England. She married Rev. Frank Symes-Thompson, an Anglican clergyman of London, and had two sons.

G14.4. Luia Juta, born in 1890, the youngest daughter, studied under Madame Albani who was at the time at the height of her fame, singing at Covent Garden, and later in Paris. She married Sir Courtney Forbes, who later became Minister to Mexico, Spain and then Ambassador to Peru. She is currently a teacher in Switzerland. They divorced in 1946, having had issue, one daughter. Sir Forbes remarried.

G15. Sarah, born in 1917, married 1) Hugh Herbert Gyle Thompson of Gerrard's Cross (died in 1972), and had issue, and 2) Dr. Hugo Stephens.

G16.1. Elizabeth, born in 1939, married in 1965 to Oliver Papps, Public Relations Director for the New Jersey Petroleum Council, and have issue, Jillian Sara and Luia Elizabeth. They live in Bernardsville, N.J.

G16.2. Robina, born in 1941, married Christopher Watson, and have issue, Timothy and Angus.

G16.3. David Thompson, born in 1943, married, and has issue.

G14.5. Jan Carel Juta, born in Cape Town in 1895. He studied Law at Christ Church College, Oxford and served in England during World War I. However, he was always keenly interested in art, and entered the art school known as *The Slade* in England, and then continued in Rome until about 1921. It was here that his career was determined by his meeting with D. H. Lawrence. While visiting Sicily with Lawrence in 1923, he painted his portrait which is today on display in the National Portrait Gallery in London. This same picture featured as the frontispiece of the classical work by Harry T. Moore, *The Life and Works of D. H. Lawrence* (1951). From Madrid in 1924, Juta went to Paris where he settled. Dur-

ing World War II he served with the British Ministry of Information between London and New
York. After the war he worked for the Department of Public Information of the United Nations. About this time he settled with his family
in Mendham, New Jersey. He was a past President of the National Society of Mural Painters
of America, and was recently re-elected (1975).

His murals have been commissioned in England, South Africa, France and the U.S.A., and
are to be found in both public and private buildings. The Cunard liners *Queen Mary* and *Queen
Elizabeth* had his murals, and several churches
in the eastern states have memorials designed by
him.

Besides the pictures to be found in the books
written by his sister (see above), the *Sea and
Sardinia* by D. H. Lawrence (1921) has eight of
his pictures, he wrote *Background in Sunshine*
(Memories of South Africa, 1972). Jan Juta is
also a lay preacher in the Episcopalian Church
and a member of several art societies.

He married in London in 1933 to Alice Hunt-
ington Marshall, who had two children from her
previous marriage. They had no issue.

G12.4. Karl Marx (also Karl Heinrich) was born in Treves
in 1818 and died in London in 1883. He became
a baptized Lutheran with his father in 1824, a
practice prevalent at that time which thereby enabled
Jews to pursue professional careers. He married in
1843 to Jenny von Westphal. He first studied juris-
prudence at the University of Bonn, and then philosophy and history at Berlin. In 1841 he obtained his
Ph.D. from the University of Jena.

Because of political activities and being the editor
of an anti-Prussian journal, Marx moved to Paris
where he stayed until 1845. Having been introduced
to Hegelian philosophy, he wrote magazine articles
which led to his expulsion from Paris to Brussels
where he remained until 1848. Here he began to pub-

lish together with Frederick Engels, who became his lifelong friend. He started a Communist magazine and his famous Manifesto appeared in 1848 which concludes with the well-known "Workers of the World, Unite!"

After visits to Vienna, a trial by jury in Cologne in 1849, and a visit to Paris from which he was again expelled, Marx settled in poverty and illness in London. The following year he was joined by Engels. In London from 1852-1861, he was a contributor to the *New York Tribune*. 1852 was also the year that two of his classic works *The Civil War in France* and *The Eighteenth Brumaire of Louis Bonaparte* appeared. During the following years he again visited Germany, and in 1866 he headed the first congress of the International in Geneva. The following year the first part of *Das Kapital* appeared, the second and third parts being published posthumously. His wife died in 1881, his daughter Jenny in 1882, and he himself the following year.

He wrote a number of other works, and is considered to be the Father of Scientific Socialism. He led a life devoted to the passionate defense of national as well as economic freedom, calling for emancipation of the Jew, Christianity and from religion generally.

Marx had six daughters, three of whom reached marriageable age.

G13.1.   Laura, married Paul Lafargue.

G13.2.   Eleanor, married the English Socialist Aveling. She, unlike her father, strongly identified herself with Judaism, but committed suicide in England in 1898.

G13.3.   Jenny, married 1872 to Charles Longuet who, at the time of his father-in-law's death, was a member of the staff of *La Justice*. After the War of 1870, he took part in the Paris Commune which led to his expulsion from France. He then lived in London, where his children were born. Four children reached adulthood.[17]

G14.1.   Jean Longuet (1876-1938), died as a result of an auto accident. He was a prominent French po-

litical socialist, lawyer and journalist, born in
London during the exile of his father there. From
1914-32 he was Deputy of the Fourth Seine District which included some important Paris suburbs. He became one of the most trusted men of
the Socialist party and an intimate friend of Leon
Blum, later Premier of France. Because of his
closeness to Russian Bolsheviks and being a
grandson of Karl Marx, he was denied entry into
the U.S.A. in 1920. The following year he joined
Leon Blum in forming a less radical political party
of Conservative Socialists and was then allowed
on a lecture tour of the U.S.A. during which he
assailed the political policies of the French war-
time Premier George Clemenceau. He was also
a member of the French Foreign Relations Committee for several terms and he vigorously declared that the Allied forces should accept Germany's peace terms following World War I and
not to make stringent demands on them. Being
an ardent pacifist, he once declared (in 1917)
at a national congress of French Socialists that
they should adopt the motto of "Peace without
victory."

He married Anita Desvaux.

G15.1.   Robert Longuet, born 1901, no issue.
G15.2.   Karl (Jean, Paul) Longuet, born 1904, married
         1949 to Simone Boisecq. He is a noted French
         sculptor of rock, marble, wood, bronze and
         steel. His works have been displayed at inter-
         national expositions and some of his pieces are
         permanently displayed, e.g. Montmesly Place,
         Creteil (Paris), in Montreuil, Chatenay-Mala-
         bry, Rosny-sous-Bois, Le Mans, Ussel, Limoges,
         Toulouse, Tours, and others. He also designed
         medallions of Karl Marx, Eluard, Leger, Schoel-
         cher, and others. He studied at the School
         Lakanal in Sceaux, the School of Decorative
         Arts and was a pupil of Niclausse and Jean
         Boucher. Since 1957 he was a member of the

French Unesco Committee. He was decorated
with the title of Knight of Arts and Letters and
received the Marmoro Portoro Award at the
Carrare International Exposition in 1957.

G16.1. Frederique, born January 1955.
G16.2. Anne Laura, born November 1958.

G14.2. Marcel Longuet, 1877-1949. He was a journalist
who had reported on the French Parliament and
toward the end of his life was a radio broadcaster.
His death was reported in the New York Times.

G15.1. Marcel-Charles Longuet.

G14.3. Dr. Edgar Longuet, M.D., born 1879 and died in
Paris in 1950 while caring for one of his patients.
He was a veteran French Socialist who resigned
from their political party in 1937 to protest its
policy of non-intervention in the Spanish Civil
War. He married Blanche Beurier.

G15.1. Paul Jean Longuet, born 1909. One of the foremost agriculturists of France who has played a
big role in politics.

He was educated at the famous School
Lycee Charlemagne in Paris and the Agriculture School of Tunis where he obtained a Diploma in Tropical Agriculture and Engineering.

From 1947-52 he was a Counsellor to the
French Union; from 1952-59 Senator for Madagascar; became (in 1959) a member of Assembly of the Province of Tamatave and of the
Senate of Malgache; in 1957 Minister of Economics to the Government of Madagascar; from
1959-63 Finance and Economics Affairs Minister to Malgache, and in 1963 their Minister
of State in charge of scientific research. The
following year he was elected Inspector General of the Aforrestry Board for development
and agricultural production, technical counsellor for the Cabinet of the Malgache President and holds the Knight of the Legion of

Honor. He is also an Officer of the National
Order of Merit, Knight of Agricultural Merit
and Grand Officer of the National Malgache
Order, amongst others.

He married in 1933 to Suzanne Denise.

G16.1.   Nelly, married Maurice Aldebert.
G16.2.   Jean-Paul Longuet.

G15.2.   Charles Longuet.
G15.3.   Frederique Longuet.
G15.4.   Jenny Longuet, died.

G14.4.   Jenny Longuet, unmarried.

G8.2.   R. Joseph Lwow, son from his father's first wife, married the
daughter of R. Isaac son of R. Moses Oppenheim. In 1724 he
occupied the position of *Rabbinatsassesor* in Eisenstadt during
the leadership of R. Meir Eisenstadt. In 1733 he became A.B.D.
of Trebitsch and remained here until his death in 1755.

G9.   R. Hirsch Lwow, *Rabbinatsassesor* of Pressburg, died in 1771.

G10.   R. Mendel Lwow.

G11.   R. Abraham Hirsch Lwow, Leader of the Pressburg (Hungary) Community where he died in 1834.

G8.3.   R. Moses Lwow, from the second wife, born in Lvov in 1704,
and died on December 28, 1757 in Nikolsburg. He left home at
the age of eight to be raised by his maternal grandfather R.
Gabriel Eskeles in Nikolsburg. In 1724 he was appointed Rabbi
of Leipnik and in 1729 he succeeded R. Jehiel Michael Hasid as
A.B.D. of Berlin. In 1730 he became A.B.D. of Frankfurt-on-
Oder where he stayed until about 1743, when he returned to
Leipnik as the A.B.D. On the death of his uncle R. Issachar
Berish Eskeles in 1753, he was appointed Landesrabbiner of
Moravia. His novellae on the Tractate of the *Talmud Rosh Ha-
Shannah* were published in 1731 in Frankfurt-on-Oder. He also
wrote to R. Jacob Poppers in 1738, which is recorded in the
Responsa work entitled *Shav Yaakov.* He was married three
times.

1. The daughter of Issachar Beer, Leader of the Nikolsburg
   Community. She died in 1727.
2. Reichele, daughter of Josel Guntzburg of Prensen, maternal

granddaughter of R. Zadok Weill of Obernheim. She died in Nikolsburg in 1748.

3. The daughter of R. Abraham, son of R. Haim of Lublin, Head of the Council of the Four Lands. She was a sister of R. Jacob Haim A.B.D. of Lublin.

G9.1. Hendel, married R. Gershon Politz (Pulitz), his second wife. His first wife Malka, daughter of Sekel Neustadt, died in Nikolsburg in 1758. They were married ten years, when her husband died on the 22nd of Elul. He was A.B.D. of Nikolsburg from 1753-72, and was succeeded by R. Samuel Shmelke Horowitz. His daughter was married to R. Haim Katzenellenbogen. (See Chapter II — Branch B — Section a — G8.)

G9.2. Wife of R. Isaac, A.B.D. of Tarnow, son of R. Jacob Haim A.B.D. of Lublin, her cousin (see above). R. Isaac died in 1769, and his wife then remarried R. Saul son of R. Aryey Lieb Lowenstamm, mentioned above (see G8.1/9/10).

G10.1. Miriam, married R. Joseph Jacob, A.B.D. of Lisk (Galicia).

G10.2. Feigel, married R. Haim son of R. Joseph Hochgelerhter. They were second cousins. (See Chapter VII—Branch B—G5.4/6.3/7.1/8.2.)

G8.4. Donna in Boskowitz.

G8.5. Hindele, married R. Joseph Eisenstadter.

G8.6. Wife of Rabbi of Chovlisk.

CHAPTER IV

DESCENDANTS OF
R. JONAH TEOMIM
(G2.1/3.3/4.1/5.9)

G5.9. R. Jonah Teomim, son-in-law of R. Meir, son of R. Saul Wahl Katzenellenbogen. His father, R. Isaiah, died in 1638, and was one of the four sons of R. Moses Aaron Teomim, son of R. Simeon Teomim-Lemel, who lived at the end of the 17th century in Prague. R. Moses Aaron's wife was Rebecca, daughter of R. Israel Horowitz and a sister of R. Phineas Halevi Horowitz. His son, Jonah, had four sons and three daughters.[1]

G6.1. R. Jacob Teomim-Shulhof, died 1703. He married Yetle, daughter of R. Anschel Shulhof. She died in 1710.

G7.1. R. Jonah Shulhof of Prague.
G7.2. R. Baruch Shulhof of Prague.

G6.2. R. Isaac Meir Teomim-Frankel, *Dokter und Rabbiner,* Rabbinical and scientific scholar. When he was eighteen years old he went to Vienna. Here he studied under R. Moses Mirles Frankel, whose daughter Sarah, he later married. After her death, Isaac remarried to a granddaughter of his father-in-law, daughter of R. Abraham (their daughter later married Isaac's brother, R. Israel). In 1670 the two families were forced to flee from the city of Vienna following the Imperial Expulsion Order which had been set for August 1st of that year. This took place during the reign of Leopold I, Emperor of Austria. Jewish homes were taken over by the city, the synagogue became Leopoldskirche and the Jewish quarter renamed Leopoldstadt. After living in Hamburg for a time, R. Isaac Teomim became A.B.D. of Zolkiev. Here he published

Ketonet Or, a commentary on *Ayin Ya'akov* (a collection of Babylonian Talmudic legends), in Amsterdam, 1684. This work also contains his genealogy and mentions the connections of his two marriages.

R. Isaac's next Rabbinical posts were A.B.D. Slutzk and later at Pinsk, where he succeeded R. Joel Halpern, son of R. Tobiah of Lissa. His signature appeared in the Records of the Land when the Council sat at Chamsk in 1683, when he was at Slutzk, and in 1695, when he was at Pinsk. His approbations were on: *Zevachei Toviah,* by R. Tobiah son of R. Samuel Gutman, Amsterdam, 1683, written in Zolkiev; *Divrei Chachamim* by R. Judah Lieb son of R. Joseph Puchbitzer, Hamburg, 1691-2, written in Chamsk; *Da'at Chochma,* one of the four books collected under the title *Kevod Chachamim,* by R. Judah Lieb Puchbitzer, Venice, 1700; *Shabatah D'Riglah* by R. Zvi Hirsch son of R. Jerachmeel Chatsch Furth, 1693, written in Slutzk; *Sefatei Chachamim* by R. Shabbtai son of R. Joseph Bass, Frankfurt-on-Main, 1712, written in 1693 when he was in Breslau; *Shmeinah Lachmoh* by R. Asher Anschel son of R. Isaac of Przemysl, Desvia, 1701, written in 1699; *Rosh Yosef* by R. Joseph son of R. Jacob of Pinczow, Keitan, 1717, written in 1700; *Kevod Chachamim* by R. Simeon Wolf son of R. Jacob of Pinczow, Hamburg, 1703, written while passing through Pinczow where he signed himself as A.B.D. Pinsk. He is recorded as "of blessed memory," thus indicating he died sometime between 1701-1702.

G7.1. R. Judah Jonah Teomim-Frankel, signed in the Records of Razinai in 1720. He married Sarah Chaya. Their son, R. Isaac Zakil Teomim-Frankel.

G7.2. R. Abraham Teomim-Frankel, mentioned in the introduction of *Dvar Moshe* by R. Moses, son of R. Ephraim Teomim. (See Branch A — G12.1/13.4.)

G8. R. Isaac (Meir) Frankel.

G9.1. R. Liebus Frankel-Teomim, A.B.D. Chartkov.

G10. R. Joseph, A.B.D. Borstein, died in 1758.

G11. R. Zvi Hirsch, A.B.D. Kalucz, married the daughter of R. Jacob of Lissa, grandson of R. Nathan, son of Chacham Zvi Ashkenazi. (See Descendants of Chacham Zvi Ashkenazi — Chapter XIII.) Their descendants constitute the Teomim Family — Branch A.

TEOMIM FAMILY

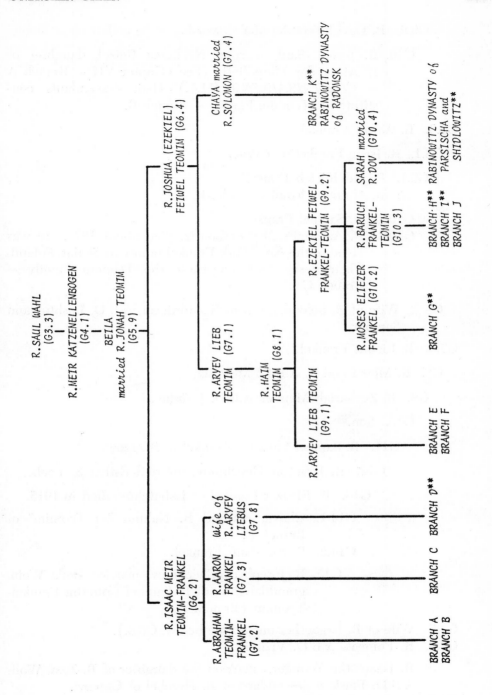

R.SAUL WAHL
(G3.3)

R.MEIR KATZENELLENBOGEN
(G4.1)

BEILA
married R.JONAH TEOMIM
(G5.9)

R.ISAAC MEIR
TEOMIM-FRANKEL
(G6.2)

R.JOSHUA (EZEKIEL)
FEIWEL TEOMIM (G6.4)

CHAYA *married*
R.SOLOMON (G7.4)

BRANCH K**
RABINOWITZ DYNASTY
of RADOMSK

R.ABRAHAM
TEOMIM-
FRANKEL
(G7.2)

R.AARON
FRANKEL
(G7.3)

wife of
R.ARYEY
LIEBUS
(G7.8)

R.ARYEY LIEB
TEOMIM
(G7.1)

R.HAIM
TEOMIM (G8.1)

R.ARYEY LIEB TEOMIM
(G9.1)

R.EZEKIEL FEIWEL
FRANKEL-TEOMIM (G9.2)

R.MOSES ELIEZER
FRANKEL (G10.2)

R.BARUCH
FRANKEL-
TEOMIM
(G10.3)

SARAH *married*
R.DOV (G10.4)

BRANCH A
BRANCH B

BRANCH C

BRANCH D**

BRANCH E
BRANCH F

BRANCH G**

BRANCH H** RABINOWITZ DYNASTY of
BRANCH I** PARSISCHA *and*
BRANCH J SHIDLOWITZ**

** = *Chassidic Dynasties*

G9.2. R. David Teomim of Prezworsk.

G10. R. Joseph Saul, married Nechama Reizel, daughter of R. Alexander Margolioth. (See Chapter VII — Branch A — G6.2/7.4/8.4/9.2/10.1/11.1.) Their descendants constitute the Teomim Family — Branch B.

G7.3. R. Aaron Frankel.

G8.1. R. Isaac Frankel of Zbariz.

G9.1. R. Judah Lieb Frankel.
G9.2. R. Abraham Frankel of Zbariz.

G10.1. R. Samuel Frankel.
G10.2. R. Aaron Frankel of Zbariz, died about 1825. He was Head of the New York Frankel family of Skalat, Poland. Their descendants constitute the Teomim Family — Branch C.

G8.2. Wife of R. Solomon, son of R. Mordecai, A.B.D. Lashtov and Sambor.

G7.4. R. Liebus Frankel.

G8. R. Meir Frankel, A.B.D. Meseritz.

G9. R. Zechariah Mendel, A.B.D. Jaroslav.

G10. Son.

G11. R. Samuel Shmelke Frankel of Rzeszow.

G12. R. Israel of Chechinov, married Esther S. Leeb.

G13. R. Eleazar Frankel of Lobatchov, died in 1915.

G14.1. Chaya, married R. Nahum Zvi Teomim[2] of Branch F.
G14.2. R. Abraham Frankel.

G15. R. Joseph of Chechinov, married Beila Wein, granddaughter of R. Samuel Ephraim Frankel-Teomim (Branch B).

G7.5. Wife of R. Israel, her uncle (see below, G6.3.).
G7.6. R. Phineas, A.B.D. Vizhniz.

G8. R. Isaac "the Younger," married the daughter of R. Zeev Wolf, A.B.D. Fiask, a descendant of R. Heschel of Cracow.
G7.7. R. Saul of Mohilev.

G7.8. Wife of R. Aryeh Liebus of Apt, son of R. Jonah A.B.D. Tarla (author of *Aleh D'Yonah*, published Furth, 1694), son of R. Moses Benjamin Zeev.

G8. R. Peretz.

G9. R. Israel of Lubartov.[3]

G10. Pearl, wife of R. Levi Isaac of Berdichev, known as the Berdichiver Rov. Their descendants constitute the Teomim Family—Branch D. Some of the descendants adopted the surname Derbarmdiger.

G6.3. R. Israel Teomim, married his niece. He published his father's book, *Kikayon D'Yonah,* in Amsterdam in 1670, and died in Zolkiev.

G7. R. Joshua Feiwel Teomim, born in Tarnograd, and died in Zolkiev in 1777. He was the author of *Kitzui Eretz*, published in Zolkiev, 1771.

G6.4. R. Joshua (Ezekiel) Feiwel Teomim, A.B.D. Przemysl, and said to have written a work entitled *Tekah Shofar.* He married Pearl, daughter of R. Ari Lieb, *Der Hoicher Reb Lieb,* son of R. Zechariah, A.B.D. of Cracow. He came to Amsterdam in 1670 where he and his brother published their father's work. His *Hagahot* appear in the 1731 Zolkiev Edition of *Taamei HaMesorah* by R. Jacob David, son of R. Isaac, A.B.D. Zausmer. His approbations were on: *Ir Chomah* by R. Abraham Judah Elijah son of R. Eliezer Lipman, Frankfurt-on-Oder, 1719, written in 1712 at Przemysl; *Brit Shalom* by R. Phineas son of R. Philta, Frankfurt-on-Main, 1718; written in 1713; *Magal HaOmer* by R. Jacob son of R. Moses HaKohen, Hamburg, 1747.

G7.1. R. Aryeh Lieb Teomim, A.B.D. Kreshov.

G8.1. R. (Haim) Joseph, was at first A.B.D. Ostrovitz and then *Darshan* of Posen. He later became A.B.D. Lublin, where R. Saul Margolioth lived. His name appears in later editions of *Ketonet Or.* He married Rachel, daughter of R. Nathan, A.B.D. Turbin, son-in-law of R. Baruch Rappoport, A.B.D. Furth, son-in-law of R. Moses Ish Zvi, A.B.D. Grodno, maternal grandson of R. Heschel of Cracow. His signature appears in various records of Lublin, where he died in 1782. (See Part III — Chapter IX.)

G9.1. R. Aryeh (Judah) Lieb Teomim, A.B.D. of Brody, author of *Gur Aryeh Yehudah*, published in Zolkiev, 1827. He is mentioned in the Responsa of R. Haim Cohen Chelek. He also wrote *Ayelet Ahavim*, Zolkiev, 1822, and *Ya'elat Chein*, Zolkiev, 1822.

G10.1. R. Ezekiel Meir Teomim-Weinberg,[4] of Bilgoray, married Golda Rachel, daughter of R. Nathan Isaac Berliner, A.B.D. Bilgoray. He was the founder of the Weinberg family — see Branch E. He died in Ostilla in 1849.
G10.2. R. Baruch Samuel Teomim, A.B.D. Brody.

G11.1. R. Meinish Mordecai of Brody, married a daughter of R. Baruch Frankel-Teomim. (See below G10.3.)
G11.2. R. Israel Teomim of Brody, founder of Branch F.

G12. R. Nathan Nata, surnamed Weinberger.

G13. R. Eleazar Weinberger.

G14. R. Asher Jonah Weinberger.

G15. Sima, married R. Meir Horowitz of Shatz-New York. (See Chapter XVI — Branch VII.)

G9.2. R. Ezekiel Feiwel (Joshua Feiwel) Frankel-Teomim, A.B.D. Ostrovitz with his father. He married the daughter of R. Issachar Ber, A.B.D. Chernowitz, son of R. Joshua Lieb, A.B.D. of Dobromil. (See Chapter XI — G7.6.) He died in 1771.

G10.1. R. Aryey Lieb Teomim of Zavichovitz, a wealthy businessman who married the daughter of R. Moses Halevi Bornstein of Zavichovitz.
G10.2. R. Moses Eliezer Frankel.

G11. R. Uri Lipman Frankel,[5] Head of the Kamader Frankel Chassidic Family. (See Branch G.)

G10.3. R. Baruch Frankel-Teomim, one of the outstanding pupils of R. David Tebele, A.B.D. of Lissa, as he mentions in his work, *Nefesh David*. He was born in 1760. He later studied under R. Judah Harif Lieber, son of R. Benjamin, A.B.D. of Cracow. His approbations to *Tzemach leAvraham* by R. Avi Hirsch, son of R. Chaim HaLevi, Warsaw, 1796, was written in 1795 when he was at

Vizhniz, where he was elected A.B.D. in 1779, succeeding R. Naftali Hirsch Margolioth, who died in 1778. He
remained there for over twenty-years until 1802. After
the death of R. Benjamin Wolf Eger in 1796, he became
A.B.D. of Leipnik in 1802. Here he wrote his most famous work, *Baruch Tam*, published by his son. His
works were: *Baruch Tam*, novellae and *pilpulim*, Lvov,
1841, with five further editions between 1878 and 1914;
Baruch SheAmar, Pietrokov, 1905, Jerusalem, 1966;
Marganita DeRav, Lvov, 1883, Pietrokov, 1930, (*Hashalem*), London, 1957; *Imrei Baruch*, Vienna, 1875, *Hagahot* on *Mishnayot* and the Jerusalem Talmud in *Turei
Even* by R. Aryeh Lieb, son of R. Asher; *Ateret Chachamim*, Responsa and novellae, Josefow, 1866 and
Padgorze, 1899; *Chidushei Baruch Tam*, London 1960,
by his two descendants, Baruch S. Shneersohn and Elhanan Halpern.

His approbation of 1822 appeared in *Toldot Avraham* by R. Abraham, A.B.D. Glogau and Ohleinov. He
remained A.B.D. in Leipnik until 1825, and died there
in 1828.

He was married twice: 1) Jochebed Rebecca,
daughter of R. Judah Parnas of Vizhniz[6] (see Landau
Family Pedigree — G8.2/9.9/10); 2) daughter of R. Zvi
Joshua HaLevi, son of R. Shmelke Horowitz (son-in-law
of his uncle, R. Phineas Horowitz, author of *Hamikneh
VeHaPele*).

G11.1. R. Joshua Heschel Frankel-Teomim, who against his
        father's wishes studied under Chassidic guidance dur-
        ing his youth. Later, his father accepted these teach-
        ings, being so impressed with the knowledge which
        he had accumulated, and even had his daughter mar-
        ry the famous Chassid, R. Haim Halberstam. Although
        his main interest was in the commercial world, R.
        Heschel was said to have accepted the position of
        A.B.D. of Komarno for a short time, so as not to break
        the family tradition which had existed for hundreds
        of years. He died in 1843. He was the head of
        Branch H.

G11.2. R. Joseph, who established a large Yeshiva in Plonsk.

His eulogy appears in *Beit Aharon* by R. Aaron of
Koyil, published Pietrokov, 1931. He married the
daughter of R. Haim Halevi Zemach of Plonsk, a descendant of the *Magen Avraham.*

G12.1. Wife of R. Zvi Hirsch, son of R. Jacob Meir Padua.
(See Chapter II — Padua Family.)

G12.2. Wife of R. Simha, son of R. Samuel Shmelke Horowitz. (See Chapter XVI.)

G11.3. First wife of R. Haim Halberstam.

G11.4. Rachel Feige, second wife of R. Haim Halberstam.
(See Sanz Chassidic Dynasty — Chapter XIV.)

G11.5. Wife of R. Meinish Mordecai Teomim of Brody. His
father was a first cousin to her father.

G11.6. Wife of R. Meir Jehiel HaLevi Kaminer, died in 1847,
from whom were descended the Gerer Chassidim —
Branch I.

G11.7. Wife of R. Zalman Goldstoff of Cracow, head of the
Goldstoff Family — see Branch J.

G11.8. Chaya, wife of R. Isaiah, son of R. Wolf Ber Schiff
of Zamoscz. From them are descended the Silberfeld and Rubinstein families. (See Chapter VII —
Branch B.)

G10.4. Sarah Teomim[9] married R. Dov, A.B.D. of White Field.
His son-in-law narrates how when newly wed, he lived
with his father-in-law, a watchmaker.

G11. Golda, married R. Jerachmeel Moses, the A.B.D. of
Parsischa (died in 1839) son of R. Jacob Isaac known
as the Holy *Yehudi* (or *Yud*).
The family later adopted the surname of Rabinowitz.

It happened once that young Jerachmeel and his father were travelling
to Rymanov and lost their way. Later after finding their road once again,
they rested at an inn, where they received some baked potatoes while
awaiting the main meal. The son, on snatching the potatoes from out of the
innkeeper's hand, was rebuked by his father. "My son," the Yehudi said,
"your hunger does not excuse your lack of good manners. Therefore
you shall sit with the driver of the coach instead of inside!"

Once Rabbi Jerachmeel was approached for advice by a tailor who had
made a suit of clothes for the local Count, but which did not fit and which
the Count refused to accept. The Rabbi counselled that the tailor remake

the suit, which, on being presented to the Count was gladly and satisfactorily accepted. From this the Rabbi taught how pride can be a hinderance; "The first suit was made careless of details because of pride, but the second was made in a contrite mood with care, thus achieving worthy workmanship."

> G12.1. R. Nathan David Rabinowitz, the Admur of Shidlowitz, was born in Parsischa in 1814 and died in Shidlowitz in 1865. He was opposed to Chassidim who stated they required a long time to prepare themselves before prayer.

As a soldier who arrives late to stand guard before the Palace daily at sunrise is punished, despite the excuse he needed time to brush his clothes, so too are we required to pray within the appointed hours, and longer preparation will be of no avail if we delay.

> In the Ethics of the Fathers we read: "Provide thyself a teacher, and get thee a companion, and judge all men in the scale of merit."
>
> R. Nathan David taught: On the death of his Rebbe, a Chassid is often hesitant to accept his new teacher. If he cannot accept him, let him then be a companion. But if he hesitates further, thinking "He may falsely think he is my Master when I only think of him as a companion, and thus he'd be having untruthful thoughts." Thus the Chassid is told to judge all men, and to believe that though he calls him Rebbe (My Master) he is seeking his friendship as a companion.

> G13.1. R. Zemach Rabinowitz, Admur of Shidlowitz, 1836-1892, married the daughter of R. Eleazar of Kozenitz.

> G14.1. R. Meir Israel Rabinowitz, died in 1926. He married the daughter of R. Noah of Piasense where he became Admur in 1910.

> G15.1. R. Jacob, succeeded his father as Admur, and perished in the Holocaust.
> G15.2. R. Zemach, also succeeded his father and, in 1931 he succeeded his uncle R. Nathan David Rabinowitz as Admur Shidlowitz.

G16. R. Zvi Menachem Rabinowitz of Warsaw, perished.

G14.2. R. Isaac Simha Rabinowitz, Admur Apt, died in 1937.

G14.3. R. Ozer Abraham Joseph Rabinowitz, Admur Rokov-Bilitz, died in 1925.

G15. R. Zemach, succeeded his father.

G14.4. R. Zvi Menachem Rabinowitz, Admur in Warsaw from 1928, perished there in the Holocaust.

G14.5. R. Nathan David Rabinowitz, 1871-1931, Admur Shidlowitz. He studied under his uncle R. Shraga Jair Rabinowitz.

G13.2. R. Phineas Rabinowitz of Kinsk, died in 1901. He married Raatza Zelda, daughter of R. Moses Naftali Katzenellenbogen. (See Chapter VIII — G9.1/10.7.)

G14.1. R. Joseph Eliezer Rabinowitz of Radom, 1862-1942, married his first cousin, daughter of R. Shraga Jair Rabinowitz of Bialberzig.

G15.1. R. Jedidiah of Radom.

G15.2. R. Benzion of Werzbinsk, married the daughter of R. Samuel Zvi of Beidozin.

G15.3. R. Alter.

G15.4. Wife of her uncle R. Haim Shraga Zvi.

G14.2. Golda Leah married R. Benzion son of R. Tuvia Horowitz (See Chapter XVI — Branch VII — G14.1/15.3/16.2).

G14.3. Malka married R. Joshua Heschel, A.B.D. Chentshin, son of R. Haim Samuel Horowitz. (See Chapter IV—Branch H — G11.1/12.3.)

G14.4. R. Elimelech Jacob Isaac Rabinowitz, married 1) the daughter of R. Hillel Brownfinkler of Radoshitz son of R. Isaac, and 2) her niece, daughter of R. Eliezer David, son of R. Hillel Brownfinkler.

G15.1. Wife of R. Haim Judah Sheinfeld, settled in England. He died in Israel in 1968.

G15.2. R. Reuben Issachar Jerachmeel Rabinowitz.

G15.3. R. Joseph Baruch Rabinowitz of Kilitz, perished.

G15.4. R. Nathan David Rabinowitz of Kilitz.

G14.5. R. Nathan David Rabinowitz of Kinsk.

G15. R. Jerachmeel Baruch Asher Rabinowitz.

G14.6. R. Haim Shraga Rabinowitz, married his niece, daughter of R. Joseph Eliezer Rabinowitz of Radom.

G14.7. R. Joseph Eliezer Rabinowitz of Radom.

G15. Wife of her uncle R. Haim Shraga Rabinowitz.

G13.3. R. Shraga Jair Rabinowitz of Bialberzig 1841-1912, author of *Aaron Eidut*. He married Dinah, daughter of R. Samuel Shmelke, son of R. Moses Lieb of Sassov.

G14.1. R. Nathan David Rabinowitz of Shidlowitz 1867-1919, named after his grandfather who died two years before his birth.

G15.1. R. Haim Israel Shalom Jekutiel of Shidlowitz, born in 1899. He married the daughter of R. Moses Bezalel Alter of Ger. The family perished. (See Chapter IV — Branch I).

G15.2. R. Jeremiah of Warsaw.

G15.3. R. Reuben Baruch, married Esther, daughter of R. Isaac Zelig Morgenstern (Admur Sokolov — See Chapter XII — Branch C). Their sons, Abraham and Jacob (married his cousin, Leah, daughter of Jacob Mendel Morgenstern).

G14.2. Wife of 1) R. Haim Eleazar Spira of Munkacs and 2) R. Haim Hager of Ottinya (died in 1934).

G14.3. Wife of R. Joseph Eliezer Rabinowitz, her first cousin.

G13.4. R. Isaac Jacob Rabinowitz of Biala, died in 1905, the author of *Divrei Binah* (Lublin, 1910) and *Yashrei Lev*. He married Rachel, daughter of R. Joshua of Sosnowiec (author of *Toldot Adam*).

G14.1. R. Nathan David Rabinowitz of Parziveh (Porisov), named after his grandfather, died in 1930. He married Leah Reizel, daughter of R. Jehiel Jacob of Kozenitz.

G15.1. Esther, married R. Abraham Jacob Shapiro of Drogobitch-Jerusalem. (See Shapiro Chassidic Family — Chapter XVII.)

G15.2. Feigle, married R. Aaron Perlow of Stolin, son of R. Israel son of R. Asher of Stolin. (See Perlow Chassidic Family — Chapter VII — G16.2, page 299.)

G15.3. R. Elimelech Moses Jehiel Rabinowitz of Parziveh.

G15.4. R. Baruch Joshua Jerachmeel Rabinowitz, Admur Parziveh-Munkacs-Holon, born in 1913. He married the daughter of R. Haim Eleazar, son of R. Zvi Hirsch Spira, Admur Munkacs, whom he succeeded, and later settled in Israel.

G16.1. R. Jacob Rabinowitz, established the Yeshiva *Darkei Teshuva* in New York.

G16.2. R. Moses Lieb Rabinowitz, Admur Munkacs in Israel where he established the Yeshiva *Minchat Eleazar*.

G15.5. Chava married R. Israel Danziger of Alexander.

G14.2. R. Meir Solomon Rabinowitz of Meseritz, 1868-1942, married the daughter of R. Isaac Barbash of Berdichev.

G15. R. Joshua Rabinowitz married the daughter of R. Samuel Bornstein of Sochotchov.

G14.3. Abraham Joshua Heschel Rabinowitz, author of *Yeshuot Avraham* (Lublin, 1931) married the daughter of R. Simeon Alter of Ger. (See Chapter IV—Branch I.) He died in 1932.

G15.1. R. Aaron Nathan David Rabinowitz, who published his father's work, married the daughter of R. Isaac Jacob Elimelech of Sochodnow.

G15.2. R. Solomon.

G15.3. Esther married R. Alter Weinberg of Slonim.

G15.4. R. Zvi.

G15.5. R. Jehiel Joshua Rabinowitz, Admur Sedlitz.

G14.4. R. Jerachmeel Jacob Zvi Rabinowitz of Sedlitz, 1878-1905. He married the daughter of R. Leibish of Ozrow.

G15.1. R. Jehiel Joshua Rabinowitz born in 1905, settled in Israel in 1946.

G15.2. R. Nathan David Rabinowitz[6a] 1900-1948, married the daughter of R. Alter of Novominsk. He settled in London in 1928.

G14.5. Motle married R. Aaron Menachem Mendel Gutterman of Radzymin. They had no issue. He died in 1934.

G14.6. Channah married R. Joseph Zvi Kalisch.

G13.5. Wife of R. Ephraim (of Nodrazin-Senna) son of R. Ezekiel of Kazimir.

G14.1. R. David Tov of Prague.

G15. R. Levi Isaac Tov, author of *Machshavot Levi*.

G14.2. R. Solomon.

G14.3. R. Jerachmeel.

G12.2. R. Jacob Isaac Rabinowitz, married the daughter of R. Dovberish Shapiro of Talust.

G13.1. R. Meir Rabinowitz, died in 1895.

G13.2. Wife of her first cousin R. Jehiel Isaiah Rapoport of Rava.

G12.3. Bracha, married R. Zvi Rappoport of Dubenka.

G13.1. R. Jehiel Isaiah Rappoport of Rava, died in 1899,

married his first cousin, daughter of R. Jacob Isaac Rabinowitz.

G14.1.   R. Jerachmeel Moses Noah Rappoport 1880-1943 A.B.D. Rava, married the daughter of R. Moses Elimelech son of R. Abraham Issachar Rabinowitz of Radomsk. (See Chapter IV — Branch K — G12.2/13.3/14.5/15.2.)

> G15.1.   David Jehiel Rappoport, born in 1902, married Channah Reizel, daughter of R. Moses Solomon Jehiel son of R. Joseph David Biderman of Lelov. (See below — G13.2/14.3.)

>> G16.   R. Jacob Ephraim Fischel Rappoport born in 1922, married Frieda Raatza, daughter of R. Dovberish Halevi Dembinsky. Their children, Moses Eliezer and Chaya Reize.

> G15.2.   R. Jacob Elimelech Rappoport.
> G15.3.   R. Abraham Akiva Rappoport.
> G15.4.   Chaya Bracha married her uncle R. Isaac Elimelech Joseph Rappoport.
> G15.5.   Deborah Gitel married R. Abraham Issachar Haim Ezekiel Shraga HaKohen Rabinowitz of the Radomsk Dynasty.

G14.2.   R. Isaac Elimelech Joseph Rappoport, married his niece, daughter of R. Jerachmeel Moses Noah Rappoport.

G13.2.   R. Ephraim Fischel Rappoport.

G14.1.   R. Jerachmeel Naftali Rappoport.
G14.2.   R. Haim Issachar Rappoport.
G14.3.   Wife of R. Moses Solomon Jehiel (Admur of Zulz), son of R. Joseph David son of R. Moses Solomon Jehiel Biederman. His first wife was the daughter of R. Aryey Lieb Ehrlich.

> G15.1.   R. Jacob Biederman.
> G15.2.   R. Eleazar Biederman.
> G15.3.   R. Israel Biederman.
> G15.4.   R. Nehemiah surnamed Gutterman.

G15.5. Wife of R. Phineas Issachar Finkler.

G16.1. Shifra married R. Samuel Aaron Shodrow-
ski. Their son R. Meir Gur Aryey Judah.

G16.2. Bracha married R. Simha Bonem son of
Abraham Moses Kalisch.

G16.3. Wife of R. Alter Jerachmeel.

G15.6. R. Menachem Mendel Biederman.

G15.7. Wife of R. David Jehiel son of R. Jerachmeel
Moses Noah Rappoport.

G13.3. R. Haim Joseph Issachar Rappoport died in
Lodz.

G12.4. Wife of R. Elimelech Shapiro of Grodzisk. (See
Chapter XVII — Shapiro Dynasty.)

G10.5. R. Isaac Teomim, A.B.D. Tiktin, married the daughter
of R. Meir Kailis (Mayerson).

G9.3. R. Haim Jonah Teomim.

G10.1. Hanale, married R. Meir Katzenellenbogen (See Katzenellenbogen Family Pedigree and K. Ellenbogen Family Pedigree — Chapter II.)

G8.2. R. David Teomim.

G7.2. R. Chaim Jonah Teomim, was successively A.B.D. of Przemysl,
and Breslau. He was the *Landesrabbiner* of Silesia from 1722-
27. He was married twice: 1) a daughter of R. David Oppen-
heim, Rabbi of Prague; 2) daughter of R. Zvi Hirsch, son of
R. Benjamim Mirls, Rabbi of Berlin. His approbation to *Yefei
Mareh* was written in 1724 at Jaroslav. He was the author of:
Aleh DeYonah, and *Kontras Rabbi Chaim,* published by R.
Abraham Yellin in Jessnitz, 1723. The former included novellae
on *Schulchan Aruch.* The 1723 Jessnitz edition of the *Yam Shel
Shlomo* by R. Solomon Luria also contains the *Kontras.*

G8.1. R. Isaac Joseph, born in 1721, A.B.D. of Slutzk and Cracow,
succeeded his father as A.B.D. of Breslau in 1754, which position he held until 1790. He died in 1793 and is mentioned in
the *Nodah BiYehuda.* R. Isaac married the daughter of R.
Samuel Zarviter. His two approbations were on: *Simlat Binyamin* by R. Benjamin Zeev, son of R. Isaac Rappoport, Dy-

hernfurth, 1788; and *She'ilat Shalom*. Besides being a well-known Rabbi, he was also the owner of a considerable business dealing in wool, linen and silk goods. He had four daughters.[7]

G9.1. Sarah, 1744-1810, married R. Saul Levin, son of R. Zvi Hirsch of Berlin, 1740-1794. She remarried to R. Wolf Eger, A.B.D. Leipnik, son of R. Akiva the Elder. (See below.)

G9.2. Edel, 1749-1818, married R. Joel Wolf Fraenckel, son of R. David, A.B.D. Berlin (author of *Korban HaEidah*).

G9.3. Rebecca, born 1749, married R. Wolf Eger, son of R. Akiva Eger the Elder, of Pressburg. R. Benjamin Wolf was born at Halberstadt, but settled in Breslau after marrying the daughter of R. Teomim. He was called to become A.B.D. Leipnik sometime after 1780, which position he held until his death. He edited his father's *Mishnat D'Rabbi Akiva* together with his brother, R. Lieb (died 1814), and added a supplement of his own, published in Furth, 1781.

G10. R. Akiva Eger, Rabbi in Halberstadt from 1814, when he succeeded his uncle, R. Lieb, until his death in 1824.

G11. R. Joseph, assistant Rabbi, died 1854.
G12. R. Jacob Egers, died 1891.

G9.4. Nache, 1752-1823, married R. Lewin Heymann, 1747-1810, of Breslau. They had two daughters and a son.

G10. Joachim Jonas Heymann, died 1845 in Breslau.

G11.1. Lea, born 1798, married Julius London (1795-1872).

G12. Auguste (1817-1896), married Weigert.

G11.2. Joseph Heymann.
G11.3. Friederike, married Henry London.
G11.4. Moritz.
G11.5. Judith Julie Manasse.
G11.6. Jacob.
G11.7. Ludwig Heymann, M.D.

G8.2. Chaya, married her first cousin, R. Zvi Hirsch, A.B.D. Zbariz, son of R. Solomon, A.B.D. Pinczow. (See below — G7.4/8.1.)

G9. Esther, married R. Alexander Sender Margolioth (died 1802), A.B.D. Zbariz, author of *Teshuvot Torat HaRaM*. (See Margolioth Family Pedigree — Chapter VII — Branch A.)

G7.3. R. Joseph (Yaski) Teomim, A.B.D. Cracow. His son records that
he wrote a collection of unpublished novellae entitled *Emek Halacha.*

G8. R. Samuel Teomim.

G9.1. R. Meir Teomim, a preacher in Lvov. He was the author
of: *Rav Peninim* comprising novellae entitled *Nofet Tzu-
fim, Me'irat Aynaim, Teivat Gomeh* and *Shoshanat Ha'
Emakim,* by his son. These were published in Frankfurt-
on-Oder in 1782. In his introduction, he also states that he
wrote *Chalukei Derech, Zemanim* (both novellae), and
HaMaggid (on Aggaddah) all unpublished. The title page
of the *Rav Peninim* mentions his two other published works,
Eliyahu Rabba and *Birkat Yosef* (Zolkiev, 1747). R. Meir
is mentioned in *Zikkaron Kahonah* by R. Isaac, son of R.
Joel Kohen Zedek, Lvov, 1863. He was a pupil of R. Phineas,
son of R. Jacob Katzenellenbogen, "the Martyr" A.B.D.
Lvov, who wrote his approbation to *Birkat Yosef* in 1741.
His wife was Gitel. He died July 10, 1773, and was succeeded by his son, R. Joseph who lived in Komarno from
1754 until then.

G10.1. R. Samuel Teomim. G10.2. R. Elijah Teomim.

G10.3. R. Joseph Teomim, born in Lvov in 1727, and died in
Frankfurt-on-Oder in 1792. He was initially a youth
teacher and educator, but on the death of his father in
1773, when he was forty-six years old, he became the
Rosh Yeshiva in Lvov. In 1782 he became A.B.D.
Frankfurt-on-Oder, where he remained until his death.
He was a scholar as well as a grammarian, linguist and
a man of general knowledge. He wrote the following
books: *Pri Megadim,* Frankfurt-on-Oder, 1775, which
appeared many times thereafter in conjunction with
many other works; *Porat Yosef,* novellae on Tractate *Yebamot,* Zolkiev, 1756; *Teivat Gomeh* and *Shoshanat Ha'amakim* in the *Rav Peninim* by his father;
Ginat Vardim, Zolkiev, 1756; *Rosh Yosef,* novellae on
the laws of Tractate *Chullin,* Frankfurt-on-Oder, 1784;
on the *Poskim* in the *Birkat Yosef* by his father.
He married Toyba, daughter of R. Eliakim. In his book
Ginat Vardim he records his entire ancestry and offspring.

G11.1. Israel.   G11.2. Frieda.

G9.2. R. Simha Nathan Teomim.

G10. R. Benjamin, married his cousin, daughter of R. Haim Joseph Teomim. Their son, R. Joseph.

G9.3. R. Haim Joseph Teomim.

G10. Wife of R. Benjamin Teomim.

G7.4. Chaya, married R. Solomon, A.B.D. Pinczow, author of *Yak'hel Shlomo,* first published in 1786 in Livorno. He was the son of R. Naftali Hirsch. His approbation appeared in *Birkat Yaakov,* a manuscript on *Choshen Mishpat.* In the *Luchot Ha'eidut,* Turin, 1867, there is a letter addressed to him by R. Jonathan Eybeschutz who also wrote his *Hesped* in his book *Ya'arot Devash* (1797-8 edition). He also wrote *Beit Shlomo,* novellae on Talmud, Pietrokov, 1827, and a manuscript on *Yalkut Shimoni.* He died in 1761.

G8.1. R. Zvi Hirsch, A.B.D. Zbariz, married his first cousin, Chaya, daughter of R. Chaim Jonah Teomim, A.B.D. Pinczow.
G8.2. Wife of R. Ari Liebus, A.B.D. Zamoscz.

G9. Wife of R. Eleazar HaKohen, A.B.D. Vaidislav, died in 1790.

G10. R. Ari Liebus HaKohen,[8] A.B.D. Neustadt, Head of the Rabinowitz Family. (See Branch K.)

G7.5. Second wife of R. Issachar Berish, son of R. Abraham Joshua Heschel of Cracow. (See Chapter IX.)

G6.5. Sarel, married 1) R. Mordecai, son of R. Heschel of Cracow; 2) R. Samuel, son of Moses Reb Mendels, A.B.D. Prague; and 3) R. Aaron Teomim, son of R. Moses. She died in 1715. In her youth she lived with her brother in Prague.
G6.6. Eidel, married R. Avigdor Karo of Vienna, Apt, Constantin and Glogau, died in 1678. He was the son of R. Samuel Phoebus, son of R. Avigdor Karo (son of the sister of Rabbi Judah Lowe).

G7.1. Zarentil, married R. Koppel Franckel the "Rich" of Vienna (died 1670). He founded the levite Franckel Family and was the son of R. Jeremiah Isaac. She was his second wife. His first wife was Vitaria, daughter of R. Simeon Zemel, grandson of R. Moses Aaron Teomim.

G7.2. Sarah, married R. Jacob, son of R. Naftali, called Jacob Isserles, of Vilna.

G6.7. Wife of R. Israel Moses Joseph Gordon. Their son, Isaac.

BRANCH A

TEOMIM FAMILY

ANCESTRY

G3.3. R. Saul Wahl Katzenellenbogen.
G4.1. R. Meir.
G5.9. Beila, married R. Jonah, son of Isaiah Teomim.
G6.2. R. Isaac Meir Teomim-Frankel died 1701/2.
G7.2. R. Abraham.
G8.   R. Isaac Frankel.
G9.1. R. Liebus Frankel-Teomim, A.B.D. Chartkov.
G10.   R. Joseph, A.B.D. Borstein died 1758.
G11.   R. Zvi Hirsch, A.B.D. Kalucz, married daughter of R. Jacob of Lissa (*Chavat Da'at*) Leverbaum son of R. Jacob Moses. (See Chapter XIII.)

G12.1. R. Ephraim Thumim,[10] A.B.D. Krisnapol, Poland.

G13.1. R. Zvi Hirsch, A.B.D. Chorostkov, author of the responsa work entitled *Eretz Zvi*, Lvov 1880. He married Gitel, and had no offspring. He died at Chorostkov in 1846.

G13.2. R. Jacob Thumim, A.B.D. Vilkatsch and later at Tarnograd, Poland. While at the latter town, the leaders of Apt offered their Rabbinical seat to him, but on the advice of R. Joshua Rokeah, the Rebbe of Belz, he declined and remained in Tarnograd. When the Jews were expelled from Poland he settled in Kolomya, where he died in 1908.

G14.1. R. Haim Hirsch Thumim of Kolomya, born 1878, author of *Zichron LeRishonim*, published Kolomya 1913.

G13.3. R. Isaac Thumim A.B.D. Krisnapol, married his cousin, daughter of R. Abraham Thumim.

G14.1. R. Abraham Thumim, A.B.D. of Krisnapol, follower of the Belzer Chassidim.

During the time that R. Ephraim Thumim was A.B.D. Krisnapol,[11] Poland, one of the local *Shochets* (butchers) returned from Belz with kosher meat which had been prepared there. Rabbi Ephraim declared this unfit which caused a stir amongst his followers and those of the Chassidic Rabbi Rokeah of Belz. When the Belzer Rebbe expressed his opinion, Ephraim replied: "You are the Rabbi of your town, and I am the leader of mine!" Some time later, the Belzer Rebbe went on a train journey from Belz, which at that time had a Jewish population of approximately 1,800, forty miles southward to Lvov. One of the larger train stations was at Krisnapol, where the train halted a number of hours. At this time, R. Ephraim's son R. Isaac was A.B.D., and the Belzer Rebbe sent a messenger to him telling that he would be visiting his town. R. Isaac went down to meet the train and after spending time together, the two families were once again reconciled.

R. Isaac's son R. Abraham, later A.B.D. of Krisnapol, studied for a number of years under R. Issachar Ber (Dov) of Belz (1854-1927/8), and became a Chassid; thus his descendants became followers of the Belzer Rebbe. R. Abraham had a son and two daughters who perished in World War II.

G15.1. R. Phineas Joseph Thumim, 1892-1958, buried in Tel Aviv. He married in 1912 to Chaya Jochebed, daughter of R. Haim Isaac Jeruchem. They settled in Israel in 1941. (See Descendants of the Heschel-Apt-Jeruchem Dynasty.)

G16.1. R. Nathan Thumim, born 1913 in Sambor, Poland. He came to the U.S.A. in 1941. In 1943 he married Rebecca (Rivke/Ruth), daughter of R. Isaac Amsel.

G17.1. Dinah, born 1944, married in 1965 to Isaac Eleazar Spira, stepson of Grand Rabbi Israel Spira, the Blozever Rebbe. (See Chapter XVII.)

G18.1. Rachel, born 1967.
G18.2. Miriam, born 1969.
G18.3. Abraham, born 1971.

G17.2. Esther, born in Zurich in 1946. In 1967 she married Isaac (Julius), son of Herschel Mariles.

G18.1. Joseph, born 1968.

G18.2. Asher Chaim, born 1971.

G17.3. Sheva, married in 1972 to Fishel Jaffe.

G16.2. R. Jacob Thumim, born 1921, married Motil Feige, daughter of R. Phineas David HaLevi Horowitz, the

Bostoner Rebbe (see Horowitz Family Pedigree—Bostoner Branch).

G17.1. Rachel Dinah born 1949, married Asher Chaim Lieberman. Their children, Sarah Sasha and Abraham Samuel Benjamin.

G17.2. Esther Gitel born 1952.

G17.3. Sheine Nechama born 1957.

G17.4. Miriam.

G17.5. R. David born 1947, married 1973 to Miriam Rochma Binah daughter of R. Moses halevi Moster. (See Chapter XVI — Branch VII — page 612 — G18.1/19/20). Their daughter Sheindel Rivke. They reside in Lakewood, N.J.

G13.4. R. Moses Thumim, A.B.D. Horodenka in Austro-Galicia, married Esther Malka, daughter of R. Solomon (died in Safed) son of Jacob Lieberman of Krakovitz, Galicia. He was the author of:

1) *Dvar Moshe,* responsa published Lvov, 1864, the introduction of this work contains his full genealogy.

2) *Ohel Moshe,* derashot and responsa, Lvov 1899, published by his son David.

3) *Orayin Talitai,* with the works of his son Naftali, Lvov 1880.

4) *Sefat Emet,* with additions by his son and grandson, Kolomya 1893.

5) *Mili DePascha,* Lvov 1905.

G14.1. R. David Thumim, born in Kolomya in 1892. He published the *Ohel Moshe* by his father and his own works are included in the *Sefat Emet* of his grandfather. He also wrote *Ma'azinim leTorah* on the life of the Chacham Zvi Ashkenazi, published Lvov 1896 and *Shem MiShimeon* on the life of Baron Rothschild, published Lvov 1920.

G15.1. Sheindel, died unmarried.

G15.2. Wife of her cousin Manes Thumim.

G14.2. R. Naftali Hirsch Thumim A.B.D. Vilkatsch, married Feige, daughter of R. Menachem Manes Lieberman. He was the author of the responsa and novellae which appeared in *Orayin Talitai* by his father. He wrote *Binat HaLevi* published in Bilgoray 1938, and settled in Lvov in his latter years where he died about 1921.

G15.1. R. Menachem Manes Thumim married his first cousin daughter of R. David Thumim. They lived in Kolomya.

G15.2. R. Abraham Thumim A.B.D. Lanka, Galicia.

G15.3. R. Beryl Thumim A.B.D. Prezworsk.

G16. Chaya married R. Shalom Leifer.

G15.4. R. Ephraim Thumim, 1877-1922, married Rachel daughter of R. Hirsch Elimelech Teitelbaum of Kolashitz.

G16. Elimelech Thumim (New York) born in 1901.

G17. Ruth Amalia Emily married Donald Sultan. Their children, Sherry, Lisa and Stanley Howard.

G15.5. R. Joseph Thumim, 1878-1962.[12] He was ordained by Rabbi Schmelkes of Lvov, Rabbi Isaac Horowitz of Stanislav (who was his great uncle) and Rabbi Weiss of Chernovitz. He married in 1893 to Sabina Rottenberg. They had seven children. From 1910-14 he was at Rozvadov, Galicia. In 1914 he came to the U.S.A. and was Rabbi of Congregation *Anshe Austria* in Boston and of Congregation *Adath Israel* from 1914-15. In 1915 he travelled to Detroit where he became Rabbi of Congregation *Beth Abraham*. He was also a Young Israel organizer, an executive officer of the Agudat Israel Movement, President of the Council of Orthodox Rabbis in Detroit and a member of the Union of Orthodox Rabbis of U.S. and Canada and the Mizrachi Movement.

He wrote *Responses to Rabbis, Commentary to Maimonides* and articles for various religious periodicals.

G16.1. Esther, born about 1900, married Harry Steinberg (Pittsburg).

G17.1. Diana, M.D., married Ira Leventer (Detroit). Their children, Mark, Jan and Robert.

G17.2. R. Nathan, born 1927, Rabbi in Dixhills, Long Island. In 1956 he married Grace, daughter of Benjamin Krane. Their children, Avery (Abraham) and Joyce.

G17.3. Herman, born 1925 (California), married Jean Magidson. Their children, Rhonda, Karen & Steven.

G16.2. Sadie, M.D. married Mr. Bloch, no issue, (Detroit).

G16.3. Earl, married and lived in Pittsburg, no children.

G16.4. Jack (Jacob), married Kathleeen, and have two adopted children (Detroit).

G16.5. Henry, lawyer in Detroit, married Alice Waze, they have an adopted son.

G16.6. Golda (Gladys), married Irwin Klar (Detroit).

G17.1. David, married and divorced, and had issue.
G17.2. Marilyn, unmarried.

G16.7. Mendel (Martin), an accountant in Cincinnati, Ohio.

G15.6. R. Jonah Thumim, succeeded his father as A.B.D. of Vilkatsch, born about 1880 and perished in 1942. He married Chaya Ashkenazi, daughter of R. Israel Ashkenazi (see below — G12.5/13.2).

G16.1. Hertz, perished.
G16.2. Joelish, of London, married Chaya Tilla, daughter of R. Issachar Dov son of Haim Jonah Halpern (see Ropshitz Horowitz-Rubin Family Pedigree — G14.1/15.3/16.5/17.4/18.1).

G17.1. David, born in 1932, married Sheila, daughter of N. Becker (Chicago).

G18.1. Dinah. G18.2. Dvorah.
G18.3. Rivke Beila.

G17.2. Nechama (Naomi) born in 1945, married Jack Ackerman (London).

G18.1. Rivke Rachel. G18.2. Meir (Mark).
G18.3. Berish (Isaachar Dov).

G17.3. Jonathan born in 1947, married in 1973 to Rivke, daughter of Jacob Dov Mannheimer (son-in-law of R. Haim Joseph son of R. Israel Jokel Teitelbaum). (See Chapter XVII.)

G14.3. Feige, married Joshua Moses Laufer.

G15.1. Four daughters.
G15.2. Solomon, married and had issue.
G15.3. Hirsch, married and had a daughter.
G15.4. Abraham, 1869-1937, died in Vienna, married Channah, daughter of Leibish Muhlstok.

G16.1. Joshua Laufer (Amsterdam), married, had no children.
G16.2. Isaac Laufer, born 1894 in Podhajce, Austro-Galicia. He came to the U.S.A. in 1949. He married Dora Sparer.

G17. Miriam, born in 1934.

G16.3. Ephraim Laufer, married, died in New York, 1953.

G17.1. Fred Laufer, married and has family.
G17.2. Walter Laufer, married and has family.

G14.4. Rebecca Necha, married R. Elimelech, son of R. Jonah son of R. Solomon Ashkenazi. R. Solomon was the brother of R. Joel Ashkenazi mentioned under G12.5. below.

G15. Blume Rosa, married R. Alexander Haim son of R. Asher Anschel Ashkenazi. R. Asher was another brother of R. Joel Ashkenazi. They were the sons of R. Moses David of Tulchev and Safed.

G13.5. Toyba Thumim, married R. Isaac (MaHaRi) Horowitz, A.B.D. Ottynia, Zurawno and Stanislav, son of R. Meshullam Issachar A.B.D. Stanislav. (Chapter XVI — Descendants of Horowitz Family — Stanislav, Branch VI.)

G12.2. R. Jonah Thumim, A.B.D. Przemysl.
G12.3. R. David Thumim.
G12.4. R. Abraham Thumim, A.B.D. Zbariz and Buczacz, author of Chesed leAvraham, responsa which were published in Lvov in 1857 and 1898. An introduction of his appears in Nachalat Yaakov by his maternal grandfather, R. Jacob of Lissa. He married the daughter of R. Zvi HaKohen Rappoport, A.B.D. Dubno son of R. Naftali Hirsch. (See Chapter VII — G6.2/7.4/8.4/9.1/10.4/11/12.1/13.3.)

G13.1. Wife of R. Isaac Thumim, son of R. Ephraim of Krisnapol.
G13.2. R. Isaac Jacob (Vienna), married and had several daughters.
G13.3. R. Moses, died in Vienna 1918/9, had no children.

G12.5. Wife of R. Joel Ashkenazi, A.B.D. Zlatchov, son of R. Moses David A.B.D. Safed (author of Toldot Adam, Jerusalem 1845), son of Asher Ashkenazi.

G13.1. Wife of R. Joel son of Isaac Babad, A.B.D. Slovita. (See Babad Family Pedigree, Branch D.)
G13.2. R. Israel Ashkenazi A.B.D. Serge, Bukovinia.

G14. Chaya, perished in the Holocaust in 1942 in the Jaworow Ghetto. She married R. Jonah son of R. Naftali Thumim.

G13.3. Wife of her first cousin, R. Hananiah YomTov Lipa son of R. Zalman Lieb Teitelbaum. (See Chapter XVII — Teitelbaum Dynasty.) R. Hananiah's mother, Rachel, was the sister of R. Joel Ashkenazi, her father.

G13.4. R. Asher Anschel Ashkenazi, 1832-95, named after his paternal great-grandfather, Admur Alesk in Stanislav, succeeding his father-in-law, R. Hanoch Mayer. (See Chapter XVII — Rokeah Chassidic Dynasty).

G14.1. R. Moses David Ashkenazi, Admur Bels (Bessarabia), Lvov, Klausenberg and Satmar, married the daughter of R. Abraham Aaron Teitelbaum. (See Chapter XVII.)

G14.2. R. Abraham Naftali Ashkenazi, Admur Alesk-Stanislav from 1887, died in 1928.

G14.3. R. Israel Ashkenazi, Admur Tolmitsch.

G14.4. R. Zvi Hirsch Ashkenazi, Admur Stanislav from 1887, and settled in Vienna in 1915 where he became known as the Rebbe of Stanislav. He married Chaya Sarah, daughter of R. Isaac Joshua Kliger of Greiding. (See Chapter XVI—Stanislav Branch). The family perished in the Holocaust, excepting one son, Meshullam.

G15.1. Reizel, married R. Haim son of R. Moses (of Zablodov) Hager.

G15.2. Freida Malka.

G15.3. R. Asher Ashkenazi, married Sosha, daughter of R. Meir Kliger of Krakowitz.

G15.4. R. Meshullam Issachar Ashkenazi, Admur Stanislav in London, married the daughter of R. Kalonymus Kalman Hakohen Yolles.

G16.1. Rachel, married R. Isaac son of R. Alexander Asher Babad of London. (See Chapter XI).

G16.2. R. Uri Ashkenazi, married the daughter of R. Asher Rosenbaum of Bucharest-Hadera.

G16.3. Sarah, married R. Moses Sofer (descendant of the *Chatam Sofer*).

G16.4. R. Zvi Hirsch Ashkenazi, married the daughter of R. Witzner.

G16.5. Malka.

G14.5. Malka Freida, married R. Isaac, son of R. Jacob Zvi Hirsch
Weilziker of Sokol, Admur Alesk-Stanislav. He perished in
the Holocaust in 1942.

G15. R. Alexander Haim Ashkenazi, 1889-1974, adopted his
mother's surname. He was a wealthy businessman from
Stanislav and lived the latter twenty-eight years of his life
in Israel. He married Blume Rosa, daughter of R. Elimelech
Ashkenazi (son-in-law of R. Moses Thumim) son of R.
Jonah son of R. Solomon (brother of R. Joel Ashkenazi of
Zlatchov).

G16.1. Rivke Necha, married R. Samuel Shmelke son of R.
Israel Klein, perished.

G16.2. Malka Freida, married Jacob Kraus of Zurich, and have
issue.

G16.3. R. Hanoch Heinich Dov Ashkenazi of Brazil, married
Zipporah, daughter of R. Fischel Sacks. They have no
issue.

G16.4. R. Elimelech Ashkenazi, born in 1915 and settled in
Israel from 1940-58. He then became the Chief Rabbi
of São Paulo, Brazil, until 1970, when he was elected
Chief Rabbi in Melbourne. He married Sarah Judith,
daughter of R. Jekutiel Zalman YomTov Lipa (Rabbi in
Frankfurt-on-Main) son of R. David Weber.

G17.1. Malka Freida Kramer, has issue (Boro Park).

G17.2. R. Isaac Ashkenazi, born in 1943, Admur Alesk-New
York, married Chavah, daughter of R. Menachem
Solomon of Karlov son of R. Moses Taubes of Kar-
lov. They have issue.

G17.3. Rivke Necha, married R. Meir Abraham Iliowitz, succeeded his father-in-law as Chief Rabbi of São Paulo.
They have issue.

G17.4. R. Jekutiel Zalman YomTov Lipa Ashkenazi, married
Freida, daughter of R. Israel Jacob son of R. Shalom
son of R. Moses Moskovitz of Shatz. They have issue.

G17.5. Rachel, married R. Jehiel son of R. Alexander Asher
Babad (mentioned above — see Chapter XI). They
have issue.

G17.6. R. Hanoch Heinich Dov Ashkenazi, married Channah, daughter of R. Issachar Berish Rubin of Kristier-
New York. (See Chapter XVI — Branch VII.)

G17.7. R. Asher Anschel Ashkenazi, married Pesel Bracha, daughter of R. Nahum Zvi Horowitz. (See Chapter XVI — Branch VII — G14.4/15.1/16.3/17/18/19.5.)

G12.6. Wife of R. Isaac Babad of Kalucz (G12 page 416).

BRANCH B

ANCESTRY

G3.3. Saul Wahl Katzenellenbogen.

G4.1. R. Meir.

G5.9. Beila, married R. Jonah, son of Isaiah Teomim.

G6.2. R. Isaac Meir Teomim-Frankel.

G7.2. R. Abraham.

G8. R. Isaac (Meir).

G9.2. R. David Teomim of Prezworsk.

G10. R. Joseph Saul, married Nechama Reizel, daughter of R. Alexander Margolioth (author of *Teshuvot Torat HaRaM*, died 1802, see descendants of Margolioth Family, Chapter VII.)[13]

G11. R. Alexander Sender Frankel A.B.D. of Prezworsk, named after his maternal grandfather, who in turn was named after his maternal grandfather (Alexander Shor).

G12.1. R. Mordecai.

G12.2. R. Joseph Saul.

G13. R. Ari Leibus, wrote an introduction to *Teshuvot Torat Ha-RaM*, responsa by his great-great-grandfather.

G12.3. R. Samuel Ephraim Zalman of Prezworsk, 1839-1922.

G13.1. R. Isaac.

G13.2. R. Ziskind.

G13.3. R. Alexander Sender Frankel, 1868-1951, married Minnie Muschel, died in New York.

G14.1. Moe Frankel, (New Jersey).

G14.2. Julius Frankel, (Riverdale, N.Y.) born 1903, married in 1937 to Hannah Levy.

G15. Richard, born 1938, unmarried.

G14.3. Joseph Frankel (Toledo, Ohio), married and had family, died 1970.

G14.4. Sam, (Florida), married and has family.
G14.5. David, (Toledo, Ohio), married and has family.
G14.6. Clara, married Mr. Kinzler (deceased). She lives in Florida.

G15. Mortimor, (New Jersey).

G14.7. Hillel, (Toledo), married and has family.
G14.8. Arthur, (Toledo), married and has family.
G14.9. Leon, (Toledo), married and has family.
G14.10. Bella, married Mr. Redlich, (New York City).
G14.11. Evelyn, married Bernard Cohn, (Lawrence, Long Island).
G14.12. Child, died in infancy.

G13.4. Sarah Yetta, married R. Hirsch Wein.

G14.1. Naftali of Boro Park, N.Y., married

1) in 1908 to Gitel, daughter of Benjamin Wolf of Dobromil, and had issue.
2) in 1966 to Chaya Sarah Weiner, daughter of Jacob Lotner of Lvov.

G15.1. Jan, born 1911, married in 1932 to R. Israel Ben David, Rabbi of Congregation *Keter Torah.*

G16.1. Aviva, born 1934, married Isaiah Drazen (Israel). Their children, David, Jenun and Elimelech.
G16.2. Sharon, born 1948, married Zush Rosenfeld (Brooklyn, N.Y.). Their children, Gita and Tuvia.
G16.3. Benjamin, born 1943.
G16.4. Simha, born 1949.

G15.2. Leah, born 1913, married in 1938 to R. Joseph son of R. Elijah Frankel-Teomim of Prezworsk (Teomim Family, Branch H).
G15.3. Shalom, born 1915, married in 1941 to Shirley.

G16.1. Rene, born 1942, married Michael Zafrani (New Jersey). They have issue.
G16.2. Daughter.
G16.3. Sheldon, born 1950.

G15.4. Boris (Berish), born 1919, married in 1941 to his first cousin Chava Frankel.

G16.1. Esther, born 1941, married in 1963 to Shalom Katz

(Brooklyn), son of Nehemiah (married the sister of R. Moses Feinstein).

G17.1. Yossi, born 1964.

G17.2. Moses Jacob, born 1969.

G16.2. Bella, born 1946, married in 1967 to Simeon Eisberg (Queens, N.Y.). Their son, Uri (Isaac), born 1970.

G16.3. Lea (Lillian), born 1954.

G16.4. Sarah, born 1947, married in 1968 to Rabbi Joel Weiss (New Jersey). Their son, Haim, born 1972.

G15.5. Joshua (Oscar), born 1922, married in 1948 to Vivian Sher.

G16.1. Moses, born 1951, married Hindi, and have issue.

G16.2. Judy, born 1954.

G16.3. Ari, born 1962.

G15.6. Zalman born 1928, married in 1954 to Vivian, daughter of Rabbi Shurkin of New York.

G16.1. Channah, born 1957.

G16.2. Ezekiel, born 1960.

G16.3. Margie, born 1963.

G14.2. Matil Wein married David Sprung, both perished in World War II.

G15.1. Zalman, born 1924 in Prezworsk (Brooklyn). Arrived in U.S.A. in 1950, married Florence Sheinowitz.

G16.1. Channah, born 1954.

G16.2. Ezekiel, born 1956.

G16.3. Margie, born 1960.

G15.2. Hirch, born 1920 (Brooklyn).

G15.3. Chaya, married Lieb Gartenlaub (Israel). Their children, Margie, Shoshanna, and Uzzi.

G14.3. Chaytche Wein born Prezworsk, married Chaim Judah (Lieb) son of Abraham Isaac Pechter.

G15.1. Zvi, born 1933, married in 1958 to Chaya Weintraub.

G16.1. Bracha Rachel, born 1959.

G16.2. Haim, born 1961.

G16.3. Toyva, born 1964.

G15.2. Pesa, married Rabbi Zvi Tewel (Boro Park, N.Y.). They have seven children.

G15.3. Channah, married Judah Schiff (Israel). Their children, Mordecai, Isaac, Esther, and Naomi.

G15.4. Sarah, married Haim Schneider (Brooklyn). Their children, Keila, Jacob, Rivke, Lieb, and Avi.

G15.5. Hennie married Menachem Rutenberg. Their children, Sheni, Sima and Lieb.

G14.4. Beila Wein (died 1942), married R. Joseph son of Abraham Abbale son of Eleazar Frankel, born Chechinov 1895, died in Israel 1967. Abraham's, sister was the wife of Nahum Zvi Teomim, Branch F.

G15.1. Zalman Frankel, born 1928, married Cynthia Zaidman, Brooklyn. They have no offspring.

G15.2. Fay, born 1927, married Haim Ginzburg (Brooklyn).

G16.1. Hischel, married Rachel, and have issue.
G16.2. Beila. G16.3. Susan. G16.4. Yossi.

G15.3. Hirsch Frankel, born 1926, married Rose Orleg. Their children, Abraham, Beila and Henny.

G15.4. Abbale Frankel, born 1933, married in 1968 to Olga Adler.

G16. Joel Zvi, born 1971.

G15.5. Chana, born 1922, married David Zucker (Brooklyn). Their children: Moses, Joshua, and Samuel.

G15.6. Chava, born 1921, married her first cousin Boris Wein.

G13.5. Reizel, married and had descendants in the U.S.A.
G13.6. Esther, married Haim Ringelheim (Brooklyn).

G14.1. Rachel (Rosa), born 1910, married in 1945 to R. Joshua Heschel son of R. Joseph Babad of Sheepshead Bay, N.Y. (See Babad Family — Branch B.)

G14.2. Anna, born 1905, married in 1931 to Arthur Bramnik.

G15.1. Ephraim Zalman (Stanley) Bramnik, born 1933, Rabbi in Fairlawn, New Jersey. He married Helen Lieberman.

G16.1. Arnold, born 1959. G16.2. Elliot, born 1962.

G14.3. Clara, born 1908, married in 1935 to Jacob Thall.

G15.1. R. Sheldon Thall, born 1935, married Judy, and has issue.

G15.2. Caroline, born 1939, married in 1959 to Arnold Gilner.

G16.1. Candy, born 1960. G16.2. Dawn, born 1962.

G15.3. Edwin, born 1943 (Akron, Ohio), married in 1967 to Helen Rubin.

G16. Kimberley, born 1973.

G14.4. Bella, 1912-1968, married Edmund Muschel. (He remarried).

G15. Rita, married Herbert Amster (Queens, N.Y.).

G13.7. Hentche, married Hirsch Feder (Brooklyn).

G14. Tilly, married Issy Greenberg (Brooklyn).

BRANCH C

THE FRANKEL-HIRSCHHORN FAMILY

ANCESTRY

G3.3. Saul Wahl Katzenellenbogen.
G4.1. R. Meir.
G5.9. Beila, married R. Jonah, son of Isaiah Teomim.
G6.2. R. Isaac Meir Teomim-Frankel (died 1701/2).
G7.3. R. Aaron Frankel.
G8.1. Isaac.
G9.2. Abraham.
G10.2. Aaron Frankel (died about 1825) of Zbariz.[14]

G11.1. Isaac Frankel of Skalat, died 1840, married Sarah Sima, daughter of Gershon, died 1890.

G12.1. Meir Judah (Liebus) Frankel of Skalat, Head of the community, known for his kindness and good deeds, married Hannah Esther, daughter of Jacob. He died in 1876 and she in 1891.

G13.1. Michael Alter studied in Tarnopol, married a daughter of the Folikov family (Russia).
G13.2. Samuel (Phillip), born in Skalat 1858. Married Pesia. In 1894 they arrived in New York to join their uncle Aaron who

came two years earlier. She died a few years later and he remarried Matil. He died July 11, 1923, and is buried in the Skalater portion of Mt. Zion Cemetery, N.Y. From the first wife:

G14.1. Elizabeth, married Hirsch Brandes.
From the second wife:
G14.2. Michael Alter. G14.3. Rose. G14.4. Sylvia.

G13.3. Hodel, married Nahum Lacks (Lax).

G14.1. Israel Lax, married Feige. Their daughter, Hodel.
G14.2. Chana Esther, married Solomon Shimmel. Their daughter, Hodel.

G12.2. Aaron Frankel of Skalat, born there in 1832, immigrated to the U.S.A. in 1892 and settled in New York. He was a successful businessman who lived to enjoy his children and grandchildren in the U.S.A. He married Yota, daughter of Judah Aryeh. He died in 1905 and his wife in 1919.

G13.1. Libe, married Menachem Mendel Judah, son of Abraham Seiden in 1877. He died in New York, July 21, 1924 and she in 1938.

G14.1. Chana, married Benjamin Kissen. No offspring.
G14.2. Avigdor (William), 1894-1971. No offspring.
G14.3. Tilly, born 1890 (Great Neck, Long Island). Married in 1912 to Charles Canter.

G15.1. Joanna, born 1916, married William Berger (Great Neck.)

G16.1. Charles Lawrence, M.D., born 1942.
G16.2. Jill Dianne, born 1951.
G16.3. Ellen, died young.

G15.2. Charles, born New York 1919, married Helen Sacks.

G16.1. Carol, married Harvey Tanenbaum (Long Island).
G16.2. Arthur, married Judy.

G14.4. Joseph, 1884-1936, married in 1914 to Celia Alexander.

G15.1. Dorothy, born 1915, married in 1935 to David H. Feldstein (died 1947). She remarried in 1965 to Louis Rosenthal (Forest Hills, N.Y.).

G16.1. Donald Martin, born 1936, married in 1958 to Barbara Grisar, later divorced.

G17.1. David, born 1960.   G17.2. Madelyne, born 1962.

G16.2. Joel Bruce, born 1943.

G14.5. Carl, died at the age of thirteen.
G14.6. Child, died at the age of eleven.
G14.7. Child, died at the age of nine.

G13.2. Toltze Frankel, died 1877, unmarried.
G13.3. Friedel Frankel married Adolf Berkelhammer.

G14.1. Isidore, dentist, died 1958.
G14.2. Irving, 1904-1969, lawyer (Westchester, N.Y.), married Phyllis.

G15.1. Allan Edward, born 1950.
G15.2. Wendy Francis, born 1952.

G14.3. Sadie (Sedonia), unmarried (New York).
G13.4. Hinde Frankel married Nathan Segal.

G14.1. Fred Segal. His daughter, Bettie.
G14.2. Lou (Miami, Florida).

G13.5. Judah Lieb (Louis) Frankel, born in 1870. He came to the U.S.A. in 1890 and settled in New York where he founded the National Cleaning Contractors Incorporated, in 1896. He was known for his generosity. He died about 1959.

G14.1. Sadie, 1896-1969, married in 1914 to Max Sweig.

G15.1. Martin (Morty), born 1915, married in 1944 to Charlotte Phillips (New York).

G16.1. Michael, born 1946.
G16.2. Jeannie, born 1943, married in 1965 to Gerald Kligman.

G17.1. Wendy, born 1969.   G17.2. Gary, born 1966.

G15.2. Carol born 1928, married in 1940 to Erwin Lurie (New York).

G16.1. Steven, born 1957.
G16.2. James, born 1951.

G14.2. Gertrude, 1900-1972, married Abraham Goodman.

G15.1. James, born 1926.
G15.2. Bernice, born 1923, married in 1941 to Norman Kramer, and had issue.

G14.3. William V. Frankel,[15] born 1904, died Rhode Island 1972. He married Selma Rentner, daughter of Maurice Rentner. He was Board Chairman and Chief Executive Officer of Warner Communications, Inc., one of the largest corporations in the U.S.A. He was also president of the National Cleaning Contractors, Inc., till 1965, having been with the company since 1926. Then he became Board Chairman. In 1966 the company was merged into the Kinney Service Corporation and became known as the Kinney National Service, of which he was chairman. In 1969, Kinney acquired Warner Bros. and became the Warner Communications. Mr. Frankel then became Chairman. He was also vice-chairman of the United Nations Day Committee, and a director of the United Jewish Appeal, the Federation of Jewish Philanthropies and the American Red Cross, building industry division.

G15.1. Andrew J., born 1932, married. His children, David E. Donna R., Eliza and Pamela E.
G15.2. Lynda, married Fred Cahill, and have issue.

G13.6. Dr. Julius (Jonah) Frankel,[16] born at Skalat May 15, 1875, and came to New York in 1890 with his brother Louis. He received his Medical degree from Cornell University in 1900 at the age of twenty-five. He married Celia Rubin, died December 7, 1945 and was buried in Mt. Zion Cemetery, N.Y. He was known as the "poor man's doctor" of the lower East Side and practiced until his retirement in 1935 as a pioneer doctor treating the poor. In his later years, he withdrew from private practice and specialized in obstetrics and gynecology. He was associated with the staffs of Beth Israel, Manhattan General, Samaritan and St. Mark Hospitals. He was the past president of the Eastern Medical Society of N.Y.C. and of the Medical Alliance.

G14.1. Harold Frankel, born 1904, New York Lawyer, former Assistant District Attorney of N.Y. County.

G15.1. Aleta, born 1933, married Bernard Frechtman, a lawyer.

G16.1. Janet, born 1959. G16.2. William, born 1960.

G15.2. Dr. Mark Edward, Orthopedic Surgeon, Tucson, Arizona, married.

G16.1. Mark, born 1963. G16.2. David, born 1964.
G16.3. Scott, born 1965.
G16.4. Lee, born 1967.

G14.2. Dr. Arthur Frankel, born 1905, New York. He was a Captain with the Army Medical Corps during World War II, and practices obstetrics and gynecology in New York. He is married and has no issue.

G14.3. Thelma, born 1907. She was a Lieutenant attached to the War Department during World War II. She married Clarence Weiner (Westchester, N.Y.).

G15.1. Julia. G15.2. Emily.

G12.3. Gute Reize Frankel, died in Skalat in 1900. She married her father's brother, Avigdor Frankel—see G11.2 below.

G12.4. Feige Frankel died Passover 1904, married Chaim Isaiah Hirschhorn, died in Skalat in 1887.

G13.1. Zelig, married Hannah, daughter of Zeev Hirschhorn. She died in 1926. Her brother Joseph's daughter Minzi, married her son Lieb—see below.

G14.1. Miriam, married Benzion Margolies of Skalat.

G15.1. Meir. G15.2. Zondel.

G14.2. Toyva, married Shemariah Greenhut.

G15.1. Herman. G15.2. Fred. G15.3. Francis.
G15.4. Victoria, married Robert Koblentz (New York). They have no offspring.

G14.3. William Hirschhorn.

G14.4. Lieb Hirschhorn, born in Skalat about 1870, came to New York in 1890 where he married his cousin Minzi Hirschhorn.

G15.1. Chaim Isaiah (Charles) (Philadelphia).
G15.2. Rose, married Joseph Himber (Philadelphia).
G15.3. Feige.

G15.4. Charney.

G13.2. Sheva (Samuel) Hirschhorn 1865-1936, coffee and tea peddler, married Clara Epstein, died 1938.

G14.1. Lieb (Louis) 1888-1940. He was a pioneer of the Tea Bag Industry. He married Milly.

G15.1. Rose, married Pat Mann (formerly Chugerman).

G16.1. Karen, married Ben Brown (Pennsylvania).
G16.2. Michael Mann (California).

G14.2. Charles, born 1890, married Lucille Rothstein.

G15.1. Patricia, born 1940. She married Richard Shein, and later divorced.

G16.1. Jeffrey, born 1962. G16.2. Gregory, born 1965.

G15.2. Sheila, born 1946.

G14.3. Max, born 1899, married in 1941 to Faye Leiderman.

G15.1. Steve, born 1942, married in 1963 to Debbi Kanter.

G16.1. Randi, born 1963.
G16.2. Michele, born 1966.
G16.3. Robert, born 1970.

G14.4. Benjamin, 1891-1967, married in 1919 to Mary Silverman.

G15.1. Marvin, born 1926, twin, married Gloria Goldin.

G16.1. Susan, born 1949.
G16.2. Carrie, born 1951.
G16.3. Ricky, born 1957.

G15.2. Sherwin, born 1926, twin, married May.

G16.1. Stanley, born 1957.
G16.2. Linda, born 1959.
G16.3. Beth, born 1968.

G15.3. Lilian, born 1923, married Arnold Steinberg (Long Island, N.Y.)

G16.1. Stuart, born 1945.
G16.2. Meryl, born 1952.
G16.3. Jeffrey, born 1951.

G13.3. Amalia Hirschhorn, married Zvi Hirsch Buxbaum (New York).

G14.1. Nathan Buxbaum, no issue.

G14.2. Haim Isaiah Buxbaum, no issue.

G14.3. Jack Buxbaum.

> G15. Charlotte, born in 1912, married Harry Grossman (Clifton, N.J.).
>
> > G16.1. Jay R. Grossman, born in 1939, married Ina Harrison and have two children. (New Jersey).
> >
> > G16.2. Leonard E. Grossman, born in 1945, married in 1968 to Judith Gerber and have a child. (New Jersey).
> >
> > G16.3. Arthur Grossman, born in 1942, unmarried (San Francisco).

G14.4. Esther, died in 1961, married in 1906 to Paul (Phineas) Fatt, died in 1960. He was the twin brother of Al Fatt below.

> G15.1. Howard Fatt, born in 1910, married Thelma Kaufman (Columbus, Ohio). Their children Amalia, Naomi and Phillip David.
>
> G15.2. Muriel, born in 1914, married in 1939 Dr. Seymour Jaslow, M.D., Medical Director of the Daughters of Miriam Nursing Home, Clifton, N.J. Their daughters Ellen, born in 1945 and Judith born in 1947.

G14.5. Yetta, married 1) Spiegelman and had two children, and 2) Harry (Hirsch) Fatt, brother of the twins above, and had a daughter. The Fatts were the owners of Homowack Lodge, Spring Glen, N.Y.

> G15.1. Jean Spiegelman, married Denman (Ellenville, N.Y.). They have no issue.
>
> G15.2. Harvey Spiegelman, married and has issue.
>
> G15.3. Florence Fatt, married Irving Blickstein, and have two daughters, Ellen and Karen.

G14.6. Beila, died 1975, Florida, married AL (Elijah) Fatt.

> G15.1. Harold Fatt, unmarried (Malibu, Calif.).
>
> G15.2. Madeleine, married John Cruser (Florida), and have issue with grandchildren.

G13.4. Hodel Hisrchhorn married Isaac Greenberg.

G14.1. Max, unmarried.

G14.2. Freddy, born 1888.

G14.3. Charles.

G14.4. George.

G14.5. Rose.

G14.6. Perl.

G14.7. Nisa.

G14.8. Minzi, married David Elijah Greenhut.

G14.9. Hannah, 1885-1967, married Jonas (Joseph) Speiser of
Skalat.

G15.1. Ephraim Avigdor Speiser,[17] born Skalat 1902, died
Philadelphia 1965. One of America's leading authorities
on the Bible and the lands and the people from which
it derived. He studied at the College of Lvov and came
to the U.S.A. in 1920. In 1923 he received his Master's
degree from the University of Pennsylvania, and his
Ph.D. from Dropsie College in 1924. In 1927 he was
visiting professor at the Hebrew University in Jerusalem and the next year the annual professor at the
American School of Oriental Research in Baghdad.

At this time, he led an expedition which surveyed
Northern Iraq and began excavations of mounds near
Mosul. From these came evidence of early trade routes
connecting Iran, China and Central Asia. Other objects
about this period, 4,000 B.C., showed links with the
Adam and Eve and Noah and the Flood stories.

He later headed expeditions for the University of
Pennsylvania and the American School of Oriental Research (A.S.O.R.).

At age twenty-nine, he was made a full professor at
the University of Pennsylvania. He served for many
years as an editor of the Journal of the American Oriental Society and the Annual of the A.S.O.R. During the
Second World War, he was chosen to serve as chief of
the Near East section of the research and analysis branch
of the Office of Strategic Services. In 1947 he published
The United States and the Near East. Professor Speiser
was also divisional chairman of the Penn. University
faculty of Humanities and was one of five faculty members named in 1964 as university professors for distinction in more than one field.

In 1954 he was chosen as a member of the board of scholars to prepare a history of the Jewish People and edited its first volume *At the Dawn of Civilization* which appeared in 1964 (Rutgers University Press). He was also editor of the new *Genesis* translation published in 1964 by Doubleday & Co.

He married in July 1937 to Sue Dannenbaum, a granddaughter of Charles Gimbel, late Chairman of Gimbel Bros., Inc.

G16.1. Joel Frederick Speiser, born in 1943, married secondly to Wendy Weiss. Their children, Danielle (from first wife), Michael and Stephen.

G16.2. Jean, born in 1940, married 1) S. D. Howard and 2) S. Polen. Their children, Sarah and David.

G15.2. Max Richard Speiser, born in 1913, married Thea Bardach (of the famous Bardach scholarly family). Their daughters, Judith (born in 1955) and Ellen (born in 1952), New York.

G15.3. Charles Stewart Speiser, died unmarried.

G11.2. Avigdor Frankel of Zbariz, born about 1815, died 1887. He was a generous man, helping the poor. He raised his two nephews, Nathan Zimmer and Isaac Greenfeld. He was Head of the Congregation, Treasurer of the *Kollel,* and helped to build the Skalater Synagogue. He married his niece, Gute, daughter of Isaac Frankel. Following the death of his parents; when he was still a boy, he was raised in his brother's home, and later married his daughter.

G12.1. Aaron (Zeev) Wolf Frankel-Teomim, 1840-1918, buried in the Skalater Plot in Mt. Zion Cemetery, N.Y. He married Beila Shifra, daughter of Joseph Altberg of Trembovla in 1858. He came to New York in 1892 with his two daughters and a son (later killed) to join his son Moritz. His wife died at Skalat in 1890.

G13.1. Moritz Frankel, 1863-1937, buried at Mt. Zion Cemetery, New York. He was the author of the genealogical work *Der Goldene Tiegel (Kur Zahav),* published New York, 1928. He married Anna Ellenberg.

G14.1. Moses (Morse) Frankel, 1881-1933, married Sophie Kalhoser.

G15.1. William (Wolf), born 1919, New York. He married:
    a) 1946, Phyllis Mann.

  G16.1. David, born 1947, Akron, Ohio.
      b) 1951, Gloria Spencer.
  G16.2. Madeleine, born 1955, twin.
  G16.3. David, born 1955, twin, Ireland.
      c) 1964, Catherine E. Krauskopf.

G15.2. Rosemary, married Eugene Becker (Silver Springs, Maryland), and they had three children.

G14.2. Joseph Frankel, 1886-1971, married in 1920 to Gussie Gerstenblith.

G15.1. Betty Rose, died young.
G15.2. Arthur, born 1920, New York, married in 1947 to Hannah Herring.

  G16.1. Bruce, born 1949.
  G16.2. Gale, born 1952.
  G16.3. Randi Beth, born 1958.

G14.3. Belle, born 1900, married in 1929 to Irving Shapiro (New York).
G15.1. David, born 1933, unmarried.
G15.2. Ruth, born 1930. She married:
    a) William Mandinach (died).

  G16.1. Mark, born 1957.
  G16.2. Barry, born 1956.
      b) Robert Welch (divorced).
  G16.3. Daniel, born 1967.

G14.4. Gertrude, born 1905, married in 1930 to Harry Filler (New York).

G15.1. Neal, born 1933, unmarried.
G15.2. Martin, born 1938 (Staten Island, N.Y.) married in 1962 to Ellen Kaufman.

  G16.1. Denise, born 1966.
  G16.2. Garret, born 1968.
  G16.3. Roth, born 1972.

G13.2. Abraham, died young.
G13.3. Hirsch, died young.

G13.4. Gershom, killed.

G13.5. Katie (Clara), married Louis Freezer.

    G14.1. Beila (Beatrice), married David Flamm and had issue, Lana.

    G14.2. Charles.

    G14.3. Mary.

G13.6. Sarah, married Lieb Held.

    G14.1. Molly, married Gus Leitner and had a son, Phillip, and a daughter.

    G14.2. Avigdor (William) Held.

G12.2. Rachel, died 1892, married her cousin Jonah son of Jonah Frankel—see below.

G11.3. Jonah Frankel, married in 1830 to Brani of Buczacz. He studied Torah under R. Abraham David A.B.D. of Buczacz, himself a descendant of Rabbi Jonah son of Isaiah Teomim. He died in 1846 at a time when his wife was pregnant with their son named Jonah after his father.

G12.1. Abraham, born 1841. He married when he was fourteen years old to Chaya daughter of Liebus Feldman of the village Ramoshpka (near Chartkov). He was able to continue his studies while being supported by his wealthy father-in-law.

G13.1. Jonah Frankel, died at Vienna in 1919.

G13.2. Israel, died 1913. His children, Haim, Abraham, Katriel and Chanze.

G13.3. Aaron of Buczacz, Galicia. His children, Lieb and Zelda.

G13.4. Joseph of Metz, married the granddaughter of R. Isaiah Shapiro *Krisrabbiner* of Chartkov. They had issue.

G13.5. Frieda, died 1919, married into the Landes Family. Their children, Abraham, Rose and Frume.

G13.6. Rose, married Haim, son of Isaac Weisbard of Janov, Galicia, where they lived until 1914 when the First World War broke out. They then moved to Budzanov and later in 1920 to Skalat where they settled.

    G14.1. Jonah of Skalat, married twice. His second wife was the daughter of Meir Yellis. Their son, Abraham Zeev, born 1906.

G12.2. Haim Frankel.

G13.1. Jonah, died in Vienna, December 14, 1914.

    G14.1. David of Vienna.
    G14.2. Dr. Emanuel, lawyer in Lvov.
    G14.3. Haim Joseph Frankel, New York, pharmacist.
    G14.4. Henry.

G13.2. Aaron of Stanislav, died in 1923.

    G14.1. Dr. Anna Meltzer of Stanislav.
    G14.2. Victoria Kremis.
    G14.3. Paulina.

G13.3. Samuel of Buczacz.

    G14.1. Haim, lawyer in Buczacz, married Toyba, daughter of Samuel Lieb Miller. Their son, Leon.
    G14.2. Abba, married Shinzi Hirschhorn of Buczacz.
    G14.3. Liebe Hinde, married in 1926 to Nathan Einleger.
    G14.4. Virginia.

G13.4. Isaac of Buczacz. His children, Haim, Feiwel, Sonya and Victoria.

G12.3. Hirsch Frankel.

    G13.1. Jonah of London.
    G13.2. Sarah of London.
    G13.3. Hinde of London.

G12.4. Jonah Frankel son of Jonah, born 1846/7, after his father's death. He married Rachel, daughter of his uncle Avigdor Frankel.

    G13.1. Dr. Amalia Frankel, born May 23, 1879 in Skalat. She received her Ph.D. in 1916. She married in 1897 to Jacob Henefeld.

    G14. Samuel, born in 1883, schooled in Tarnopol, died young.

G12.5. Minzi, married Moses Mordecai Miller of Buczacz. She died there in 1907.

    G13.1. Jonah.
    G13.2. Samuel Lieb, died in Buczacz 1910.

        G14.1. Edel, died in Vienna 1915.
        G14.2. Toyva, married Haim son of Samuel Frankel.
        G14.3. Moritz of Vienna.

G13.3. Deborah Pines, died in Kremnitz in 1923. Her daughter, Brani.

G12.6. Hinde Anderman, died 1885.

G13.1. Deborah, married Mendel Engelstein. Their sons, Aaron and Fischel.

G13.2. Golda Eiszler of Stanislav. Her children, Enoch, Hinde and Mazia.

G13.3. Malka Kaufman of Stanislav. Her children, Feiwel, Alexander and Deborah.

G11.4. Feige, married Gershon.

G12.1. Hodel, married Ziskind Rosenbaum of Skalat.

G13.1. Leah, married Joseph Shmirer of Zbariz. Their children, Isaiah, Gershon, Mendel, Esther, Rebecca and Yente.

G13.2. Feige, married Moses Brandeis of Skalat.

G14.1. Hirsch, born Skalat, settled in New York, married Elizabeth, daughter of Phillip Frankel.

G14.2. Sarah, married Alter Brazach of Skalat.

G12.2. Charne.

G11.5. Deborah Frankel married Moses Judah Greenfeld. She died in Skalat 1849.

G12.1. Isaac of Skalat, orphaned as a child and raised by his uncle Avigdor. He died in Skalat 1902.

BRANCH D

DESCENDANTS OF
LEVI ISAAC OF BERDICHEV

ANCESTRY

G5.9. R. Jonah son of Isaiah Teomim (son-in-law of R. Meir son of Saul Wahl).

G6.2. R. Isaac Meir Teomim-Frankel.

G7.8. Wife of R. Aryeh Liebus of Apt.

G8. R. Peretz.

G9. R. Israel.

G10. Pearl wife of Levi Isaac, 1740-1810. He was one of the most famous of the third generation of the Chassidic movement. He was the son of Meir, Rabbi of Hoshakov (Galicia). He married the daughter of a rich contractor and moved to his father-in-law's home in Lubartov (Poland) where he studied under R. Joseph Teomim. In 1766, he studied under Dov Ber. He succeeded R. Samuel Shmelke Horowitz of Nikolsburg as Rabbi of Richwal, then Zelechow, and became the *Zaddik* of Zelechow. In 1775, he became Rabbi of Pinsk and Berdichev in 1785 until his death. He was the founder of Chassidism in central Poland. While Rabbi of Pinsk, he engaged in a debate with the *Mitnaged* R. Abraham Katzenellenbogen of Brest.[18] They met near Warsaw, in 1781 and in 1784 Katzenellenbogen circulated a letter of his arguments against Chassidism. Levi Isaac did not establish a dynasty.

He was the author of *Kedushat Levi*, published Slavuta 1798, Zolkiev 1806 and Berdichev 1811, with supplements by his sons.

G11.1. R. Israel of Pikov, died 1818, called Dermbarmdiger. He was the author of *Toldot Yitzchak ben Levi*.

G12.1. R. Samuel Shmelke.

G13. R. Elimelech of Berdichev.

G14. R. Levi Isaac.

G15. R. Joseph Lieb Perl of Rizchov, 1847-1910.

G12.2. R. Mattithiah Ezekiel.

G13. R. Phineas, married Feige, daughter of Ezekiel of Karlin.

G14. R. Mattithiah Ezekiel.

G15. R. Simeon Dov, married the daughter of R. Aaron Friedman of Buhusi. (See chapter XV.)

G12.3. R. Moses, married Shasya Sarah, daughter of Eliezer Lieber of Keidan.

G11.2. R. Meir of Berdichev, died 1806. He was the author of *Keter Torah*.

G12.1. Esther Rachel, married R. David Aryeh Lieb (died 1849) of Nodverna, son of R. Zvi Hirsch Maged (author of *Tzemach Hashem LiTzvi*, published Berdichev 1818).

G13. R. Meir.

G14. R. Zvi Haim Maged of Tetsch, published *Keter Torah* by
Meir son R. Levi Isaac his ancestor, at Satmar (Rumania)
in 1933, and reprinted in London, 1957.

G15. R. Aaron Maged.

G12.2. R. Joseph of Berdichev, published *Kedushat Levi* in 1811.

G12.3. Wife of R. Ezekiel son of R. Aaron Jampoller (Landau). (See
Chapter X — G8.3/9.3/10.2/11.2/12.2.)

G11.3. R. Dov Ber, died 1823.

G12. R. Levi Isaac.

G11.4. Wife of R. Joseph Bunem Wallis.

G12. R. Jekutiel Zalman.

G11.5. Wife of R. Nathan of Kozenitz.

BRANCHES E AND F

TEOMIM AND WEINBERG FAMILIES

ANCESTRY

G3.3. R. Saul Wahl Katzenellenbogen.

G4.1. R. Meir.

G5.9. Beila, married R. Jonah, son of R. Isaiah Teomim.

G6.4. R. Joshua (Ezekiel) Feiwel.

G7. R. Aryeh Lieb, A.B.D. Kreshov.

G8. R. (Haim) Joseph, A.B.D. Lublin.

G9.1. R. Aryeh (Judah) Lieb, A.B.D. Brody (*Gur Aryeh Yehudah*).

G10.1. R. Ezekiel Meir Weinberg — Branch E.

G10.2. R. Baruch Samuel Teomim, A.B.D. Brody — Branch F.[19]

BRANCH E

G11.1. R. Zvi Hirsch Joseph of Bilgoray.

G11.2. R. Jonah of Jaroslav.

G11.3. R. Saul of Bilgoray.

G11.4. Wife of R. Dov Berish, son of R. Eliezer (of Lublin — see below),
A.B.D. Gorai and Tomashov.

G11.5. Esther (died 1869), married R. Samuel Eli (Elijah) who died in
1878, son of R. Eliezer Schwerdscharf of Lublin (died 1888), author

Damesek Eliezer, published Kolomya, 1843, son of R. Dov Berish Halpern, A.B.D. Lublin. They were descended from R. Jehiel Heilprin, author of *Seder HaDorot* (died about 1746). His Ethical Will appears in *Tirosh VeYitzhar* by his grandson, R. Zvi Ezekiel Michelson.

G12.1. Gitel, married R. Jonah Haim Kranenberg. Their son, R. Ezekiel Meir of Balkovia.

G12.2. Frieda, married R. Isaac Harmon of Bilgoray.

G12.3. R. Moses Zvi Schwerdscharf.

G12.4. R. David Tebele Schwerdscharf of Bilgoray (Lublin District), died in 1878, married Gitel Ginendel, daughter of R. Moses Jacob, son of R. Mordecai Zeev, son of R. Meshullam Zalman Ashkenazi. (See Ornstein-Ashkenazi Pedigree — Chapter XII — Branch E.)

G13.1. R. Moses Jacob Schwerdscharf of Kolomya, author of: *Da'at Linvonim,* Munkacs, 1898, a history of Polish Jewry; *Geza Tarshishim,* Lvov 1905, on the lives of R. Haim Hager, R. Israel Friedman and R. Naftali Zvi Horowitz; *Hadrat Tzvi,* Sighet 1909, genealogy; *Keter Melucha,* Kolomya 1909, on the occasion of the sixtieth Jubilee of Emperor Franz Josef; *Nachalat Yesharim,* Sighet 1903; *Torat Ha'amim,* Kolomya 1890; *Tikun Olam,* Kolomya 1906. He is mentioned in *Tirosh VeYitzhar* by his brother-in-law, R. Zvi Ezekiel.

G14.1. Tirzah (Regina), married Isaac Hellering. She was born in 1884 and he in 1882. They met in Kolomya, and married about 1908. They perished with their family in the Holocaust.

G15.1. Israel Hellering. G15.2. Hilda. G15.3. Giesella.

G15.4. Toni (her twin, Edward).

G15.5. Edward Hellering, born in 1910, married in Israel in 1947 to Rachel Fixler. They live in Cleveland.

G16.1. Margaret, born 1948, married Mark B. Ermine and have a son, Jason Ian.

G16.2. Ruth, born 1950, married Barry A. Rosenthal, and have a daughter, Stacy Lynn.

G14.2. Raatza, and a brother, all perished. Raatza had a daughter, now married in Israel, Hinda Leiter.

G13.2. Dov Berish of Lublin, married and had issue.

G13.3. Hinde Sarel, died in Warsaw in 1904, married R. Zvi Ezekiel, son of R. Abraham Haim Michelson, her first cousin.

G13.4. R. Isaac Nathan of Zaklikov, mentioned in *Tirosh VeYitzhar* by his brother-in-law, R. Zvi Ezekiel.

G13.5. Liebe Reizel, married R. Moses Gelernter, A.B.D. of Revitz and Marad, son of R. Israel, author of: A Commentary on *Tehillim* (Psalms) entitled *Hazhir Hashalem*, Pietrokov 1905; *Imrei Moshe, Biurim* and *Hagahot*, Lublin 1937; *Vayitzav Moshe*, Bilgoray 1934.

G13.6. Deborah, married R. Isaac Honigbaum of Kazimir, as his second wife.

G13.7. Esther, married R. Samuel Honigbaum of Bilgoray, son of R. Isaac Honigbaum (G13.6) as his first wife. They had issue, some of whom survived the Holocaust.

G12.5. Hannah Beila, married R. Abraham Haim Michelson (died 1857), son of R. Jacob Jehiel Michael Klausner of Pietrokov. (See Berliner Family Pedigree — Chapter XII — Branch C.)

G12.6. Zlata, married R. Zeev Wolf Lvov of Komarno.

BRANCH F

G10.2. R. Baruch Samuel Teomim, A.B.D. Brody.

G11. R. Israel of Brody, died young.

G12. R. Abraham Teomim, A.B.D. Zbariz, Pomarin and for forty years, A.B.D. Zalischick. He was the author of many works, published and unpublished, many of which were lost during the two World Wars. Those published are: *Avel Katan (Kaved)*, funeral oration for R. Shalom Joseph,[20] son of R. Israel Friedman, Lvov, 1851; *Avel Gadol*, funeral oration for R. Israel Friedman,[21] Lvov, 1851; *Beit Avraham; Birkat Avraham*, on the Talmud; *Birkat Avraham*, Responsa; Responsa at the end of *Nechmat Yosef* by his grandson, R. Joseph Thumim; *Nachal Dimah*, funeral oration for R. Joshua Rokeah,[22] Zlotchiki, 1894.

He was married twice, marrying two sisters: 1) daughter of R. Isaac Dov, who died, having no issue; 2) Breindel Yota, daughter of R. Isaac Dov Heizler of Buczacz, grandson of R. Isaac Dov Margolioth, A.B.D. Yazlivitz (brother of R. Meir, son of R. Zvi Hirsch), son of R. Zvi Hirsch, A.B.D. Yazlivitz. She had issue.

G13.1. R. Zeev, succeeded his father as A.B.D. Zalischick.

G13.2. R. Nahum Zvi, called Zida Thumim[23] the *Yunger Rov* (Younger Rabbi) having been Rabbi of Zalischick for six years during his father's life time, became A.B.D. of Lobatchov, as requested by his father, the post of A.B.D. Zalischick transferred to his brother, R. Zeev. He was the author of: *Zayit Ra'anan; Anaf Etz Avot;* a Responsum which appears in *Nechmat Yosef* by his son. During his Rabbinate at Lobatchov he completed the study of Talmud with his pupils and followers seven times, and forty-nine times for *Mishnayot.* When he reached *Kedoshim* (one of the Tractates) and commenced the Mishna *Zevachim,* he collapsed and died at the *Klaus* in 1929. He married Chaya, daughter of R. Eleazar Frankel of Lobatchov (died in 1915). She died during the Holocaust of World War II.

G14.1. R. Isaac Dov Thumim, married Gitel, daughter of R. Nahum. Both perished during World War II. He was a publisher.

G15.1. R. Mordecai Lipa,[24] born in 1910, married Malka, daughter of R. Elijah Frankel-Teomim, A.B.D. Przworsk. Both perished during World War II. (See Branch H.)

G15.2. R. Eleazar, perished during World War II.

G15.3. R. Abraham, perished during World War II.

G14.2. R. Joseph Thumim, 1888-1967, left Poland in 1933 for London, England, where he was Rabbi of the East End Potaver Synagogue until 1936 when he came to the U.S.A. Here he was known as the *Kalbisher Rov.* He was the author of: *Motiv U'Mfarek,* New York, 1954; Responsa, *Nechmat Yosef,* New York, 1949. He was married twice: 1) in 1911 to Rebecca, daughter of R. Isaac Bratspies; 2) in 1946 to Chaya Jochebed (whose first husband was R. Phineas Joseph, son of R. Abraham Thumim — see Branch A).

G15.1. David Elimelech Thumim, born 1912, perished in 1943.

G15.2. Feige, born 1920, perished in 1943.

G15.3. Leah, born 1914, married in 1939 to R. Isaac Joel Rabinowitz, the New York Manistretcher Rov of the Linitz-Koritz Family. (See Chapter XV.)

G14.3. Channah Thumim, born in Lobatchov, perished during World War II. She married Gedaliah Lieberman (died in 1920).

G15. Abraham, perished during World War II.

BRANCH G

KAMADER CHASSIDIC FAMILY

ANCESTRY

G3.3.   R. Saul Wahl Katzenellenbogen.
G4.1.   R. Meir.
G5.9.   Beila, married R. Jonah, son of R. Isaiah Teomim.
G6.4.   R. Joshua (Ezekiel) Feiwel.
G7.   R. Aryeh Lieb, A.B.D. Kreshov.
G8.   R. (Haim) Joseph, A.B.D. Lublin.
G9.2.   R. Ezekiel Feiwel, A.B.D. Ostrovitz.
G10.2. R. Moses Eliezer.
G11.1. R. Uri Lipman Frankel.

G12. R. Shraga Feiwel, A.B.D. Ruska.

G13. R. Samuel Frankel, called Samuel Kamader, born in 1814, died
   in 1884. He was one of the foremost Chassidic Rabbis of Hungary, who studied under R. Haim Halberstam of Sanz and was
   appointed by him Rabbi of Darag. He wrote *Amarei Shofar*,
   Biurim and Novellae, Munkacs, 1888, Ihel, 1932, and Jerusalem,
   1940.

G14.1. R. Meir of Rotsfurt.
G14.2. Wife of R. Jacob Zvi Weisman, A.B.D. Savslau.
G14.3. Wife of R. Zeev Citron, who succeeded his father-in-law,
   died in 1927.

G15.1. R. Ezekiel Shraga Citron, Rabbi of Entash.
G15.2. Wife of R. Zvi Hirsch Friedman, A.B.D. Hatseg, son of
   R. Menashe Simha, A.B.D. Savronetz.

G11.2. R. Isaac Frankel, A.B.D. Krali.
G11.3. R. Baruch Frankel of Kralov.

BRANCH H

DESCENDANTS OF
R. BARUCH (the *Baruch TaM*) FRANKEL-TEOMIM'S SON

G10.3. R. Baruch Frankel-Teomim.
G11.1. R. Joshua Heschel, A.B.D. Komarno, died in 1843.

G12.1. R. Jacob Isaac Frankel-Teomim, A.B.D. successively of Naharayov, Miyechov, Kchoncz, Prezworsk and Chechinov, all towns in Galicia.

G13.1. R. Joshua Heschel, died 1894, A.B.D. of Naharayov and Lobatchov, married Beila, daughter of R. Eleazar, Rabbi of Mariampol and Rohatyn, son of R. Meshullam Issachar Horowitz. (See Chapter XVI — Stanislav Branch VI — G14.3/15.5.) Of their children, a few died young.

G14.1. R. Elimelech Frankel-Teomim,[25] born in Lobatchov in 1884, and perished about 1943 in the Holocaust. He was A.B.D. of Javorow, Poland and the author of *Hafla'ot Nedarim*, published in Bilgoray in 1936. He married Reizel Chaya Shifra, daughter of R. David Menachem Meinish Babad[26] (1865-1938).

G15.1. R. Joel Moses, perished with his family in World War II.

G15.2. R. Meshulam Issachar, perished with his family during World War II.

G15.3. Toyba, unmarried, perished in World War II.

G15.4. Jochebed, married R. Abraham, son of R. Tuvia Horowitz (Rabbi of Shendeshov, Galicia) of the Ropshitz Chassidic Dynasty. They also perished during World War II. (See Chapter XVI — Branch VII — G14.2/15.3/16.1/17.1.)

G15.5. R. Joshua Heschel, born 1905, settled in Tel Aviv after the war, married twice. His first wife was Channah, daughter of R. Menashe Horowitz, his first cousin, R. Abraham's sister.

G16.1. Shalom, married and has issue.

G16.2. David, married and has issue.

G15.6. Jacob Isaac Frankel of Manhattan, New York, born in 1917. He married in 1943 to Gitel (Gertrude), daughter of Abraham Wolf. They arrived in the U.S.A. in 1948.

G16.1. Elimelech, born 1946, married in 1971 to Ilana Yezelsky. Their son, David Menachem, born in 1972.

G16.2. Shifra, born in 1949 (twin).

G16.3. Jochebed, born in 1949 (twin), married in 1969 to Abraham Stein. Their children, Zurit, born in 1970 and Noam Meshullam, born in 1971.

G14.2. R. Elijah Frankel-Teomim,[27] born 1877, was A.B.D. Prezworsk from about 1924 until his death on Yom Kippur, 1943 while he was visiting in Rohatyn. He was the author of Responsa *Nachalat Avi*, published in Bilgoray, 1937. He married Reizel, daughter of R. Abraham Abbale Ingber, a descendant of the Chacham Zvi Ashkenazi.

G15.1. R. Joseph Frankel, born in 1907. He left Poland in 1940 and arrived in the U.S.A. in 1941. He currently resides in Brooklyn. He was one time Rabbi of the Bikur Cholim Synagogue in Brooklyn. He married in 1938 to Leah (Lillian), daughter of Naftali, son of R. Hirsch Wein, himself a descendant of the Teomim Family — see Branch B.

G16.1. Reizel, born, 1941, married in 1961 to R. Mendel Kaufman (of the Babad Family — see Babad Family — Branch C).

G16.2. Joshua Heschel Frankel, born 1945, M.S. in Biology.

G15.2. Malka, married R. Mordecai Lipa, son of R. Isaac Dov, son of R. Nahum Zvi Thumim. (See Teomim Family — Branch F.) They both perished during the Holocaust.

G15.3. R. Jacob Isaac, married Toyba, daughter of R. Menachem Mendel Babad, Rabbi of Gurahamo, Rumania. (See Babad Family — Branch B.) They both perished in the Holocaust.

G15.4. Joshua Heschel, married the daughter of R. Isaac Lieb Ernberg. He perished with his family in the Holocaust.

G15.5. R. Abraham Abbale, married Frieda, daughter of R. Menashe Horowitz, Rabbi of Jolin, son of R. Elijah, son of R. Naftali Haim, son of R. Meir Horowitz. (See Chapter XVI — Branch VI — G14.1/15.3/16.1/17.1/18.)

G15.6. Feige, married R. Mordecai, son of R. Abraham Heller. They perished in the Holocaust.

G15.7. Hinde Mirl, was the second wife of R. Isaac Halevi Steinberg, Rabbi of Jaroslav — Tel Aviv, son of R. Shemariah, A.B.D. Premyslan, Galicia. R. Isaac's mother was a great granddaughter of R. Joshua Heschel Teomim of Komarno. (See below — Teomim Family — Branch H — 12.4/13.1/14.1.)

G15.8. Frieda Hena, married R. Isaac, son of R. Moses Bergman of Stanislav. His first wife was Martel, daughter of R. Abraham Ingber, (his mother's sister). They perished in the Holocaust.

G14.3. R. Baruch Frankel of Sanok, married into the Kaner Family.

  G15.1. Daughter. Her daughter, married Bretler (Tel Aviv).
  G15.2. R. Joshua Heschel, perished in the Holocaust.
  G15.3. R. Ezekiel, perished in the Holocaust.

G14.4. R. Joseph of Sanz, perished in the Holocaust.
G14.5. Malka, married R. Joshua Heschel Parnes, perished in the Holocaust.

G12.2. R. Ezekiel Shraga Frankel-Teomim, A.B.D. of Klasni and Viyel-litchka, author of *Divrei Yechezkiel*, published by his grandson Simha as appears in the introduction which he wrote, Padgorze in 1909. This was reprinted in New York by his descendant Aaron Elimelech Haim Frankel-Teomim. R. Ezekiel died in 1885.

  G13.1. R. Phineas, A.B.D. Chechinov, married Reizel, daughter of R. Ezekiel Halberstam of Sieniawa. (See Chapter XIV — Branch A — G14.1/15.3.)

    G14.1. R. Samuel Shmelke Azriel Frankel-Teomim, A.B.D. Klasni and Viyellitchka, died in 1934. He married Sarah, his first cousin. She died in 1913. His second wife was Yita, daughter of R. Naftali Halberstam of Keshanov. She was married before this. (See Chapter XIV — Branch C — G14.3/15.1/16.4.)

      G15.1. Toyba Rachel, married R. Aaron, son of R. Elisha of New York (Gorlice Branch of Halberstam Family).
      G15.2. Yochebed Reize, married Naftali Zvi Samuel, son of R. Eleazar Halevi Rosenfeld of Ospinzi (son-in-law of R. Haim Halberstam of Sanz).
      G15.3. Ezekiel Shraga, killed in 1944, married Rivke, daughter of R. Meir, Admur Linsk, son of R. Abraham Haim Horowitz (Ropshitz Horowitz-Rubin Family Pedigree — G14.3/15.2/16.1). Their entire family perished in the Holocaust.
      G15.4. R. Phineas Aryey Liebish, succeeded his father as A.B.D. Klasni. He married Rachel, daughter of R. Haim Parnas of Yasliska. He was killed on Yom Kippur 1941, and their entire family perished in the Holocaust. R. Haim Parnas of Yasliska was the son-in-law of R. Abraham Shalom, son of R. Ezekiel Shraga Halberstam. (See Chapter XIV — — Branch A — G14.1/15.5/16.3.)

G15.5. Haim Baruch Frankel-Teomim.

G15.6. David Frankel-Teomim.

G15.7. Frume Beila, married R. Menachem Mendel, A.B.D. Malitsch, son of R. Naftali Horowitz (Ropshitz Horowitz-Rubin Family Pedigree — G14.2/15.1/16.1).

G13.2. R. Simeon Alter Frankel-Teomim, A.B.D. Padgorze and Cracow, born in 1850 and died 1st day of Passover, 1901. He married Sarah Gitel, daughter of R. David Halberstam of the Keshanov Branch. (See Chapter XIV — Branch C — G14.3 /15.7.)

G14.1. Nechama, married R. Joseph Moses, son of R. Nahum Zalman Shneerson (A.B.D. of Cherkassi). They perished in the Holocaust.

G15.1. R. Baruch Simeon (Jerusalem). He was Rosh Yeshivah of Chebin. He married Reizel, daughter of R. Berish Weidenfeld of Chebin.

G16.1. Joseph Moses, married Rivke, daughter of R. Elhanan Halpern, son of R. David, son of R. Mattithiah Haim Halpern.

G16.2. R. Nahum, married daughter of R. Eichenstein of Zhidachov.

G15.2. Deborah Leah, married R. Isaac, son of R. Shem Klingberg (Zalishitz Rov, Boro Park, Brooklyn).

G16. Nechama, married R. Mordecai Rokeah, son of R. Abraham Simha Rokeah. (See Chapter XVII.)

G14.2. Ruchama Frankel-Teomim, married R. David, A.B.D. Pshezlov, son of R. Abraham Haim (A.B.D. Plotsch) Horowitz. (See Ropshitz Horowitz-Rubin Family Pedigree — G14.1/ 15.6/16.2/17.1.)

G14.3. Chaya Frankel-Teomim, married R. Mattithiah Haim Halpern. He was the son of R. Abraham Judah Uri, whose grandmother was the daughter of R. Asher Isaiah Rubin of Ropshitz. (See Chapter XVI — Branch VII.)

G14.4. R. Simha Frankel-Teomim of Cracow, A.B.D. Skavin, perished in 1942. He married his first cousin, Miriam, daughter of R. Naftali, son of R. David Halberstam. She died in 1937. He published the *Divrei Yechezkiel* in 1909 by his grand-

father. He remarried to Yita (her third marriage) daughter
of R. Naftali Halberstam, his first wife's sister.

G15.1. R. Simeon Alter, A.B.D. Skavin, born in Cracow 1902,
perished in 1945. He married Beila, daughter of R. Aaron
Elimelech Shnieur Zalman, son of R. Mordecai Dov Twersky of Hornistopol. She perished in 1943. (See Chapter
VII—Branch B — G9.6/10.4/11.2/12/13/14 /15/16.1/17.2.)

G16.1. Sarah Gitel, killed in 1943.

G16.2. R. Moses, killed in 1943.

G16.3. Aaron Elimelech Haim, born in Cracow, came to the
U.S.A. in 1950 and settled in New York. He married
Malia Sarel, daughter of Avi Zins. They have no chil-
dren.

G15.2. Rivke, married R. Joshua Feiwel, her first cousin. (See
below.)

G15.3. Reizel, married R. Reuben Horowitz. She remarried to R.
Joseph Hirsch. They perished in the Holocaust. She had
one child from her first marriage.

G16.   Sarah, married Meilich Kornreich.

G15.4. Chaya, married R. Menashe Unger (divorced). She remarried to R. Moses Haim Lowe, A.B.D. Pietrokov. They
perished in the Holocaust.

G16.1. Samuel Isaac Lowe, perished in the Holocaust.

G16.2. Naftali Lowe (surname changed to Lavi), was the
Press Secretary for General Moshe Dayan.

G16.3. R. Israel Meir Lowe, Rabbi of Tel Aviv.

G14.5. R. Jacob Frankel-Teomim, (1867-1929) A.B.D. Padgorze,
succeeding his father. He married Yita (died 1917), daughter of R. Moses, son of R. Ezekiel Halberstam. (See Chapter
XIV — Branch A — G14.1/15.2/16.2.)

G15.1. R. Joshua Feiwel Frankel-Teomim, 1892-1942, A.B.D.
Padgorze after his father's death in 1929, married his first
cousin, Rebecca, daughter of R. Simha Frankel-Teomim,
A.B.D. Skavin.

G16.1. R. Simeon Ezekiel Frankel-Teomim, born in Karlsbad
in 1914, settled in Israel in 1950 and became the Rabbi
of Kiryat Ono (near Tel Aviv, Israel). He married Gitel,

daughter of R. Isaiah, son of R. Nahum Englard. (See Chapter IV — Branch K — G13.3/14.3/15.4.)

G17.1. Isaiah, born in 1949, married Malka, daughter of R. Abraham Landau (the Strikover Rabbi).

G17.2. Rivke born in 1942, married R. Israel David Feigenblatt.

G15.2. R. Ezekiel Shraga Frankel, died in New York 1967. He married and had no children.

G15.3. Miriam, married R. Haim, son of R. Jacob Samson Kaner (son-in-law of R. Ezekiel Shraga Halberstam of Sieniawa). R. Haim Kaner is the Kossover Rov.

G15.4. Rachel, married R. Moses Steinberg (Broder Rov, New York), son of R. Shemariah Steinberg (Premyslaner Rov). They are descendants of R. Joshua Heschel, A.B.D. Komarno, son of R. Baruch Frankel-Teomim. (See below G12.4/13/14.1/15.2.)

G15.5. Channah, married her first cousin, R. Asher Halpern (Dembitzer Rov, New York). See page 614.

G12.3. Sarah Frankel-Teomim, wife of R. Haim Samuel, A.B.D. Chentshin, son of R. Eleazar, son of R. Mordecai Zeev, son of R. Zvi, son of R. Jacob Isaac Horowitz (the "Seer of Lublin").

G13.1. R. Joshua Heschel Horowitz, succeeded his father at Chentshin. He married Malka, the daughter of R. Phineas, son of R. Nathan David Rabinowitz. (See Descendants of R. Joel Ashkenazi Katzenellenpogen;[28] also Chapter IV — G6.4/7/8/9.2/10.4/11/12.1/13.2/14.3.) R. Joshua Heschel died in the Holocaust in Auschwitz.

G14.1. R. Joseph Baruch, A.B.D. of Chentshin, married the daughter of R. Phineas Isaiah Taub. He perished with his five children in the Holocaust.

G14.2. R. Nathan David, married Leah Epstein. They perished in the Holocaust with four children.

G15. Frieda, married and divorced Zoher (Tel Aviv).

G16.1. David. G16.2. Joshua Heschel.

G14.3. Deborah Pearl, married R. Joshua, son of R. Isaac Glikman, son of R. Asher, son of R. Naftali Rubin. (See Ropshitz Horowitz-Rubin Family Pedigree — G14.4/15.4/16.1/17.4/18.1/19.1.)

G14.4. Channah Gitel, perished with her family in the Holocaust.

G13.2. Channah Bracha, married R. Jacob Joshua Frankel.

G14. Bella Rachel, married Elijah Haim Huberland.

G15. Joshua Huberland, married his first cousin, Esther, daughter of R. Isaiah Shapiro of Grodzisk. (See Chapter XVII — Shapiro Dynasty.) They live in New York.
Channah Bracha married again to R. Elimelech Shapiro of Grodzisk, and had issue. (See Chapter XVII.)

G13.3. R. Eliezer Horowitz, died in 1917, married Chatche, daughter of R. Moses Joseph Teitelbaum. (See Chapter XVII.)

G14.1. R. Baruch Kalonymus Dov Horowitz of Pilitz.
G14.2. R. Liebish, married the daughter of R. Ephraim Ganzweig, perished.

G13.4. R. Shalom Horowitz of Chentshin, died in 1918.
G13.5. Wife of R. Isaac Solomon of Zelichov-Keletz.
G13.6. Mirl Reize, married R. Abraham Solomon Epstein of Ozrov.

G14. R. Moses Jehiel Epstein, Admur Ozrov-Chentshin, author of *Eish Dat* and *Be'er Moshe*.

G12.4. Wife of 1) R. Israel Mendel Wechsler,[29] and had issue, and 2) the Rabbi of Stry (East Galicia).

G13.1. R. Moses Wechsler of Tarnow, a prominent businessman who died there about 1901-2. He married Friedel, daughter of R. Benjamin Zeev Lesser, son of R. Menachem Mendel Lesser (author of *Shuvah Shemachot*, published Przemysl, 1878).

G14.1. Sarah, second wife of R. Shemariah (Rabbi of Premyslan, Galicia), son of R. Abraham Halevi Steinberg, A.B.D. of Brody. He escaped to Pomojan and died there in 1940.

G15.1. R. Isaac Steinberg (from first wife) 1888-1967. He married 1) Sarah, died in 1930, daughter of R. Alter Dov Shprung, and 2) Hinde Mirl, daughter of R. Elijah Frankel-Teomim. (See above — G12.1/13.1/14.2.) R. Isaac was the A.B.D. of Jaroslav and later A.B.D. of Tel Aviv.

G16.1. R. Moses Steinberg, born in 1909, Rabbi of Kiryat Yam, Israel, and author of *Torat HaTor*, published in Tel Aviv in 1959 and *Torat HaGer*. He married Ginah, daughter of R. Abraham Gleicher.

G17. Dr. Abraham Steinberg, M.D., born in Germany after the War and married Lynne, daughter of R. Weinberg of Boston. They have a son Isaac, born in 1972.

G16.2. Abraham Steinberg (from second wife) of Tel Aviv, born in 1939, and married in 1957 Channah, daughter of R. Eliezer Landau.

G17.1. Elijah, born in 1959.
G17.2. Shemariah, born in 1962.

G15.2. R. Moses Steinberg (from second wife), born 1903, came to U.S.A. in 1947 (Broder Rov, New York). He married another descendant of R. Joshua Heschel Frankel-Teomim, A.B.D. Komarno, Rachel, daughter of R. Jacob, son of R. Simeon Alter (A.B.D. Padgorze) Frankel-Teomim. (See above — G13.2/14.5/15.4.) They had no children.

G15.3. R. Meir Steinberg (from second wife), 1905-1971, A.B.D. Chartkov and London. He was a member of the London Rabbinate. He married Channa, daughter of Uri Schechter of Auschwitz.

G16. Hindel (Henrietta), married Vivian Kelley, engineer (London). They have two sons.

G15.4. R. Baruch Steinberg (from second wife), 1900-1941, Chief Rabbi and Army Chaplain in Poland. He was killed at Katyn in Russia among the 14,000 officers of the Polish Army killed by the Russians. He died unmarried.

G15.5. Reize, married Solomon Herbst of New Sanz.

G16.1. Moses, married, died.
G16.2. Wolf, died unmarried.
G16.3. R. Usiel (London), married the daughter of R. Israel Aryeh Lieb the Premyslan Rov, son of R. Ephraim Zalman Margulies (Margolioth) of Lanka.

G17.1. Shlomo Herbst, married the daughter of Rabbi Gabel (Boro Park, Brooklyn). They have two sons.
G17.2. Aryeh Lieb Herbst.

G14.2. R. Israel Menachem Mendel Wechsler of Tarnow, 1864-1926, married Frumet, daughter of R. Jehiel Meir Tannenbaum. (See Chapter XVI — G9/10.10/11.4.)

G15.1. Aryey Lieb Wechsler, perished with his wife, Ita and three sons.

G16. Hinde, married Emil Kessler, M.D. (France). Their daughter, Anette, is married to John Balatra.

G15.2. Reizel Bindiger. She remarried Wolf Engel. They perished in the Holocaust.

G15.3. Wolf (Benjamin Zeev Wechsler) married Elisheva Zucker, perished with their family.

G15.4. Sheindel, married Lazer Innfeld, perished with their two sons.

G15.5. Chantsche, married Abraham Mandelbaum, perished with their three children.

G15.6. Joshua Heschel, died in 1917 unmarried.

G15.7. Abraham Baruch, married Nellie Frankel, perished with their family.

G15.8. Jochebed, married Isaac Gross, perished in the Holocaust.

G15.9. Moses Wechsler, born in 1903, and settled in Israel in 1934 (Jerusalem). He is one of the directors of the Lewin-Epstein Publishing House. He married Ronnie, daughter of Benjamin Zeev Engel.

G16.1. Dr. Israel Menachem Wechsler, born in 1934, Plastic Surgeon, married Dinah Brevdo. Their children, Sharon and Yael.

G16.2. Orah (Zipporah) born in 1935, married Michael Zak. Their children, Dafna, Tamar and Isaac.

G16.3. Uziel Wechsler, born in 1942, married Daniela Rasin. Their children, Gabriela and Jonathan.

G16.4. Benjamin Zeev Wechsler, born in 1946, married Ruth Eliav (Liebling). Their children Mishael and Mattia.

G14.3. Joshua Heschel Wechsler, died before the War. His family perished.

G14.4. Abraham Baruch Wechsler, died before the War. His family perished.

G14.5. Benjamin Zeev (Wolf Lazer) Wechsler, married Ethel Mandel.

G15.1. Moses, killed, married Lana, daughter of Joseph Nathanson.

G16.1. Samuel Wechsler (Belgium — New York). His children, Baruch Joseph, Esther and Ricky.

G16.2. Reizel, married Moses Aftergood (Boro Park, Brooklyn). Their daughter, Channah Rivke.

G15.2. Wife of R. Michael Hollander, Dayan of Tarnow.

G14.6. Jochebed, married Eliezer David Lazer of Tarnow, perished with his wife and family in the Holocaust.

G15. Hendel, came to the U.S.A. in 1952, married Joseph Wolf. Their son, Moses.

G14.7. Chantsche, married Moses Sheinberg. The entire family perished in the Holocaust.

G14.8. Naatsche, married Fishel Schrot. The entire family perished in the Holocaust.

G14.9. Rivke, married Mendel Herzog. The entire family perished in the Holocaust.

BRANCH I

GER CHASSIDIM — ALTER FAMILY

ANCESTRY

G3.3.   R. Saul Wahl Katzenellenbogen.
G4.1.   R. Meir.
G5.9.   Beila, married R. Jonah, son of R. Isaiah Teomim.
G6.4.   R. Joshua (Ezekiel) Feiwel.
G7.   R. Aryeh Lieb.
G8.   R. Joseph.
G9.2.   R. Ezekiel Feiwel.
G10.3. R. Baruch Frankel-Teomim, died in 1828.
G11.6. His daughter, wife of R. Meir Jehiel Kaminer[30] of Chentshin who died in 1847. Responsa of his appear in *Baruch She'amar* by his father-in-law.

G12. R. Judah (Yudel) Kaminer, died in 1894, married Hadassah, daughter of R. Moses Haim Rothenberg, brother of R. Isaac Meir, son of R. Israel, A.B.D. Ger.

G13. Jochebed Rebecca, married her third cousin, R. Judah Ari Lieb, son of R. Abraham Mordecai Alter of Ger. R. Judah Ari Lieb's great-grandfather, R. Israel was a disciple of R. Levi Isaac of

Berdichev. His son, R. Isaac Meir Rothenberg (1789-1866) had studied under R. Israel Hofstein, the Maggid of Kozenitz, R. Simha Bonem of Parsischa and R. Menachem Mendel of Kotsk. R. Isaac Meir lost thirteen of his children during his lifetime. He was the author of *Chidushei HaRIM*, first published in Warsaw in 1875. His *Hesped* (funeral oration) appears in *Marom Ha-RIM*, Warsaw 1892. His son, R. Abraham Mordecai, was the father of R. Judah Ari Lieb Alter (G13.).

R. Judah Ari Lieb was born in 1847 and died in 1905. He became Admur of Ger in 1870, and was the author of *Sefat Emet*, the first edition appearing in Pietrokov-Cracow 1905-8.

G14.1. R. Abraham Mordecai Alter of Ger, 1866-1948. He was the last of the Ger Dynasty in Poland. He married Rhoda, daughter of R. Noah Shachor of Biala. (His son, R. Abraham, was married to the daughter of the Kotsker Rabbi, Israel Morgenstern — see Chapter XII). He was one of the founders of the Agudat Israel, and visited Israel many times. He escaped from Ger to Warsaw and reached Israel in 1940. He died at the height of the siege of Jerusalem in 1948. He is buried in *Yeshivat Sefat Emet*.

  G15.1. R. Meir of Warsaw, married the daughter of R. Liebus, son of R. Naftali Hirsch Berliner. (See Chapter XII — Berliner Family Pedigree.)

  G15.2. R. Isaac, died young, married the daughter of R. Baruch Kaminer.

  G15.3. R. Israel, born 1892, married the daughter of R. Jacob Meir Biederman. (See G14.6 below). He is the present Rebbe of Ger.

  G15.4. R. Simha Bonem, married his first cousin, daughter of R. Nehemiah Alter.

  G15.5. Wife of R. Isaac Meir Alter, son of R. Moses Bezalel. They were first cousins.

  G15.6. Wife of R. Solomon Yasakovitz.

  G15.7. Wife of R. Isaac Fishel Heina (grandson of the *Zichron Shmuel*).

  G15.8. Deborah Matil, married R. Isaac Meir Levine.

G14.2. R. Moses Bezalel Alter, married the daughter of R. Simcha Chaim of Warsaw.

  G15.1. R. Isaac Meir, married his cousin. Their son, Lieb.

G15.2. R. Abraham Mordecai, married the daughter of R. Saul Moses Silverman of Verishov.

G15.3. R. David, married Feige, the daughter of R. Azriel Meir Eger of Lublin.

G15.4. R. Joel, married the daughter of R. Nehemiah Alter. They were first cousins.

G15.5. Leah, married her first cousin, R. Abraham Issachar Alter.

G15.6. Hadassah.

G15.7. Frimitsche.

G14.3. R. Nehemiah Alter of Warsaw, married the daughter of R. Zvi Morgenstern of Lomaz and Kotsk, brother of R. Israel Morgenstern of Kotsk. (See above G14.1.)

G15.1. Solomon. G15.2. Liebel. G15.3. R. Menachem.

G15.4. Yota Hena, married R. Bonem.

G15.5. Feige, married R. Joel Alter.

G15.6. Jochebed, married R. Yudel Katz.

G15.7. Hadassah, married R. Abraham Isaac Silman.

G15.8. Toyba, married R. Aaron Citron.

G14.4. R. Menachem Mendel Alter, Rabbi of Pavianitz and Kalicz, married the daughter of R. Abraham Issachar Rabinowitz of Radomsk (*Chesed LeAvraham*). (See Chapter IV — Branch K — G11/12.2/13.3.) He remarried the daughter of R. Moses Frivis.

G15.1. R. Abraham Issachar, Rabbi of Pavianitz, wrote *Meir Einei HaGolah*. He married his first cousin, Leah, daughter of R. Moses Bezalel Alter.

G15.2. R. Haim Eliezer, married daughter of R. Enoch Vaidislovski.

G15.3. R. Isaac Meir. G15.4. R. Mordecai.

G15.5. Feige, married R. Benjamin Eliezer Yustman.

G15.6. Jochebed Ita, married R. Lieb, son of R. Isaac Meir Alter.

G15.7. Rebecca Beila, married R. Haim Eliezer Horowitz, A.B.D. Elchtov.

G14.5. Feigle Alter, married R. Zvi Hanoch HaKohen Levine, A.B.D. Bendin. He died in 1935.

G14.6. Wife of R. Jacob Meir, son of R. Bezalel Biederman.

G15. Wife of R. Israel, son of R. Abraham Mordecai Alter.

BRANCH J

DESCENDANTS OF

ZALMAN GOLDSTOFF
(SON-IN-LAW OF R. BARUCH FRANKEL-TEOMIM)

G10.3. R. Baruch Frankel-Teomim.

G11.7. Gitel, married Zalman Goldstoff, one of the Leaders of the Cracow Community.[31]

G12.1. Leibish Goldstoff.

G13.1. Joseph Goldstoff of Cracow, married Rosalia Rakover, sister of Ephraim.

G14.1. Hinde, perished in the Holocaust, married her first cousin, Zalman son of Ephraim Rakover.

G15. Fredericka, born 1914 came to the U.S.A. in 1947. She married Alex Greenberg (New York). Their children, Helen married Leonard Goodman (and have issue) and Steven Greenberg.

G14.2. Haim, perished with his wife and two daughters in the Holocaust.

G14.3. Golda, married and perished in the Holocaust.

G14.4. Lola, married and perished, together with one child. Another daughter Miriam survived, and married Jacob Katz (Haifa). They have issue, Azar and Yael.

G14.5. Regina, married Meir Kogan of Chernovitz. They had four children. One son,

G15. Professor Abraham Kogan was born in Kishinev in 1921. He settled in Israel where he joined the Aeronautics Department of the Haifa Technion in 1953 and became a full Professor there in 1962. He has devised methods of desalinization of sea water without the use of metallic heat exchange. He married the daughter of Dr. Emanuel Velikovsky of Princeton University. They have issue, Meir and Rivke.

G14.6. Zalman Goldstoff, married Mirl, daughter of R. Phineas Horowitz of Bohorodezany. (See Chapter XVI — Branch VI — G14.3/15.3/16.2/17.1.)

G15.1. Salik, perished.

G15.2. Clara, married Benzion Katz (Benshalom). He was born in Sanok in 1907 (Galicia) and studied at the University of Cracow, where he taught Hebrew Language and then emigrated to Palestine in 1940. From 1941-63 he was Director of the Jewish Agency's Youth and HeChalutz Department. In 1964 he was elected the Dean of the Tel Aviv University, which position he occupied until his death in 1968. He was the author of a number of books and the translator of works in Persian, Arabic and Greek.

G16. Amnon Katz.

G15.3. Eva, married Dr. Lazar Golomb (Medicine) of London.

G16. Pearl, married.

G14.7. Leo Goldstoff, lives in Vienna and Israel, and was married twice.

G15.1. Joseph (John) Goldstoff, lives in Israel, is married and has issue.

G15.2. Gerta, married and lives in England with two children.

G13.2. Leah Goldstoff, perished in the Holocaust, married Mordecai Schwartz (died 1928). They lived in Padgorze (near Cracow) and Vienna.

G14.1. Rebecca, eldest, married twice. Her second husband was Dr. Bernard Salomon (who had first married her sister Golda). They had issue, Junia, perished.

G14.2. Golda, first wife of Dr. Bernard Salomon (her second husband).

G15.1. Ludwig (Lieb) Salton (New York).

G15.2. Ulek, perished.

G14.3. Hendel, died before the War, married Herman Bergman who perished.

G15. Albert Bergman, lives in Rome and Vienna and has issue, Harry.

G14.4. Abraham, died young.

G14.5. Reizel, unmarried, perished.

G14.6. Zisl perished, married Dr. Hugo Rosenfeld. He remarried and lives in London. Their son Mordecai (Martin) perished.

G14.7. Ella, born 1906, married Abraham Polyocan, came to the U.S.A. in 1950.

G15.   Mark, born 1938, married Maxine Dworkin (New York) and have issue, Nicol Aviva.

G12.2. Feiwel Goldstoff, married the daughter of Haim Freilich of Cracow.

G13.1. Baruch Goldstoff 1849-1911. He had seven children.

G14.1. Moses Goldstoff, eldest 1865-1928. His two children Akiva and Manya perished with family in the Holocaust.

G14.2. Chaya Leah 1873-1942, perished, married Asher, son of Abraham Kalman Rozler of Sanok.

G15.1. Solomon Rozler 1897-1970 (New York), married Beila (Bertha) daughter of R. Mordecai son of R. Moses David Ashkenazi. They had no issue.

G15.2. Moses Menachem Rozler, Ph.D., born 1898, came to the U.S.A. in 1951. Married Minke Atlas.

G16.1. Thea, born 1939, married Joshua, son of R. Haim Jacob[32] Safrin (Komarno Rov) and have issue, Lisa and Eliezer in New York. (See Chapter XVII — Eichenstein Dynasty — G1/2.3/3.1/4.1/5.4/6.1/7.9.)

G16.2. Rebecca, born 1946, married Moses Schreiber (Fifth generation descendant of the *Chatam Sofer*, R. Moses Schreiber of Pressburg). They have issue, Asher and Akiva.

G16.3. Helen (Chaya Leah), born 1951, married Moses Selig Neuman and have issue, Zipporah.

G15.3. Joshua Ezekiel Shraga Feiwel Rozler, married Sarah Werner. They perished in the Holocaust with two children.

G15.4. Manya, Ph.D. Psychology, married Moses Gitter (New York).

G16.1. Dr. Kurt Gitter, born 1937 (New Orleans), married Mildred Heiman, and have issue, four children.

G16.2. Dorothy, married David Harman Ph.D., Philosophy, son of Abraham Harman (born 1914, Israeli Representative to the United Nations 1950-3, Consul-General to New York 1954-5, Ambassador to Washington 1959-68 and

President of the Hebrew University in Jerusalem). They have issue, Dama Channah and Orev Solomon.

G15.5. Rose, Ph.D. Philosophy, married Leo Shabo (New York), no issue.

G14.3. Haim Goldstoff 1874-1957, married Chanah Biegeleisen. He died in Jerusalem.

G15.1. Solomon Zalman Goldstoff, married the daughter of R. Berish Weidenfeld (Chebiner Rov). They have no issue.

G15.2. Joshua Ezekiel Shraga Goldstoff of Antwerp. Married Esther, daughter of Nahum Heller. They perished without issue.

G14.4. Isaac Goldstoff 1876—Holocaust, married the daughter of Jacob Weinberger of Dukla, but had no issue.

G14.5. Feiwel Goldstoff, perished with his wife and family.

G14.6. Hanoch Goldstoff, perished with his wife and one son. Another son survived.

G15. Baruch Goldstoff (Ramat Gan).

G14.7. Gitel, died 1928, married 1) Beryl Manzon, and had issue who perished, 2) R. Hager of Vizhniz later divorced and 3) R. Aaron Rokeah (Belzer Rebbe) later divorced.

G12.3. Jacob Goldstoff.

G13.1. Baruch Goldstoff, died in Cracow 1916, buried in Padgorze.

G14.1. Israel Tobias Goldstoff 1876-1931, in Cracow, married Eva (Chava) Majer.

G15.1. Samuel Goldstoff (New York), born in 1916, and came to the U.S.A. in 1950. He married in 1947 to Gitel (Gusta) daughter of Haim Goldfinger. They have issue, Hyman Tobias.

G15.2. Beryl Goldstoff (Pittsburgh). He had three daughters. One married Byron and had issue David Byron (New York).

G15.3. Zalman Goldstoff, died in 1939 (Holland). His son, Joseph Goldstoff.

G13.2. Feiwel Goldstoff, father of Ephraim, father of Hirschel Goldstoff of Amsterdam.

BRANCH K

RADOMSK CHASSIDIC DYNASTY

ANCESTRY

G3.3.   R. Saul Wahl Katzenellenbogen.

G4.1.   R. Meir.

G5.9.   Beila, married R. Jonah Teomim.

G6.4.   R. Ezekiel Feiwel Teomim.

G7.4.   Chaya, married R. Solomon, A.B.D. Pinczow.

G8.2.   Wife of R. Ari Liebus, A.B.D. Zamocz.

G9.   Wife of R. Eleazar HaKohen.[33]

G10.   R. Ari Liebus HaKohen, surnamed Rabinowitz, A.B.D. Neustadt.

G11.   R. Dov Zvi Rabinowitz, A.B.D. Vlostzov, died in 1839.

G12.1. Sarah, died 1830, married R. Joseph Grandman of Kinsk.

G12.2. R. Solomon Rabinowitz, 1800-1866. He became the Rebbe of the
town of Radomsk from 1834 until his death, and the Founder of
that Chassidic Dynasty, as well as being one of the leaders of Polish Chassidism. He was a disciple of R. Issachar Ber of Radoshitz.

Once when R. Menachem Mendel of Kotsk heard that R. Solomon had
become a **Rebbe** he commented how he was truly suited for such a title.
He explained this with a saying: "Words which emerge from one man enter
the hearts of others." The "Radomsker" would always make sure that before he reproached another, he himself was certain that fault was not within his own heart.

In his youth he was already discerned as a prodigy. The young man
used to go with his companions to visit Rabbi Meir of Apt. Once when the
Rabbi observed the youth, he bade the companions never to bring him to
visit again. But when they had returned to their town of Vlostzov and then
went again to Apt, the young Solomon was so insistent on going, they decided to take him as far as a small village outside Apt. The Rabbi then
asked them where the lad was and they answered: "You had requested us
not to bring him here again." "My reason," replied the Sage, "is that this
youth is a greater Saint (Zaddik) than I am, and it is absurd that you visit
me when he lives in your home town."

He was the author of *Tiferet Shlomo*, published in Warsaw in
1867-9.

G13.1. R. Aryey Liebus Rabinowitz, 1823-90. His sons, R. Israel, R. Ezekiel, R. Itamar and R. Eleazar.

G13.2. R. Zvi Meir Rabinowitz, the A.B.D. of Radomsk, died there in

1902. He married 1) the daughter of R. Elijah of Modziz, and 2) the daughter of R. Gershon Halevi Landau of Kaminsk. He was the Rabbi for some thirty-six years.

G14.1. R. Moses Haim.

G14.2. R. Israel Phineas succeeded his father as A.B.D. Radomsk.

G14.3. R. Abraham David, died in 1885 as a young man, author of *Migdal David*.

G14.4. R. Emanuel Gershon, A.B.D. Demblin, married the daughter of R. Israel of Modziz.

G14.5. R. Jacob.

G14.6. R. Isaac Mordecai, A.B.D. Plovna, died in 1938, author of *Ohel Shlomo*, published in Pietrokov, 1924, containing the novellae of his grandfather, R. Solomon; *Siach Yitzchak* (in *Beit Shlomo*), published Pietrokov, 1927; *Da'at Mordecai*, published by his son in Keidan, 1939; and *Ateret Shlomo*, published in Pietrokov, 1926.

G15.   R. Zvi Meir Rabinowitz, author of *Reb Yaakov Yitzchak Mi-Pasischa (Parsischa)*, published in Pietrokov, 1932; *HaMaggid MiKoznitz*, published Tel Aviv, 1947; and *Reb Simha Bonem MiPasischa*, published in Tel Aviv, 1945. These all deal with the history and biography of Chassidism and its Rabbis.

G14.7. R. Joshua Nahum Rabinowitz of Jerusalem, married the daughter of R. Berliner.

G14.8. Wife of R. Moses Mendel.

G13.3.   R. Abraham Issachar Rabinowitz, 1843-1892, Admur of Radomsk, married the daughter of R. Menachem Mendel Landeberg. He was the author of *Chesed LeAvraham*, published Pietrokov, 1893-6.

G14.1. R. Solomon Rabinowitz.

G14.2. R. Ezekiel Rabinowitz, Admur Radomsk, died 1910, the author of *Keneset Yechezkiel*, published in Bendin, 1913.

G15.1.   R. Solomon Hanoch Rabinowitz, 1883-1942, the last Admur of Radomsk. He perished with his wife, Esther, daughter of R. Moses Elimelech Rabinowitz (his uncle), his daughter, and son-in-law.

G16.   Reizel, married R. Moses David, son of R. Nathan Nahum Rabinowitz (See G14.3. below). They were first cousins and perished in the Holocaust in the Warsaw Ghetto.

G15.2. R. Elimelech Rabinowitz, A.B.D. Shidlov.

G15.3. Wife of R. Elimelech Rabinowitz, her cousin (See below G14.3/15.2).

G15.4. Wife of R. Moses Twersky of Krosna (See Chapter VII — Branch B).

G14.3. R. Nathan Nahum Rabinowitz, Admur of Zavertza and Krimilov, married Judith, daughter of R. Joseph Blumfeld.

G15.1. R. Moses David Rabinowitz, married his cousin, Reizel (above). They had a child who died young, and they themselves perished in the Holocaust. He was the author of novellae which were published together with those of his father-in-law entitled *Shivchei Kohen,* published in 1953.

G15.2. R. Elimelech Rabinowitz of Zavertza.

G15.3. R. Hanoch Rabinowitz.

G15.4. Esther Frumet, married R. Isaiah Englard of Sosnowiec.

G16.1. R. Abraham Issachar Englard, born 1911, married 1) Sarah, daughter of R. Mordecai Joseph Eleazar Leiner. (See Berliner Family Pedigree — page 450 — G13.2.) He lives in New York (Crown Heights) as the Sosnowitzer Rov, with his second wife and children.

G16.2. R. Jacob Englard, born 1920, unmarried.

G16.3. Gitel, married R. Simeon Ezekiel son of R. Joshua Feiwel Frankel-Teomim. (See Chapter IV — Branch H — G11.1/ 12.2/13.2/14.5/15.1/16.1.)

G15.5. Chaya Sarah, married R. Isaiah, son of R. Elimelech Shapiro of Grodzisk. (See Chapter XVII — Shapiro Dynasty.)

G15.6. R. Abraham Rabinowitz.

G15.7. R. Jacob Rabinowitz.

G15.8. Friedel, married Hanoch Bornstein of Sochotchov. They have family in Israel.

G14.4. R. Jacob Joseph Rabinowitz, 1873-1902, A.B.D. Klavozk and Breznitz, author of *Emet LeYaakov.*

G14.5. R. Moses Elimelech Rabinowitz, died young, married Mincha, daughter of R. Meir David Mordecai Biederman (of the Lelov Family — see Chapter XVI — Branch I).

G15.1. Esther, married her first cousin, R. Solomon Hanoch Rabinowitz.

G15.2. Zipporah, married R. Jerachmeel Moses Noah Rappoport

of Rava. (See Chapter IV — G6.4/7/8/9.2/10.4/11/12.3/13.1 /14.)

G15.3. Yente, married R. Menachem Mordecai, son of R. Jacob Joshua Frankel. Their daughters—Chaya, married Aaron Weinberg, and Feige Gitel married Moses Weinberg, two brothers. They live in Tel Aviv. R. Jacob Joshua was a son-in-law of R. Haim Samuel Horowitz of Chentshin. (See Chapter IV — Branch H.)

G15.4. Leah, married R. Nathan Eliezer Shapiro, perished in the Holocaust.

G15.5. Hanoch Rabinowitz.

G14.6. Wife of R. Menachem Mendel Alter of Pavianitz (son of the Rebbe of Ger — See Chapter IV — Branch I — G13/14.4).

G14.7. Wife of R. Abraham son of R. Menachem Kalisch of Amshinov.

G14.8. Wife of R. Mordecai Mendel of Atvosk.

G13.4. Wife of R. Lipman Litmanowitz of Kotsk.

G13.5. Wife of R. Israel Brann.

G13.6. Wife of R. Jehiel Luria (died in Safed).

CHAPTER V

A.

DESCENDANTS OF

R. SOLOMON ZALMAN KATZENELLENBOGEN
(G3.3/4.2/5.1)

MEISELS, MIRKES, LEVINE, EISENSTADT AND REINES FAMILIES

G6.1. Wife of R. Abraham, son of R. Elijah Kalamankes (of Lvov), son of R. Abraham (of Lublin) Jaffe, of Cracow, who died there in 1652. Abraham was a first cousin to R. Joel Sirkes, the *BaH* of the same family as the *Levush* (R. Mordecai Jaffe).

G7. R. Zvi Hirsch Kalamankes of Cracow.

G8. R. Judah Lieb A.B.D. Eidlitz.

G6.2. Wife of R. Simha Bonem (of Mohilev), son of R. Judah Lieb (of Cracow), son of R. Simha Bonem Meisel (son-in-law of R. Moses Isserles, the *ReMa* of Cracow). His father R. Judah was a seventeenth century printer and author in Cracow.[1]

G7. R. Solomon Zalman Meisel(s) A.B.D. Mohilev,[2] who married the daughter of R. Joseph, son of R. Simha A.B.D. Mohilev. He succeeded his father-in-law when the latter left to become Judge at Posen. (See Chapter III—Descendants of R. Naftali Hirsch Gunzburg, G6.6/7.)

G8. R. Judah Lieb Mirkes A.B.D. Mir, married the daughter of R. Zvi Hirsch, son of R. Gershon of Prague (a descendant of the *Tosfot YomTov*, R. Lipman Halevi Heller).

G9.1. R. Israel Mirkes A.B.D. Minsk, died in 1813, married Mira,

daughter of R. Joseph A.B.D. Slutzk and Helusk. He wrote a
number of approbations to various works.

G10.1.   R. Zvi Hirsch Mirkes, succeeded his father in 1813 as
A.B.D. Minsk.

G10.2.   R. Judah Lieb, was A.B.D. together with his brother in
Minsk.

G10.3.   R. Saadiah Isaiah Mirkes.

G10.4.   R. Michael Mirkes, A.B.D. Dvoretz. On his death, he was
eulogized by R. Abraham, son of R. Asher of Minsk. The
eulogy appeared in *Amud HaYemani* published in Minsk,
in 1811.

G10.5.   Wife of R. Menachem Eliezer (of Vilna), son of R. Levi,
author of *Ateret Rosh* and *Yair Kanoh*, published in Vilna
in 1862. He was a pupil of R. Elijah, the Gaon of Vilna,
and later settled in Minsk where he died in 1807.

G9.2.   R. Solomon Zalman Mirkes,[3] first elected A.B.D. Mir and later
at Franfurt-on-Oder (about 1771) and then finally at
Königsberg, where he died. He wrote a number of approbations and was the author of *Derosh HaHesped*, Königsberg
1769; *Shulchan Shlomo*, Frankfurt-on-Oder 1771; *Shar-
sharot Ha-avotot*, Frankfurt-on-Oder 1771; *Kisei Shlomo*
and *Mattato Shel Shlomo*. He married the daughter of R. Haim
HaKohen A.B.D. Smorgen.

G10.1.   R. Zvi Hirsch of Minsk.

G11.   R. Solomon Zalman of Slutzk.

G10.2.   Shprintze, married R. Benjamin Wolf, son of R. Asher
Gunzburg of Vilna. He died in 1788, some three years be-
fore his father. His wife died in childbirth, that same year.
R. Asher's father, R. Kalonymus Kalman was the son of R.
Isaac, son of R. Asher Gunzburg (a brother of R. Naftali
Hirsch Gunzburg, mentioned above G7).

G11.1.   R. Solomon Zalman, married Liebe Gitel, daughter of R.
Abraham Berish of Brody.

G11.2.   Mirke, married R. Saul, son of R. Moses (A.B.D. Helusk) Levine of Karlin.

G12.1.   R. Moses Isaac Levine of Karlin.

G12.2.   R. Zeev Wolf Levine.

G12.3.   R. Solomon Zalman Levine, married the daughter of

R. Jacob Aaron Luria of Minsk, son of R. Judah Luria.

G12.4. R. Ari Lieb Levine.

G12.5. Chaya, married 1) R. Gad Asher, son of R. Joshua, son of R. Shalom Rokeah (See Rokeah Family Pedigree); 2) R. Aaron Luria of Pinsk.

G12.6. Vita, married R. Jacob Naftali Hirsch Berenstein of Lvov.

G12.7. Achsa, married R. Jacob Meir, son of R. Haim Padua, A.B.D. Brest, a descendant of the Katzenellenbogen family (See Chapter II — Branch A — G10.2/11/12.)

G12.8. Dinah, married R. Dovberish Levine. (See Chapter VII—Descendants of R. Ari Lieb Katz—G6.2/7.4/8.4/9.1/10.2/11.1.)

G10.3. Reina, married R. Moses, surnamed Reines, after his wife's name. They were the founders of the Reines family. See below for their descendants.

G9.3. R. Joshua, married the daughter of R. Shalom Rokeah (A.B.D. Tiktin), son of R. Eleazar (A.B.D. Amsterdam) Rokeah. (See Rokeah Family Pedigree.)

G10. R. Zeev Wolf, died in 1814.

G9.4. Leah, married R. Michael A.B.D. Kletsk and Mir,[4] son of R. Meir Eisenstadt (1670-1744, known as the *MaHaRaM* Eisenstadt). Novellae of his can be found in *Ketonet Or* to which he wrote an approbation (published Frankfurt-on-Oder 1754).

G10.1. R. Moses Eisenstadt, A.B.D. Kletsk, married Finkel, his first cousin, daughter of R. Eleazar (his father's sister).

G11.1. R. Michael Eisenstadt, succeeded his father as A.B.D. Kletsk, and married the daughter of R. Jacob Uri of Vilna. (See Gunzburg Family Pedigree—Chapter III).

G12. R. Moses Jacob Eisenstadt A.B.D. Kletsk.

G13. Daughter, married R. Meir. (See below G10.3/11.1 12.3.)

G11.2. R. Eleazar Eisenstadt, community leader of Kletsk.

G11.3. R. Solomon Zalman.

G11.4. Malka, married R. Joseph David A.B.D. Mir.

G11.5. Sarah, married 1) R. Simeon, son of R. Asher Gunzburg

of Vilna (See G9.2/10.2 above) and 2) R. Eliezer
A.B.D. Helusk.

G10.2. R. Solomon Eisenstadt of Brest.

   G11. Itke, married R. Abraham of Sokolov.

      G12. Motel, married R. David.

G10.3. R. Zvi Hirsch Eisenstadt A.B.D. Lubetsch and Mir. He,
like his brother R. Moses, married his first cousin, daughter
of R. Eleazar.

   G11.1. R. Elimelech Eisenstadt of Lida.

      G12.1. R. Elijah Akiva Eisenstadt A.B.D. Lida.
      G12.2. R. Zvi Hirsch of Trispoli.
      G12.3. R. Meir, married the daughter of R. Moses Jacob
              A.B.D. Kletsk. (See above G9.4/10.1/11.1/12/13.)
      G12.4. R. Abraham.
      G12.5. R. Eleazar.

G9.5. Shprintze, married R. Joseph, son of R. Bezalel, son of R.
Naftali HaKohen Katz. (See Chapter V, Branch B—Katz Family Pedigree G5/G6/G7.1/8.1.)

REINES FAMILY

ANCESTRY

G3.3.   R. Saul Wahl.
G4.2.   R. Abraham Wahl Katzenellenbogen.
G5.1.   R. Solomon Zalman Katzenellenbogen.
G6.2.   Wife of R. Simha Bonem of Mohilev.
G7.   R. Solomon Zalman Meisels.
G8.   R. Judah Lieb Mirkes.
G9.2.   R. Solomon Zalman Mirkes, died in 1773.
G10.3. Reina, married R. Moses, surnamed Reines, after his wife's name.
G11.   R. Haim Reines, a Dayan in Vilna during the life of R. Elijah, the
        Vilna *Gaon*.

G12.   R. Solomon Naftali Reines, born in Vilna in 1797, and died in Karlin,
        near Pinsk in the district of Minsk in 1889. As a young man, he
        joined the *Back to Palestine Movement,* which had been started
        among the disciples of the *Gaon* of Vilna. He settled in Safed where

he established a Hebrew Printing Press. During the unrest of 1834, his home and press were destroyed by the local inhabitants of the town. In 1837 he represented the Ashkenazi *Kollel* in Europe. While he was in Warsaw, he received news that all the members of his family had perished as a result of an earthquake in Safed which had occurred on January the first of that year. The quake took the lives of over four thousand Jews there.

R. Solomon then settled in Karlin, where he had been in business previously, remarried, and had issue.

G13.1. R. Isaac Jacob Reines, born in Karlin on October 27 (9th Cheshvan), 1839. He was first taught by his father, then under R. Jehiel Halevi of Karelitz, and finally at the Yeshiva of Volozhin (in 1855) and Eisheshok until 1857. He was ordained by R. Samuel Avigdor and R. Eleazar Moses Horowitz of Pinsk. Two years later, he married Elke Rachel, the daughter of R. Joseph Rosen (Reisen) of Hordok, and, as was the custom, he studied further while living with his father-in-law who, in 1862, became A.B.D. of Telz in Lithuania, and later of Slonim in Poland.

By the time he was twenty-one, he had completed a number of works, yet unpublished. Some of his writings were printed in the *Eidut BeYaakov* by his father-in-law. Reines became A.B.D. of Shukian in 1867 and of Shwentsian, in the district of Vilna in 1869, where he remained for sixteen years.

From his youth, he acquired secular knowledge, particularly in languages, logic and mathematics. Thus his work *Chotam Tochnit* (Mainz, 1880; Pressburg, 1881), which was a condensation of a larger manuscript, *Derech HaYam*, contained the logical principles of *Halachah* (Law), and a methodology of the Talmud. Although the most Orthodox felt it to be almost heretical, and condemned him, the *Maskilim* were greatly impressed. In the 1882 meeting of Rabbis and other Jewish leaders at St. Petersburg, he was unsuccessful in having a new system of Talmudic study accepted, which would have included the teaching of Russian and secular sciences. Consequently, that same year, he established his own Yeshiva, which was denounced by the Hebrew Press. The Government was also informed, and he was put for a while in a Czarist prison. Because of financial difficulties and the Jewish opposition, the Yeshiva was closed down by the authorities, having lasted for four years.

My father, of blessed memory, moreover, was wise to detect blemishes

where others did not discern them. For example, he found fault with the
heads of the Yeshivoth in his day who kept their pupils from the study of
secular knowledge and the acquisition of the language of their country. As
a result the Yeshivah graduates grew up without the ability to find a place
in society and to cope with the practical problems as useful citizens. . . .
As a result of their maladjustment, many became contumacious; some de-
generated to depravity and heresy. My father, of blessed, memory, tried to
convince his colleagues, at the Rabbinic conference in St. Petersburg, that
the time had come to introduce in the Yeshivoth the study of the Russian
language and the newly awakening Holy Tongue. Seeing that no one paid
attention to him, nay, that he was opposed on all sides, he went ahead and
did a novel thing. He founded a Yeshivah (first in Schwenzian and later in
Lida); he invited great masters of Torah and piety, among them the Gaon
Poliatchek, of blessed memory renowned by his appellation "The Meichecher
Illuy," as well as excellent instructors in Hebrew and Russian. The Rabbis
fumed and fulminated, and refused to forgive for his double crime—depart-
ing from the methods and actions of other Rabbis, and for introducing
secular subjects in Yeshivoth, in which only sacred studies should be pursued.

(Introduction to *Or Chodosh Al Zion.*)

In 1885 he became A.B.D. of Lida, where he remained until
his death in 1915. Here in 1905, he was able to open a new Yeshiva
which included secular education, and attracted many students.
R. Reines is however most known for his establishing the *Mizrachi*
Movement in 1901, which combined Herzl's political Zionism
with a spirit of Orthodoxy. He attended the Zionist Congresses,
and it was after the fifth congress that he formed the splinter
Mizrachi Movement when Zionist radicals threatened to turn
Zionism away from religion. The following year on March 4-5,
1902, he held the first Mizrachi Conference in Vilna. In 1903 he
sponsored the Uganda project at the Sixth Zionist Congress for
the establishment of a Jewish State.

In yet another matter was my father distinguished from his colleagues.
When Doctor Herzl appeared on the Jewish scene a new, strange and alien
personality in the camp of Israel—and created a movement and an organic
change in outlook, a much found expression in the new term Zionism, the
Rabbis instituted inquiries and investigations to determine the character of
this writer, and his antecedents. After much debate and argumentation they
arrived at the unanimous conclusion that Zionism was an abnegation and
denial of the belief in the coming of the Messiah, an essential principle of
faith, and that the authors and leaders of the new movement were all her-
etics, men without the flavor or savor of religion. They issued proclamations,
warning the people by spoken and printed word disseminated in all Jewish

communities to stay away from these wicked men. Not one among the great
and renowned Rabbis as much as expressed the slightest opposition to this
decision—all were in complete agreement; not a dissenting voice was heard,
except the voice of my father, of sainted memory.

After closely examining the positive and negative aspects of the movement, the constructive and subversive elements, he came to the conclusion
that those who took up the sword against Zionism, declaring it a forbidden
movement, had acted without vision and understanding. They had no right
to condemn as transgressors all who followed or joined it.

He determined to come out openly against the detractors of the Zionist
movement from the Orthodox camp. His family, his relatives and friends
pleaded with him not to do anything that might rouse the Rabbis and pietists
against him, not to become a man of strife and contention to all his colleagues.
He was adamant. He traveled to the Zionist Congress. Hardly three years had
passed when he succeeded in launching the Mizrachi, and in surrounding
himself with Rabbis and Scholars and writers, men of piety, men of action,
and thanks to his exertions and influence, the Mizrachi Movement spread
throughout the lands of the Diaspora and Eretz Israel.

It became a highly activating force in Judaism and Zionism, as we see
today, to the great joy of those who love Torah, Israel and Eretz Israel.

(*Or Chodosh Al Zion.*)

He also wrote *Nod Shel Dema'ot* (published in 1890), which
was reprinted in 1934 in Jerusalem, by his son, with a full family genealogy. The 1904 edition was published in Vilna by Mordecai Katzenellenbogen (see Chapter VIII). His other published works include, *Or Chodosh Al Zion*, Vilna 1902; *Or Le'
Arba'ah Asar*, Pietrokov 1913; *Or Shivat HaYamim*, Vilna 1896;
Orah VeSimha, Vilna 1896; *Orim Gedolim*, Vilna 1887; *HaAra-
chim*, New York 1926, published by his son; *Shnei HaMe'orot*,
Pietrokov 1913; *Sha'arei Orah*, Vilna 1886; and *Sha'arei Orah Ve-
Simha*, Vilna 1899.

G14.1.   R. Moses Reines, the second son, born in 1870 and died on
         March 7, 1891. He was the author of *Ruach HaZeman*, pub-
         lished in *Otzar HaSifrut; Netzach Yisrael*, Cracow 1890; *Aksani'
         ut Shel Torah*, Cracow 1890; and *Dor VeChachmav*, Cracow
         1890.

G14.2.   R. Abraham Dov Ber Reines, born in 1868 and died in Israel
         in 1955 as the result of an automobile accident. He succeeded
         his father as A.B.D. Lida until he left for the U.S.A. about
         1925. He settled in New York where he established a Yeshiva
         in memory of his father and also the R. Isaac Jacob Reines

Publication Society. This society published a number of works including *Sefer Ha'Arachim* (Lexicon of Homiletics) in 1926 which R. Abraham edited. He also reprinted the *Nod Shel Dema'ot* by his father in 1934. He married Fridel, daughter of R. Moses Samuel of Borrisov, author of *Yedei Moshe* (Pietrokov 1899), son of R. Zvi Horowitz.

He was the author of *Chatzer ADaR*.

G15.1. Reichel, born in 1890, perished in the Holocaust. She married in 1911 to David Friedland, a wealthy Zionist from Lodz.

    G16.1. Chava, married Israel Aaronson of Haifa. Their son, Joseph, a lawyer, married.

    G16.2. Schachna Friedland, Professor of Music in Brussels, Belgium. He married twice, without issue.

    G16.3. Moshe and Tamara, perished.

G15.2. Sarah Leah, married in 1912 to R. Solomon M. Schlifer (Shlifer or Schliefer), 1889-1957, son of R. Jehiel Michael, A.B.D. of Aleksandrovka, Ukraine. He studied under R. Isaac Jacob Reines and was ordained in 1907. He later married Reines' granddaughter and succeeded his father in Aleksandrovka, where his wife and a son died of starvation during the civil war after the 1917 revolution. He made his living as an accountant, but settled in Moscow as secretary to the Great Synagogue Congregation, and later their Rabbi and chairman. In 1928 he was forced to leave the rabbinate because of the Bolshevik antireligious policies, and again became an accountant in Moscow. He was one of the few leaders of the Soviet Jewish community to survive the Stalin regime.

In 1940 he was designated by the Soviet Government to take over the Chief Rabbinate of Moscow, where he remained until his death. During World War II, he helped many refugees who fled to Moscow. He was held in respect even by some official circles, so that, in 1956, he received permission for the first time to reprint, with some omissions, three thousand prayer-books which he called *Siddur Ha-Shalom* (i.e. the prayer-book of peace, as opposed to *Siddur HaShalem,* the complete prayer-book, as is customary). He also opened the only legally established Yeshiva, *Kol Yaakov,* some three months before his death, and re-established relations between Soviet and American Jewry. On June 25, 1956, he received a five-man delegation of the Rabbinical Council of America which came to study the conditions of Soviet Jewry, which included R. David Hollander of Mount Eden Center, Bronx, New York; R. Hershel Schacter of Mosholu Jewish Center, Bronx, and R. Samuel Adelman of Newport News, Virginia.

He remarried after the death of his first wife. The Soviet Government sent a delegation to pay its respects to his widow on the occasion of his death, which was also reported in the New York Times, April 2, 1957.

From his first wife, two sons, Michael and Isaac Jacob, died young. He had no issue from his second wife.

G16.1. Moses, killed in Berlin during World War II while serving in the Russian army.

G16.2. Golda, married in Moscow in 1933 to Emanuel Machlin, and settled in Israel in 1972.

G17. Jacob (Yasha) Machlin, born in 1936, married Fani Fradkin. Their daughter, Leah.

G15.3. Reina Reines, died in 1972, married Dr. Aaron Scheflin, M.D. They had no issue.

G15.4. Chaya Zipa, born in 1898, perished in the Holocaust in 1944. She married her second cousin, Solomon Bick (see below).

G15.5. Dr. Nechama Sinegubko, married Mordecai Sinegubko, died in childbirth.

G15.6. R. Dr. Chaim Wolf (Zeev) Reines, born in 1903. He received his Ph.D. from the University of Berlin, and settled in the U.S.A. He was a professor and lecturer at the Hebrew Teachers College and the Catholic Dusquesne University in Pittsburgh. He later settled in New York. He was married, but had no issue, and was the author of seven books, published between 1935 and 1972, and some thirty.articles which appeared in various Hebrew, English, Yiddish and German publications.

G15.7. Hinde (Ayalah), born in 1904, married in 1930 to Menachem Isaac Silverman, a prominent Zionist and educator.

G16. Eliezer Silverman, born in 1934, an educator (Portchester, New York).

G15.8. R. Eliezer Reines, 1905-72, died in Philadelphia.

G16. Sarah Rivke, married in 1955 to Morris Smith. Their children, Daniel, Perez and David.

G15.9. Rebecca, died unmarried in 1917.

G15.10. Maasha, born in 1910, married in 1935 to R. Abraham Johanan Levy, Rabbi of *Congregation Machne Yisrael* in Brooklyn.

G16.1. Rachel, born in 1936, married in 1955 to R. Asher Lemel Ehrenreich. Their children, Joseph, Naftali Jacob, Esther, Hinde Liba and Israel Haim.

G16.2. Samuel Levy, born in 1938.

G16.3. Channah Yita, born in 1940, married in 1960 to R. Samuel Haim HaKohen Lax. Their sons, Shlomo, Isaac Jacob, Joseph and Simeon.

G16.4. Florence, born in 1944.

G15.11. Feige, unmarried (Lakewood, New Jersey).

G14.3. Gela, married R. Aaron Rabinowitz. He succeeded his brother-in-law about 1925 as A.B.D. of Lida. They perished.

G15.1. Elimelech, perished.

G16. Dr. Moses Rabinowitz, a Major in the Russian Army during World War II.

G15.2. Joseph Rabinowitz.

G15.3. Rachel, perished, married Zvi Timkevitz of Warsaw. He settled in Detroit. One son perished.

G15.4. Elke, married R. Avigdor son of R. Israel Cyperstein of Pinsk (born in 1903). He studied under R. Moses Mordecai Epstein (1863-1933), who was the rabbi and director of the famous Yeshiva at Slobodka, near Kovno. In 1923 R. Epstein founded the Yeshiva in Hebron. In 1925 R. Avigdor was among the Slobodka students who went to study in Hebron with R. Nathan Zvi Finkel. During 1928, R. Epstein became the Hebron Yeshiva director, but because of the Arab attacks, moved the Yeshiva to Jerusalem. At this time R. Avigdor had returned to Poland on a visit and was thus saved from possible death. He then studied for two years at the Mir Yeshiva. He succeeded his father-in-law as A.B.D. Lida which position he held for seven years, until the family was forced to flee at the outbreak of World War II to Shanghai. Here he remained until the end of the war and came to the U.S.A. in 1946, settling in New York as one of the heads of Yeshiva Isaac Elchanan (part of Yeshiva University). He held this post for twenty-five years until he settled in Israel in 1972. He was also a leading member of the American Mizrachi Movement, and is currently a leader of the world Mizrachi. Most recently R. Cyperstein was chosen chairman of the board of the *Yad HaRav Herzog,* the famous Talmudic Research Center in Jerusalem. He also served for a two-year period as Chief Rabbi of Argentina.

G16.1. R. Nathan Zvi Cyperstein, born in Vilna 1932. He came to the U.S.A. via China in 1946 and married Sarah Bakst. Their children, Aaron Israel, Miriam, Eli and Tova. He is a lawyer.
G16.2. Batya, born in Lida in 1936, married Benjamin Lampert, a lawyer. They settled in Bnei Brak (Israel).
G16.3. Shulamit, born in 1941.
G16.4. Nechama (Naomi), born in China in 1946, married R. Noam Gordon, Professor of Mathematics, City College, New York. Their children, Yehuda, Gitel and Israel.

G15.5. Nechama, Frodel and Sarah, perished in the Holocaust.

G13.2. Aryey Lieb Reines, a merchant in Pinsk.

G14.1. Haim, Velvel and Moses.
G14.2. Saul Reines, 1886-1947, came to the U.S.A. in 1907 where he married Leah, daughter of Meir David Goldstein in 1913. He was a close friend of the stage and cinema actor, Paul Muni.

G15.1. Leon (Judah Lieb) Reines, named after his grandfather, born in 1914, married Esther Puro. Their daughter, Sheila.
G15.2. Irving (Isaac Jacob) Reines, born in 1920, married Phyllis Weiner. Their children, Eric and Stacey.
G15.3. Harriet, unmarried (New York).
G15.4. Madelaine, married Morris Bernstein, and have two children.

G14.3. Reina, unmarried, died in 1972.
G14.4. Galia, married Bennie Berman, no issue.

G13.3. Miriam (Mira), died in Pressburg in 1926, married R. Abraham son of R. Jacob Bick of Mohilev, as his second wife. He had children by his first wife. After he remarried he travelled to Turkey and Palestine where he suffered the pogroms under the Turkish

rulers. His eldest child was born in Turkey (Israel Bick). He was
also the author of a number of works, of which *Ohel Yosef* was
published in Jerusalem in 1869, as part of his *Ohel Moed; Biku-
rei Aviv,* Lvov 1873; *Yesod Ohel Moed,* Lvov 1876; *Moda Le-
Binah BeMikra,* Jerusalem 1881; and *Pri HaAretz,* Jerusalem
1882. Having returned to Europe he settled in Pressburg where
he published *Beit Yaakov,* 1890; *Pri HaAretz,* 1890; *Beit Avraham,*
1890; *and Archei Alai,* 1891. He died impoverished in 1903 and
was buried in Pressburg.

The following story is related in Lubavitcher literature about
R. Abraham Bick.

It was the custom for the Lubavitcher Rebbe (R. Shalom DovBer
Schneersohn, 1866-1920) to rest after his midday meal. Once, he was reclin-
ing in a restless manner, with a vacant stare, and appeared to be in "another world." His son (R. Joseph Isaac Schneersohn, 1880-1950, father-in-
law of the present Lubavitcher Rebbe) became alarmed, and attempted to
arouse his father by noisily pacing the room and moving the furniture, but
to no avail.

When it was already late, the Rebbe awoke confused, and perplexed as
to the day of the week. Having gained his composure, he prayed the evening service, but strangely incorporated the liturgy reserved for the High
Holidays, much to the bewilderment of his son.

The following morning the Rebbe asked his son for their money, but
being destitute, he pawned his silver cane and gave his father the money.
The Rebbe then went, leaving his son at home. After a while, delivery-men
began to arrive with parcels of female apparel from different stores. The son
thought his father had bought gifts for their family. When evening came,
the Rebbe returned and bade his son hastily pack for a train journey to the
city of Pressburg (where R. Abraham Bick had died). On their arrival, it
was the custom to hire a wagon, but on this occasion, the Rebbe insisted they
walk.

They stopped a young Yeshiva student who was hurrying by, and asked
of him the way to the hotel. He was rather abrupt, whereupon the Rebbe
rebuked him, so that the lad then guided them to the hotel, where the owner
(R. Abraham Bick) had died the day before (in 1903) which corresponded
to the time of the Rebbe's restless afternoon sleep. At home, the widow and
three daughters were sitting *Shiva.*

After a short rest the Rebbe and his son visited the local Yeshiva, where
they engaged in learning with the students, and in particular with one bright
pupil. Thereafter they paid a condolence call to the widow who was now
poor, without even having decent clothes for her daughters. Their conversation drifted to marriage, whereupon the Rebbe offered his help. He chose
the young man he had met in the street and the bright Yeshiva student for

two of the daughters and reassured the mother that he had ample new clothes for them all. Thereafter the Rebbe and his son departed and returned home.

Five years later (in 1908), R. Joseph Isaac Schneersohn revisited Pressburg and learnt that all three daughters were now happily married. The one husband his father had chosen was now the A.B.D. of a nearby town (R. Newman of Alt-Ofen) and the other a principal of a school (Wolf Newman).

> Note: the facts of this story have been confirmed by grandchildren of R. Bick, some seventy years after the event occurred.

G14.1. Israel Bick of Pressburg, married in 1919 to Martha Strauss. They perished.

    G15.1. Edith, born in 1919, came to the U.S.A. in 1937. She married Arthur Stern and had a son, Jerry, born in 1948.

    G15.2. Armin, born in 1923, married Doris Schmidt (New Jersey). Their son, Martin.

G14.2. Arno Bick of Michelstadt, settled in Israel. He married Rosa Bravman.

    G15.1. Alfred Bick, married and has issue (Ramat Gan, Israel).

    G15.2. Ilse, died unmarried.

    G15.3. Norbert Bick, married and has issue (Cleveland, Ohio).

G14.3. Isaac (Ignatz), married Mira Mannheimer (New York).

    G15. Inga, married Eric Isler (Connecticut). Their sons, Robert and Frank.

G14.4. Solomon Naftali Bick, named after his maternal grandfather, born in 1896, and married his second cousin, Chaya Zipa, daughter of R. Abraham Dov Reines (see above).

    G15.1. Mirka and Jacob, perish in the Holocaust.

    G15.2. Sarah, born in Lodz, and settled in the U.S.A. after the Holocaust. She married Morris Berkowitz, and was the authoress of *Where are my Brothers?*, published in New York in 1965.

        G16.1. Cecilia (Zipa), born in 1947, a college graduate, married in 1971 to Reubin Margules. Their daughter, Julie.

        G16.2. Florence, born in 1948, a music teacher.

        G16.3. Shelley, born in 1953, cum laude graduate from Barnard College, New York.

G14.5. Azriel Bick of Vienna. He and his family perished.

G14.6. Mordecai (Martin) Bick of Brünn, the youngest son, died unmarried in Vienna.

G14.7. Chaya (Kate), married R. Dr. Joseph Newman, *Oberrabbiner* in Alt-Ofen (Obuda) in Budapest.

   G15.1. Sarah, eldest child, died unmarried.

   G15.2. Abraham Newman of London, married.

   G15.3. Simha Newman of London, married.

   G15.4. Benzion Newman of London, married.

   G15.5. Judith Rethi of Budapest.

   G15.6. Yehudah Newman, Professor of Meteorology, married Chavah Szenesh, Jerusalem), and have issue.

   G15.7. R. Isaac Jacob Newman, the *Papa Rov* of the Belz Chassidim in Montreal. He married twice, his first wife having perished in the Holocaust.

G14.8. Nechama (Nettie), married Wolf Newman, perished in the Holocaust.

   G15.1. Sarah, married 1) Mr. Parcel, perished, and had issue, and 2) Mr. Roth. Their daughter, Edith, married and lives in Israel.

   G15.2. Gela, married Joseph Engel, perished.

   G15.3. Professor Jacob Newman, born in Pressburg, Czechoslovakia in 1914, where he studied at the Yeshiva College. He emigrated to England in 1939 and obtained his M.A. from the University of Manchester in 1945. Shortly thereafter he was elected as a researcher and part-time lecturer in Criminology at the University of Liverpool. He held Rabbinical positions in Petrzalka (1936-38), England and in 1951 went to South Africa as National Rabbi to the Country Communities. He settled in Johannesburg where, besides serving as Rabbi of the Northern Suburbs Hebrew Congregation, he was Professor of Post-Biblical Jewish Literature, University of Pretoria and Vice-Principal of the Johannesburg Rabbinical Seminary. In 1969, having received his D.Litt., Rabbi Newman returned to the study of criminology and received his M.A. with distinction in that field. In 1970 he settled in Cape Town, where besides serving as a community Rabbi, he lectured in three departments at the University of Cape Town, including Sociology and Social Work. He was widely consulted for his great knowledge in juvenile crime, delinquency and antisocial problems. In 1974 he settled in Israel.

He is the author of many articles on criminology in various journals, and his published works include: *Semikhah (Ordination)*, 1950; *Judaism in the Home*, 1956; *Speak Unto the Children of Israel*, 1957; *With Ink in the Book*, 1957; *A Guide to Judaism for the Young*, 1959; *Nahmanides*, 1960; *Early Halachic Sources*, 1965; *The Eternal Quest*, 1965; *Towards Light; Ingathering;* and four works in Hebrew, *Biur Halachah*, 1964; *Maayan Yaakov; Iyyun Halachah;* and *Baalot HaShachar.*

He married in 1952 to Zelda, daughter of Rev. R. A. Myburg, and has four sons, Nahum Zeev, Avron, Gavriel and Hillel Yehuda.

G15.4. Leah, married Otto Marchfeld of Vienna. Their only son died as the result of an accident in Israel.

G15.5. Abraham, perished unmarried.

G14.9. Foga (Flora), youngest child, married Joseph Halevi Lefkowitz of Pressburg. They perished.

G15.1. R. Abraham Lefkowitz, 1918-1965, Principal of an Elementary School in Israel. He was the author of *biurim* and *chiddushim,* called *VaYosef Avraham,* on the *Revid HaZahav* by R. DovBer son of R. Judah Trevis, published New York, 1967. He married Sarah Katzburg.

G16.1. Zipporah, married R. Raphael Posen of Jerusalem, and have four sons.

G16.2. Ayalah, married Dayan, and have issue.

G16.3. Miriam and G16.4. Rivke.

G15.2. Toby, born in 1919, married in 1946 to Aaron Samuel Gewurz. They came to the U.S.A. from Belgium in 1951 and settled in New York.

G16.1. Foga, born in 1947, married Jacob Zvi Weiss (Toronto). Their children, Deborah, Pearl and Joseph.

G16.2. Jekutiel Dov, born in 1953.

G15.3. Mordecai, born in 1921, married Reize Fettman (Bnei Brak). Their children, Judah (married with issue), Zipporah (married) and Sarah.

G15.4. Jonah, born in 1923, married Judith Kalisch (New York).

Their children, Reuben (married Leah Fischel and have issue), Joseph (married Channah Fleischman and have issue), Sarah (married Saul Zabel and have issue), Zvi Hirsch (married Leah Silverman and have issue), Samuel (married Leah Lowe and have issue), Foga (married Yehiel Stern) and Menachem.

G15.5. Geli, born in 1924, married Mordecai Stern (Tel Aviv). Their children, Joseph, Moshe and Yechezkiel.

G15.6. Chavah, born in 1923, married Alexander Klein (Paris). Their children, Esther, married Clive Rosenfeld of London, and have issue, and Joseph Klein.

G15.7. Sarah, born in 1930, married Nathan Sweetbaum (Los Angeles). Their children, Elizabeth and Judith.

G13.4. Deborah, born in Pinsk, married Fischel Fix of Dvinsk. They settled in Uniontown, Pa. A number of children died young.

G14.1. Mayer Fix of Cleveland, Ohio, married and had a daughter Dorothy (married).

G14.2. Rachel, married Aaron Hilbrom (New York), having no issue.

G14.3. Israel Fix, married and had two daughters, Gertrude (married) and Lillian (married).

G14.4. Reina, born in Dvinsk about 1905, married Reuben Okin.

G15.1. Leo (Leibel) Okin, born in 1922, married and has issue, Phyllis (married Mesh Rack), Margaret, Sandra and Helaine. They live in Seattle, Wash.

G15.2. Jerry (Jeremiah) Okin, born in 1925, married and has issue, Ellen Deborah, Pauline and Phillip. They live in Fair Lawn, N.J.

B.

DESCENDANTS OF
R. NAFTALI KATZ (G3.3/4.6/5.2)

KATZ, PARNAS, ELLENBERG AND FINKELSTEIN FAMILIES

ANCESTRY

G3. R. Saul Wahl.

G4. R. Judah Katzenellenbogen.

G5. Dinah, married R. Naftali Katz, son of R. Isaac, son of R. Samson (son-in-law of the *MaHaRaL* of Prague). R. Naftali's uncle, R. Haim, was the A.B.D. of Posen, and his aunt, Chavah (Eva), was married into the well-known Bacharach family. She was the mother of R. Haim Jair, son of R. Samuel Abraham Bacharach.

R. Naftali was a prominent Rabbinical figure and was elected successively the A.B.D. of Prussitz, Nikolsburg (in Merrin) and Pinsk (in Lithuania). He later became A.B.D. of Lublin at the same time that R. Abraham Joshua Heschel of Cracow was the head of the city's Yeshiva. Together they wrote an approbation to *Damesek Eliezer*, written by R. Eliezer, son of R. Samuel of Apt, written in 1645. The book was published in Lublin in 1646. They also wrote an approbation to the first edition of the *Yoreh Deah* of 1646.

R. Naftali's wife, Dinah, was later remarried to Rabbi Heschel of Cracow, after R. Naftali's death in 1649, some twenty-five years after the death of his father, R. Isaac. He was the author of *Peirot Genosar* and *Yam Kineret*. These works were published by his grandson, R. Naftali Hirsch Katz of Frankfurt. R. Naftali is also mentioned in the *Or Chayim* by the *TaZ* (R. David Halevi), and his responsa appear in *Chut Hasheini*.

G6. R. Isaac Katz,[5] Darshan of Prague and later A.B.D. of Stefan in Volhynia. He also was elected Darshan of Lublin and married a certain Edel.

G7.1. R. Naftali Hirsch Katz, who succeeded his father as A.B.D. of Stefan, was born in the mid-seventeenth century. He married Esther Sheindel, daughter of R. Samuel Shmelke, son of R. Meir Zak (of Lvov), whom he succeeded as A.B.D. of Ostrow on the death of his father-in-law. Some four years later, in 1691, he was elected A.B.D. of Posen, in which year he and his wife presented a bronze candelabra to the Great Synagogue of Ostrow. This gift was still used by the community in the twentieth century (as recorded in 1907 by R. Biber in *Mizkeret leGedolei Ostraha*). Its inscription ran:

And when the ark came to rest; the honor of our teacher and Rabbi, Naftali son of Isaac Katz, A.B.D. of our congregation . . . he and his wife Sheindel, daughter of the pious Joseph Samuel Shmelke, A.B.D. of our congregation who ministered here many years, donated this candelabra to the synagogue to kindle a perpetual light of remembrance, in the year 1691.

In his younger years, R. Naftali wrote the following approbations: *Beit Hillel* by R. Hillel, son of R. Naftali Hirsch, published Dyhernfurth, 1691, written in 1690; *Derachei Moshe HaAruch* by R. Moses, son of R. Israel Isarel, with additions by R. Jochanan

Kremnitzer, published Sultzbach, 1692, written in 1692; *Ir Binyamin* by R. Benjamin Zeev, son of R. Samuel Darshan, published Frankfurt-on-Oder, 1698, written in 1694; *Beit Yaakov* by R. Jacob, son of R. Samuel, published Dyhernfurth 1696, written in 1695; Passover Haggadah with Commentary entitled *Chaluke De-Rabanan,* published Amsterdam 1695; *Berit Mateh Moshe* published Berlin, written in 1700; *Avek Soferim* by R. Abraham son of R. Levi, published Amsterdam 1704, written in 1703; *Or Yisrael* by R. Israel, son of R. Aaron Jaffe, published Frankfurt-on-Oder, 1702, written in 1702; *Beit Yehudah* by R. Judah son of R. Nissan, published Dessau 1698, written in 1698; *Bigdei Aharon* by R. Aaron, son of R. Moses Teomim; published Frankfurt-on-Main 1710/1; *Binyan Shlomo* by R. Solomon Zalman, son of R. Judah Lieb Katz, published Frankfurt-on-Main 1708; *Yalkut Shimeoni,* written in 1708. In 1704 R. Naftali spent Rosh HaShanah (New Year) in Amsterdam, where he wrote another approbation to *Tikunei HaZohar* in 1706.

In the approbation to *Divrei Zikkaron* written in 1704, he signed himself: "Naftali HaKohen Horowitz." In the same year he was elected A.B.D. of Frankfurt-on-Main. Here he spent a number of years with the community, but in 1711, a fire broke out in the city's Jewish Quarter. This disaster was attributed to the Rabbi and the rumor was that it had started in his very house. The local townsfolk were up in arms about the incident, and to prevent being thrown into jail, R. Naftali and family were forced to flee the city to Poland. His later approbations were thus signed by him as: "The light, saved from the Fire, Naftali HaKohen."

About 1713, he returned to settle once again in Ostrow, where his son, R. Bezalel was A.B.D. at the time. R. Naftali became known as the "Rabbi (Rov) of Posen" and was held in the highest esteem. In the minutes of the Jewish Community of Ostrow of 1717, it is recorded that he had been sent honey at a time he was entertaining visitors. In the same year, his son R. Bezalel died and the father delivered the eulogy, which aroused much admiration and respect from the city's mourners. He remained in Ostrow until after the Festival of Shavuot (Pentecost) of 1718, when he left on a visit to the Holy Land to accept the position of Nasi or President of the Safed Community. On route, in 1718, he participated in the Jaroslav meeting of the Council of the Four Lands which approved the book *Birkat Yaakov.*

He was also instrumental in having R. Abraham Kahane become A.B.D. of Ostrow. He visited his mother's grave in Stefan on his journey to Israel. That same year he reached Constantinople where he wrote a further approbation to *Tikunei HaZohar* (see above) shortly before the Rosh HaShanah of 1719. For unclear reasons he remained in Constantinople and died there in 1719.

He was the author of *Birkat Yehud* in two parts — a) *Smichut Chachamim* and b) *Kedusha Uvracha*, both published together at Frankfurt-on-Main in 1704 (a third portion remained unpublished); *Yam Kineret*, Responsa to which were added his father's *Peirot Genosaur*; unpublished manuscripts, *Et Mosphaihen* and *Maggid Niflaot Hashem; Shaar Naftali,* Prayers and supplications, published by his pupil, R. Asher, in Berlin in 1757; *Beit Rachel,* Prayers and supplications, published Amsterdam in 1741; *Shaar HaHacannah,* Prayers for the sick, published Lublin, 1719; and *Tzavaat Naftali,* published Berlin 1729 by his grandson R. Samson Katz. Many other manuscripts were lost.

G8.1.   R. Bezalel Katz, succeeded R. Joel Halpern as A.B.D. Ostrow in 1710. He married the latter's daughter, Menucha. He was known as "Der Rabbi Reb Bezalel." He wrote an approbation to the *Pnei Moshe,* by his first cousin, R. Moses Katz, and together with his father, to the *Shelah* by R. Isaiah Horowitz in 1717. He died young in 1717 and was eulogized by his father. His wife never remarried and the minutes (Pinkas) of the Ostrow Community mentions sending honey to "the widow of Rabbi Bezalel" and also "on the occasion of the visit of her son (Nachman) from Lvov." She died in 1757 and was buried next to her brother, R. Mordecai Halpern.

G9.1.   R. Isaac Katz, successor of R. Judah Lieb, son of R. Asher Anschel (of Pinczow), A.B.D. of the Ostrow Klaus, when he left to become A.B.D. of Slutzk. His first wife was the daughter of R. Judah Lieb Ettinge, A.B.D. Lvov, but they had no children. R. Isaac studied in Lvov under R. Jacob Emden, son of the Chacham R. Zvi Hirsch Ashkenazi (see his descendants). R. Jacob Emden's first wife, Rachel, was R. Isaac's first cousin, and he mentions R. Isaac in his book *Megillat Sefer.*

R. Isaac then remarried to the daughter of R. Judah Lieb, son of R. Asher Anschel whom he had succeeded as A.B.D. of the Ostrow Klaus. He also died young in 1734 and was eulogized by R. Haim HaKohen of Lvov. He was buried next to his grandfather, R. Joel Halpern.

G10.1. R. Joel Katz, A.B.D. Antonin and then of Stanislav,
married Rebecca, daughter of R. Dovber A.B.D. Chartkov,
son of R. Abraham Segal, A.B.D. Horochov and Lvov.

G11.1. R. Isaac Katz, as a child was very clever and was considered a wonder-child by the Rabbis of his generation.
When he was twelve years old, he accompanied his father to Stanislav when he was offered the Rabbinical
post there, and the following year, when he was thirteen,
he married the daughter of R. Zvi Hirsch Margolioth
A.B.D. Meseritz. (See Chapter VII—Margolioth Family—G7.4/8.4/9.3.)

Isaac studied hard and had a widespread fame by
the time he was fourteen when he was elected A.B.D.
Koretz. Here he was consulted far and wide. His wife's
second cousin, R. Ephraim Zalman Margolioth (See
Chapter VII), was his pupil. About this time, the Klaus-
School of Ostrow was rebuilt and R. Isaac was invited
to become the new head. He was, however, reluctant to
leave Koretz and no less than three times every year, the
representatives of Ostrow requested his acceptance of
the Rabbinical Seat that had been occupied by his forefathers. Eventually, it seems, he accepted, as is borne
out by the approbations he wrote to various works. R.
Isaac was also a pupil of R. Dovber, the Maggid of
Meseritz.

He was the author of *Brit Cahonat Olam* published
in Lvov by his brother, R. Meshulam in 1796 and *Zikkaron Cahonah*, Responsa published in Lvov in 1863. He
died at the age of thirty-five and was buried in Koretz.

G12. R. Israel Katz, A.B.D. Levo. He wrote many works
which he willed to have buried with him. He had three
daughters, one of whom was

G13.1. Sarah, great-grandmother of the wife of R. Menachem Mendel Biber, author of the historical work
on the Jews of Ostrow, *Mizkeret LeGedolei Ostraha*, published in 1907.[6]

G11.2. R. Meshulam Katz, A.B.D. Zuranow and Koretz, succeeding his brother R. Isaac there. He later became
A.B.D. Lvov. He published his brother's work and was

the author of *Petach Nidah; Gufei Halachot;* and *Ikar Tosfot YomTov.* He died in Lvov in 1810.

G11.3.   R. Judah Lieb Katz, A.B.D. Ohlechov and Stry.

G10.2.   Wife of R. Nahum A.B.D. Zausmer.

G9.2.   R. Nachman Katz, married the daughter of R. Haim HaKohen Rappoport A.B.D. Lvov. He became a member of the Chevra Kaddisha in 1741 and later one of the leaders of the Ostrow community. He died in 1774 (on the 4th of Iyar) and was buried in Ostrow.

G10.1.   R. Joel Katz, A.B.D. Yachov and later a teacher in the Ostrow-Klaus. He died in 1801.

G10.2.   Wife of R. Aryey Judah Lieb, son of R. Phineas, son of R. Saul (A.B.D. Lodmir), and one of the leaders of the Ostrow Chevra Kaddisha. Their sons were R. Samuel and R. Simha.

G10.3.   Sheindel, married R. Perez Moses Parnas of Dubno (died in 1808), son of R. Menachem Meinish (died 1782), son of R. Avigdor Parnas. She died in 1802.

G11.1.   R. Haim Nachman Parnas,[7] named after his maternal grandfather, was born in Dubno and died in 1854. He married Sarah, the daughter of R. Ephraim Zalman Margolioth of Brody (See Chapter VII—Margolioth Family). She died in 1808, a year after he had lost his father. R. Nachman then decided to leave Dubno and settled in the city of Vilna, known as "Jerusalem of Lithuania" because of its Jewish population and scholarship. He remarried Rosel, daughter of R. Aryey Lieb, son of R. Ber (called "Leibele Reb Berish").

It was his practice to study wrapped in his *Tallit* (prayer shawl) and to wear his *Teffilin* (Phylacteries) until midafternoon each day in the House of Study (*Beit Hamidrash*) of his father-in-law. The rest of the day was spent at home studying. By means of his extreme diligence, he achieved a masterly understanding of both Halacha and Kabalah. He delivered daily discourses on *Alfasi* before the leaders of the Vilna Community in the *Beit Hamidrash.*

In 1850, R. Haim Nachman established a Yeshiva in Vilna where, at prayer, he followed the "*Ari* Rite" (*Ari* was R. Isaac Luria, the famous Cabalist of Safed), and every Shabbat, before reading of the Law, he studied the *Zohar* on the relevant section. He took an active interest in communal affairs and was himself highly esteemed. For many years he administered the distribution of Vilna's philanthropic funds, including those for indigent Jews residing in Israel.

He wrote his genealogy in the Lvov Edition of *Megaleh Amukot,* in 1795, written originally by his ancestor, R. Nathan Shapiro of Cracow. His approbations appear in a number of contemporary works. He also concerned himself with the needs of the community as a whole and of the individuals in it and because of his grasp of worldly matters, many turned to him for advice on their problems. He was buried in Vilna.

G12.1.   R. Abraham Parnas, 1815-1893, was one of the Vilna leaders of the community to greet Sir Moses Montefiore when he visited their city in 1846. Sir Moses sent him a silver goblet as a gift. R. Abraham died on his birthday at the age of seventy-eight years. He was buried next to his father who had died some thirty-nine years before, and next to his uncle, R. Ezekiel Landau, who had been A.B.D. Vilna and died in 1870.

His first wife was Chaya Beila (died 1840) daughter of R. Isaac Eliasberg and bore him his first two sons, and his second wife, Feige, daughter of R. Haim Ratner, bore him one more son.

   G13.1.   R. Isaac Parnas, married Sarah (died 1861), daughter of R. Shalom Ezekiel Luria. He died in Dubno in 1872.

   G13.2.   R. Liebel Parnas (died in Minsk in 1875), married Rikle (died 1887), daughter of R. Mordecai Zadok Marshalkovitch of Dubno. (See Chapter VII — Branch A — G6.2/7.4/8.4/9.1/10.4/11/12.1 and Chapter XVI — G10.9/11.3/12.1/13.3.)

   G13.3.   R. Jacob Parnas, Gabbai of the Vilna Community.

G12.2.   R. Elijah Parnas of Plotsk, died in 1870.

G12.3.   Perel, married R. Isaac Levi, son of R. Joseph Zakheim. Isaac died in 1878, and his wife in 1880.

G12.4. Wife of R. Aaron Moses Padua, son of R. Jacob Meir Padua, descendants of R. Saul Wahl. (See Chapter II — page 37 — G10.2/11/12.)

G11.2. Wife of R. Aryey Lieb Ellenberg, son of R. Zvi Hirsch. (See Below G8.6/9.4/10/11.1/12/13.2.)

G9.3. R. Joseph Katz, married Shprintze, daughter of R. Judah Lieb Mirkes, A.B.D. of Mir. (See Chapter V — Branch A — G6.2/7/8/9.5.)

G9.4. Wife of R. DovBerish, son of R. Samuel of Ostrow, one of the leaders of the Ostrow community's Chevra Kaddisha. (See Chapter XI — G7.1/8.2/9.3/10.1.)

G10.1. R. Zvi Hirsch Katz.

G10.2. Sarah, married R. Asher Anschel, son of R. Judah Lieb (A.B.D. of the Ostrow-Klaus, Slutzk and Pinsk). (See G8.4/9.2/10 below.) R. Asher's sister was married to R. Isaac Katz, son of R. Bezalel Katz (See above G7.1/8.1/9.1.) He was the author of *Baruch Mibanim Asher,* published Zolkiev, 1749; *Korban Asham,* remained unpublished; and *Otat Lemoadim,* published Zolkiev 1752. He died 1777.

G9.5. First wife of R. Moses Rokeah, (A.B.D. Zlatchov), son of R. Eleazar Rokeah (A.B.D. Amsterdam)—see Rokeah Family Pedigree. (His second wife was the daughter of Chacham R. Zvi Hirsch Ashkenazi).

G9.6. Wife of R. Joseph Landau, A.B.D. Klymnatov, son of R. Judah Landau. He is mentioned in his brother R. Ezekiel Landau's *Noda BiYehudah.* (See Landau Family Pedigree — Chapter X — G8.3/9.1.)

G8.2. R. Phineas Isaac Katz, A.B.D. Fulda and Kremsier, who wrote an approbation to *Damesek Eliezer.*

G9. R. Samson Katz, who published the Ethical Will of his grandfather in Berlin, 1729. He includes his father's Novellae at the end of this edition, as well as his own Novellae.

G8.3. R. Jacob Mordecai Katz, A.B.D. Brody and Posen. He wrote an approbation to the Responsa *Even HaShoham.* He married the daughter of R. Meshullam (son-in-law of R. Abraham Joshua Heschel of Cracow). (See his descendants — Chapter IX — G6.9.)

G9. Rachel, wife of R. Jacob Emden, son of the Chacham R. Zvi Hirsch Ashkenazi. (See his descendants — Chapter XIII — G8.10.)

G8.4. R. Samuel Shmelke Katz, A.B.D. Breslau, named after his maternal grandfather, R. Samuel Shmelke Zak of Ostrow. In Breslau, he wrote an approbation to *Yafe Mareh*, Legends of the Jerusalem Talmud, by R. Samuel, son of R. Isaac Jaffe-Ashkenazi and published Berlin 1724-6 (third edition).

G9.1. R. Joseph Katz, married Shprintze, daughter of R. Judah Lieb Mirkes. (See Chapter V — Branch A — G7/8.)

G10. Wife of R. Samuel mentioned in the introduction of *Agudat Azov* by R. Jacob Israel, son of R. Zvi Stern, published Zolkiev 1782.

G9.2. R. Haim Katz of Glogau.

G10. R. Naftali Hirsch Katz, A.B.D. of the Ostrow-Klaus and later A.B.D. of White Field. He then succeeded R. Abraham Meshulam Zalman Ashkenazi, son of the Chacham R. Zvi Hirsch Ashkenazi on the latter's death in 1777. (See descendants of R. Zvi H. Ashkenazi — Chapter XIII — G8.7.)

He wrote a number of approbations. He married Rebecca Gitel, daughter of R. Mordecai, son of R. Judah Lieb A.B.D. of the Ostrow-Klaus. R. Judah Lieb's[8] son, R. Asher Anschel and his daughter were also intermarried into the Katz family. He died in 1796 and his wife in 1795.

G11.1. R. Asher Anschel Katz, named after his maternal great-grandfather, a member of the Ostrow Chevra Kaddisha, and one of the leaders of the community.

G11.2. R. Abraham Katz, also mentioned in the minutes of the Chevra Kaddisha of Ostrow.

G11.3. R. Aaron Samuel Katz, A.B.D. Stefan, where he succeeded his father-in-law, R. Joseph Joel Halpern. He then became A.B.D. of the Ostrow-Klaus and after that, A.B.D. of Jampol. In his latter years he was A.B.D. White Field. All his manuscripts were burnt after which he wrote and published *Even HaRosha* and *VeTzivah HaKohan*, White Field 1823; and *Yarim Rosh*, a commentary on Midrash Rabbah, published Berdichev 1811. He died in Ostrow in 1814 and his wife Miriam Rikel in 1807.

G12. R. Haim Moses Katz, died young.

G13. R. Naftali Hirsch Katz, who published his grandfather's work *VeTzivah HaKohan,* together with his great uncle R. Moses Katz. He married the daughter of R. Isaac Zvi, son of R. Dovber (A.B.D. of Meseritz) son of R. Naftali Hirsch (A.B.D. Dubno), son of R. Zvi Hirsch (A.B.D. Halberstadt). (See Chapter VII — Branch B — G6.3/7.4/8.2/9.6/10.3/11/12.)

G11.4. R. Joseph Nachman Katz.

G11.5. R. Isaac Katz, died in Ostrow, 1819.

G11.6. R. Moses Katz, published his father's work *VeTzivah HaKohen,* together with his grandnephew.

G11.7. R. Meir Katz.

G8.5. R. Shaltiel Katz.

G8.6. Shprintze, married R. Jacob (A.B.D. Posen) son of R. Isaac (A.B.D. Posen). He succeeded his father-in-law when the latter left Frankfurt-on-Main for Posen, following the devastating fire that occurred there. He wrote a number of approbations between the years 1649-1729. He is mentioned in the *Keneset Yechezkiel,* written by R. Ezekiel Katzenellenbogen A.B.D. Altona-Hamburg-Wandsbeck. (See descendants of R. Joel Ashkenazi-Katzenellenbogen — Chapter VIII.)

G9.1. Wife of R. Isaac Dovber (A.B.D. Yazlivitz, son of R. Zvi Hirsch Margolioth (1637-1737), author of *Be'er Yitzchak.* Part of his responsa are to be found in the *Meir Netivim* by his brother, R. Meir Margolioth. (Published Polna, 1791). (See Ornstein-Ashkenazi — Chapter XII — Family Pedigree G8/9.1.)

G10. R. Samuel Margolioth A.B.D. Zalischick.

G11. Wife of R. Ari Liebish Brodie A.B.D. Kreshov. (See Ornstein-Ashkenazi Family Pedigree G8/9.3/10.2/11.1.)

G9.2. R. Abraham.

G10. R. Solomon Zalman of Kremnitz A.B.D. Greiditz.

G9.3. R. Isaac, Dayan (Judge) of Posen.

G9.4. Wife of R. Ephraim Fischel, Parnas or Head of the Council of the Four Lands, son of R. Aryey Lieb of Cracow.

G10. R. Jacob A.B.D. Lodmir. He married the daughter of R. Saul Katzenellenbogen A.B.D. Pinczow (great-grandson of R. Saul Wahl). See Chapter II.

G11.1. R. Solomon Zalman Lieberman A.B.D. Brody, married the daughter of R. Simha HaKohen Rappoport of Grodno.

G12. R. Zvi Hirsch Lieberman, A.B.D. Lokatch, author of *Chemdat Tzvi*, published Mohilev 1825. He wrote an approbation to *Mayyim Yechezkiel* by R. Ezekiel Katzenellenbogen of Altona.

G13.1. R. Jehiel Lieberman, A.B.D. Lokatch.

G14. R. Moses.

G15. R. Isaachar Ber, Admur and A.B.D. Torbin.

G16. R. Jacob Weissbrot, A.B.D. and Admur Kroshnik.

G17. R. David Joseph Weissbrot, Admur Kroshnik.

G13.2. R. Aryey Lieb Ellenberg, married the daughter of R. Perez Moses Parnas. (See above G8.1/9.2/10.3/11.2.)

G14.1. R. Simha Nathan Ellenberg A.B.D. Moshzisk and later of Lvov, where he died in 1859. He married the daughter of R. Baruch Roth (son-in-law of R. Israel, son R. Simha Rappoport).

G15. R. Zvi David Ellenberg, married daughter of R. Moses Sofer (Schreiber), the *Chatam Sofer*.

G16.1. R. Jacob Ellenberg of Krasna.
G16.2. R. Solomon Zalman Ellenberg of Lvov.

G14.2. R. Abraham Finkelstein of Lublin.

G15.1. Chaya, married Joseph Hirsch Wahl of Lublin.
G15.2. Hinde, married R. Ephraim Berliner (See Berliner Family Pedigree G9.2/10.1/11.4).
G15.3. R. Moses Zvi Finkelstein of Brest, married Chanah Feige, daughter of R. David Lieb Chamsky. (See Ornstein-Ashkenazi Families — G9.1/10.1/11/12.)

G16.1. R. Mordecai Finkelstein of Brest.

G16.2. R. Meshullam Zalman Finkelstein of Brest.

G16.3. Rachel, married R. Isaac son of R. Israel Meisels (A.B.D. Sedlitz).

G16.4. R. Dov Finkelstein of Brest-Warsaw.

G9.5. Wife of R. Aryey Lieb (of Posen), son of R. Abraham (Reb Haim of Lublin), son of R. Haim (son-in-law of R. Benjamin Wolf Halpern).

G10. Sheindel, married R. Joshua Heschel (A.B.D. Dombrovo), son of R. Menachem Meinish, son of R. Jacob Jokel Horowitz. (See Horowitz Family Pedigree — Chapter XVI — G9/10.9/11.1/12.)

G8.7. Eidel, wife of R. Saadiah Isaiah Katzenellenbogen. (See Katzenellenbogen Family Pedigree — Chapter II.) He was the son of R. Saul of Pinczow, mentioned above (G8.6/9.4/10).

G8.8. Wife of R. Zeev Wolf Mirls,[9] son of R. Meshulam Zalman Mirls, A.B.D. Altona-Hamburg-Wandsbeck. R. Zeev's sister was the wife of the Chacham R. Zvi Hirsch Ashkenazi.

G9. Minke, died 1736, married R. Mordecai, son of R. Abraham Takles of Lissa, A.B.D. Berlin. He died 1743.

G8.9. Keila, married R. Judah Lieb, son of R. Gabriel (A.B.D. Nikolsburg). Both died young. (See Chapter IX — Branch A — G8.6.)

G9. R. Haim, who was raised and educated by his maternal grandfather, R. Naftali Hirsch Katz.

G8.10. Wife of R. Moses, son of R. Eleazar of Cracow.

G7.2. R. Judah Lieb Katz, A.B.D. Plotsk.

G7.3. R. Isaiah Katz, Judge in Brody.

G8. R. Menachem Meinish Katz.

G9. Wife of R. Meir Horowitz, the *MaHaRaM* of Tiktin. He was the progenitor of the large Horowitz family, recorded in Chapter XVI.

CHAPTER VI

BRANCH A

ANCESTRY

G3.3. Saul Wahl.
G4.7. Feiwel Wahl.
G5.1. Wife of Strelisker.
G6. Joshua Strelisker.
G7. Ber Strelisker.[1]

BRANCH B

DESCENDANTS OF

R. JACOB SHOR (G3.3/4.8/5) SON OF R. EPHRAIM ZALMAN SHOR
HEILPRIN, SHOR AND ADLER FAMILIES

G5. R. Jacob Shor, married Channah daughter of R. Isaiah son of Moses
Reb Lazers of Vilna.

G6.1. R. Zvi Hirsch Shor.
G6.2. Yente, married R. Saul, son of R. Moses Katzenellenbogen of Pinc-
zow. (See Chapter II.)
G6.3. Rebecca, married R. Abraham Dess of Brody (died there in 1715).
G6.4. Wife of R. Eliezer Lipman (A.B.D. Tarnograd) son of R. Isaac
(A.B.D. Tiktin) Heilprin.[2] She died in Brody.

G7.1. R. Israel Heilprin, was originally the A.B.D. of the town of Zaslav where he wrote an approbation to *Chakei Derech* in 1728
by R. Moses Yekutiel Kaufmann published in Dyhernfurth in
1747. About the year 1728 the A.B.D. of Ostrow, R. Abraham

265

Kahana, left and R. Heilprin was invited to accept the Rabbin-
ical position. As a young man, he was betrothed to the daughter
of R. Shabtai Kohen (the *ShaCh*, died 1662) but later married
Reize daughter of R. Isaac Krakover A.B.D. of Brody son of R.
Issachar Berish. (See Chapter XI—Babad Family Pedigree—
G7.1/8.4.)

G8.1. R. Lipman Heilprin of Medzibeh.
G8.2. R. Zalman Heilprin of Zaslav, married the daughter of the
Rabbi of Pinsk.
G8.3. R. Mordecai Heilprin A.B.D. Zaslav and later of Kremnitz. In
1787, he wrote an approbation to *Sefat Emet* published in
Lvov in 1788. He settled in Israel where he died and was
buried. He married the daughter of R. Jacobke of Brody and
Prague (who was also the father-in-law of R. Ezekiel Landau
—See Landau Family G8.3/9.3).

G9. Deborah, married R. Hirsch.

G8.4. R. Jacob Heilprin of Lodmir.
G8.5. R. Isaac Heilprin A.B.D. Sokol.
G8.6. R. Joel Heilprin A.B.D. Leshnov.

G9.1. R. Eliezer Lipman Heilprin.

G10. R. Ephraim Heilprin of Jerusalem.

G11. R. Alexander Samuel Heilprin, author of *Rosh HaMiz-
beach,* published in Lvov in 1883, in which he mentions his father and grandfather in the introduction.

G9.2. Rachel Deborah, married R. Phineas Halevi Horowitz, the
prominent Chassidic leader and A.B.D. of Frankfurt (author
of the *Hafla'ah* which mentions his wife's ancestry). He was
also a descendant of the Katzenellenbogen family. (See
Horowitz Family Pedigree—Chapter XVI—G10.8/11.4.)

G8.7. R. David Heilprin, succeeded his father on the latter's death.
At that time the son of the Chacham R. Zvi Ashkenazi, R.
Abraham Meshullam Zalman was the A.B.D. of the commu-
nity "Klaus." He wrote approbations to *Birkat Yosef* by R.
Joseph Teomim in 1741 (published in Zolkiev in 1747); *Mish-
chat Aharon* in 1743; *Maftei'ach HaOlamit* in 1745, and a
number of others at this time. He married Rosa, daughter of
R. Haim son of R. Benjamin (author of *Ir Binyamin*). His

Ethical Will *Darkei Tzion* (together with his son's, R. Issachar Berish), was published in Polna in 1798. The last twenty years of his life he spent in the town of Zaslov where he died in 1765. His wife died in 1770.

G9.1. R. Issachar Berish Heilprin, married the daughter of R. Jehiel A.B.D. of Kovle.

G9.2. R. Isaac Heilprin, died 1770 and was buried next to his parents.

G9.3. Rosa, died young.

G7.2. Wife of R. Elijah A.B.D. Wilkomir son of R. Meir A.B.D. Krotoschin.

G8. R. Jacob Halevi Shor A.B.D. Karoz, married the daughter of R. Ezekiel Katzenellenpogen A.B.D. Altona-Hamburg-Wandsbeck. (See Chapter VIII—G4.2/5.2/6/7.2/8.4.)[3]

G9.1. Wife of R. Joseph Moses Simha (A.B.D. Zmigrad, Lentchov and Onsdorf) son of R. Zvi Hirsch Rappaport (A.B.D. Mir —See Chapter III—Branch D—G6.2/7.4).

G9.2. R. Abraham Halevi Shor A.B.D. Emden, married the daughter of R. Meir Gunzburg A.B.D. of Vizin (See Chapter III— Branch D—G6.2/7.1/8.1/9.8).

G10.1. R. Isaac Halevi Shor of Emden, later settled in Vilna after his father's death and lived with R. Elijah Pesseles whose daughter he married. After her death, he remarried the daughter of R. Haim Halevi Landau A.B.D. Podkamon (See Landau Family Pedigree—G8.1/9.2/10.6). She died in childbirth in Vilna in 1779.

G11. R. Ezekiel Halevi Landau (adopted his mother's maiden name),[4] born in Vilna in 1779 and married his cousin Chaya Sarah daughter of R. Liebele Berish (their mothers were sisters). His wife died in 1841 and he remarried. His first marriage was in 1793 when he was only fourteen and at which time he received the blessings of the Gaon of Vilna, R. Elijah. He studied under R. Haim of Volozhin and later became the A.B.D. of Vilna. He died there in 1870 at the age of ninety. Both his children died during his lifetime.

G12.1. R. Haim Landau, married the daughter of R. Hirschel Zalkinds. He died in 1846.

G12.2. Elke (died in Warsaw in 1829), married R. David
Halevi Epstein[5] of Warsaw (died there in 1872),
son of R. Simeon Zemmel Epstein. He was the
author of *Kinman BeShem* as a part of *Ayin Avraham* by R. Abraham Shick, published in Königsberg 1848, and *Minchat Yehudah*.

G13. R. Isaac Epstein of Vilna, died in Berlin in 1892,
married the daughter of R. Haim Halevi Horowitz
of Vilna.

G14. Wife of R. Zechariah Isaiah Hakohen Yolles of
Lvov (died in 1852), author of *Dovber Meisharim* published in Lvov in 1831, *Zecher Yisha-
yahu* published in Vilna in 1882; and *Eit Ledaber*
published in Lvov in 1834. He was the son of R.
Mordecai Zvi Yolles.

G10.2 R. Jacob Jokel Halevi Shor A.B.D. Anikatch.

G11. R. Saul Halevi Shor of Keidan.

G12. Zessle, married R. Abraham Katzenellenbogen. (See
Chapter VIII—G8.5/9/10/11.)[6]

G6.5. Wife of R. Judah Lieb of Krotoschin, died in 1740.[7]

G7. R. Jacob Benjamin Frankel, Rabbi of Hanau where he died December 3, 1791. His first position to the Rabbinate was in Obernik
in Poland and settled in Hanau in 1758, serving as the community
leader for thirty-three years. He married 1) Esther, daughter of
R. Joel of Wronke. She died in 1779. 2) Schonle, daughter of
Nathan. She died in 1788.

G8.1. R. Michael Frankel, died in Hanau, November 22, 1838. He
married 1) Reichel, daughter of R. Zvi Hirsch and granddaughter of R. Abraham Abush Lissa (died 1764 or 1768, the
Chief Rabbi of Frankfurt-on-Main, and author of *Birkat Avraham*). 2) Breinche, daughter of Abraham Stern of Hanau.

G9. Esther, married Kalmann Kohn. She died in Hanau in 1816.

G8.2. Hanale, married R. Samuel of Gelnhausen.

G9.1. Rebecca, married R. Abraham Berend son of R. Issachar
Berish in Hanover. He died in 1807 and she remarried
Ephraim Mayer. She died in 1861.

G10. Samuel Mayer, a follower of R. Nathan Adler mentioned below.

G8.3. Rebecca, married R. Mordecai Marcus Adler, Chief Rabbi of Hanover.[8] She died in Hanover in 1858 at the age of ninety-two years.

I remember her telling me a story about the Rothschilds (recalls her grandson Marcus Nathan Adler),[9] who were friends of her husband Rabbi Mordecai Adler. One winter night early in the 19th century they were disturbed by a loud knocking at their street door. Rabbi Mordecai looked out of the window and asked what was wanted. The answer was: "Oh, it is R. Mayer and R. Amschel Rothschild passing through Hanover. We want the Rabbi to *bensch* us and give us his blessing." When they had been made welcome and had received their blessing, they confided to their friends the mission they were engaged on. It was to interview a prince who was about to entrust them with his wealth. She first became acquainted with Sir Moses Montefiore in 1847 and thereafter he never went abroad without first paying her a visit.

> Rabbi Adler was the son of R. Baer Adler of the city of Frankfurt. He was first Dayan there and later the Rabbi of Hanover for some fifty-two years until his death in 1834. His father was a first cousin to R. Nathan Adler (1741-1800) known as the "Chassid." His novellae appeared in *Leshon Zahav* published in Offenbach, 1822. The couple had six children.

G9.1. Benjamin Adler, died childless.

G9.2. Heinemann Adler, married and had six children.

G9.3. R. Baer Adler (1785-1866), married Esther, daughter of Hirsch Moses Worms, whose brother Benedict Moses Worms, was the father of Baron Solomon, the father of Baron Henry de Worms (See Chapter II—Branch III). His novellae, those of his father and brother, R. Gabriel Adler, were also printed in *Leshon Zahav* (1822). They had ten children.

G10.1. Henrietta, married Moritz Budge. He died in 1872.

G11.1. Max Budge.

G11.2. Heinrich (Henry) Budge. In 1867 he formed a brokerage firm in New York with Jacob Henry Schiff and Leo Lehmann (all originally of Frankfurt). They did not get on well and in 1872 when Budge returned to Europe on the death of his father, the firm was dissolved. He later returned to New York and was again associated with Schiff.[10]

G10.2. Joel Adler, married his first cousin Esther, daughter of R. Gabriel Adler. Their son was Max Adler, and his son in turn was Joachim Isaac Adler.

G9.4. R. Gabriel Adler, Chief Rabbi of the Schwarzwald in Oberdorf, married Blumle daughter of R. Phineas Katzenellenbogen A.B.D. of Ettingen. (See Chapter II—Section D—Branch I.)

G9.5. Hundchen, married Jacob Budge. They had two daughters, one was,

G10. Wife of R. Dr. Treuenfels A.B.D. Stettin.

G9.6. Chief Rabbi Nathan Marcus Adler, 1803-1890. He was named after his second cousin the Cabalist and Chassid R. Nathan Adler. By virtue of his German birth at a time when Hanover was under British Rule, he was a British subject. He received the broadest of educations at the Universities of Gottingen, Erlangen, Wurtzburg and Heidelberg. Here he learned Hebrew, Theology, and Classical and Modern Languages. In 1830 he became the Rabbi of Oldenburg and within a year was elected the Chief Rabbi of Hanover. In 1842 the Chief Rabbi of London, R. Solomon Herschell (a descendant of the Katzenellenbogen Family as well), died. For three years the seat of the Rabbinate remained open because it was a time of schism within the London community, but after fifteen candidates were submitted, Rabbi Adler was elected on July 9, 1845. In 1855 the inauguration of Jews' College took place with Rabbi Adler as its first president, thus establishing the first school for training Jewish ministers and teachers. Dr. Adler was also very active within the synagogal administration devoting time to the provincial communities as well, thus helping to establish the United Synagogue and being recognized as the first Chief Rabbi of the British Empire, including its colonies overseas. He was also the founder of the Hospital Sabbath which aimed at collecting money for the hospitals. In 1872, on the illness of the Prince of Wales, he sent a copy of a prayer he wrote to the

Princess for which she was greatly thankful and wrote a letter of thanks to him.[11] He also had copies of the Jubilee Service specially bound and sent to the Queen and the Prince of Wales. His most important work was *Netinah la-Ger,* a commentary on the Targum Onkelos, published in Vilna in 1874. Others include Hebrew Prayers recited during critical episodes in English history, *Sermons* in English and German, including his installation address in London, *The Jewish Faith* and *The Bonds of Brotherhood.* His other works in Hebrew were *Derashot, Responsa, Chiddushim* (Novellae) and *Ahavat Yehonathan.* He translated the *Cuzari* (by Judah HaLevi) into German and edited *Sefer Yaer* in connection with the *Netinah la-Ger.*

He married twice: 1) Henrietta, daughter of Hirsch Moses Worms, the sister of Esther Worms who married his brother Baer Adler. She lived from 1800-53 and they had five children, the eldest, Marcus N., Sarah, Jeanette, Mina and the youngest, Dr. Hermann; and 2) Celestine Lehfeld (1821-91) and had Elkan N., Rebecca and Ida.

A week before his death, only a few days after his eighty-seventh birthday, the London Jewish Chronicle announced his failing health, thus somewhat preparing the Jewish Community for his death, a few days later.

The venerable Chief Rabbi passed a quiet night preceeding his death, his three sons and two daughters never leaving his bedside since they had been summoned to Brighton by Mr. Pocock, his medical attendant. . . . Throughout his last illness he retained perfect consciousness and did not omit to perform his daily devotions with his wonted regularity; even insisting upon continuing his usual Talmudical studies, almost to the last hour of his life.[12]

It was early morning. He arose from bed and his faithful servant, Joseph van Gelder, helped him to bathe and to dress. Then, clad with his Talith and Tephilin, his children around him, he bade them intone the morning service. At the Shema prayer, his voice was heard, and with the word "The Lord is one" on his lips, he expired.[13]

G10.1. Sarah Adler (died in 1907), the eldest daughter, married Henry Solomon (1813-91).[14] Both are buried in the Jews' Cemetery, Willesden, London. They had ten children.

G11.1. Sidney Solomon, died in 1898, unmarried.

G11.2. Jeanette, married Carl Jacob.

    G12.1. Henry (Harry) Jacob, died, unmarried.

    G12.2. Emily (Emmy), married Ernest Alex Myer (killed in action in 1915), no issue.

    G12.3. Eugene Jacob, married Essie Goodman.

G11.3. Florence Solomon, married Simeon Lazarus son of Lewis Lazarus (founder of Lewis Lazarus and Co., one of the leading merchants in metals, and who joined with others to establish the London Metal Exchange). He, with his brother, used to report market quotations, fluctuations, etc. to the national press.

    G12.1. Frank Lazarus, married Dorothy Cahn.

        G13. Allan Lazarus, married and has a daughter and son, Marc.

    G12.2. George Maitland Lazarus, Barrister-at-Law, served in the Royal Artillery during the First World War, and after demobilization joined the family business. He married Mary Ann (Molly) Lewis.

        G13.1. Barbara, married Tim Simon and they have three children.

        G13.2. David Maitland Lazarus, head of "Save and Prosper" (a Unit Trust Group), married and has children.

        G13.3. Joan, married Dr. Solomons (Obstetrics, Dublin) and they have children.

    G12.3. Dorothy, married Stanley Samuel Cohen (son of Alderman Louis Cohen of Liverpool, 1846-1922, head of the departmental chain of stores, Lewis's Ltd.). Stanley was a lieutenant-colonel in the British Army.[15]

        G13.1. Margot, married Ronald Montagu Simon.

           G14. Timothy Simon, married Doreen Beebe, have a son, Matthew, and a daughter, Merula, married Richard Frankel and have three children.

G13.2. Fay, married Michael Jacobs and had three children, Anne, David and Nicholas.

G13.3. Jill, married Stanley da Pinna Weal and have a son and daughter.

G11.4. Rebecca Solomon, married Raphael Lewisohn, a member of the Lewisohn Family of New York[16] who were pioneers in the development of extensive copper-mines throughout the U.S.A. She died about 1930.

G12.1. Beatrice, married 1) Humphrey Michael Myer and had issue, and 2) Eric Coveney.

G13.1. Jasmine Ruth, married Eric Feldorf.

G13.2. Ewart Myer, married and had two sons, Jonathan and Rodney (married and has issue).

G12.2. Claude Lewisohn, married late in life (about age sixty) and died in 1968.

G11.5. Frances Solomon, died about 1950, married her cousin Henry Josiah Solomon, died about 1923.[17]

G12.1. Harold Josiah Solomon born in England in 1886 and died in Switzerland in 1930.[18] He entered the British Army and distinguished himself during the First World War and was subsequently promoted to Lieutenant-Colonel. He was a daring cavalry officer with great physical activity which characterized his life until a few years before his death, his health was impaired by an accident. After the war, he resigned his position and became the director of commerce and industry in the Palestine Administration under the Commissionership of Sir Herbert Samuel. He left the civil service in 1922 to become the director of the Palestine Potash Company. He was also for a time, governor of the Haifa Technion, director of the Anglo-Palestine Club, and council member of the Anglo-Jewish Association and of the Domestic Board for Palestine. He married in 1919 to Flora Berenson.

G13. Peter Solomon, married and had two daughters.

G12.2. Arthur Ewart Solomon, stockbroker, married Rachel Mendoza.

G13.1. Wendy, married Michael Greenly and had three children.

G13.2. Bruce Solomon, married and has two children.

G13.3. Rodney Solomon.

G12.3. Gladys Henriette, born 1892, married in 1917 to John Lewisohn.

G13.1. Ivor Lewisohn, married Elizabeth Prince and had three daughters.

G13.2. Anthoy Clive Leopold Lewisohn, judge, married and has two sons.

G13.3. Leonore, married Malcolm Mendoza, and have issue, Miles Mendoza.

G11.6. James (Jacob) Henry Solomon, stockbroker, married in 1897 to Caroline (born in 1875) daughter of Alfred Louis (died in 1903) son of Louis Cohen (died 1882).

G12. Violet Maud Solomon, born in 1901, married in 1921 to John (Jack) Sebag-Montefiore (1892-1972)[19] son of Arthur (1853-95) son of Sir Joseph Sebag-Montefiore and Adelaide Cohen (sister to Alfred Louis Cohen). Arthur was thus a first cousin to Violet's mother.

G13.1. Hazel Sebag-Montefiore, unmarried.

G13.2. Myrtle, married David Ellis Franklin (born 1919), a banker, son of Ellis Arthur (born 1894, a director of the publishing company Routledge & Kegan Paul) son of Arthur Ellis Franklin (born 1857, compiler of the genealogical work *Records of the Franklin Family*, Second Edition London, 1935). Their children, Nigel, Veronica, Shirley and Stephen.

G13.3. Harold Sebag-Montefiore (born in 1924), Conservative member of the Greater London Council and President of the Anglo-Jewish Association (London). He married in 1967 to Harriet daughter of Benjamin Harrison Paley of New York. Their daughter is Jennifer.

G13.4. John Sebag-Montefiore, died during World War II.

G13.5. Patrick Sebag-Montefiore.

G13.6. Anthony Sebag-Montefiore.

G11.7. Gertrude Solomon, (died in 1964), married in 1889 to Hermann Henry Myer (died 1909).

G12.1. Muriel Hilda, married Edgar Henriques Samuel.

G13.1. Brenda Samuel, sculptress, died about 1938, unmarried.

G13.2. Denis Edgar Samuel, married Sheila Merriman, and had issue, Martin (married and has two children), Patricia and Stephen.

G13.3. Audrey Violet Samuel.

G12.2. Henry D. Myer, born in 1892, married Louie Ruth Solomon.

G13.1. Dulcie Rosalind, married Victor Michaelis Halsted, and had three children, Edward David Michaelis Halsted (an actor), Naomi Susan Halsted and Hilary Anne.

G13.2. Richard H. Myer, married Barbara Rigal. Their sons: Jonathan, Andrew and Nicholas.

G13.3. Aline Verity, married 1) Arthur Gerald Furst and had a son, David Furst, and 2) Vladimir (Edward) Schneerson, who has two children from a previous marriage.

G13.4. Yvonne Gwyneth, married Edwin David Greenbaum (Wyncote, Pa.), and have issue: David, Jeffrey and Jennifer.

G12.3. Ruth Evelyn, married Major Joseph Bernard Solomon (cousin to Louie Ruth G11.7/12.2 above).

G13.1. Andrew Bernard Solomon.

G13.2. Phillipa Gertrude, married in 1950 to Captain Roger Carol Michael Nathan, the Second Lord of Churt, born in 1922. He succeeded his fa-

ther in 1963, on the latter's death. The First
Lord Nathan, Harry Louis, was a prominent
soldier and politician, hero of World War I,
M.P., Minister of Civil Aviation (1946-58),
author and was raised to the peerage in 1940.[20]
His son Roger served in World War II (1939-
45), has been an associate member of the Bar
Association of the City of New York (since
1957), is Director of J. W. French & Company,
Ltd. and has a number of other memberships.
Their children: Jenny (married); Nicola; and
Rupert Harry Bernard Nathan (born in 1957).

G13.3. Susan, married Michael Welman, banking executive, and have issue, Sarah and Mark.

G11.8. Arthur Henry Solomon (changed his name to Arthur Henry), married in 1918 to Margaret Lewis.

G12.1. Bryan David Henry, married Pamella Cohen and
had three sons.

G12.2. Miles Henry (killed at Arnhem in 1944) married
and had a daughter, Caroline Ann.

G11.9. Amy Josefa Solomon (died about 1954), married her first cousin Berthold Israel. (See below—
G10.3/11.)

G11.10. Mortimer Henry Solomon, died 1929/30, unmarried.

G10.2. Jeanette Adler, second eldest daughter, married R.
Asher Anschel Stern (1820-88),[21] Chief Rabbi of Hamburg and son of R. Meir Stern. As a child of eleven
years he went to Fulda where he studied under R.
Zekel Wormser and later under R. Isaac Dov Bamberger A.B.D. of Wurzburg. He became the A.B.D.
of Hamburg in 1851. In 1855 he went to London
where he met his future wife and later the same year
married her. The marriage service was conducted in
Hamburg by his father-in-law. Here he was a close associate of the city mayor and held a position in the
senate. He was held in high esteem by Jew and Gen-
tile alike and held his office longer than any previous
Rabbi there, some thirty-seven years until his death

on 28th Adar. During his life he was involved in an
argument as to the purchase of a new cemetery and
led him to publish three books on this subject. After
his death the leading Rabbis of his generation had
their responsa on this matter printed in *Ohelsdorfer
Bergrafnisplatz* published in Hamburg in 1889.

G11.1. R. Naftali Stern, 1870-1943. He came to New York
in 1938 and is buried there.[22] He married Eva daughter of Professor Lehman Marx of Darmstadt.

G12.1. Anschel (Arthur) Stern, born in 1905, married
Dora Loebenberg (New York). Their daughter,
Jeanette (named after her great-grandmother),
born in 1945.

G12.2. Jeanette, born in 1906, died in Frankfurt in childbirth about 1927. She was married to Dr. Marcus
Hirsch, son of Wolf son of Marcus son of R. Samson Raphael Hirsch.

G12.3. Herbert (Joseph) Stern, born in 1909, married
Riva Ziff (New York). Their daughter is Aviva,
born in 1952.

G12.4. Walter (Judah Nathan) Stern, born in 1911, married Mildred Simon (New York). Their daughter is Evelyn.

G12.5. Vera (Mindel), born in 1918, married Max Straus
(New York).

Their children: Meyer Straus, Herbert Straus
(married Rachel Strauss and have a son, Meir
Aaron) and Beatrice (born 1953).

G11.2. Meir Stern, died young.

G11.3. Sarah, married Gustav Baer. Their children included Dr. Walter Baer, married, but died in London about 1966 without issue; Erna, married a cousin Baer, and had issue, and died about 1966. Her
son is Shmuel Baer (Jerusalem) and his family. The
other children of Sarah were Gertrude, Harriet and
the youngest, Jeanette.

G11.4. Deborah, married Nahum Loeb (perished in Theresienstadt) and had a daughter, Edith, who lived in
Israel where she was married.

G11.5. Shulamit, (1859-1940), married Abraham Hollander (of Altona). Their sons: Asher (Arthur); Arnold, unmarried; and Anton, married (died 1974).

G11.6. Zila, married Martin Joelson. They had issue, perished in the Holocaust.

G11.7. Rachel (died in 1930), married Gustav Gluckstadt.

G12.1. Herman, perished.

G12.2. David, married Gustele Mayer.

G12.3. Fanny.

G12.4. Max Gluckstadt.

G12.5. Rudolf Gluckstadt (1872-1939), died in Bolivia. He married in 1920 to Hannah, daughter of Wilhelm Moeller and his wife Sarah (daughter of Isaac son of R. Samson Raphael Hirsch.) She lives in New York.

G13.1. Ruth, born in 1921, married Samuel Grosz (New York).

G14.1. Ari Grosz, born in 1947, married Gitti Spielman (Brooklyn). Their daughter, Shoshana, born in 1972.

G14.2. Rachel, born in 1948, married in 1970 to R. Yitzchok Goodman (New York). He is a teacher in the Hudson County Yeshiva (Union City, N.J.). Their daughter, Chavah, born in 1973.

G13.2. Elisabeth, born in 1923, married Martin Belski (Israel). Their children: Ruby and Dan.

G11.8. Rebecca Stern, married Moritz Major, had no issue.

G11.9. Yetche (1856-1917), married Rabbi Dr. Michael Cahn (born in Hildesheim in 1849 and died in Fulda in 1920).[23] He graduated from the Hildesheimer Rabbinical College in Berlin, and then served for a year in the community of Samter, and in 1877 he was nominated to become "district rabbi of the region and community rabbi of the Fulda community." At the time of his appointment the community was about five hundred strong out of a total population of 13,000 inhabitants. He married Yetche in 1878 and they had twelve children, two of whom died at birth. He retired in 1919 when the Jewish population had increased to 1,200 members.

Rabbi Cahn was the inventor of the *"metzitza* tube" for the use of hygienically sucking up the blood at the ritual of Brit Milah (circumcision) which was designed in consultation with the prominent surgeons of his day, Virchow, von Bergmann and Pettenkofer. It is now in use world-wide. He played a great part in the local Fulda Jewish School and the educational system.

He helped to reorganize the ritual slaughter and the sale of meat according to the new halachic interpretations, improved the mikveh (ritual bath) and supervised the writing of Torah scrolls and Tefillin. These latter were approved by all the European Rabbis and those of Eastern Europe in particular. During World War I he helped families whose heads had gone to serve and attended to the needs of the Jewish prisoners-of-war. When several provinces were threatened with the outlawing of ritual slaughter, he appealed to the son of the then Chancellor, Prince Bismarck, and was successful in influencing him to pass a law safeguarding ritual slaughter.

In 1882, the blood libel brought against the community of Tisza-Eslar in Hungary prompted Rabbi Cahn to appeal to Bishop Kopp, who later became the Archbishop of Mainz, and received a reply from him "that there is no basis in the Jewish religion for the assumption that Jews might ever have used Christian blood for ritual purposes nor is it supported by history, and that accusations of this kind, whatever the circumstances, must definitely be regarded as criminal lies." Later when R. Samson Raphael Hirsch of Frankfurt, whose teachings he ardently upheld, established the *Freie Vereinningung für die Interessen der orthodoxen Judentums,* R. Cahn became a leading member of the organization. It was designed to safeguard the interests of orthodox Jewry.

G12.1. Rabbi Dr. Leo Cahn (born in Fulda in 1889 and died in Bnei Brak in 1958). He was the district Rabbi from 1919-1938, as his father's successor. He was also concerned with education and the literal observance of the Law. He was considered an excellent orator. In Israel which he reached via England having left Germany in 1938 following the *Kristallnacht,* he did not accept any Rabbinical position, but was a teacher and director of a Secondary School. He was married to Leah (of the Auerbach family), and they had four children, married into other prominent families in Jerusalem.

G12.2. Gotthelf Cahn (lived in Altona), married and had issue. Of his daughters, one married Beer (London), another married Berkowitz (Bnei Brak) and a third married Van Ments (Haifa).

G12.3. Wife of Rabbi Dr. J. Lorsch, Deputy Rabbi of Fulda, and later Rabbi in Frankfurt.

G10.3. Mina Adler, married Jacob Israel. He was the son of Nathan Israel (1782-1852) who founded in 1815 a dry goods business in Berlin which became one of the largest department stores of that city. Their family was prominent as well in Jewish Communal affairs. They had six children, only one of whom was still living in 1909,[24] Berthold Israel, who ran the business until the rise of the Nazis who confiscated their possessions before the World War II. He later died of a heart attack. He married his first cousin, Amy Josefa Solomon (see above G10.1/11.9), and had three children.

G11. Berthold and Amy Israel.

G12.1. Viva, married George Prins, a leading diamond merchant. They had a daughter, Vivian, who was married.

G12.2. Herbert Israel, born about 1904, settled in New York and died while on a holiday in Italy about 1964.

G12.3. Wilfred (Wilfrid) Israel, 1899-1943,[25] who assisted his father in the Berlin company and re-

mained in Germany until 1939 having helped the
Jews there, and settled in England. He helped establish together with his father the Kibbutz of
HaZoreah and the youth Village of Ben Shemen.
In England he was a member of the Jewish Colonization Association and a prominent communal
worker and philanthropist. He died together with
Leslie Howard when their plane was shot down
by the German Luftwaffe in 1943 as they were
returning from a Youth Aliyah Mission to Portugal. He did not marry. His art collection was
bequeathed to Kibbutz HaZoreah where it is displayed in the Wilfrid Israel House for Oriental
Art and Studies.

G10.4. Marcus N. Adler, eldest son, M.A., born in Hanover
in 1837 and died in London in 1911. He studied at the
University College in London and was the actuary for
the Alliance Assurance Co. from 1857-92. He was a
member of Jews' College council and the Jewish High
School for Girls council, and president of the Stepney
Jewish School from 1863 until his death. He was a
Fellow of the Royal Statistical Society, a founder of
the London Mathematical Society and vice-president
of the Institute of Actuaries. He was one time secretary of Sir Moses Montefiore and author of works on
archaeology, Jewish history, life assurance and political economics. His books include *Chinese Jews* (Oxford, 1900), *The Itinerary of Benjamin of Tudela*
(translation, Oxford, 1907) and a genealogy of his
family, *The Adler Family* (London, 1909). He married 1) Fanny Myers and 2) Emma Kisch.[26]

G11.1. A son, died young.

G11.2. Hetty, married Levy.

G11.3. Phoebe, married Caro. Their children: Walter, Nor-
bert, Harry and Fanny. There are no descendants
alive today.

G11.4. Blanche, married May.

G12. Fanny, married Moore. Her children: May (married Walter Leon, a relative, but had no issue) and
Richard (no issue).

G11.5. Myra, married Kisch. Their children Eve (died unmarried), Oliver (died in World War II) and John
Kisch (married and has three daughters).

G11.6. Herbert M. Adler, born in London 1876 and died
there in 1940. He was educated at St. John's College, Cambridge and practiced as a barrister until
1915. In 1911 he succeeded his father as director
of the Stepney Jewish Schools and retired in 1939.
In 1922 he was appointed first director of Jewish
education by the committee of the Jewish War
Memorial. He was co-editor of *The Service of the
Synagogue* (1904), an author of *A Summary of the
Law Relating to Corporations* (London, 1903) and
Jewish Prayer Book (1922). He married Octavia
and had issue.[27]

G12.1. Aletta Adler, unmarried.
G12.2. Robin Adler, married and has issue.

G13.1. Simon Adler, unmarried.
G13.2. Andrea, married Harris and had a daughter,
Anna Louise.

G11.7. Constance, married Lesser. Their children: Pamella,
Charles and Harry.

G10.5. Rabbi Dr. Hermann Adler, Chief Rabbi of the United
Hebrew Congregations of the British Empire. He was
the second son, born in Hanover in 1839 and educated
at University College School and University College,
London, and later at Prague and Leipzig, where in
1862 he received his PhD and the following year his
Rabbinical Diploma by the Chief Rabbi Rappoport of
Prague. From 1862-4 he was principal of Jews' College and then became Rabbi of the Bayswater Synagogue, and in 1879, on his father's declining health,
he was appointed assistant Chief Rabbi and Chief
Rabbi in 1891, on his father's death. His influence was
very widespread and he was recognized socially as
the representative of the Jewish community. He therefore received an honorary LL.D. from St. Andrew's
University (in 1899), D.C.L. from Oxford University
(in 1909), and C.V.O. conferred upon him the same

year by King Edward VII. His written works were *Course of Sermons on the Biblical Passages Adduced by Christian Theologians in Support of the Dogmas of Their Faith* (London, 1869), *Anglo-Jewish Memories* (1909) and a number of articles which appeared in various journals. He was a supporter of the colonization of Palestine which he visited in 1885, and of the rights of Russian Jewry, participating in conferences in Berlin (in 1889) and in Paris (in 1890). He was an opponent of Reform Judaism. He married Rachel Joseph and had three children.[28]

G11.1. Henrietta (Nettie, 1868-1950) Adler, public social worker and educator, who wrote articles on child welfare. She died unmarried.

G11.2. Rev. Solomon Alfred Adler (1876-1910).[29] He was the Rabbi of the Hope Place Synagogue in Liverpool from 1902-4 and then left for the Hammersmith and West Kensington Synagogue where he remained until his early death at the age of thirty-four years. He was unmarried.

G11.3. Ruth (1872-1952), married in 1895 to Alfred Eichholtz (1870-1933).[30] He became a Fellow of Emmanuel College, Cambridge and lecturer in Anatomy and Physiology from about 1894-8. Then he was the Chief Medical Inspector of H.M. Ministry of Education. His children adopted the name of Eccles.

G12.1. David Eccles, born in 1906, unmarried, retired Professor Emeritus of the Classics' Department at Bristol University.

G12.2. Hubert Eccles, born in 1899, married Sybil Albu. He held a commission in H.M. Forces.

G13. Jonathan Eccles, born in 1926, married Priscilla Whiting. He held a commission in H.M. Forces, and had issue, Sarah, born 1955 and Julian, born 1957.

G12.3. Robert Eccles (1896-1957), lawyer and partner in the firm Adler (E.N.) and Perowne. He also held a commission in H.M. Forces. He was married twice: 1) Enid Albu and had two daughters, and 2) Cesira Buran, and had a daughter. His first wife remarried and became Enid Balint, a well-known psychoanalyst.

G13.1.   Barbara, born in 1928, married Ralph Clark, and have issue, Susan born 1954, Judith born 1956, Rachel born 1959 and Michael born 1962.
G13.2.   Jill, born in 1930, married Alexander Oldham, and have issue, Frances born 1956, Jacqueline born 1959 and Peter born 1962.
G13.3.   Mariangela, born 1955.

G10.6.   Elkan Nathan Adler, 1861-1946, unmarried. He was educated at London University where he received his B.A. and M.A. In 1930 he received the honorary Doctorate of Hebrew Law from the Jewish Theological Seminary in New York. This Seminary acquired his vast collection of manuscripts which he had collected on travels throughout the world in 1923. He was a member of the Board of Deputies, of the Council of the Anglo-Jewish Association, Jews' College, the Joint Foreign Commission, the Royal Institute of International Affairs, a Fellow of the Royal Historical Society and the author of a number of books, including *About Hebrew Manuscripts* (London, 1905), *Jews in Many Lands* (Philadelphia, 1905), *Jewish Travellers* (London, 1930) and *History of the Jews in London* (Philadelphia, 1930).

G10.7.   Ida (died in 1933), married Magnus Schaap.[31] Of their seven children, only one married. They changed the surname to Sharp. The unmarried were Marion (1882-1968), Sophie (1883-1962), Ethel (1886-1927), James (1889-1943), Nathan (born 1891) and Cecil (1892-1966).

G11.   Leo Sharp, 1884-1946, married Vera Geffen. Their children: two daughters (one is married) and a son, Peter Sharp (married, with a son and two daughters).

G10.8.   Rebecca (died in 1890), married Harry Heilbut.[32] They had three sons. He remarried and had issue (perished in the Holocaust).

G11.1. Nathan Heilbut, died in New York in 1969, unmarried.

G11.2. Ernst Heilbut, married and perished in the Holocaust with two sons, Robert and Fred. A third son,
Harry (surnamed Hashavit) is married and has two
sons, Gideon and David (now married) in Tivon,
Israel.

G11.3. Otto Nathan Heilbut, 1890-1970 (buried in New
Jersey). He was in the cotton import-export business in New York where he settled in 1940. He married Bertha Lewinsky. Their sons are Anthony
(born 1940) and Wilfred (D.D.S. born 1943) of
New York.

BRANCH C

Descendants of

R. SOLOMON ZALMAN Son of R. Eliezer Lipschutz

Lipschutz Family

Ancestry

G3.3. R. Saul Wahl.

G4.9. Geila, married R. Benjamin Lipschutz.

G5.3. Wife of R. Solomon Zalman Ravardo.

G6. R. Eliezer.

G7. R. Solomon Zalman Lipschutz, adopted the family name of his
great-grandfather R. Benjamin Lipschutz.

G8.1. R. Ephraim Lipschutz. A responsum of his appears in the
works of his brother.

G8.2. R. Eliezer Lipschutz, A.B.D. Ostrow (about forty years) and
Neuwied. Author of *Siach Hasadeh, Damesek Eliezer, Heishiv Reb Eliezer,* all published in Neuwied in 1749.

G9.1. R. Solomon Zalman Lipschutz.

G9.2. R. Judah (Judel) Lipschutz.

G9.3. R. Israel Lipschutz (died 1748), A.B.D. Ostrow, Cracow,
and Neuwied. He was a pupil of R. Ezekiel Katzenellenbogen of Altona-Hamburg-Wandsbeck. It was he who originally signed the famous "Get" (Divorce Bill)[33] in Cleves
in August 1766, which sparked a heated controversy and

dispute throughout Europe as regards its legality. The point
in question was whether a certain Isaac was insane or not.
Israel, feeling that he was, had granted a "get." However,
the Frankfurt-on-Main courts declared this "get" invalid,
and requested Rabbi Lipschutz to advise the wife not to
rely on the "get" and not to remarry. In 1766, Israel sent
a responsum to Frankfurt clarifying his decision to validate
the "get." Because the Beth Din of Frankfurt still did not
agree, the case was presented to the leading Rabbinical
authorities who included scions of the Katzenellenbogen
family—R. Naftali Hirsch of Schwabach and his brother R.
Eliezer of Alsace, who supported Rabbi Lipschutz. He was
married to their niece, Rebecca.[34] Israel was the author of
Or Yisrael, published in Cleves 1770, responsa which include
many letters of correspondence on the Cleves Divorce Case.

G10.1. R. Solomon, published his father's work.
G10.2. R. Gedaliah Lipschutz, died 1826. He was A.B.D. Chad-
zicz and Obrizizk (near Posen). He married Keila,
daughter of R. Zvi Hirsch Halevi. He was the author of
Regel Yeshara, published Dyhernfurth 1776; *Chumrei
Matnita,* Berlin 1784; *Knesset Yisrael,* published Breslau
1818; and extracts of several works published by his son
Israel.

G11. R. Israel Lipschutz, born 1782 and died September 9,
1860, A.B.D. Dessau and Danzig. He led an ascetic life,
frequently fasting three days in succession and studying
incessantly. He was the author of *Tiferet Yisrael,* Hanover 1830, a Mishnaic commentary in which he applied
his own nomenclature to the various Orders; *Zerach
Yisrael Bederech Ketzarah;* Manuscripts of Torah, Talmud, and others, published in *Ateret Tiferet* by Eisenstadt, Vilna 1877; and his Ethical Will, Königsberg 1861.

G12. R. Baruch Isaac Lipschutz, born in Dessau and died
in Berlin 1877. He was a Rabbi of Landsberg and then
district Rabbi in Mecklenburg-Schwerin, but was
obliged to resign from both positions as a consequence
of congregational disputes. He settled in Hamburg
and was the author of *Torat Shmuel, ein Erbauungs-
buch fur Israeliten,* published Hamburg 1867.[35]

CHAPTER VII

A.

DESCENDANTS OF

R. ARI LIEB (G3.3/4.10/5) SON OF R. MOSES KATZ

MARGOLIOTH, BLOCH, RAPPOPORT FAMILIES
TWERSKY (OF MAKAROV) AND PERLOW
CHASSIDIC DYNASTIES

G5. R. Ari Lieb Katz.[1]

G6.1. R. Zeev Wolf Katz A.B.D. Lomaz and later of Brest. He married Rachel the daughter of R. Abraham (Abba Mori) son of R. Jacob (A.B.D. Vienna).

    G7.1. R. Zvi Hirsch A.B.D. Vislovitz, married the daughter of R. Moses Dovrushes, Parnas of Lublin.

        G8. R. Zeev Wolf A.B.D. Modly, married the daughter of R. Moses son of R. Joseph Gunzburg (author of *Leket Yosef*).

    G7.2. Frodel, married R. Jacob son of R. Jehiel Michael Halpern (A.B.D. Berjan, author of *Beit Yaakov*), A.B.D. Zovnitz.

        G8. R. Solomon Isaac Halpern, A.B.D. Tarnopol.

    G7.3. Wife of R. Solomon son of R. Abraham Abbale son of R. Solomon of Zolkiev, A.B.D. Slutzk.

G6.2. Wife of R. Mordecai Liebus son of R. Israel (A.B.D. Brest, son-in-law of R. Abraham Halpern of Lublin) son of R. Moses (author of *MaHaDuRa BaTRa*, and son-in-law of R. Samuel *MaHaRaSHa* Edels).

288

G7.1. R. Abraham Abbale, elected A.B.D. Zolkiev in 1699, author of
a number of approbations. He married the daughter of R. Isaac
of Zolkiev.

G8. Wife of R. Avigdor of Jerusalem, where he was buried.

G7.2. R. Israel Eiser, Parnas of Lublin.

G8.1. R. Meir, died in Lublin in 1800.

G8.2. Wife of R. Naftali Hirsch son of R. Moses (of Brody) A.B.D.
Zolkiev. He wrote a number of approbations.

G8.3. Rebecca, married R. Moses Phineas, son of R. Abraham, son
of R. Haim (son-in-law of R. Benjamin Wolf the son of R.
Abraham Halpern—See G6.2 above). Moses Phineas was
A.B.D. Zbariz and Zolkiev and the *Ne'eman* (Trustee) of the
Council of the Four Lands. He wrote the following approba-
tions to *Porat Yosef*, by R. Joseph Teomim, in 1741 and 1756;
Birkat Yosef by R. Joseph Teomim, in 1746; *Beer haTov* by
R. Moses of Zolkiev in 1746; *Neta Sha'ashu'im* by R. DovBer
son of R. Nathan of Pinsk, Zolkiev in 1748; *Shaarei Binyamin*
by R. Benjamin Zeev son of R. David Ashkenazi in 1752 in
Zolkiev; *Mitznefet Bad* by R. Alexander Ziskind, son of R.
David Kantshiger in 1757, Zolkiev; and *Tsemach Menachem*
by R. Menachem Nachman son of R. Jekutiel Zussman Katz
in 1761, Zolkiev.

He was also one of the Rabbis who signed at Zolkiev in
1751 against R. Jonathan Eybeschutz and he was the last
Parnas of the Council of the Four Lands shortly before its
dissolution by the Polish Government in 1764.

G9.1. R. Joseph Landau, 1726-1801 A.B.D. Posen, author of *Zichron She'erit Yosef*. He married the daughter of the great
Talmudist R. Ezekiel Landau, and his father-in-law mentions him a number of times in his famous work, the *Noda
BiYehuda*. (See Landau Family Pedigree.) He was considered to be very wealthy and influential.

G10.1. R. Judah Landau, A.B.D. Wladowa, author of *Beit Yehudah*, published in Lvov, 1831. He married Elke,
daughter of R. Moses son of R. Naftali Hirsch of Satanow.

G11. R. Isaac of Wladowa, author of *Minchat Yitzchak*, published together with his father's work in 1831. He was
buried in Jerusalem.

G10.2. R. Phineas, married the daughter of R. Benjamin Braude A.B.D. Grodno.

    G11.1. R. Eleazar Landau, adopted his great-grandfather's family name for his own, was A.B.D. Walkavisk.

    G11.2. R. Liebe, married R. Zvi Hirsch Ratner of Minsk (son of R. Haim David Ratner).

G9.2. R. Samuel Polkenfeld, A.B.D. Bilgoray, where he wrote a number of approbations. He later became A.B.D. Tarnopol and then Przeworsk. After his brother's death, he became A.B.D. Posen. He was the author of *Beit Shmuel Acharon* published in Nodvahar 1806 and married Rachel Hadassah, daughter of his uncle R. Zvi Hirsch of Lublin (his father's brother).

G7.3. Wife of R. Isaac Rappoport A.B.D. of the Ostrow Klaus, son of R. Moses Meir Rappoport of Lvov.

    G8.1. Wife of R. Judah Lieb A.B.D. of the Ostrow Klaus, and later A.B.D. Slutzk and Pinsk, son of R. Asher Anschel. He married Zelda.

        G9.1. R. Asher Anschel, author of *Baruch MiBanim Asher,* published Zolkiev 1749 and *Korban Ashir*. He was at first Judge (dayan) of Ostrow and later A.B.D. Slonim where he wrote a number of approbations. He married Sarah, daughter of R. Dovber, son of R. Samuel Jokels of Ostrow.

        G9.2. R. David, author of *Otot Lemoadim*.

G7.4. Veitel (died in Zolkiev in 1739), wife of R. Alexander Sender, son of R. Ephraim Zalman Shor, author of the well-known Rabbinical work *Tevuot Shor,* published in Zolkiev, 1733, together with *Bechor Shor,* entitled *Simlah Chadashah*. Alexander died in 1737 and was buried in Zolkiev.

    G8.1. R. Zalman.

    G8.2. Wife of R. Samuel Shmelke, son of R. Moses (of Zlatchov) Rokeah. (See Rokeah Family Pedigree.)

    G8.3. Deborah, married R. Israel, son of R. Isaac Babad (See Babad Family Pedigree). Founders of the Brodsky Family Pedigree.

        G9. R. Alexander Sender Haim, married his second cousin (see below, G10.3)

    G8.4. Hinde, born 1696, married R. Menachem Meinish of Zolkiev, son of R. Isaac (A.B.D. of Javorow) Margolioth.

G9.1. Wife of R. Abraham Yekutiel Zalman Rappoport (called Pereles) of Brody, where he died on the second day of Jewish New Year 1798, son of R. Moses (A.B.D. of Tarnopol).

G10.1. Sarah (died 1796), married R. Zvi Hirsch Horowitz, author of *Machaneh Levi*. (See Horowitz Family Pedigree Branch III, and Below — G9.2/10.2/11.1/12.1.)

G10.2. Beila, married R. Zvi Hirsch, son of R. Dovber of Vilna. He died about 1817/8.

    G11.1. R. Dovberish, married the daughter of R. Saul Levine of Karlin. (See Chapter V — Branch A — G6.2/7/8/9.2/10.2/11.2/12.8.)

    G11.2. R. Abraham Yekutiel Zalman, married the daughter of R. Eiser of Sokolov. He died in Vilna in 1839.

    G11.3. Rikel, married R. Isaac Israel Eiser of Vilna, called Reb Isaac Zalmans.

    G11.4. Hanale, married R. Abraham Jacob Landau, son of R. Samuel son R. Ezekiel (*Noda BiYehuda*). (See Landau Family Pedigree.)

    G11.5. Wife of R. Nathan Michael Sheinfinkel of Karlin.

G10.3. Reizel, married second cousin R. Alexander Sender Haim Shor (See descendants of R. Abraham J. Heschel of Cracow — Part III — G7.1/8.1/9.2/10.1). Head of the Brodsky Family.

G10.4. R. Moses Rappoport, married daughter of R. Meir (A.B.D. Holfin).

    G11. R. Naftali Hirsch Rappoport, died in 1830, married daughter of R. Simha, son of R. Benjamin Rappoport.

        G12.1. Zvi Hirsch, R. of Dubno, author of *Ezrat Kohanim*, married Dinah Reizel, daughter of R. Mordecai Zadok, son of R. David (of Dubno) Marshalkovitch. (See Chapter XVI — G10.9/11.3/12.1/13.3/14.5.)

            G13.1. R. David Eliezer Rappoport, died as a young man and his novellae appeared in his father's book, Vilna-Zhitomir 1845-1866.

            G13.2. R. Jacob Moses Rappoport. His novellae appeared in his father's book.

G13.3. Wife of R. Abraham Teomim A.B.D. Buczacz, author of *Chesed LeAvraham.* (See Chapter IV — Branch A.)

G12.2. R. Simha Rappoport (mentioned in the *Chesed Le-Avraham.*)

G13. R. Meir A.B.D. Borstein, also mentioned in the *Chesed LeAvraham.*

G10.5. Wife of R. Abraham Hirsch (Liebus) Horowitz, son of R. Isaac Hamburger (See Chapter XVI — G11.3/12.4). He died in 1803.

G9.2. R. Mordecai Margolioth.[3]

G10.1. R. Alexander Sender Margolioth, married Sarah Esther, daughter of R. Zvi Hirsch A.B.D. Zbariz, son of R. Solomon of Pinczow. (See Teomim-Frankel Family Pedigree — page 182.) He succeeded his father-in-law at Zbariz as A.B.D., where he wrote an approbation to *Mincha Chadasha* by R. Isaac Shor, in 1774, published in Alexnitz in 1774. Alexander then became A.B.D. Satanov, where he died on Rosh Chodesh Tevet in 1802. He left behind many works in manuscript, published as *Teshuvot HaRaM,* in Warsaw in 1859.

G11.1. Nechama Reizel, married R. Joseph Saul Teomim. (See Teomim-Frankel Family Pedigree — Branch B.)
G11.2. R. Samuel Margolioth A.B.D. Stry and Dulczawka.
G11.3. R. Mordecai Margolioth A.B.D. Satanov, where he succeeded his father.
G11.4. R. Naftali Zvi Hirsch Margolioth of Lvov.
G11.5. R. Aryey Liebus Margolioth A.B.D. Zmigrad.
G11.6. Deborah, married R. Uri Shraga Feiwel Bloch, founder of the Bloch Family of Bialystok and later in Israel and South America. (See Bloch Family Pedigree — Chapter VII, below.)
G11.7. Wife of R. David Landau, A.B.D. Sanz for forty years.
G12. R. Baruch Landau, A.B.D. Sanz, died there in 1847.

G10.2. R. Menachem Meinish Margolioth A.B.D. Dynowitz, died in 1829. He married the daughter of R. Aaron Rabinowitz, A.B.D. Levertov, son of R. Eliakim Getzel of Levertov. R. Getzel was also the father-in-law of R. Jacob Moses Leverbaum (Chapter XIII) and of R. Mordecai Zeev Ornstein (Chapter XII — Branch E).

G11.1. R. Ephraim Zalman Margolioth of Brody 1760-1828. He died in Brody where he lived most of his latter days in study. He was independently wealthy and never accepted a Rabbinical position. His wife was a sister to the wife of R. Wolf Ber Schiff (See Chapter VII — Branch B). He was the author of numerous works, including *Beit Efraim; Rosh Efraim; Olelat Efraim; Yad Efraim; Shem Efraim; Mateh Efraim; Zerah Efraim; She'erit Efraim,* and *Sha'arei Efraim* (published respectively at Lvov 1809, Lvov 1809, Lvov 1884, Dubno 1820, Berdichev 1826, Zolkiev 1835, Lvov 1853 and Dubno 1820). A funeral oration on the death of R. Menachem Nahum Twersky (father of R. Mordecai, founder of the Twersky-Chernobyl Chassidic Dynasty) appeared in Lvov 1899, entitled *Dim'at Efraim.* He was also the author of a genealogical work which traces the families Landau, Margolioth, Ettinge and others, entitled *Ma'alot Ha-Yochasin* (Lvov 1900). *Mikneh VeKinyan* is a collection of Responsa dealing with the sale of leavening on the eve of Passover (published Zolkiev 1865). Many other works were left in manuscript. R. Margolioth owed his wealth to the successful Banking House which he established in Brody. He was thus able to establish a Yeshiva as well, of which he was the head. Here he was recognized as a leading authority and his Yeshiva produced many famous Rabbinical scholars. His funeral oration was published by R. Solomon Kluger in Zolkiev 1834 under the title *Ein Dimah.*

G12.1. Wife of R. Jacob Joshua, son of R. Zvi Hirsch (*Machaneh Levi*) Horowitz. (See Horowitz Family Pedigree-Branch III.) He is mentioned in the Responsa of his father-in-law, *Beit Efraim.*

G12.2. Sarah, first wife of R. Haim Nachman Parnas of Vilna. (See Chapter V — Branch B — Descendants of R. Naftali Katz — page 257.)

G12.3. Wife of the son of R. Zvi Hirsch David (A.B.D. Cracow), son of R. Isaac (A.B.D. Cracow) Halevi. Zvi died in 1852. (See Lowenstamm Family Pedigree — Chapter XII — page 438 — G9.2.)

G12.4. Wife of R. Benjamin Wolf (Zeev) Low 1775-1851, successively R. of Rosprza, Amshinov, Kolon (1812-26), Nagytapolcsany (1826) and Verbo (1836). He was the author of *Sha'rei Torah* (1821 first part; 1851 Vienna second part), third part published by his son in 1872. He was a great Talmudist, son of R. Eleazar Low (*Shemen Rokeah* 1758-1837). They divorced and R. Benjamin married the daughter of R. Isaac Landau of Auschwitz.

G11.2. R. Eliakim Getzel Margolioth.

G12.1. R. Joel Margolioth.

G12.2. R. Moses Margolioth of Brody, married his cousin, daughter of R. Haim Mordecai Margolioth.

G13.1. R. Mordecai.

G13.2. R. Eliakim Getzel of Cracow.

G14.1. R. Abraham Margolioth.

G14.2. Wife of R. Shmelke Shenker.

G14.3. Wife of R. Shakna Landau.

G14.4. Wife of R. Saul Kroll.

G13.3. Mindel, married R. Issachar Berish Freilich.

G12.3. R. Haim David Margolioth, married his cousin, daughter of R. Haim Mordecai Margolioth.

G13. Deborah, married R. Zvi Hirsch Halberstam A.B.D. Kosiatyn. (See Halberstam Family — Chapter VII — Branch B — G7.4/8.2/9.6/10.4/11.4/12.)

G11.3. R. Jacob Margolioth.

G11.4. R. Haim Mordecai Margolioth A.B.D. Dubno and author of *Sha'arei Teshuva*, which remained unfinished due to his untimely death in 1818. His brother, R. Ephraim Zalman, later completed the work. He established his own printing office in Dubno.

G12.1. R. Menachem Meinish Margolioth A.B.D. Mazev, Porisk and Horochov, married Gitel daughter of R.

Jacob Aryey (of Kobly) son of R. Mordecai Shapiro (A.B.D. Nechshov).

G13.1. R. Haim Mordecai Margolioth, A.B.D., Dobyasser, married his cousin, the daughter of R. Nahum (of Makarov) Twersky, son of R. Mordecai of Chernobyl (See Below G10.4/11.4/12/13.2/14.4.)

G13.2. R. Ephraim Zalman Margolioth II,[4] A.B.D. Mazev and Trisk, married Sheine Reizel and Malka, daughters of R. Abraham (A.B.D. Trisk) Twersky (also a son-in-law of R. Jacob Aryey Shapiro mentioned above). Ephraim died in 1886.

G14.1. Feige Mintze, married R. Isaac Meir (of Zinkov) son of R. Samuel Heschel. (See Heschel Family Pedigree — G11.1/12.1/13.1/14.1.)

G14.2. Chaya, married R. Shalom Joseph (of Husyatin) son of R. Mordecai Shraga Friedman. (See Friedman-Ruzhin Chassidic Dynasty.)

G14.3. Sheva, married R. Abraham Dov (of Rotmistrivka) son of R. Menachem Nahum Twersky.

G14.4. Jochebed, married R. Moses (of Choristkov) son of R. Mordecai, son of R. Moses Twersky.

G14.5. Gitel, married R. Nahum, son of R. David (of Makarov) Twersky. See below.

G12.2. R. Zvi Hirsch Margolioth, married Ita Deborah daughter of R. Simha Asher (of Vitebsk) son of R. Gershon Gunzburg. (See Chapter III — Branch D — Gunzburg Family Pedigree — G7.1/8.3/9.1/10.1.)

G12.3. Wife of R. Moses Margolioth of Brody, her first cousin (above).

G12.4. Wife of R. Haim David Margolioth, her first cousin (above).

G12.5. Wife of R. Nahum son of R. Solomon of Lodmir, son of R. Moses of Lodmir, son of R. Solomon of Karlin. (See Friedman Dynasty — G12.1.)

G13. R. Gedaliah.

G14.1. R. Uri Aaron of Kalicz.

G14.2. R. Moses of Stanislav, perished in World War II.

G11.5. R. Alexander Sender Margolioth of Brody.

G10.3. Wife of Rabbi Isaac Wolf son of R. Judah Lieb Berenstein (Descendants of R. Abraham Joshua Heschel of
Cracow — See Chapter XI — G7.1/8.3/9.1/10.1).

G10.4. Rechel, married R. Phineas A.B.D. Kollevan.[5]

G11.1. R. Moses A.B.D. Sadagora, author of *Pnei Moshe,*
published in Koretz 1817-8.

G11.2. R. Sender Samuel A.B.D. Horochov.

G11.3. R. Avigdor A.B.D. Horev.

G11.4. R. Mordecai A.B.D. Dubenka and Koretz.

G12. Wife of R. Jossel Horowitz, 1782-1818, son of R. Jacob
Isaac of Lublin, known as the *"Chozeh* of Lublin."

G13.1. Blume, died unmarried.

G13.2. Hinde Motil, married R. Nahum Twersky, 1805-
1851 (Makarov), founder of the Makarov Branch
of the Twersky Chassidic Dynasty, son of R.
Mordecai of Chernobyl (1770-1837).

G14.1. R. Jacob Isaac Twersky of Makarov (died in
1892), married Zipporah, daughter of R. Samuel Abba of Slovita.

G15.1. R. Moses Mordecai Twersky of Makarov
(died 1920), married Chavah, the daughter
of R. Joshua Rokeah of Belz, the Second
Rebbe (See Rokeah Chassidic Dynasty).

G16.1. R. Zvi Aryey of Berdichev (died 1938),
married Malka, daughter of Jehiel Heschel
of Krolevets. (See Chapter XV — G11.1/
12.1/13.4.)

G17. R. Simha Lerner (Tel Aviv).

G16.2. Motil, married R. Samuel Abba Hager of
Horodenka (Kossov-Vizhniz.)

G16.3. R. Samuel Abba, married Rikel, his first
cousin, daughter of R. David Twersky of
Makarov.

G16.4. Malka, married 1) R. Zusia Moril and 2)
R. Sander Ginsberg.

G16.5. Feige, married R. Aaron Nahum Rokeah of Magrov.

G16.6. Hannah Rachel, married R. Abale Ungvar.

G16.7. Ziporah, married R. Zilbiger of Jaroslaw.

G15.2. R. David Twersky of Makarov-Kiev (died 1902), married Feige, daughter of R. Abraham Twersky of Trisk.

G16.1. R. Nahum Twersky of Makarov — Zavil (died 1926 in New York), married Gitel, daughter of R. E. Z. Margolioth of Mazev, son of R. Menachem Meinish. (See above — G11.4/12.1/13.2/14.5.)

G16.2. R. Nisim Judah Lieb A.B.D. of Pokshinowitz-Kielce (died 1941), succeeded his uncle R. Mordecai of Kazmir.

G16.3. Rickel, married her cousin R. Samuel Abba, son of R. Moses Mordecai.

G16.4. Reizel, married R. Judah Aryey Perlow of Wladowa, son of R. Jacob of Novominsk.

G16.5. Sarah, married Abraham Jacob, son of R. Zvi Ponitz.

G16.6. Zida, married R. Haim Gerson Manzon.

G15.3. R. Isaiah Twersky of Makarov (died 1919), married Chaya Sarah, (died 1920) daughter of R. Haim Menachem Heschel of Zinkov.

G16.1. R. Abraham Joshua Heschel Twersky of Kiev, married daughter of R. Jerachmeel of Kozenitz.

G16.2. R. Isaac Jacob Twersky (1896-1945), married Sima, daughter of R. Joshua Heschel Rabinowitz of Manisterich, Admur Makarov-Chicago-Kiev. (See Chapter XV — Branch B — page 544 — G15.3.)

Their children include Chaya Sarah, married Solomon Drillman, Margolia Rachel, married Gershon Schulman; and Isaiah Twersky.

G15.4. Chaya, married R. Israel Zvi, R. Baruch

Meir Twersky of Azranitz, R. Joseph Rabinowitz and R. Zvi of Ulanov.

G14.2. Chaya, and
G14.3. Zivia Sheine.
First and second wives of R. Asher (of Stolin)
son of R. Aaron (of Karlin) Perlow (see below.)
G14.4. Eidel, married R. Mordecai son of R. Menachem Menish Margolioth (G11.4/12.1/13.1 —
above).

G9.3. R. Zvi Hirsch Margolioth A.B.D. Meseritz.

G10. Wife of R. Isaac son of R. Joel son of R. Isaac Katz. (See
Chapter V — Branch B.)

THE PERLOW CHASSIDIC DYNASTY
(of STOLIN-KARLIN)

ANCESTRY

G3.3.   R. Saul Wahl Katzenellenbogen.
G4.10. Wife of R. Moses Katz.
G5.   R. Ari Lieb Katz.
G6.2.   Wife of R. Mordecai Liebus.
G7.4.   Wife of R. Alexander Sender Shor.
G8.4.   Hinde, married R. Menachem Meinish Margolioth.
G9.2.   R. Mordecai Margolioth.
G10.4. Rechel, married R. Phineas A.B.D. Kollevan.
G11.4. R. Mordecai A.B.D. Dubenka-Koretz.
G12.   Wife of R. Joseph Horowitz of Turstein (1782-1818).
G13.2. Hinde Motil, married R. Nahum Twersky (1805-1851).
G14.2. and
G14.3. Wives of R. Asher (1827-73) the second (of Stolin), son of R.
Aaron[6] (1801-72) the second (of Karlin) Perlow. R. Asher's third
wife was the daughter of R. Elimelech Shapiro of Grodzisk. He
succeeded his father, but died a year later at Drogobitch.

G15.1. Chanah, married R. Mordecai of Kazmir (died 1917), son of R.
Abraham (of Trisk) Twersky, (son of R. Mordecai of Chernobyl,
founder of the Twersky Dynasty). He was the author of *Ma'amar
Mordechai*.
G15.2. Wife of R. Moses of Stefan, son of R. Baruch (of Stefan), son of

R. Mordecai (of Korostyshev), son of R. Moses (of Korostyshev, and son of R. Mordecai of Chernobyl).

G15.3. R. Israel Perlow of Stolin (1869-1922) died in Leipzig and was buried in Frankfurt-on-Main. He was orphaned at the age of four years and as a teenager became the Admur of Karlin-Stolin. He married Bracha Sheindel, his first cousin (daughter of R. David [of Zlatopoli] son of R. Johanan [of Rotmistrovka] Twersky). He was known as the *Yenuka MiStolin*.

G16.1. R. Asher Perlow, perished in 1942, married daughter of R. Mordecai, son of R. Menachem Nahum, son of R. Isaac Twersky (of Skvira, son of R. Mordecai (of Chernobyl, founder of the Dynasty).

G16.2. R. Aaron Perlow, perished 1942, married Feigle, daughter of R. Nathan David Rabinowitz of Parziveh. (See Chapter IV — G9.2/10.4/11/12.1/13.4/14.1/15.2.)

G16.3. R. Moses Perlow perished 1942, married daughter of R. Phineas, son of R. Isaac Joel Rabinowitz (of Kantikoziba).

G16.4. R. Jacob Haim Perlow, Admur of Stolin, came to New York in 1929, died in 1946 and was buried in Detroit. He married Chanah, daughter of R. Abraham Joshua Heschel Eichenstein (of Chodorov).

G16.5. R. Abraham Elimelech Perlow, 1892-1942, Admur of Karlin, married Chava, daughter of R. Mordecai Joseph Twersky (brother of Bracha Sheindel — G15.3 above).

G16.6. R. Johanan Perlow of Lutsk 1900-1955. He succeeded his father as Admur of Lutsk in 1922. He survived the Holocaust and came to the United States in 1947 as the leader of the Karlin-Stolin followers, after the death of his brother, R. Jacob Haim, in 1946. He was reinterred two years after his death in Tiberias. He married the daughter of R. Simeon Solomon Brandwein. His daughter's son, R. Baruch Meir Jacob Shochet (born in 1954) is the present leader of the Karlin-Stolin Chassidim.

G16.7. Chavah, married R. Shalom, son of R. Jacob Moses Safrin, Admur of Komarno (died 1929). (See Chapter XVII — Eichenstein-Safrin Dynasty.)

G16.8. Wife of R. Shalom (of Apt), son of R. Issachar Dov Rokeah of Belz. (See Rokeah Dynasty.)

G16.9. Wife of R. Abraham Jacob, son of R. Isaac Mordecai Shapiro of Gvoditz. (See Shapiro Chassidic Dynasty.)

G16.10. Wife of R. Abraham Elimelech, son of R. Israel of Grodzisk.

BLOCH FAMILY PEDIGREE

ANCESTRY

G3.3.   Saul Wahl.

G4.10.   Daughter, married Moses Katz.

G5.   Ari Lieb Katz.

G6.2.   Daughter, married Mordecai Liebus.

G7.4.   Daughter, married Alexander Sender Shor.

G8.4.   Hinde, married Menachem Meinish Margolioth.

G9.2.   Mordecai Margolioth.

G10.1.   Alexander Sender Margolioth.

G11.6.   Deborah, married Uri Feiwel Bloch[7] of Vilna.

G12.1.   Aaron Zeev Bloch.

G12.2.   Noah Bloch,[8] one of the leaders and philanthropists of Vilna, died
         in 1809. His daughter married R. Levi son of R. David Rokeach.

G12.3.   Samuel Menachem Meinish Bloch.

G12.4.   Alexander Sender Bloch, named after his maternal grandfather born
         1809 and died in Bialystok in 1848. He married Malka Reizel,
         daughter of Isaac Zabludowsky of Bialystok, one of the city's wealth-
         iest leading Jews. Pictures of Sender and Malka can be found
         in the book on Bialystok published in New York by the Bialystoker
         Center (N.Y.).[9]

   G13.1.   Noah David Bloch of Bialystok, married Teiwel, daughter of
            Shalom Zabludowsky. Their daughter, Ulde, married Abraham
            Walkavisky.

   G13.2.   Benzion Bloch of Bialystok. His children: Isaac; Jonah; Pesha,
            married Neumark; and Leah Deborah.

   G13.3.   Esther Zlata, married twice. Her first husband was Tanhum
            Broda of Tiktin. Their daughters: Teiwel married Michael Dillan,
            and Pesha, married Zvi Hirsch Rosenthal. Esther's second hus-
            band was Mordecai Haim Heilprin of Bialystok. Their children:
            Alexander; Israel; Feiwel; David; Deborah, married Press; and
            Feige.

   G13.4.   Sheine Chaya, married Benjamin Heilprin (died Bialystok 1882)
            son of Jacob Koppel of Bialystok.

      G14.1.   Feiwel Heilprin, settled in the U.S.A. His children: Koppel in
               Warsaw; Alexander; Leibel; and Feigel.

      G14.2.   Alexander Heilprin in Vitebsk.

G14.3. Pesha, married Mordecai Wolff of Bialystok. Their children: Koppel; Alexander; Nathan of Bialystok; Joseph Benjamin; and Sarah Rebecca.

G14.4. Rachel, married Abraham Arkin in Warsaw. Their children; Gedalliah and Sonya, married Samuel Doshevsky in Warsaw.

G14.5. Feigel, married Moses Zeev Swinn of Lodz. Their daughter, Motte, married Mordecai Heilprin of Lodz.

G14.6. Blume, married Abraham Abba Lipschutz of Bialystok. Their children; Alexander Sender of Bialystok; Uri Judah Lieb of Warsaw; Deborah; Rachel; Pesha; and Isaac Elchanan.

G13.5. Sarah Elke, married Menachem Nahum Zausmer of Bialystok.

G14.1. Zvi Hirsch Zausmer. His sons: Saul (Sigfried) and Lieb (Leon).

G14.2. Asher Anschel Zausmer of Lodz.

G14.3. Channah Feige, married Isaac Baresh of Bialystok. Their children: Alexander; Samuel; Anschel; Beila; and Deborah.

G14.4. Wife of Yudel Luria of Pinsk.

G14.5. Friede, married Levin.

G14.6. Esther, married Zalman Meirach of Bialystok.

G13.6. Rachel, married Abraham Hakohen Zussman of Ostrow. Their children: Feiwel; David; Etta; and wife of Jacob Shenberg.

G13.7. Riva, married Moses Wahl. Their sons: Alexander and Shraga Feiwel.

G13.8. Pesha, married Haim Pines of Razinai.[10]

G14.1. Ari Lieb Pines of Bialystok.

G14.2. Samuel Pines of Bialystok.

G14.3. Shraga Feiwel Pines of Bialystok.

G14.4. Noah Pines.

G14.5. Moses Pines of Warsaw.

G14.6. Meir Pines of Bialystok.

G14.7. Mordecai Pines.

G14.8. Aaron Pines.

G14.9. Isaac.

G14.10. Golda, married Aaron Blumethal of London.

G14.11. Deborah, married Moses Eiser Kabrunki of Lodz.

G13.9. Rashke, married Moses Eiger of Vienna. Their sons: Alexander and Joseph.

G13.10. Hinde, married Moses Rattner of Mohilev.

G13.11. Chavah, married Samuel Eli Kagan of Vitebsk.

G13.12. Chishe, married Jacob Zelkin of Smolensk (grandson of R. Isaac Joel Rabinowitz, the Rebbe of Manisterich — See Chapter XV).

G13.13. Shraga Feiwel Bloch of Bialystok.[11]

G14.1.   Alexander Joseph Bloch of Lodz, married Rachel. He was in the textile manufacturing business and died before the war. One son, Feiwel survived the Holocaust and two daughters perished. One, Hela, was a schoolteacher who survived in the Lodz Ghetto in 1942. Later she went to live with her uncle Alexander Susskind Kohen in Warsaw, where they perished.

G14.2.   Deborah, married Moses Rutenberg of Vitebsk. He died young.

G15.1.   Lipa, a renowned communist activist during Czarist times. After the Russian Revolution he was named Commissionar. His mother lived with him during the time of Stalin's first purge and he died during this period.

G15.2.   Clara, married Segelowicz, looked after her mother in Warsaw on the death of her brother until the Holocaust when they and her daughter, Marinka, perished.

G15.3.   Malka Reizel, married and both died young. Their son, Mische, died young and a daughter, Ada, survived. She married Schkeidi and they live in Israel with their two children and grandchildren.

G14.3.   Zlate, married Alexander Susskind Kohen in Warsaw. He was the co-writer of the Yiddish daily of Warsaw called *Der Moment* and was also a translator of Yiddish to French and English. Their son, Professor Feiwel Kohen, was a prominent physician in the U.S.S.R.

G14.4.   Pesha, married Moses Zeev Fraenckel of Bialystok. Their children: Abraham Ber, Rachel, married Axelrod; and Feigel. They all perished with the family in the Holocaust.

G14.5.   Taibel, married Ephraim Prowalski, a lumber merchant in Warsaw. His son, Joseph, was a lawyer and his children perished in the Holocaust.

G14.6.   Feigel, married and separated early after. She lived in Warsaw with her sister, Zlate, and perished with the family in the Holocaust.

G14.7.   Tuvia (Tewel) Bloch, married Keila Steinberg. They settled in Argentina in 1938.

G15.1.   Joel Bloch, born 1907/8, married in Argentina in 1927 to

Liebe Judowski. She died in the late 1960's and he lives in Tartagal, Santa Fe (Argentina).

G16.1. Clara.

G16.2. Eugenia (Doctor Medicine), married Felipe Alperovich (Orthopedic Surgeon, Utica, N.Y.). They have three children.

G16.3. Alexander Bloch, lawyer (San Martin de la Argentina), married Flora. They have issue: Veronica (born 1970) and Tewel Sebastian (born 1972).

G15.2. Felix Bloch, arrived in Argentina about 1932 where he was in the textile business. Married Rebecca (Rita) Ponieman, and settled in Israel in 1974.

G16.1. Clarisa, born 1939, unmarried, settled in Israel in 1962.

G16.2. Victor Bloch, born 1943, married Dina Schatzki (Kfar Saba, Israel).

G16.3. Graciela, married Yitzchak Altallef (Jerusalem). Their son is Tewel Ariel (born 1972).

G15.3. Guenia, married in 1938 to Jacob Niseliches (changed to Sinai). He lived in Israel and after their marriage in Argentina, they returned to Israel (currently Tel Aviv). He is in metallurgy production in Holon.

G16.1. Ezekiel Sinai, married Ilana Grossman. Both are engineers.

G16.2. Lior Sinai, born 1949, married and has a daughter.

B.

DESCENDANTS OF

R. MEIR WALSCH
(G3.3/4.12, SON-IN-LAW OF SAUL WAHL)

BUBER, HALBERSTAM, HOCHGELERHTER, RUBINSTEIN, SHLICHTER
AND SILBERFELD FAMILIES
TWERSKY CHASSIDIC DYNASTY OF HORNISTOPOL

G4.12. Pesia, married R. Meir Walsch.

G5.4. Miriam, married R. Simeon Rappoport, A.B.D. of Yazlivitz, son of R. Abraham (Shrentzel) Rappoport (author of *Eitan HaEzrachi*) of Lvov.

G6.1. R. David Rappoport of Brody.

G6.2. Wife of R. David Halevi.

G6.3. Gela, married R. Moses Phineas Harif,[12] the first Chief Rabbi
of both the urban and suburban communities of Lvov, where
he died on September 17 (26 Elul), 1702, son of R. Israel. He
was elected the A.B.D. there, following the departure of R. Zvi
Hirsch, son of R. Zechariah Mendel, to Lublin. In the Rabbinical
world he was known as the *MaHaRaM Harif*. His signature appears in the minutes of the Council of the Four Lands at Jaroslav in 1686. R. Moses was the author of Talmudic annotations
and additions to the Talmudic Tractate *Gittin*, which were
mentioned in the *Tiv Gittin* by R. Ephraim Zalman Margolioth
(published in Koretz in 1819). Margolioth mentions that he obtained R. Moses Harif's manuscript. Harif is mentioned in the
works of contemporary Rabbis and he wrote approbations to:
Nachalat Azriel at Jaroslav in 1685, by R. Azriel Ashkenazi, published in Frankfurt-on-Oder in 1691; *Toldot Yitzchak*, in
1687; the Responsa *Beit Yaakov* at Jaroslav in 1692; *Nachalat
Haim* in 1687 by R. Haim son of R. Joshua Halevi, published in
Wilmersdorf in 1713; *Ashlich* in 1698, published in Dyhernfurth
in 1727; *Pnei Moshe* by R. Moses, son of R. Isaiah Katz, published in Wilmersdorf in 1716; *Beir Hillel* published in Dyhernfurth in 1691; *Tzintzenet Menachem* published in Berlin in
1720; and *Gevurat Anashim* by R. Shabtai, son of R. Meir
HaKohen published in Dessau in 1697.

G7.1. Wife of R. Moses Haim, son of R. Eliezer, A.B.D. Lvov-Ko-
marno.

G8.1. R. Eliezer.

G9. R. Abraham.

G10. Leah, married R. Wolf Ber (Zeev Dov) Schiff, born
in Zamocz in 1761), author of *Minchat Zikkaron*, published in Cracow in 1894, son of R. Zvi Heilprin. In his
youth he studied under R. Solomon, son of R. Moses
of Chelm, (author of *Merkavat HaMishna*) and later
in the yeshiva of R. Judah Lieb Margolioth (author of
Peri Tevuah). His second wife was Sheindel, sister of
the wife of R. Ephraim Zalman Margolioth of Brody.
They married in 1807. He died in Cracow in 1847. Head
of the Silberfeld-Rubinstein-Buber-Schlichter Family
(see below).

G8.2. R. Jacob Isaac, A.B.D. Zamocz, died in 1771.

  G9.1. R. Joseph Hochgelerhter[13] A.B.D. Zamocz. He was the author of *Mishnat Chachmim,* published in Lvov in 1792. He married his niece, Zipporah (see below).

    G10.1. R. Isaac Hochgelehrter, author of *Zichron Yitzchak,* published in Lvov in 1800, A.B.D. Chelm.

    G10.2. R. Haim Hochgelehrter, 1769-1809, A.B.D. of Grubieszow, married Feigel, daughter of R. Isaac, son of R. Jacob Haim of Lublin. (See Chapter III — Branch E — G6.5/7.2/8.3/9.2/10.2.)

      G11. R. Moses Jacob Hochgelehrter of Cracow, married Eidel Pesel, daughter of the philanthropist Eliakim Getzel Rakover of Cracow. He died in 1840.

      G12. Esther Feigel, married Michael Cypres, community leader and philanthropist in Cracow.

        G13. Zipporah, married R. Haim Lieb Horowitz, A.B.D. of Cracow. (See Chapter XVI — Branch VI — G13.1/14.3/15.3/16.1.)

    G10.3. Feigel, married R. Moses, son of R. Zvi Hirsch Zamocz (1740-1807, A.B.D. of Glogau) A.B.D. of Tomashov.

  G9.2. Chaya, married her uncle, R. Jacob Haim, son of R. Abraham of Lublin. (See Chapter III — Branch E.) She remarried R. Saul Lowenstamm, A.B.D. Amsterdam on the death of her husband in 1769.

    G10.1. R. Isaac, A.B.D. Trani.

      G11. Feigel, married her second cousin, R. Haim, son of R. Joseph Hochgelehrter.

    G10.2. Zipporah, married her uncle, R. Joseph, son of R. Jacob Isaac Hochgelehrter of Zamocz.

  G9.3. Esther, married the A.B.D. of Ravni.

  G9.4. Hadassah, married R. Eliezer Landau, A.B.D. Turbin. (See Landau Family Pedigree — Chapter X.)

G7.2. R. Israel of Lvov, died in 1730.

G7.3. R. Zvi Hirsch Harif, A.B.D. Jaworow, died 1737.

G7.4. Wife of R. Naftali Hirsch Ashkenazi, A.B.D. Kobly and then of Lvov, died in 1712.

G8.1. R. Israel Ashkenazi, A.B.D. Kobly, Tiktin and Lublin. He
married the daughter of R. Baruch Rappoport of Furth.

G8.2. R. Zvi Hirsch surnamed Halberstadt, where he was A.B.D.,
married Yente, the daughter of R. Simha Rappoport. He
was the author of Responsa entitled *Ateret Tzvi*, published
in Lvov in 1804. Other Responsa can be found in *Makom
Shmuel* and *Keneset Yechezkiel*. He wrote numerous approbations to books of his contemporaries. He died in Halberstadt in 1747.

G9.1. R. Solomon Dov Halberstadt, A.B.D. Glogau. He married
the daughter of R. Jacob Joshua of Cracow (author of
Pnei Yehoshua).

G10. R. Aaron Joshua Elijah Halberstadt, A.B.D. Koenigs-
berg and later of Ravitz. He wrote a number of approbations and left a manuscript of Novellae. He died
in 1846.

G9.2. R. Abraham Halberstadt, A.B.D. Ravitz.

G9.3. R. Samuel Halberstadt, A.B.D. Hagenau, and later Dayan
of Halberstadt.

G9.4. R. Simha Halberstadt, A.B.D. Sokol and Dessau.

G10.1. R. Israel, A.B.D. Sokol.

G10.2. R. Mordecai, A.B.D. Komarno.

G9.5. Wife of R. David of Lublin.

G9.6. R. Naftali Hirsch Halberstadt, A.B.D. Kobly and Dubno.
He died in 1770. He married Frodel, daughter of R. Jacob,
son of R. Isaac Babad. (See Chapter XI — page 406 —
G9.4.)

G10.1. R. Zeev Wolf Halberstadt, A.B.D. Dubno. He married
Ita, daughter of R. Nachman Heilprin, A.B.D. Brest.

G10.2. R. Zvi Jacob, A.B.D. Podkamin, married Reizel,
daughter of R. Isaac Horowitz (known as the "Hamburger" — See Chapter XVI).

G10.3. R. Dovber, A.B.D. Meseritz.

G11. R. Isaac Zvi.

G12. Wife of R. Naftali Hirsch Katz (See Chapter V —
Branch B — G8.4/9.2/10/11.3/12/13).

G10.4. R. Moses, A.B.D. Satanow, married the daughter of
R. Isaac, son of R. Zvi Hirsch Landau (A.B.D. of

Cracow). (See Landau Family Pedigree — Chapter
X — G8.2/9.6.)

G11.1. R. Simha Halberstadt, A.B.D. of Brody, married the
daughter of R. Isaiah, son of R. Meir Horowitz
(A.B.D. Tiktin — See Horowitz Family — Chapter
XVI). R. Isaiah's father-in-law, R. Haim Landau,
was a first cousin to R. Simha's mother. (See Landau Family Pedigree.)

G12.1. R. Aryey Liebus Halberstam, A.B.D. of Tarnograd, died 1838. He married Miriam, daughter of
R. David Ashkenazi, A.B.D. of Tarnograd (a descendant of the Chacham Zvi — See Chapter
XIII).

G13.1. R. Haim, surnamed Halberstam, founder of the
Chassidic Dynasty of Sanz. For his descendants see Chapter XIV.

G13.2. R. Avigdor Halberstam of Dukla, married the
daughter of R. Abraham Haim Horowitz of
Lyzhansk, son of R. Naftali of Ropshitz. (See
Chapter XVI — Branch VII.)

G14.1. Wife of R. Aryey Lieb (her cousin) son of
R. David Halberstam of Keshanov. (See
Chapter XIV — Branch C.)

G14.2. Wife of R. Moses David Teitelbaum of Walowa. (See Chapter XVII.)

G13.3. Wife of R. Joseph Babad, author of the *Minchat
Chinuch*. (See Chapter XI — Branch C.)

G13.4. R. Moses Halberstam, A.B.D. Sborow (Galicia).

G14. Blume Liebe, married R. Haim Eleazar Waks,
A.B.D. successively of Tarnograd, Kalicz (from
1862-81) and Pietrokov (son of R. Abraham
Judah Liebus Waks). He was the author of
Nefesh Chaya, published in Pietrokov in
1876-7.

Rabbi Waks was born in Tarnograd in 1822
and died in 1889. He married twice and had
issue from both wives.[14]

G15.1. Riva, married R. Simha Shnor.

G15.2. Esther married 1) R. Azriel HaKohen
        Bloss and 2) R. Liebish (Liebus) Berliner
        or Warsaw. (See Chapter XII — Branch
        C — G9.2/10.1/11.3/12.1/13.1.)
        They had issue, descendants of whom live
        in Israel today.

G15.3. Yota, married R. Moses Frivess.

G15.4. Gitel, married 1) R. Eliezer Baumgold and
        2) R. Naftali Unger.

G15.5. Rikel, married 1) R. Mendel Auerbach
        and 2) R. Mendel Baumgarten. They per-
        ished in the Holocaust.

G15.6. R. Abraham Moses Waks, married Zviah,
        daughter of R. Jacob Engelman.

G15.7. Jochebed, married R. Uri son of R. Zuss-
        man Eybeschutz of Pietrokov. (See Chap-
        ter XI — G7.4/8/9/10/11.2.)

G15.8. Sarah, married R. Joseph (1878-1936) son
        of R. Menachem (died in 1917) and suc-
        ceeded his father as Admur of Amshinov
        in 1917.

    G16.1. R. Jacob David, died in Warsaw in 1942.
            He and his family perished in the Holo-
            caust.

    G16.2. R. Isaac Kalish, the Amshinover-New
            York Rebbe (Brooklyn).

G11.2. R. Zvi Hirsch Halberstadt, A.B.D. Constantin, mar-
        ried Judith, daughter of R. Meir (A.B.D. Constan-
        tin), son of R. Jacob Emden (See Descendants of
        Chacham Zvi Ashkenazi — Chapter XIII — G9.14
        /10.2). He succeeded his father-in-law on the lat-
        ter's death.

    G12. R. Isaac Halberstadt, A.B.D. Constantin, died in
          1838.

    G13. Beila, married R. Jehiel Michael Auerbach (1785-
          1856), A.B.D. Korima, son of R. Menachem Men-
          del Auerbach.[15]

        G14. R. Meshullam Zusia Isaac Auerbach, A.B.D.

Talomitz, married Sterna Rachel, daughter of
R. Jacob Israel Twersky (Rabbi of Cherkassi).
He was born in 1819 and died in 1882. She died
in 1845. His second wife was the daughter of
R. Haim Hager of Kossov. R. Twersky was the
son of the founder of the Twersky Dynasty, R.
Mordecai of Chernobyl.

G15. R. Mordecai Dov (1839-1903), (adopted the
surname Twersky), Admur of Hornistopol,
married Reitze (died 1918), daughter of R.
Haim Halberstam of Sanz (See Chapter
XIV — G14.8). He was the author of *Emek
She'elah* (Pietrokov 1906), *Chibur Leta-
harah, Turei Zahav* (Jerusalem 1936), *Emet
Hachochmah* (Satmar 1928), *Peleh Yo'etz,*
and edited *Emet Hatefillah* by his grandfather, R. Jacob Israel Twersky.

G16.1. R. Aaron Elimelech Shnieur Zalman
Twersky of Krosna in Galicia (1862-
1924), married the daughter of R.
Moses Horowitz of Rozvadov, son of R.
Eliezer Horowitz of Dzikov. (See Chapter XVI — Branch VII — G14.1/15.6/
16.5.)

G17.1. R. Moses Twersky of Krosna was born
in 1895 and perished in the Holocaust. He married the daughter of R.
Ezekiel Rabinowitz of Radomsk. (See
Chapter IV — Branch K.)

G17.2. Beila, married R. Simeon Alter,
A.B.D. Skavin, son of R. Simha
Frankel-Teomin. (See Chapter IV —
Branch H — G12.2/13.2/14.4/15.1.)

G16.2. R. Haim Moses Twersky (1866-1933)
of Hornistopol, married the daughter of
R. Nahum Twersky of Rotmistrovka.

G16.3. R. Benzion Judah Lieb Twersky of
Hornistopol (1868-1951), married the
daughter of R. Isaac Joel Rabinowitz of

Kantikoziba. (See Chapter XV.) He
was successively at Hornistopol, Kiev,
Antwerp, Tel Aviv, Chicago.

G17.1. R. Jacob Israel Twersky, Admur
Hornistopol — Milwaukee, married
the daughter of R. Benzion Halberstam of Bobov. (See Chapter XIV —
Branch B — G14.2/15.3/16.1/17.1.)

G17.2. R. Menachem Nahum Twersky, author of *Midor el dor,* published in Tel
Aviv in 1967.

G17.3. R. Moses Meshullam Zusia Twersky,
died in 1920, married the daughter of
R. Simha Issachar Dov Halberstam.
(See Chapter XIV — Branch A —
G15.4.)

G16.4. R. Baruch Dov Twersky of Kalinkowitz
and Vienna (1875-1925), married the
daughter of R. Solomon Zalmina of
Roshkov. (See Chapter XV — Heschel
Family — G10.1/11.1/12.1/13.3/14.5.)

G11.3. Elke, married R. Judah, A.B.D. Wladowa, son of
R. Joseph Landau. (See Chapter VII — Branch A
— G6.2/7.2/8.3/9.1.)

G11.4. R. Ezekiel,[16] surnamed Halberstam, married the
daughter of R. Menachem Mendel Rubin of Linsk
(father of the founder of the Ropshitz Chassidic
Dynasty — See Chapter XVI).

G12. R. Zvi Hirsch Halberstam, A.B.D. of Kosiatyn, married Deborah, daughter of R. Haim David, son of
R. Eliakim Getzel Margolioth. (See Margolioth
Family Pedigree — Chapter VII — G6.2/7.4/8.4/
9.2/10.2/11.2/12.3.)

G13.1. R. Getzel Halberstam, A.B.D. Zbariz.

G13.2. R. Moses Lipa of Brody, married Pesha, daughter of R. David Haim Brecher.

G14.1. Anna Sarah Halberstam, unmarried, died in
Philadelphia in 1894.

G14.2. Zvi Hirsch (Harry) Halberstam, born in Brody in 1867, was the only son and immigrated to the U.S.A., arriving in Philadelphia on January 3, 1891. The trip from Bremen to the United States took him no less than six months and two days. He married in 1894 to Sarah, daughter of David Horowitz, in Philadelphia. They settled in Johnsonburg, Pennsylvania, where they operated a dry goods store. They had seven children. After a brief period in Springfield, Massachusetts, following World War I, the family settled in Torrington, Connecticut where Harry was in the automobile business until his retirement in the late 1920's. He died there in 1945 and his wife died in 1949.

G15.1. Morris L. Halberstam, 1896-1963, married Maye Gaber in 1923.

G16.1. Doreen, born in 1925, married in 1950 to Seymour Cyge. Their sons: Richard (born in 1951) and Charles (born in 1953).

G16.2. Betsy, born in 1930, married in 1954 to Marvin Deutsch. Their adopted daughter is Caren.

G15.2. Dr. Charles A. Halberstam, 1898-1950, B.A. (1923) and M.D. (1927). He married Blanche Levy in 1929. He practiced in New York and taught at the Flower and Fifth Avenue Hospitals in New York, and served in the U.S. Army in both World Wars.

G16.1. Dr. Michael Joseph Halberstam, born in 1932, B.A. (Harvard 1953), M.D. (Boston University 1957). He married in 1958 and later divorced in 1974. There are two adopted children, Charles and Eban. He was the author of *The Pills in Your Life* and is a frequent contributor to medical journals and national magazines. The family resides in Washington, D.C.

G16.2. David L. Halberstam, born in 1934, graduated from Harvard, B.A. in 1955. In 1960 he was with the Washington Bureau of the New York Times and the following year the correspondent to the Congo and to Vietnam in 1962. In 1964 he shared the Pulitzer Prize for Journalism for his reporting of the Vietnam War and he also received the George Polk Memorial Award for Foreign Reporting. In 1962 he received the Page One Award. He was also the New York Times correspondent to Paris and Warsaw, where in 1965 he met and married the Polish actress, Elzbieta Czyzewska (Tchizevska). They resided in New York City. He was the author of *The Noblest Roman, The Making of a Quagmire* (1965), *Ho, One Very Hot Day*, (1967), *The Unfinished Odyssey of Robert Kennedy,* and *The Best and the Brightest,* and is a frequent contributor to national magazines and a lecturer at colleges and universities.

G15.3. Betty Halberstam (1899-1974), unmarried, worked as an assistant clerk of the Lichfield Connecticut Court and died in Torrington.

G15.4. Eugene Halberstam, born in 1900, worked with his father and brother, Morris, in the automobile business and married in 1925 to Edythe Pincus of Torrington. In his later years he worked for the Metropolitan Life Insurance Company and retired in 1959. They live in Tucson, Arizona.

G16.1. David Halberstam, born in 1926, served in the United States Navy in World

War II. In 1950 he received his B.S. and his M.S. the following year from Northwestern University. In 1952 he married Joan Kaplan in Danbury, Connecticut and he resides now with his family in Spring Valley, New York. He is currently the Director of the Corporate Financial Analyses Department of the Singer Company, and before that was the Vice-President and Controller of the Burt Art-Randall Division of Textron in 1970-1971, and was with Union Carbide from 1951 to 1970, becoming Product Manager of their nonwoven products in 1969-1970. Besides his experience in financial analysis and control, marketing and engineering, he is the holder of two patents. Their children are Michael Harry (born 1953), Robert Charles (born 1955) and Nancy Esther (born 1959).

G16.2. Libby Halberstam, born in 1927, married Harold Kotok in Danbury, Connecticut in 1946. Their children: Sherry, born in 1947, received her B.A. in 1969 and married Robert M. Cohen in 1971; Jannifer, born in 1949, received her B.A. in 1971; Irvene, born in 1951; and Bethany, born in 1960.

G15.5. Bertha Halberstam, 1903-1965, unmarried, lived and died in Torrington.

G15.6. Lillian Halberstam, born in 1907, married Dr. T. J. Hirschberg in 1950. He died in 1961 and they had no issue.

G15.7. Laura Halberstam, born in 1910, graduated from Central Connecticut College in 1949 and is currently a public schoolteacher in West Hartford, Connecticut. She married in 1946 to Max Rubin. Their daughter, Sara Elizabeth, was born in

1951, received her B.A. in 1973 from
Cornell University and married Phillip
Saffrey in 1974.

G14.3. Gitel (1865-1941), married to Morthre
Hersch Rottenstreich. He was a Hebrew
teacher in Galicia and they emigrated to the
United States in 1908. The couple had elev-
en children, only a few of whom survived
to adulthood. She remarried later in life.

G15.1. Tessie Cohen Freed, died in 1971. She
had one daughter, who died in 1973 and
left two sons, Glen and Gerald Guthrie,
married with family.

G15.2. Pearl Konigsberg, died at the age of thirty,
had two sons and four daughters, married
with grandchildren.

G15.3. Lou Roth (shortened from Rottenstreich),
of Cleveland, Ohio. His son is Joel.

G15.4. Clare, married to Harry Bliden. They live
in Florida.

SILBERFELD-RUBINSTEIN-BUBER-SHLICHTER FAMILY PEDIGREE

G11.1. R. Isaiah Zvi Schiff,[17] married Chaya, daughter of
R. Baruch Frankel-Teomim. (See Chapter IV —
G6.4/7.1/8.1/9.2/10.3/11.8.)

G12.1. Reali, married R. Samuel Zangwill,[18] A.B.D.
Przemysl, son of R. Aaron Nathan Heller, A.B.D.
Kreshov and Frampol.

G13.1. R. Isaiah Zvi Heller, A.B.D. Frampol, published the *Ateret Zekeinim* by his great-grandfather, R. Baruch Frankel-Teomim (Josefow,
1866). He died in 1905.

G13.2. R. Zeev Dov Heller.

G13.3. Jochebed Rebecca (died in 1917), marred 1)
R. Samuel Hakohen Weichman of Kreshov
(died in 1892), and 2) R. Benjamin Krischer
of Sanz.

G14.1. Gitel (died in 1932), married R. Abraham Shalom (of Stropkov), son of R. Ezekiel Halberstam (of Sieniawa). (See Halberstam Chassidic Dynasty — Chapter XIV — Branch A.) He remarried her niece, Chaya Shlichter (see below).

G14.2. Hena (died in Israel, Kfar HaRoeh in 1943), married R. David Shlichter (died in 1941) of Komarno.

G15.1. R. Samuel Haim, perished in 1942, Dayan (Judge) in Komarno.

G15.2. R. Baruch Shlichter, born in 1896, (adopted the surname Yosher), first Chief Rabbi of Acco. He lives in Jerusalem and is the author of some twenty-one small books (in Hebrew) on various subjects, including the history of Komarno, entitled *Beit Komarno* (1974).

G16.1. Nahum Yosher.
G16.2. Gabriel Shlichter.
G16.3. Mayijah, married Moshe Shelhon.

G15.3. Chaya, second wife of R. Abraham Shalom Halberstam of Stropkov. She perished with her only son Joseph Yom Tov in Auschwitz in 1942.

G15.4. R. Israel Joseph Shlichter, perished in Tarnow with his wife, Leah, daughter of R. Haim Weichman of Komarno, and their children, Rebecca and Zeev Dov.

G15.5. Rachel.

G15.6. Toyba Matil, married Eliezer Afner.

G15.7. Mindel Nechama, married R. David Menachem Meinish Babad. (See Chapter XI — Branch D.)

G12.2. Rebecca, wife of R. Solomon Zaly Silberfeld of Cracow.[19]

G13.1. Reizel (1848-1918), second wife of R. Mordecai, son of R. David Zvi Rubinstein. His first wife was Pesel, daughter of R. Jacob Jokel (son of R. Zeev Wolf, son of R. Joshua, son of R. Nathan A.B.D. White Field) Horowitz of Brody. (See Horowitz Family Chapter XVI — G10.9/11.3/12.2/13.2.) He was the son of R. Solomon Rubinstein mentioned below.

G13.2. Gitel (Augusta), wife of Naftali Hirsch (Horace) Rubinstein, son of R. Aryey Lieb Rubinstein, mentioned below.

G13.3. Chaya Silberfeld, married Liebish Splitter, a furrier in Scheveningen, Holland.

G14.1. Haim Splitter.
G14.2. Twins, David and Azriel of Antwerp.

G13.4. Wolf Ber (Bernhard) Silberfeld. He lived in Coleraine, Australia, eighty miles from Melbourne, where he was described as a sheepfarmer and merchant, as well as being an occultist. His niece, Helena Rubinstein, lived with him when she first arrived in Australia.

G14. Eva, only child married Louis Levy. She died in 1947.

G15. Theo. H. Levy, married in 1922 to Doris Sampson. As a young man in 1919 after World War I in which he served as Captain, he returned to Australia via New York where he was met by and stayed with Helena Rubinstein for a short while. They had a son Keith of the Royal Australian Navy who was killed in action in 1945, and a daughter Sheila, married, with issue.

G13.5. Aryey Lieb (Louis) Silberfeld, lived in Merino, Australia, died childless.

G13.6. John Silberfeld, died in 1913. He emigrated about 1885 to Australia, but later returned to Europe where he settled in Antwerp about the turn of the century. He married Caroline Weiner, died in 1918.

G14.1. Jack, died unmarried.
G14.2. Helena Sardeau (1899-1969)[20] married

George Biddle. She was a painter, graphic artist and author. Her sculptures are in the Whitney Museum of American Art, the Metropolitan Museum of Art, the Smithsonian Institution, the Tel Aviv Museum, and others. She came to the United States in 1914 from Antwerp and was naturalized in 1933.

G15. Michael Biddle, born in 1934 in New York. Married to Elizabeth Gurbeck, they have no issue.

G14.3. Matilda (Tilly), married Kane in New York.

G15. John Kane, unmarried, in Panama.

G14.4. Regina, married Johler, New York.

G15.1. Andrew, died young.
G15.2. John Silson, adopted his mother's maiden name. He was an M.D. and died in New York in 1972 without issue.
G15.3. Sylvette, married Howard Meyer, (lawyer), in New York. Their children are Jonathan, Franklin and Andrew.

G14.5. Victor Silson, born in 1895, settled in the United States and lives in New York. Like his wife Mala Kolin, his second cousin, he was also part of the "family corporation" of the Helena Rubinstein cosmetics firm. They have no issue.

G11.2. Gitel Schiff, married R. Solomon Rubinstein (son of R. Mordecai of Zolkiev), a prominent publisher in the town of Zolkiev. His father was a printer in partnership with Mayerhofer until 1797 when he and his son Solomon continued on their own. He wrote an unpublished manuscript entitled *Kiddush HeChadash* and is mentioned several times in the Responsa work *Shoel U'Meishiv* by R. Joseph Saul Halevi Nathanson. (See Chapter XII Branch E — G9.2/10.5/11.2.)

G12.1. R. Aryey Lieb Rubinstein.

G13. Naftali Hirsch (Horace) Rubinstein, married his fourth cousin, Gitel (Augusta) Silberfeld (see above G11.1/12.2/13.2). Through their daughter, Helena, are descended the family of the cosmetics firm of Helena Rubinstein.

G14.1. Helena,[21] the eldest of eight daughters was born in Cracow in 1872 and attended the University there and later spent a few years studying Medicine at the University of Zurich. Having abandoned her medical career, she decided to leave Cracow and its prospective suitors in marriage and went to join her uncles in Australia, who had already settled there about 1885. She arrived there in 1890 with a jar of face cream that had been supplied by her mother and made for the family by their Hungarian physician, Dr. Lykusky. Initially she lived with her uncle Bernhard Silberfeld and his wife in Coleraine, some eighty miles from Melbourne. Here she learned to speak English and attended school. After some time Helena decided to move to the "big city" of Melbourne where she hoped to open a shop to sell her "mother's cream" which was shipped out to her from Cracow. She had been struck by the poor complexion of the Australian women due to the constant exposure to sunlight and was convinced that her cream would be the answer to their problem. At the turn of the century she was living in St. Kilda where she worked as a café waitress and invited her two sisters, Manka and Ceska, and also Dr. Lykusky to join her in producing the cream locally.

The next step in expansion was to sail for London in 1894 so that by 1902 she was said to have accumulated $100,000 in capital. Here she married in 1908 to the Amer-

ican-born newspaper reporter, Edward J.
Titus (originally Morgenbesser) who had
been stationed in Melbourne and then also
went to London. The same year she was
named the best dressed woman of the year
and lived with her husband and a private
Viennese woman doctor in the Mayfair man-
sion that once belonged to the third Marquess of Salisbury. In 1909 her first son, Roy,
was born and three years later, Horace, the
child of a brief reconciliation of her marriage which eventually ended in divorce. In
1913 the family moved to Paris and two years
later, as a result of the World War, she was
persuaded to return with her husband to the
U.S.A. They arrived in New York in 1915
where she opened a Maison de Beaute in
Manhattan. In 1916 her husband separated
from her and, following the Armistice in
1918, he returned to Europe. She visited him
frequently in Paris where he published a literary magazine in English *This Quarter,*
making the transatlantic journey four or five
times a year.

Back in the U.S.A. Helena began to open
beauty salons across the country but met
with much opposition and rivalry with the
already established Elizabeth Arden. In
1928 she sold two-thirds of her business to
Lehman Brothers and went into semi-retire-
ment. She was now fifty-six years old. Following the failure of Lehman Brothers, she
was able to buy back control for less than
a quarter of the amount she had sold for, a
move which was the best she ever made in
a business enterprise. In 1938 she divorced
Edward Titus and the same year married
Prince Artchie Gourelli-Tchkonia of Georgia
(U.S.S.R.). He was twenty years her junior.
They spent much of their time in Paris until
his death in 1955. Three years later she was

saddened again by the death of her younger
son Horace.

During her married years Helena, who
was known as Miss Rubinstein, the Madame,
or Princess Gourelli as she liked to be called,
ran seven homes in France, London, Buenos
Aires, Mexico, New York and Greenwich,
which were museum-like with priceless
pieces and paintings. She created the Helena Rubinstein Foundation in 1953 which
gave funds to health, medical research and
child rehabilitation organizations. It also
supported the America-Israel Foundation
and provided Israelis with art scholarships.
In Israel she opened up a Helena Rubinstein
factory and also attended the official opening of the Helena Rubinstein Pavilion in Tel
Aviv in 1959.

Although she controlled the corporation
and almost completely ran the lives of her
employees which included members of her
family, she was mainly concerned for the
betterment of her relatives by supporting
their education and giving them positions in
her corporation. In this way it was more of
a "family affair." Thus her two sisters who
originally joined her in Australia occupied
positions in London (where Ceska was the
President) and in New York (where Manka
helped open the business in 1915). In New
York her nephew, Oscar Kolin, was the executive vice-president and his sister, Mala
Rubinstein, was her "heiress apparent" and
later, in 1970, became executive vice-president. Another niece, Marcelle Beilin, and a
second cousin, Leah Yarcho, managed the
corporation in Buenos Aires. Two other second cousins, Regina Garrett (and her husband) and her brother, Mark Rubinstein,
managed the Australian branch. Her son,
Roy Titus, was the chairman of the board

SILBERFELD-RUBINSTEIN-BUBER-SHLICHTER FAMILY

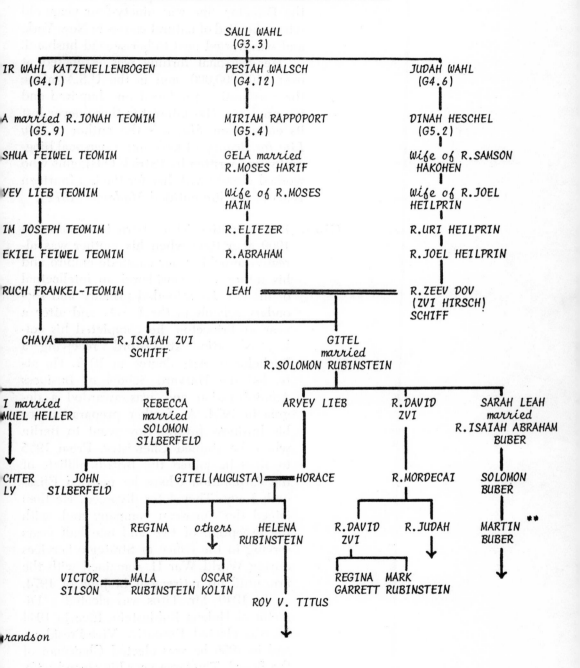

SAUL WAHL
(G3.3)

IR WAHL KATZENELLENBOGEN   PESIAH WALSCH   JUDAH WAHL
(G4.1)   (G4.12)   (G4.6)

A married R.JONAH TEOMIM   MIRIAM RAPPOPORT   DINAH HESCHEL
(G5.9)   (G5.4)   (G5.2)

SHUA FEIWEL TEOMIM   GELA married   Wife of R.SAMSON
                                 R.MOSES HARIF   HAKOHEN

VEY LIEB TEOMIM   Wife of R.MOSES   Wife of R.JOEL
                                 HAIM   HEILPRIN

IM JOSEPH TEOMIM   R.ELIEZER   R.URI HEILPRIN

EKIEL FEIWEL TEOMIM   R.ABRAHAM   R.JOEL HEILPRIN

RUCH FRANKEL-TEOMIM   LEAH ════════════ R.ZEEV DOV
                                                       (ZVI HIRSCH)
                                                       SCHIFF

CHAYA ══════ R.ISAIAH ZVI   GITEL
              SCHIFF   married
                                      R.SOLOMON RUBINSTEIN

I married   REBECCA   ARYEY LIEB   R.DAVID   SARAH LEAH
MUEL HELLER   married   ZVI   married
                     SOLOMON   R.ISAIAH ABRAHAM
                     SILBERFELD   BUBER

CHTER   JOHN   GITEL(AUGUSTA)══════HORACE   R.MORDECAI   SOLOMON
LY   SILBERFELD   BUBER

         REGINA   others   HELENA   R.DAVID   R.JUDAH   MARTIN   **
                           RUBINSTEIN   ZVI   BUBER

VICTOR ══ MALA   OSCAR   REGINA MARK
SILSON   RUBINSTEIN KOLIN   GARRETT RUBINSTEIN

                           ROY V. TITUS

randson

and on her death on April 1, 1965, became
the Director. She was ninety-four years old
when she died of natural causes in New York,
and was buried next to her second husband.

Her personal fortune was estimated at
over $100,000,000, and in the U.S.A. alone
the corporation produced one hundred and
ten products. Her interest in these never lost
its enthusiasm. She was the author of *My
Life for Beauty* (1966) and a personal biography was written by Patrick O'Higgins who
worked closely with her for the last fourteen
years of her life entitled *Madame* (1971).

G15.1. Roy Valentine Titus, born in London in
1909 at a time when his mother was already launching her cosmetic empire and
his father was considered an intellectual
of his era. He attended primary and secondary schools in the U.S.A. and after a
year at Princeton, he completed his college education at Oxford, receiving a
Bachelor of Arts degree in 1932. He attended the Harvard School of Business
Administration and was awarded a degree in 1934. As further preparation for
his business future, Roy went to Berlin
where he studied Chemistry. From 1935
to 1938 he joined the British affiliate of
the corporation where he married Elizabeth Levy. They later divorced. He then
joined the American company and, with
the exception of two and one half years
serving in the Office of Strategic Services
during World War II, remained with the
firm until his retirement in June of 1974.

In 1940, Mr. Titus was elected a Director of Helena Rubinstein, Inc.; in 1944
he was elected Executive Vice-President,
and in 1956 he was elected Chairman of
the Board. The same year his second wife,

Marie Behr, whom he had married two
years earlier, died. He remarried again in
1957 having an only daughter from this
marriage. On the death of his mother in
1965, Mr. Titus became the Director of
the firm and in 1970, he was elected
Chairman of the Executive Committee.
His fourth marriage was to Niuta Grod-
zins and they currently live in New York.
Following his retirement, he established
the Roy V. Titus Company on Fifth Avenue in Manhattan.

Roy Titus always maintained a warm relationship with the many employees of Helena Rubinstein, Inc. Like his mother before him, he supervised the numerous facets of his firm with an "open-door" policy and was
always available for conferences or consultations with his associates. He
believed that strong executives make a successful company and once he put
a man in a job he respected him and relied on his judgment in his area of
responsibility. Although he had regard for lines of authority in business,
Mr. Titus did not stand on ceremony. He maintained an unusual direct,
straightforward and honest manner toward all employees in every echelon.
Known to be an excellent judge of people, Roy Titus never let his personal
feelings affect his business relationships.

A man with a sharp, "uncluttered" mind and a keen sense of humor, the
retired Chairman of the Executive Committee of Helena Rubinstein, Inc. is at
the same time a sensitive, gentle person. He still is known for his concern
with the personal triumphs and tragedies of most of his former firm's employees. This human side of Roy Titus inspires a loyalty and closeness felt
by all those who know him or have worked for him.

His bright, alert mind makes Mr. Titus seem an impatient person at
times. He has been known to become restless if a conference wastes time
getting to the point or if a conversation wanders from the business at hand.
His ability to think matters through swiftly enables Roy Titus to make decisions, yet he often weighs those decisions carefully and long before acting on them.

Strongly involved in civic interests, Mr. Titus serves on the Board of the
Children's Blood Foundation, The Film Society of Lincoln Center and the
Board of Governors of the Tel Aviv Museum. He is also Chairman of the
Board of the Helena Rubinstein Foundation.[22]

G16. Helena Titus, born in 1958.

G15.2. Horace Titus, born in London in 1912. He
came with his family to New York in 1915.

He was married twice; his first wife, Evelyn Schmitka, bore him a son, Barry, and a daughter, Toby. They married and had issue. Horace died in April 1958.

G14.2. Pauline Rubinstein, second child, married Hirschberg and lived and died in Paris.

G15. Marcelle, lived in Buenos Aires where she was part of the family concern, but later settled in Paris. She married 1) Beilin, and had two sons, and 2) Hose De Barros (Paris). Her two sons have issue.

G14.3. Rosalia (Rosa), third child, lived in Poland where she married Oppenheim. Three children perished in the Holocaust.

G15. Gisele, married Dr. Dezajac, M.D., Buenos Aires. They have two children.

G14.4. Regina, fourth child, married Morris Kolin. She perished in the Holocaust.

G15.1. Oscar Kolin, New York Helena Rubinstein Cosmetics. Married Berte Ancel.

G16.1. Diane (Didi), married Corbin, divorced. Has two adopted children.

G16.2. Jacqueline, married 1) Levin and 2) John Herrmann (divorced).

G17. Edward Levin (New York).

G15.2. Henry Kolin, Toronto, married Meta Guttman.

G16.1. Mary, married Dr. Michael Levitt, M.D.

G16.2. Twins, Michael and Pamella, married Michael Sendrovitch (Toronto).

G15.3. Mala,[23] born in Cracow and as a teenager went to her aunt in Paris, where she was raised and trained from her youth in the cosmetics field as an apprentice to her aunt, "Madame Rubinstein." She later took charge of the Paris Salon until the mid thirties when she was needed to help in New York. Her first project was to learn "all" about the American woman and the American market. This she accomplished by criss-crossing the country—speaking with thousands of women to discover for herself the American woman's beauty needs, interests, desires and the many factors influencing the cosmetic market. As the Helena Rubinstein company grew in the United States, Miss Rubinstein was active in every area of management. Special assignment and "keeping-in-touch" trips took her more often to distant points. No matter how demanding the pressures of business, she was able to contribute most meaningfully through her expert knowledge of cosmetics. For example: creating special camouflage make-up for disfigured servicemen who were awaiting completion of plastic surgery; developing grooming and beauty programs for hospitalized women; working with the blind on practical make-up techniques. She lectured untiringly at schools, universities and women's organizations. She was, and is, in constant demand to speak on television programs consequently reaching millions of women nationally and internationally.

By the time Helena Rubinstein died in 1965, she had passed her scepter of responsibility to those who would lead the company to even greater heights. Miss Rubinstein, her "heiress apparent" became "cosmetic queen," a member of the Board of Directors and assumed the title of Senior Vice-President. In 1970 she was appointed Executive Vice-President.

She received the Humanitarian Award

from Children's Asthma Research Institute and Hospital and was always concerned with youth and education. She was chosen by Harper's Bazaar as one of 100 women in the United States "Most In Touch With Our Times"; was awarded by the Greek Government the Order of Merit which had previously been awarded to Madame Curie; has received the Cosmy Award of Achievement from Cosmetic Fair and the Golden Order of Merit from the Japanese Red Cross; and in celebration of its Golden Anniversary, the London Chelsea Flower Show bestowed upon Miss Rubinstein the singular distinction of naming a rose in her honor. She is the author of *Mala Rubinstein Book of Beauty*. She married her second cousin, Victor Silson. (See above — G13.6/14.5.) They have no children.

G15.4. Leon, perished in the Holocaust.

G15.5. Rachel, married Shalev, Israel.

G14.5. Stella Rubinstein, fifth child, married 1) Oscestowitcz and 2) De Bruchard. She was President of the French Corporation.

G15. Andre Oscestowitcz, Paris.

G14.6. Cecilia (Ceska, Cesiu), sixth child, born about 1883 and died about 1967. She lived in London and was married to an Australian, Cooper. They managed the family corporation in England, and had an adopted child.

G14.7. Manka (Manya), seventh child, born in 1885, lived variously in Australia, France and the United States. She, together with her sister Helena, opened the business in New York in 1914. She now lives in New York. She married 1) Vincent Czerwinsky and had a son; 2) Bernard Bernard (Immerdauler, of Vienna); and 3) Ephraim P. Adir, who died.

G15. John Bernard, New Orleans, married twice.

G16. Patricia, married Fred DeLaura (Long Island). Their children are Manka and Ricky.

G14.8. Erna Rubinstein, youngest child, born 1886, lives in New Jersey. She married Max Michelson, socialist writer, lecturer and contributor to Yiddish periodicals.

G15.1. Horace Michelson, born 1919, lawyer in New York. He married Gertrude Rosen. Their daughters: Martha (1953-1973) and Barbara, born in 1955.

G15.2. Henry Michelson, born 1909, M.D. in Paterson, New Jersey. He married Marion Duester. Their children are Robert and Janet, who married Jacques Reed (Bethesda, Maryland). Their children are Jacky and Jeremy.

G15.3. Micheline (Lee), married Max Liebman, Reston, Virginia. Their sons are Michael and George.

G15.4. Gertrude, married August Eckel, Chicago.

G16.1. Margaret, married Robert Goertz, Princeton, New Jersey.

G16.2. John, married Barbara and has a son born in 1973.

G12.2. R. David Zvi Rubinstein[24] of Zolkiev, married Pesel, daughter of R. Jacob Jokel Horowitz of Brody. (See Chapter XVI — G10.9/11.3/12.2/ 13.2.) They had one child.

G13. R. Mordecai Rubinstein, born 1844 in Zolkiev. He married 1) the daughter of R. Israel Kahane, A.B.D. Zolkiev, and had two sons and a daughter. She died in 1876, and he remarried 2) Reizel Silberfeld, his fourth cousin (see above G11.1/12.2 /13.1). They had three sons and one daughter. After his first marriage he settled in Lvov where he published and sold books, including the publication of the works of his great-grandfather, R. Schiff. He was also the Reader of the Law (Baal Koreh) in the Synagogue of R. Joseph Saul Halevi Nathanson (mentioned above G11.2), the Chief Rabbi there with whom he was a close associate. After his second marriage, R. Mordecai settled in Cracow from where in 1907 he went to Palestine and settled in Jerusalem. Here he published *Nitei Ne'emanah* in 1908, which contains full details of his family genealogy. He died in 1917, and his wife, Reizel, died the following year.

He was also the author of *Givat Shaul* published in Lvov in 1875; *Ayeh Sofer,* published in Cracow in 1884; *Geviat Ari,* published in Cracow in 1880; *Derush Leprakim,* published in Cracow in 1889, (reprinted by his son, R. Judah Rubinstein, with an appendix *Kontras,* New York 1972); *Commentary on the Passover Haggadah,* published in Cracow in 1882; and *Mar Deror.*

The children from his first wife are:

G14.1. Salomon Rubinstein, socialist and editor of a Zionist paper in Brünn (Austria). He lived in St. Garlin, Switzerland. He married and had issue.

G14.2. R. Gedalliah Zvi Rubinstein,[25] A.B.D. Zbariz from 1893 for some thirty years until his death in 1926. (He was born in 1865). He married twice, secondly to a daughter of R. Meir Hakohen Glass, A.B.D. Rohatyn. He wrote *Mispar Gadol,* published in Cracow in 1882 and was one of the founders of the Mizrahi organization in East Galicia.

G15.1. Sarah, married R. Moses Alter Rotler, A.B.D. Tarnoruda.

G15.2. R. Israel David Rubinstein, A.B.D. Tomashov-Marzovietsk 1890-1926, married the daughter of R. Isaac Meir Kanal, Chief Rabbi of Warsaw. He was a lecturer in

Talmudic Studies at the Rabbinical Seminary *Tachkemoni* in Warsaw.

G16.1. Professor Abraham Rubinstein (Bar Ilan University, Israel), born in 1912, professor of Chassidism, married and has issue.

G16.2. Zahava, married Aaron Birenfeld (Tel Aviv).

G16.3. Others perished.

G15.3. Dreizel, settled in Jerusalem and married R. Joseph Joshua Lauber. Their children adopted the surname Eliav.

G16.1. Pinhas Eliav, Ambassador of Israel to the United Nations as Director of Political Affairs.

G16.2. Professor Mordecai Eliav (Bar Ilan University, Israel), Professor of Jewish History. He married twice.

G15.4. Rivka.

G15.5. Pessiah.

G15.6. Lieb.

G15.7. Meir.

G14.3. R. Abraham Haim Rubinstein, perished in the Holocaust.

G14.4. Chaya, married R. Joel Ehrman of Rava-Rushka, perished.

G15.1. Shifra, married Joseph Joshua Lieberman, son of Shalom, son of Haim Elijah Lieberman (of Alesk Family).

G15.2. Daughter (in Beersheba).

From his second wife:

G14.5. R. Isaac Rubinstein, 1888-1944, perished with his wife, Dreizel, daughter of Miriam Frankel of Lvov, last Chief Rabbi of Vienna.

G15.1. Simon Rubinstein, chess champion.

G15.2. Rivke, married, lives in Haifa with her family.

G14.6. R. David Zvi Rubinstein, perished.

    G15.1. Rivke (Regina), married Fred Garrett (Australia). She was sent by Helena in 1928 to study in her salon and laboratory until 1938. The following year she left for Paris and in April of 1939 she arrived in Australia to work for the corporation as Managing Director of Australia and New Zealand with her husband. They retired in 1966.[26]

    G15.2. Mordecai (Mark) Rubinstein, manager in Sydney, Australia.

    G15.3. Dr. Baruch Rubinstein of the Educational Department in Israel, died in 1974.

    G15.4. Others perished.

G14.7. R. Naftali Rubinstein, perished, Professor in the Hebrew Gymnasium in Cracow.

G14.8. Leah, married Kalman Blum, perished.

G14.9. R. Judah Rubinstein, born in Cracow in 1898. He studied and married in Jerusalem to Esther, daughter of R. Abraham Menachem Preiss of Jerusalem in 1918. He later settled in Brooklyn, New York in 1922. He was a prominent contributor to many periodicals, author and genealogist.

    G15.1. Leah, 1920-1968, lived in Argentina (she managed Helena Rubinstein in Buenos Aires). She married Jehudah Yarcho. Their daughter is Gitel.

    G15.2. Helena (Chaya), born in 1922, married Jerome Greenberg, (New Jersey). Their daughters are Gail (Gitel) and Michelle (Malka).

    G15.3. Ruth (Rebecca), born in 1931, married Merrit (Moses) Rosenthal, D.D.S. (Staten Island, New York). Their children are Mark (Mordecai) and Gail (Gitel).

G14.10. Stella Rubinstein, Professor of Medieval Art at the Sorbonne in Paris. She married Pro-

fessor Ernest Weil (Paris). They had no issue.

G14.11. Wolf Ber Rubinstein, perished in Cracow.

G12.3. Sarah Leah (Frieda Sarel),[27] married R. Isaiah
        Abraham Buber (died in Lvov in 1870) son of
        R. Joseph Zvi Halevi. The family claimed de-
        scent from the two prominent Rabbis, R. Lip-
        man Halevi Heller (Tosfot YomTov) and R. Ben-
        jamin Aaron (Masa'ot Binyamin).

G13.1. Simha Buber of Lvov.
G13.2. Moses Buber of Lvov.
G13.3. Solomon Buber, [28] Galician scholar and editor
        of Hebrew works, born in Lvov on February 2,
        1827. His father, who was well-versed in Tal-
        mudic literature and Jewish philosophy, taught
        him secular education and obtained profes-
        sional teachers for his religious education. He
        married at twenty to Adele (Udel) and en-
        tered the commercial world becoming "Han-
        delskammerath" and auditor of the Austro-
        Hungarian Bank, the National Bank and the
        Galician Savings Bank. He was also on many
        Jewish community committees in Lvov and
        was one of their leaders for close to half a cen-
        tury. He became a wealthy merchant and
        owned a large estate. During his youth he was
        influenced by the writings of Nahman Kroch-
        mal, S.L. Rappoport and Zunz.

        Being a researcher by nature he became
        particularly attracted to Midrashic literature
        resulting in the commentary on *Pesikta de Rab
        Kahana* published by the Mekize Nirdamim
        Society, Lyck (Lutsk), 1868, and in German
        (Leipzig) in 1884. Other Midrashic works sim-
        ilarly edited appeared between 1883 and 1902
        numbering some fifteen in all. He distin-
        guished himself in other fields as well, includ-
        ing the biography on the grammarian Elias
        Levita, Leipzig, 1856, *Anshei Shem* (biogra-
        phies and epitaphs of the leaders and Rabbis

of Lvov from 1500-1890), Cracow, 1895 and *Kiryah Nisgavah* (biographies of the leading Rabbis of Zolkiev), published Cracow, 1903. He further wrote ten more books between 1885 and 1901 and his knowledge of Jewish history and literature is displayed in the additions to the works of others and his numerous contributions to magazines. For his services he received the title of "Imperial Councillor." He had two sons.

G14. Kalman (Karl) Buber, married and divorced in 1880 and remarried in 1892.

G15.1. Nelly, wife of R. Markus (Mordecai Zeev) Braude, maternal grandson of R. Zvi Hirsch Ornstein of Lvov. (See Chapter XII — Branch E.)

G15.2. Martin Buber,[29] born on February 8, 1878. Because his parents divorced when he was only three years old, he was educated and raised by his grandfather in Lvov where he learned Talmud, literature and the ways of Chassidism whose Rabbis and leaders he became exposed to. At the age of thirteen he drifted away from formal Judaism but remained a deeply religious man. At seventeen he entered the University of Vienna to study philosophy and the history of art, and later at the Universities of Berlin, Zurich and Leipzig. In 1901 he received his Ph.D. in Vienna.

In 1900 at the University of Leipzig, he was first exposed and later became deeply involved in the Zionist movement founded by Theodor Herzl. Buber became the editor of the Zionist journal *Die Welt* in 1901 and later helped found the Judische Verlag (Jewish Publishing House). One of the journalists was a Roman Catholic, Paula Wrinkler (who wrote novels under the pen name of Georg Munk).

They later married, and she converted to Judaism and died in 1958 in Israel.

Buber dropped out of active Zionism after he felt more urgently a need for spiritual revival than the political nationalhood concepts of Herzl. He then devoted his time studying the literature of the Chassidim and their Zaddikim (Sages) and lived among them in Poland. He found their folklore profound in its simplicity and wrote a number of books about them.

After his retreat he again became active in journalism, editing *Der Jude* from 1919-1924 and *Die Kreatur* from 1926-1930 (together with two others). At this time (1923-1933) he was Professor of Comparative Religion at the University of Frankfurt-on-Main. After being dismissed from his post by the Nazis, he settled in Palestine in 1938 where he immediately became Professor at the Hebrew University in Jerusalem. He retired in 1951 and held the title of Professor Emeritus of Social Philosophy at the Hebrew University. The same year he visited the U.S.A. and his lectures here were later published as *Eclipse of God* and *At the Turning*.

The Union Theological Seminary bestowed the Universal Brotherhood Award on him and the Hebrew Union College of Cincinnati, the Honorary Doctor of Letters. Being a non-conformist, he opposed the execution of the Nazi Adolf Eichmann in Israel. On the occasion of his 85th birthday in 1963 about three hundred students staged a torchlight parade to his house, a simple abode in the Talbieh district of Jerusalem. Here he lived with his granddaughter, Barbara Goldschmid as his secretary and housekeeper. At the end of 1963 Buber flew to Amsterdam to receive the $28,000 Erasmus Award, one of Europe's highest prizes. He was also nominated by the late Dag Hammarskjold for a Nobel Prize and some weeks before his death, he received the Freedom of Jerusalem Award. He was the author of over 700 books and papers. His religious philosophies influenced Protestant theologians as well, as Reinhold Niebuhr once called him "the greatest living Jewish philosopher." He believed in religion as an experience and not as a dogma. His death on June 14, 1965 was received throughout the Jewish world with deep regret and tributes were paid to him by leading conservative Rabbis, his disciple and closest friend Professor Shmuel Hugo Bergman, and others, as was reported extensively in the New York Times. He was buried in West Jerusalem, homage being paid by thousands of students, professors, politicians, clergymen, tourists and admirers. He was eulogized by Premier Levi Eshkol and his friend Professor Bergman.

G16. and G17. Two children: a son, Rafael Buber, and a daughter, Mrs. Eva Strauss-Steinitz. They in turn had four children and eight grandchildren.

CHAPTER VIII

Lvov and was also the Head of the Yeshiva. He died there on February 28 (13th Adar), 1660. His name appeared a few times in the Records of the Council of the Four Lands. He is mentioned in the *Eitan HaEzrachi* by R. Abraham, son of R. Israel Jehiel Rappoport (published in Ostrow in 1796) in the year 1645. He married the daughter of R. Benjamin Aaron of Slonik, the author of *Masa'ot Binyamin* and *Seder Mitzvot Nashim.*[3]

G6.   R. Abraham Katzenellenpogen, Dayan in Brest.

G7.1.   Wife of R. Asher, son of R. Saul Gunzburg (See Chapter III— Branch D—G6.2/7.2). He is mentioned in the Responsa *Keneset Yechezkiel* of his brother-in-law when he wrote to him for his opinion of the problem of Agunah (a married woman who wants to remarry but cannot obtain definite proof of her husband's death).

G7.2.   R. Ezekiel Katzenellenpogen was born in 1668 or 1669,[4] he himself having been uncertain of the fact, and grew up in Brest, where he studied under R. Mordecai Susskind son of R. Moses Rothenberg who lived there until about 1691. He was first A.B.D. of the town of Zitel, then A.B.D. Razinai. In 1707 he was called to Keidan and to Altona in 1714 where he served the community for thirty-five years until his death. This last position was secured for him through the efforts of Issachar Kohen, an influential member of the Altona Congregation. In return, Ezekiel later secured the Rabbinate for his son-in-law, R. Jacob Emden, at Keidan. Nevertheless, R. Emden seems to have been prejudiced against R. Ezekiel whom he describes as a man of very low moral character, an ignoramus and a poor preacher.

The Community at the time was under Danish Rule, the salary he was to receive being five hundred kroner from the Altona members, two hundred from the Hamburg members and a smaller amount from the Wandsbeck members over a three-year period. This was recorded in the Community Records in 1713. He married Esther, the daughter of R. Solomon Zalman, who was the son of R. Joel of Brest (the grandson of R. Joel Sirkes, called the *BaCh*). She died in 1748, and was buried in the Königstrasse Cemetery in Altona (Tombstone No. 3072). Her husband was the author of *Keneset Yechezkiel* published in Altona in 1732, *Mayim Yechezkiel* published in 1786, *Tefillot le-Yartzheit* published in 1727, and *Tzava'at*

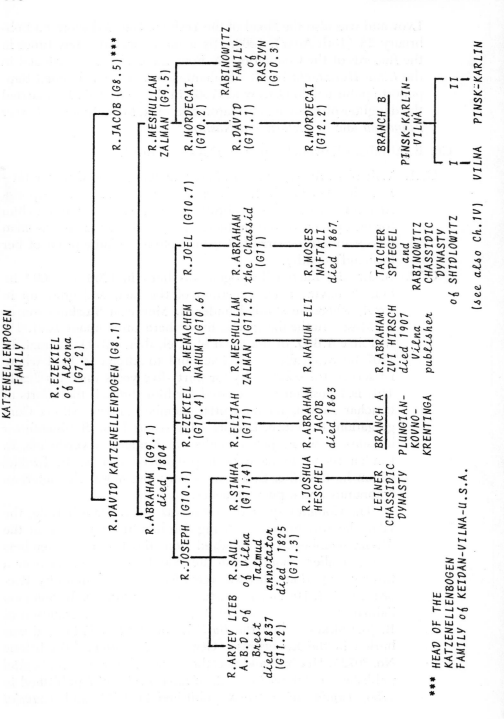

Yechezkiel (His Ethical Will) published in 1750 (and again in 1871 by a descendant—See below G8.1/9.1/10.6/11.2/12/13) and *Me'orer Zikkaron* published in 1727. In his works he mentions a manuscript *Lechem Yechezkiel* which was not published. Another manuscript *Tal Orot* containing precepts about mourning can be found as a supplement to a handwritten Siddur (Prayer-book) which was used by the Jewish Community of Fredericia and dated 1780. He wrote numerous approbations. He died in Altona, July 9 (23rd Tammuz), 1749 and was buried next to his wife (Tombstone No. 3073).

G8.1.   R. David Katzenellenpogen, A.B.D. of Keidan after his father had left for Altona in 1714. His signature in the Records of the Council of the Four Lands appeared in 1751 at the meeting of Mir. Sometime after 1726 the Gaon (R. Elijah) of Vilna, while still a child, studied under him for several months in Keidan, having been brought there by his son, R. Abraham, who had been visiting Vilna and saw the wonder-child prodigy. He died about 1756. He married the daughter of R. Solomon, son of R. Israel (A.B.D. of Birz and Zamocz). R. Solomon's wife was the daughter of R. Meshullam Zalman Neumark, A.B.D. of the Triple Community of Altona-Hamburg-Wandsbeck (died in 1706).

G9.1.   R. Abraham Katzenellenpogen, born about the beginning of the seventeenth century and was in Vilna in 1726 where he met the child Elijah of Vilna. In 1746 he wrote an approbation to *Beit Avraham* by R. Abraham HaKohen as the A.B.D. of Slutsk. He signed in the Records of the Council of the Four Lands at Mir (as did his father in 1751) the proposition to excommunicate R. Jonathan Eybeschutz (See Chapter III re Eybeschutz-Emden Affair), which decision was reversed at the next meeting in Jaroslav in 1753). He wrote numerous approbations which suggest he became the A.B.D. of Brest about 1760 and held the position there for forty-four years until his death in 1804. His last approbation was written in 1787. His son and grandson also held the Rabbinical post in Brest. His funeral oration appeared in *Rei'ach HaSadeh* published in Sokolov in 1795 and writen by R. Eliezer Halevi of Pinsk. He appears to have married twice: 1) the daughter

of R. Joseph Etkes of Vilna, and 2) the daughter of R.
Simha Rappoport A.B.D. of Lvov.

G10.1.   R. Joseph Katzenellenpogen, succeeded his father as
         A.B.D. of Brest in 1804. He wrote approbations to
         Pnei Aryey written in 1778 (published in Amsterdam,
         1790), and *Halacha Pesukah* written in 1782 (pub-
         lished in Sokolov, 1787). He visited Keidan in 1782
         where he signed in the Community Records. He mar-
         ried Achsah, the daughter of R. Simha Halevi, A.B.D.
         of Slonim. She died in 1772. (See Chapter XII—G6.4/
         7.1.)

G11.1.   R. Meshullam (Yekutiel) Zalman Katzenellenpogen
         of Lublin, where he died as a young man in 1786.

G11.2.   R. Aryey Lieb Katzenellenpogen succeeded his fa-
         ther at Brest and held the Rabbinical Post until his
         death in 1837 (August 13) when he was succeeded
         by his relative R. Jacob Meir Padua. (See Chapter
         II—Section B.) He left no written works, but was
         considered one of the greatest Rabbis of his gen-
         eration. He wrote numerous approbations and his
         signature is second on a resolution adopted by the
         convention that assembled in Vilna in 1818, by order
         of the Czar Alexander I, to select three Jewish dep-
         uties to reside in St. Petersburg as representatives
         for the Jews.

G11.3.   R. Saul Katzenellenpogen (usually Katzenellenbo-
         gen in books), born about 1770 in Brest. He first
         lived at Plotsk and then Vilna where he became a
         disciple of the Gaon of Vilna, and became one of
         the city's assistant Rabbis. He was a prominent
         communal leader and he enjoyed great popularity.
         Stories about him appear in *Eivel Kaved* by A. B.
         Lebensohn (Vilna-Grodno 1825) and *Givat Shaul*
         by a relative R. Zvi Hirsch Katzenellenbogen (Vilna
         1825). A Synagogue was named after him, the *Beit
         Shaul Klaus*. He is the author of annotations which
         first appeared in the Vilna Edition of the Babylo-
         nian Talmud and subsequently. He wrote several
         approbations between 1787 and 1824, and several
         of his novellae can be found in *Netivot Olam* by

R. Zvi Hirsch Katzenellenbogen (Vilna, 1822). He died in Vilna January 12 (22nd Tevet), 1825 and his funeral oration was delivered by R. Abraham Abbale and was printed in his *Beit Avraham* (published at Sedilkov, 1937).

G11.4.   R. Simha Katzenellenpogen A.B.D. of Zablodov, also known as Simha Joel.[5]

G12.   R. Joshua Heschel Katzenellenpogen of Brest.

G13.   R. Simha Joel Katzenellenpogen of Brest.

G14.   R. Zvi Hirsch Katzenellenpogen A.B.D. of Slovochitz, from 1864 until his death in 1890. He married Gitel, daughter of R. Mordecai Kligsberg. She died in 1905.

G15.1.   Yota, born in Brest in 1849, died in 1906, married in 1865 to R. Jacob Leiner, 1824-78, Admur of Izbica, and a Chassidic leader, son of R. Mordecai Joseph Leiner. He was the author of *Beit Yaakov*, published Warsaw 1890. He died in 1878, his father in 1854.

G16.1.   R. Jeruchem Meir Leiner, born in 1875, died about 1940. He was the author of annotations entitled *Meir Ayin* which were published in *Galgulay Neshamot* by R. Menachem Azaraiah of Pono, Lublin edition 1907. The end of this book gives his full genealogy. He also published a commentary *She'erit Yosef* in *Seder Olam*.

G16.2.   Ruchama, born 1866, married R. Pesach Joshua Kligsberg.

G16.3.   R. Mordecai Joseph Leiner, born in Radzyn in 1869, lived in Lublin.

G16.4.   Alta Toyba, married R. Mordecai Judah Epstein of Kobryn.

G16.5.   R. Gershon Hanoch Leiner (1839-1891) Admur of Radzyn, author of *Sidrei Tehoroh, Orchot Chayim, Petil Techeilet*.

G17. R. Mordecai Joseph Eleazar, died 1929, married 1) daughter of R. Meshullam Margolioth of Pinczow (See Chapter XII—Branch C), and 2) daughter of R. Solomon Cohen of Kroshnik.

G18.1. R. Samuel Solomon Leiner, born in 1910 and perished in 1942 in the Holocaust. He was successor to his father at Radzyn.

G18.2. Chavah, married Jacob Groman of Warsaw.

G19. Daughter, married Greenberg and has family.

G18.3. Toyba, married Zvi Guraryey.

G19. Chaya, married R. Nahum Goldsmit. They settled with their family in Bnei Brak (Israel).

G18.4. Sarah, first wife of R. Abraham Issachar England,[6] of Sosnowiec-New York. (See Radomsk Chassidic Family Pedigree — Chapter IV — Branch L — G12/13.3/14.3/15.4/16.1.)

G16.6. R. Joshua Heschel Leiner of Chelm.

G17.1. R. Haim Simha Leiner of Lodmir.
G17.2. R. Obadiah Leiner.
G17.3. R. Gedaliah Leiner of Chelm.
G17.4. R. Chananiah Leiner of Lodz.
G17.5. R. Jeruchem Leiner of Lodz.
G17.6. Wife of R. Moses Isaac Glicksman of Sedlitz.
G17.7. Wife of R. Mordecai Lieb Groman of Warsaw.

G16.7. Gitel Rosa, married R. Moses Haim Sochochowsky of Boskowitz.
G16.8. Sheindel, married R. Akiva Tennenbaum.

G16.9. Channah, married R. Solomon Klepis.

G15.2. R. Simha Joel Katzenellenpogen, married his cousin, the daughter of R. Samuel Dov Leiner, Admur Boskowitz (his father's brother).

G15.3. Chaya, married R. Moses Isaac.

G10.2. R. Moses Katzenellenbogen.

G10.3. R. Ephraim Katzenellenbogen of Sislowitz (Shaulai).

G11. R. Abraham of Shaulai.

G10.4. R. Ezekiel Katzenellenbogen A.B.D. of Sislowitz (Shaulai), wrote an approbation to *Mar'ot HaTzova'ot* by R. Moses Zeev A.B.D. Bialystok, published in Grodno, 1810.

G11. R. Elijah Katzenellenbogen of Vilna.

G12. R. Abraham Jacob Katzenellenbogen died in Plungian in 1863. He wrote an original manuscript of the family genealogy in Vilna in 1843 and was the Progenitor of a large family through two children, many of whom settled in South Africa (See Branch A below—Katzenellenbogen Family of Plungian-Kovno-Kretinga).

G10.5. R. David Katzenellenpogen A.B.D. of Walkavisk, married the daughter of R. Judah Lieb A.B.D. Zaner (son of R. Simha Tiktiner).

G10.6. R. Menachem Nahum Katzenellenpogen A.B.D. Birz, married 1) Rachel, daughter of R. Isaac (Hamburger) Horowitz (See Chapter XVI — page 559—G12.5) and 2) Rachel, the widow of R. Jacobke, son of R. Ezekiel Landau (See Landau Family Pedigree — G8.3/9.3/10.2).

G11.1. R. Zeev Wolf Katzenellenpogen, died in Slutzk in 1747.

G11.2. R. Meshullam Zalman Katzenellenbogen.

G12. R. Nahum Eli (Elijah) Katzenellenpogen (usually Katzenellenbogen) the Trustee of the Vilna Community (i.e. their Treasurer and Chief Secretary).

G13. Abraham Zvi Hirsch Katzenellenbogen 1835-1907.[8] He settled in Vilna in 1885 where he was also the Community Trustee and a publisher of books. He married into a wealthy and prominent Vilna family, his wife being a daughter of R. Isaac Judah Lieb, son of R. Shemariah Rabinowitz. Among those books he published is the *Zava'at Yechezkiel*, the Ethical Will of his ancestor R. Ezekiel of Altona, and *Sha'arei Rachamim* (Vilna 1871) the introduction of which gives his family ancestry. At the end of the Ethical Will, which was published in 1871, he announces "This dear book and all types of similar nature, from different publishers, old and new, can be found for sale in my book store."

G14. Isaac Judah Lieb Katzenellenbogen, continued to publish in Vilna, at times printing books with his cousin, Mordecai Katzenellenbogen (See Branch B below), e.g. the book entitled *Kol Omer Kerah* published in 1913 by Mordecai, was printed by Isaac J. Lieb.[9]

G10.7. R. Joel Katzenellenbogen A.B.D. Kamarovka. In 1786 he is recorded as becoming a member of the Brest Community Council. His descendants became Chassidic followers. This must have been a traumatic event to his family,[10] especially since his father R. Abraham Katzenellenpogen of Brest had vehemently opposed Chassidism and violently attacked the leading Chassidic Rabbi Levi Isaac of Berdichev (See Chapter IV Branch D).

G11. R. Abraham Katzenellenbogen, known as "the Chassid," A.B.D. Trespoli and Shidlowitz.

G12. R. Moses Naftali Katzenellenbogen A.B.D. Kreshov and Tarnograd, died in 1867. Responsa of his can be found in the *Divrei Chayim* by the Sanzer Rabbi Haim Halberstam and *Nefesh Chaya*, by R. Haim Eleazar Waks. He had a number of children[10a]

G13.1. Channah Binah, married R. Abraham Jacob A.B.D. Zamocz.

G14. R. Aryey Lieb Taicher A.B.D. Tarnograd.

G15. Mordecai Zvi Taicher of Tarnograd, published *Pnei Yitzchak* by R. Isaac Harif in Jaroslav in 1905.

G13.2. Raatza Zelda, married R. Phineas (the Kinsker Rov) son of R. Nathan David Rabinowitz (Shidlovtzer Rov). (See Chapter IV — G6.4/7/8/9.2/10.4).

G13.3. Esther Toyba, married R. Moses Spiegel.

G14. R. Naftali Aryey Spiegel A.B.D. Cheshov (near Lublin), born 1869 and died in the U.S.A. in 1949 (buried in New Jersey). He married Sarah the daughter of R. Jacob Isaac Unger (maternal grandson of R. Jacob Isaac Horowitz, known as the Chozeh or Seer of Lublin).

G15.1. R. Moses Menachem Spiegel, married, lives with family in New York, (Brooklyn).

G15.2. R. Phineas Elijah Spiegel, married Baasha, daughter of R. Baruch Mordecai Burstein.

G16. Moses Spiegel, married Bracha, daughter of Avigdor Lerer (Brooklyn).

G9.2. R. Joel Katzenellenpogen A.B.D. of Shinova and Yartchov. He wrote an approbation to *Asifat Yehudah* published in Frankfurt-on-Main in 1763, and *Ohel Moshe* published in Zolkiev in 1754. He married Yara, daughter of R. Haim, son of R. Simha Rappoport, A.B.D. Lvov.

G10. R. Dov Berush, published the *Mayim Yechezkiel* by his grandfather in 1786.

G9.3. R. Israel Katzenellenpogen A.B.D. of Walkavisk, wrote two approbations.

G9.4. R. Shalom Katzenellenpogen A.B.D. Ashatiz.

G9.5. R. Meshullam Zalman Katzenellenpogen A.B.D. Keidan as his father's successor about 1756, where he signed in the Community Records in 1758, 1760, 1762 and 1770. He wrote approbations to *Beit Yaakov Eish* published in Frankfurt-on-Main in 1765 and *Tiferet Yisrael* published in Sokolov in 1773.

G10.1. R. Menachem Nahum Katzenellenpogen, succeeded
his father as A.B.D. Keidan. His signatures in the
Community Records are dated from 1770-1778. He
wrote an approbation to *Tiferet Yisrael* published in
Frankfurt-on-Main in 1774.

G11. R. Moses Mordecai Katzenellenpogen A.B.D. Keidan
who signed the Community Records between 1782-
1795. He wrote an approbation to *Sha'ar Rachamim*
in 1783.

G10.2. R. (Moses) Mordecai Katzenellenpogen.

G11.1. R. David Katzenellenpogen A.B.D. Wilki (near
Kovno).

G12.1. R. Meshullam Zalman of Yanoshak.
G12.2. R. Mordecai Katzenellenpogen of Wilki and Linkowe. He married Malka and in 1806 left Lithuania for Bucharest in Rumania leaving his wife and
son behind.[11] He was the Progenitor of a large
family today mainly in South Africa, England and
the U.S.A.—See Branch B below, Katnezellenbo-
gen Family of Pinsk-Karlin-Vilna.

G11.2. R. Nahum Katzenellenpogen A.B.D. Wilki.

G10.3. Bathsheba, married R. Nathan Nata Rabinowitz
A.B.D. Raszyn (Zamocz District).

G11. R. Dov (Zeev) Ber Rabinowitz of Kelem, succeeded
his father as A.B.D. Raszyn.

G12.1. R. Meshullam Zalman Rabinowitz.
G12.2. R. Mordecai Rabinowitz, married Sarah, daughter of R. Jehiel Michal, son of R. Aaron Gordon
of Vilna (who was the Medical Doctor to the
Polish King John Sobieski III, who ruled from
1670-1696).

G13.1. R. Samuel Rabinowitz of Karlin, married the
daughter of R. Gad Asher Rokeah (adopted
his mother's maiden name) son-in-law of R.
Joshua Mirkes of Pinsk. (See Chapter V—
Branch A and the Rokeah Family Pedigree.)

G13.2. Channah Pesel, married R. Michal Endelman of Warsaw.

G13.3. R. Moses Rabinowitz of Vilna, where he was known as "Moshel Klemer,"[12] the seller of medicinal drugs, and was one of the first to help establish a Home for the Poor, the Old and the Weak. He died in 1877. His wife was Feigel (died in 1889) daughter of R. Samuel (Jonas) Broda. They were buried in Vilna.

G14.1. R. Gershon Rabinowitz, died in 1887 in Vilna.

G14.2. R. Mordecai Rabinowitz (1827-1891),[13] married Chaya, daughter of R. Haim Lieb Sachor (son-in-law of R. Jacob Berlin, father of R. Naftali Zvi Judah Berlin the *Natziv* of Volozhin and Head of the famous Yeshiva established there). R. Mordecai was the author of *Divrei Chaim* published in Vilna in 1891, *Shalom Mordecai* published in Vilna in 1890, *Mar D'Ror* and *Rav Chesed.*

G14.3. Sarah Henna, married R. Judah son of R. Abraham son of R. Israel, son of R. Abraham son of R. Jehiel Michal Gordon (R. Jehiel's daughter Sarah is mentioned above as the wife of Sarah Henna's paternal grandfather).

G8.2. R. Feiwel Katzenellenpogen.

G8.3. Mirl, married R. Isaac son of R. Israel (A.B.D. Hanau). She died in 1734.

G8.4. Wife of R. Jacob Halevi Shor A.B.D. Karoz (See Chapter VI — Branch B — G6.4/7.2/8).

G8.5. R. Jacob Katzenellenpogen of Keidan. President of the Community Council.

G9. R. Joel Katzenellenpogen of Keidan.

G10. R. Mordecai, who was martyred.

G11. R. Abraham ("Kailis") Katzenellenbogen of Keidan, died in 1849. He married the daughter of R. Saul Halevi of Keidan, son of R. Jacob Jokel Halevi (See above — G8.4).

G12.1. R. Saul Katzenellenbogen, known as Saul Kei-
        daner,[14] lived in Vilna and married the daughter
        of R. Moses Judah Grommer. He was a wealthy
        merchant there as well as a learned scholar and
        died in Vilna at the age of forty-eight in 1868.

G13.1. Mordecai Katzenellenbogen of Vilna, owned a
        wholesale and retail chinaware store on *Nie-
        metskaya Ulita* (German Street) in the Vilna
        Ghetto.
G13.2. Feiwel (Feitel) Katzenellenbogen.
G13.3. Rachel, married her first cousin, Meir Aaron
        Katzenellenbogen.
G13.4. Abraham Katzenellenbogen, married Rebecca
        Kahn, owner of a textile business on the Jews
        Street of the Vilna Ghetto.

G14.1. Ephraim.
G14.2. Moses, died young.
G14.3. Rachel.
G14.4. Anna Katzenellenbogen, Professor of Math-
        ematics at Moscow University.
G14.5. Joshua Selig, surnamed Katz, born about
        1877 and died in 1951 (buried in New Jer-
        sey). He came to the U.S.A. about 1906, and
        married the following year to Lena Srolis-
        conn.

G15.1. Barbara, born 1908, married in 1934 to
        Joseph Lubin (Long Island).

G16.   Edward Lubin, born 1943, married Ann
       Einhorn. Their daughter, Alison Rachel,
       born in 1972.

G15.2. Bart (Beryl) Katz, born in 1912, married
        in 1935 to Alice Lang (New York). Their
        son, Robert Katz, born in 1937.

G14.6. Uriah Katzenellenbogen, born in Vilna. He
        left there in 1910 for Warsaw and later lived
        in the vicinity of Shaulai. He frequently vis-
        ited Vilna and published there a book en-
        titled *Lito* together with E. J. Goldsmith

(1913). In May 1915, when the Jews were expelled from the Kovno Province, he spent a few days in Vilna and eventually, after many wanderings, reached New York in 1937. Here he later published a larger edition of his previous book on the history of the Lithuanian Jews *Lite*. He was married twice, having issue from the first wife.

G15.1. Moses (Misha), surnamed Allen, married and has two children, Marsha and Neil (Toronto).

G15.2. Abraham (Brasha), surnamed Bogen (Montreal), unmarried.

G12.2. (Son) Katzenellenbogen.

G13. Meir Aaron Katzenellenbogen of Vilna, owner of one of the largest textile factories in Lithuania and White Russia, married his first cousin Rachel Katzenellenbogen.

BRANCH A

KATZENELLENBOGEN FAMILY OF PLUNGIAN-KOVNO-KRETINGA

ANCESTRY

G1. R. Meir Katzenellenbogen.
G2.1. R. Samuel Judah.
G3.2. Wife of R. Joel Ashkenazi Katzenellenpogen.
G4.2. R. Abraham Ashkenazi.
G5.2. R. Jacob.
G6. R. Abraham.
G7.2. R. Ezekiel Katzenellenpogen.
G8.1. R. David.
G9.1. R. Abraham.
G10.4. R. Ezekiel.
G11. R. Elijah Katzenellenbogen.
G12. R. Abraham Jacob Katzenellenbogen, died in 1863, on 9th Shvat, in Plungian.

G13.1. Saul of Vilna.

G14. Abraham Jacob of Shaulai, author of a handwritten pedigree of his family (in 1886), the original having been dictated by his grandfather.

G13.2. Ezekiel,[15] married Guta (?) Columbus.

G14.1. Isaac, born 1845 in Kovno. He immigrated to South Africa, arriving at Cape Town sometime before the Boer War. He settled in Cape Town, was a member of the Roeland Street Synagogue, and is buried in the Old Cape Town Jewish Cemetery (Maitland). He died in 1921. His wife was Freda, 1851-1929, daughter of Benjamin Tetz of Memel. Her sister married her husband's brother.

G15.1. Charles (Ezekiel) of Plungian, born in 1879. He settled in Wolseley in the Cape Province (South Africa), where he established a trading store together with a Mr. Frank Fish. He also supplied meals to all main-line trains passing from Johannesburg to Cape Town and vice versa as in those days there were no dining saloons. He married about the year 1905 in Cape Town to Eda Cohen, 1880-1962. The couple are buried in the small Jewish Cemetery of the Ceres Congregation in the Cape Province. Charles died in 1931.

G16.1. Lionel (Lieb), 1909-1958. Married out of faith to N. Binge in 1930.

G17.1. Dion, born 1934.
G17.2. Edith, born 1941.
G17.3. Charlotte, born 1950.

G16.2. Minnie, born 1911. Married to David Samson in 1932.

G17.1. Charles (Ezekiel), born 1934. Married in 1964 to Joan Rock. Their son, Stanley, born 1965.
G17.2. Eric, born 1939. Married in 1962 to Sheila Levin. Their children are Jeffery, born 1963 and Dorothy, born 1966.
G17.3. Felicity, born 1945. Married in 1967 to Beryl Berman.

G16.3. Millie, born 1912. Married in 1937 to Gershon Batten.

G17.1. Farrol Charles, born 1939. Married in 1961 to Cynthia Israel. Their children: Seale, born 1962; Lauren, born 1965; and Joanne, born 1966.

G17.2. Peggy, born 1942. Married in 1965 to Sydney Juter. Their daughter, Adele, born 1967.

G17.3. Barbara, born 1950.

G16.4. Pauline, born 1919. Married in 1945 to Simmy Lewis.

G17.1. Rhena, born 1950.

G17.2. Hazel, born 1957.

G16.5. Isaac (Sakkie), born 1921. Succeeded his father at Wolseley where he runs a general store and hotel. Married in 1947 to Peggy Katz.

G17.1. Graham, born 1948.

G17.2. Charles, born 1950.

G17.3. Ruth, born 1954.

G17.4. Judith, born 1958.

G15.2. Abraham Jacob 1871-1938. Buried in Cape Town. He ran a store at Wolseley which included the sale of patent medicines. He married in 1899 to Ray Smulian, 1880-1965.

G16.1. Laura (Lottie) 1900-1965. Married to Barney Ezer.

G17.1. Colin, married to Sylvia Blumberg.

G17.2. Seymour Aubrey, born in 1934. Married to Chippie Falkenstein. Their sons are Robert and David.

G17.3. Eilene. Married to Hymie Marks.

G16.2. Bennie, born 1902. He was an accountant in Johannesburg. Married in 1934 to Flora Starfield. Both died in 1973 (May).

G17.1. Ronald Farrel, born 1936.[16] Dip Law (Rand): Hotelier and Law Consultant involved with Tourism; educated at Parktown B.H.S., Wits University. Married in 1959 to Shelley Samuels. His children are Laurin, born 1960; Steven, born 1962; and Dana, born 1963.

G17.2. Joan, born 1948, married Martin Orkin.

G16.3. Adolf (Abe) 1903-1959. Married in 1934 to Phyllis Miller (Salkinder).

G17.1. Robert, born 1938. Lives in Germiston, Transvaal. Married in 1962 to Jeanette Silver.

G17.2. Pamella, born 1947. Married.

G16.4. Helen, born 1910. Married in 1934 to Benjamin Smiedt.

>   G17.1. Adele, born 1940. Married 1960 to Teddy Swirsky. Their children are Melony, born 1961; Jill, born 1962; and Paul, born 1967.
>   G17.2. Pam, born 1946.

G15.3. Goodman of Pretoria, Transvaal, born 1890. Married in 1912 to Maisie Melman, born 1894.

>   G16.1. Laurence of Rustenberg, Transvaal, born 1913. Married in 1945 to Florence, daughter of Jackson Goldberg, sister of Cecile married to Charles Perel (See G15.6/16.3 be-below).
>
>   >   G17.1. Ivan, born 1948.
>   >   G17.2. Merlene, born 1951.
>
>   G16.2. Leon, born 1916. Married in 1940 to Jessie Belshitz.
>
>   >   G17.1. Peter, born 1942.
>   >   G17.2. Ruth, born 1944.
>
>   G16.3. Phyllis, born 1919. Married in 1940 to Reuben Miller.
>
>   >   G17. Sandra, born 1952.

G15.4. Leah, died in 1942. Married in 1898 to Isaac Fine.

>   G16.1. Benjamin Fine, born 1902, married Pauline Koppelowtiz in 1935. They had no children.
>   G16.2. Matthew Fine, born 1909, married Jean Lipshitz in 1939.
>
>   >   G17.1. Leon Gerald, born in 1943, married Brenda Sakinovsky in 1966. M.B. Ch. B. (U.C.T. 1966). Their daughters Michal, born 1968 and Dana.
>
>   >   G17.2. Sandra Ruth, born 1948.
>
>   G16.3. Barney Fine, born 1900, married Miriam Schlosburg, daughter of Joseph in 1928.
>
>   >   G17. Carmel, married Lionel Blumberg of Swellendam. Their children are Izette and Laurence.
>
>   G16.4. Myer Fine, married Bertha Urisohn in 1939.
>
>   >   G17.1. Penelope, born 1941.
>   >   G17.2. Lester, born 1948.

G16.5. Harry Fine 1903-1939, married his first cousin Minnie Dembovsky in 1932. (See below G15.5/16.1.)

  G17. Arthur Michael, born 1933. Married Denise Lasofsky in 1960. Their daughters are Roslyn, born 1961 and Janine, born 1966.

G15.5. Hilda, married Abraham Micah Dembovsky.

  G16.1. Minnie, married Harry Fine, her cousin (G15.4/16.5 above).
  G16.2. Tilly, married Dr. Harold Lee.

    G17.1. Ginger, married Mavis Lazarus. Their son is Howard.
    G17.2. Alan.
    G17.3. Mack.

  G16.3. Ray, married Dr. Horace Segal of Port Elizabeth.

    G17.1. Alistair, married.
    G17.2. Charlene, married Dennis Terespolsky. They have three children.
    G17.3. Michael.

  G16.4. Sylvia, married Dr. Burjack of Johannesburg.

    G17.1. Patricia, married.
    G17.2. Michael.

  G16.5. Eve, married Max Malamed. They live in the U.S.A.

G15.6. Millie, married Israel Perel of Somerset West, Cape.

  G16.1. Benjamin, married Mary Immelman.

    G17. Vivian, married Anne Joy.

  G16.2. Abraham Perel, married Bertha Segal.

    G17.1. Sandra.
    G17.2. Michael, married.

  G16.3. Charles Perel, married Cecile Goldberg, daughter of Jackson (thus a sister of Florence, married to Laurence Katzenellenbogen). (See G15.3/16.1 above.)

    G17.1. Anne.
    G17.2. Melvyn.

  G16.4. Minnie, married Michael Allen.

G17. Charles Allen.

G15.7. Becky, married Moses David (Morris) Bloch, brother of
         Nathan Bloch, Director of Bloch and Co., Wholesalers in
         Cape Town.

G16.1. Reuben, unmarried.
G16.2. Ethel, married Samuel Robin.

G17.1. Enid.
G17.2. Monica.

G16.3. Sydney Bloch, married. He has four children.

G15.8. Hoda, born 1904, married Louis Kaplan.

G16.1. Harry, of Port Elizabeth, died in 1967, married Sally Edel-
         son.

G17.1. Freda, married Gamsu of Potchefstroom.
G17.2. Howard Kaplan, married.

G16.2. Gertie, married Lou Troube of Kimberley.

G15.9. Esther, 1884-1951, married in Cape Town in 1909 to David
         Michaelovsky (1882-1955) of Wellington, Cape Town.

G16.1. Ray, born in 1911, married in 1934 to Harry Atlas of Cape
         Town.

G17.1. Reva, born in 1935, married Jack Marcuson. Their chil-
         dren are Melany, born in 1958; David, born in 1959; and
         Jonathan, born in 1961.
G17.2. Charna, born in 1943, married Melvyn Levitt.
G17.3. Lesley, born in 1950.
G17.4. Selwyn, born in 1939, married Brenda Davidson. Their
         son, Adrian, born in 1965.

G16.2. Aaron Michael, 1910-1967, married Anne Cohen. They had
         no children.
G16.3. Abraham Jacob, born in 1913, married Pearl Orolowitz.
         They have two adopted children: Morris, born in 1952,
         and Michael, born in 1958.
G16.4. Meyer, born in 1915, married Bella Peltz.

G17.1. Alan, born in 1954.
G17.2. Estelle, born in 1966.

G16.5. Ethel, born in 1923, married Hyman Casper of Wynberg, Cape.

G17.1. Harry, born in 1948.
G17.2. Eric, born in 1953.
G17.3. Seymour, born in 1954.

G14.2. Elijah Dov Ber, died at Kretinga in 1924. He married Ita, daughter of Benjamin Tetz, in 1865. She died in 1920.

G15.1. Herman (Hirsch) Katzenellenbogen, 1877-1943, of Pretoria, South Africa. He married Freda, daughter of Moses (Morris) Schlosburg (1883-1958). He established a large wholesale firm in Pretoria of the same name which is still run by members of the family today.

G16.1. Morris (Boysie), 1906-1926.
G16.2. Helene, 1902-1956, married Maurice Balzam, died in 1960.

G17.1. Maurice, born in 1928, married in 1947 to Joe Bernstein. They settled in England. Their children are Jared, born in 1948, and Hermonine and Danita, twin sisters, born in 1952.
G17.2. Seymour, unmarried.

G15.2. Nathan Katzenellenbogen, born about 1892, died in 1962. He is buried in Kiriat Shaul Cemetery, Israel. He married Rachel, daughter of Israel Schlosburg, a cousin to Freda above. She died in 1961 and is also buried in Kiriat Shaul.

G16.1. Motla Joyce, born in 1913. Married twice—in 1937 to Solomon Frank, and then to Norman Hanson. She had two daughters by her first husband.

G17.1. Natalie, born in 1941, married in 1963 to Eli Bendor. Their children are Anat, born in 1964 and Yuval, born in 1966.
G17.2. Vivian, born in 1943, married in 1963 to Dr. Hillel Halkin. Their children are Amir, born in 1964 and Michaele, born in 1966.

G16.2. Carmel, 1909-1967, married in 1931 to Harry Phillips.

G17.1. Sharon, born in 1932. Married in 1954 to Professor Eugene Kark, Department of Surgery, Mount Sinai Hos-

pital, New York (resigned there in 1973). Their children
are Vanesa, born in 1963 and Eden, born in 1966.

G17.2.   David, born in 1933.

G17.3.   Jonathan, born in 1945.

G16.3.   Hannah, married Sam Jaff of Johannesburg.

G17.1.   Janet, born in 1941, married in 1959 to Ralph Bernstein
(Inbar). Their sons are Yaron, born in 1961 and Dan
Michael, born in 1965.

G17.2.   Stephen, born in 1943, married in 1968 to Naomi Pel-
ham.

G17.3.   Nicholas, born in 1946.

G16.4.   Ita, born in 1922, married in 1942 to David Pinshow. They
settled in Kfar Shemariahu, Israel.

G17.1.   Lesley, born in 1945. Married to Avner Yaniv in 1966.
Their daughter is Carmel, born in 1967.

G17.2.   Barry, born in 1947.

G17.3.   Gabi, born in 1954.

G15.3.   Rebecca, 1883-1955, married Samuel Ludwin, died in 1919
in Moscow.

G16.1.   Dorrik, Dr. 1897-1963, married in 1940 to Genia Glazer.

G17.1.   Haia, born in 1942, married to Joe Shapiro in 1963. Their
daughter is Dorit, born in 1966.

G17.2.   Samuel Ludwin-Katzenellenbogen, born in 1944, M.B.
Ch.B. (Witwatersrand) in 1967.

G17.3.   Tamar.

G17.4.   David, together with his twin, born in 1949.

G16.2.   Franya, born in 1901, married in 1930 to Morris Tooch.

G17.1.   Ita, born in 1931, married in 1952 to Neville Malkinson.
Their children are Robin, born in 1957 and Dana, born
in 1960.

G17.2.   Samuel, born in 1934, married in 1960 to Rachel Nach.
Their children are Mark, born in 1961; Darrin, born in
1963; and Neil, born in 1967.

G16.3.   Benjamin, born in 1903, married Irene Berkowitz. They
had no issue.

G16.4. Slava, 1910-1947, married in 1939 to Emil Biss. Merlin, born in 1942.

G16.5. Sana, born in 1913, married Benjamin Dorfan. They settled in Givat Shapiro, Israel.

G17.1. Samuel Dorfan, born in 1932, married Toby. Their children are Aviva and Ethan.

G17.2. Ella, married Colin Gorfil. They have a daughter, Shelley.

G17.3. Lynne, married Mervyn Wolff.

G17.4. Manny Dorfan.

G15.4. Leah (Lena) 1867-1940, married in Kretinga to Lieb Hirschowitz, died about 1903.

G16.1. Moses, Dr. died in California, U.S.A. about 1948. He was born about 1887 and married Sonya. Their daughter is Ruth.

G16.2. Child died in infancy.

G16.3. Gita, born 1889, killed during Second World War. She was a dentist and married in 1915 to Dr. Saul Traub.

G17.1. Uri, born 1925. Perished in World War II.

G17.2. Lova (Leon), born in 1916, Engineer. He married in 1962 to Sonya Chanin.

G16.4. Yetta, born about 1895. Married to Dr. Grisha Rabinowitz. Their daughter is Ella.

G16.5. Edward Hirschowitz. He immigrated to South Africa where he changed his surname to Katzenellenbogen about 1910. He was born in 1898, and married in 1922 to Tilly Ludman. They settled in Pretoria. Her sister Ada married Robert, a brother of Rachel Schlosburg, wife of Nathan Katzenellenbogen.

G17.1. Lionel Katzenellenbogen, born in 1923, married in 1946 to Annette Levy. He is Group Merchandising Manager of Baby Land (South Africa) in Pretoria. Their children are Lynn, born in 1948; Barbara, born in 1950; and Mark, born in 1957.

G17.2. Elliot Katzenellenbogen, Dr., born in 1925, married in 1951 to Shulamit Krinski. Their children are Ron, born in 1952; Dan, born in 1955 and Nir, born in 1956.

G17.3. Karin, born in 1928, married in 1949 to Dr. Ivor Fix.

Their children are Gail, born in 1950; Alan, born in 1953; and Brett, born in 1955.

G16.6. Mina, 1909-1937, married Boris Schlesin. Zara, married Eric Moskow.

G16.7. Malka 1905-1955, married Pavel Bossin in 1951.

G16.8. Benjamin, born in 1903.

G14.3. Judah Lieb Katzenellenbogen, born in 1850, died 1933. He married about 1870 in Kretinga to Hannah Emdin, died about 1923. He was the author of a handwritten pedigree scroll, in possession of his grandson, Joseph Katzenellenbogen of Johannesburg.

G15.1. Solomon Zalman, 1878-1949, from Bronkhorstspruit, Transvaal. He died unmarried and was buried in Pretoria.

G15.2. Jacob (Yekel), 1890-1964, from Bronkhorstspruit, Transvaal. He died unmarried and was buried in Cape Town.

G15.3. Joshua Selig, 1880-1949, buried in Pretoria.

G15.4. Malka, married Saul Israelowitz. They and their three children, Joshua, Hannah and Rosa, perished during the Second World War.

G15.5. Abraham Ezekiel Katzenellenbogen, 1876-1949. He arrived in South Africa by ship in 1893 from Kretinga and left from Cape Town northwards to Southern Rhodesia where, in 1908, he married Bertha Shawzin.

G16.1. Leonard Shawzin (adopted his mother's name). He was born in 1911 and is a director of the Cape Town branch of Truworths Ltd. He married in 1940 to Stella Cohen.

G17.1. Gail, born 1944, married in 1965 to Tony Hoberman. Their child is Nicol.

G17.2. Daryl, born 1949.

G17.3. Karin, born 1946.

G16.2. Moses (Maurice) Nellen (he shortened his original surname), born in 1913. Formerly a Cape Town Cardiologist. He married twice: in 1947 to Rosa Laurence, who died in 1953, and by whom he had two children—Jan Charles Frederick, born in 1950 and Gideon Asher, born in 1952 —and then to Felicity Sandelson (Lister).

G16.3. Joseph (Jose) Katzellenbogen, born 1918,[17] educated S.A.C.S., Cape Town, University of Cape Town (B. Com.), a director of the Johannesburg branch of "Truworths." He married in 1952 to Jessica Schneider.

G17.1. Tessa, born 1953.
G17.2. Jonathan Charles, born 1955.
G17.3. Peter, born 1957.
G17.4. Mark David, born 1958.

G16.4. Emily, born 1919, married in 1931 to Jack Jowell.

G17.1. Jeffery Lionel, born 1939. Married in 1964 to Frances, daughter of the Progressive Party Parliamentary Representative, Helen Suzman (South Africa). Their daughter is Joanna, born 1967.
G17.2. Roger Mark, born 1942.

G14.4. Saul Katzenellenbogen of Berlin.

G15.1. Siegfried.
G15.2. Myrtle.

G14.5. Herman Katzenellenbogen (Chatzke) of Berlin. He died in Sweden.

G15.1. Arthur, born in 1902 in Berlin, unmarried. Immigrated to South Africa and lives in Cape Town.
G15.2. Daughter.

G13.3. Wife of Isaac Segall.

G14. Helen, 1870-1947, married in 1890 to Zvi (Herman) Wolpert.

G15.1. William, born in 1893, married in 1928 to Sarah Suzman.

G16. Lewis Wolpert, Professor at Middlesex Hospital, born in 1929, married in 1961 to Elizabeth Brownstein.

G17.1. Miranda, born 1962.
G17.2. Daniel Mark, born in1963.
G17.3. Jessica Sarah, born in 1966.
G17.4. Mathew William, born in 1967.

G15.2. Fanny, 1892-1962, unmarried.
G15.3. Ulrich, born in 1895, married Sadie Davidson.

G16.1. Hiliary, married Max Canard.

G17.1. Stephen.
G17.2. Joan.

G16.2. Raymond, married Zelma.

G15.4. Jenny, married twice. Her first husband was J. Shor.

BRANCH B

KATZENELLENBOGEN FAMILY OF
PINSK-KARLIN-VILNA

ANCESTRY

G1.   R. Meir Katzenellenbogen.
G2.1.   R. Samuel Judah.
G3.2.   Wife of R. Joel Ashkenazi Katzenellenbogen.
G4.2.   R. Abraham Ashkenazi.
G5.2.   R. Jacob.
G6.   R. Abraham.
G7.2.   R. Ezekiel Katzenellenpogen.
G8.1.   R. David.
G9.5.   R. Meshullam Zalman.
G10.2.   R. (Moses) Mordecai.
G11.1.   R. David.
G12.2.   R. Mordecai Katzenellenbogen.
G13.   R. Joel Isaac Katzenellenbogen.

Joel Isaac was born in 1798 in the little Lithuanian town of Linkowe, where his father, Mordecai, was Rabbi. When the boy was only eight years old, his father left him and his mother, Malka, and for various reasons, went to Bucharest in Rumania. His mother noticed that he was a brilliant child and, while still very young, brought him to Vilna, a great center of Jewish learning, the "Jerusalem" of Lithuania. Here he entered the Yeshiva of Rabbi Mordecai Meltzer. As time passed by, young Joel gathered much in Rabbinical knowledge, and his teacher adopted him as his own son. When he left the Yeshiva, he went to study in the Beit HaMidrash (Study House) of Rabbi Elijah, known as the Gaon (Genius) of Vilna.

By the age of his Bar-Mitzvah (thirteen), his reputation was known throughout the city of Vilna, and he was highly praised by its learned men and Rabbis. He was once approached to deliver a discourse on *Pilpul d'Oraita* in the Great Vilna Synagogue. On that day, the Shul was packed to capacity with many learned men, listening to this wonder child. Among them was his former teacher, Rabbi Meltzer, as well as Rabbi Ablai Passovler. So brilliant was his oration that now he was held in even higher esteem than before.

By the age of eighteen, many sought him as a husband for their daughters. Eventually, Joel married Frume Toyba, a daughter of Abraham Abba Halevi Horowitz, a wealthy businessman from the town of Kelem. Joel's undemanding wife served him for twenty-five years of married life, enabling him to study the Law without ever having to worry about financial troubles. They were blessed with two sons.

His first offer to a Rabbinical call was as Rabbi of Kelem which, much to his father-in-law's regret, he declined. Instead, he went to the town of Salent where he studied further under Rabbi Zvi Salenter. During the three years he spent there, the two men became very close friends.

Meanwhile, his father-in-law again requested him to accept the Rabbinical post in Kelem. This time, Joel hid himself in a wagon of roaming paupers, and ended up in Novhardek. Here he was welcomed by the city elders and went to study under Alexander Ziskind. Once again, his brilliance captured the hearts of all those who heard him. Rabbi Ziskind was so impressed that he willed his post of Head of the Beth Din of Novhardek to be given to Joel on his death.

Joel, however, continued his wanderings and reached Karlin, where he was taken into the home of Chaya Luria, a rich and generous lady. Here he became a close friend of her son, Joshua Heschel Rokeah. He remained in Karlin but on the death of his father-in-law, financial embarrassment caused him to accept the position of Rabbi of Sad. On the death of Rabbi Ziskind, he initially accepted the Rabbinical post there, but then changed his mind, feeling that the duties demanded of him would then hinder his further study. He did, however, later accept positions at Zausmer and then Semiatetz. Here he introduced great improvements to the city and became beloved by Jews and Gentiles alike.

His latter days were spent in Novo (New)—Alexanderowski, where he was Chief Rabbi for six years. On his resignation, he held a great farewell banquet and settled in Tashenowitz, where he taught but did not accept any position. He passed away at the age of eighty-two on November 23 (22nd of Cheshvan) 1890. He was buried in Czechanowitz, in the Grodno District.[18]

He was the last of a long line of Rabbis and his work entitled *Zerah Yitzchak* was published by his son Abraham Abba Katzenellenbogen in Warsaw in 1898, some seven years after his father's death.

Joel Isaac, during his lifetime, had been greatly upset by the tragic death of his other son, Samuel Michal, by the Cholera plague of 1872. He had intended to publish a work entitled *Beit Shmuel* ("The House of Samuel"), a work dealing with the Laws of Mourning. But this was not realized.

The work, like other Rabbinical Responsa, is a collection of questions addressed to the Rabbi, and the answers he gave on points of Jewish Law. The basic form is according to the "Four Turim" (or "Rows"), as first compiled by Rabbi Jacob, son of Asher, of the fourteenth century. The four include:

1. Orah Chayim (Way of Life)   —Daily life, Sabbath, Fasts and
                                        Festivals.

2. Yoreh Deah (Teacher of   —dietary laws, ritual cleanliness,
   Knowledge)   teachers, study, charity, sickness,
                                        death, mourning, etc.

3. Eben HaEzer (Stone of Help)   —marriage laws.

4. Choshen Mishpat (Breastplate   —civil and criminal law.
   of Judgment)

This work lacks Responsa of the fourth type with six, seven and three chapters for the first three sections which, together with an index, totals 164 pages. The book opens with an introduction by the author's son, many of whose descendants are now living in the U.S.A. There are also a number of Approbations (Letters of Rabbinical Approval) by Rabbis of that generation. They include Rabbi Haim Soloveitchik, who was considered the greatest Talmudist of his generation. He was the grandfather of Rabbi Joseph Ber Soloveitchik, Head of the Isaac Elchanan Seminary (Yeshiva University, New York) and a foremost American Orthodox Rabbi today.

When, in 1764, the Council of the Four Lands was dissolved, its decrees and decisions no longer held effect upon East European Jewry. Thus, later Family descendants dropped the "p" and returned to using the original name. But name changing did not end there. Further abbreviations of this longest of all Jewish surnames gave rise to names such as Katz, Katze, Katzen, and Bogen in our immediate branch, and Kay, Nellen, Allen, Katzenell, and a variety of spellings for Katzenellenbogen itself, in other branches of the family.

The long line of Rabbis ended its era with the death of Joel Isaac in 1890. A new generation of printers and publishers took its place, the first, his son, Abba, who in 1898 published the *Zera Yitzchak*. In the generation of his grandchildren, this was even more prominent. All of his six grandsons were in printing or stationery, one way or another. The family was to be found in Europe, Africa and America. Lithuanian control was under Mordecai, who published and printed in the Vilna Ghetto from 1870 onwards. His store was to be found on the *Yiddische Gass* (Street of the Jews) and from here supplies went abroad to his brother, Judah Meir in New York (who was also printing books of his own at that time), and to his two brothers-in-law (both in South Africa), Beinkinstadt in Cape Town and Kawarsky in Johannesburg. Abraham Abba and Samuel were in printing on Manhattan's Lower East Side. Judah Meir became a co-founder of the Hebrew Publishing Company on Delancey Street, which continues to supply Jewish books and religious articles for some seventy-three years. A daily prayerbook published by the company was named after him. Samuel was later the founder of the Gem Press (on Park Avenue, New York), which is still managed by his sons today. Grandsons Michal and Chuntche were in the stationery line in New York.

After Rabbinics and Printing, the family entered its third phase of evolution. That of utilizing the best of what the New World, away from the Ghetto ties, had to offer. Thus, with his great-grandchildren in Australia, England, Russia, Israel, South Africa, and the U.S.A., the world of academics and business takes the leading role.

The family today, besides college graduates and university graduates, counts among this generation no less than three university professors, of Economics, of Art History and of Communication Arts and Sciences.

He had two sons who were the progenitors of large families.[19]

G14.1. Samuel Michal Katzenellenbogen — Branch I.
G14.2. Abraham Abba Katzenellenbogen — Branch II.

BRANCH I (first son)
(VILNA)

G14.1. Samuel Michal Katzenellenbogen, died as a young man of cholera in an epidemic in 1872. He was married to Rosa, the daughter of Rabbi Isaac Judah Lieb Rabinowitz (1806-1853), one of the most prominent Jews of the City of Vilna. R. Judah was the author of *Darkei Teshuva* (The ways of repentance), published by his only son in New York in 1909. He was the son of Shemariah Rabinowitz. Rosa died when she was over ninety years old.

G15.1. Mordecai Katzenellenbogen, born in Vilna in 1858 and died there in March of 1934 (corresponding to the 5th of Nissan). His father died when he was only fourteen. His mother's sister had married into another branch of the Katzenellenbogen family. Her husband, uncle Abraham Zvi Hirsch, was Treasurer of the City's Charities, and had continued in the printing line when he settled in Vilna. It was under his influence that his

nephew Mordecai established himself in printing as well, and
later became one of the city's leading booksellers and publishers, working at times independently, or with the famous
printing Romm family (under the "widow and sons Romm"),
or with his cousin, Isaac Judah Lieb K., son of his uncle Abraham Zvi Hirsch. He purchased the copyright to print various
works, notably those of the famous Hebrew novelist and journalist, Peretz Smolenskin (1842-1885) from his widow. His collected works of fiction were published in Vilna in 1901, including one hundred of his personal letters. At the turn of the century, Mordecai went to the U.S.A. where he helped his brother,
Judah Meir, establish the Hebrew Publishing Company. After
his death, the Vilna bookshop continued to thrive under the
management of his family, notably his son Isaac, until a decade
later, the city of Vilna and its Ghetto fell into the hands of the
Germans. From 1870 onwards, he had continued to supply all
types of books and religious articles to Europe, England, South
Africa and the U.S.A.

He married Deborah, daughter of Raphael Beinkinstadt. She
died about 1936/7.

G16.1. Celia (Zilia), the eldest, married Isaac Friedman, son of
the Rabbi of Antokol. Their children: Sophie, Ossip and Raphael, named after his maternal grandfather.

The Rabbi of Antokol (a small town adjacent to Vilna)
was R. Benjamin son of R. Zvi Friedman, who died in 1918,
having served the community some forty years.

G16.2. Sonya (Sarah), born about 1888, married in Vilna in 1906
to Boris (Baruch son of Mendel) Rosenstein. They lived
initially in Vilna, but at the outbreak of World War I, they
fled to Bialystok, losing much of their possessions, where they
settled and remained until they perished in the Holocaust
of World War II.

G17.1. Rachel, born October 2, 1907, studied as a pharmacist in
Belgium, where she married Saul Szapiro.[20] They survived
the Holocaust and after the war went to South Africa.
Later they divorced, she returning to Belgium with her
son, and he remaining with the two daughters.

G18.1. Dorette, born October 31, 1932. She studied at the Cape
Town Medical School as a radiographer. She married in

1953 to Bertie Coopersmith (born October 4, 1930). Some years later they immigrated to England and settled outside London, in Ealing. Their children: Claude, born March 15th, 1954, and Jennifer, born September 9th, 1955.

G18.2. Adele, born December 24, 1933. She married in Cape Town to Roger Adlington (and had a daughter), and secondly in Paris to Pierre de Vigier. Their daughter is Jeanine, born in 1959.

G18.3. Raphael, born December 26, 1936, also studied to become an architect, married in Belgium in 1966 to Elaine Segers (later separated). Their son is David Baruch Samuel (Bernard Simon), born in 1967.

G17.2. Emanuel, born in Vilna, April 11, 1909. In 1926 he immigrated via Danzig and England, to Cape Town, South Africa, arriving there on the Union-Castle Ocean liner "Glengorm Castle." At first he was employed by his great-uncle, Moses Beinkinstadt, and worked in his bookstore. Later he became an accountant and bookkeeper, and then went into the dress business in Johannesburg. In Cape Town, he met Annie, daughter of Samuel Marine (born June 5, 1910), and on June 15, 1938, they married in Johannesburg. They returned to settle in Cape Town, where he went into the cement roof-tile business and was the director of the company called "Eagle Cement and Marble Works."

G18.1. Mervyn (Mordecai, after his great-grandfather), born in Cape Town, April 3, 1939. He received an Accountancy Diploma, and married on October 10, 1966 in Port Elizabeth to Bettina Ketellapper. They settled in Cape Town. Their children: David, born April 30, 1969; Shaun, born August 14, 1972; and Jason (Jochanan) born February 8, 1974.

G18.2. Sandra (Sarah, after her grandmother), born February 8, 1943. She received a teacher's diploma, and settled in Israel, where she married in 1970 to David Hadad (later separated). Their daughter is Tali, born in Israel, 1970.

G18.3. Neil (Nachum), born in Cape Town,[21] October 31, 1944. Received his Medical Doctorate from the University of Cape Town in 1967 (M.B.Ch.B.). He married in

Johannesburg on January 14, 1968 to Mavis (Ita) Joyce daughter of Otto (Moses) Naumann. She was born in Johannesburg, October 19, 1944. Their children: Joel, born June 26, 1969, Tel Hashomer, Israel; Ari, born May 21, 1971, Cleveland, Ohio; and Moshe Baruch, born September 5, 1975, Elizabeth, New Jersey.

G18.4. Brenda (Bracha), born July 17, 1953, married in Jerusalem, August 16, 1973, to Steven (Chanoch) Abelman of Port Elizabeth, South Africa. Their sons: Akiva, born July 18, 1974 and Asael, born December 5, 1975.

G17.3. Samuel, born in 1917. He was married but perished with his wife and child during the Holocaust. He was a journalist.

G17.4. Raphael (named after his grandfather), born in 1919, and died of diphtheria in 1923.

G16.3. Samuel Katzenellenbogen, married and exiled to Siberia during the Russian Revolution.

G16.4. Tanya (Frume Toyba), named after her paternal great-grandmother, was born about 1893 and died in Cape Town in 1955. She married Samuel Tarshish. They immigrated to South Africa in 1928.

G17.1. Ethel, born in 1926, married David de Keyser, later divorced. She settled in London taking an active role against South African "apartheid" policy.

G17.2. Jack, born in 1920, unmarried, South Africa. Had to serve prison sentence for active anti-Government demonstrations.[22]

G16.5. Anna, married Haim Lafski (a cousin of Boris Rosenstein, her sister's husband). He was the son of Aaron Lafski, a member of the prominent family of that name in Vilna.

G16.6. Isaac Katzenellenbogen.

G16.7. Zeena, married Lazer Apatoff of Vilna. The Apatoff family was one of the more prominent in Vilna, with a large number of family members.

G16.8. Nachum, married Rosa.

G16.9. Fanya, married into the Eizov family. They settled in Cracow.

G16.10. Sander Katzenellenbogen.

G16.11. Bertha.

G15.2. Judah Meir (Jacob) Katzenellenbogen, was born in Vilna in 1865 (in the month of Cheshvan), and died in New York on April 9, 1920 (the 7th day of Passover). He lies buried in the Washington Cemetery, Brooklyn. There is a discrepancy between the Hebrew and English dates on the tombstone as regards his age at death. This is correctly fifty-four years.

He arrived in the U.S.A. about 1885 and established a bookstore at 66 Canal Street, on Manhattan's Lower East Side, which became a meeting place for Jewish scholars. He also began printing his own books. In 1900, with the help of his brother Mordecai, who came from Vilna for a visit, he became the co-founder of the Hebrew Publishing Company which originally had premises at No. 34 Eldridge Street, and later at 77-79 Delancey. As company president, he was the first to publish Jewish music, thereby putting Jewish theater on a firmer foundation, and also, the first to publish Jewish-Hebrew dictionaries in New York. He married Ida Willenefsky, who died in 1941, and was buried next to her husband. His death was an event of great mourning and the funeral, headed by New York's Chief Rabbi, Rabbi Margolies, was attended by thousands of people.

G16.1. David Hirsch, born in 1891, died on December 3, 1924, having served in the First World War. He lies buried next to his parents. He married Eva Jacobs (died in 1966), and had a son. She later remarried to Isidore Wexler.

G17. Judah (Jud) Wexler, adopting his stepfather's name. He was born on March 12, 1922 and obtained a B.S. in Pharmacy. He settled in Florida. He married in 1947 to Sydelle Leichter. Their daughter is Donna (Deborah), born May 19, 1951.

G16.2. Ethel, born in 1894 and died July 8, (25th Tammuz), 1953. She married Moe (Moses) Salwen, died in 1947. They are buried in the Montefiore Cemetery, Long Island.

G17.1. Ernest Daniel, born January 31, 1920 (B.A., M.B.A., Univ. Michigan), married in Detroit 1942 to Leona Gallow, born in 1918 (B.A. Education, Univ. Michigan). They settled in El Cerrito, California.

G18.1. Clifford Eric, born November 9, 1946 (B.S., Univ. California), married in San Francisco in 1968 to Gail Goldberg, born 1947.

G18.2. Monette, born June 20, 1948 (B.A., M.L.S., Univ. California), married in San Francisco in 1970 to Joel B. Meredith, born 1944. The daughter is Melanie Lynne, born January 20, 1973.

G17.2. Judith (Judy) Marian, born June 22, 1923 (B.A.), married in 1955 to Bernard Feder (C.P.A.), Engelwood Cliffs, New Jersey. Their daughter is Elizabeth, born July 8, 1958.

G17.3. David Judah, born August 24, 1926, married in 1949 to Barbara Wynn. They settled in Rockville Centre, Long Island. Their children: Ira Mitchell (Isaac Moses), born April 3, 1952; Ethel, born May 19, 1955; Susan, born April 17, 1958; Marcy Ilene, born March 22, 1960; and Seth Andrew (Shlomo Asa), born March 22, 1966.

G16.3. Reitze (Rose), born January 18, 1896, married twice: 1) in 1924 to Joshua Dubin, and 2) in 1934 to William Raskin. She died in 1974.

G17. Joseph Raskin, born February 17, 1935, married in 1958 to Rochelle Eybeschutz. Their children: William, born March 16, 1960, and Isabel, born September 1, 1962.

G16.4. John Isidore (Jonah Isaac), born in 1900. He shortened his name to Katze, and settled in Los Angeles. He was married twice. His second wife, Ethel Sellers, had a son from her previous marriage. They had no issue.

G16.5. Leah (Lillian), born in 1901, married in 1924 to Jacob Bernard Rosenfeld, died in 1971. They lived in Brooklyn, N.Y.

G17.1. Judah Meyer, born August 25, 1925 (B.A. 1949), married in New York in 1953 to Rhoda Katz (B.A. 1947). They live in New York. Their sons: Joel Benjamin (Judah), born May 17, 1957, and Mark (Moshe) Raphael, born November 27, 1964.

G17.2. Mordechai, born February 1, 1930 (B.A. 1951, Ll.B. 1954), married in 1963 to Susan Comora (M.A. 1956). They live in New York. Their children: Michael John (Johanan), born December 9, 1966, and Amy Ruth, born June 24, 1969.

G16.6. Gertrude (Goldie, Gwyn), born 1907, married Harry Laitin (deceased). They had no issue.

G16.7. Samuel, died in New York in infancy.

G15.3. Abraham Abba Katzenellenbogen, born in Vilna in 1867, the third son of Samuel Michal. He was first married to Gitel (Gita) Zauberblatt, and settled in Grodno, where they had three daughters. In the late teens of this century, after the death of his wife in 1916, he immigrated to the U.S.A., and established a printing shop at No. 187 Division Street on Manhattan's Lower East Side. In New York, he remarried to Taube Agar, and they also had three daughters.

Abba suffered from Asthma, and spent his latter years in Lakewood, New Jersey, where he died on the first day of Passover (15th Nissan), April 17, 1927. He was buried in the small local Jewish Mt. Sinai Cemetery, only three streets away from where he lived, and close by the Synagogue "Sons of Israel." After his death, his second wife and daughters went out to the west coast, and settled in San Francisco.

From first wife:

G16.1. Anna, married a Dr. Sluzky (Sluzkin) in Moscow. They had issue.

G16.2. Fania, born January 1, 1904 in Grodno. She later went to Rome, Italy, where she married in 1926 to Romolo Pieroni (a Catholic of Jewish descent).

G17.1. Sonia, born in Rome July 30, 1929, and married there on August 28, 1949 to Moshe Dobrejcer. They immigrated to Australia, and settled in Melbourne. Their children: Doris E., born April 2, 1953, married 1974 to William Benet; Leah, born June 27, 1956; Anna, born May 17, 1958; and Gary, born December 1963.

G17.2. Three brothers, two in Rome, each married with four children, and one in Melbourne, with three daughters.

G16.3. Bertha, born August 3, 1913 in Grodno. She immigrated to Palestine as a young lady. She later married Theo Gunther, and they settled in Nicosia, Cyprus, and in 1967 settled in Australia. They had no issue.

From second wife there are three children whose whereabouts are unknown.

G15.4. Leah, born in Russia and died in Johannesburg, South Africa in 1937. She married Jacob Kawarsky (1870-1926).

G16.1. Jenny (Ginger), born January 7, 1898, married in 1926 to Wilf Stern (deceased).

G17. Natalie born May 9, 1932, married in 1956 to Zelig Genn. Their children are: Shala, born July 16, 1957 and Clive, born August 14, 1960.

G16.2. Dora, born January 29, 1900, married in 1930 to Harry Cantor.

G17. Isabelle, born April 17, 1932, married Simon Margolis. Their sons are Lawrence and Robin.

G16.3. Lottie, born April 2, 1902, died April 5, 1952, married in 1923 to Willie Barnett.

G17. Daphne, born April 18, 1926, married Alec Mailer. Their children are Clifford and Linda.

G16.4. Samuel, born January 15, 1904, died October 19, 1969, married in 1946 to Victoria (Vicky) Selley. They had no issue.

G16.5. Sayde, born October 2, 1905, died July 16, 1967, married Joe Goldstein (deceased). They had no issue.

G16.6. Barney, born January 5, 1907, married in 1950 to Dorothy Hattersly. They had no issue.

G16.7. Louis (Lulu), born February 24, 1916, married in 1953 to Hilda Goodman. They had no issue.

BRANCH II (second son)

(PINSK — KARLIN)

G14.2. Abraham Abba Katzenellenbogen of Pinsk, a prominent Jewish city in the Government of Minsk (Russia). It was noted for its large number of Jewish factories, tanneries, sawmills, shipyards and foundries. The total Jewish population during his lifetime was about 18,000 out of 28,000. He settled in its suburb of Karlin which became known as one of the strongholds of Hassidism with its followers of the Perlow family of Rebbes, until 1870, when they removed to nearby Stolin.

In Karlin, Abba, named after his maternal grandfather, supplied the cutlery and crockery at weddings, and also had his father's Responsa, the *Zerah Yitzchak* published at Warsaw in 1898. He died in 1914, shortly after his daughter, Minnie, had sailed from New York to Russia to fetch him, but was compelled to turn back at the outbreak of World War I. He was married twice, and had issue from both. His second wife was Dinah Pomerance.

G15.1. Michal Katzenellenbogen, born in Russia in 1868 and died in Pasadena, Calif. on February 17, 1922 while visiting his sister and brother-in-law there. He was buried in the Mt. Judah Cemetery in Brooklyn. Like other members of the family, he had a modest stationery store at 52 Canal Street on Manhattan's Lower East Side during the 1910's, in partnership with his brother Samuel. He was already in the U.S.A. at the time his father published the *Zerah Yitzchak,* and wrote a letter home to his father in 1897, saying: ". . . how great is my joy at the publication of the Responsa 'Zerah Yitzchak' . . . that the memory of our father will be thus remembered forever." He was the eldest child from his father's first wife. He was married twice, his second wife was Ettie Pomerance, who had a child from her previous marriage.

G16.1. Joel Isaac (Jules Irwin), shortened his name to Bogen, was born in New York City on September 19, 1903, the son of his father's second wife. He was named after his father's grandfather, author of the *Zerah Yitzchak,* who had died some thirteen years before. Jules was a brilliant scholar, and received his B.S. at Columbia University in 1922, his M.A. in 1924, and his Ph.D. in 1927. That same year, on September 24th, he married Victoria Gombert. In his early years, he was a reporter for the New York Journal of Commerce and, later became one of its leading editors. During 1924-5, he was an instructor for foreign trade at New York University, and then, successively, Assistant Professor (in 1927-9), Associate Professor (1929-1932), and Professor from 1932 onwards. In 1963 he was Chairman of the Banking and Finance Department and Research Professor of Finance. During his lifetime, he had also been a Consultant Economist for the Savings Bank Trust Company (1947), technical advisor of the sub-committee of the Senate, on the Committee on Banking and Currency (1930-31), and was the author of:

1. *The Anthracite Railroads* (1927).
2. *Analysis of Railroad Securities* (1928).
3. *Investment Banking* (1929, 1937, with H. P. Willis).
4. *Corporation Finance* (1930).
5. *The Banking Crisis* (1933, with Marcus Nadler, 1895-1965, his lifelong friend).
6. *The New Tax Program* (1935).

7. *Money and Banking* (1936, with M. B. Foster, M. Nadler and R. Rodgers).

8. *Security Credit* (1960, with H. E. Kroos).

Jules was also a contributor to articles on banking, business finance and taxation in the New International Year Book from 1937 onwards.

He died in New York on May 17, 1963, and was buried in the Cemetery of the Sephardic Congregation, of which he had been a member, the "She'erith Israel."

G17.1. Mitchel Arthur (Michael Abba), born in 1931, named after his paternal grandfather and great-grandfather. He married in New York in 1971 to Myung Nun Lee. Their son is Jules Lee, born November 13, 1973.

G17.2. Stephen David, born in 1934.

G17.3. Vivian Marie, born in 1944. Received an M.A. in Fine Arts from Columbia University. Married in 1966 to Jeffrey Gorden (New York).

G16.2. Mason (Nathan) Bogen, 1906-1966, buried in the She'erith Israel Cemetery. He married in 1942 to Shirley Sokol (ow), later divorced. She remarried to Harold Sherry. Mason was from the second marriage and had one child. Their daughter is Arleen, born December 24, 1949.

G16.3. Daughter from the first marriage.

G15.2. Samuel Katzenellenbogen, born in Pinsk in 1879 and came to U.S.A. in 1897, where he settled in New York. He married in 1898 to Eva Mickalitsky (died in 1958) of Pinsk. At the beginning of the century, he was a furrier, but because of seasonal variations of his earnings, he went to work with his brother Michal on the Lower East Side. Then, later, like others of the family, he established a printing firm for himself, which became known as the "Gem Press," finally located on Park Ave, New York (established in 1938). It is still managed by members of his family. He died on July 3, 1934, and was buried in the Mt. Judah Cemetery, next to his brother Michal. (His sons adopted the surname of Katz).

G16.1. Feigel (Frances, Fanny), 1899-1966, buried in Mt. Hebron Cemetery, Queens. She was married twice, secondly to Louis Burstein. They had no issue.

G16.2. David (Dunny) Katz, 1901-1955, married Marion Stolwein. They had no issue. (He was buried in the Katz Family Plot, Beth El Cemetery, Paramus, N.J.)

G16.3. Menashe (Max), born December 8, 1903, married twice: 1) in 1927 to Lillian Goldstein, and had issue. 2) in 1953 to Rose Gottfried (Davis). He retired from the Gem Press in 1970.

    G17.1. Marilyn, born March 15, 1930, married in 1947 to Stanley Hookman (Lt. Colonel, San Antonio, Texas). Their son is Laurence, born May 22, 1956.

    G17.2. Susan, born June 17, 1935, married in 1958 to Lesley Gamza (Cranford, New Jersey). Their children: Lori, born April 3, 1957, and Alan, born November 23, 1959.

G16.4. Beila (Blanche), 1906-1971, married Joseph Falk in 1930.

    G17. Sandra, born in 1937 (M.A.).

G16.5. Nathan, born in 1909, married in 1936 to Leah Cohen.

    G17. Steven, born in 1939.

G16.6. George (Joseph), born August 10, 1910, married in 1942 to Emma Krigler (Rockland County, New York).

    G17.1. Gary, born August 20, 1947.
    G17.2. Peter, 1951-3.
    G17.3. Deborah, born August 21, 1956.

G16.7. Irving (Isaac), born in 1917, married Anna Zimmerman (Long Island).

    G17.1. Samuel, killed in a plane crash, 1959.
    G17.2. Walter, born 1942, married Maxime. Their son is Samuel, born 1971.
    G17.3. Donna, born in 1944, married Paul Ivory. Their sons are Paul II, Steven and Andrew.
    G17.4. Bruce, born in 1946, married Barbara.
    G17.5. Laurence (Larry) and Lynn, twins born in 1948. Laurence married Eilene Brady.

G16.8. Libby (Lillian), born in 1920, married in 1940 to Phillip Gullo (Nassau County, N.Y.).

    G17.1. Steven, born in 1943, married in 1962 to Christine Badomi. Their sons: Phillip, born in 1964, and Jason, born in 1968.

G15.3. Malka Sarah (Manya, Minnie) Katzenellenbogen, born in Pinsk in 1874, and immigrated to the U.S.A. at the age of sixteen. The following year, 1890, she married Julius Cassileth, a furrier, in New York City. In their latter years they lived in Pasadena, California, where their brother Michal was visiting at the time of his death in 1922. Julius also died there on May 22, 1929, and was buried in the Montefiore Cemetery (Long Island). Minnie died on December 15, 1954, and was also buried there.

G16.1. Son, died in infancy.

G16.2. Frume Toyba (Mathilda, Tilly), named after her grandfather Abba's mother (wife of Joel Isaac K.). She was born in New York on November 22, 1895. She was married twice: in 1915 to Alexander Encherman (died in 1965) whom she later divorced, and, secondly, in 1929, to Max Prown (died in 1969). They settled in Red Bank, New Jersey. She had issue from both husbands.

G17.1. Claire Iris (Chaya Itzig), born July 5, 1916, married in 1939 to Benjamin Emanuel Lobell (Manhattan).

G18.1. Judith (Judel Rochel) born January 9, 1942 (A.A.) She married in 1964 to Jerrold F. Heller, D.D.S., later divorced. Their son is David Alexander, born February 6, 1967.

G18.2. Robert David (Reuben YomTov), born January 29, 1945 (B.A.).

G17.2. Robert Encherman, born August 20, 1918 (B.A.). He married in 1947 to Carolmae Baehr (B.A.), (Merrick, Long Island). Their children: Susan, born July 31, 1950; William, born February 7, 1953; and Nancy, born August 12, 1957.

G17.3. Jules David Prown, born in Freehold, N.J., March 14, 1930. In 1947, he graduated from Peddie School and four years later, received his B.A. (Lafayette College), followed by a M.A. and his Ph.D. in 1961. He married on June 23, 1956 to Shirley Ann Martin, and settled in Orange, Connecticut. From 1957-8, Jules was Director of the Historical Society of Old Newbury, Newburyport, Mass. From 1967-71, he was Asst. Professor of Art History, and from 1971 on, Full Professor at Yale University (New Haven). From 1963-8, he was Curator of the Garvan and related Collections of American Art at the University Gallery, and Director of the Paul Mellon Center for British Art and British Studies from 1968. He was a visiting lecturer at Smith College in 1966-7, on the visiting committee of the American Paintings of the Metropolitan Museum of Art (New York City) from 1968, and a member of the advisory commission of the National Portrait Gallery in Washington in 1969. Besides being a member of various historical and art societies, he was the author of *John Singleton Copley* (2 Volumes, 1966), and *American Painting from its Beginnings to the Armory Show* (1969).

Their children: Elizabeth Anderson, born August 9, 1957; David Martin, born November 18, 1959; Jonathan, born January 20, 1959; Peter Cassileth, born March 20, 1963; and Sarah Peiter, born November 23, 1967.

G16.3. Marion, born March 30, 1899, married in New York in 1920 to Alvin Rosenberg.

G17.1. William Joseph, born August 11, 1920, married in 1942 to Geraldine Zuck (Hewlett, Long Island).

G18.1. Jane Roberta, born November 18, 1944, married in 1966 to Steven Verona (DDS). Their sons are Brett Alan, born October 16, 1969, and Bryan Scott, born April 4, 1972.

G18.2. Peter Milton, born July 11, 1955.

G18.3. Susan Helen, born May 2, 1957.

G17.2. Wynn Michael Reynolds (Merwin Rosenberg) of Tappan, New York, born January 14, 1923. Received his Ph.D. from Columbia University in 1957. In 1968 he became Professor of Communication Arts and Sciences at Bronx Community College, New York.

G16.4. Max Cassileth, born June 17, 1897, married in New York in 1918 to Beatrice Goodman. They settled in Los Angeles.

G17.1 Edith, born March 31, 1919 in New York, married in Los Angeles to Benjamin Lane. Their sons: Steven, died in a car accident in Los Angeles on February 28, 1969, and Robert, born December 26, 1946.

G17.2. Joyce, born December 3, 1922 in New York, married in Los Angeles to Benjamin Morrison. Their sons: James (Jimmy) born September 28, 1947, married to Luz Elena Calleros in 1971 in Los Angeles, and Thomas, born December 27, 1948.

G17.3. Roberta, born September 16, 1931 in New York, married in Los Angeles to Leonard Freedman. Their sons are Jeffrey, born July 11, 1953, and Ronald, born February 15, 1957.

G15.4. Jacob (Chana, Chuntsche) Katzenellenbogen, born in Pinsk on January 18, 1882, the youngest son of his father Abba and his second wife, Dinah Pomerance. He left Russia in 1901 to join his brothers in New York. Here he was in various stationery businesses, and in 1903, married Fanny Levy (died in 1958). He spent many years away from his wife and children, but returned home where he died on January 9, 1962. He was buried in the Kaye Family Plot of the New Montefiore Cemetery, Pine Lawn, Long Island. During his lifetime, he shortened his surname to Katzen, and his children adopted the name of Kaye or Kay.

G16.1. Dinah (Diana), born February 12, 1904, married Abraham Pinchuck.

G17.1. Robert, born April 15, 1928, unmarried (Monticello, N.Y.).

G17.2. Toby (Thelma, Terry), born October 16, 1931, married in 1951 to Harry Broderson (Brooklyn). Their children are Jacki Sue, born October 28, 1956, and Richard Dennis, born March 18, 1953.

G17.3. Martin, born March 3, 1940, married 1) Phyllis (later divorced) and had issue, and 2) in 1965 to Leah Rosen. Their children: Curt, born February 6, 1960; Abraham, born April 17, 1967; and Grace, born July 25, 1970.

G16.2. Murray (Meir Mendel) Kaye, born in 1905, unmarried (Brooklyn).

G16.3. Irving Kaye (Isaac), born in 1907. Married twice but had no issue. Retired to Florida.

G16.4. Benjamin Kay, born in 1909, married to Barbara Shebroe. They had no issue (Brooklyn).

G16.5. Emanuel (Mannie) Kaye, born January 19, 1911. He married twice: 1) in 1935 to Janet Casin, later divorced, and had issue, and 2) in 1965 to Judith Zigler, died in 1973 (Fort Lee, New Jersey).

G17.1. Jeffrey, born October 22, 1940, married in 1961 to Helaine Appelman. Their children are, Stacey, born June 8, 1965, and Meryl, born January 2, 1963.

G17.2. Richard, born April 28, 1943.

G16.6. Estelle, born May 20, 1913, married to Irvin Paul (later separated).

G17.1. Emanuel, born December 31, 1937, married twice: 1) Frances Hamilton and had issue, and 2) in 1961 to Barbara Konefal and had issue. Their children: Scott, born March 24, 1959; Kandee, born June 29, 1962; Guy, born December 24, 1963; and Todd, born October 7, 1967.

G17.2. Allan, born February 16, 1941, married Gail (Edison, N.J.). Their children are Steven and Randye.

G17.3. Ronald.

G16.7. Abraham, born February 23, 1915, married in 1939 to Selma Medvin (Spring Valley, N.Y.).

G17.1. Barry Dennis, born February 8, 1941, married in 1963 to Beverly Walder. Their children: Lisa Michelle, born August 20, 1965; Jody Lynne, born March 25, 1969; and Lori, born April 13, 1972.

G17.2. Craig, born November 19, 1944, married in 1967 to Carol Norman. Their children are Ian Scot, born July 15, 1969, and Alicia Daryl, born April 26, 1972.

G17.3. Stewart Curt, born January 25, 1955.

CHAPTER IX

RABBI ABRAHAM JOSHUA HESCHEL OF CRACOW
AND THE FAMILY BACKGROUND

ONE of the outstanding Talmudic scholars of his day, R. Heschel was first a teacher in Brest-Litovsk, where his father, R. Jacob was A.B.D. and head of the Yeshiva. Then, in 1630, his father was appointed A.B.D. of Lublin and head of their Yeshiva. R. Heschel followed on, and again assisted his father until the latter's death in 1644. He then became head of the Yeshiva. At this time, Rabbi Naftali Katz was in Lublin and became the A.B.D. after R. Jacob. R. Naftali was married to Dinah Katzenellenbogen, Heschel's mother's first cousin. Together, R. Naftali and R. Heschel gave their approbation on *Damesek Eliezer*. When R. Naftali died in 1649, R. Heschel became his successor having waited only five years for the position since his father's death. He had also lost his first wife, the daughter of R. Moses Lazers of Brest, and remarried his second cousin, Dinah, the former wife of R. Naftali Katz. The story goes that she had desired this second marriage to this *Gaon* (Genius), who was accustomed to study and visit in her father's house years before. She was known as Dinah *de Gedole* (the great) for her knowledge of Jewish Law.

R. Heschel remained at Lublin for four years and was then called to the post of A.B.D. of Cracow and head of their Yeshiva, succeeding the famous *Tosfot YomTov*, Rabbi YomTov Lipman Halevi Heller, who died there in 1654.

He wrote approbations to *Amarot Tehorot*, at Lublin, published there in 1645; *Maggid Meisharim*, at Lublin in 1646; *Yoreh Deah*, at Lublin in

1646, published at Cracow; *Damesek Eliezer,* together with R. Naftali Katz in 1645; *Peirush* on *Massorah* in 1645, published at Amsterdam in 1650; and *Choshen Mishpat* at Gremnitz in 1654.

R. Heschel was wealthy as well as being very pious, and his reputation attracted numerous students, among whom were R. Shabbtai, son of Meir HaKohen; R. Aaron Samuel Koidanover; R. David Halevi (author of *HaTaZ*) and his son, R. Samuel; R. Gershon Ashkenazi and R. Hillel of Brest Litovsk. His method of teaching was of the didactical type of Talmudic study, known as *Pilpul.* His renown as a legal authority spread far and wide and questions were addressed to him from all over Europe. When he did give decisions, often reluctantly, they were brief, logical and to the point.

During the years of unrest between 1648 and 1649, while at Lublin, the Cossacks under Bogdan Chmielnicki began their blood-thirsty massacre against the Jews, particularly of the Ukraine, Volhynia and Podolia. R. Heschel was obliged to flee from Lublin to the district of Merrin and then to Austria where he was again safe. During this period it has been estimated that between one hundred thousand to three hundred thousand Jewish souls perished in various towns and cities. As a result, many women lost their husbands and the problem of *Agunah* (a woman legally, according to Jewish law, restricted from remarrying until definite proof of her husband's death was obtained) arose. In many such cases R. Heschel was approached for his decision.

One such case involved a certain R. Jacob Ashkenazi, his sister's son and father of the famous Chacham Zvi, who was married in Vilna to Nechama, daughter of R. Ephraim HaKohen, A.B.D. of Vilna. In a Chmielnicki raid on the city of Vilna in 1648, R. Jacob was captured by the enemy, having been separated from his wife and her family during their flight from the city. Their belief was that he had perished, but his life had been spared by the Cossacks. Nechama and her father settled in Trevicz in Merrin, and on the evidence of research into the events of her husband's tragedy, the officials of Vilna concluded that he had died. When he was thus approached, R. Heschel permitted her to remarry. To everyone's surprise R. Jacob returned six months later very much alive. R. Heschel thereafter resolved never again to give legal decisions in these matters.

After these troubles he was commissioned by the Polish communities to solicit financial aid from the wealthier Jewish communities of Austria, Bohemia and Moravia for the victims of the Cossack massacres. R. Heschel was also said to have received an audience with the Austrian Emperor.

He died in Cracow in 1663.

His works were: Commentaries on *Sefer Mitzvot Gadol,* by R. Moses of Coucy, published Kopost in 1807; Novellae on *Baba Kamma, B. Metzia* and *B. Batra* in *Toldot Aharon* by R. Aaron Kelniker, his student, published Lublin in 1682; *Chidshei Halachot,* Offenbach 1723; 600 homilies on the Torah in *Hanukat HaTorah* by E. J. Erosh, published in 1900, and gathered from different 17th and 18th century Rabbinical sources; Responsa in the works of others, e.g. *Asifat Zekeinim, Teshuvot Geonei Batra,* and *Amudei Shitim;* Novellae and a commentary on *Shulchan Aruch* in manuscript at Oxford.

THE CHILDREN AND GRANDCHILDREN OF
R. ABRAHAM JOSHUA HESCHEL
OF CRACOW[1]

G6.1. R. Eliezer, A.B.D. Dubno from 1715-19, succeeding R. Isaac, son of R. Saul Gunzburg. Head of the Landau Family Pedigree. (See this section — Chapter X.)

G6.2. R. Mordecai, married Sarel, daughter of R. Jonah, son of R. Isaiah Teomim. (See Teomim Family Pedigree — Chapter IV.)

G6.3. R. Issachar Berish of Cracow, *Parnas* (President) of the Council of the Four Lands. He died in 1690 in Cracow. He wrote approbations to the Bible in German, published in Amsterdam by Atias, written in 1677 while he was presiding over the Council at Jaroslav Fair, *Zerah Avraham,* written in 1683, and *Ketonet Or,* published by R. Isaac Meir Frankel in 1684. His signature appears fifth in the letter sent to his nephew, R. Moses, son of R. Abraham, author of *Tiferet le Moshe.* It appears that he was married twice, and possibly three times: first to the daughter of R. Mordecai Yollis of Cracow; second to the daughter of R. Joshua Feiwel Teomim (see Chapter IV); and third to the daughter of R. David (died 1698), son of R. Shabtai Kohen (author of *HaShach,* who died in 1662). R. Berish was head of the Babad Family. (See Chapter XI.)

G6.4. R. Saul lived at first at Lublin with his father, R. Heschel, until the latter's death in 1663. Then he went to Brest, from whence his mother came. (Both of R. Heschel's wives came from Brest.) Here he was elected the head of the city's *Yeshiva-Klaus* in 1680, and then A.B.D. Keidan in 1685, where his signature appeared in the Minutes of the Rabbinical Council. His next Rabbinical post was A.B.D. of Brest, where he wrote approbations to: *Shabta D'Rigla* by R. Zvi Hirsch, son of Jerachmeel, in 1691, published in Furth in 1693; *Divrei Chachamim* by R. Judah Lieb Puchweitzer in 1692, while he presided at the Chamsk Council of the Four Lands meeting, published in Hamburg in 1692-93; and *Shem Shmuel* by R. Samuel, son of R. Moses, in 1698, published in Frankfurt-on-Oder in 1699. In 1698 R. Saul was called to become A.B.D. of Opatow (Apt) and the Cracow District, where he wrote five more approbations to *Ohil Yaakov* by R. Jacob, son of R. David Shapiro, in 1698, published in Frankfurt-on-Oder in 1719; *Magen Avot* to the *TaZ*, in 1700; *Maginei Shlomo* by R. Joshua, son of R. Joseph in 1700, published in Amsterdam in 1715; *Brit Mateh Moshe,* a Haggadah Commentary, in 1700; and *Kevod Chachamim* by R. Judah Lieb Puchweitzer in 1700 when he was at the Jaroslav Council of the Four Lands meeting, published in Venice in 1700.

In 1701 R. Saul became A.B.D. of Cracow where he wrote another five approbations to *Rosh Yosef,* by R. Joseph of Zulz, in 1701; *Lekach Tov,* by R. Eliezer Lipman of Zamocz in 1701, published in Frankfurt-on-Oder in 1705; *Chemdat Tzvi,* in 1704; *Naftali Sheva Retzon,* by R. Naftali Hirsch Gunzburg in 1705, published in Hamburg in 1705; and *Ir Binyamin,* by R. Benjamin Zoa son of R. Samuel Darshan, in 1709, published in Furth in 1722. R. Saul was also a member of the Rabbinical Councils of Krinek (near Grodno) and Zulz, in 1687 and 1700 respectively, where he signed in the Minutes.

His responsa are found in the works *Yad Eli* (No. 18); *Shavot Yaakov* (No. 107); and *Rema* (at the end). He was finally offered a position of A.B.D. Amsterdam in 1707, to succeed R. Moses Judah son of R. Kalonymus Kohen, but on his way there he died at Glogau. He was married to the daughter of R. Ari Lieb, A.B.D. Cracow, son of R. Zechariah Hanavi (the Prophet). His four children were the founders of large Rabbinical families. (See Descendants of R. Saul Heschel — Chapter XII.)

G6.5. Wife of R. Abraham, son of R. Jacob Jokel, son of R. Samuel, son of R. Helman (the brother of R. Bezalel, father of the *MaHaRal* of Prague).

G7. R. Moses, who as a young man first studied under his grandfather, R. Heschel, in Brest, where he later established his own Yeshiva. He was the author of Novellae *Tiferet leMoshe,* published by his grandson in 1776 at Berlin; and also *Hagahot* on the Talmud in 1673. He was A.B.D. Grodno and signed at the Meeting of the Council of the Four Lands at Zulz (1673), Zablodov (1676), Chamsk (1679) and Luntchne (1681). He wrote approbations to *Migdal David* in 1674 at Grodno, and *Kanah Chochma* in 1679 at Chamsk.

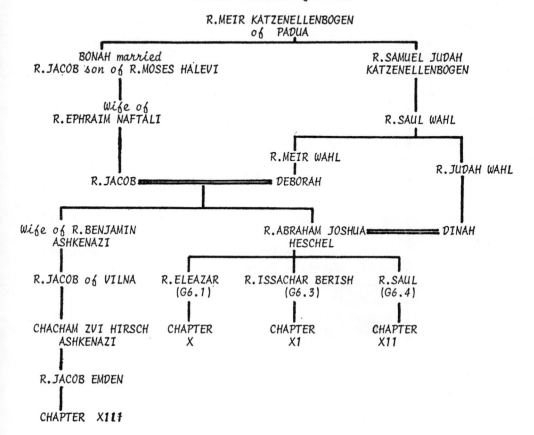

DESCENDANTS OF R. ABRAHAM
JOSHUA HESCHEL of CRACOW

R. MEIR KATZENELLENBOGEN
of PADUA

In 1680 he was called to become head of the Yeshiva in Cracow, but died the following year before he could ascend to the post. He married Nechama, daughter of R. Benjamin Mirels. She died at Grodno in 1742 and was eulogized by R. Samuel, A.B.D. Amdor (author of *Teshuvot Shmuel*). The eulogy appears at the end of the work by her husband. Her grandson wrote a lamentation on her which he published at Grodno. He died in Grodno on April 28, 1681.

G8.1. R. Haim of Grodno, married the granddaughter of R. Israel Swincher, A.B.D. Lutzk.

G9. R. Solomon, who published his grandfather's *Tiferet leMoshe* in 1776. He wrote an approbation to *Sha'arei Binyamin* by R. Benjamin Zeev Ashkenazi in 1752, published in Zolkiev in 1752. He

was one of the Rabbis of Lithuania at the Mir Council who denounced R. Jonathan Eybeschutz.

G8.2. Wife of R. Baruch Rappoport[2] (son of R. Moses Meir of Lvov),
initially A.B.D. in Vilna for a while, succeeding R. Hillel Halevi
who died in 1706. He became A.B.D. Furth at this time, succeeding R. Eliezer Heilprin, who died in 1700, and of Grodno
in 1715 upon the departure of his uncle, R. Simha Rappoport
for Lublin. This position had also been held by his father-in-
law. He wrote a number of approbations in these different
towns. His responsa appeared in the *Or Ne'elam* and *Shem
Ya'akov,* and his written works were left unpublished. He was
an opponent of Nehemiah Hayun (1714), R. Moses Haim Luzzatto (1735) and R. Isaiah Bassan. He died in 1746.

G9.1. R. Aryey Lieb Rappoport, a wealthy merchant, contemporary
of R. Haim David Azulai (who received some stories from him
about his revered father), and later A.B.D. Schneitich and
Heilzfeld (Wurzburg district). He wrote an approbation with
his father to *Me'adeni Yom Tov* (Furth 1744), to *Chochmat
Shlomo* (Sulzbach 1755). He married Esther, the daughter of
R. Gompel Emrich of Vienna. She died in Frankfurt-on-Main
in 1768.

G10. R. Isaac the Scribe.

G11. R. Jonah Rappoport of Nodvahar, wrote approbations to
the three books published there in 1794 by R. Joseph To-
wetz. They were *Or Machamim* (4th edition), *Yesod
Emunah* (5th edition) and *Ma'amar Ha'acheirto* (4th
edition).

G9.2. R. Zvi Hirsch Rappoport, A.B.D. Wallerstein and Homburg.
He wrote an approbation (as did his brother) to *Chochmat
Shlomo* in 1752 and to *Reishit Chochmah,* which was pub-
lished in Furth. He died in 1763.

G10.1. R. Isaac Rappoport, Dayan of Lissa, later succeeded his
father in Wallerstein and was then A.B.D. of Bonn. He
also wrote an approbation to *Reishit Chochmah* in 1762,
and to some other works as well. He died in Rheindorf
in 1788.

G10.2. Simha Bonem Rappoport, A.B.D. Wurzburg, Markbreit,
Wallerstein and Bonn (Cologne district). After his mar-

riage he settled in Heilzfeld and later succeeded his uncle
R. Aryey Lieb Rappoport as Chief Rabbi of the Wurzburg district. He became A.B.D. Markbreit and finally accepted the post of A.B.D. Wallerstein where his father and
brother had been previously. He was a renowned scholar
and much of his correspondence is included in the works
of his contemporaries. He wrote *Chidushei RaShBatz* and
Parparat RaShBatz. He died in 1816.

G11. R. Samuel of Kellin.

G9.3. R. Wolf Rappoport of Furth.

G10. R. Isaac Rappoport, A.B.D. Leipnik. He married when he
was eighteen to the daughter of R. Gershon, son of R. Moses
Pollitz, A.B.D. of Nikolsburg. He was the author of *Meah
Derushim,* which was left unpublished. He died in Leipnik.

G11. R. Benjamin Zeev Rappoport, born in 1754, and married
in 1771 to the daughter of R. David Boskowitz. He wrote
Simlat Binyamin, Simlah Shri'ah, Eidut LeYisrael and
others. He died in 1837.

G12. R. Mendel Rappoport, who published his father's
books.

G9.4. Wife of R. Samuel Shapiro.
G9.5. Wife of R. Israel, A.B.D. Offenbach and Hanau, son of R.
Naftali Hirsch Ashkenazi, A.B.D. Kobly. (Rabbi Israel's
brother, R. Zvi Hirsch Halberstadt, was the ancestor of the
Halberstam Chassidic Dynasty and Family.)
G9.6. Wife of R. Nathan Nata, A.B.D. Torbin. A responsa of his can
be found in *Beit Avraham* by R. Abraham, A.B.D. Tarla.

G10. Wife of R. Joseph, son of R. Aryey Lieb Teomim. (See Teomim Family.)

G9.7. Wife of R. Isaac Oppenheim, son of R. Ber, A.B.D. Pressburg.

G10.1. R. Haim Oppenheim, A.B.D. Dressnitz.

G11. R. Dov Ber, A.B.D. Eybeschutz.

G12.1. R. Haim Oppenheim, 1833-91 A.B.D. Merrin (Prus-
sia).
G12.2. R. David Oppenheim. His son, R. Joachim.
G12.3. Hinde, married R. Isaac Hirsch Weiss, died in 1905.

G10.2. R. Ber Oppenheim succeeded his brother as A.B.D. Dress-nitz and was the author of the responsa *Mei Bor,* published in Vienna in 1829. A responsum to him can be found in the *Ateret Chachamim* by R. Baruch Frankel-Teomim of Leipnik.

G6.6. Esther, married R. Nathan Nata, son of R. Isaiah of Hildesheim (son-in-law of R. Nathan Shapiro, author of *Megalleh Amukot*). She died in 1668 in Cracow.

G7. R. Isaiah, A.B.D. Kobly. He wrote a number of approbations between 1712-1724.

G8. R. Zechariah.

G9. R. Israel Pineles of Lvov. He and his father are mentioned in the *Megalleh Amukot,* by his ancestor, published in Lvov in 1795.

G6.7. Wife of R. Aaron Zvi Hirsch Hakohen.

G7.1. R. Moses Hakohen, pupil of R. Abraham Broda, author of *Asifat HaKohen,* published in Amsterdam in 1731.

G8. R. Joshua Heschel, whose novellae appear in his father's work.

G7.2. R. Isaac Joshua Heschel Hakohen, whose novellae appear in his brother's work.

G8. R. Abraham, A.B.D. Tarla, Neeman (trustee and second in command) of the Council of the Four Lands, author of *Beit Avraham* and *Get Kasher.* He wrote an approbation to *Tavnit HaBayit* in 1745.

G7.3. R. Nathan Nata Hakohen, whose novellae appear in his brother's work.

G7.4. Blume, married R. Isaac, son of R. Abraham Hakohen. He is mentioned in the *Nodah BiYehudah* by R. Ezekiel Landau.

G6.8. Karindel, married R. Shraga Feiwel. She died in childbirth in 1675 in Cracow.

G6.9. Wife of R. Meshullam.

G7. Wife of R. Mordecai, son of R. Naftali Katz A.B.D. Ostrow. Mordecai was A.B.D. Brody and then Posen. (See Chapter V — Katz Family.)

G6.10. Feige, married R. Naftali Hirsch, son of R. Benjamin Wolf. He
was successively A.B.D. Pinczow and Lublin, where he died in
1682, and his wife in 1691. He wrote approbations to: *Leket Shmuel*
in Pinczow, 1673; *Aderet Eli* in Lublin, 1678; *Kanah Chochmah*,
by R. J. L. Puchweitzer in Jaroslav, 1680; *Divrei Chachamim* by
R. J. L. Puchweitzer in Jaroslav, 1680; *Beit Yehudah* by R. Judah
of Kalicz, in 1680; *Zerah Avraham* in 1680; and *Olat HaTamid* in
1680. R. Naftali is mentioned in *Birkat HaZavach* and *Yedei Moshe*
(by his pupil, R. Moses Joseph of Zulz). He signed in the Minutes
of the Council of the Four Lands at Lentchov in 1681.

G6.11. Hesia (born after her father's death), was the second wife of R.
Meir, son of R. Benjamin Wolf A.B.D. Apt and Lublin, succeeding
R. Simha Rappoport at Lublin.

  G7. R. Aryey Lieb of Buczacz and head of the Lvov Community. He
married Jochebed, daughter of R. David of Zamocz.

G6.12. Wife of R. Samson HaKohen.

  G7. Daughter, married R. Joel Heilprin[3] of Zamocz, the elder, author of
Nifolot Elohim, published in Zolkiev 1710.

    G8. R. Uri Heilprin.

      G9. R. Joel Heilprin.

        G10. R. Isaiah Heilprin.

          G11. R. Zvi Hirsch of Zamocz, married the daughter of R. Alex-
ander Ginsburg.

            G12. R. Zeev Wolf Schiff, whose daughter, Gitel, married R.
Solomon Rubinstein. (See Chapter VII — Branch B —
G7.1/8.1/9/10.)

CHAPTER X

LANDAU FAMILY PEDIGREE

ANCESTRY

G3.3. Saul Wahl Katzenellenbogen.

G4.6. Judah Wahl.

G5.2. Dinah, married R. Heschel of Cracow.

G6.1. R. Eliezer, A.B.D. of Dubno.

G7. Wife of R. Zvi Hirsch Landau (died in 1714), who was known as R. Hirsch Witeles and a delegate to the Council of the Four Lands. He was the son of R. Ezekiel Landau (a judge in Apt, and his wife Witush, daughter of Isaac Harif—hence the name Witeles), son of R. Benjamin Wolf. The family was of Levite origin, hence known as Segal-Landau.

G8.1. R. Abraham Landau, the A.B.D. of Apt the early 1700s, where the family had been prominent for some three generations. He was mentioned in the Community Records during 1711 and 1747.

G9.1. R. Joseph Landau, A.B.D. of Neustadt where he wrote an approbation to *Keter Aharon* written in 1781, which was a commentary to *Keter HaOlam* by R. Aaron son of R. Moses of Zablodov, Zolkiev Edition of 1782. He was also mentioned in the Apt Records of 1727 when he became a member of the Chevra Kadisha.

G10.1. R. Zvi Landau, A.B.D. Sanz.

G10.2. R. Eleazar Landau, A.B.D. Turbin, mentioned in the Apt Records of 1794. He married Hadassah, daughter of R. Jacob Isaac A.B.D. Zamocz. Their daughter, Rebecca.

G9.2. R. Haim Landau, A.B.D. Podkomin. In his younger years he lived at Brody where he wrote approbations to *Shevet MiYisrael* in 1772, and *Tiferet Yisrael* in 1773. He must have become the A.B.D. of Podkomin about 1774/6, because the following year he wrote an approbation to *Be'er Yitzchak*, stating he was in that town, and also to *Agudat Azov* in 1782 and *Ohel Rachel* in 1788. He married the daughter of R. Jacob Babad. (See Chapter XI — G7.1/8.2/9.5.)

G10.1. R. Jacob Landau of Brody, married two daughters of R. Ezekiel Landau.[1] (The fathers were first cousins—See Below G8.3/9.3/10.7.)

G11. R. Judah Landau, known as Reb Judel Shmelkes after his father-in-law, R. Samuel Schmelke Hakohen, whose daughter Hinde Rachel he married. R. Samuel was the A.B.D. of Ostrow where he died in 1798. R. Judah Landau succeeded his father-in-law as the A.B.D. of Ostrow on the latter's death, and remained there until his death in 1839. His tombstone records his maternal grandfather, R. Ezekiel Landau, the A.B.D. of Prague.

G12. Wife of R. Benjamin Zeev Wolf Landau. (See below G8.4 /9.2/10.1/11.)

G10.2. Rechel, married R. Samuel son of R. Haim Shabtelis of Vilna. She died in Vilna on the eve of the Jewish New Year 1839, and he at the end of 1818. The family adopted the surname Landau, but were not Levites.[2]

G11.1. R. Abraham Jacob Landau, died as a young man in 1828, and was buried in Vilna.

G12. R. Samuel Landau (1821-45), named after his paternal grandfather, married Rechel the daughter of R. Isaac A.B.D. of Volozhin. She died in 1854. R. Isaac was also the father-in-law of R. Naftali Zvi Judah Berlin (the *Natziv*, died in 1893), and of R. Eliezer Isaac Fried (A.B.D. Volozhin, died in 1853—see below).

G13.1. Wife of R. Haim Hillel Fried, son of R. Eliezer Isaac. He had the *Chut HaMeshulash* by his father printed in Vilna in 1882, and died in 1910.

G13.2. R. Yekutiel Zalman Landau, Rabbi of Vitebsk and in

1878 was elected A.B.D. of the Chassidim at St. Petersburg. He died in 1895.

G11.2. R. Isaac Elijah Landau (1801-77). He was born in Vilna and studied under R. Yarberger and R. Smorgener. In 1818 he married Reitze Frodel, daughter of Mordecai Zadok Marshalkovitch of Dubno. She died in 1868. (See Chapter XVI — G10.9/11.3/12.1.)

He settled in Dubno where, with his father-in-law's help, he was able to carry on a prosperous business and became known as a great scholar and preacher. On Saturdays and holidays he used to preach in the synagogue where he attracted large crowds. Because of his eloquence, he was chosen by the communities of Volhynia as a member of the Rabbinical Commission appointed by the emperor in 1861. This was held at St. Petersburg where he remained for five months. In 1868 he was called to Vilna as a preacher and Dayan (judge) which offices he held until his death. In Vilna he established a kosher kitchen for the Jewish soldiers. He was a prolific writer, a recognized authority and was solicited by many writers to write approbations to their books.

His first work was *Me'aneh Eliyahu* published in Vilna in 1840. His other works are *Berurei HaMadot, Petashgan* (published Vilna, 1872-5), *Dubar Shalom* (published Warsaw, 1863), *Mikra Sofrim, Kiplayim LeTushya* (published Vilna, 1869), *Derushim lechol Chaftzeihem* (published Vilna, 1871), *Achrit leshalom* (on the Haggadah, published Vilna, 1871), *Lishmoah Belimudeihem* (published Vilna, 1876), Commentary on *Mechilta* (published Vilna, 1844), *Kol Shaon* (published Vilna, 1871), *Ramat Shemuel* (published in 1873), and other commentaries.

G12.1. R. Samuel Landau.

G12.2. Miriam, married Mordecai Zvi Hirsch son of R. Jacob Reb Liebelis. Their son, Samuel.

G11.3. R. Eleazar Landau, born in Vilna in 1805, and named after his father's brother R. Eliezer (or Eleazar) son of R. Haim, who died earlier the same year. He was the author of *Damesek Eliezer* (Vilna, 1865) and died in Grodno in 1883. He married Reizel Hadassah, daughter of R. Haim Brodie[3] (author of *Torah Or*).

G11.4. Wife of R. Jacob Fischel Myerson of Tiktin.[4]

G11.5. Frodel, married R. Zvi Hirsch Simchowitz of Minsk (son of R. Haim).

G11.6. Gitel, married R. Samuel son of R. Jedidiah Lipman Ellisberg of Eyvenitz.

G10.3. Wife of R. Isaiah son of R. Meir Horowitz.[5] (See Chapter XVI — G9/10.2.) Their daughter was the mother of R. Liebus, the father of R. Haim Halberstam, Founder of the Sanz Chassidic Dynasty.

G10.4. R. Abraham Isaac Landau, married the daughter of R. Jacobke Landau. (See below G8.3/9.3/10.2/11.4.[6])

G11. R. Eleazar Landau.

G12. Marcus Landau, born in Brody in 1837. He began his career as a merchant in Brody (from 1852-69) and Vienna (from 1869) but in 1878 he began to devote his life to the study of literature and became a leading Austrian historian. In 1871 he had received his Ph.D. from the University of Giessen, and besides writing numerous books, he also contributed essays, memoirs and articles to German and Italian periodicals and newspapers. During his life he made repeated visits to Italy.

G10.5. R. Naftali Hirsch Landau, married Elke, daughter of R. Isaac ("Hamburger") Horowitz.[7] (See Chapter XVI — G10.9 /11.3/12.9.)

G10.6. Channah, second wife of R. Isaac Halevi of Emden. (See G8/9.2/10.1 — page 267.)

G9.3. R. Dov Ber Landau, mentioned in the Records of the Apt Chevra Kaddisha in 1727-28.

G9.4. R. Jacob Landau, A.B.D. Lobatchov, married the only child of R. Moses Ziskind Rutenberg A.B.D. of Altona-Hamburg-Wandsbeck.[8]

G10.1. R. Ziskind Landau.

G10.2. Wife of R. Isaac, A.B.D. Lobatchov.

G10.3. R. Naftali Landau.

G9.5. R. Naftali Hirsch Landau, married Nechama Sarah, daughter of the Chacham Zvi Ashkenazi[9] who lived in Apt. After her husband was killed there, she left Apt and went to rejoin her father in Amsterdam where she later died. (See Chapter XIII — G8.4.)

G8.2. R. Isaac Landau, born in Apt where he was elected A.B.D. in
       1719. He wrote an approbation to *Derash Moshe* in 1721, and in
       1724 he attended the meeting of the Council of the Four Lands at
       Jaroslav. The same year he wrote an approbation to *Yafe Mareh,*
       and in 1729 he became the A.B.D. of Zolkiev where he wrote ap-
       probations to *Gur Aryey* (published in Amsterdam, 1733), to *Beit
       Halevi* (published Zolkiev, 1732) and in 1733 to *Beit Lechem
       Yehudah* (Zolkiev, 1733). Thereafter, he became A.B.D. of Lvov
       in 1734. Here he again wrote approbations, in 1736 to *Beit Shmuel,*
       in 1741 to *Torah Or,* and to a number of others until about 1754
       when he was elected the A.B.D. of Cracow where he wrote an
       approbation in 1757 to *Mitznefet Bad,* and others, until his death
       there in 1768. He was involved with the Eybeschutz-Emden Af-
       fair (see Chapters III and XIII) and corresponded with R. Eye-
       beschutz. He married the daughter of R. Simha Doctor of Lvov
       (who was the physician to the Polish King John Sobieski and died
       in 1702).

G9.1. R. Aryey Lieb Landau, Judge in Apt where he is mentioned in
       the Community Records in 1727, 1730 and 1746. He also at-
       tended the meeting of the Council of the Four Lands at Zulz
       in 1742 as the representative from Lvov, and wrote an approba-
       tion to *Sha'arei Binyamin* in 1752 published in Zolkiev the same
       year.

G9.2. R. Jacob Landau, A.B.D. Tarla and then at Tarnopol, men-
       tioned in the Community Records of Apt in 1720. He attended
       the Jaroslav meeting with his father in 1724 and wrote an ap-
       probation there to *Yafe Mareh.* Like his brother, R. Aryey Lieb,
       he wrote an approbation to *Sha'arei Binyamin* in 1752 and to
       other works until 1773. A responsum of his can be found in *Bat
       Einai* by R. Issachar Dov, published in Dubno in 1798.

  G10. Reize, married R. Isaac ("Hamburger") Horowitz. (See Chap-
        ter XVI — G10.9/11.3.) Their children are fully recorded else-
        where, but of his seventeen children, four daughters married
        back into the Landau family. (See below and above.)

G9.3. R. Asher Landau.

G9.4. R. Zvi Joseph Landau,[10] A.B.D. Greiding and, like his father,
       was a supporter of R. J. Eybeschutz and signed in his favor in
       1751 with the other leaders of Zolkiev. He died there in 1766.

  G10.1. R. Alexander Sender Landau, A.B.D. Brody.

G10.2. R. Hirsch Landau of Zmigrad.

G10.3. R. Abraham Landau of Cracow.

G10.4. Vita, married R. Hillel son of R. Liebus of Karov.

G9.5. Wife of R. Joseph Ittinge (author of *Luchot HaEidut*), A.B.D. Rohatyn, son of R. Judah Lieb of Lvov.

G9.6. Sarah Rebecca Sheindel, married R. Moses (A.B.D. Satanov) son of R. Naftali Hirsch (A.B.D. Dubno). They were the ancestors of R. Haim Halberstam, founder of the Sanz Chassidic Dynasty. (See Chapter VII — Branch B — G7.4/8.2/9.6/10.4.)

G9.7. Wife of R. Moses Phineas, son of R. Abraham son of R. Haim of Lublin.

G9.8. Wife of R. Nathan Nata (A.B.D. Ropshitz, and a nephew of R. Jonathan Eybeschutz).

G9.9. Wife of R. Baruch Parnas.

G10. R. Judah of Vizhniz.

G11. Jochebed Rebecca, first wife of R. Baruch Frankel Teomim. (See Chapter IV — G6.4/7/8/9.2/10.3.)

G8.3. R. Judah Landau,[11] mentioned in the Records of the Apt Community in 1709 until 1737 and died there at the end of that year (13th Kislev). He married Chaya, daughter of R. Eleazar A.B.D. of Dubno, son of R. Issachar Berish of Cracow. (See Chapter XI — G7.7.)She died in Apt in 1740.

G9.1. R. Joseph Landau, A.B.D. Klymnatov, married the daughter of R. Bezalel Katz A.B.D. Ostrow (See Chapter V — Branch B — G7.1/8.1/9.6.) He was mentioned in the *Noda BiYehudah* (see below).

G9.2. Wife of R. Mordecai son of R. Lieb A.B.D. Cracow.

G9.3. R. Ezekiel Landau, born in Apt on October 8, 1713. He was taught by his father and R. Isaac Segal of Lodmir as a child. Later he studied under the Rabbis of Brody and Vladimir and from 1734 to 1745 he was the Judge (Dayan) of the Brody Jewish Community, and in 1745 was elected the A.B.D. of Jampol where he wrote an approbation to *Maftei'ach Haolamit* by R. Raphael Emanuel, published that year at Zolkiev. In 1752 he wrote an approbation to *Sha'arei Binyamin;* in 1753 to the *TaZ* commentary on the *Shulchan Aruch* and the Talmudic commentary *Even HaEzer;* and in 1757 to *Meil Tzadakah* at which time he witnessed the siege of the city of Prague where he was the A.B.D. at that time, having been invited there in 1754. The state of the Jewish Community at this time was very miserable, having been expelled from Bohemia in 1745, and allowed to return in limited numbers, and then the fire of 1754 which destroyed a large part of their ghetto. R. Landau, however, remained in the city at this time to serve as their Rabbi until his death on April 29 (15th Iyar) 1793.

Like the other Rabbis of his generation he was involved in the Eybeschutz-Emden affair, and was noted for his tactful answer given to the Rabbis who consulted him on this matter. He adopted the attitude that the amulets (see Chapter III — Lwow Family) may have been falsified, thus giving the accused R. Eybeschutz a way of exculpating himself. It was this reply that attracted the community of Prague to invite him to become their leader.

In the famous divorce case of Cleves validated by R. Lipschutz (see Chapter VI — page 285 — G9.3 and a number of other leading Rabbis mentioned elsewhere in this book, R. Landau took sides with these other Rabbis against the Frankfurt Rabbis, so that in 1769 they were so enraged with him they declared that neither he nor his sons should ever be elected to the Frankfurt Rabbinate. He wrote a number of other approbations.

R. Ezekiel was greatly respected, a man of great amenity of character and widely consulted on Jewish matters, and also by the government of the time. He was strict in ritual matters, but for the sake of peace, he would sometimes sanction things which he did not approve of. He was a lover of the Haskalah (Enlightment) Movement but saw great dangers in the German translation of the Bible by Moses Mendelssohn (see Chapter III). As a student of Cabbalah, he was versed in mysticism. Nevertheless he strongly opposed the rise of Chassidism.

In a conflagration of 1773 he lost most of his manuscripts and was thus induced to have those works which were spared published, and to add to them his new productions. His most famous work is the collection of responsa entitled *Noda BiYehudah* (published in Prague in 1776 during the reign of Maria Theresa), *Derush Hesped* (a funeral oration on the death of Maria Theresa), Prague, 1781; *Shevah VeHoda'ah* (1790); *Mar'eh Yechezkiel* (published by his son R. Samuel in 1830); and others including a number of commentaries on the Talmud which still appear today in the volume of the Vilna Talmud. He married Liebe, daughter of R. Jacobke of Prague.

G10.1. R. Israel Landau, the third son, married twice. His first wife was the daughter of the A.B.D. of Stachev, son of R. Zechariah Mendel Frankel (A.B.D. Jaroslav). They had two sons, Eleazar and Joshua, after which they divorced. She remarried R. Moses Chasid of Ropshitz, and her two sons went to live with her and their stepfather. His second wife was the daughter of R. Baruch Benedict A.B.D. Leeuwarden (from 1841-86), and they had a son Moses. He was the author of *Chok leYisrael* published in Prague in 1798. He was a pupil of R. Israel Zamocz, and from 1782 worked as a Hebrew printer in a Christian firm. In 1793 he reprinted R. Abraham Farissol's *Iggeret Orchot Olam* and in 1794 his father's *Dagul Mervavah*. His *Chok leYisrael* was a translation of Maimonides' *Sefer HaMitzvot*.

G11.1. R. Eleazar Landau (from his father's first wife), born in 1778, and was educated by his stepfather R. Moses Chasid in Ropshitz. In 1791, shortly before his thirteenth birthday, he and his brother Joshua went to Prague to study under their famous grandfather R. Ezekiel Landau. On the occasion of his Bar-Mitzvah he delivered a sermon to the community which was considered to be wonderful and which made his grandfather extremely proud.

His first marriage was to Hinde, daughter of R. Menachem Mendel of Lvov, where he remained after the marriage and devoted his time to Rabbinical studies. In 1805 the seat of the Lvov Rabbinate became vacant and the community preferred to choose R. Jacob Ornstein as their leader, which led to much enmity later between these rabbis. R. Landau became the A.B.D. of Sternberg, and on the death of his first wife he married Rivele daughter of R. Aryey Lieb Bernstein of Brody, the former wife of R. Samuel Nirenstein of Brody. He settled in Brody where he engaged in business and became the A.B.D. in 1829 while R. Aryey Lieb Teomim, the incumbent Rabbi there was sick and bedridden, and was not told of this appointment so as not to aggravate his ailing condition. However, R. Landau died before him in 1831, from the cholera epidemic. He was the author of *Yad HaMelech* published in

Lvov in 1826. His novellae on the Babylonian Talmud appear in the Vilna Edition of the Talmud. A number of his works were left in manuscript. His responsa can be found in the second series of the *Noda BiYehudah* (with a reply to R. Samuel son of R. Ezekiel Landau, his uncle), in *Mei Be'er* (Vienna, 1829) by R. Ber Oppenheimer and *Zecher Yeshayahu* (Vilna, 1881) by R. Zechariah Isaiah Yolles.

G12.1. R. Judah Lieb Landau of Brody, married 1) the daughter of R. Issachar Horowitz of Warsaw, and 2) the daughter of R. Mendel Landau of Mohilev.

  G13. R. Eleazar Landau (1842-1905), author of *Zichron Eleazar* published in Brody in 1906.

G12.2. R. Moses Landau of Cracow and Pinsk.

  G13. R. Eleazar Landau, married Sarah, daughter of R. Solomon Zalman son of R. Meir Hakohen Zussman. (See Chapter XIII — page 480 — G13.4/14.4.)

G12.3. R. Zeev Wolf Landau of Kovno, published the *Derushei HaTzelach*, a collection of sermons by his great-grandfather, R. Ezekiel Landau, in Warsaw, 1899. He married the daughter of R. Joshua Heschel, A.B.D. of Lublin.

G12.4. Wife of the Rabbi of Jassy.

G12.5. Wife of R. Samuel Perez, son of Zalman Posner of Warsaw.

G12.6. Wife of R. Mordecai Zeev Ornstein.[12] (See Chapter XII — page 460 — G11.)

G12.7. Wife of R. Heschel Sheinfinkel.

G11.2. R. Moses Landau, born December 28, 1788 and died in Prague May 4, 1852. He studied at the Yeshiva in Prague and later established a Hebrew and Oriental printing press there. His chief merit as a typographer, for which his press became famous, lay in the fact that he always personally supervised the correction of the works that were published so that they were printed almost without a mistake.

In 1819 he was elected superintendent of the Jewish school in Prague, and shortly thereafter one of the com-

munity members of the board of directors. In 1849 he was
elected the alderman, and a member of the Stadrat (city
council) the following year. His own literary contributions
include a volume of poems *Amaranten* published in 1820;
Bikkurei HaIttim, an almanac for the friends of Hebrew
literature; an Aramaic Talmudic Dictionary published in
Prague in 1819-24 which contains valuable observations
and numerous treatises of a philosophical, historical, ar-
cheological and geographical character; *Marpe Lashon,*
a collection of all the foreign words found in Rashi, the
Tosfot, Maimonides and the *Rosh,* published in Prague
in 1829-31; and others, including his own edition of the
Bible printed in Prague in 1833-37.

In his will he left his Hebrew library to the orphan
asylum which he had established, and his other Oriental
works to a Jewish Theological Seminary to be founded in
the future.

G12. Hermann Landau, publicist in Prague, died about 1890.[13]

G11.3. R. Joshua Landau, A.B.D. Radom.

G10.2. R. Jacobke Landau, named after his maternal grandfather,
born in 1745 or 1750, lived at Brody where he was a prosperous merchant, and died in 1822. Novellae which he wrote
can be found in the *Noda BiYehuda* by his father. In 1784
he wrote an approbation to the Bible. He married 1) Rachel
daughter of of R. Isaac ("Hamburger") Horowitz (see Chapter XVI — G10.9/11.3/12.5) and 2) Reize, daughter of R.
Issachar Berish Yellis of Medzibeh.

G11.1. Wife of R. Haim Gedalliah of Waldorka and White Field.[14]

G12. Wife of R. Nechemiah, A.B.D. Bechov, son of R. Jacob
Isaac (the Holy *Yehudi*) of Parsischa. R. Nechemiah Jehiel
died in 1853. (See Chapter IV — G6.4/7/8/9.2/10.4.)

G13.1. R. Haim Gedalliah of Bechov, 1833-1904, married the
daughter of R. Nathan Lieb, son of R. Mendel of
Rymanov.

G14.1. R. Nathan Aryey, Admur Izbiza. His son-in-law, R.
Benzion Zucker of Turstein.

G14.2. R. Nechemiah, Admur of Chelm.

G14.3. R. Jacob Isaac, perished in 1940.

G13.2.   R. David of Zilkovke.

G13.3.   R. Bezalel, married the daughter of R. Jekutiel of Sassov.

G13.4.   R. Jacob Isaac, succeeded his father as Admur Bechov, but died a few years later.

G11.2.   Reize, married 1) R. Eleazar Landau (his first wife was the daughter of R. David Heilprin A.B.D. Ostrow), nephew of R. Haim Landau A.B.D. Podkomin, and had a son, Isaac, and 2) R. Aaron Hakohen Jampoller, and had two other sons.

G12.1.   R. Isaac Landau, married the daughter of R. Israel author of *Sha'arei Mishpat.*

G12.2.   R. Ezekiel Landau of Berdichev, married the daughter of R. Meir son of R. Levi Isaac of Berdichev, the Chassidic Leader. (See Chapter IV — Branch D — G10/11.2.)

G13.   Wife of R. Moses halevi Ettinge, A.B.D. Yormilintz.

G11.3.   R. Judah Landau (from his father's second wife) of Brody, died in 1841. He married the daughter of R. Solomon Lipschutz A.B.D. Slutsk.

G12.1.   Wife of R. Haim Ephrati of Odessa.

G12.2.   R. Menachem Meinish Landau.

G12.3.   R. Eleazar Landau.

G12.4.   Berish Landau of Brody.

G11.4.   Rebecca Nissel, married R. Abraham Isaac Landau. (See above — G8.1/9.2/10.4.)

G10.3.   R. Samuel Landau, the Chief Dayan and A.B.D. of Prague succeeding his father, where he died at an advanced age on October 31 (28th Tishrei) 1834. He was the champion of orthodoxy and when, at the end of the eighteenth century, the Austrian Emperor planned the establishment of Jewish Theological seminaries (as his nephew R. Moses Landau had envisioned), he was opposed, which led to his publication of his *Shivat Tzion* (Prague, 1827). He also published *Mar'eh Yechezkiel* written by his father, and his own novellae, homilies and discourses can be found in the *Ahavat Tzion* and *Doresh leTzion* by his father.

In 1830 he delivered a sermon praising Mendelssohn's
Bible translation for its good German, and suggested that the
fathers decide that when their sons reach the age of ten,
whether to teach them Talmudic studies or secular educa-
tion. His father's *Ahavat Tzion* contains four of his sermons.
He married Hindche, daughter of R. Uri Feiwel, A.B.D.
Lissa and Hanau, (died in 1770) son of R. Samuel Helman
(A.B.D. Metz).

G10.4. Friede,[15] married R. Joseph (the Holy); A.B.D. Jaworow and
Posen. (See Chapter VII — Branch A — G6.2/7.2/8.3/9.1.)

G10.5. Wife of R. Zalman, son of R. Meir Pressberg of Vienna.

G10.6. Wife of R. YomTov, son of R. Ephraim Vehli.

G10.7. Yarit (died 1773), first wife of R. Jacob son of R. Haim
Landau A.B.D. Podkomin. (See G8.1/9.2 above.)

G10.8. Mirl, second wife of R. Jacob.

G8.4. R. Ezekiel Landau, mentioned in the Apt Community Records of
1711 to 1731. He wrote an approbation to *Tavnit Ot Yosef* in 1747.
He married the daughter of R. Menachem Mendel of Cracow.

G9.1. R. Benjamin Zeev Wolf Landau, mentioned in the Apt Community Records from 1716 to 1745. He was the A.B.D. of Kreshov
and married the daughter of R. Jacob son of R. Meir Horowitz.
(See Chapter XVI — G10.9/11.2.)

G9.2. R. Joseph Landau, mentioned in the Apt Community Records
from 1716 to 1756 where he was the head of the *Klaus*. He then
became the A.BD. at Zolkiev and lastly A.B.D. of Brody. He
wrote approbations to *Beit Avraham* and *Mitznefet Bad* in 1752
and 1757 respectively.

G10.1. R. Jacob Simha Landau, A.B.D. Apt, mentioned in the *Ma'on
HaBerachot* by his younger brother.

G11. R. Benjamin Zeev Wolf Landau,[16] A.B.D. Ostrow, known to
the community as Reb Wolf Reb Judeles. In his later years
he went to settle in Safed in Palestine where he died. He
married the daughter of R. Judah Landau. (See above G8.1/
9.2/10/11/12.)

G12. R. Jacob Landau of Ostrow.

G13. R. Mordecai Landau, born in Ostrow in 1848, and married when he was sixteen to the daughter of R. Baruch
Skomirowsky of Zhitomir with whom the couple lived

until Mordecai was thirty years old, having spent the years entirely devoted to religious studies. He and his sons were later involved in the wood processing industry and owned a large area of forest. In 1900 he was afflicted with severe rheumatism of his legs which was not improved with medical therapy. He died two years later in 1902, and was buried in Zhitomir.

G14.1. R. Moses Landau.
G14.2. R. Judel Landau.
G14.3. R. Haim Landau.

G10.2. R. Israel Jonah Landau, (died in 1824), A.B.D. of Kempen (Posen District), the author of *Ma'on HaBerachot* (published Dyhernfurth, 1816). He wrote an approbation in 1810 to *Mishnat Reb Eliezer*. He married Gitel, daughter of R. Samuel of Lubertov.

G11.1. R. Aryey Lieb Landau, married the daughter of R. Isaac Meisels A.B.D. Koretz.
G11.2. R. Joseph Samuel Landau, succeeded his father as A.B.D. Kempen on the latter's death and remained there until his death in 1837. He was the author of *Mishkan Shilo* (published Breslau, 1837) printed as part of *Kur HaBechinah* which included his Ethical Will.

G12. Wife of R. Ezekiel, son of R. Isaac Landau (of Wladowa). (See Chapter VII — Branch A — G6.2/7.2/8.3/9.1/10.1.)

G11.3. R. Abraham Aaron Moses Landau.
G11.4. Hannah, married R. Mordecai Zeev Ashkenazi who succeeded his father-in-law in 1837 as the A.B.D. of Kempen. (See Chapter XII — page 457 — G9.1/10.2/11.1.)
G11.5. Nehsa Feige, married R. Abraham Aryey, mentioned in the introduction of his father-in-law's book.

G10.3. R. Aryey Liebus Landau A.B.D. Koretz.
G10.4. R. Alexander Sender Landau of Brody.
G10.5. R. Eliezer Landau.

CHAPTER XI

BABAD FAMILY — ITS BEGINNINGS

G5. R. Heschel of Cracow.

G6.3. R. Issachar Berish.[1]

G7.1. R. Isaac, A.B.D. Berjan and then Brody, where he died in 1704.

G8.1. R. Mordecai Yollis of Brody, who signed in the Minutes of the Council of the Four Lands in 1742 when the Council met at Tishvicz. In 1743 he travelled to Frankfurt-on-Oder for a market day visit, where he died in the month of Tammuz.

G9.1. R. Menachem Mendel of Brody, who approved, with the Rabbis of Lvov, the publication of *Sha'arei Binyamim*, by R. Benjamin Zeev, son of R. David Ashkenazi, published at Zolkiev in 1752.

G9.2. R. Israel (called Levitzer), who occupied the second highest position in the Council of the Four Lands, i.e. *Ne'eman* (Trustee — the treasurer and the secretary). He married Deborah, the daughter of R. Alexander Sender Shor, author of *Tevu'ot Shor*, son of R. Ephraim Zalman Shor.

G10.1. R. Alexander Sender Haim, adopted his mother's name Shor, and married Reizel, the daughter of R. Abraham Jekutiel Zalman Rappoport of Brody. (See Chapter VII — G7.4/8.4/9.1.)

G11.1. R. Israel Isaac.

G12. Esther Gitel, married R. Zvi Hirsch Horowitz of Berdichev.

403

G11.2. R. Meir (Shor) Brodsky. Head of the Brodsky Family Pedigree.[2] See Babad Family — Branch F.

G10.2. Veitel, married R. Samuel Shmelke (died 1793), son of R. Moses, son of R. Eleazar Rokeah. From this union are descended the Belz Chassidic Dynasty, established by R. Shalom Rokeah of Belz, son of R. Eliezer Rokeah (their grandson). (See Chapter XVII.)

G9.3. R. Jehiel, A.B.D. Jolkamin.

G10. R. Isaac.

G11. R. Elijah.

G12. R. Aryey Liebus, author of *Ironot HaBusam*.

G8.2. R. Jacob (Yollis) of Brody, who signed at Tishvitz in the Council of the Four Lands, as coming from Tarnopol. He d:.' :- 1748. He married Reizel, the daughter of R. Samuel Halevi of Meseritz. She died in 1767. They had three sons and four daughters. R. Samuel was the son of R. Abraham, A.B.D. Rzeszow, and the maternal grandson of R. Joshua of Cracow, (author of *Pnei Yehoshua* — See Berenstein Family Pedigree in this section).

G9.1. R. Issachar Berish, named after his great-grandfather, called "Reb Yekels," mentioned in the introduction of the Responsa *Birkat Yaakov*.

G10. R. Zvi Hirsch of Brody, who approved the Pentateuch Edition of 1774, and who is mentioned in the *Or Chadash* by R. Eleazar, son of R. Eleazar Kallir, published in Frankfurt-on-Oder in 1776.

G11. Wife of R. Moses (Zvi Hirsch) Goldes of Slonima.

G9.2. R. Isaac Babad ("Sons of the Av Beth Din" — B.A.B.A.D.) of Brody. He approved the appearance of the work *Sha'arei Binyamin,* published in 1752 (see G7.1/8.1/9.1 above), together with the Rabbis of Brody in 1752. His wife's name was Reala.

G10.1. R. Joshua Heschel Babad,[3] 1754-1838, initially A.B.D. Budzanow and from 1801, of Tarnopol. He left Lublin in 1828 after a short stay because of a dispute with the *Mitnagdim* there. He returned to Tarnopol where he remained until his death. A reply to him by R. Jacob of Lissa appears at the end of his *Nachalat Yaakov*. He was the author of *Sefer Yeho-*

shua, Responsa, published Zolkiev, 1829. He married the daughter of R. Israel Eiser, son of R. Mordecai Reb Leibish, son of R. Israel Eiser (A.B.D. Lublin), son of R. Moses (author of *Mahadura Batra*).

G11.1. R. Abraham Ari Babad, A.B.D. Mikulonitz — head of the Babad Family — Branch B.

G11.2. R. Moses Babad, A.B.D. Przeworsk, married Toyba.

G12.1. R. Joseph Babad, 1800 — 1874, died in Tarnopol. He was successively A.B.D. Bohorodezany, Zbariz, Sniatyn and Tarnopol. He was the author of the well-known *Minchat Chinuch,* published first Lvov, 1869. It contains a commentary on the *Sefer HaChinuch* — the 613 Jewish Laws. The Vilna edition of 1923 had additions by R. Meir Simha of Dvinsk and other Rabbis. An extant responsum appears in *Kovets Teshuvot* (1850), a supplement to his *Minchat Chinuch* (1952 edition). Two responsa are addressed to him by his grandfather and two from R. Joseph Joel Deutsch, when he was Rabbi and A.B.D. Zbariz and Sniatyn. He is head of the Babad Family — Branch C.

G12.2. R. Haim Babad, A.B.D. Mikulonitz — head of the Babad Family — Branch D.

G10.2. R. Nathan Babad of Rava, A.B.D. Jaworow.

G11.1. R. Isaac (Babad) Grossfeld of Rzeszow.

G12. R. Joseph Simha Grossfeld of Dobrowitz.

G11.2. R. Abraham Babad, A.B.D. Bisk.

G12.1. R. Issachar Dov, A.B.D. Bisk, succeeding his father there in 1845. After the First World War he settled in Vienna. He wrote a commentary *HaHashlomo* to the *Minchat Chinuch* by his cousin (Shulsinger edition, 1952).

G12.2. R. Shalom Jacob of Bisk.

G13.1. R. Moses, A.B.D. Bruzdovitz.

G14. R. Abraham, A.B.D. Przemysl.

G13.2. R. Zondel, A.B.D. Sterotz.

G10.3. Beila, second wife of R. Isaac Horowitz, A.B.D. Altona-Hamburg-Wandsbeck. See below G9.6.

G9.3. R. Samuel, known as Reb Yekels of Brody.

G10.1. R. Dov Ber of Ostrow, who flourished during the lifetimes of R. David Heilprin and R. Abraham Meshullam Zalman, son of the Chacham Zvi Ashkenazi. They were also both A.B.D. of Ostrow. He married the daughter of R. Bezalel HaKohen (died in 1717), son of R. Naftali H. Katz (author of *Smichut Chachamim*), A.B.D. Ostrow. (See Chapter V — G6/7.1/8.1/9.4.) He was one of the members of the *Chevra Kaddisha*, and there is a record of honey being sent to him in their minutes book in 1736, (Cheshvan).

G11.1. R. Zvi Hirsch, one of the leaders of the *Chevra Kaddisha*, who signed in their minutes book in 1749.

G11.2. Sarah, married R. Asher Anschel, A.B.D. of Ostrow. He was the son of R. Judah Lieb, A.B.D. of the Ostrow *Klaus*, Slutsk and Pinsk, himself a son-in-law of R. Isaac, son of R. Moses Meir Rappoport.

Asher was accustomed to arise to study at midnight. One Friday night, it is told, when he was prevented from studying due to the darkness, he went to the home of a mother who had just delivered a baby, where a light was burning, and with book in hand, he studied until morning.

He wrote approbations in Ostrow to *Mafligei Reuven*, in 1754, by R. Mordecai Gompel, son of Reuben, published in Zolkiev in 1775 and *Shevet MiYisrael*, in 1743, by R. Jacob Israel, son of Zvi Stern, published in Zolkiev in 1772.

He died in 1777 and left no offspring.

He was the author of *Baruch MiBanim Asher*, published in Zolkiev in 1749, a homiletic commentary on the Torah, the title being a quotation from Deut. XXXIII, 24. His ancestry to R. Moses of Lublin (known as the *Mahadura Batra*) is recorded in it; *Otot leMoadim*, Zolkiev in 1752, novellae and festival laws; *MeiAsher Shmeinah Lachmoh*, left unpublished; and *Korban Ashir*, left unpublished.

G10.2. R. Joseph.

G10.3. Wife of R. Joseph Jacob Horowitz, A.B.D. Alexnis, son of R. Isaac Horowitz (known as the "Hamburger" — See Chapter XVI, and also G9.6 below).

G9.4. Frodel, married R. Naftali Hirsch, A.B.D. Kobly and Dubno,

son of R. Zvi Hirsch Halberstadt. (See Chapter VII — G7.4/
8.2/9.6 — page 306.)

G9.5. Wife of R. Haim, son of R. Abraham Landau, A.B.D. Podkomin.
(See Landau Family Pedigree — Chapter X.)

G9.6. Reize, married R. Isaac "Hamburger" Horowitz, son of R. Jacob
Horowitz, his first wife. He was A.B.D. of the Triple Commu-
nity of Altona-Hamburg-Wandsbeck (died in 1767). (See
Chapter XVI.)

G9.7. Wife of R. Berish, son of R. Heschel, A.B.D. of Dubno.

G8.3. Wife of R. Zeev Wolf, A.B.D. Skalat (in the Tarnograd District).

G9.1. R. Issachar Berish, *Parnas* of Frankfurt.

G10.1. R. Aryey Judah Lieb Berenstein, A.B.D. of Zbariz and Gali-
zian. He is mentioned in the approbation of *Augudat Azov*
by R. Jacob Israel, son of R. Zvi Stern, A.B.D. Kremnitz
(died in 1788), published in Zolkiev in 1782.

G11. R. Isaac Wolf Berenstein.

G12. Wife of R. Menachem Meinish Chajes.

G13. R. Meir Chajes, a highly esteemed banker, who lived in
Florence, Italy for fifteen years before settling in Brody.

G14. R. Zvi Hirsch Chajes, born in Brody in 1805 and died
in Lvov in 1855. He was head of the Chajes Family
— Babad Family — Branch E.

G10.2. R. Zvi Hirsch of Brody.

G11. R. Haim of Brody, married Rebecca, daughter of R. Samuel
Halevi Ittinge of Brody.

G12. R. Israel Menachem Mendel, A.B.D. Trevolla. He was the
author of *Bigdei Kavod*, published by his son as part of
Bigdei HaKodesh by his father-in-law, R. Joseph Moses
Simha, son of R. Zvi Rappoport.

G8.4. Reize, married R. Israel, son of R. Eliezer Lipman Heilprin, A.B.D.
Tarnograd. (See Chapter VI — Branch B — G6.4/7.1.)

G7.2. R. Joshua Heschel, A.B.D. Tarla.

G8.1. R. David, A.B.D. Dobrowitz.

G9.1. R. Mendel, A.B.D. Kazanhordek, married the daughter of R.
Aaron of Dvirhordek.

G9.2. Wife of R. Isaac Jehiel Michael.

G10. Wife of R. Eliezer, A.B.D. Helusk.

G8.2. Wife of R. Jacob, A.B.D. Glogau, Brody and Hamburg, son of R. Meir Horowitz, A.B.D. Tiktin. (See Chapter XVI.)

G7.3. R. Moses, called "Doberishes" after his wife, Deborish, daughter of his uncle, R. Meir, A.B.D. Opatow (Apt) and Lublin, from Meir's first wife (daughter of R. David, son of R. Samuel Halevi, *HaTaZ*, 1586-1667).

G8. R. Saul of Chelm.

G9. Sarel, married R. Dovberish, A.B.D. Vlatchek.

G10. R. Isaac.

G11. R. Jacob Zvi, A.B.D. Ershid.

G12. R. Benjamin.

G13. R. Moses Nahum Jerusalimski,[4] A.B.D. Kamenka, author of the Responsa, *Minchat Moshe,* published in Warsaw, 1882. He was born in 1855 and died in 1914. He became Rabbi of Kamenka in 1880, of Ostroleka in 1901, and of Kielce in 1902. He was among the first Polish Rabbis to support the Chovevei Zion Movement. He also wrote *Beer Moshe,* Responsa (Warsaw, 1901); *LeShad Ha-Shema* on the *Rambam* (Warsaw, 1881); and *Birkat Moshe,* Responsa (Lvov, 1886). Extracts of his diary during World War I appeared in *Sefer Kilz* (1957).

G7.4. Wife of R. Solomon, son of R. Jehiel Michael, son of R. David, (A.B.D. Apt).

G8. R. Issachar Berish, married the daughter of R. Simeon Wolf.

G9. R. Solomon Zalman, A.B.D. Poznov, married the daughter of R. Zvi Hirsch of Pietrokov.

G10. R. Eleazar Poznovsky of Pietrokov.

G11.1. R. Abraham Zvi Hirsch of Pietrokov, author of the Responsa *Brit Avraham,* published in Dyhernfurth in 1819.

G11.2. Wife of R. Uri Eybeschutz.

G12. R. Zussman of Pietrokov.

G13. R. Uri Eybeschutz, married Jochebed, daughter of R. Haim Eleazer Waks.

G7.5. Esther, wife of R. Gabriel Eskeles — Founder of the Eskeles Family Dynasty — See Babad Family — Branch A.

G7.6. Wife of R. Joshua Lieb, A.B.D. Dobromil.

G8. R. Issachar Ber, A.B.D. Chernowitz.

G9. Wife of R. Ezekiel Feiwel Teomim. (See Chapter IV — G6.4 /7/8.)

G7.7. R. Eliezer, A.B.D. of Dubno.[5]

G8. Chaya, married R. Judah, son of R. Zvi Hirsch Landau. They were the parents of the prominent R. Ezekiel Landau, author of *Noda BiYehudah*. (See Chapter X — G8.3/9.3.)

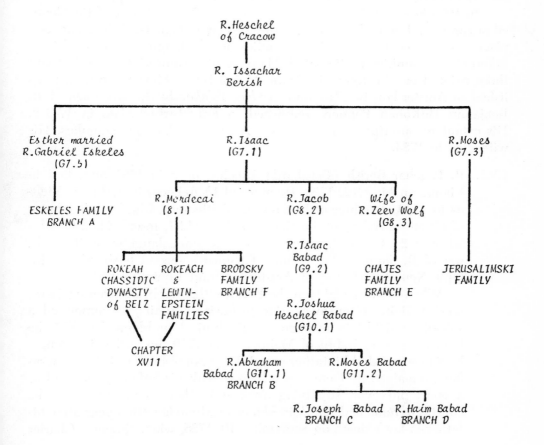

BABAD FAMILY

Later Descendants

BRANCH A

ESKELES FAMILY

R. Gabriel Eskeles[6] (G7.5 above), was born in Cracow and studied as a child under R. Aaron Samuel Kaidanover (1614-76) of Cracow. His father, R. Judah Lowe (Lieb), was the son of R. Haim son of R. Sini (Sinai). This R. Sini was a brother of R. Judah Lowe, known as the *MaHaRaL* of Prague, and creator of the *Golem*. As he became better known, R. Gabriel was called simply "Gabriel of Cracow." He was firstly A.B.D. of Olkusz, from 1684 to 1693, and then of Prague (from where his ancestors had come), from 1693 to 1698. From here he went to Metz until 1709, and finally became A.B.D. of Nikolsburg from 1709, until his death on February 2, 1718. His full title was *Landesrabbiner* of Moravia, and he was also the head of the Nikolsburg Yeshiva, sharing the office with R. David Oppenheim.

In 1698 he was a delegate representing the Posen district of the Council of the Four Lands, held at the Jaroslav Fair in Galicia. This event took place every three years in different cities at which the leading Rabbis of different communities participated. Many of his manuscripts were lost and those printed can be found in *Panim Meirot* by R. Meir Eisenstadt, published in Amsterdam in 1715, and in *Shav Ya'akov* by R. Jacob son of R. Benjamin HaKohen Poppers, published in Frankfurt-on-Main in 1741-2. His extant manuscripts were on *Pirkei Avot*, Novellae and Homilies. His wife died in 1734.

G8.1. R. Issachar Berish (Bernhard) Eskeles, born in 1691 and died in Vienna on March 2, 1753. He married 1) Rebecca Eva, died in Vienna in 1749, daughter of R. Samson Wertheimer, Chief Administrator of Financial Affairs of the Emperors Leopold I, Joseph I and Charles VI, and 2) Channah, niece of his first wife, daughter of R. Wolf, son of R. Samson Wertheimer. Channah's second husband was Joseph Neumark-Hartog of Amsterdam and Königsberg.

When he was eighteen, he became the Rabbi of Kremsir (Kromeriz). Being often away, due to business affairs, he appointed a substitute Rabbi to manage the Rabbinical problems. In 1717, he is mentioned as Rabbi of Mainz and in 1719, he settled in Vienna, having succeeded his father as A.B.D. of Nikolsburg in 1718. R. Bernhard remained in Vienna as a banker with his father-in-law, and as a court purveyor, supplying arms and other commodities for the court. He remained *Landesrabbiner* of Moravia until a year after his father-in-law's death on September 10, 1725, when Emperor Charles

VI named him as successor to R. Samson Wertheimer as *Landes-rabbiner* of Hungary as well. Working on behalf of the Jews of Moravia, he managed to have annulled a decree by Empress Maria Theresa imposing taxes upon the Jews in 1742, and in 1744-5, another decree, that of banishment of the Jews from Moravia and Bohemia. He also established the Eskeles-Stiftung, a foundation for Torah teaching to children and providing for poor brides. His novellae on the Talmudic tractate *Berachot* remained unpublished.

G9.1.   Margarethe, 1741-2, died in Vienna.
G9.2.   Esther, 1750-2, died in Vienna.
G9.3.   Leah (Eleanore), 1752-1812, died in Vienna. She married, and later divorced Meir Fliess of Berlin. They were involved in a Prussian spy scandal.
G9.4.   Bernhard Eskeles, born posthumously in 1753, and died in 1839. He became one of Austria's outstanding financiers. He started out in Amsterdam and, having lost his father's legacy, he returned in 1774 to Vienna. Here, in 1800, he married Cecily (Cecilia, 1760-1836), the widow of Benjamin (Simha Bonem) Wulff of Dessau. (See Chapter III — Mendelssohn Family.) She was a daughter of Daniel Itzig.

Bernhard went into partnership with his wife's brother-in-law, Nathan von Arnstein, and founded the Austrian National Bank in 1816. He was ennobled in 1797, became a baron in 1822 and was the only Austrian Jew to be invited to the Paris Sanhedrin convened by Emperor Napoleon I in 1806. His wife made their home a meeting place for the high society, mainly during the Vienna Congress. Although they remained Jews, they had their children baptized in 1824, having then been married for twenty-four years.

G10.1.   Maria Anna Cecilia Bernhardine, 1801-1862, died in Munich. She married in 1825 to Count Franz von Wimpffen (1797-1870).

G11.1   Heinrich Wimpffen, 1827-96, Consul-General, married in 1865 to Baroness Kamilla Webersfeld (died in 1898). They had no issue.
G11.2.   Alfons Wimpffen, 1828-66, Colonel, married in 1860 to Countess Caroline Lamberg.

G12.   Caroline, 1861-1902, married in 1884 to Count Moritz Vetter von der Lilie (1856-1945).

G13. Franz Vetter von der Lilie, 1885-1958, Ambassador, married in 1930 to Stephanie of Stutterheim (1894-1940), and secondly in 1949 to Elma Ubaldini della Carda (1889-1964). He had issue from his first wife.

G14. Peter Vetter von der Lilie, born in Baden-Baden in 1932.

G11.3. Viktor Wimpffen, 1834-97, married in 1860 to Baroness Anastasia Sina (1838-89).

G12.1. Hedwig, 1861-92, married in 1881 to Count August Zichy.

G13.1. Maria, born in 1883.
G13.2. Theodora, born in 1886, died before 1920.
G13.3. Anastasia, born in 1891, married in 1917 to Count George Szechenyi.

G12.2. Siegfried Wimpffen, 1865-1929, owner of large estates in Hungary, married in 1892 to Countess Franziska Stockau (1873-1933).

G13.1. Maria, 1894-1969, married in 1920 to Count Friedrich Silva-Tarouca.

G14.1. Karl, born in 1921, killed in Vienna in 1945.
G14.2. Helene, born in 1923.

G13.2. Georg, 1896-1968, died in Chicago, Ill., married in 1926 to Countess Jacqueline Zichy (born in 1903).

G14.1. Maria Franziska, born in 1927.
G14.2. Maria Anna, born in 1928.
G14.3. Maria Theresia, born in 1929, married in Chicago, Ill., in 1952 to Joe Dressel.
G14.4. Jacqueline, born in 1930, married George Rippstein (Scottsdale, Arizona).
G14.5. Joseph Wimpffen, born in 1933, married in 1968 to Ray Post (Chicago, Ill.).
G14.6. Elisabeth, born in 1935, married in Chicago in 1952 to Tibor Csukasy (Chicago, Ill.).
G14.7. Notburga, born in 1936.
G14.8. Agnes, born in 1938, married in 1962 to Sonnath Chatterjee (East Lansing, Michigan).
G14.9. Georgine, born in 1939, died in Chicago, Ill. in 1966.
G14.10. Peter Wimpffen, born in 1941.

G13.3. Simon Wimpffen, born in 1897.

G13.4. Franz Wimpffen, born in 1899, married in 1927 to Katharina Shiffera and after her death in 1961, to Vera Wahl. He had issue from the first wife.

G14.1. Siegfried Wimpffen, born in 1928, married in 1958 to Baroness Antoinette Adamovich.

G15.1. Franz Michael, born in Vienna in 1959.
G15.2. Alexandra, born in Vienna in 1960.

G14.2. Johanna, born in 1936, married in 1957 to Prince Otto Windisch-Graetz.

G14.3. Friederike, born in 1938, married in 1960 to Baron Carlo Bach.

G15.1. Carlotta, born in Vienna in 1961.
G15.2. Alberto, born in Vienna in 1963.

G13.5. Friedrich Wimpffen, born in 1900.

G13.6. Viktor Wimpffen, born in 1902, owner of Kainberg Castle in Styria, married in 1949 to Baroness Desiree Kellersperg. They have no issue.

G13.7. Eveline, born in 1905, married in 1926 to Count Rudolf Zichy.

G14.1. Maria, born in 1927, married Count Clemens Walderdorff in 1949.

G15.1. Wilderich, born in 1951.
G15.2. Philipp, born in 1952.
G15.3. Madeleine, born in 1955.
G15.4. Maria Anna, born in 1957.
G15.5. Josef, born in 1960.

G14.2. Jacob Zichy, born in 1928.

G14.3. Heinrich Zichy, born in 1929, married in 1953 to Micheline Warson.

G15.1. Friedrich, born in Vienna in 1954.
G15.2. Heinrich-Michael, born in Vienna in 1955.
G15.3. Maria Alexandra, born in Vienna in 1957.

G14.4. Eveline, born in 1930, married in 1950 to Count Leopold Hartig.

G15.1. Georg, born in Vienna in 1951.
G15.2. Maria Elisabeth, born in Vienna in 1952.
G15.3. Christoph, born in Vienna in 1954.
G15.4. Gabriele, born in Vienna in 1957.

G14.5. Clara, born in 1932.
G14.6. Friedrich Zichy, 1937-51.
G14.7. Zenaide, born in 1953.

G13.8. Hedwig, born in 1906, married Baron Gottfried Korb von Weidenheim.
G13.9. Johann, born in 1911, married in 1934 to Susanne Sranyi.

G14.1. Eva, born in 1935.
G14.2. Otto Wimpffen, born in 1938, married in Chicago, Ill. in 1962 to Verlea Miller.

G15.1. Stefan, born in Chicago, Ill. in 1965.
G15.2. Susanna, born in Chicago, Ill. in 1966.

G14.3. Johann Wimpffen, born in 1951.

G12.3. Simon Wimpffen, 1867-1925, married in 1890 to Countess Karoline Szechenyi. They had no issue.

G11.4. Maria Wimpffen, 1842-1918, married in 1867 to Baron Friedrich Gagern (1842-1910).

G12.1. Alfons Gagern, 1867-1909, Doctor of Law, married in 1899 to Luise Matti.

G13.1. Josefa, born in 1900.
G13.2. Gabriele, 1903-1918.

G12.2. Heinrich Gagern, 1868-1900, Doctor of Law.
G12.3. Marie, 1870-1947, married in 1893 to Lt. Colonel Karl Spies. They had no issue.
G12.4. Friedrich Gagern, 1872-1952, a Catholic clergyman.
G12.5. Franz Gagern, 1876-1932, married in 1920 to Countess Emma Mikes. They had no issue.
G12.6. Ernst Gagern, 1878-1954, Admiral, married in 1906 to Baroness Marie Luise Maltzahn.

G13. Marietta, born in 1907.

G10.2. Baron Denis (Daniel) Eskeles, born in 1803 and died in Vienna in 1876. He inherited the firm established by his father, but went bankrupt in 1859. He married in 1831 to Emilie (Wilhemina) Baroness Brentano-Cimarolli (1809-80). Her father was the banker, Baron Karl Brentano-Cimarolli. They had six daughters.

G11.1. Helene Maria Cecilia, 1837-99, married in 1853 to Baron Ludwig Gablenz-Eskeles (1814-74).

G12.1. Dionys, born in 1856, Lt. Colonel, married in 1897 to Anna Zelzer.

G13. Heinrich Gablenz Eskeles, 1898-1940.

G12.2. Heinrich Gablenz-Eskeles, 1857-1926, Colonel.
G12.3. Mathilde 1859-89, married in 1877 to Baron Gustav Acton. They had no issue.

G11.2. Mathilde, born in 1839, married in 1857 to the French Ambassador Marquis Joseph de Gabriac (1831-1903).
G11.3. Emilie Maria, 1841-1917, married in 1862 to Baron Theodor Raule (1830-84). They had no issue.
G11.4. Malvine Henrietta, 1842-1918, married in 1859 to James Ritter von Baertling (1817-94), Military General.

G12.1. Alice, born in 1863, married in 1888 to Heinrich Ritter von Plessing. (1852-1913).

G13.1. Gottschalk, born in 1889.
G13.2. Konrad, born in 1890.
G13.3. Heinrich, born in 1894.

G12.2. Hugo James Baertling, born in 1865.

G11.5. Bernardine Seraphine, 1845-79, married in 1865 to Giovanni Marchese Canigiani de Ceschi born in 1834. They had no issue.
G11.6. Maria Flora Cecilia, 1849-1930, married in 1867 to Count Wulhelm Saracini de Belfort (1831-1907).

G12.1. Paride, 1867-1936, married in 1908 to Anastasie Zechany.

G13. Maria de Belfort, born in 1909.

G12.2. Luisa, born in 1876, married in 1915 to Major Friedrich Lorber.

G8.2. R. Joachim (Jacob) Eskeles,[7] married his second cousin (see G8.4/9.2/10 below).

G9. R. Loeb Eskeles of Shaffa, died in 1763.

   G10.1. Edel.
   G10.2. R. Jacob Moses Gabriel Aaron Eskeles.
   G10.3. Bondel, married R. Wolf, son of R. Solomon Turnau in Prague.

G8.3. Rebecca Bella, married R. Aaron Moses Ezekiel Lwow (or Lember-ger). See Lemberger-Marx Family — Chapter III.
G8.4. Rosa, married R. Phineas Katzenellenbogen of Boskowitz. (See Chapter II). She remarried R. Elias, son of R. Abraham Lichtenstadt (died in 1758).

   G9.1. Rosa, died in 1797, married Juspa Gokesch (Joseph) of Frank-furt-on-Main.[8]
   G9.2. Moses Lichtenstadt.

     G10. Hinde Rachel, married her second cousin Jacob, son of R. Gabriel Eskeles (see above).

G8.5. R. Teibele Eskeles, married and had issue, Miriam and Jochebed.
G8.6. R. Judah Lieb Eskeles (died young), married Keila Katz. (See Chapter V — Branch B — G8.9.)

BRANCH B

G11. R. Abraham Ari Babad, A.B.D. Mikulonitz, Galicia.

   G12. R. Isaac Babad, A.B.D. Kalush, married the daughter of R. Zvi Hirsch Teomim of Borstein. (See Chapter IV — Branch A.)

     G13.1. R. Hirsch Babad.

       G14.1. R. Menachem Mendel Babad, A.B.D. Gurahamo, died in 1926.

         G15.1. Toyba, married R. Jacob Isaac, son of R. Elijah Frankel-Teomim. (See Chapter IV — Branch H.)
         G15.2. R. Abraham Moses Babad, Rabbi of Jebelia (near Tel Aviv).

     G13.2. R. Moses Babad, 1860-1916, A.B.D. Lvov, married Deborah, daughter of R. Abraham Menachem Steinberg of Brody.

       G14.1. Dr. Jacob Babad, born in 1895 (Rehovot, Israel), married Jeanette David of Amsterdam.

         G15.1. Sheula, born in 1933, married Professor Aviezer Frankel, Department of Mathematics, Weizmann Institute. They have issue.

G15.2. Channah, married Asher Feldman. They have issue.

G15.3. Professor Yair Babad (Professor of Mathematics — Chicago, Ill.) They have issue.

G15.4. Elisha Babad, Lecturer in Psychology at the Hebrew University in Jerusalem.

G14.2. Dr. Shemariah Babad (Ramat Aviv, Israel). He was born in 1900 and married in 1932. They settled in Israel in 1933.

G15.1. Naomi, born in 1937, married Arman Madjar. Their children, Tali, Michal and Ilan.

G15.2. Michael Babad, born in 1939.

G14.3. Abraham David Babad, perished.

G14.4. Samuel Babad, perished.

G14.5. Miriam, married Abraham Solomon Zeidman, perished.

G13.3. R. Jacob Babad, died in 1916, married the daughter of R. Alexander Halpern, A.B.D. Lvov, author of the work *Rosh Ha-Mizbeach.*

G14.1. R. Phineas David Babad, married, perished in the Holocaust. He had issue, and a daughter settled in Tel Aviv.

G14.2. R. Joseph Babad, born in Golagura in 1875. He was A.B.D. of Kalush, where his grandfather had been the A.B.D., but fled from the Germans during World War II and reached England via Amsterdam. He settled in Manchester and died there in 1944. He was also one time Rabbi of Vienna. He married Sima Vita, daughter of R. Haim Samuel Dreizner of Lvov.

G15.1. Rachel, remarried to Joel Wlodawer of Manchester. They have no issue.

G15.2. R. Joshua Heschel Babad, born in 1900. He came to the U.S.A. in 1940. He married Rosa (Rachel), daughter of Haim Ringelheim (see Frankel-Teomim Family — Chapter IV) and was a member of the Jewish Theological Seminary of New York. They have no issue.

G13.4. Channah, married her first cousin, R. Jacob, son of R. Jonathan Horowitz (a son-in-law of R. Zvi Hirsch Teomim of Borstein, mentioned above). Their grandchildren include the Mermelstein Family (Brooklyn, N.Y.), Professor Simeon Yawetz of Haifa, and David Blum of Tel Aviv.

BRANCH C

G12.1. R. Joseph Babad,[9] 1800-1874. He was the author of the popular Rabbinical work called *Minchat Chinuch*, by which he is popularly known. He was married three times. His second wife was the sister of R. Haim Halberstam of Sanz and his third, the daughter of R. David Hager of Zablodov (son-in-law of R. Moses Lieb of Sassov).

G13.1. R. David Meir Babad, A.B.D. Sniatyn, later *Dayan* (Judge) of Safed in Israel, where he died.

G13.2. R. Moses Babad, A.B.D. Przemysl.

G14. R. Joshua Heschel Babad, A.B.D. Solitza.

G15.1. R. Shalom Babad.

G15.2. R. Samuel Shmelke Babad.

G15.3. R. Moses Babad, born in Jassy, Rumania in 1881, married Sarah Rost, and perished in the Holocaust about 1941. He was the Rabbi of a Vienna Congregation.

G16.1. R. Joseph Babad, born in Lobatchov in 1908.[10] He obtained his Ph.D. in Vienna in 1933 and was Rabbi at the Theological Seminary there in 1935, the year he married Pelke Rathaus. He came to the U.S.A. in 1940 and settled in Chicago, Ill. From 1952 on, he was Dean of the Students and Professor of Hebrew Languages and Literature at the Hebrew Theological College in Chicago. He was the author of *History of Jews in Medieval Carinthia*.

G17.1. Ada (Adina), married Abraham Morduchowitz (Monsey, New York), and have three children.

G17.2. Rachel, married Abraham Bruckenstein (Chicago, Ill.), and have three children.

G16.2. Dr. Frederick (Feiwel) Babad, M.D., born in 1913. He studied Medicine at the University of Vienna, finishing in 1938. Because of the situation in Germany he left for the U.S.A., but returned to obtain his degree in Vienna in 1947. He married in 1942 to Lissa Gratsch, and settled in Trenton, New Jersey.

G17.1. Dr. Joshua Babad, M.D., born in 1945, married.

G17.2. Melvin, born in 1949.

G15.4. Toyba, born about 1880 and perished in 1944, married R.
Moses, son of R. Abraham Bergman. He was Rabbi of Jassy
and later of Jassina (later called Korosmezo). They had one
daughter.

G16. Gitel, born in 1902, married in 1929 to Chaim Schneier (died
in Vienna in 1938). She came to the U.S.A. in 1949, and
died in New York in 1973. They had an only son.

G17. R. Arthur (Abraham) Schneier, born in Vienna in 1930,
and came to the U.S.A. in 1947. He married in 1958 to
Donna F. Makovsky, and they have two children, Marc
(born 1959) and Karen (born 1962). He is the Rabbi of
the Park East Synagogue *Zichron Efraim* in New York.

G13.3. R. Joshua Babad.
G13.4. R. Shalom Babad.
G13.5. R. Simeon Babad, born in 1839, and elected A.B.D. of Tarnopol
on his father's death in 1874. He held the position until his death
in 1909. He married Rachel, daughter of R. Haim Babad of
Brody. They had fourteen children, most of whom died young.
He wrote glosses to the *Minchat Chinuch* by his father.

G14.1. Joseph, died unmarried in 1909.
G14.2. Sarah, married her first cousin, R. Moses Hornstein. He died
young.
G14.3. R. Joshua Heschel Babad, born in 1867, A.B.D. Tarnopol until
he died in 1919, having succeeded his father there. He married
Leah, daughter of R. Aryey Judah Liebus, son of R. Joseph
Hananiah Lipa Meisels (A.B.D. Przemysl).

G15.1. R. Joseph Hananiah Lipa Babad, born 1891. His wife and
three children perished in the Holocaust. He settled in New
York, and died in 1975.
G15.2. Hena, married R. Jacob Shalita,[11] the last A.B.D. of Tarnopol
before the Holocaust. He was the A.B.D. together with his
father-in-law from 1912, and the only Rabbi there as leader
on the latter's death in 1919. He was born in 1896 in Jawo-
row, son of R. Benzion Shalita. They perished with their son,
Simeon, in 1943.
G15.3. Gitel married R. Joseph, son of R. Joshua Heschel Babad.
They perished.
G15.4. Rachel, married R. Uri, son of R. Menachem Mendel Kauf-

man. He was Rabbi of the *Chasam Sofer* Synagogue in New York.

G16.1. R. Mendel Kaufman, born 1935, Rabbi of New Haven (Connecticut) Young Israel Synagogue for many years and currently Rabbi in New York. He was the author of a commentary on the *Peri Megadim* (see introduction to the Teomim Family Pedigree), published in New York in 1970. He married in 1961 to Reizel, daughter of R. Joseph, son of R. Elijah Frankel-Teomim of Przeworsk. (See Teomim Family Pedigree — Branch B.) Their children are Lifchy, born in 1962; Uri, born in 1964; Gitel, born in 1968; and Elijah, born in 1972.

G16.2. R. Joshua Heschel (Harry J.) Kaufman, Rabbi of Young Israel Congregation in Montreal, Canada, formerly of Washington, D.C. He married Gitel, daughter of Rabbi Small of Chicago, Ill. Gitel is the niece of Rabbi HaGaon Moses Feinstein of New York.

G17.1. Sima Leah, married in 1971 to Jeruchem Lacks (Brooklyn, N.Y.). They have issue.
G17.2. Uri Kaufman.
G17.3. Eliahu Kaufman.

G13.6. Wife of R. Jacob Hornstein.

G14.1. R. Moses, married his cousin, Sarah Babad.
G14.2. R. Joseph Hornstein, married Pearl Sneh, had issue of whom,

G15. Jacob Hornstein (New York), married Sarah, daughter of Samson Fischer of Vienna. They had seven children.

G13.7. Chavah from the third marriage, died young about 1879. She married R. Samuel, son of R. Dovberish (author of *Derech Ha-Melech*), son of R. Samuel HaKohen Rappoport (A.B.D. Lvov).

G14.1. R. Joseph Haim Rappoport, A.B.D. Rava-Ruska (near Lvov), married Toyba, daughter of R. Jacob Koppel Brenner of Stanislav. Five children perished in the Holocaust, Moses, Dov Berish, Chava, Pesel and Griena.

G15.1. David Simha Rappoport, married Miriam.

G16.1. Moses Rappoport (Montreal).
G16.2. Aryey Liebish Rappoport (Brooklyn, N.Y.).

G15.2. R. Isaac Meir Rappoport (Prager Rabbi of New York), born in 1898, married 1) Leah Malka, daughter of R. Abraham Weiss, and 2) Liebe Raatza, daughter of Asher Rubin. (See Chapter XVI — G17.2 — page 605).

G16.1. Dov Berish (Bernard), born 1924, married Chaya Steinberg.

G17.1. Malka Esther, married in 1973 to Samuel Zvi Reider (New York).

G17.2. Abraham Haim.

G16.2. Eidel, married Moses Ezekiel, son of R. Abraham Mordecai Levi Isaac Samuels.

G17.1. Shlomo (Miami, Florida), married and has two children.

G17.2. Shraga Feiwel (Israel), married.

G17.3. Leah Malka; 4. Asher; 5. Dov Berish; 6 Elimelech.

C16.3. Samuel, unmarried, died in Auschwitz.

G16.4. Chava, died before the War.

G14.2. R. Joshua Rappoport, Rabbi of Chorostkov, married Beila, daughter of R. Judah Aryey Lieb Babad. They perished.

G13.8. Hinde, married R. Jacob son of R. Reuben Poppers (Papers). His first wife was Dreizel Rappoport by whom he had three sons, Issachar Shamai, Zvi Uri and Haim.

G14.1. R. Joseph Poppers, A.B.D. Brody, author of *Mincha Chadasha*, died in 1941. He married Sarah, daughter of R. Israel Kaminer.

G15.1. R. Ezekiel Shraga Poppers, succeeded his father as A.B.D. Brody, married Pesha, daughter of R. Judah Aryey Lieb Babad, A.B.D. Padolovochisk. They perished in the Holocaust.

G15.2. R. Judah Ari Poppers, perished.

G15.3. Hadassah, married her cousin, R. Dovberish Poppers of Tarnopol, perished.

G15.4. Hinde, Jochebed and Dreizel, all perished.

G14.2. R. Joshua Heschel Poppers. His son, Zvi Hirsch Poppers (Ph.D., formerly of New York).

G14.3. R. Moses Poppers, married his niece, Dreizel, daughter of R. Haim Poppers of Tarnopol. They perished with their children. One son, Dovberish, married his cousin Hadassah.

G14.4. Miriam, married R. Menachem Mendel Sneh of Lvov, perished with their family.

G14.5. Gitel, perished.

G14.6. Toyba, married Isaac Langson.

BRANCH D

G12.2. R. Haim Babad, A.B.D. Mikulonitz.

G13.1. R. Moses (twin of R. Joshua Heschel below), Rabbi of Mikulonitz.

G14.1. R. Simeon Babad, born about 1859 and died in 1935. He was the Rabbi of Jaworow and Budzanow, and married Leah, the daughter of R. Shalom Mordecai Schwadron, died in 1911, known as the *MaHaRaSHaM* of Borjan in Galicia. R. Simeon succeeded his father-in-law as Rabbi of Borjan in 1911.

G15.1. R. Jacob (Yankel) Babad, 1888-1972. He came to the U.S.A. in 1946, and was married to Esther Sheindel, daughter of R. Simha, son of R. Nathan Goldberg (The *Gaon of Limanov*). R. Simha's sister was married to R. Haim Isaac Jeruchem. (See Chapter XV — Heschel-Jeruchem Family Pedigree.)

G16.1. Shalom Mordecai (Markus) Babad,[12] born in 1913 at Sanok. He came to the U.S.A. in 1948, and married Judith, daughter of Solomon Grawer.

G17.1. Solomon, born in Antwerp in 1946. He married Miriam Rachel Ehrman. Their children, Rivke, born in 1970, Jacob, born in 1973, and Leah Gitel, born in 1976.

G17.2. Rachel, born in 1953, married Mordchai Preiserowicz.

G16.2. Reizel, married Moses Englander (Brooklyn, N.Y.).

G17.1. Toyba, married Samuel Weksler (Antwerp). Their children, Ricky, Joseph and Estelle.

G17.2. Helen, married Jack Nash. He is the president of Oppenheimer & Co., Inc. Their children, Pamella and Joshua (New York).

G17.3. Israel, married Caryl Ruth, daughter of Sam Schechter.

G16.3. Rachel, married 1) Leibel Pluczenik, and had issue, and 2) Moshe A. Sheinbaum, as his second wife. He is the president of Shengold Publishers (New York), publishers of this book.

G17.1. Shimon S. Pluchenik, married Esther, daughter of Eliezer (Louis) Glick. Their children, Betty, Leah, Aryeh Leib, and Yaakov Avraham.

G17.2. Mirl Pluchenik.

G16.4. Riva (Rivke), married David Kertzner, perished in the Holocaust.

G15.2. Esther Gitel, perished in 1943, married to Haim Bari.

G16. Malka (Mali), married Wolf, son of Isaac Balminger (Israel).

G14.2. R. Joshua Heschel Babad, who succeeded his father as A.B.D. Mikulonitz.

G15. R. Joseph Benzion Babad, A.B.D. Mikulonitz, perished in the Holocaust.

G14.3. Rachel, married R. Joseph, son of R. Isaac Joshua Kliger, the Rabbi of Greiding. (See Horowitz Family Pedigree — Branch VI — G15.6 et seq.)

G14.4. Toyba, married R. Joseph Babad. (See below G12/13.2/14.4.)

G13.2. R. Joshua Heschel Babad, A.B.D. Strzyzow and later of Podwoloczyska, died in 1892. He married Gitel, daughter of R. Alexander Asher Margolioth.

G14.1. R. David Menachem Meinish Babad[13] of Brody, 1865-1937. He succeeded his father as A.B.D. Strzyzow in 1892 and in 1894, on the death of his father-in-law, R. Moses Landau, A.B.D. Jaworow and Lyzhansk, he took his place in Jaworow. He held this position until 1911. The rest of his life was spent in Tarnopol. He participated in the Rabbinical Conferences in 1925 and 1927 in Cracow and Lvov, and was a close associate of the Belzer Rebbe (R. Issachar Dov Rokeah — see Rokeah Family Pedigree). He was the author of Chavatzelet HaSharon, published in Bilgoray in 1931. He married 1) Leah, daughter of R. Joel M. Landau, Rabbi of Jaworow, and had issue; 2) his niece, Chaya, daughter of R. Joseph Babad; and 3) Mindel Nechama, daughter of R. David Shlichter. (See Chapter VII — Branch B — Shlichter Family.)

G15.1. Reizel Chaya Shifra, married R. Elimelech, son of R. Joshua Heschel Frankel-Teomim. (See Chapter IV — Branch H.)

G15.2. Pesha, married twice, secondly to Aaron Schney.

G16.1. Reala, married R. Naftali Hirsch Landau, A.B.D. Borstein.

G16.2. Beila, married R. Uri Shraga Feiwel, A.B.D. Poznov.

G15.3. Beila, perished in Tarnopol in 1943, married R. Uri Shraga Feiwel, A.B.D. Budzanow, son of R. Jacob Zvi Babad. They had no issue.

G15.4. Sima, married her first cousin, R. Joshua Heschel, son of R. Aryey Lieb Babad. They perished in the Holocaust.

G15.5. Jochebed, married R. Abraham Horowitz.

G14.2. R. Shalom Babad, A.B.D. Varicz (near Belz), perished in the Holocaust.

G15.1. Frumet, married R. Solomon Langener of Toronto (The Strattoner Rebbe), and have issue.

G15.2. Pesha, married R. Abraham Mordecai Ashkenazi, A.B.D. Varicz, and had issue.

G14.3. R. Judah Aryey Liebus Babad,[14] known as the "Padolovochisker Rebbe," married Milka, daughter of R. Reuben David, son of Abraham Joshua Heschel Ephrati. They had ten children.

G15.1. R. Joshua Heschel Babad, A.B.D. of Tarnopol, succeeding his father-in-law, R. Meinish Babad, whose daughter, Beila, he married. They perished in the Holocaust.

G15.2. Beila, married R. Joshua Rappoport (A.B.D. Chorostkov). They perished.

G15.3. Pesha, married R. Ezekiel Poppers.

G15.4. Raatze, married R. Michal Ashkenazi.

G15.5. Wife of R. Moses Lustig.

G15.6. Reuben David Babad; 7. Alexander Asher Babad; 8. Haim, perished; 9. Ezekiel; and 10. Sima. All perished.

G14.4. R. Joseph Dov Babad, born in 1875, R. of Mikulonitz, suceeding his father-in-law there. He married Toyba, daughter of R. Moses, son of Haim Babad. (See above G12/13.1/14.4.)

G15.1. Chaya, second wife of her uncle, R. Meinish Babad, of Tarnopol. (See above.)

G15.2. R. Abraham Moses Babad,[15] known as the "Sunderlander Rabbi." He was born in Mikulonitz in 1908. From 1932 to 1933 he was acting Rabbi of Mikulonitz, and then emigrated to England in 1936. In the same year he married his second cousin, Chaya, daughter of R. Israel Aryey Margolioth (Margulies). He was Principal of the *Or Yisrael* Yeshiva in

London from 1937 to 1939, and Rabbi of the *Ohavei Emeth* Synagogue there from 1937 to 1941. From 1942 to 1947 he was at the *Adath Yisrael* Congregation in Edgware, and then settled in Sunderland as head of the community until his death in 1969. Besides being a vice-chairman of the Agudat Israel Movement in Great Britain and a member of its World Executive, he was also active in other societies dealing with the rescue of Polish Jewry, and was a contributor to Rabbinical and political journals.

G16.1. Beila Bracha, born in 1938, married R. Bezalel Simha Menachem Benzion Rabinowitz, and have issue.

G16.2. R. Joseph Dov Babad, born in 1949, married in 1970 to Chaya, daughter of R. Abraham David Horowitz, and have issue (London).

G15.3. Reize, married R. Baruch Redlich, perished in the Holocaust. He was A.B.D. Mikiloyev.

G15.4. R. Alexander Asher Babad, perished.

G14.5. R. Isaac Babad, 1870-1929, A.B.D. of Tartakov, married Beila Bracha, daughter of R. Mordecai, son of Reuben David Ephrati. (See G14.3 above.)

G15.1. R. Joshua Heschel, A.B.D. Tartakov, born in 1906, and perished with his family in the Holocaust. He married the daughter of R. Isaac Rubin, Rabbi of Jaworow.

G15.2. Pesha, married R. Israel Aryey, son of Ephraim Zalman Margolioth (Margulies).

G15.3. R. Alexander Asher (Osias) Babad, born in 1910. He was the Dayan (Judge) of Walowa and later Chief Judge in Budapest. He settled in the U.S.A. in 1947, and lives in New York. He married 1) Rachel, his second cousin, daughter of R. Aaron (of Walowa), son of R. Israel Jacob Jokel Teitelbaum, and had one son, and 2) Pearl Feige, daughter of R. Jehiel Greenzweig, in 1946 in Budapest.

G16.1. R. Isaac Babad, born in 1937 (London), married Rachel, daughter of R. Meshullam, son of R. Zvi Hirsch Ashkenazi. Their children, Pearl, Kalman Joshua Heschel, Shalom and Mordecai Samuel. (See Chapter IV — Branch A.)

G16.2. Rachel Miriam, married Shalom Mendelowitz (Monsey, N.Y.). Their children, Beila Bracha, Menachem Zeev, Rivke Frieda, Channah Mirl, and Jehiel Zelig.

G16.3. R. Jehiel Babad[16] (New York), born in 1948, married in 1967 to Rachel, daughter of R. Elimelech, son of R. Alexander Haim Ashkenazi of Melbourne (Australia). R. Alexander was a first cousin to R. Meshullam Ashkenazi mentioned above (G15.3/16.1). Their children, Isaac, born in 1969, and Gitel Rivke, born in 1972. (See Chapter IV — Branch A.)

G16.4. Haim Joshua Heschel Babad, born in 1949, married in 1968 to Ethel, daughter, of Meshullam Zalman Glanz of Brooklyn. Their children, Chanoch, born in 1970, and Beila Bracha, born in 1972.

G16.5. Channah, married Abraham, son of R. Baruch Nathan Halberstam. (See Chapter XIV — Branch C.)

G16.6. Mordecai Babad.

G16.7. Naftali Meir Babad.

G15.4. Meir Babad, unmarried.

G15.5. Raatza, married R. Shalom Rokeah of Krisnapol.

G15.6. Sarah Rebecca, married R. Phineas Reiner, A.B.D. Lodmir.

G15.7. Sima, married R. Joel, son of R. Aaron (A.B.D. Borjan) Halpern.

G15.8. Blume, married R. Moses, son of R. Joseph Kliger. (See Chapter XVI — Branch VI — Stanislav.)

G14.6. Raatza, married R. Nachman (A.B.D. Helitch and Koslov), son of R. David Horowitz. (See Chapter XVI — Branch VI — Stanislav — G14.3/15.5/16.1.)

G14.7. Toyba, married R. Abraham (A.B.D. Strzyzow), son of R. Samuel Babad, (G13.3/14.3 below). They were first cousins, and perished in the Holocaust.

G13.3. R. Samuel Babad, A.B.D. Sander-Vishne (near Galicia-Hungary border).

G14.1. Wife of R. Aaron (of Walowa), son of R. Israel Jacob Teitelbaum. (See Chapter XVII.) Their daughter married R. Alexander Asher Babad (G13.2/14.5/15.3 above).

G14.2. R. Uri Liebus Babad, succeeded his father as A.B.D. of Sander-Vishne.

G15. R. Samuel Babad, Rabbi of Danzig.

G14.3. R. Abraham Babad, A.B.D. Strzyzow, married his first cousin, Toyba Babad.

G13.4. R. Isaac Babad, A.B.D. Sassov.

G14. Son.

G15. R. Joel Babad, A.B.D. Slovita, married the daughter of R. Joel (A.B.D. Zlatchov), son of R. Moses David (A.B.D. Tulchev-Safed) Ashkenazi. (See Chapter XVII — Teitelbaum Family and Chapter IV — Branch A.)

G13.5. Wife of R. Shrentzel. Their son, R. Solomon Shrentzel.

G13.6. Wife of R. David, son of R. Eleazar Horowitz. (See Chapter XVI — Branch VI — Stanislav — G14.3/15.5.)

BRANCH E

THE CHAJES FAMILY

ANCESTRY

G8.3. Wife of R. Zeev Wolf.

G9.1. R. Issachar Berish.

G10.1. R. Aryey Judah Lieb Berenstein.

G11. R. Isaac Wolf Berenstein.

G12. Wife of R. Menachem Meinish Chajes, a wood merchant in Brody, later settled in Florence and Leghorn, Italy.

G13. R. Meir Chajes, a banker in Florence, associated with the banking firm Berenstein-Chajes and Company, later called Meir Chajes and Son.

G14.1. R. Zvi Hirsch Chajes,[17] born in Brody in 1805, and died in Lvov in 1855. He studied under R. Ephraim Zalman Margolioth as well as other scholars, and was ordained at the age of twenty-two. He then became A.B.D. of Zolkiev, where he befriended the philosopher, Nahum Krochmal. He was elected A.B.D. of Kalicz in 1852, and returned to Zolkiev shortly before his death. He remained an Austrian subject throughout his life. Of his five sons, all except one, Isaac, were merchants. He was the author of *Torat Nevi'im, Ateret Tzvi, Mavoh HaTahmum, Darkei Hora'ah*, a collection of responsa, *Amarei Binah, Minchat Kena'ot, Hagahot* on the Talmud and various articles in the works of others.

G15.1. Leon Chajes, born in Zolkiev in 1828, and died in Vienna in 1891.

G16. Dr. Adolf Chajes, Lawyer in Padgorze, author of *Ueber die Hebräische Gramatik Spinoza's,* (Breslau, 1869).

G17. Wife of Moritz Skaler of Stanislav.

G15.2. Haim Joachim Chajes, born in Zolkiev in 1830, and died in Lvov in 1886.

G16.1. Hannah, married her first cousin, Max Chajes. (See below.)

G16.2. Dr. Herman Chajes M.D., died in Vienna in 1928.

G16.3. Miriam, married Dr. Adolf Shritter.

G16.4. Sophie, married Professor Dr. Salomon Frankfurter (1856-1941). He was a prominent Austrian librarian, pedagogue, classical philologist and archaeologist. He obtained his Ph.D. in Vienna, in 1883. The following year he became an officer of the Vienna University Library and its director from 1919 until 1923. He was also the author of numerous works, and the uncle of the U.S. Supreme Court Justice, Felix Frankfurter, who died in 1965.

G15.3. Solomon Chajes, born in Zolkiev in 1835.

G16.1. Adolf.

G16.2. Max, married his first cousin, Hannah Chajes (above).

G16.3. Hirsch Perez Chajes, 1876-1927, a child prodigy, born in Brody and became a noted Rabbi and scholar. He was also a Zionist leader and studied at the Jewish Theological Seminary in Vienna and later at the University there. He became Rabbi of Trieste in 1912, Deputy Rabbi of Vienna in 1918 and later their Chief Rabbi. He was reburied in Tel Aviv in 1950. He was the author of Hagahot on the Talmudic Tractate *Berachot,* published in Breslau in 1911; *Ma'amarim Le-Zichron,* published Vienna, 1933; notes added with an introduction to *Peirush Mesechet Mashkin,* by R. Solomon, son of Hayetom, published in Berlin in 1909; and a commentary on the book of Psalms, Kiev, 1908.

G15.4. Wolf Chajes, born in Zolkiev in 1845, and died in Danzig in 1901.

G16. Dr. Beno Chajes, Professor of Medicine in Berlin.

G15.5. R. Isaac Chajes, 1842-1901, A.B.D. Brody. He was born in Zolkiev and died in Brody.

G16.1. Hirsch Perez Chajes.

G16.2. Saul Chajes, 1884-1935, born in Brody, and worked at the library and archives of the Vienna Jewish Community. He was a foremost East European bibliographer and his most important work was *Otzar Beduyei HaShem* (1930, reprinted 1967).

G16.3. Another son, and three daughters.

G15.6. Yita Shifra, born in Zolkiev in 1837, and died in Lvov in 1858.

G14.2. Son.

G15. Markus Chajes.

G16.1. Ludwig Chajes, killed in World War I in 1915.

G16.2. Isaac Chajes, perished in the Holocaust.

G16.3. Two sisters, Genia and Dora, perished.

G16.4. Dr. Josef Chajes, M.D., born in Lvov in 1875 and died in Jerusalem in 1944. He studied medicine in Vienna and later became the Chief of Gynecology of the Jewish Hospital in Lvov. In 1926 he moved to Vienna, and in 1934 to Jerusalem and the following year to Tel Aviv, Israel. He married in 1908 to Valerie Roth in Lvov. She was a noted concert pianist and settled with her sons in Detroit.

G17.1. Dr. Richard Chajes, M.D., died in Detroit, 1966. He practiced medicine in Israel and settled in Detroit in 1953, where he joined the staff of Brent and Plymouth General hospitals. His two daughters, Daria and Mila.

G17.2. Julius Chajes, born in Lvov in 1910. When he was about six, he began to play the piano with his mother as his teacher, and then under Anna and Lola Niementowska and Severyn Eisenberger at the Institute of Music in Lvov. He wrote his first composition and gave his first piano recital at the age of nine, and the following year continued his studies in Vienna with Richard Robert, Angelo Kessissoglu, Julius Isserlis and the couple Moritz Rosenthal and his wife Hedwig Kanner-Rosenthal. He wrote his first string quartet when he was thirteen, and played his *Romantic Fantasy* (Piano Concerto) with the Vienna Symphony Orchestra when he was fifteen. He studied at the University of Vienna and at the Vienna Conservatory of Music, and in 1933 he was the Honor Prize winner at the First International Competition for Pianists in Vienna. In 1934 he went with his parents to Palestine and was appointed head of the piano department at the Music College in Tel Aviv. The famous Rose Quartet performed two of his string quartets at a farewell recital in Vienna. For the next two

years he conducted the Jerusalem Male Chorus and researched ancient Hebrew music. In 1937 he was awarded
two prizes by the Juedischer Kulturbund in Berlin for a
composition of his.

In December 1937 he came to New York and began
to perform over the Columbia Network and in three So-
nata recitals in New York Town Hall. In 1940 he moved
to Detroit as music director of the city's Temple Beth El,
taught at the Institute of Musical Art and then as music
director of Detroit's Jewish Community Center. A few
years later he joined the Piano Faculty of Wayne State
University and founded the Jewish Community Center
Symphony Orchestra. Today he is established as an extraordinary composer and pianist through his concerts and
radio work and as an eminent piano teacher. His students
have won many competitions. Chajes has toured extensively and his published compositions included chamber
music, choral works, songs, and opera, a cello Concerto,
a symphonic poem, two piano Sonatas, and a Piano Concerto. Many of his compositions are in the repertoire of
leading musicians, and his songs *Adarim* and *Palestinian
Nights* are in the repertoire of almost every Jewish concert singer.

Chajes married 1) Shulamit Silber in 1934, divorced in
1940, 2) Marguerite Schieber-Kozenn, divorced in 1964
and 3) Annette Schoen-Loring.

G18. Jeffrey H. (Yosef Hillel), born in 1965.

BRANCH F

THE BRODSKY FAMILY

G7.1.   R. Isaac.

G8.1.   R. Mordecai Yollis.

G9.2.   R. Israel.

G10.   R. Alexander Sender Haim, adopted the surname Shor.[18]

G11.2.   R. Meir Shor, adopted the surname Brodsky, from the name of his
         hometown Brody. He settled in Zlatopol (Kiev District) where he

married Miriam Itel, daughter of R. Jonah of Zlatopol. They had five sons, all of whom became wealthy and were considered the richest Jewish family in Russia of the nineteenth century.

G12.1. Wife of R. Moses Charal of Zlatopol.
G12.2. Israel Brodsky, 1823-89, was the wealthiest of the five brothers, and settled in Kiev where he was famous for his philanthropy.

G13.1. Leon (Leibish) Brodsky of Kiev.
G13.2. Lazar (Eliezer) Brodsky of Kiev. The two were owners of twenty-two sugar factories and three refineries making them the leading sugar producers in Russia. They were also councilors of commerce and received decorations from the Russian and French (Legion of Honor) Governments.

G12.3. Abraham Brodsky, 1816-84, settled in Odessa in 1858. He was also very prominent in the sugar industry and other large enterprises. He was for many years the most influential member of the Odessa city council and vice-mayor for many years. He gave much to charitable and educational institutions, and founded important benevolent societies in Odessa and Zlatopol. He died in the latter city.

G13. Samuel Brodsky, 1846-96, married the daughter of the author and journalist Ossip (Joseph) Rabinovitch. He was appointed a member of the Odessa city council.

CHAPTER XII

BRANCH A
LOWENSTAMM AND AUERBACH FAMILIES

G6.4. R. Saul,[1] son of R. Heschel of Cracow.

G7.1. R. Isaac Joshua Heschel, A.B.D. Breslau, and afterwards succeeded R. Baruch Kahane Rappoport as A.B.D. Vilna from 1712 on. He was named after his grandfather. He wrote approbations to: *Korban HaEidah,* a commentary on the Jerusalem Talmud, by his brother-in-law, R. David, son of R. Zvi Hirsch Mirls, published Dessau, 1743; *Mira Dachya* on Rashi, in 1712; *Brit Shalom,* in 1713; and *Gaon Tzvi,* by R. Zvi Hirsch Horowitz. He married a daughter of R. Simha Dokter of Prague, and then Reizel, daughter of R. Hirsch Mirls, son of Benjamin, who was the widow of R. Haim Jonah Teomim (see Teomim Family Pedigree — Chapter IV). He died in Vilna on September 9 (26th Elul), 1749, and his wife in Berlin in 1764.

Jekutiel, the physician of Vilna, son of Lieb Gordon, who had studied in Italy, wrote to him at Vilna in 1729 from Padua, expressing his enthusiasm for R. Moses Haim Luzzatto. This appears in Jacob Emden's *Torat HaKena'ot,* published in Amsterdam in 1752.

G8. Chaya, married R. Simha Halevi, A.B.D. Slonim, son of R. Jekutiel Zalman Halevi, A.B.D. Drogobitch.

G9. Achsa, married R. Joseph, A.B.D. Brest, son of R. Abraham Katzenellenbogen, A.B.D. Brest. (See Descendants of R. Joel Ashkenazi Katzenellenbogen — Chapter VIII — G7.2/8.1/9.1/10.1.)

433

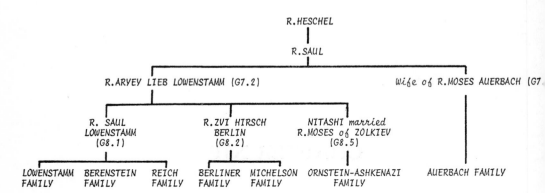

DESCENDANTS OF R.SAUL SON OF
. R.ABRAHAM JOSHUA HESCHEL OF CRACOW

R.HESCHEL

R.SAUL

R.ARYEY LIEB LOWENSTAMM (G7.2)   Wife of R.MOSES AUERBACH (G7

R. SAUL   R.ZVI HIRSCH   NITASHI married
LOWENSTAMM   BERLIN   R.MOSES of ZOLKIEV
(G8.1)   (G8.2)   (G8.5)

LOWENSTAMM   BERENSTEIN   REICH   BERLINER   MICHELSON   ORNSTEIN-ASHKENAZI   AUERBACH FAMILY
FAMILY   FAMILY   FAMILY   FAMILY   FAMILY   FAMILY

G7.2. R. Aryey Lieb Lowenstamm,[2] born about 1690 in Cracow, and
died on the seventh night of Passover (April 2), 1755. He married
in 1707 to Miriam, daughter of the Chacham Zvi Hirsch Ashkenazi,
a distant relative. (See his descendants.) She died in 1757. He
accompanied his father-in-law to Amsterdam, but later went to
Poland where he was appointed A.B.D. Dukla, and then of Tarnopol in 1720. Because this position had been obtained by his influential relatives with governmental support, he was not received
favorably, and left to become A.B.D. Rzeszow from 1724-1728. He
then went to Glogau from 1734-1739 as their leader, where he was
involved in the dispute with regard to R. Moses Haim Luzzatto,
against whom he issued a ban in 1735, and about whom Jekutiel,
the physician, had so enthusiastically written to his uncle R.
Isaac Joshua Heschel, A.B.D. Breslau and Vilna. He was elected
A.B.D. Amsterdam in 1740, where he remained for fifteen years
until his death there.

He was also mentioned in the minutes of the Council of the
Four Lands, and like his cousin, R. Zvi Hirsch Berlin, was actively
involved in the Emden-Eybeschutz affair.

He was invited to be A.B.D. Prague in 1751, but did not accept this position. His brother-in-law, R. Jacob Emden, in his
Megillat Sefer, describes Aryey as a man of mediocre abilities,
whose scientific attainments were not above the practical require-
ments for the Rabbinical Office.

He wrote approbations to: *Toldot Yaakov*, in 1724; *Yafe
Mareh*, in 1724; The Bible with three *Targumim* published at Dyhernfurth; *Mira Dachya*, in 1734; the Frankfurt-Berlin Edition of

the Talmud; *Hishta'arot Melech HaNagav,* in 1735; *Kehilat Shlomo,* in 1740 while at Glogau; *Netzach Yisrael,* in 1740; *Korban Aharon,* in Dessau in 1742; and to the *Tur Even HaEzer* in 1746.

He published the second edition of the Responsa of the *ReMa* (Moses Isserles) to which he added his own notes and annotations (*Kontras Acharon*), in 1711, together with Shemariah, son of Jacob of Grodno; and wrote Responsa in *Ma'amar Mordecai* by R. Mordecai of Düsseldorf, published in Bruenn in 1790; Responsa in *Divrei David,* by R. David of Meldola, published in Amsterdam, in 1753; Novellae in *Pnei Moshe* (on the Jerusalem Talmud); Responsa in the *Binyan Ariel* by his son, in Amsterdam in 1778; Responsa with those of his father-in-law's *Chacham Zvi.*

His funeral orations were delivered by his brother-in-law, R. Jacob Emden (in the *Sha'agat Aryey*), and by his brother-in-law, R. Abraham Meshullam.

G8.1. R. Saul Lowenstamm,[3] named after his paternal grandfather, was born in 1717 while his father was serving as A.B.D. Rzeszow. He married the daughter of R. Abraham Kahana, A.B.D. Dubno, whom he succeeded as Rabbi there on his death in 1749. Previously, he had been A.B.D. Lakacz (Hungary). In 1754 he signed in the minutes of the Council of the Four Lands at the Jaroslav meeting. On his father's death in 1755, he succeeded him as A.B.D. of Amsterdam's Ashkenazi Community, where he devoted much time to the *Beit HaMidrash* established by his father. He wrote many approbations, most while he was serving in Amsterdam, between the years 1756 and 1790. The generosity of his congregation enabled him to build a new house which he occupied on June 22, 1778. He remained as A.B.D. of Amsterdam for some thirty-five years until his death in 1790. Some time after 1769 he married the widow of R. Jacob Haim, A.B.D. Lublin. (See Chapter III.)

He was the author of: *Binyan Ariel,* published in Amsterdam in 1778; Responsa in *Or HaYashir, Or Yisrael, Zichron Yosef,* and *Noda BiYehudah;* and Novellae on the *Mishnayot* and *Torah* entitled *Chatzer Chadasha,* published in Amsterdam in 1765.

G9.1. R. Jacob Moses Lowenstamm, born in 1747, A.B.D. Filehne (Poznania) and Cleves. In 1793 he succeeded his father as A.B.D. of Amsterdam, where he remained until his death there in 1815.

He wrote approbations to *Yesod Olam,* published by R. Baruch of Sokolov, and *Dagul Mervavah,* by R. Ezekiel Landau.

He married his first cousin, Sarah, daughter of R. Zvi Hirsch Berlin, and she died in 1802. He then remarried Chaya, widow of Meir Marx (grandfather of Karl Marx), daughter of Moses Lwow (or Lemberger). (See Chapter III.)

His sermons, given while he was serving at Filehne, entitled *Chiluk BePipula D'Oraita,* were published in the *Binyan Ariel* by his father.

G10.1. R. Jehiel Aryey Lieb Lowenstamm, A.B.D. Leeuwarden, who died during his father's lifetime in 1807, and was buried in Amsterdam. He married Rebecca, daughter of R. Abraham Gedaliah, A.B.D. Copenhagen.

G10.2. R. Naftali Lowenstamm of Amsterdam.

G10.3. R. Abraham Nachman Lowenstamm of Amsterdam, died in Apt.

G10.4. Rebecca Reizel, married R. Samuel Berenstein, head of the Berenstein Family. See this Section — Branch B.

G10.5. Hinde, married R. Naftali Zvi Hirsch, A.B.D. Shoval.

G10.6. Esther Frieda, married her sister's husband's brother, R. Joseph Berendt, son of R. Issachar Berish (A.B.D. Hannover). See G10.4.

G9.2. R. Ari Lieb Lowenstamm, married Channa, daughter of his relative R. Jacob Emden.

G10. Daughter, married R. Reich.[4]

G11. R. Isaiah of Terevo.

G12. R. Meir of Terevo, friend of the Chassid, R. Naftali Zvi of Ropshitz, founder of one of the Chassidic sects in Galicia. (See Horowitz-Rubin Ropshitz Family Pedigree.)

G13. R. Saul Reich, one of the pupils of R. Naftali of Lyzhansk.

G14. R. Aryey Liebus Reich of Lyzhansk, married the daughter of R. Kalonymus Zeev of Brody, grandson of R. Eliakim Getz, A.B.D. Hildesheim.

G15. R. Kalonymus Zeev Wolf Reich of Brezov.

G16.1. R. Jacob of Brezov.

G16.2. R. Abraham of Vienna.

G16.3. Wife of R. Lieb Grestler of Vienna.

G16.4. Wife of R. Gershon Frieder of Przeworsk.

G16.5. Wife of R. Haim David Reich of Blozov.

G16.6. Wife of R. Joseph Zimet of Jasla.

G16.7. Wife of R. Bezalel Oberlander of Sanek.

G16.8. Wife of R. Michael Millinger of Charna.

G9.3. Wife of R. Meir Jacob, son of R. Phineas Horowitz, A.B.D. Frankfurt-on-Main. Some of Meir's novellae appear in the *Hafla'ah* by his father. (See Horowitz Family Pedigree.)

G9.4. Wife of R. Eleazar, A.B.D. Zalozhtsy, son of R. Isaac Horowitz (A.B.D. Altona-Hamburg-Wandsbeck). (See Horowitz Family Pedigree.)

G9.5. Wife of R. Abraham Kahana, A.B.D. Brecztiz.

G10. R. Jacob Kahana of Vilna, died in 1826. He was the author of *Gaon Yaakov,* a commentary on the Talmud, published by R. Rafael Nathan Rabinowitz, Lvov, 1863, and arranged the work *Eliyahu Rabba* by R. Elijah the *Gaon* of Vilna, whose niece, the daughter of his brother R. Issachar Ber, he married. He lies buried between R. Elijah, son of Moses Kramer, and R. Hillel, A.B.D. Vilna.

G8.2. R. Zvi Hirsch Berlin (Berliner), 1721-1800. Founder of the Berliner Family. See this Section — Branch C.

G8.3. Esther, married R. Saul Halevi, A.B.D. The Hague, born 1711 and died in 1784. He served the Dutch community for thirty-seven years, during which time he was said never to have slept on a bed. He wrote approbations to: *Ateret Rosh,* in 1765; *Ha-Aruch Mashach,* in 1767; *Margarita Shapira,* in 1767; *Ahavat Chesed,* in 1776; *Binyan Ariel,* by his brother-in-law, R. Saul in 1778; *Okolides deHague,* in 1779; *and Mispar Tzva'am,* in 1784. His Responsa are found in: *Or Yisrael.* On his death, three eulogies appeared in *Chut Yair; Givat Shaul,* by R. Isaac Tirkheim; and *Pardes David,* by R. David Dishbeck.

G8.4. Sarah Leah, married R. Isaac Halevi, son of R. Mordecai, son of R. Joshua Halevi Reizes. R. Joshua was killed in Lvov in 1728. R. Isaac was first A.B.D. Leshnov, Chelm and then Cracow. He wrote a number of approbations in 1756 and 1757 at Leshnov, in 1769, 1773 and 1776 at Chelm, and in 1780, 1781,

1785, 1786, 1788 and 1798 at Cracow. His works can be found in *Keter Kahunah* and *Peri Tevuah,* which contain his responsa, and Novellae left in manuscript. He died in Cracow in 1799.

G9.1.   R. Mordecai Halevi, became A.B.D. Zalozhtsy as a young man and later on A.B.D. of Tiktin, where he died in 1817. He married Gitel, daughter of R. Jacob Jokel Kahana Shapiro of Leghorn, a descendant of R. Isaac, son of R. David Shapiro of Cracow. He wrote an approbation to his son's *Asifat Geonim* in 1806.

G10.1.   R. Aryey Lieb Halevi, succeeded his father as A.B.D. Tiktin where he remained for twenty-one years and died in 1837. His wife was Sarah, daughter of R. Joseph of Tiktin, died in 1853. He published *Asifat Geonim,* Responsa and Sermons, in Bialystok in 1806 with his father's approval; and Responsa by his grandfather R. Heschel.

G11.   Deborah, the third wife of R. Abraham, son of R. Joseph Zakheim of Vilna. (See Chapter XVII — Rokeah Family — *not* Dynasty) R. Abraham was a son from his father's first marriage.

G10.2.   Miriam Mindel, married R. Joseph Hakohen Meizes of Lvov.

G9.2.   R. Zvi Hirsch David Halevi, A.B.D. Cracow. During this period R. Moses Solomon Zalman of Warsaw was called to the post of A.B.D. Cracow. However, the community was divided under him and he went to settle again in Warsaw, acting as A.B.D. of Cracow, with R. Zvi David as the community Rabbi under him. After his death, R. Zvi David assumed full responsibility as A.B.D. Cracow. He died there in 1832.

G10.   Son, married the daughter of R. Ephraim Zalman Margolioth of Brody. (See Margolioth Family Pedigree — Chapter VII.)

G8.5.   Nitashi, married R. Moses of Zolkiev, grandson of R. Naftali Hirsch of Zolkiev, author of *Or Yekarot.* They were the progenitors of the Ornstein-Ashkenazi Family Pedigree. See this Section — Branch E.

G8.6.   Wife of R. Zvi Hirsch, A.B.D. Lublin, son of R. Saul, A.B.D. Lublin son of R. Meir Margolioth A.B.D. Ostrow.

G9.1. R. Joshua, married the daughter of R. Eliezer of Pietrokov.

G10. R. Abraham Margolioth, author of *Brit Avraham,* a commentary on the Bible, Pietrokov, 1899.

G9.2. R. Isaac Zalman. His son, R. Saul Krakover of Lublin.

G7.3. Wife of R. Joshua, son of Meir Falk, *Darshan* of Posen. His approbation to *Ayin Yaakov,* published in Berlin, was written in 1708.

G7.4. Wife of R. Moses, son of R. Menachem Mendel Auerbach of Krotoschin,[5] *Parnas* of Posen. R. Menachem, 1620-1689, was the founder of the Polish Branch of the well-known Auerbach Rabbinical Family. He was the author of *Ateret Zekeinim,* A.B.D. Rausnitz (Moravia) and then A.B.D. of Krotoschin. He was the son of R. Meshullam Zalman (Solomon) Fischhof-Auerbach of Vienna, son-in-law of R. Judah Lieb Rofeh (the Doctor) *Ma'or Katon,* A.B.D. Vienna (and one of the famous physicians of the Viennese branch of the Lucerna Family). R. Zalman was among those expelled during 1670, and settled in Posen. The grandson, R. Moses, was the first to sign a list of Rabbis approving the publication of *Even HaShoham* and *Me'irat Einayim* in 1773.

G8. R. Menachem Mendel Auerbach (the Younger), succeeded his grandfather as A.B.D. Krotoschin, and was leader of the Council of the Four Lands. His wife was the daughter of R. Isaac, Parnas of Posen and Krotoschin, son of R. Samuel Katzenellenbogen, who, according to family tradition, helped to finance the destitute Swedish King Charles XII after his Russian defeat, so that he could reach home. He wrote approbations to *Shtei Ha-Lechem,* in 1733, *Even HaShoham, Me'irat Einayim* and *Or Chachamim* by R. Benjamin, son of R. Saul Katzenellenbogen, A.B.D. Samter and Krotoschin. (See Chapter II.)

He died in the mid-eighteenth century, and left Responsa and extant manuscripts.

BRANCH B

BERENSTEIN FAMILY

ANCESTRY

G3.3. R. Saul Wahl.
G4.6. R. Judah.
G5.2. Dinah, married R. Abraham J. Heschel.

G6.4.   R. Saul Lowenstamm.

G7.2.   R. Aryey Lieb, died in 1755.

G8.1.   R. Saul, died in 1790.

G9.1.   R. Jacob Moses, died in 1815.

G10.4. Rebecca Reizel, died in 1835, married R. Samuel Berenstein,[6] who
        was born about 1767 in Hannover where his father, R. Issachar
        Berish, and grandfather, R. Aryey Lieb (author of *Pnei Aryey*), had
        been Rabbis, and died December 21 (4th Tevet), 1838. R. Aryey
        Lieb was in turn, the son of R. Jacob Joshua (author of *Pnei Ye-
        hoshua*), A.B.D. Cracow, Lvov and Frankfurt. R. Samuel was for
        many years A.B.D. Groningen in Holland, and probably the first
        Rabbi of Holland to preach in the Dutch language. He later be-
        came A.B.D. Leeuwarden, where he remained until 1815, when
        he was elected to succeed his father-in-law, R. Jacob Moses, as
        A.B.D. of Amsterdam's Ashkenazi community.

        Although it is said that he was often in conflict with his father-
        in-law because of his liberal ways, R. Samuel was under no suspi-
        cion as regards his Talmudic orthodoxy. R. Moses Sofer of Press-
        burg (author of the famous Rabbinical *Chatam Sofer*), addressed
        him in the highest of terms reserved for only the most pious sages,
        as is seen in a responsum to him in that work, dated 1819.

        R. Samuel's only literary remains are his sermons which ap-
        peared in *Ha-Me'assef*, 1809; *Leereden*, mentioned by Kayserling
        in *Jüdische Literatur;* and a sermon of 1832, in the British Museum.

G11.   R. Issachar Ber Berenstein, born in Leeuwarden in 1808 and died
        in The Hague on December 13, 1893. He was *Dayan* (Judge) of
        Amsterdam at the time of his father's death in 1838, and kept that
        office for more than ten years. He did not secure the position of
        A.B.D. Amsterdam, that post remaining vacant for a quarter of
        a century. In 1848 he became A.B.D. The Hague, succeeding R.
        Joseph Asher Lehmans who died in 1842. He remained in this of-
        fice for forty-five years during which time he contributed much to
        the building up of communal institutions, such as an orphan asylum
        and a Jewish hospital. He was also the organizer of a Jewish his-
        torical and literary society. His services were recognized by the
        Dutch Government, and he was decorated with the Insignia of the
        Order of the Golden Lion. His death was mourned by the entire
        population of the Dutch capital, so highly honored and respected
        he was.

BRANCH C
BERLINER FAMILY
MORGENSTERN CHASSIDIC DYNASTY OF KOTSK

ANCESTRY

G3.3. R. Saul Wahl.

G4.6. R. Judah Wahl.

G5.2. Dinah, married R. Abraham Joshua Heschel.

G6.4. R. Saul Lowenstamm.

G7.2. R. Aryey Lieb Lowenstamm, died in 1755.

G8.2. R. Zvi Hirsch Berlin (also known as Hirschel Levin,[7] or the Reverend Hart Lyon). He was born at Rzeszow in 1721. In his youth he studied under his father and went with him to Amsterdam in 1740 when he was nineteen years old. He developed knowledge of Talmud, Hebrew Grammar, Jewish History, Philosophy, Physics and Geometry. He also took part in the Emden-Eybeschutz controversy, siding with R. Emden, his maternal uncle. After his father died in 1755, he was elected to the post of Chief Rabbi of the Great and Hambro Synagogues of the Ashkenazi community in London. Under the command of his uncle, R. Emden, he accepted in 1758. On route, he stopped in The Hague, where he wrote an approbation to *Meivin Chidot* in 1757, by R. Joseph, son of David Heilbronn (published Amsterdam, 1765).

In London he became known as the Rev. Hart Lyon and was painted by the famous artist, J. Turner. He remained in London for seven years, and left because he was prevented from publishing a defense of *Shechitah* (Ritual Slaughtering) in reply to an attack by Jacob Kimchi in 1764 and also because he was dissatisfied with the state of Talmudic studies there. He became A.B.D. of Halberstadt, and also head of the Yeshiva there until 1770, when he became A.B.D. of Mannheim, and three years later, A.B.D. of Berlin. In Berlin he wrote approbations to: *Tiferet Yisrael,* by R. Israel Jaffe of Sokolov, in 1774, published in Frankfurt-on-Oder in 1774; *Or Chadash* (on Tractate *Pesachim*) by R. Eleazar, son of Eleazar Kallir, published in Frankfurt-on-Oder in 1776; *Yesod Olam,* a manuscript in his library, in 1777, by R. Isaac, son of Joseph HaYisraeli, published by Baruch, son of Jacob Sokolover, Berlin, 1777;

Sidrei Tahara in 1783, by R. Zvi Hirsch, son of Simha Bonem Rappoport in Rodelheim, 1783; *Shivim Panim,* by R. Abraham HaKohen,
son of Jehiel HaKohen, of Lisk, in 1783; and *Mispar Tzva'am,* by R.
Zvi Hirsch Mirles, published in Berlin, 1789.

In 1785 he was requested to become A.B.D. of Metz, after the
death of R. Aryey Lieb, son of Asher (known as Lion Asser), the
author of *Sha'agat Aryey,* published in Frankfurt-on-Oder, in 1755
but he did not accept. He was a close friend of Moses Mendelssohn, and even wrote an approbation to his German translation
of the Bible. When the Prussian Government requested R. Zvi Levin
to write in German an account of Jewish commercial and matri-
monial law, he asked Mendelssohn to compose it under his supervision. It was entitled *Ritualgesetze der Juden,* published in Berlin
in 1778. The friendship drifted when Levin attempted to prevent
the publication of Naftali Hirsch Wessely's *Divrei Shalom ve-Emet,*
which appeared in Berlin in 1782. When Mendelssohn defended
Wessely, Levin sent in his resignation, but did not however act on
it, and remained in Berlin until his death in 1800. He married 1)
Golda, daughter of R. David Tebele HaKohen, died in Berlin in
1794, and 2) Shprintze (in 1797), when he was seventy-eight years
old. She was the daughter of R. Abraham (of the family of the
Chacham Zvi). After his death some three years later, she remarried R. Zobel Eger, A.B.D. Braunsweig.

Levin supported and defended his son, Saul Berlin in the dispute
in which he was involved, especially with regard to the forged Responsa *Besamim Rosh,* published in Berlin in 1793. He was the
author of: *Ateret Zekeinim,* only in manuscript; *Hagahot,* in manuscript on *Sefer Yochasin, Sefer Hachinuch, Kaftor ve-Perach, Sefatei
Yeshanim; Minchat Ahavah,* published in Rotterdam in 1811; and a
commentary on Mishna *Lechem Shnaiyim* (on *Pirkei Avot*), published together with his uncle R. Emden in Berlin, 1834. A poem
written by him can be found in the *Binyan Ariel,* by his brother, R.
Saul Lowenstamm. (See Lowenstamm Pedigree above.) His Responsa can be found in those of *Ma'amar Mordecai,* by R. Mordecai
of Düsseldorf, son of Eliezer Halberstadt, published in Bruenn,
1790, and *Beit Ephraim,* by R. E. Z. Margolioth of Brody. Poems,
entitled *Nachalat Zvi* in *HaMaggid* (Nov. 14, 1870) and *Hagahot*
on the Vilna Edition of the Talmud were published by his descendant, R. Zvi Ezekiel Michelson. (See Michelson Pedigree.)

G9.1. R. Saul Hirschel,[8] born in 1740, when his father was nineteen.

When he was twenty, he was ordained by some of the greatest Rabbis of his time. When he was twenty-eight, he was already serving as A.B.D. of Frankfurt-on-Oder and the Province of Schlesin. Some time before 1782, becoming disenchanted with the "antiquated Rabbinical authority," he retired from the Rabbinate, and settled in Berlin where he joined the Haskalah Movement, whose members were admirers of Moses Mendelssohn. Unlike his father, he supported Naftali H. Wessely at a time when he was most violently opposed by the most emminent German Rabbis. He wrote a satire *Ketav Yosher*, published in 1794, after his death, in which he sharply criticized the educational methods, superstitions and customs which had spread among the people during his life time. It was also meant as an attempt to have Wessely's *Divrei Shalom ve-Emet* become Rabbinically accepted.

He travelled in 1784 to Italy, ostensibly to seek a cure for his rheumatism, but conceivably to meet the Wessely Rabbinical supporters. In Italy he wrote a pamphlet against R. Chaim Joseph David Azulai's *Birkat Yosef*, which appeared in Leghorn in 1772. Becoming interested in manuscripts, R. Berlin edited *Or Zaruah* written by R. Isaac, son of Moses of Vienna, which appeared in 1862. He also wrote *Mitzpeh Yokta'el*, published in Berlin in 1789, where he used a pseudonym of Obadiah, son of Baruch Ish Polonia (of Poland), which contained a criticism on the *Torat Yekutiel* by R. Raphael, son of R. Yekutiel Susskind Kohen, A.B.D. of Altona-Hamburg-Wandsbeck. The book caused a great stir among the Rabbis, including Berlin's father, who placed a ban upon it and its author.

When his father discovered the identity of its author, he tried to protect his son. Before this storm subsided, R. Saul Berlin published another controversial book, *Besamim Rosh*, in Berlin in 1793, together with comments entitled *Kassa deHarsna*. Although he claimed that he had only added notes to a manuscript by a certain R. Asher, son of Jehiel, R. Saul was strongly doubted, and because of its strong leniencies, he was labelled as an atheist. His father managed to save face somewhat in these affairs. He also was the author of *Arugat Habosem*, on his *Besamim Rosh* (Berlin), which appeared the same year, and *Teshuvat Shaul*, published in Berlin in 1789, and which contained a letter by his father to one of his pupils concerning the ban placed on his son's work, *Mitzpeh Yoktael*, which had appeared the same year. He wrote an approbation to *Kochav Yaakov*, written in 1762.

After wandering from country to country, R. Saul went to London in 1794 to become their Ashkenazi Chief Rabbi, then being about fifty-four years old, but he died before entering office on November 16 (23rd of Cheshvan), 1794 in London. His wife was Sarah, daughter of R. Isaac Joseph Teomim. (See Chapter IV.)

G10.1. Miriam.

G10.2. Hena, married 1) Abraham Hertz of Jessnitz and 2) Isaac, son of Meir Jaffe of Berlin.

G10.3. R. Aryey Lieb, A.B.D. of Dubenka and Breslau. He was educated by his maternal grandfather, R. Teomim. At the age of fifteen he had written two works, *Mekor HaBeracha* on the 613 Jewish Laws, and *Eilat Ohavim* on the Mishna, which remained in manuscript.

G9.2. R. Abraham David Tebele Berliner[9] of Pietrokov, married Zlate, daughter of R. Eli, son of Hirsch Parnes. He died in Pietrokov in 1831.

G10.1. R. Aryey Lieb Berliner, became known as "Liebish Reb Tebeles." He married 1) Chavale, daughter of R. Manly Reb Wilfs of Kinsk and 2) Gitel, daughter of R. Benjamin Frankel of Linsk. Gitel was the widow of R. Abraham Joel, son of R. Zvi Joshua, son of Shmelke Horowitz. (See Chapter XVI — Branch I — G11.2/12/13.1.) Gitel's brother was R. Zeev Wolf Frankel, A.B.D. Przeworsk and Rzeszow.

G11.1. R. Zvi Hirsch Berliner of Pietrokov, married Malka, daughter of his father's second wife, Gitel, and her former husband, R. Abraham Joel Horowitz.

G12.1. Chava, married R. Michael Michelson of Pietrokov. He was the progenitor of the Michelson Family. See below in this Chapter — Branch D.

G11.2. Wife of R. Abraham Katz of Pietrokov, son of Jekutiel Zalman of Cracow, son of Eleazar Hakohen.

G12.1. R. Eliezer Zvi Hakohen, died in Chentschin, 1869.

G13.1. David Tebele Rosenblum of Radom.
G13.2. Saul Rosenblum of Zalshin.
G13.3. Dov Berish Rosenblum of Zvolhin.

G11.3. R. Saul Berliner of Pietrokov, married the daughter of R. Nathan, A.B.D. of Lotamirsk.

G12. R. Naftali Hirsch Berliner of Dambia.

G13.1. R. Liebus Berliner of Warsaw, married the daughter of R. Haim Eleazar Waks, A.B.D. of Kalicz. (See Chapter VII — Branch B — G9.6/10.4/11.1/12.1/13.4/14.)

G14. Wife of R. Meir, son of R. Abraham Mordecai Alter of Ger. (See Chapter IV — Branch I.)

G13.2. Wife of R. Israel Moses, son of R. Jehiel Meir Lipschutz (A.B.D. of Gastinin). R. Israel was the Chassidic Rabbi (Admur) of Proskorov (Prushkov) and died in Warsaw in 1918. He was the author of *MaRoM HaRim*, published in Warsaw in 1892.

G14. R. Menachem Mendel Lipschutz, died in 1934 in Warsaw.

G13.3. Wife of R. Jacob Rosepkowitz of Ozorkov.

G14. Wife of R. Zvi Hirsch, son of Isaac Peretz Michelson. (See Michelson Family Pedigree below.)

G11.4. R. Ephraim Berliner of Lublin, married Hinde, daughter of R. Abraham Finkelstein. (See Chapter V — B — Descendants of G8.6. Also Ornstein-Ashkenazi Pedigree.)

G12.1. Abraham Berliner of Kiev and Warsaw.
G12.2. Zlate, married Alter Weltchler of Lublin.
G12.3. Sima, married Zalman Glass of Lodmir.
G12.4. Toyba, married Feiwel Tuvia of Belz.

G11.5. Wife of R. Meir Rubin, A.B.D. Tomashov.
G11.6. Rechele, married R. Jacob Moses Posner, a follower of the Chassidic Rebbe, R. Menachem Mendel of Kotsk. He was also the owner of a large textile factory in Zagerez (near Lodz) which employed many of the "Kotsker" Chassidim.

G12.1. R. Hirschel Posner.

G13.1. Wife of R. Nathan Heinsdorf of Zagerez.
G13.2. R. Liebish Posner of Lodz.

G14. Wife of the Chassidic Rabbi, Isaac David of Chechanov-Warsaw.

G12.2. Wife of R. Hertzel, A.B.D. Ashetsk.

G12.3. Chava, married R. Isaac (Phineas) Zelig Halevi Frankel
        of Zagerez, born in 1818, son of Moses Isaac Heisreck
        (son-in-law of Baruch Gliksman whose name the family
        adopted).

  G13.1. Zlate, married R. Abraham Hirsch Gliksman of Lodz,
          born in 1838.

    G14. Phineas Zelig Gliksman, author of *Tiferet Adam*, on the
          life of his parents, published at Lodz in 1923/24. He
          also wrote: a biography of R. Eliakim Getz, published
          in Lodz in 1936; a biography of R. Zeev Lipshitz and
          R. Abraham Landau with a history of the Rabbis of
          Ozrokov, published in Lodz in 1934; a biography of R.
          Hirsch of Tomashov, published in Lodz in 1932; *Ir Lisk
          ve Chachmeha*, the Rabbis of Lisk, published in Lodz
          in 1927; *HaRav Shel Simcha*, a biography of R. Moses
          Nehemiah HaKohen, published in Lodz in 1930; and
          a biography in *Rofdunei Bitfuchim* by R. Elaikim Getz,
          published in Lodz in 1937.[10]

  G13.2. Jochebed, married the Chassidic Rabbi, Admur Kotsk
          (Kock), Rabbi Israel Haim Morgenstern,[12] son of the
          second R. of Kotsk, R. David, son of R. Menachem
          Mendel of Kotsk, founder of the Family. Mendel was
          a pupil of the Seer of Lublin, Rabbi Jacob Isaac, and
          after studying in Tomashov, settled in Kotsk where he
          died in 1859. His son, R. David, was unable to keep
          his father's adherents together, and they became fol-
          lowers of his own pupil, the Rebbe of Ger (Alter Fam-
          ily mentioned in Chapter IV). R. David died in 1873.

          R. Israel Haim was born in Kotsk in 1842 and mar-
          ried in 1857. His wife died in 1896. He was the author
          of *Shalom Yerushalayim*, published in Pietrokov in 1925.
          He died in 1905.

          On the death of his first wife, he married his niece
          Bishke, daughter of his sister, Nechama (who married
          R. Abraham Gorfinkel of Pilev) and had four other
          children.

  G14.1. R. Zvi Hirsch Morgenstern, succeeded his father as
          Admur Kotsk and was the author of *Ateret Tzvi*, pub-

lished in Warsaw in 1934, which included the *Ma'aseh HaMenorah* by his father. He died in 1925.

G15.1. R. Moses Baruch Morgenstern of Gribov-Wladowa.
G15.2. R. Joseph Aaron Morgenstern.
He had three children, of whom Esther married Gelernter, and David settled in Philadelphia.
G15.3. R. Jacob David Morgenstern.
G15.4. Esther and 5. Chava, married Silman.

G14.2. R. Isaac Zelig Morgenstern, Admur and A.B.D. Sokolov, died in 1939, when he was about seventy-four, having served in Sokolov for forty-two years. He was a leader of the Agudas Israel Movement and married Chaya Hinde, daughter of Mordecai Schoenfeld of Pinczow, who died in 1942.

G15.1. R. Jacob Mendel Morgenstern, A.B.D. Wengrau, married in 1902 to Rachel, daughter of Moses Tannenbaum of Werzbenik (Werzbinsk). He perished in 1939 aged about fifty-two years. Three children died young.

G16.1. R. Solomon, Admur Kotsk-London-Chicago, where he died. He married Chava, daughter of Joshua Soroka. They had a daughter (married) and two sons, Dr. Mendel Morgenstern and Dr. Sidney Morgenstern (born in 1928, received his M.D. in 1949, and currently resides in Chicago).
G16.2. Jochebed, married and perished.
G16.3. Toyba Liebe, died in 1974, married R. Jacob David Baruch, Admur Varka-New York, son of R. Abraham Moses Kalish. Their children, Mendel, Isaac Bunim and Shoshana (Rosa).
G16.4. Israel, married and perished.
G16.5. Leah, married her first cousin, Jacob Rabinowitz.
G16.6. Esther 7. Bracha 8. Rechel, all unmarried, perished.
G16.9. Abraham Morgenstern, youngest son, settled in Chicago. His children, Chaya (Vivian), Menachem (New York) and Deborah (Debbie), all married.

G15.2. Esther, married R. Reuben Baruch, son of R. Nathan David son of R. Shraga Jair Rabinowitz. (See Chapter IV.)

G15.3. Toyba, married secondly Pesach Schneier of Korev-Warsaw (who was married firstly to Chava, daughter of R. Zvi son of R. David Morgenstern of Kotsk). They had issue, four children.

G15.4. Rachel, married R. Aryey Lieb son of R. Azriel Meir Alter Eiger, Admur Lublin (descendants of R. Akiva Eiger, the Younger, who died in 1837). Four children perished and a son survived the Holocaust.

G16. R. Menachem Mendel Eiger of Williamsburg, Brooklyn, married with issue.

G15.5. R. Moses David Morgenstern of Sokolov, where he officiated with his father, married Feige, daughter of R. Alter of Jechlin. Three children perished.

G16.1. Pearl, married Lieb Newman (Chicago), and have four children.

G16.2. Mendel Morgenstern (Tel Aviv), married and has seven children.

G15.6. R. Benjamin Paltiel Morgenstern, Admur Sterdin, died in 1945. He married Deborah Toyba, daughter of R. Joseph Kalish of Amshinov. Their family of six children perished.

G15.7. Beila Ruchama, married in 1918 R. Nachum Mordecai Perlow, Admur Novominsk-New York, where they settled in 1929.

G16.1. R. Baruch David Perlow (Chicago), born in 1921, married Frieda Malka, daughter of R. Heinich son of R. Abraham Joshua Heschel Twersky, Maliner Rebbe, and have issue, Isaac Zelig, Feige Hinde and Joseph.

G16.2. R. Jacob Perlow, born in 1921, Rosh Yeshiva of the *Beis Medrash Al Shem HaRav Shlomo Breuer* (Washington Heights, New York), married Judith, daughter of R. Abraham son of R. Joshua Heschel son of R. Issachar Dov Eichenstein, Ad-

mur Zhidachov-Chicago. (See Chapter XVII —
Eichenstein Dynasty — G2.5/3.1/4.1/5.3/6/7/8.)
Their children, Feige Dinah, twins Joshua Heschel
and Alter Israel Simeon and Sarah Channah.

G16.3. R. Alter Israel Simeon (Brooklyn, New York),
born in 1937, married Breindel, daughter of R.
Moses Naftali son of R. Noah Zvi Ullman, and
have issue, Joseph, Chaya Hinde, Aaron, Miriam
Reizel, Sarah Esther and Deborah.

G15.8. Jochebed, married Avigdor son of Solomon Jakobo-
witz of Lodz.

G16.1. Rechel, married Feldman (Tel Aviv), and have
issue.

G16.2. Israel (Tel Aviv), married and has issue.

G15.9. Rivke, married R. Aaron Israel son of R. Samuel
Bornstein of Sochotchov. They settled in Tel Aviv.
One son perished and the other, David, lives in
Beersheba, Israel.

G15.10. Sarah, married R. Benjamin Morgenstern.

G15.11. Leah (Tel Aviv) married Jacob Greenberg, member of the Israeli Knesset. Their daughter, Rachel.

G14.3. R. Moses Mordecai Morgenstern, died in Warsaw in
1929.

G14.4. R. Joseph Morgenstern, Rabbi in Kotsk, died in 1939.
He succeeded his brother R. Moses Mordecai as Admur Kotsk in 1929, where he had served since 1924.
They both died childless, and the position then went
to R. Joseph Fisch, step-son-in-law of R. Joseph's second wife, who was also his nephew. (See below).

G14.5. Glicke, married 1) R. Abraham Shachor, son of R.
Noah, and 2) R. Nahum Meir Halevi Fisch of Chentschin.

G15.1. Chantsche 2. Rachel 3. Abigail.

G15.4. R. Joseph Asher Zelig Fisch, Rabbi in Gribov,
then Strikov, and in 1939 succeeded his uncle R.
Joseph Morgenstern as the last European Admur
of Kotsk. He married the daughter of R. Simha Jair
Rosenfeld of Pietrokov.

G14.6. Nechama Zeena, married Heinich Bloss of Warsaw, and had nine children.

G14.7. Beila Rochma, married R. Eliezer Shalom Epstein A.B.D. Porrisov, and had five children.

G12.4. Wife of Zvi Kirschbaum.

G13. Noah Kirschbaum of Lodz, married Dinah, daughter of Samuel Goldstein.

G14. Jacob Kirschbaum of Lodz,[11] settled in Israel in 1963. He was the author of *From Jerusalem to Jerusalem* and other books.

G10.2. R. Isaac Nata Berliner, A.B.D. Gourai and Bilgoray, married the daughter of R. Avigdor Meisels, A.B.D. Bilgoray, son of R. Zvi Hirsch Meisels, son of R. Samson, A.B.D. Zalkowitz. There is a Responsum to R. Isaac from R. Z. E. Michelson in the latter's *Tirosh VeYitzhar* (No. 58).

G11.1. Golda Rachel, died in 1885, married R. Ezekiel Meir Frankel-Teomim (Weinberg), died in 1849. He was the son of R. Aryey Lieb Teomim of Brody. (See Teomim Family Pedigree Chapter IV — Branch E.)

G11.2. Wife of R. Nahum Plost, A.B.D. Bilgoray.

G11.3. Dovberish Berliner; 4. Lipa Berliner; 5. Yedidi Berliner; 6. Zvi Hirsch Berliner of Bilgoray.

G10.3. Rachel, married R. Elyakim Getzel of Cracow, son of Mordecai Horowitz of Cracow.

G11.1. Golda, married Isaac Maize of Cracow, author of *TZafnat Penah.*

G11.2. R. Raphael Eli Horowitz of Cracow, married the daughter of R. Saul Landau.

G11.3. R. Shmelke Horowitz of Plotsk.

G11.4. R. Saul of Cracow.

G11.5. Wife of R. Jehiel Margolioth of Pinczow.

G12. R. Meshullam Margolioth of Pinczow.

G13.1. Getzel Margolioth, married the daughter of Meyer Mendelssohn of Warsaw.

G13.2. Wife of R. Mordecai Joseph Eleazar Leiner, son of R. Gershon Chanoch Leiner of the chassidic family of Radzyn-Izbica. (See Chapter VIII — G7.2/8.1/9.1/10.1/ 11.4/12/13/14/15.1/16.5/17.)

G9.3.   Solomon Hirschel (Herschell), born in 1762 in London while his father was serving there as Rabbi, but was raised on the continent from the age of two years when his father left England. He married in 1779 at the age of seventeen to Rivke Kennisberg, who was born in 1762 as well.

After his Polish and German education, he became A.B.D. of Przemysl in Prussia in 1793. Then he returned in 1802 to England to become A.B.D. of the Ashkenazi Great Synagogue, succeeding R. David Tebele Schiff, who had in turn succeeded R. Hirschel's father in 1765. The position had however been vacant for some ten years. Like his predecessor, R. Hirschel was acknowledged by the provincial communities and was thus the first officially recognized Chief Rabbi of the British Empire, his authority also extending to British Colonies overseas. He was of the old "European Style" Rabbis, with imperfect knowledge of English. He preached in Yiddish and unlike his controversial brother, R. Saul, left virtually no literary remains.

After his death, his library was passed on to the London *Beth Hamidrash*. It included some important manuscripts, which were catalogued by A. Neubauer, published in Oxford in 1886. His portrait can be found in the National Portrait Gallery in London. He died on October 31st (Rosh Chodesh Kislev), 1842, and his wife in 1832.

G10.1. R. David Tebele Berliner of Jerusalem, where he was murdered in 1851. He married the daughter of R. Isaac, son of Jonah Reich, and settled in Jerusalem in 1838.[13]

G11.   Wife of R. Haim Johanan Zvi Hirsch, son of R. Mordecai Slonek, a pupil of R. Moses Schreiber. He came to Jerusalem with his father-in-law in 1838.

G10.2. R. Saul Berliner of Posen, born in 1799. He married Frodel, daughter of R. Jacob Shapiro of Krotoschin. While visiting his parents in 1832, his mother died and after mourning for her, he died the same year.

G10.3. R. Ephraim London of Tysmenitsa, married the daughter of R. Mordecai Roller, A.B.D. Cladrow.

G10.4. R. Zvi Hirsch Berliner in Jerusalem.

G9.4.   Sarah, married her first cousin, R. Jacob Moses Lowenstamm.

G9.5. Reizel, married R. DovBer Ginzburg, A.B.D. Russia.

G9.6. Beila.

G9.7. Zipporah Frodel, married R. Meir Segal Hozen, father-in-law of R.
       Zvi Hirsch, son of R. Dovberish A.B.D. Hannover.

BRANCH D
MICHELSON FAMILY

ANCESTRY

G3.3.   R. Saul Wahl.

G4.6.   R. Judah.

G5.2.   Dinah, married R. Abraham Joshua Heschel.

G6.4.   R. Saul.

G7.2.   R. Aryey Lieb Lowenstamm, died 1755.

G8.2.   R. Zvi Hirsch Berlin, died 1800.

G9.2.   R. Abraham David Tebele Berliner, died in 1831.

G10.1. R. Aryey Lieb Berliner.

G11.1. R. Zvi Hirsch Berliner.

G12.1. Chava, married R. Michael (Klausner) Michelson.[14] His ancestry
        appeared in *Ma'amar Mordecai*, published by his grandson, R. Z.
        E. Michelson, at Pietrokov, in 1907. It mentions his connections to
        Katzenellenbogen, Isserles and Sirkes Families.

G13.1. R. Abraham Haim Michelson, died in 1857. He married Hannah
        Beila, daughter of R. Samuel Eli Schwerdscharf. (See Chapter IV
        — Branch E.) R. Abraham was the author of *Ohel Avraham*, on
        the life of Rabbi Abraham Field, Pietrokov 1911. He contributed
        to *Dover Shalom*, where he is also called Simha Bonem, Przemysl,
        1910.

  G14.1. R. Zvi Ezekiel Michelson, born 1853 and perished at Treblinka
          in the Holocaust of 1942, at which time numerous manuscripts
          of his in three large chests were lost. He married his first cousin,
          Hinde Sarel, daughter of R. David Tebele Schwerdscharf. (See
          Chapter IV — Branch E.) She died in 1923. He was a child
          prodigy, orphaned at an early age, and thus obliged to move
          from one place to another until he was offered to become Rabbi
          of Zamocz in 1884. He refused the position, and became Rabbi
          of Karsinbrod the same year. After becoming Rabbi of Plonsk

in 1893, he was known as the "Plonsker Rav." In 1922 he was
elected a member of the Warsaw Rabbinical Council where he
engaged in many communal activities.

He was a prolific writer as shown by the number of works
below. He was an outstanding authority of family genealogy and
was thus a biographer and bibliographer as well. He also wrote
works of *Halacha, Aggadah* and History. The 1907 Lublin edition of *Gelgulei Neshamot* by Menachem Azariel of Pono contains a pedigree of the R. Jeruchem Meir Leiner. This connects
back to the Katzenellenbogen family, and was written by R. Zvi
Ezekiel. His works include (the better known first): *Degan Shamayim,* appended to *Ein HaBedolach,* by R. Israel Jonah Landau, Pietrokov 1901, (a Commentary of Talmud. Landau was
Rabbi of Kempen, from whom Zvi's wife was descended); *Beit
Yechezkiel,* Responsa, Pietrokov, 1924; *Pinot Habayit,* Halachic
Responsa and novellae, Pietrokov, 1925; *Tirosh VeYitzhar,* Re-
sponsa, Bilgoray, 1936; *Siddur Beit HaOtzar,* 1931; *Divrei Ha-
Shirah,* Responsa appended to *Shirat Yisrael* by R. Israel Jonah
Landau, Jerusalem, 1897; *Tzemach HaSadeh,* appended to
Tzemach leAvraham by Zvi Hirsch, son of Haim HaLevi of
Plonsk, 2nd edition, Warsaw 1935; Additions to *Aleh DeYonah*
by R. Israel Jonah Landau, Warsaw 1934; *Divrei Gedolim,* published by R. Zvi Ezekiel, with an introduction by him, Pietrokov, 1933. Biographies were: R. Gershon of Koyal in *Beit Aharon,*
Pietrokov, 1931; R. Meshullam Zalman Ashkenazi in *Beit Meshullam,* Pietrokov, 1905; R. Joseph Teomim in *Notrikon,* Bilgoray, 1910; R. Simha Bonem of Parsischa in *Niflaot HaYehudi,*
Bilgoray, 1908; R. Zvi Hirsch Levin of Berlin in *Tzava Rav,* Pietrokov, 1907; R. Jeruchem Meir Leiner in *Gelgulei Neshamot*
by Menachem Azariah of Pono, Lublin, 1907; R. Alexander Ziskind Kahana in *Torat HaKohen,* Warsaw, 1939; R. Shabbetai
Bass, R. Phineas of Korets, R. Solomon Ganzfried, R. Jacob Aryeh of Radzymin and the Margolioth Family.

G15.1. R. Abraham Simha Bonem Michelson, wrote notes to the
        Shemen Tov by his ancestor, R. Samuel Shmelke Horowitz,
        published Pietrokov, 1905.

G15.2. R. Samuel Shmelke Phineas Michelson,[15] *Mohel* (Ritual Cir-
        cumciser) in Cape Town, South Africa. He is mentioned in his
        father's Responsa *Tirosh VeYitzhar* in a letter addressed from
        Warsaw on July 10, 1934. He was born in Poland in 1878 and

married in England in August of 1909 to Violet, daughter of Adolf Fryde who was a close friend of his uncle, Nathan Michelson. The two men had met in Johannesburg some years before the marriage. In 1911 they returned to settle in Cape Town. Rev. Samuel Michelson retired to Salisbury, Southern Rhodesia in his latter years, where he died on June 3, 1973.

G16. Victor David Michelson, born in London in 1912, came to South Africa in 1916. He married firstly to Geraldine Konigsfest of Vryheid, Natal, and secondly (in 1942) to Miriam Ash. He was Director of Public Relations to the State of Israel Bond Organization in Montreal and also a journalist in Montreal until 1969. He then returned to South Africa and is currently living in Johannesburg.

G17. Adele, born in 1936, married (later divorced) Avraham Zion in 1966. She worked at one time for the Israel Delegation to the United Nations Organization, and also as a secretary to Professor Rabbi Louis Rabinowitz, formerly of South Africa. She currently lives in South Africa. Her daughter, Daniella, was born on June 3, 1967.

G15.3. Rebecca, married R. Meir Shulvass. He is mentioned in the Responsa of his father-in-law, addressed to him while living in Tel Aviv, written in 1936.

G16. R. Dr. Moses Avigdor Shulvass,[16] born in Plonsk in 1909, and was ordained as a Rabbi by the Tachkemoni Rabbinical Seminary in Warsaw in 1930. In 1934 he received his Ph.D. degree from the University of Berlin, and lived from 1935 to 1947 in Israel where he was active as a lecturer, editor and author. He wrote *The Jews in Wuerzburg During the Middle Ages* (1934), *Bibliographical Guide to Jewish Studies* (1935), and *Rome and Jerusalem* (1944). In 1948 he immigrated to the U.S.A. and was Professor of Rabbinic Literature and Jewish History at the Baltimore Hebrew College until 1951, when he joined the College of Jewish Studies in Chicago (later called Spertus College of Judaica) as Distinguished Professor of Jewish History and then Chairman of the Graduate Studies Department. His other published books are *Chapters from the Life of Samuel David Luzzatto* (1951), *Jewish Life in Renaissance Italy* (1955), *In the Grip of Centuries* (1960), *Between the Rhine and the Bosphorus* (1964) and *From East to West*

(1971). He was Visiting Lecturer in History at the Harry Fischel School for Higher Jewish Studies, Yeshiva University in 1949, and Lecturer in Hebrew at the Ner Israel Rabbinical College in Baltimore from 1949 to 1951. He was also contributor to and editor of scholarly and literary journals in English, Hebrew and Yiddish. He was also past and present member of many religious, Jewish and historical societies and is listed in the *Who's Who in World Jewry, Who's Who in American Education, Contemporary Authors,* and others. He married in 1935 to Celia Cemach and has two daughters, Phyllis and Ruth.

G15.4. Wife of R. Joshua Heschel Levinstein, mentioned in the Responsa of his father-in-law, addressed to him January 13, 1939 from Warsaw.

G15.5. Chava, married R. Abraham Nathan Ellberg, A.B.D. Warsaw and Sanek, mentioned in the Responsa of his father-in-law.

G16. R. Judah (Yehuda) Ellberg,[17] born in 1912, married in 1948 to Tehilla Feinerman. Their children, Nathan and Eve (Montreal).

G14.2. Nathan Isaac Michelson of Tysmenitsa, died in Cape Town, South Africa. He married the daughter of R. Saul Horowitz (1831-1912) A.B.D. Tysmenitsa, author of *Besamim Rosh HaChadashot*, son of R. Meshullam Issachar Horowitz, A.B.D. Stanislav (1808-1888). (See Horowitz Family Pedigree.)

Nathan and his wife, Esther divorced. She went to live in Cracow, where she died in 1908, and he on January 25, 1916.

G15.1. Meshullam (Sam) Michelson, died unmarried in the U.S.A.

G15.2. Abraham Haim Michelson, born in Tysmenitsa in 1884 and died in New York in 1961. He became an American citizen in January of 1915, and was married to Ida Sachs.

G16.1. Nathan, born in 1920, married in New York in 1950 to Rae Salem. Their children, Robert, born in 1954 and Carol, born in 1957.

G16.2. Maurice, born in 1923, married in 1946 to Caroline Jacknowitz. Their children, Richard, born in 1953 and Ellen, born in 1950.

G16.3. Esther, named after her grandmother, married Emanuel Strauss. Their daughters (all married), Edith, Laureen and Janet.

G14.3. Rebecca, married R. Samuel Strauss of Krilev.

G13.2. R. Isaac Peretz Michelson.

G14. R. Zvi Hirsch Michelson, married the daughter of Jacob Rosepkowitz. (See Berliner Family Pedigree — G11.3/12/13.3 above.)

G13.3. Wife of R. Isaiah Zeev Follman of Pietrokov. (See Chapter III —
G9.2/10/11.4/12.1/13.4.)

G13.4. Wife of R. Gershon Poznowsky of Pietrokov.

G13.5. R. Solomon Michelson of Pietrokov.

G13.6. Wife of R. Gedalliah Ginzburg of Pietrokov.

G13.7. Wife of R. Moses Auerbach of Kalicz.

G12.2. Friedke, married R. Kalonymus Kalman, son of R. Liebus, A.B.D.
Piletz.

BRANCH E

ORNSTEIN, ASHKENAZI, ETTINGE AND BRAUDE FAMILIES

ANCESTRY

G3.3. R. Saul Wahl.

G4.6. R. Judah Wahl.

G5.2. Dinah, married R. Abraham Joshua Heschel.

G6.4. R. Saul Lowenstamm.

G7.2. R. Aryey Lieb Lowenstamm, died in 1755.

G8.5. Nitashi, married R. Moses of Zolkiev,[18] died in 1764, son of R. Joseph,
son of R. Chanoch Heinich, descendants of the *TaZ*, R. David Halevi.
He was known as "Rabbi Moshe ben Reb Joskes." They had two
sons and a daughter.

G9.1. R. Meshullam Zalman Ashkenazi, A.B.D. Pomarin, died as a young
man at the age of twenty-four. He married Reizel, his first cousin,
daughter of R. Aryey Lieb Auerbach, A.B.D. Stanislav. She then
remarried R. Meir Harif, A.B.D. Ostrow and Lvov, son of R. Zvi
Hirsch Margolioth, A.B.D. Yazlivitz, who was also her first cousin. (See Chapter V — Branch B — G8.6/9.1.)

G10.1. Ita Ashkenazi.

G11. R. Meshullam Zalman of Dubno, named after his maternal
grandfather.

G12. Wife of R. David Lieb Chamsky of Brest-Litovsk.

G13. Channah Feige, married R. Moses Zvi, son of R. Abraham Finkelstein (of Lublin). They were descendants of Rabbi Moses Isserles (known as the *ReMa*) and also of the Katzenellenbogen Family. (See Chapter V — Finkelstein Pedigree — Branch B — G8.6/9.4/10/11/12/13.2/14.2.)

G10.2. R. Meshullam Zalman Ashkenazi, the posthumous son, became A.B.D. of Cazimir and Naselsk. In 1826 he was elected A.B.D. of Lublin, which post he held for seventeen years, until his death at an old age on May 1 (Rosh Chodesh Iyar), 1843. His wife, Genendel, was the daughter of R. Joseph Mendelsberg of Cazimir, a friend of the "Maggid of Kozenitz."

He wrote an approbation to *Reach Nichoach* by R. Azriel, son of Elijah, published in Warsaw 1840. His Responsa appear in *Zichron Tzvi Menachem* by R. Zvi Menachem Meisels, published in Przemysl in 1873 and he also wrote glosses to the 1869 edition of the Vilna Mishna.

G11.1. R. Mordecai Zeev Ashkenazi, A.B.D. Kempen.

G12.1. R. Moses Jacob Ashkenazi, died in Memel in 1844 when he was about thirty-five years old.

G13. Gitel Genendel, married R. David Tebele Schwerdscharf. (See Chapter IV — Branch E.)

G12.2. Hannah, married R. Israel Jonah, son of Joseph Landau. (See Landau Family Pedigree.)

G11.2. R. Joshua Heschel Ashkenazi, who succeeded R. Berish, son of R. Moses Ashkenazi (a distant relative descended from the Chacham Zvi Ashkenazi) as A.B.D. Lublin in 1853. He remained there until his death on February 10 (2nd Adar Rishon), 1867. His wife was the daughter of R. Benjamin Braude, A.B.D. Grodno. During the reign of Czar Alexander II, a new Yeshiva was opened in Lublin, on which occasion R. Joshua delivered a sermon. This speech was translated into Polish and was highly praised by the Polish Officials. Because of this, he was made an honorary citizen.

He wrote an approbation to *Ohel Yaakov* by R. Moses, of Dubno, in 1859. He also wrote an approbation on the appearance of the Vilna Edition of the Talmud, when there was rivalry with the Slovita Edition.

Although his manuscripts were destroyed in a fire in

Grodno, some Responsa can be found in *Noda BaShearim* by R. Berish Ashkenazi, whom he had succeeded, published in Warsaw in 1859.

G12. R. Benjamin Ashkenazi, 1824-1894, settled in Grodno where he was the leader of communal affairs and a prominent philanthropist. He initiated the building of a hospital and old-aged home which earned him the title of "honorary citizen." In 1882 he was sent as a delegate to the Rabbinical Convention at St. Petersburg. In 1883 he was one of the few Jews officially present at the Coronation of Czar Alexander III in Moscow, and in 1884 was appointed Chairman of the Committee on Prisons of the Grodno Government.

G10.3. R. Aryey Lieb Ashkenazi, studied under his stepfather, R. Meir Margolioth, in Ostrow. He married the daughter of R. Abbale, son of Pesach Cohen, when he was thirteen years old. Later he studied under his uncle, R. Mordecai Zeev Ornstein. His signature appeared a number of times in the Pinkas (Minutes) of the Ostrow community. He died in 1806 and was buried in Ostrow.

G11.1. R. Mordecai Zeev Ashkenazi, married Rachel, daughter of R. Mordecai Zadok Marshalkovitch of Dubno. (See Chapter XVI — Introduction — G9/10.9/11.3/12.1/13.3.)

G11.2. R. Meshullam Zalman Ashkenzai, married the daughter of R. Hirsch Kazmirer.

G11.3. R. Saul.

G11.4. Wife of R. Solomon Zalman Kahane, known as Zalman Gottes, son of R. Abraham Aryey Lieb Sheines (A.B.D. Berdichev, and author of *Or HaNe'erav*).

G11.5. Wife of R. Haim Halberstadt, son of Zvi Jacob. (See Chapter VII — Branch B — G6.3/7.4/8.2/9.6/10.2.)

G9.2. R. Mordecai Zeev Ornstein,[19] known as the "Great Rabbi Mordecai Zeev" to distinguish him from his grandson of the same name. He was firstly A.B.D. of Satanow and Kamenka. Later he became A.B.D. of Jampol and some time before 1774 he succeeded R. Solomon, son of Moses of Chelm, as A.B.D. of Lvov.

R. Mordecai was inclined toward Chassidism, and was said to have studied for a time under R. Dov Ber, the *Maggid* of Meseritz. Although he did not publish any Halachic works, his novellae were quoted by his descendants, and his approbations were numerous, written between the years 1770 and 1786 while he served at both Jampol and at Lvov.

He died in 1787 in Lvov.

G10.1. R. Jacob Meshullam Ornstein, 1775-1839. His father died when he was still in his teens, too young to succeed him as A.B.D. of Lvov, and thus, for the first time in about a hundred years, this position was given to another, not of his family.

He married the daughter of R. Zvi Hirsch, son of Naftali Hirsch Wahl of Jaroslav (in Galicia). Here he spent his youth and was supported by his father-in-law until the latter's death.

Jacob was proposed as his successor, but he declined because there was some disagreement within the community over this matter. Instead, in 1801 he became A.B.D. of Zolkiev, the town in which his grandfather (died 1764) had lived.

Later, in 1805, he became A.B.D. Lvov, which position he held until his death, some thirty-four years later, in 1839. He was both wealthy and independent. The rise of Chassidism and the Haskalah Movements caught him in the middle. Although he professed to be a *Mitnagid* (i.e. opposer of Chassidism), he nevertheless opposed the Haskalah Movement very resolutely. He distrusted the circle of *Maskilim* of his city, which included men such as Solomon J. Rapoport and Nahum Krochmal. Rapoport's sharp criticism of Ornstein's work *Yeshuot Yaakov*, which appeared in 1809, led to the latter issuing a ban of excommunication against him and the *Maskilim* leaders in 1816. This ban was found one day on the door of the Lvov Synagogue and its writing was attributed to his proud and haughty son, R. Mordecai Zeev, who was a strong supporter of his father. The text refers to the "sins" of the *Maskilim* studying German and other books, including the Bible with Moses Mendelssohn's commentary.

Ornstein was later publicly compelled to rescind the ban when its content, translated into German, was made known to the Austrian Government. Although he was labeled the "Great Inquisitor of Galicia" by his opponents, R. Jacob was one of the greatest Halachists of his day.

His great work, *Yeshuot Yaakov* contains novellae on the *Shulchan Aruch*, published in parts in Zolkiev in 1809 and 1828. They were all published together with additions from

his manuscripts and glosses by his grandson, R. Zvi Hirsch in
Lvov, in 1863. He also wrote Responsa by the same name published in Pietrokov in 1906. Other Responsa appeared in *Yad
Yosef* and *Mayim Chayyim,* and a Torah Commentary which
appeared in 1907.

G11. R. Mordecai Zeev Ornstein, considered to be a haughty personality who was the strong supporter of his father. Because
of his high self-esteem, he refused to accept any but the highest of Rabbinical positions, until finally, after many years, he
was invited to the post of A.B.D. of Przemysl in Galicia. However, he died before entering office in Lvov on October 28,
1837. His Responsa and novellae appear in the *Yeshuot Yaakov*
by his father. He also wrote *Moreh LiTzdakah,* published in
Lvov in 1854.

G12. R. Zvi Hirsch Ornstein, born in Lvov. His first Rabbinical
calling was A.B.D. of Brest Litovsk in 1855, where he succeeded R. Jacob Meir Padua (also a Katzenellenbogen descendant), whose great-granddaughter he later married. He
remained there until 1874, when he was ordered to leave by
order of the Russian Government on the grounds that he was
a foreign national. In reality, the officials feared him because
of the respect and admiration the people had for him. He
then began to face times of hardship, having been deprived
of all his wealth, and was compelled to accept any vacant
position that came along. He returned to Galicia, where he
was elected A.B.D. of Rzeszow from 1874-5, and then at
Lvov in 1875. Here he succeeded the husband of his second
cousin, Edel, R. Joseph Saul Nathanson. (See below.) He
remained here for thirteen years until his death on March
21 (9th Nissan), 1888.

Unlike his father and grandfather, he was tolerant of the
Maskilim and even succeeded in attracting them while he
was at Lvov. At the same time he was disliked by the Chassidim.

Realizing the Austrian Government's intention of introducing compulsory general education, he attempted to
change the old *cheder* method of learning and its organization, but failed in his efforts.

His wife, Achsa, the daughter of R. Jehiel Benzion, son
of R. Meir Kristianpoller, both of whom had been the A.B.D.

of Brody, was also the granddaughter of R. Aaron Padua. (See Chapter II — B — Branch A.)

Some of his novellae and Responsa were published in the second edition of his grandfather's *Yeshuot Yaakov*. His son-in-law, R. Aryey Lieb Braude, published part of a collection of his Responsa which was entitled *Birkat RaZaH* under the name *Milchamot* in Lvov in 1889.

G13. Channah, wife of R. Aryey Lieb Braude, son of Abraham Joseph son of Haim. R. Lieb succeeded his father-in-law as A.B.D. Lvov, and died in 1928.

   G14.1. Michael Braude.

   G14.2. R. Mordecai Zeev (Markus) Braude,[20] born in Lodz in 1869, and died in Haifa October 18 (25th Tishrei), 1949. He married Nelly, daughter of Karl, son of Solomon Buber (and a sister of the philosopher Martin Buber). He studied at the University of Freiberg until 1898, and was an active Zionist and attended the First Zionist Congress in 1897 at Basel (Switzerland). He subsequently attended many other such Congresses. He was also a member of the Polish Senate, and settled in Palestine in 1940, where he died. His family currently resides in Haifa. A full biography of his life (in Hebrew) was published by the Zionist Histadrut in Jerusalem in 1960. It includes his memoirs.

G10.2. Wife of R. David Berish of Berjan,[21] son of R. Abraham Solomon Halpern of Rohatyn. He wrote an approbation to *Or Pnei Moshe*.

 G11. Wife of R. Aryey Liebus halevi Nathanson of Berjan, author of *Beit El*, published in Lvov in 1875.

   G12.1. R. Joseph Saul Nathanson, A.B.D. Lvov, married his second cousin, Eidel, daughter of R. Isaac Aaron Ettinge. (See below — G10.5/11.2.)

   G12.2. R. Solomon Zalman Nathanson of Berjan.

G10.3. Malka, married R. Abraham Abbish Ashkenazi of Brody.

G10.4. R. Moses Joshua Heschel Ornstein, A.B.D. of Radwill and Tarnograd, author of *Yam HaTalmud*, published in Lvov in 1825. In its introduction, he writes that he left other unpublished manuscripts.

G11. R. Samuel Jacob Ornstein, died without issue. His novellae appear in his father's *Yam HaTalmud.*

G10.5. Esther, married R. Isaac Aaron, son of R. Naftali Hirsch Ettinge [22] (also Ettinger). R. Naftali was A.B.D. of Lvov.

G11.1. Mordecai Zeev Ettinge, born in 1804, and died on June 30 (2nd Tammuz), 1863. He married Manya, daughter of R. Kalman Lipes. He worked and studied for many years together with his brother-in-law, R. Joseph Saul Nathanson. His own Responsa collection, *Ma'amar Mordecai* was published in Lvov in 1852. Together with R. Nathanson he published: *Mafrishei HaYam* (on the *Yam HaTalmud* by his uncle), Lvov, 1825; *Magen Gibborim*, part one, Lvov, 1834 and part two, Zolkiev, 1839; *Me'irat Einayim*, Vilna, 1839; *Ner Ma'aravi* on the Jerusalem Talmud, Pietrokov, 1889-90; and annotations to the Vilna edition of the Talmud. He wrote numerous approbations, and left unpublished manuscripts.

G12.1. R. Isaac Aaron Ettinge, born in Lvov in 1827. He distinguished himself with his intellectual activity and industry, and was invited to several rabbinical positions in Galicia. However, being independently wealthy, he declined until finally, in 1868, he accepted the post of A.B.D. of Przemysl for two years. Later he succeeded his relative, R. Zvi Hirsch Ornstein, in Lvov in 1888. He was consulted by both the mitnagdim and Chassidim, and he was regarded as the leader of Galician Jewry by the Government. The Austrian government officially recognized him as the *Nasi* (President) of Palestine. His novellae were published in the *Ma'amar Mordecai* of his father, and his Responsa *MaHaRI Halevi* were published in Lvov in 1893. He wrote numerous approbations. A responsum to him can be found in the *Tirosh VeYitzhar* by R. Michelson.

He died in Lvov on January 16 (7th Tevet), 1891, having been there only three years.

G13.1. Wife of R. Joshua son of R. Haim Mordecai Zussman. (See Chapter XIII — G8.10/9.14/10.1/11.3/12.1/13.3.)

G13.2. R. Solomon Ettinge, married Sima, daughter of R. Ephraim Zalman, son of R. Abraham Abba Zvi Zuss-

man. (See Chapter XIII — G8.10/9.14/10.1/11.3/12.1
/13.3.)

G13.3. Naftali Ettinger, merchant in the Lvov district, owner
of a farm with a mill. He married into the Landau Rabbinical family of Cracow. One son died young, another,
Leo, settled in France and perished with his wife in the
Holocaust. A daughter also married, died at an old age
in Nice.

G14. Max (Mordecai) Ettinger,[23] named after his great-grandfather, born in Lvov in 1874. Although the family was
raised in the Jewish orthodox tradition, his mother was
more worldly with an understanding for music, and was
his first teacher. Because of the illness and opposition
of his grandfather, the Chief Rabbi of Lvov, Max was
only able to devote himself entirely to music after the
latter's death in 1891. In 1900, he enrolled as a student
at the Akademie den Tonkunst in Munich and devoted
himself to musical composition. Here he studied under
Ludwig Thuille and Joseph Rheinberger, and others. He
was also a choirmaster in Saarbrücken and Lubeck. From
1933 onwards he settled in Switzerland with his residence
in Ascona, but spent much time in Zurich occupied with
his musical career. A complete catalog of his works was
compiled by Emil Jucker. Aside from chamber-music
and songs, his chief works are: oratorios, *Weisheit des
Orients, Das Lied von Moses, Königin Esther, Jiddisch
Lebn,* and *Jiddisch Requiem;* operas, *Judith* (1921),
Juana (1923), *Clavigo* (1926), *Fruhling's Erwachen*
(1928), *Dolores* (1931) and *Der Dybuk* (1947). He
wrote some twenty Yiddish and Hebrew songs with
piano accompaniment.

He married Josi Krisak, having no issue, and died on
July 19, 1951 in Basel, and she some eleven days later.
He was eulogized by his close friends Saul Hurwitz and
Hermann L. Goldschmidt.

G12.2. Wife of R. Joseph, son of R. Saul son of R. Lieb Popirna
(A.B.D. Lisk).

G13. Hinde, died in 1921, married R. Nahum, son of R. Mena-

chem Mendel Follman of Warsaw. (See Chapter III —
Follman Family — G9.2/10/11.5/12.4.)

G12.3. Channah, married R. Tuvia, son of R. Uri Ber Gunzberg
of Vilna. (See Chapter III — Branch A — G11.1/12.7.)

G11.2. Eidel, married her second cousin, R. Joseph Saul halevi
Nathanson, son of R. Aryey Liebus (author of *Beit El*). R.
Saul was born in Berjan, and settled in Lvov where he was
known as the "Lemberger Rabbi." He wrote some works with
his brother-in-law, R. Mordecai Zeev Ettinge. His own works
were very numerous (about thirty in all), which included
Responsa (*Yad Yosef* and *Yad Shaul*, Lvov, 1851, *Sho'el
U'Meishiv*, Lvov, 1869); annotations (to *Noda BiYehuda,
Mizbeach Kaparah, Chacham Zvi, Seder HaDorot, Sifri,* and
others); various novellae and commentaries.

After twenty-five years of collaboration with his brother-
in-law, the two drifted apart because of a difference of opinion regarding the baking of Passover Matzah by machinery.
He wrote a total of three hundred approbations. In 1839, he
was offered the position of Head of the Lvov Yeshiva succeeding his great uncle, R. Jacob Ornstein. He only took office in 1857 where he remained for eighteen years until his
death in 1875. He had no issue.

G10.6. Wife of R. Isaac Nirenstein of Jaroslav.[24]

G11. Nechama, married R. Zvi Ozer, son of R. Asher Anschel Zausmer (A.B.D. Stry).

G12. R. Menachem Nahum Zausmer of Bialystok, married the
daughter of R. Alexander Sender, son of R. Uri Shraga Bloch
of Bialystok. (See Chapter VII — Bloch Family.)

G13.1. Zvi Hirsch Ozer Zausmer of Bialystok. His sons, Saul
(Siegfried) and Lieb (Leon).

G13.2. Asher Anschel Zausmer of Lodz, married the daughter
of R. Jacob Meir Beilin.

G13.3. Channah Pesha, married Isaac Barash of Bialystok.
Their children, Alexander, Samuel, Beila and Deborah.

G13.4. Wife of Judah (Yudel) Luria of Pinsk.

G13.5. Frieda, married Levine.

G13.6. Esther, married Zalman Weirach of Bialystok.

G10.7. Wife of R. Judah son of R. Naftali Hirsch Brodie. She was his mother's first cousin.

G9.3. Leah Dreizel, married R. Aryey Lieb, A.B.D. Stanislav, son of R. Mordecai Auerbach, A.B.D. Bomberg and Kremnitz.

G10.1. Gitel, married R. Haim, son of R. Uri.
G10.2. Wife of R. Naftali Hirsch Brodie-Ashkenazi, A.B.D. Mikulonitz, son of R. Isaac Ashkenazi of Brody.

G11.1. R. Aryey Liebus Brodie, A.B.D. Kreshov, married the daughter of R. Samuel of Zalischik, son of R. Isaac Dov Berish Margolioth of Yazlivitz. (See Chapter V — Branch B — page 261 — G9.1/10.)
G11.2. R. Judah Brodie, married the daughter of R. Mordecai Zeev Ornstein.
G11.3. R. Eliezer Lipman Brodie, A.B.D. Kamenetz.
G11.4. Sarah, married R. Mordecai Rubinstein. Their son, R. Solomon Rubinstein. (See Chapter VII — Branch B.)
G11.5. Wife of R. Abraham Kahana of Brody, son of R. Zeev Wolf.
G11.6. Yota, married R. David halevi Brotsheiner.

CHAPTER XIII

DESCENDANTS OF
THE CHACHAM ZVI HIRSCH ASHKENAZI
INCLUDING THE RAPPOPORT AND ZUSSMAN FAMILIES

ABBI Zvi Hirsch[1] was born in Merrin (Moravia) in 1660 to his father, R. Jacob Ashkenazi, who had been assumed dead following the Chmielnicki Raid on the city of Vilna in 1648, (see introduction to the Descendants of R. Abraham Joshua Heschel of Cracow), and his mother, Nechama, daughter of R. Ephraim Hakohen, A.B.D. of Vilna, author of *Sha'ar Ephraim*. R. Jacob followed his father-in-law to Bodin (Alt-Ofen) with his family. R. Zvi thus received his education in his youth from his father and grandfather and later studied under R. Elihu Cobo in Salonica, where he investigated Sefardic methodology. On his return journey to Alt-Ofen he spent some time in Constantinople where his learning earned him his title of *Chacham* ("Genius").

He married the daughter of a prominent citizen of Alt-Ofen, but she was killed with her daughter in 1686 by a cannon shot and he was compelled to flee. At this time his parents were taken captive by the Prussians. He reached Sarajevo where he became A.B.D. and in 1689 he returned to Germany where he married for the second time to Sarah (who died in 1719), daughter of R. Meshullam Zalman Mirls Neumark, A.B.D. of Altona-Hamburg-Wandsbeck.

When the Chacham Zvi, in his earlier days, was rabbi of a German town, he was requested to write an approbation to a manuscript in accordance with the prevailing custom. Enraged at finding that the author was a follower of the False Messiah, Shabbatai Zvi, he threw the manuscript into the fire.

467

Because this was against German law, he was compelled to flee with his family to Poland. Though he possessed a number of gold coins, he was forced to spend one each day to sustain his large family. With only one gold coin left, his discouraged wife bemoaned the dismal future, to which her husband said: "If you have so little faith in the Lord, I shall secure a divorce, for you lack the fortitude of a Rabbi's wife."

Some hours later he was visited by the elders of the Amsterdam congregation who invited him to become their Rabbi. The Chacham quickly changed his hasty decision against his wife and obtained an annulment from the Rabbis.

Once the head of the Rothschild family, Mayer Amshel in Frankfurt, passed the Chacham Zvi on the street. He offered the great Rabbi a donation of money which the latter refused, despite his destitute state following his dismissal from his earlier Rabbinical post. Mayer Rothschild thereupon dropped the piece of money to the ground and on pronouncing it *hefker* made it the property of anyone else. Thereupon the Chacham Zvi picked up the money and blessed the man with great future success— which indeed transpired as the famous Rothschild name and wealth has been world renowned.

In 1690 the Chacham Zvi became head of the *Klaus* (study-house) of the Altona Congregation, which became a famous house of learning. Many pupils flocked to learn from him. Because of receiving a very small salary he was compelled to seek a livelihood in various pursuits.

After the death of his father-in-law in 1706 he was installed as A.B.D. of the triple community jointly with R. Moses, son of R. Alexander Rothenberg. Because of friction he resigned and returned to his *Klaus* in 1709, but soon after in January of 1710 he was elected A.B.D. of the Ashkenazic community of Amsterdam, where he received a free residence and a generous salary. Within a few years conflicts arose within his congregation, which became progressively worse.

His son, R. Jacob Emden, recorded this story in his *Megillat Sefer*, (Warsaw 1896):

> When I gained a little understanding I felt father's suffering, his pain and shame because of the people who wished to deprive him of his livelihood and degrade him of his honor. After this he became very ill with pleurisy on account of an excess of bile, caused on account of the dispute at Altona. The doctors had already given him up but my sisters and I fasted on his account on the Monday and Thursday of one week when I was only twelve years old. When my father was appointed Rabbi of the Ashkenazic congregation at Amsterdam the time of my wanderings and exile commenced. . . .

Now this is what happened. The sins of the community led to the coming of Satan to make the world chaotic; namely the evil spirit and poisonous serpent, the abominable hypocrite Hayun who confused the holy congregation of Sephardim and Ashkenazim alike. The heart of all the people was divided in two, those who went to the right and those who went to the left. Yet, at the beginning, the entire congregation of Sephardim to a man were true to their Father in Heaven, and it was they who awakened and roused love against which the whole wealth of a man is esteemed with contempt. They came to my father, of blessed memory, to consider the case of this hypocrite and man of violence, to investigative his impure and worthless book; wishing to depend primarily on the authority of my father, knowing him to be an absolutely reliable person possessed of wisdom and understanding. . . .

So they gave him the book of Hayun for a certain time to examine, since it had reached them only for a little while by dint of great stratagems. And they placed the sword in father's hands to execute justice against that enemy of the Lord who had thought to replace Judaism by his imaginary new faith; and who set out to remove Israel from the traditions of their fathers, as was finally proved in all the courts of Israel from East to West. They all thanked my father and teacher of blessed memory, for being zealous on behalf of the Lord, and issuing a stern verdict against that troubler of Israel, to remove him from the boundaries of Israel. Afterwards many more of his abominations were revealed. For he did the deeds of Balaam and polluted the Holy Land; the very world cannot contain all that he has done, as has already been set out in print in various pamphlets and sheets.

Yet at that time Satan was advancing among the members of the holy congregation of Sephardim, and all but in their very sight. After they came back and took the book of abomination from my father of blessed memory, they accepted his words and accordingly undertook to drive the disgusting Hayun out of their synagogue; but then they reconsidered and set out to destroy all that they had built; their hearts turned against father, they turned their backs upon him and did not wish to hearken unto him any more about executing justice upon that man. And after they had already done as my father of blessed memory counseled, and very shamefully thrust Hayun forth from their synagogue, they changed their minds and admitted him to their congregation, entreating him with great honor. . . .

Ever since the community had been established, he [Hayun] said, the Ashkenazim had been abject and submissive before the Sephardic congregation of Amsterdam, because of the leading position of the latter with their wealth, their pedigree and greatness; while they also had precedence in time, since scarcely had Holland become a free kingdom on its own than the forced-convert Sephardim fled from Spain and established themselves in Amsterdam. . . .

But the Ashkenazim who had come there were poor compared to them, since they were unimportant as regards wealth and greatness in those days; and now what nightmare was this where the lower ones were on top and the upper ones below!

The man spoke after this fashion and stole their hearts which had been whole with the Lord to begin with, by reason of his smooth foreign tongue and flattery; so that their minds turned to follow him when he said: Although the law may not be so, the time requires this, so that you may protect the honor of yourselves and our chief congregation by not accepting the decision of the Ashkenazic Rabbi, but by repenting of all that you have already done. . . . All this chapter and the stratagems and instruments and strange and bitter falsehoods which came about at that time have already been made known to those who are still alive and well remember this evil mishap, which is not yet as far back as fifty years. Also many works and pamphlets were written and published at the time of this grave war which lasted a full year. . . . Actually, it was this incident which led me to write this book in order to proclaim the wonders and loving kindness of His blessed Name; for the new is as the old, the father reveals his truth unto his children and all that happened to the fathers befell the sons; a thing which cannot be written in full detail. Therefore I shall not deal further with this incident which occurred more than forty years ago. . . . For that which befell my father of blessed memory befell me in the case of Rabbi Jonathan Eybeschutz, an absolute parallel, so that which befell the father also befell the son.

After R. Ashkenazi was deserted by all but a few friends he resigned his office and fled in 1714 from Amsterdam, and after leaving his wife and children in Emden, proceeded to London at the invitation of its Sephardic congregation at which time his portrait was painted. From here, having declined to accept the Rabbinate in London, he returned to Emden and then via Hanover, Halberstadt, Berlin and Breslau to Lvov where he succeeded R. Simha HaKohen Rappoport in 1717 but died some months later on May 2 (2nd day Rosh Chodesh Iyar) 1718.

He was the author of responsa entitled *Chacham Zvi*, published Amsterdam, 1712.

G8.1.   Miriam, wife of R. Aryey Lieb, son of R. Saul Lowenstamm A.B.D. Amsterdam. (See Descendants of R. Abraham Joshua Heschel-Lowenstamm Family Pedigree.)

G8.2.   Rachel, married R. Isaac A.B.D. Neshov, Slovitz and Bialy, (brother of R. Michael Eisenstadt A.B.D. of Kletsk—See Eisenstadt Family Pedigree), son of R. Meir *MaHaRaM* Eisenstadt (author of *Panim Me'Irot* 1670-1744).

G8.3.   Second wife of R. Moses A.B.D. Zlatchov, son of R. Eleazar

(A.B.D. Amsterdam) Rokeah (see Rokeah Family Pedigree). From them are descended the Shapiro and Rokeah-Belz Chassidic Dynasties. R. Moses' first wife was the daughter of R. Bezalel son of R. Naftali Katz (*Smichut Chachamim* — Chapter V).

G8.4. Nechama Sarah, married R. Naftali Hirsh, son of R. Abraham Landau (Chapter X-G8.1/9.5). Her husband was killed in Apt and she returned to Amsterdam where she was buried.

G8.5. Daughter, died young in Amsterdam.

G8.6. R. David Ashkenazi, A.B.D. Yarchov, died in 1757.

  G9. R. Meshullam Zalman Ashkenazi A.B.D. Dobromil and Pomarin died in 1775.

    G10. R. David Ashkenazi A.B.D. Tarnograd.

      G11. Miriam, wife of R. Aryey Liebus Halberstam. (See Chapter VII — Branch B — G5.4/6.3/7.4/8.2/9.6/10.4/11.1/12.1.)

G8.7. R. Abraham Meshullam Zalman Ashkenazi A.B.D. Ostrow, author of *Divrei Rav Meshullam*, published Koretz 1783. He was the youngest of his father's five sons, born in Altona. He was orphaned as a baby and adopted by his brother-in-law, R. Aryey Lieb Lowenstamm, and his brother, R. Jacob Emden, arranged his marriage to the daughter of R. Josefa of Ostrow under whom R. Abraham studied. He was later elected A.B.D. of the *Klaus* (study house) in Ostrow and he succeeded R. David Halpern as A.B.D. Ostrow. He remained the Rabbi there for forty years from 1737 until his death in 1777.

  G9.1. R. Zvi Hirsch, married the daughter of R. Joseph Joel Halpern A.B.D. Stefan. He published his father's work in 1783. He was first A.B.D. Berdichev and then succeeded R. Naftali Hirsch HaKohen as A.B.D. of the Ostrow *Klaus* in the year his father died.

  G9.2. R. Aaron, who signed in the minutes of Ostrow (*Pinkas*) a number of times.

  G9.3. R. Haim of Ostrow.

  G9.4. Wife of R. Naftali Rokeah of Brody, son of R. Moses (A.B.D. Zlatchov). They were first cousins.

G8.8. R. Ephraim Ashkenazi, died in 1772.

  G9. Batya Zvia, the third wife of her uncle, R. Jacob Emden.

G8.9. R. Nathan Ashkenazi of Brody.

  G9.1. R. Zvi Hirsch Ashkenazi, A.B.D. Bornstein.

G10. R. Mordecai Ashkenazi of Ornstein.

G11. R. Moses Ephraim Ashkenazi, A.B.D. Kalicz, died in 1828.

G12. R. Zalman Ashkenazi.

G13. R. Samuel Ashkenazi,[2] married Rachel, daughter of R. Meir (A.B.D. Zinkov), son of R. Abraham Joshua Heschel (A.B.D. Apt). (See Heschel Chassidic Dynasty.)

G14.1. Wife of R. Joseph (died 1847), son of R. Isaac (died 1865), son of R. Jehiel Michael Halevi Heilprin, all Admur of Brezna. R. Jehiel, who died in 1848, was the founder of the Brezna Chassidic family and a first cousin to R. Dan of Radwill, mentioned in Chapter XV (Heschel Family — G10.1/11.2.)

G15.1. R. Abraham Samuel Heilprin of Brezna, died in 1918, married the daughter of R. Mordecai of Zovhil (a distant relative). He was Admur Brezna.

G16.1. Second wife of R. Issachar Dov Rokeah (her second cousin), the third Belzer Rebbe.

G16.2. R. Isaac Heilprin, died in 1939, married the daughter of R. Mordecai Twersky, Admur Loyev. (Chapter XV — Heschel Dynasty G10.1/11.4/12/13.2/14.1.)

G17.1. R. Aaron Heilprin, 1889-1943. His wife and three daughters survived the Holocaust.

G17.2. R. Jehiel Michael Heilprin, perished in 1942.

G16.3. R. Nahum Joshua Heilprin of Dombrovitz, perished in 1942 with his family.

G16.4. R. Joseph Heilprin, Admur of Sarni, died in 1918. He had moved to Kiev in 1914 but later returned to Sarni.

G15.2. R. Jehiel Michael Heilprin (1843-1916), Admur Koretz.

G16.1. R. Baruch Josefow, died 1936, married the daughter of R. Mordecai Lerner. He established himself in Dubno.

G16.2. R. Joseph Jerusalimsky of Kishinev, perished with his family in 1941. He was Admur Kishinev for over 40 years.

G16.3. R. Eliezer Halevy, Admur of Koretz, perished there in 1942 with his family and some 500 Jews.

G15.3. R. Meir Heilprin, died in 1914.

G14.2. Rebecca Miriam, married R. Joshua, son of R. Shalom Rokeah the Belzer Rebbe. (See Chapter XVII.)

G14.3. Wife of R. Mordecai (of Loyev), son of R. Menachem Nahum Twersky of Chernobyl. (See Chapter XV — Heschel Dynasty — G10.1/11.4/12/13.2.)

G14.4. First wife of R. Abraham Joshua Heschel (of Skvira), son of R. Isaac Twersky of Skvira. (See Chapter XV — Skvira [Twersky] Chassidic Dynasty.)

G9.2. Jacob Moses Leverbaum, A.B.D. Zbariz. He married the daughter of R. Eliakim Getzel of Levertov. R. Getzel was also the father-in-law of R. Mordecai Zeev Ornstein (see Chapter XII — Branch E).

G10. R. Jacob, surnamed Lisser[3] after the town of Lissa (Prussia) where he was A.B.D.

His wife was a daughter of R. Benjamin Wolf Shapiro. In his youth R. Jacob was a pupil of R. Meshullam Egra. He became the A.B.D. of Kalicz and later of Lissa. Here he taught R. Akiva Eger the Younger who lived there from 1770-1791. He later returned to Kalicz where he lived for ten years. He died at Stry May 25, 1832. His most important works were *Chavat Da'at* (Lvov 1799); *Mekor Chayim* (Zolkiev 1807); *Netivot HaMishpat* (Dyhernfurth, Lvov and Zolkiev 1809); *Torat Gittin* (Frankfurt-on-Oder 1813); *Beit Yaakov* (Grubeschow 1823); and *Kehillat Yaakov* (Lvov 1831). He also wrote commentaries on Ecclesiastes, Lamentations and the Song of Songs, a compendium of laws *Derech HaChayim* (Zolkiev 1828) and a commentary on the Passover Haggadah and ritual.

G11. Wife of R. Zvi Hirsch, son of R. Joseph Frankel-Teomim. (See Frankel-Teomim Family Pedigree — Branch A.)

G9.3. R. Ephraim Ashkenazi of Brody.

G10. R. Moses David Ashkenazi.

G11. R. Naftali Zvi Ashkenazi Chachamovicz, published the *Nachalat Yaakov* by his second cousin, R. Jacob of Lissa. He married the daughter of R. Joseph May of Lvov (1764-1810), son of R. Michael May. R. Joseph May (or Mai) succeeded with his brother R. Jehiel Michael to the printing house established by their father at Dyhernfurth. He was the son-in-law of R. Isaiah Berlin (Pick), Rabbi of Breslau.

G8.10. R. Jacob Israel Emden,[4] born in Altona, June 4, 1697 and died there April 19, 1776. In the Rabbinical world he was called Yawetz (from the initials of his name Jacob son of Zvi) and officially in historical records he is called Jacob Herschel.

Until he was seventeen he studied under his father, first at Altona and then in Amsterdam from 1710-14. His father was then forced to flee, leaving the family in Emden. The following year when he was eighteen, R. Jacob married Rachel, daughter of R. Mordecai son of R. Naftali HaKohen Katz of Ungarish-Brod (Broda) in Moravia, where he went to continue his studies under his father-in-law.

He became well-versed in Talmudic literature, Kabbalah, grammar and Latin and Dutch languages. He also acquired a knowledge of philosophy, but later opposed this subject, even stating that the *Moreh Nevuchim* (Guide to the Perplexed) by R. Moses Maimonides was not written by him. He spent three years in Broda as a private instructor in Talmud and then began to deal in gems and jewelry. This necessitated his travelling around from town to town. During these years his life was marked by the tragic deaths of a number of his children. He did not accept any Rabbinical post until 1728 when he visited his father in Amsterdam and subsequently became the A.B.D. of Emden from which town he became known. It was a maritime town in the Prussian Province of Hanover.

In 1733 he returned to Altona where he was allowed by the Chief Rabbi, Ezekiel Katzenellenpogen (See Chapter VIII) who had been there since 1712, to open his own private synagogue. From the King of Denmark, who ruled Altona-Hamburg-Wandsbeck at that time, he obtained permission to establish a printing press.

By nature R. Emden was outspoken and fiery, quick-tempered and said to be of a jealous disposition. The situation in Altona did not help to improve these matters. He considered, it seemed, every successor of his father, the Chief Rabbi of Altona-Hamburg-Wandsbeck until 1709, as an intruder, perhaps feeling that he should have become the community's spiritual leader. Instead, his father had been forced to leave, with R. Moses Susskind Rothenberg remaining there until his death in 1712, to be followed by R. Ezekiel Katzenellenpogen. Thus his relationship with R. Ezekiel was strained from the beginning. He openly called Katzenellenpogen an ignoramus, a poor preacher and criticized his Halachic decisions. Despite the conflicts within the community, he was still allowed by the Chief Rabbi to maintain his private synagogue.

Following the death of his first wife in 1739, he became ill and depressed. Even the burial of his wife caused a further conflict to the community and himself. He was offered in marriage the daughter of R. Samuel Helman of Metz and Mannheim, with the promise to become the A.B.D. of Glogau, but he did not accept. Instead he remarried a wealthy widow, daughter of R. Hirsch of Halberstadt. After this wedding he had troubles with her family in regard to her dowry. She died in 1743, and he married a third time to his niece, Batya Zvia, daughter of R. Ephraim Ashkenazi. At about the same time he had recovered his health sufficiently so as to write and print books. His controversial *Siddur Amudei Shamayim* first appeared in 1745 which was quickly denounced, despite the approbation of the Chief Rabbi of the German communities.

R. Emden was known to have been a vehement opposer of the followers of the false-messiah, Shabbatai Zvi (1626-76), who had been proclaimed the King and Messiah on the Jewish New Year of 1665 by his followers. His father had also been involved with these sectarians whom he had also opposed. Thus when, in 1750, Rabbi Jonathan Eybeschutz was called to Altona to succeed R. Katzenellenpogen who had died, R. Emden turned against him as well, accusing the new Chief Rabbi of being a Shabbataian follower. This was due to one of R. Emden's pupils, Joseph Prager, who in 1751, showed R. Emden an amulet which R. Eybeschutz had written for a woman in childbirth, and R. Emden saw within the script Shabbataian allusions. On February 4, 1751 R. Emden, from the pulpit of his synagogue, publicly denounced him without reference to his name. But the community leaders supported their Chief Rabbi and named R. Emden a caluminator. Even Emden's closest friend, Moses Chajes, head of the Portuguese community, turned against him. For fear of his life, he fled in May that year to his brother-in-law, R. Aryey Lieb Lowenstamm, then Chief Rabbi of Amsterdam. (See Chapter XII.) He remained here for a year until King Frederick of Denmark, in June 1752, allowed him to return to Altona and fined the community one hundred thalers. In August R. Emden returned to his synagogue and printing press. However, in 1756, the King and the Senate of Hamburg officially recognized R. Eybeschutz as the Chief Rabbi of the United Congregations of the Triple Community. But even though the Royal support and the Rabbinical decision of the Council of the Four Lands voted in favor of R. Eybeschutz, R. Emden never gave in, even after R. Eybeschutz's death in 1764. This Council had met at Jaroslav in 1753.

In 1772 R. Emden again came into public notice when the Duke of Mecklenburg-Schwerin withdrew the permission formerly given to the Jews to bury their dead immediately. When his opinion was consulted, he referred them to Moses Mendelssohn, the philosopher from Dessau (See Chapter III), whose opinion agreed with the duke's order. He had also had a dialogue with Mendelssohn about the Seven Commandments of the Sons of Noah in 1774. He died in Altona two years later. His first wife Rachel, his second wife Sarah, and his third wife Batya Zvia (Rachel) died in 1739, 1743 and 1804 respectively. His third wife was buried next to him in the Konigstrasse Cemetery in Altona. His first wife had died in childbirth and was named after her mother. (See Chapter V — Branch B for her lineage.)

R. Emden was the author of numerous works, mainly polemics and Rabbinical. These include the Polemics *Torat HaKena'ot* (Amsterdam, 1752—biographies of Shabbatai Zvi, and criticisms of Nehemiah Hayun, R. Eybeschutz and others), *Edut BeYaakov, Shimmush, Shebirat Luchot HaAven* (Altona, 1759—a refutation of R. Eybeschutz's *Luchot HaEidut* which appeared in 1755) and others. The Rabbinical works include *Lechem Shamayim*, Responsa *She'elat Yawetz, Siddur Tefillah* and others which include unpublished manuscripts, some of which are kept in the Library of Columbia University, New York. His autobiography *Megillat Sefer* was published in Warsaw in 1896.

G9.1. R. Solomon Zalman, second son, A.B.D. Podhajce, later in London.

G9.2. Zvi, named after his grandfather, was born in Brody where he died young.

G9.3. Zvi, named after his deceased brother was circumcised amidst great celebration with the aged R. Ezekiel Katzenellenpogen as *Sandek* (Godfather), but he too died young in 1740.

G9.4. Son from his second wife, also died young.

G9.5. Mordecai, from his third wife, died in infancy in 1748.

G9.6. Levi, born in 1753, circumcised by his father but died in infancy in 1754.

G9.7. Joseph, died young in 1758.

G9.8. R. Judah, born in 1750, died in 1775 and buried in Altona.

G9.9. Esther, from first wife, born in 1736, married but had no children and died in 1763.

G9.10. Mamala, died young.

G9.11. Nechama, from second wife, born in 1742, married R. Abraham, son of R. Baruch. She died in 1775.

G9.12. Daughter, died at age six years, and another died young in 1763.

G9.13. Channah, born 1755, from this third wife, married R. Wolf Hollander. She died in 1831. According to another source she was married to R. Aryey Lieb, son of R. Saul, son of R. Aryey Lieb Lowenstamm. (See Lowenstamm Family Pedigree.)

G9.14. R. Meir Emden, A.B.D. of Constantin was R. Jacob Emden's first son, born in 1717 at Brody. He went with his father to Emden, where he studied for some three years and then studied under his grandfather Chacham Zvi. He married a daughter of a wealthy merchant of Lissa, the town of his famous nephew R. Jacob Lisser, and they had two daughters. He wrote responsa which can be found in the *Divrei Rav Meshullam* by his father's brother, R. Abraham Meshullam Zalman.

G10.1. Miriam married R. Dovberish, A.B.D. of Medzibeh, son of R. Aryey Lieb (A.B.D. Prezworsk — died in 1759), son of R. Haim HaKohen Rappoport (A.B.D. Lvov).

G11.1. R. Haim Rappoport, A.B.D. Ostrow, and author of the responsa *Mayim Chayim* (published posthumously by his son), succeeded R. Bezalel Margolioth there in 1822. He occupied this position for seventeen years until he resigned in 1838 and was succeeded by his son, R. Jacob, and died the following year. He married about 1790 to Ziporah, daughter of R. Abbale, son of R. Pesach, son of R. Solomon

Zalman Cohen of Ostrow, (and he was thus also known as R. Haim Tzipores). She died in 1843. Another daughter of R. Abbale was married to R. Aryey Lieb, son of R. Meshullam Zalman Ashkenazi (A.B.D. Pomarin). (See Orstein-Ashkenazi Family Pedigree — G8/9.1/10.3.) R. Abbale died in 1812.

G12.1. R. Jacob Rappoport, A.B.D. Ostrow after his father, published his father's responsa.

G13.1. R. Moses Rappoport, 1820-1845. His novellae are found in his grandfather's responsa work.

G13.2. R. Meir Rappoport, 1825-53. His novellae are also found in his grandfather's responsa work.

G12.2. R. Jekutiel Zisel Rappoport of Minsk, married 1) Sarah, daughter of R. Zeev Wolf, and 2) Feigel, daughter of R. Jacob, A.B.D. Karlin.

G13.1. R. Jacob Rappoport of Minsk, married daughter of R. Jacob Jokel son of Liebel Reb Berish of Vilna.

G13.2. R. Wolf Rappoport of Minsk, married his first cousin, daughter of R. Hirsch Saltzman. (Their mothers were sisters.)

G13.3. Rachel, married R. Israel Meisels, A.B.D. Zulz.

G13.4. Malka, married R. Jacob, son of R. Samuel Eliasberg of Eunitz.

G13.5. Feigel, married R. Jonah, son of R. Meir HaKohen Zussman. (See below G11.3/12.1/13.1.)

G12.3. Wife of R. Dovber, son of R. Mordecai Zalman Halperson of Zaslov.

G11.2. R. Meir Rappoport, mentioned in his brother's responsa.

G12. Wife of R. Saul Issachar HaKohen Rappoport.

G13. R. Meir Menachem Rappoport, A.B.D. Rzeszow.

G11.3. Wife of R. Solomon Zalman HaKohen Zussman of Ostrow. Head of the Ostrow Zussman (Sussman) Family Pedigree.

G12.1. R. Meir Zussman (died 1860), married Jochebed, daughter of R. Meir of Tiktin. She died in 1833.

G13.1. R. Jonah Zussman of Warsaw, married daughter of R. Jekutiel Zisel Rappoport. (G11.1/12.2/13.5 above.)

G13.2. R. Dov Berish Zussman, married the daughter of R. Simeon Zemel Halevi Epstein of Warsaw. (Zemel died in 1855.)

G13.3. R. Abraham Abba Zvi Zussman, died 1884 in Ostrow. He married his sister-in-law, Jaret, daughter of R. Jacob Joshua Horowitz, (son of R. Zvi Hirsch *Machaneh Levi*). (See below and Horowitz Family Pedigree — Branch III.)

G14.1. R. Ephraim Zalman Zussman, married his first cousin, Jochebed, daughter of R. Shalom, son of R. Aaron Luria (see G13.6/14 below).

G15.1. R. Shalom, named after his maternal grandfather, married the daughter of R. Moses Berenstein.

G15.2. R. Meir, married the daughter of R. Jacob Ettinge of Homin.

G15.3. R. Moses Aaron, married the daughter of R. Nathan, son of R. Isaac (Hamburger) Horowitz. (See Horowitz Family Pedigree Introduction.)

G15.4. Sima, wife of R. Solomon, son of R. Isaac Aaron Ettinge (See Ettinge Family under Ornstein-Ashkenazi Family Pedigree G9.2/10.5/11.1.)

G15.5. Beila (died 1903), married R. Isaac Kalman, son of R. Jacob Meshullam Frankel-Teomim. He is mentioned at the beginning of *Mizkeret Le Gedolei Ostrow* (Biber, Berdichev 1907), one of the main sources of the Zussman Family genealogy.

G14.2. R. Haim Mordecai Zussman of Ostrow, died young in 1881. He married his first cousin, Jochebed, daughter of R. Solomon Zalman Zussman. (See below G13.4/14.3.)

G15.1. R. Joshua, maried the daughter of R. Isaac Aaron Ettinge. (See Ettinge Family under Ornstein-Ashkenazi Family Pedigree — G9.2/10.5/11.1/12.1.)

G15.2. R. Samuel Shmelke.

G15.3. R. Nahum.

G15.4. Wife of R. Mordecai Ettinge.

G14.3. R. Jacob Joshua Zussman, named after his maternal grandfather, R. Jacob Joshua Horowitz.

G14.4. R. Moses Zussman.

G13.4. R. Solomon Zalman Zussman (died 1881) of Ostrow, married his sister-in-law, Dreizel, daughter of R. Jacob Joshua Horowitz (see G13.3 above). (See Horowitz Family Pedigree — Branch III.)

G14.1. R. Ephraim Fischel Zussman, married his relative, the daughter of R. Saul Rokeah (son-in-law of R. Jerachmeel, son of R. Samuel Shmelke Horowitz — See Horowitz Family Pedigree — Branch III).

G14.2. Sima, married R. Shmelke, son of R. Saul Rokeah, her sister-in-law's brother.

G14.3. Jochebed, married her first cousin, R. Haim Mordecai Zussman. (See above — G12.1/13.3/14.2.)

G14.4. Sarah, married R. Eliezer, son of R. Moses, son of R. Eliezer Landau (A.B.D. Brody). (See Landau Family Pedigree — page 397 — G12.2/13.)

G13.5. R. Haim Zussman, died without offspring.

G13.6. Feige, wife of R. Aaron Luria of Minsk (brother of R. David Luria).

G14. R. Shalom Luria, married his first cousin, Jochebed, daughter of R. Ephraim Zalman Zussman. (See above — G13.3/14.1.)

G13.7. Miriam, second wife of R. Aaron Luria above.

G13.8. Reizel, married twice. Her second husband was R. Aryey Liebus, son of R. Alexander Sender Landau (died in Ostrow in 1889).

G12.2. R. Zvi Zussman of Ostrow.

G12.3. Wife of R. Joseph Zvi Meizes of Ostrow.

G11.4. Wife of R. Jacob Rappoport of Medzibeh, son of R. Zalman Pereles of Brody. R. Jacob's sister was married to R. Aryey Lieb, son of R. Isaac (Hamburger) Horowitz (see Horowitz Family Pedigree Introduction).

G12. Judith, married R. Isaac Lieb, son of R. Jehiel Michael Zetil.

G11.5. R. Zvi Ari Rappoport.

G12. Wife of R. Saul Issachar Berish Bick, A.B.D. Medzibeh.
G13. R. Zvi Ari Bick.

G14.1. R. Haim Jehiel Michal Bick.

G15. R. Haim Jehiel Michal Bick of Medzibeh-New
York. Reprinted *Mohr U'Ketziah*. (Grossman's 1953,
New York) by R. Jacob Emden.

G16. R. Moses Zvi Bick of New York, married and has
issue.[5]

G14.2. R. Simha Bick.

G15. R. Isaac Bick.

G16. R. Saul Bick of New York.

G10.2. Judith, married R. Zvi Hirsch (1717-1791) Halberstadt,
A.B.D. of Constantin, succeeding his father-in-law, R. Meir,
son of R. Jacob Emden. He was the son of R. Moses (A.B.D.
Satanov), son of R. Naftali Hirsch (A.B.D. Dubno). (See
Chapter VII — page 308 — G11.2.)

CHAPTER XIV

HALBERSTAM CHASSIDIC DYNASTY OF SANZ

AIM,[1] son of R. Aryey Lieb Halberstam, was born in 1792 in the town of Tarnograd where his father was the A.B.D. His paternal ancestry was recorded in Chapter VII — Branch B, and his maternal ancestry in Chapter XIII. His mother, Miriam, was the daughter of R. David Ashkenazi of Tarnograd, a descendant of the Chacham Zvi Ashkenazi. In his youth young Haim studied in the *Cheder* which was also run by his father. From birth, he was a sickly child. Once when he was brought to the *Chozeh* (Seer) of Lublin, the sage prophesied a great future for the child and that he would be blessed with a long life. As he grew, he remained with a limp in one leg. Under the influence of the *Chozeh* he became a *Chassid*. He also studied under R. Naftali Zvi, founder of the Ropshitz Dynasty, R. Zvi Hirsch of Zhidachov, R. Zvi Hirsch of Rymanov, R. Shalom, founder of the Belz Dynasty, and R. Israel, founder of the Ruzhin Dynasty.[2]

Even in his youth he prayed with great fervor and used to stamp his feet on the floor. Once his master, the Ropshitzer's wife, said to her husband: "Why do you not tell him to only stamp with his healthy and not his lame foot?" The Rabbi replied: "If I knew that he was aware which foot he stamped, I would have told him."

The son of R. Baruch Frankel-Teomim,[3] R. Joshua Heschel of Komarno, who was also influenced by the Chassidic leaders of the generation, first introduced R. Haim (who had adopted the surname of Halberstam) to his father. The latter, at first strongly opposed to Chassidism, was later to choose R. Haim as his son-in-law through two of his daughters. However, his daughter was reluctant to marry someone with a deformity. R. Haim

483

requested to speak to her alone in private. What was spoken remains a secret unto this day, but after that they were married and had eight children. The couple remained with R. Baruch Frankel-Teomim in Leipnik for a year. In 1830 he was elected A.B.D. of Sanz and the following year became the Admur there. His first wife died about 1860/1 and he remarried her sister, but they had no issue.

In 1861/2 he married a third time to Rachel, daughter of R. Jehiel Zvi Unger of Tarnow (son of R. Mordecai David of Dombrovo — See Chapter XVII — Unger Dynasty) and had six more children.

The Yeshiva he established at Sanz was run on the scholarly old style tradition of Poland and thus attracted both Chassidim and Mitnagdim. He was strict in matters of learning and observance and unlike the other *Tzaddikim* of that period, his religious "court" was modest and discreet, devoid of splendor and luxury. Because of his resentment of the "royal style" living of the Friedman Chassidic Dynasty, a controversy arose between the two groups of Sanz and Sadagora. When R. Dov Ber of Leovo, youngest son of R. Israel Friedman of Ruzhin, renounced Chassidism, R. Haim Halberstam issued a letter in which he openly criticized the way of life of the Sadagora Chassidim. This led to much conflict, following which a Ukrainian Rabbinical Convention called for Haim's excommunication and even demanded that he be handed over to the Russian Authorities. Various Rabbinical authorities attempted to intervene without success. After several years the dispute settled down. R. Dov Ber later returned to Chassidism.

R. Haim Halberstam of Sanz was the author of *Divrei Chayim* (published at Zolkiev, 1864, and Lvov, 1875). He had a profound knowledge of Talmud and the commentaries, the Midrashim and Medieval philosophical literature. He was also an exponent of the ecstatic mode of prayer which he developed from his youth, developed Chassidic melody and opposed asceticism. He died in 1876.

His first father-in-law said of him: "Despite my son-in-law's deformed (crooked) leg, he has a clear and brilliant (straight) mind." In response to being asked if the miracles recorded in the books about the Zaddikim were true, the Sanzer Rebbe replied: "I am unable to vouch for the written record, but I am sure a true Zadik can, unless contrary to Divine Will, achieve whatever he desires."

When he was old, he once came across a weeping apple-vendor in the market place. She bemoaned the fact that none came to buy, and if this continued, she would be ruined. Thereupon the great Sage took her place and called out: "Fine apples to buy." Within a short while the news spread across town so that all the apples were sold, the people considering it a great honor to buy from the revered and famous Rabbi.

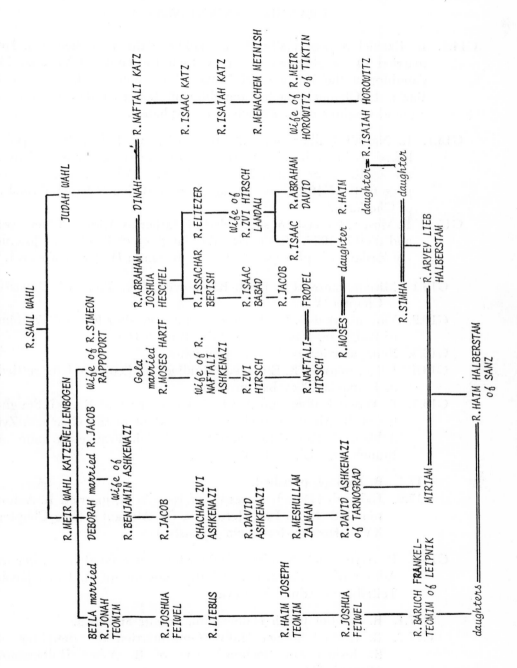

ANCESTRY of R. HAIM HALBERSTAM of SANZ

BRANCH A (SIENIAWA)

G14.1. R. Ezekiel Shraga Halberstam, 1813-96, Admur of Sieniawa. He married 1) daughter of R. Aryey Lieb Lipschutz of Vizhniz, 2) daughter of the Rabbi of Holshitz, 3) daughter of R. Judah Zvi Razla, 4) Channah Rachel, daughter of R. Hirsch Ramraz and 5) a granddaughter of R. Elimelech of Lyzhansk.

G15.1. R. Naftali Halberstam, 1834-64, author of *Ilah Shlucha*, published by his father. He married 1) Frume, daughter of R. Aaron son of R. Asher Isaiah Rubin (Chapter XVI — Branch VII — page 603 — G16.1), and 2) daughter of R. Jacob Israel Twersky of Cherkassi.

G15.2. R. Moses Halberstam, succeeded his father as Admur of Sieniawa and died in 1920. He married the daughter of R. Phineas Joseph (of Zaslav) Shapiro (son-in-law of R. Haim Hager of Kossov).

G16.1. Miriam, married R. Jacob Rabinowitz. (See Radomsk Dynasty — Chapter IV.)

G16.2. Yita, married R. Jacob son of R. Simeon Alter Frankel-Teomim of Padgorze. (See Chapter IV — Branch H.)

G16.3. Beila, married without having issue.

G16.4. Feige, married R. Elimelech Bindiger of Sieniawa, later settled in Rumania. They had no issue.

G16.5. R. David Halberstam A.B.D. Sokolov, married Rachel, daughter of R. Abraham Ingber, a descendant of the Chacham Zvi Ashkenazi. Her sister married R. Elijah Frankel-Teomim of Branch H. (Chapter IV.)

G17.1. R. Ezekiel, perished.

G17.2. Deborah (Dora), currently of New York, married R. Aaron son of R. Haim Isaac Jeruchem (of Altstadt). (See Chapter XV — Heschel-Jeruchem Dynasty.)

G16.6. R. Aryey Lieb Mordecai Halberstam, succeeded his father as Admur of Sieniawa, married the daughter of R. Israel Jacob Teitelbaum, Admur Walowa.

G17.1. R. Jekutiel Judah Halberstam, Admur Sieniawa.

G17.2. R. Ezekiel Shraga Halberstam, married the daughter of R. Joshua (of Bochnia), son of R. Asher Halberstam (Branch C).

G16.7. Chaya Channah, married R. Jacob Samson Kaner, A.B.D. Chechoyv, died in 1941.

G17.1. Miriam Jochebed, married R. Jacob Elimelech son of R. Ezekiel Paneth, perished with family in 1944.

G17.2. Sosha, married R. Mendel A.B.D. Desh, son of R. Ezekiel Paneth (brother of R. Mendel above). They perished in 1944.

G18.1. Ezekiel, perished.

G18.2. Leah, married R. Moses son of R. Haim Hager, the present leader and Admur of Vizhniz-Bnei Brak.

G17.3. R. Baruch Kaner-Halberstam 1895-1953, Admur Sanz who died in New York after living there only five weeks. He married the daughter of R. Shalom son of R. Aaron Halberstam A.B.D. of Sanz (see Branch D) and succeeded him there in 1935. They had no issue.

G17.4. R. Haim Kaner, died in New York in 1968, married his first cousin, the daughter of R. Jacob Frankel-Teomim. (See above.)

G18.1. Rachel, married 1) R. Jacob Jokel Weidenfeld (no issue), and 2) R. Menashe Levertov. Their children, Channah and Rebecca.

G17.5. R. Abish Kaner, Admur Botosani-Haifa, born in 1894, married the daughter of R. Moses Joseph of Solitza.

G17.6. Sarah Deborah, married R. Jacob Joseph (Vaslui-Tel Aviv) son of R. Dov Halpern. (See Chapter XV—page 525—G17.1.)

G17.7. Zipporah, married R. Eliezer Yolles (Montreal).

G18.1. Zvi Hirsch Yolles, married and has issue (Brooklyn).

G18.2. Leah, married R. Phineas Menachem Mendel Rokeah son of R. Zvi Elimelech of Birch (Jamaica, New York).

G17.8. Sheindel, married 1) R. Asher Anschel son of R. Israel son of R. Henoch Ashkenazi (had issue), and 2) R. Samuel Elijah halevi Epstein (New York).

G18. Moses Ashkenazi married Leah Lefkowitz. Their son, Jacob Joseph.

G16.8. Wife of her first cousin, R. Aryey Lieb, son of R. Ezekiel Shraga Halberstam.

G15.3. Reizel, married R. Phineas son of R. Ezekiel Shraga son of R. Joshua Heschel Frankel-Teomim. (See Chapter IV — Branch H.) He was the A.B.D. of Klasni.

G15.4. R. Simha Issachar Dov (Ber) Halberstam, Admur Chechinov, died in 1914. He married Frieda, daughter of R. Joshua Rokeah, the second Belzer Rebbe (See Chapter XVII), and was the author of *Divrei Simcha.*

    G16.1. R. Ezekiel Shraga Halberstam 1900-43, the last Admur of Chechinov, married the daughter of R. Hananiah YomTov Lipa Teitelbaum. (See Chapter XVII — Teitelbaum Dynasty G12.1 /13.1.) The entire family perished.

    G16.2. Rebecca Miriam, married R. Meshullam Zusia Twersky. (See Chapter VII — Branch B — G7.4/8.2/9.6/10.4/11.2/12/13 /14/15/16.3/17.3.)

    G16.3. Channah Rachel, married R. Aryey Lieb son of R. Isaac Tuvia son of R. Meir Rubin. (See Chapter XVI — Branch VII — Rubin Dynasty — page 609 — G18.4.)

G15.5. R. Abraham Shalom Halberstam 1854-1940, Admur Stropkov,[4] married 1) Gitel (died in 1932), daughter of R. Samuel Weichman, and 2) her niece, Chaya, daughter of R. David Shlichter of Komarno. (See Chapter VII — Branch B.)

    G16.1. Chava, married R. Mendel son of R. Meir Horowitz. (See Chapter XVI — Branch VII — Horowitz Dynasty — page 599 — G18.2.)

    G16.2. R. Menachem Mendel, Admur Stropkov-New York, died in 1954 and was buried in Israel. He wrote *Divrei Menachem.*

        G17.1. Wife of R. Moses Aaron son of R. Jehiel Nathan Halberstam (Branch E).

        G17.2. R. Haim Halberstam, married Rebecca, daughter of R. Aryey Lieb Rosenfeld (Branch H).

    G16.3. Wife of R. Haim Parnas of Yasliska.

        G17. Rachel, married R. Phineas Aryey Lieb son of R. Samuel Shmelke Azriel Frankel-Teomim. (Chapter IV — Branch H — G12.2/13.1/14.1/15.4.)

    G16.4. Wife of R. Issachar Ber son of R. Liebish (Admur Apt, died in 1929) son of R. Joseph Zechariah Lipschutz. (See Chapter XVII — Teitelbaum Dynasty — page 675 — G15.)

G16.5. YomTov Joseph Halberstam, only child from the second marriage, perished.

G15.6. R. Aryey Lieb Halberstam, Admur Tarnow, died in 1930, married his first cousin, daughter of R. Moses Halberstam.

G16.1. R. Zvi Hirsch Halberstam, married Frieda, daughter of R. Meir son of R. Mendel Horowitz. (See Chapter XVI — Branch VII — page 600 — G18.5.) They perished in the Holocaust. He was the Admur of Sambor.

G16.2. R. Nahum Ephraim Halberstam, married his first cousin, Raatza, daughter of R. Naftali son of R. Samuel Rubin. (See Chapter XVI — Branch VII — page 604 — G18.4.) He was the Admur of Tarnow succeeding his father.

G17.1. Rachel Miriam, perished.
G17.2. Feige, married R. Hananiah YomTov Lipa Teitelbaum, the Nierbatur Rabbi of New York. (See Teitelbaum Dynasty Chapter XVII — G12.2/13.1/14.4/15.2.)

G16.3. R. Ezekiel Shraga Halberstam, Admur Przemysl.

G15.7. Feige Beila, married R. Mendel, Admur Fristik and Dukla, son of R. Aryey Lieb Halberstam. (See Branch C.)

G15.8. Wife of R. Naftali (of Vizhniz), son of R. Samuel son of R. Aaron Rubin. (See Chapter XVI — Branch VII — page 603 — G17.1.)

G15.9. Wife of R. Ezekiel Bindiger of Bartfeldt (Bardiyov).

BRANCH B (BOBOV)

G14.2. R. Meir Nathan Halberstam, married Beila, daughter of R. Eliezer Horowitz of Dzikov, son of R. Naftali Zvi, founder of the Ropshitz Dynasty. (Chapter XVI.)

G15.1. Wife of R. Haim Eliezer son of R. Jacob Isaac Unger, Admur Radlov. (See Unger Dynasty — Chapter XVII.)

G15.2. First wife of R. Naftali (of Malitsch), son of R. Jacob Horowitz. (See Chapter XVI — Branch VII — page 594 — G16.1.)

G15.3. R. Solomon Halberstam, 1847-1906, Admur of Bobov, married Rebecca, daughter of R. Joshua son of R. Shalom Rosenfeld. (See branch H.)

G16.1. R. Benzion Halberstam, 1873-1941, succeeded his father as Admur of Bobov.[5] He was known for his musical compositions.

He married 1) Tirzah, daughter of R. Naftali son of R. Judah Horowitz (see Chapter XVI — Branch VII — page 594 — G16.1/17.3), and 2) Chaya Friedel, daughter of R. Shalom Eliezer son of R. Haim Halberstam, his second cousin (Branch F — G15.3).

G17.1. Leah Deborah, married R. Jacob Israel son of R. Benzion Judah Lieb (of Hornistopol) Twersky of Milwaukee, and have issue.

G17.2. Rebecca Beila, married 1) R. Ezekiel Shraga son of R. Isaac Isaiah Halberstam of Chechoyv (Branch G), and 2) R. Haim Perlman of Brooklyn (no issue).

G17.3. R. Solomon Halberstam, leader and present Admur of the Bobover Chassidim in New York, born in 1906. He founded the village of Bobov near Bat Yam in 1958. He married 1) Rachel, daughter of R. Haim Jacob Teitelbaum of Limanov, his first cousin, and 2) Friedel, daughter of R. Aryey Lieb (of Tomashov) son of R. Isaac Tuvia Rubin (see Chapter XVI — Branch VII — G14.4/15.3/16.2/17.3/18.4/19.5). From his first wife he had one son, and six children from his second marriage.

G18.1. R. Naftali Zvi Halberstam, married Hessa, daughter of R. Joseph son of R. Ezekiel Paneth (mentioned above). (Branch A — G14.1/15.2/16.7/17.1 — R. Joseph was a brother to R. Jacob Elimelech Paneth.)

G19.1. Rachel, married Joshua son of R. Mordecai David Rubin.

G19.2. Rivke.

G18.2. R. Benzion Halberstam, married in 1974 to the daughter of R. Menachem Mendel son of R. Israel Jeshurun Rubin. (See Chapter XVI — Branch VII.)

G18.3. Esther.

G18.4. Sarah, married Jacob Israel Jeshurun son of R. Shabtai son of R. Haim Meisels. R. Shabtai's wife was a sister of R. Mordecai David Rubin (G18.1/19.1) above.

G18.5. Malka.

G18.6. Deborah Leah, married Jonathan Benjamin Goldberger.

G18.7. Nechamah, married Haim Jacob Tauber.

G17.4. Nechamah, married 1) R. Moses son of R. Feiwel Stempel of Cracow, died in 1941, and had two children, and 2) R.

Joshua Meir son of R. Raphael son of R. Israel (of Sassov) Freshwater of London, and had two sons.

G18.1. Samuel Judah Stempel, married Rachel, daughter of Solomon Kleinman.

G18.2. Shoshana, married Zeev (Kohen) Stern, London.

G18.3. Benzion, (of London), married the daughter of R. Weinberger (Long Island).

G18.4. Solomon Freshwater (of Lakewood, N.J.), married the daughter of R. Gedalliah Shorr, the head of the Yeshiva *Torah Va-Das* (Lakewood, N.J.).

G17.5. Bracha, married 1) R. Solomon son of R. Zvi Hirsch son of R. Isaac Tuvia Rubin (see Chapter XVI — Branch VII) and had a son, and 2) Judah Lemberger (New York) and had a daughter.

G18.1. Haim Zvi Rubin (Brooklyn).

G18.2. Miriam.

G17.6. R. Haim Joshua, 1912-1943, married Leah (born in 1908), daughter of R. Baruch son of R. Moses son of R. David Halberstam of Keshanov (Branch C). She came to the U.S.A. with her sons in 1946.

G18.1. R. Baruch David Halberstam, born in 1936, married Achsah, daughter of R. Haim son of R. David Meisels. (See Teitelbaum Dynasty—Chapter XVII.) Their children: Moses Joshua (born in 1959); Benzion Dov (born in 1961); and Rechel Breindel (born in 1965).

G18.2. R. Jacob Joseph Halberstam, born in 1938, married Sarah, daughter of R. Aaron Teitelbaum. Their son, Haim Joshua (born in 1960).

G17.7. R. Ezekiel David Halberstam, married the daughter of R. Jehiel son of R. Meir (of Dzikov) Horowitz of Pokshavnitz. R. Jehiel's wife was a daughter of R. David Halberstam of Keshanov. (See Branch C and Chapter XVI — Branch VII.)

G18.1. Jehiel Halberstam, married Yente, daughter of R. Aaron Teitelbaum and have nine children.

G18.2. Haim Halberstam, married Adina (Eidel Binah), daughter of R. Isaac Liebes. (See Chapter XVI — Branch VI.) Their children: Meshullam Issachar Joseph, Benzion Abraham Jacob and Zipporah Leah.

G18.3. Benzion, married Frieda, daughter of R. Shraga Feiwel son
of R. David Halberstam of Keshanov (Branch C), and
have two children.

G18.4. Solomon Halberstam.

G17.8. R. Moses Aaron Halberstam, unmarried, perished.

G17.9. Raatza, married R. Israel Weitz, with family (London).

G17.10. Gitsche, married Motil Lipschutz. Their sons, Benzion and
Shalom Eliezer.

G17.11. Malka, married R. Israel Jacuber, with family (London).

G16.2. Wife of R. Haim Jacob Teitelbaum of Limanov. Their daughter, Rachel, was the first wife of her cousin R. Solomon Halberstam of Bobov. (See Teitelbaum Dynasty — Chapter XVII.)

BRANCH C (KESHANOV)

G14.3. R. David Halberstam, 1821-1894, Admur Keshanov, married 1)
Achsah, and had issue (R. Joseph Zeev and R. Aryey Lieb), and 2)
Leah Zissah Zinz. The order of birth of the other sons was; third,
R. Moses and fourth, R. Naftali.

G15.1. R. Naftali Halberstam (died 1925), Rabbi in Keshanov together
with his nephew R. Joseph Elimelech Halberstam, until 1908
when he alone was the Rabbi. He married the daughter of R.
Abraham Joshua Heschel of Tulst.

G16.1. Wife of R. Haim Jacob Rosenfeld.

G17. Rachel, married Hirsh Tauber (Brooklyn).

G18. Haim Jacob Tauber, married Nechama, daughter of R. Solomon Halberstam of Bobov. (See Branch B. — G16.1/17.3/
18.7.)

G16.2. R. Menachem Mendel Halberstam, Admur Keshanov.

G17.1. Wife of Judah Reiner (Brooklyn).

G17.2. Wife of Benjamin Schachner (Brooklyn).

G17.3. Wife of Billet (Brooklyn).

G17.4. Wife of Kalickstein.

G16.3. Miriam, first wife of her first cousin R. Simha (A.B.D. Skavin)
son of R. Simeon Alter Frankel-Teomim. (See Chapter IV —
Branch H — G11.1/12.2/13.2).

G16.4. Yita, second wife of R. Simha Frankel-Teomim, her third husband. Her first marriage which ended in divorce was to R. Zalman Lieb son of R. Moses David Teitelbaum (Lapishiver Rov), and her second marriage was to R. Samuel Shmelke Frankel-Teomim, a first cousin to R. Simha mentioned above. (See Chapter IV — Branch H.)

G15.2. R. Moses Halberstam, died in 1915 married 1) the daughter of R. Israel Meilich son of R. Joseph (of Dombrovo) Unger, and had issue, and 2) the daughter of R. Mordecai Zalman A.B.D. Zhitomir.

G16.1. R. Baruch Halberstam (from first marriage), died in Keshanov in 1917. He married Rechel Breindel, daughter of R. Abraham Haim son of R. Menachem Mendel Horowitz. (See Chapter XVI — Branch VII — page 599 — G17.1.)

G17.1. Frieda.

G17.2. Matle, married Elchanan Joseph Herzman (Brooklyn).

G17.3. Mishket, perished.

G17.4. Abraham Haim, perished in a Russian prison.

G17.5. R. David Halberstam, born in 1899, escaped to Vienna and came to the U.S.A. in 1941, the Admur Keshanov-New York. He married Riva, daughter of R. Haim Jeruchem. (See Chapter XV — Jeruchem Family — G15/16.3.)

G18.1. R. Baruch Nathan Halberstam, married Chaya. Their children: Feiwel; Toyba Rachel, married Haim David Blum; and Abraham, married the daughter of R. Asher Isaiah Babad. (See Chapter XI.)

G18.2. R. Moses Halberstam, married Hinde, daughter of R. Eleazar son of R. Mordecai son of R. Zvi Elimelech Spira. (See Chapter XVII.) They have issue.

G18.3. R. Shraga Feiwel Halberstam, married Matil Leah, daughter of R. Samuel Haim Paneth. Their children: Haim Samuel; Baruch Abraham; Rechel Breindel; Frieda (married Benzion son of R. Ezekiel David Halberstam of Bobov, Branch B); and Rachel (married Joseph Mordecai Eichenstein).

G18.4. Miriam, married Ezekiel son of R. Elisha Horowitz of Monsey, N.Y. and have issue.

G17.6. Leah, born in 1908, married R. Haim Joshua son of R. Benzion Halberstam of Bobov (Branch B).

G16.2. R. Joseph Elimelech Halberstam (from first marriage), died in 1867. He married Ethel, daughter of R. Abba Ingber. He was Rabbi in Keshanov together with his uncle, R. Naftali Halberstam.

G17.1. R. Aryey Lieb Halberstam.

G17.2. Hinde, married her first cousin R. Joseph son of R. Jacob Israel Halberstam.

G17.3. Feige, married her uncle R. Samuel son of R. Abba Ingber.

G17.4. R. Jehiel Michael Halberstam, perished in 1941, married Miriam, daughter of R. Abraham Hanoch Zilbiger of Chechinov.

G18. Haim David Halberstam, born in 1928, married Reizel Golda Ehrman.

G19.1. Jehiel Michael Dov, married Jochebed Rivke, daughter of R. Mordecai Dov son of R. Elisha Halberstam of Gorlice (Branch E).

G19.2. Miriam, married Shlomo Zalman Schon (Lakewood, N.J.).

G19.3. Israel Meir Halberstam.

G16.3. R. Jacob Israel Halberstam, (from second marriage).

G17.1. R. Joseph Halberstam, married his first cousin, Hinde, daughter of R. Joseph Elimelech Halberstam. She was the President of the WIZO Organization in Israel.

G17.2. R. David Halberstam.

G17.3. R. Lieb Halberstam, perished.

G17.4. Hella, married Joseph Tarchevsky (lawyer, Germany) and have a daughter.

G17.5. Pearl, married Moses Bank (New York) and have issue.

G17.6. Lotka, married Alexander Zilberman (Israel) and have two daughters.

G16.4. R. Aryey Halberstam, married Hentche, daughter of Menachem Mendel Parnes. He was Leader of the community of Gorlice. They perished in the Holocaust.

G17.1. David Halberstam, born in 1911 (Montreal), married and has issue, Miriam (born in 1950) and Sarah (born in 1951).

G17.2. Rebecca, married R. Samuel Abraham Zeldenreich, and have issue.

G17.3. Pearl, married her first cousin, R. Markus Halberstam (New York). They have issue. (See Branch C.)

G16.5. Channah, married David May (Israel) and have issue.

G16.6. Deborah, married R. Lieb Halberstam, father of Markus (mentioned above).

G15.3. R. Joseph Zeev Halberstam, married Zipporah, daughter of R. Menachem Mendel son of R. Asher Isaiah Rubin. (See Chapter XVI — Branch VII.) He was Admur Keshanov, succeeding his father in 1894.

G16.1. R. Aaron Halberstam,[6] 1865-1942, author of *Mutzal MeiHaeish* and *Meged Shamayim*. He married 1) Rebecca Rachel (1865-1881), daughter of R. Alter Meir David Halevi Rothenberg (see Rokeah Dynasty — Chapter XVII) and had one son, and 2) Deborah, daughter of R. Joshua Isaac Kliger A.B.D. Greiding, and also had issue. (See Chapter XVI — Branch VI — page 584 — G16.4.)

G17.1. R. Menachem Benjamin Benzion Halberstam (from first marriage), 1881-1951, the Admur Sanz-Brooklyn. He published the *Mutzal MeiHaeish* in New York in 1955. He married the daughter of R. Abraham Haim Rothenberg of Vaidislav.

G18.1. R. Jacob Moses Halberstam, died in 1975.

G19. Abraham Rothenberg.

G18.2. R. Isaac Shalom (Irving) Rothenberg-Halberstam, 1911-74. Rabbi of the Mapleton Park Hebrew Institute (Brooklyn). His children, Aaron and Zipporah Yitta.

G18.3. Abraham (Tony) Rothenberg (Germany).
G18.4. Alter (Arthur) Halberstam (Germany).
G18.5. Regina (Rivke), married Elimelech Trokenheim (Brooklyn).

G19.1. Abraham Trokenheim, married with three sons.
G19.2. Vivian, married Shi Ostrov, and have issue.

G18.6. Golda, married Jack London.

G17.2. Wife of R. Joel Moses Pinter.

G18. R. Isaac Joshua Pinter (Brooklyn).

G16.2. R. Asher Halberstam A.B.D. Bochnia.

G17. R. Joshua Halberstam, perished.

G18. Wife of R. Ezekiel Shraga son of R. Aryey Lieb Mordecai
Halberstam of Sieniawa. (See Branch A.)

G16.3. R. Naftali Zvi Hirsch Halberstam A.B.D. Galisk, married the
daughter of R. Moses Rokeah of Korev. (See Chapter XVII.)

G17. R. Lieb Halberstam, Admur Galisk, married Deborah, daughter of Moses Halberstam. (See above G14.3/15.2/16.6.)

G18.1. R. Mendel Halberstam, succeeded his father as Admur
Sanz, perished in the Holocaust.
G18.2. R. Mordecai (Markus) Halberstam, Kempner Rabbi, New
York, maried Pearl, daughter of R. Aryey Halberstam. They
were first cousins. (See above.)

G19.1. Naftali Zvi Halberstam.
G19.2. Hentche (Helen), married Jacob Moses Poupko.
G19.3. Malka, married Zeev Guggenheim.

G15.4. Wife of R. Shalom son of R. Jacob Isaac son of R. Haim Meir
Jehiel Shapiro. (See Chapter XVII.)
G15.5 Miriam, wife of R. Jehiel, (of Pokshavitz), son of R. Meir (of
Dzikov) Horowitz. (See Chapter XVI — Branch VII — page 587
— G16.4.)
G15.6. Wife of R. Eleazar (of Rzeszow), son of R. Elimelech Weissblum.
(See Shapiro Dynasty — Chapter XVII.)
G15.7. Sarah Gitel, married R. Simeon Alter Frankel-Teomim A.B.D.
Padgorze. (See Chapter IV — Branch H — G12.2/13.2.)
G15.8. Hinde, married R. Moses Joseph son of Jekutiel Judah Teitel-
baum of Ihel-Sighet. He was a brother of R. Hananiah YomTov
Lipa Teitelbaum. (See Chapter XVII.)
G15.9. R. Aryey Lieb Halberstam, Admur Dukla. He married his sec-
ond cousin, daughter of R. Avigdor Halberstam, Admur Dukla,
whom he succeeded. (See Chapter VII — Branch B.)

G16.1. R. Menachem Mendel Halberstam, died in 1926, Admur
Dukla and Fristik, married Feige Beila, daughter of R. Ezekiel
Shraga Halberstam of Sieniawa. (See Branch A.)

G17.1. R. Chunah, 1900-42, Admur Kolashitz, married the daughter
of R. Moses son of R. Baruch Halberstam of Gorlice (Branch

E). He and his family perished. He wrote *Bein HaShemashot* and *Divrei Chunah.*

G17.2. R. David Halberstam, Admur Chebin, married Malka, daughter of R. Eleazar Rosenfeld. He and his family of ten children perished.

G17.3. R. Ezekiel Shraga Halberstam, A.B.D. Dukla, published the *Divrei Yechezkiel* and perished with his family.

G17.4. Channah Miriam, married her first cousin, R. Ephraim David son of R. Jehiel Nathan Halberstam (Branch E). He was the Admur of Mishlenitz-Yashlisk.

G17.5. R. Avigdor Halberstam, married Channah Rachel, daughter of R. Naftali Rubin. (See Chapter XVI — Branch VII — page 605 — G18.11.)

G17.6. R. Haim Baruch Halberstam, succeeded his father as Admur Fristik.

G16.2. Wife of R. Jehiel Nathan son of R. Moses Halberstam of Bardiyov. (See Branch E.)

BRANCH D (SANZ)

G14.4. R. Aaron Halberstam, 1824-1906.

G15.1. R. Samuel Shmelke Halberstam of Dukla.

G15.2. R. Aryey Lieb Halberstam, A.B.D. of Gribov and New Sanz, born in 1852.

G16.1. R. Mordecai Zeev Halberstam of New Sanz-Gribov.

G17. R. Baruch Halberstam, Admur Gribov, married the daughter of R. Sinai son of R. Baruch Halberstam of Gorlice. (See Branch E.)

G18.1. Wife of R. Simha Felsenburg.

G18.2. R. Naftali Halberstam, Admur Gribov-New York.

G16.2. Wife of R. Abraham Haim son of R. Moses David Teitelbaum.

G16.3. Wife of R. Avigdor Zvi son of R. Jehiel Nathan Halberstam. (See Branch E.)

G16.4. R. Phineas Shemariah Halberstam, married Zipporah, daughter of R. Naftali son of R. Judah Horowitz of Malitsch (see Chapter XVI — Branch VII).

G15.3. R. Shalom Halberstam of Piekla, A.B.D. of Sanz, died in 1935,

married the daughter of R. Meir (of Dzikov) son of R. Eliezer
Horowitz (See Chapter XVI — Branch VII — page 590 — G16.8).

G16. Wife of R. Baruch Kaner. (See Branch A — G15.2/16.7/17.3.)

G15.4. Wife of R. Israel Jacob Jokel Teitelbaum of Walowa, his second
wife. (See Teitelbaum Dynasty — Chapter XVII.)

G15.5. Wife of R. Moses Halberstam of Bardiyov, her first cousin. (See
Branch E.)

BRANCH E (GORLICE)

G14.5. R. Baruch Halberstam, 1826-1906, Admur Gorlice, married the
daughter of R. Zalman Lieb Teitelbaum (author of the *Yitav Lev*).

G15.1. R. Moses Halberstam, 1850-1904, Admur Bardiyov, married his
first cousin, the daughter of R. Aaron Halberstam of New Sanz.
They had twenty-one children.

G16.1. R. Samuel Halberstam, married Pesel, daughter of R. Meir
Lipschutz of Janow. They perished in the Holocaust. (See
Chapter XVII — Teitelbaum Dynasty — G11.2/12.2/13.1.)

G17.1. R. Haim Berish (Dov) Halberstam, 1891-1971, married
Sarah, daughter of R. Joseph son of R. Zvi Elimelech Spira
of Birch. (See Spira Dynasty — Chapter XVII.)

G18.1. Chaya Frieda, married R. Ezekiel Shraga son of R. Issachar
Dov Halpern. (See Chapter XVI — Branch VII — Horowitz
Family — page 589 — G18.3.)

G18.2. R. Zvi Elimelech, perished.

G18.3. R. Israel Meir Halberstam, married, and has issue in Israel.

G17.2. R. Jekutiel Judah Halberstam.

G18. Rachel Feige, married R. Nahum Zvi son of R. Jacob Isaac
Horowitz-Pentzer. (See Chapter XVI — Branch VII.)

G16.2. R. Aryey Lieb Halberstam, born in 1870, became Admur Mu-
shina in 1904 and perished in the Holocaust. He married the
daughter of R. Samuel Rokeah of Sokol. (See Rokeah Dynasty
— Chapter XVII.)

G17. R. Menachem Mendel Halberstam, married in 1910 to Hena,
daughter of R. Isaac Isaiah Halberstam. (See Branch G.)

G18. R. Aaron Joshua, perished with family.

G16.3. R. Isaac Halberstam, married Channah, daughter of R. Joshua son of R. Zvi Elimelech Spira of Blozov. (See Spira Dynasty — Chapter XVII.)

G17.1. R. Haim Moses Halberstam married twice. His second wife was Mirl, daughter of R. Abraham David Rubin. (See Chapter XVI — Branch VII — page 608 — G18.1/19.1.) They had no issue.

G17.2. R. Baruch Halberstam, married Hena, daughter of R. David son of R. Joseph Spira of Dynow. (See Chapter XVII — Spira Dynasty.)

G18.1. David Halberstam, married with issue.

G18.2. Isaac (Isidore) Halberstam, married with issue, California.

G17.3. R. Joseph Halberstam, married Beila Friedman.

G18.1. Channah, married Ari Gertz.

G18.2. David, married and has issue.

G18.3. Leah.

G17.4. R. Tuvia Halberstam, married Channah Asenath, daughter of R. Zvi Elimelech Rokeah of Birch. (See Rokeah Dynasty — Chapter XVII.)

G18.1. Rivke, married Joshua Abramson.

G18.2. Joshua.

G18.3. Miriam.

G16.4. R. Jehiel Nathan Halberstam, 1865-1933, Rabbi of Old Sanz, and became Admur Bardiyov in 1904. Married the daughter of R. Aryey Lieb son of R. David Halberstam of Keshanov. (See Branch C.)

G17.1. R. Avigdor Zvi Halberstam, Rabbi of Old Sanz from 1904, born in 1884 and perished in the Holocaust.[7] He married the daughter of R. Aryey Lieb (of Gribov), son of R. Aaron Halberstam. (See Branch D.)

G17.2. R. Ephraim David Halberstam, married the daughter of R. Menachem Halberstam of Fristik. (See Branch C.)

G17.3. R. Jekutiel Judah Halberstam, Admur Gorlice.

G17.4. R. Jacob Halberstam, married the daughter of R. Tuvia of

Stryzow, son of R. Abraham Haim Horowitz of Shendeshov.

G17.5. R. Ezekiel Shraga Halberstam.

G17.6. R. Moses Aaron Halberstam, married the daughter of R. Menachem Mendel son of R. Abraham Shalom Halberstam of Stropkov. (See Branch A.)

G17.7. Wife of 1) R. Haim Joseph son of R. Jekutiel son of R. Samuel Halberstam (her first cousin), and 2) R. Dov Lifshitz (Israel).

G17.8. Wife of R. Chunah Zvi Rubin, Admur of Old Sanz (page 604).

G17.9. Miriam, married R. Moses Israel Holtzstock.

G16.5. R. Jekutiel Halberstam.

G16.6. R. Joshua Halberstam, born in 1896, perished with his family. He married the daughter of R. Judah Zvi son of R. Issachar Berish Eichenstein of Dolina, and succeeded him as Admur in 1911. (See Chapter XVII — Eichenstein Family Dynasty.)

G17. R. Haim Isaac Halberstam of Slotopeno.

   G18.1. Wife of R. Joel.

   G18.2. Wife of R. Zvi son of R. Abraham Halberstam of Ridnik. (See Branch E.)

G16.7. Wife of R. Chunah son of R. Mendel Halberstam of Kolashitz. (See Branch C.)

G16.8. Chaya, married R. Ephraim son of R. Aryey Lieb Halberstam of Gribov. (See Branch D.)

G16.9. Sarah, married R. Naftali Hirsch son of R. Moses Eliakim (Admur Dombrovo). (See Chapter XVII — Unger Dynasty.)

G15.2. R. Elisha Halberstam, 1860-1941, Admur Gorlice, succeeded his father in 1906. He married his first cousin, the daughter of R. Mordecai Dov Twersky of Hornistopol.

G16.1. R. Menachem Mendel Halberstam (died in the U.S.A. in 1964), Admur Gorlice-Ropshitz, married Channah Mindel, daughter of R. Menashe Mariles of Ropshitz. (See Chapter XVI — Branch VII.)

   G17. Leah, married R. Meshullam Zusia (Sigmund) son of R. Moses Twersky, Talnoyer Rebbe of Philadelphia. (See Chapter XV — Heschel Dynasty — G11.1/12.1/13.4/14.6.)

G16.2. R. Naftali Haim Halberstam, perished in 1943.

G17.1. Pesel, married R. Samuel son of R. Joshua Haim son of R. Menachem Teitelbaum (Admur Gorlice). (See Chapter XVII.)

G17.2. Raatza, married Tuvia son of R. Naftali son of R. Israel Jacob Teitelbaum of Walowa. Her father and his mother were first cousins. (See below — G15.6/16.1.)

G17.3. Wife of Abraham Ganzvi (Gansweig), (Queens, New York), and have issue.

G17.4. Judith, married Israel Lieber (Brooklyn), and have issue.

G17.5. Alter Halberstam, married and has issue.

G16.3. R. David Moses Halberstam, Admur Dynow-New York, married Beila, daughter of R. Joseph of Dynow son of R. Zvi Elimelech Spira of Birch. They had no issue.

G16.4. R. Aaron Halberstam (New York), married Toyba Rachel, daughter of R. Samuel Shmelke son of R. Phineas Frankel-Teomim, A.B.D. Klasni. (See Chapter IV — page 218 — G14.1.)

G17.1. Sarah, married Naftali son of R. Baruch son of R. Abraham Frankel. Their daughters, Slavie and Jochebed. (See Chapter XVI — Branch VII — page 598 — G19.)

G17.2. Samuel Shmelke Halberstam, born in 1934, married Rivke Haltzer (New York). Their children: Shlomo, Sarah, David and Leah.

G16.5. R. Mordecai Dov Halberstam.

G17. Jochebed Rebecca, married Michael son of R. Haim David Halberstam. (See Branch C.)

G16.6. R. Baruch Halberstam (Bnei Brak), married Gitel Pischan.

G16.7. R. Ezekiel Shraga Halberstam, Admur Gorlice-New York.

G17. Alta Zipporah, perished.

G16.8. Miriam Leah, married into the Safrin family, perished in 1943.

G16.9. Nechamah, married.

G16.10. Bracha, married R. Baruch Moses Parnes.

G17. Wife of R. Isaac Jacob Sekula (Brooklyn).

G16.11. Feige, married R. Isaac son of R. Elimelech (Tysmenitsa-Lancut) Spira-Kuten. (See Chapter XVII — Spira Dynasty — G3.2 /4.3/5.2.)

G15.3. R. Sinai Halberstam, 1870-1941,[8] Admur Zmigrad, married in 1917

to the daughter of R. Naftali of Malitsch, son of R. Judah Horowitz. (See Chapter XVI — Branch VII — page 594 — G17.2.)

G16.1. R. Israel Halberstam, Admur Zmigrad-New York (Brook-
        lyn), married and has issue.
G16.2. R. Jacob Halberstam, (died in 1967), Admur Chakov-New
        York-Jerusalem. He established the Yeshiva *Divrei Chayim* in
        Jerusalem. He married Eidel Dinah, daughter of R. Shalom
        (Admur Shatz-London) son of R. Moses son of R. Joel (Ad-
        mur Shatz) Moskovitz. R. Shalom was married to his first
        cousin, Shlamtze, daughter of R. Meir son of R. Joel Mos-
        kovitz. Shlamtze's brother was R. Jacob Moskovitz mentioned
        below (G16.11).

G17.1. R. Naftali Halberstam, succeeded his father as Admur
        Chakov in 1967, married and has three daughters.
G17.2. R. Moses Halberstam, married the daughter of R. Hillel
        Schlesinger (Jerusalem). They have seven children.
G17.3. Chaya, married R. Joshua son of R. Alter Jacob Israel Wag-
        schal. (See Chapter XVII — Shapiro Dynasty.)
G17.4. Feige, married R. Joshua Malavicki, and have six sons (Jeru-
        salem).
G17.5. Meir Halberstam of Netanya, married, and has six children.
G17.6. R. Naftali Halberstam, Admur Chakov-Sanz-Jerusalem, mar-
        ried, and has three daughters.
G17.7. Rechel, married R. Shalom Eizkowitz, and have fourteen
        children (New York).
G17.8. Miriam, married R. Moses Deutsch, and have eleven chil-
        dren (London).

G16.3. R. David Halberstam of Sosnowiec, married the daughter of
        R. Ezekiel Rabinowitz of Radomsk. (See Chapter IV.)
G16.4. Wife of R. Baruch son of R. Mordecai Zeev Halberstam of New
        Sanz-Gribov. (Chapter XIV — Branch D.)
G16.5. R. Aryey Lieb Halberstam, Admur Zmigrad-Bnei Brak.
G16.6. R. Baruch Halberstam, married the daughter of R. Berish
        Weidenfeld of Chebin, perished.
G16.7. R. Haim Halberstam A.B.D. Ospinzi, married the daughter of
        R. Joshua Phineas Bombach (A.B.D. Ospinzi), perished.
G16.8. R. Abraham Abbish Halberstam of Satmar, perished.
G16.9. R. Aaron Halberstam of Zmigrad, married the daughter of R.
        Haim Baruch Hager of Vizhniz, perished.

G16.10. R. Ezekiel Halberstam Admur Ridnik, perished.

G16.11. Wife of R. Jacob Moskovitz, Admur of Shatz-Haifa, son of R. Meir of Shatz. He died in 1957.

G15.4. R. Shalom Halberstam Admur Niska, perished with family.

G15.5. R. Zvi Hirsch Halberstam, Admur Ridnik, died in 1918, married the daughter of R. Israel Horowitz of Bernov. (See Chapter XVI — Branch VII.)

G16.1. Wife of R. Silverman.

   G17. R. Moses Silverman (Brooklyn).

G16.2. R. Jekutiel Judah Halberstam, born in 1904, the Admur Klausenburg. He married the daughter of R. Hain Zvi Teitelbaum of Sighet. She and their eleven children perished in the Holocaust, but he survived and re-established his court in Williamsburg (Brooklyn, N.Y.). In 1956 he founded Kiriat Sanz near Netanya, Israel, and three years later he, with some fifty of his followers, settled in Israel.

G16.3. R. Abraham Halberstam, Admur Ridnik.

   G17. R. Zvi Halberstam, succeeded his father as Admur Ridnik-Los Angeles. He married the daughter of R. Haim Isaac son of R. Joshua (of Dolina) Halberstam. (See Branch E.)

      G18. Hesia, married R. Haim Jacob son of R. Menashe Horowitz. (See Chapter XVI — Branch VII.)

G15.6. Jochebed Rebecca, the eldest daughter, married R. Aryey Lieb of Ridnik, son of R. Jeruchem Teitelbaum of Tarnow-Jerusalem. R. Lieb was Rabbi in Kreshov, and died in 1921 in Berlin.

G16.1. Pesel, married R. Naftali son of R. Menashe Teitelbaum (See Chapter XVII — Teitelbaum Dynasty).

G16.2. Benjamin, 1891-1961, adopted his mother's surname Halberstam, married Alta Dreizel, daughter of R. Jacob Epstein of Ozrov son of R. Judah Aryey. (See Chapter XVI — Branch VII — page 593 — G16.1/17.3.)

   G17. Jacob Lieb Halberstam (Ph.D. Psychology, New York), born in 1928, married Sarah Leah, daughter of Haim Joseph Pasternak. They have five children.

G16.3. Miriam, wife of R. Phineas Joseph Dachner (Shapiro). (See

Chapter XVII — Teitelbaum Dynasty — G11.2/12.1/13.2/14.2.)

G17.1. Frieda, married R. Moses Aryey Freund (Dayan in Jerusalem.

G17.2. R. Sinai Dachner, perished.

G17.3. R. Jeruchem Dachner, perished.

G17.4. R. Dov Ber Dachner (Belgium), no issue.

G17.5. R. Jacob Simeon Dachner (Brooklyn, N.Y.), married and has
issue, Israel, (married) and Jochebed, (married, Montreal).

G15.7. Wife of R. Moses Lieb son of R. Solomon Spira of Stryzow.

BRANCH F (ROTSFURT)

G14.6. R. Shalom Eliezer Halberstam, 1862-1944,[9] married Miriam Sarah,
daughter of R. Mordecai Dov Twersky of Hornistopol. (See Chapter VII — Branch B.)

G15.1. R. Haim Halberstam A.B.D. Satmar, married secondly the daughter of R. Baruch Rubin of Rizdoviz. (See Chapter XVI — Branch
VII.) Six children of the first marriage perished.

G15.2. R. Zusia Halberstam of Rotsfurt, perished in 1944, married 1) the
daughter of R. Naftali Teitelbaum of Nierbatur, and 2) the
daughter of R. Judah Ehrlich.

G16.1. Raatza, married R. Joel Beer (Sao Paulo), and have nine children.

G16.2. Sima, married R. Joseph Katz (New York), and have ten children.

G16.3. Jochebed Rebecca, married R. Meilich Reinman (New York).
Their daughter, Sarah Rachel, married Jacob Asher son of
Moses Moster. (See Chapter XVI — Branch VII.)

G15.3. Chaya Friedel, married R. Benzion Halberstam of Bobov as his
second wife. (See Branch B — G15.3/16.1.)

G15.4. Udel, married R. Isaac Zvi Rotenberg of Kasani. Their three
daughters perished.

G15.5. Rachel Sima, married R. Haim Zvi son of R. Hananiah Yom-Tov
Lipa Teitelbaum of Sighet. (See Chapter XVII.)

G15.6. Channah, married R. Menachem Mendel son of R. Shalom Rosenfeld (Admur Kamenka). (See Chapter XVI — Branch VII.) They
perished in 1944.

BRANCH G (CHECHOYV)

G14.7. R. Isaac Isaiah Halberstam, 1864-1943,[10] Admur Chechoyv-Cracow, married 1) Frieda, daughter of R. Jehiel of Krelevets, son of R. Zusia Heschel (see Heschel Dynasty — Chapter XV), and 2) Esther, daughter of R. Jacob Zvi (Admur Porisov), son of R. Joshua Asher Rabinowitz son of the *Holy Yud.* (See Chapter IV — page 175 — G9.2/10.4.) 3) Hinda Bindiger nee Parnes.

From his first marriage:

G15.1. R. Haim Halberstam, eldest child, 1882-1956, Admur Chechoyv-New York. He arrived in the U.S.A. about 1924. He married in 1899 to Mirl, daughter of R. Menashe Mariles, Rabbi of Ropshitz. (See Chapter XVI — Branch VII.)

G16.1. R. David Joshua Halberstam of Sosnowiec, 1900-1943, perished in Auschwitz. He married in 1922 to Feigel Jochebed, daughter of R. Isaac Rubin (adopted the surname of Glikman). R. David Joshua Halberstam was the A.B.D. of Old Sosnowiec. She also perished with her children, Jehiel (1930-43) and Shifra Channah Henia (1934-43). Another child, Asher, died in infancy. One son survived the Holocaust.

G17. Menachem Mendel Halberstam, born in Sosnowiec in 1926, married in 1950 to Mina (Mindel), daughter of R. Zvi Elimelech Rokeah (Admur Birch-New York — See Rokeah Dynasty — Chapter XVII.) Their children: David (born in 1951); Feigel Jochebed (Fay) (born in 1954); and Bracha (born in 1964).

G16.2. R. Simeon Halberstam, married Channah Asenath, daughter of R. Shalom son of R. Issachar Dov son of R. Moses Rokeah (of Karov). They perished with their children, Leah, Deborah and Menashe. (See Chapter XVII — Rokeah Dynasty.)

G16.3. Five others, died in infancy.

G15.2. Rechel Deborah (of Kiev), married R. Haim Isaac (1886-1943) son of R. Abraham Joshua Heschel Twersky (of Loyev). (See Chapter XV — Heschel Dynasty — G10.1/11.4/12/13.2/14.1/15.1 /16.1.) R. Haim Isaac died in a Soviet prison in the course of the Stalinist persecutions of Jewish clergymen.

G15.3. Hena, married in 1910 to R. Menachem Mendel Halberstam. (See Branch E — G15.1/16.2/17.)

G15.4. R. Jacob Zvi Halberstam, born about 1896/7 in Cracow, and became A.B.D. of Sucha (near Cracow) in 1923. He married in
1914 to Chaya Sarah, daughter of R. Eleazar son of R. Joshua
Rosenfeld. They perished with his father in 1943. (See Branch
H.) The children who perished were Haim (1920-43), Malka
(1924-43), Rivke Hena (1926-43) and Joshua Shalom (1932-43).

G16.1. Deborah, born in 1923, came to the U.S.A. in 1946 and married in 1953 to Zvi Elimelech (Meilich) son of R. Judah Joshua
son of R. Mordecai Spira. (See Chapter XVII — Spira Dynasty.)

G16.2. Sima, born in 1931, came to the U.S.A. in 1946 and married in
1954 to Jacob Preisser. Their children: Jonathan Zvi, Uriel and
Chaya Malka.

G16.3. Baruch Halberstam, born in 1934 (twin). Perished in 1943.

G16.4. Asher Halberstam, born in 1934 (twin), married in 1967 to
Renee Engel (London). Their children: Jacob Zvi, Moses
Baruch, Haim Isaac and Menachem.

G16.5. Ezekiel David Halberstam, born in 1935.

G15.5. R. Ezekiel Shraga Halberstam of Cracow, born in 1905. He
married in 1923 to Rebecca Beila, daughter of R. Benzion Halberstam of Bobov. (See Branch B.) He perished in the Holocaust.

G16.1. Solomon, died in infancy.

G16.2. Esther, married in 1951 to Aaron Nussbaum (Toronto). Their
children, Reizel, Sarah and Ezekiel.

BRANCH H (ROSENFELD FAMILY)

The main Rosenfeld Lineage stems from R. Shalom Rosenfeld (died
in 1851), son of R. Jacob Joseph (of Rava). He was a pupil of the Belzer
Rebbe, R. Shalom Rokeah, and a close friend of the Sanzer Rebbe, R. Haim
Halberstam. (Their children later married.) He was the Rabbi of Yaritchov
and Kamenka and died young. His son was R. Joshua Rosenfeld (died in
1896) who married the daughter of R. Zvi Hirsch of Driscopolia (a brother-
in-law of R. Shalom of Belz). The genealogy of his son, R. Shalom Rosenfeld is given in Chapter XVI — Branch VII by virtue of his marriage to the
daughter of R. Abraham Horowitz of Shendeshov, and the genealogy of his
other son, R. Eleazar Rosenfeld is given here.

G14.13. Friedel, married about 1880 to R. Eleazar Halevi Rosenfeld[11] of Ospinzi (later called Auschwitz) where he became the Rabbi. He was born about 1861, and his wife in 1863. He perished in the Holocaust in Sosnowiec. He was the Admur of Ospinzi (also Oswiecim) from 1907, and lived in Israel from 1936-9. She died during World War I.

G15.1. R. Haim (Alexander) Rosenfeld, born about 1882, married Chaya, daughter of R. Isaac Tuvia Rubin, his first cousin (see below). He and his family perished in the Holocaust. He succeeded his father as Admur Ospinzi.

G16.1. R. Naftali Hirsch Rosenfeld, Admur Newmarket, married Hannah, daughter of R. Haim Jacob son of R. Shalom Rosenfeld. Their fathers were first cousins. (See Rosenfeld Family in Chapter XVI — Branch VII.) They and their children perished.

G16.2. Sheindel, married R. Abraham Joshua son of R. Isaac Rosenfeld. Their fathers were first cousins. (See Chapter XVI — Branch VII.) They had no issue.

G16.3. Rebecca Hena, married R. Abraham Joshua son of R. Benzion Ornstein.

G16.4. Friedel. G16.5. Miriam.

G15.2. Sheindel, married R. Aryey Lieb son of R. Haim Baruch Rosenfeld. They were first cousins. He was Admur Zasla.

G16.1. Moses Ezekiel. G16.2. Haim Baruch.

G16.3. Rebecca, married R. Haim son of R. Menachem Mendel Halberstam. (See Branch A — G15.5/16.2/17.2.)

G15.3. R. Shalom Rosenfeld, married his first cousin Hannah Golda, daughter of R. Shalom son of R. Joshua Rosenfeld of Kamenka. (See Chapter XVI.)

G16.1. Sheindel, married R. Naftali Freund.

G16.2. Malka. G16.3. Haim.

G16.4. Frieda, married R. Joseph David Rubin, Admur Sassov-New York. (See Chapter XVI — Branch VII — page 606 — G17.1/ 18.1. His second wife.)

G15.4. Hannah Golda, married R. Asher son of R. Hanina Horowitz of Ulanov. (See Chapter XVI — Branch VII — page 596 — G16.3.)

G15.5. Miriam Rechel, married her first cousin, R. Jonah, son of R. Menachem Mendel son of R. Eleazar Baron. She died young and he perished in the Holocaust.

G16.1. Haim, married and perished.

G16.2. Sheindel Mirl, married R. Samuel son of R. Haim Baruch of Vizhniz, son of R. Naftali Rubin. (See Chapter XVI — Branch VII — page 604 — G18.2/19.2.) Their children perished.

G16.3. R. Abraham Joshua Heschel Baron (Jerusalem), married Rebecca Ehrlich. They have eleven children, some of whom are married and have issue.

G15.6. R. Naftali Zvi Samuel Rosenfeld, married Jochebed, daughter R. Samuel Shmelke Azriel Frankel-Teomim of Klasni. He was Rabbi in Ospinzi. (See Chapter IV — Branch H.)

G16. Friedel, married Naftali Wietschner (New York) and have issue.

G15.7. Chaya Sarah, married R. Jacob Zvi son of R. Isaac Isaiah Halberstam. (See Branch G.)

G15.8. Malka Deborah, married R. David son of R. Menachem Mendel Halberstam. (See Branch C — G15.9/16.1.)

CHAPTER XV

BRANCH A

RUZHIN CHASSIDIC DYNASTY (FRIEDMAN FAMILY)

Including

VIZHNIZ DYNASTY (HAGER FAMILY) AND
VASLUI DYNASTY (HEILPRIN FAMILY)

ANCESTRY

G3.3. Saul Wahl.

G4.1. Meir Wahl Katzenellenbogen.

G5.2. R. Moses of Chelm.

G6.6. R. Saul of Pinczow.

G7.5. R. Ephraim Zalman Katzenellenbogen.

G8. Matil, second wife of R. Meir, A.B.D. Tiktin, son of R. Samuel Horowitz. (See Horowitz Family Pedigree — Chapter XVI — G9.)

G9. R. Dovberish Horowitz.

G10. R. Meshullam Feiwel Horowitz of Kremnitz,[1] author of *Mishnat Chachamim,* published in Ostrow, 1796. Approbations to his book were written by prominent Rabbis of his generation including R. Ezekiel Landau and R. Saul of Amsterdam.

G11. Henia, married R. Abraham the "Angel" (*HaMalach*), 1739-1776, son of R. Dovber the Maggid of Meseritz (died 1772), the disciple and successor to the great Rabbi Israel son of Eliezer (known as the *Baal Shem Tov* — the founder of the Chassidic movement).

It is related that once a fire broke out in the house of the young Dovber's father. On hearing his mother cry, the child asked his mother why she grieved so over the loss of their home. She replied it was not the house but their family tree record that was consumed in the flames. "I shall make a new family tree starting with me," came the child's reply. And indeed the family down until today is an unbroken chain of the most respected Rabbis throughout their generations.

On his wedding night, it is said, R. Abraham, on entering the wedding room was so awe-inspiring and his voice so fearful, that his wife fainted and remained so until morning. The following night she was filled with courage and endured his magnificence. In the course of time the couple had two sons, after which they lived apart again. They were married twelve years. After his death, his widow once dreamed she ascended to Heaven where she saw the face of her deceased husband. "O friends, know that my wife holds grievance against me for we lived apart on earth, and I ask forgiveness," he said. His widow cried out "Thou art forgiven," and she awoke with a consoled heart. In another dream, the deceased Sage appeared to R. Nahum Twersky of Chernobyl who had offered his hand in marriage to his widow. So she did not remarry but lived in poverty and went to settle in Israel where no one knows where she lies buried to this day.

G12.1. R. Israel Haim of Lodmir, married twice. His first wife was the daughter of R. Solomon of Karlin and they had one child. His second marriage was to the daughter of R. Gedaliah Rabinowitz of Linitz. (See below.)

G13. Deborah, married R. Jehiel Michael of Zovhil (1786-1856), son of R. Moses of Zovhil (died 1831), son of R. Jehiel Michael of Zlatchov.

G14.1. R. Mordecai Goldman.

G15.1. Solomon Goldman of Zovhil-Jerusalem.
G15.2. Wife of R. Samuel Brejan.

G14.2. R. Jehiel Michael of Zovhil.

G15.1. Wife of R. Phineas Rokeah of Noveria. (See Chapter XVII.)
G15.2. Wife of R. Jacob Israel Karff.

G12.2. R. Shalom Schakna, 1766-1803, married Chavah, daughter of R. Abraham, son of R. Zvi Hirsch of Berdichev. He lived in Probisht. Both his parents died when he was still young, and he grew up in the house of R. Nahum Twersky of Chernobyl.

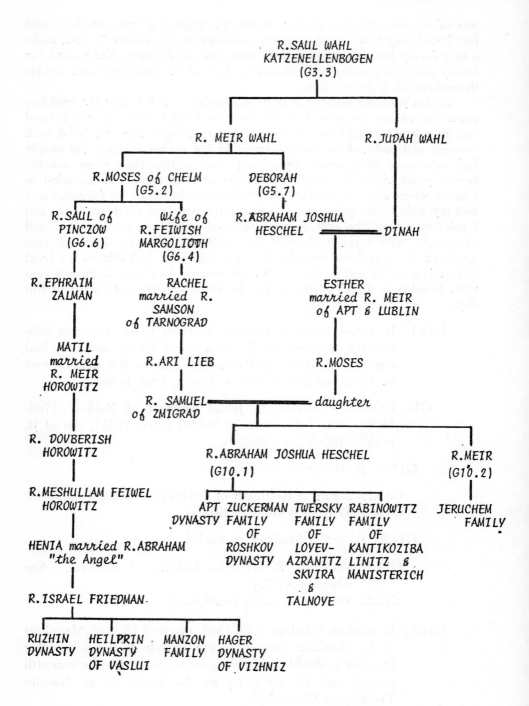

R.SAUL WAHL
KATZENELLENBOGEN
(G3.3)

R. MEIR WAHL   R.JUDAH WAHL

R.MOSES of CHELM   DEBORAH
(G5.2)   (G5.7)

R.SAUL of   Wife of   R.ABRAHAM JOSHUA
PINCZOW   R.FEIWISH   HESCHEL ═══════════ DINAH
(G6.6)   MARGOLIOTH
                  (G6.4)

R.EPHRAIM   RACHEL   ESTHER
ZALMAN   married R.   married R. MEIR
                 SAMSON   of APT & LUBLIN
                 of TARNOGRAD

MATIL
married   R.ARI LIEB   R.MOSES
R. MEIR
HOROWITZ

                 R. SAMUEL ═══════════ daughter
                 of ZMIGRAD

R. DOVBERISH
HOROWITZ
                      R.ABRAHAM JOSHUA HESCHEL   R.MEIR
                      (G10.1)   (G10.2)

R.MESHULLAM FEIWEL
HOROWITZ   APT   ZUCKERMAN TWERSKY   RABINOWITZ   JERUCHEM
                     DYNASTY FAMILY   FAMILY   FAMILY   FAMILY
                                OF   OF   OF
HENIA married R.ABRAHAM   ROSHKOV   LOYEV-   KANTIKOZIBA
    "the Angel"   DYNASTY   AZRANITZ LINITZ &
                                        SKVIRA   MANISTERICH
                                          &
R.ISRAEL FRIEDMAN   TALNOVE

RUZHIN   HEILPRIN   MANZON   HAGER
DYNASTY   DYNASTY   FAMILY   DYNASTY
            OF VASLUI   OF VIZHNIZ

In his youth he was fond of showing off and instead of devoting time
to his studies, would wander off into the woods. Nevertheless he became
a leading Rabbi among the Chassidim of his generation. Much as in his
youth his stepfather, Rabbi Nahum, had found him vain, so now he ad-
monished him against living in such luxury, as if he were the aristocratic
Prince of the Exile. He responded with a parable: "Once a hen hatched
some goose eggs which had been placed in her nest. Thus the chicks believed they were hens, but when they came to a pond, they immediately
jumped into the water, causing much alarm to their hen-mother. They reassured her of their ability to swim without any difficulty."

G13.1. R. Abraham, 1787-1813.

G13.2. R. Dovber, died young, was engaged to the daughter of
         R. Levi Isaac of Berdichev (Chapter IV).

G13.3. R. Israel Friedman,[2] Founder and Head of the Ruzhiner
         Chassidic Dynasty, 1797-1850. He was considered to
         have had outstanding qualities as a child, and when his
         father died leaving him an orphan at six years of age,
         he went to live with his brother, R. Abraham.

         He married when he was thirteen to Sarah (died in
         1849), daughter of R. Moses Levi Ephrati (Head of the
         Yeshiva of Berdichev), son of R. Eliezer (Head of the
         Yeshiva of Karlin). On the death of his brother, he be-
         came the Chassidic leader and rapidly became a great
         leader, establishing a splendid "court" and lived in
         great luxury and splendor, having moved from Probisht
         to Ruzhin. This was in 1813. When he travelled it was
         in a carriage with silver fittings, drawn by four horses
         and accompanied by an entourage of attendants. The
         downtrodden Russian Jews flocked to him as a new and
         great leader, soon to be followed by non-Jews and in-
         tellectuals, officials and noblemen, who had heard of his
         reputation. The authorities however became suspicious
         of this new "King of Jews" which, in 1838, led to the
         accusation of his implementing the death of two Jew-
         ish informers, and he was put into a Kiev prison for
         twenty-two months, following which the charges were
         dropped. However, his "Royal" aspirations were still
         felt to be threatening, and because of constant police
         surveillance, he left for Kishinev, Bessarabia where he
         was no better off. Because his followers heard that he
         was to be banished to Siberia, they smuggled him into

Rumania where he spent a short while in Jassy, and then
into Bukovina in Austro-Hungary where he established
his court again in Sadagora in 1841, and was joined by
his family who received permission to leave Russia. The
court was founded on an estate called Zolotoi-Potok
which had been purchased for him by his followers. He
also became a Turkish citizen and the family held, and
still holds the title of "citizen of Jerusalem" (Jerusalem
then being under Turkish rule). Pilgrimages were made
to visit him from all over Russia and Poland, and he had
a profound influence upon Rumanian Chassidism. His
court or palace was constantly filled with the sound of
music and dancing. He was appointed the head of the
Volhynia *Kollel* in Israel in 1825 on the death of R.
Heschel of Apt, and helped those Jews in Israel finan-
cially, including the establishment of the *Tiferet Yisrael*
Synagogue (also called the Nissan Bak Synagogue,
which was destroyed in 1948, and is now being rebuilt)
in 1872.

Although he left no written works; his teachings
were published in *Irin Kadishin, Beit Yisrael, Tiferet
Yisrael, Kenesset Yisrael, Pe'er Yisrael,* and others. He
remarried the widow of R. Zvi of Rymanov.

G14.1. R. Shalom Joseph Friedman, 1813-51, made Sadagora
his Chassidic Center, and died in Leipzig. He married Blume Reizel, daughter of R. Dan Yungerlieb of
Radwill. He was the first child and had four children.

G15.1. R. Isaac Friedman, 1834-96, founder of the Buhusi
Dynasty, and the main propagator of Rumanian
Chassidism. He married Sheina Rachel, daughter of
R. David Hager of Zablodov, son of R. Menachem
Mendel of Kossov.

G16.1. R. Israel Shalom Joseph Friedman, 1863-1923,
Admur Buhusi, succeeding his father. He married the daughter of R. Moses Abraham Zuckerman of Roshkov.

G17.1. Wife of R. David of Jassy, son of R. Mordecai
Zusia Twersky. He died in 1918.

G17.2. Wife of R. Menachem Mendel Friedman of Buhusi, her cousin.

G16.2. R. David Friedman of Buhusi, died in 1889. He married the daughter of R. Abraham Joshua Heschel Heschel of Medzibeh.

G17.1. R. Menachem Mendel Friedman of Buhusi, died in 1943, married his first cousin (G16.1/ 17.2 above).

G18. Jochebed Feige, married her first cousin R. Isaac, son of R. Shalom Joseph Friedman of Buhusi.

G17.2. R. Shalom Joseph Friedman of Spikov, 1878-1920, married the daughter of R. Mordecai of Spikov, son of Menachem Twersky (page 547).

G18.1. R. David Friedman of Ploesti, 1898-1941, married the daughter of R. Aaron Twersky of Azranitz. They perished in the Holocaust.

G18.2. R. Isaac, Admur Buhusi, born in 1903. He was an active Zionist and did much to help Rumanian Jewry in the Holocaust period. He settled in Israel in 1950, and resides in Tel Aviv. He married his cousin Jochebed Feige, daughter of R. Menachem Mendel Friedman.

G19. Shoshana, married Dr. Israel Friedman, Ph.D. (Israel), son of R. Jacob of Pascani. (See below G16.4/17.1.)

G16.3. R. Abraham Joshua Heschel Friedman, Admur Adjud, died in 1940. He married 1) daughter of R. Nahum Friedman of Stefanesti, (they were second cousins — see below G14.3), and 2) the daughter of R. Zalman Horstein.

G17. R. Menachem Nahum Friedman, 1873-1933, Admur Itcani. He married Miriam, daughter of R. Israel, son of R. David Moses Friedman of Chartkov. (See below G14.5.) He was the author of works on philosophy, *Ha-emet veHasheker, Ha-Chalom vePetirono* and *Omer Man.*

G16.4. R. Moses Judah Lieb Friedman, Admur Pascani, died in 1947. He married his first cousin, daughter of R. Nahum Dov Friedman of Sadagora.

G17.1. R. Jacob David Friedman, 1892-1955, Admur Pascani, died in Jaffa. He married the daughter of R. Phineas (of Zinkov), son of R. Haim Menachem Heschel of Apt, his first cousin.

G18. Dr. Israel Friedman, Ph.D., married his cousin Shoshana above.

G17.2. R. Isaac Friedman.

G18. Israel, married Zipporah, daughter of R. Haim Meir Hager. (See Hager Dynasty this chapter.)

G17.3. R. Israel Friedman, married the daughter of R. Haim Dov Heilprin. (See G14.7/15.1/16.)

G18.1. Wife of Milgrom (Tel Aviv).

G19. Michael Milgrom (Antwerp) and Haim Dov.

G18.2. Wife of Engelsberg (Antwerp).
G18.3. Wife of Bornstein (Tel Aviv).

G17.4. Wife of R. Aviezer Zelig Shapiro, her first cousin (see below G16.10).

G16.5. R. Jacob Friedman, 1878-1957, married the daughter of R. Israel, son of R. Mordecai Shraga Friedman of Husyatin. He succeeded his father-in-law as Admur of Husyatin in 1949. The whole family settled in Israel in 1937. He wrote *Ohelei Yaakov.*

G17.1. R. Isaac Friedman, 1900-1968, Admur Husyatin, and was buried in Tiberias.
G17.2. Nechama Gitel Miriam, married R. Jacob Joshua Heschel Balminger.

G18. Mordecai Shraga Balminger, married Raya, daughter of R. Shalom Heschel, son of R. Isaac Meir Heschel of Kopzynce. They have issue.

G16.6. Esther, married R. Israel, son of R. Abraham Jacob Friedman of Sadagora.

G16.7. Wife of 1) R. Haim Meir Jehiel, son of R. Elimelech Shapiro of Grodzisk (Shapiro Chassidic Dynasty), and 2) R. Shalom, son of R. David Heilprin of Vaslui, her second cousin. (See below G14.7.)

G16.8. Jochebed, no issue.

G16.9. Pesia Leah, married R. Haim Hager. (See below — G14.9/15.1/16.2.)

G16.10. Sheba, married R. Haim Meir Jehiel Shapiro (Shapiro Chassidic Dynasty).

G16.11. Chavah, married R. Mordecai Zusia of Hozales, son of R. Menachem Nahum Twersky of Trisk.

G16.12. Malka, married R. Phineas, son of R. Haim Menachem Heschel of Zinkov.

G16.13. Bracha, married R. Aaron, son of R. David Twersky of Skvira.

G16.14. Chaya Shifra, married R. David Aaron of Zorek, son of R. Jacob Lieb Twersky of Trisk. They perished in the Holocaust.

G17. Wife of R. Abraham Joshua Heschel Twersky of Makhnovka. (See Skvira Dynasty at the end of Chapter XV.)

G15.2. R. Nahum Dovber Friedman of Sadagora, 1843-83, buried in Vienna, married his first cousin Pearl, daughter of R. Abraham Jacob Friedman of Sadagora.

G15.3. Rachel Leah, married her uncle R. David Moses Friedman.

G15.4. Bathsheba, married her first cousin, R. Nahum Mordecai Friedman of Chartkov.

G16.1. R. Shalom Joseph Friedman of Melnitz, married 1) his first cousin, Chavah, daughter of R. Israel Friedman of Sadagora and 2) daughter of R. Joseph of Zlatopoli, son of R. David Twersky.

G17. R. Moses Aaron Friedman, married the daughter of R. Samuel Phineas Shapiro.

G16.2. Gitel, married R. Moses Judah Lieb Friedman of Pascani, her first cousin.

G14.2. R. Abraham Jacob Friedman, 1819-1883, succeeded his father as Admur of Sadagora in 1850. He married Miriam, daughter of R. Aaron Perlow, Admur of Karlin. (See Perlow Chassidic Dynasty.) In 1856 he was arrested and spent fifteen months in jail. They had seven children who were progenitors of Chassidic families at Sadagora, Chernovitz (Chernovtsy), Rymanov and Boyan (which also spread to Leipzig and Lvov). The dynasty ended in 1971 in New York.

G15.1. R. Solomon Friedman of Sadagora, 1843-81, married 1) daughter of R. Zvi of Rymanov and 2) Feigle, daughter of R. David Heilprin, his first cousin, and had issue.

G16.1. Chaya Leah, married R. Nahum Mordecai, son of R. Israel Moses Friedman of Chartkov (G14.5 /15.2/16.2 below).

G16.2. Miriam, married her first cousin, R. Israel Friedman of Leipzig-Boyan.

G15.2. R. Isaac Friedman, 1849-1917, Admur of Boyan, founder of the Boyaner Dynasty in Bukovina. He married Malka, daughter of R. Johanan of Rotmistrovke, son of R. Mordecai Twersky of Chernobyl. He died in Vienna.

G16.1. R. Menachem Nahum Friedman, 1869-1936, Admur of Chernovitz. He married his second cousin, the daughter of R. Mordecai Shraga Friedman of Husyatin. He was the author of *Devarim Nichumim* and *Zeh Yenachamenu*.

G17.1. R. Aaron Friedman of Boyan-Chernovitz, died in 1941. He married the daughter of R. Haim Hager of Ottinya. (See below G14.9/15.1/ 16.2.)

G17.2. R. Mordecai Shraga Friedman of Boyan-Chernovitz, died in 1942. He married the daughter of Israel, son of R. Baruch Hager. (See below G14.9/15.1/16.1/17.11.)

G17.3. Wife of R. Moses of Boyan-Cracow, son of R. Shalom Joseph Friedman. (See below G14.6/15.2.)

G16.2. R. Israel Friedman of Leipzig, 1879-1951, buried in Safed. He settled in Israel in 1939, and lived in Tel Aviv. He married his first cousin, daughter of R. Solomon Friedman of Sadagora.

G17.1. Wife of R. Isaiah Shapiro. (See Shapiro Dynasty.)

G17.2. Wife of R. Mordecai Shraga Heschel. (See Heschel Dynasty.)

G16.3. R. Abraham Jacob Friedman of Lvov, 1886-1942. He married the daughter of R. Mordecai of Leovo. They perished in the Holocaust.

G16.4. R. Mordecai Solomon Friedman, 1891-1971, Admur and last of the Boyan Dynasty, died in New York, and was buried in Jerusalem. He married Chava, daughter of R. Israel Shalom Heschel of Apt. She died some three months before him. They came to the U.S.A. via Vienna in 1926. He was also the founder of the *Ruzhiner* Yeshiva in Jerusalem and Bnei Brak.

G17.1. Israel Shalom Joseph Friedman, born in 1912, married the daughter of Joseph Haim Luckstein. They live in New York. He works in the Social Services, Department of Welfare.

G17.2. Isaac Friedman, real estate agent in New York, married Judith Gottesman. Their daughters, Emily, Barbara and Paula.

G17.3. Malka (Mimi), married Menachem, son of Joseph Brayer. He is a psychologist at Yeshiva University. Their children David, Nechama and Israel Abraham.

G16.5. Miriam, married R. Dovber, son of Israel Friedman of Chartkov. Their fathers were first cousins.

G15.3. R. Israel Friedman, 1852-1906, Admur of Sadagora, succeeding his father in 1883. He married 1) in 1868 to Esther, daughter of R. Isaac Friedman of

Buhusi from whom there were three sons and 2)
Bathsheba, daughter of R. Shalom Joseph Friedman,
his first cousin, having further issue.

G16.1. Moses, died aged eleven years.

G16.2. R. Aaron Friedman, 1876-1912, Admur Sadagora, succeeding his father in 1906. He married
in 1896 to Sarah Sheindel, daughter of R. Shalom Joseph, son of R. Mordecai Shraga Friedman
of Husyatin. He was the author of *Kedushat
Aharon*.

G17.1. R. Mordecai Shalom Joseph Friedman, Admur
Sadagora, born in 1897, and succeeded his fa-
ther at Sadagora, and later at Przemysl in
1912. He married Mirl Mira, daughter of R.
Israel Shalom Joseph, son of R. Abraham
Joshua Heschel Heschel of Apt. They settled
in Tel Aviv in 1939. He was the author of
Kenesset Mordecai.

G18.1. R. Abraham Jacob Friedman, born in 1929,
leader of the Sadagora Chassidim in New
York until 1973, when he settled in Israel.
He married in 1953 to Ciporah, daughter of
R. Joseph Aryey, son of R. Ephraim Fischel
Feldman (descendants of the *Tosfot Yom-
Tov*, R. Lipman Heller).

G19.1. Chava Yuta Hadassah, born in 1954, married Samuel Zanwill Scharf (descendant
of the *Tosfot YomTov*). They have issue.

G19.2. Israel Moshe, born in 1956.

G19.3. Elisheba, born in 1957.

G18.2. Israel Friedman, born in 1921, married in
1949, and has issue, Daniel, Joel and Abigail.

G16.3. R. Shalom Joseph Friedman of Chernovitz, 1879-
1935. He married Sheindel, the daughter of R.
Baruch, son of R. Menachem Mendel Hager (see
below G14.9).

G17. Dr. Haim Baruch Friedman, Ph.D., married, and
lives in Haifa. They have issue.

G16.4. R. Abraham Jacob Friedman of Sadagora, 1884-1961. He lived in Vienna, and settled in Israel in 1939 (Tel Aviv). He married Blume Reizel, daughter of R. Isaac Meir, son of R. Abraham Joshua Heschel Heschel of Apt. He was a leader of the Agudat Israel Movement.

G17. Sarah, married R. Israel Shalom Joseph, son of R. Abraham Joshua Heschel Heschel of the Apt Family. (See Heschel Dynasty — G11.1/12.1/13.3.)

G16.5. R. Isaac Friedman of Rymanov, 1886-1928, died in New York. He married Sarah Deborah, daughter of R. Asher Isaiah of Rymanov, son of R. Meir Horowitz of Dzikov. (See Chapter XVI — Branch VII.)

G17.1. Israel Friedman, died in New York in 1967, married Channah, daughter of Tuvia Fleishman.

G18.1. Dinah, married R. Mendel Hirsch, and have issue, Zahava, Israel, Atara and Haim Jacob.

G18.2. Irving (Isaac) Friedman, married Shirley Haas, and lives in Brooklyn. Their son Israel. He is National Public Relations Director of the United Jewish Appeal.

G17.2. Shprintze, married Joseph hakohen Goldhirsch, New York. They have no issue.

G16.6. R. Solomon Haim Friedman of Sadagora, born in 1887, married the daughter of R. Samuel Hornstein (a descendant of R. Naftali Katz, the *Smichut Chachamim*). They settled in Tel Aviv, and had issue — two daughters with families.

G16.7. R. Judah Zvi Friedman of Sadagora, 1887-1951, married the daughter of R. Haim Aaron, son of R. Israel Friedman of Chartkov.

G16.8. Zipporah, married R. Isaac Mordecai, son of R. Aviezer Zelig Shapiro. (See Shapiro Dynasty.)

G16.9. Chavah, married R. Shalom Joseph, son of R. Nahum Dov Friedman of Sadagora.

G16.10. Rachel, married R. Solomon, son of R. Nahum Mordecai Friedman of Chartkov.

G15.4. Ruchama, married her first cousin, R. Israel Friedman.

G14.3. R. Menachem Nahum Friedman, 1823-68, Admur Stefanesti, Rumania.

G15.1. R. Abraham Mattithiah Friedman, 1848-1933, succeeded his father as Admur, and married the daughter of R. Isaac Reich (son-in-law of R. Asher Isaiah Rubin, Admur Ropshitz. (See Chapter XVI — Branch VII.) They had no issue.

G15.2. Wife of R. Abraham Joshua Heschel Friedman, Admur Adjud. (See above G14.1/15.1/16.3.)

G14.4. R. Dov Friedman of Leovo, 1827-75. He married the daughter of R. Mordecai Twersky of Chernobyl, but had no issue. He was the most controversial member of the family, also described as a tragic figure. At first Admur of Husi (Rumania), Seuleni (Ukraine) and finally Leovo (Rumania). In 1869 he turned against Chassidism and published an attack against them which led to a conflict and battle of literature between the two great Chassidic families of Ruzhin and Sanz (Friedman and Halberstam respectively). He left home, and lived with one of the *Maskilim* in Chernovitz. This became known as the Sanz-Sadagora conflict, the Ruzhiners being accused of living in royal and pompous luxury, with excommunications and recriminations on both sides. Dov of Leovo later repented of his attack, but the conflict only ended with the death of R. Haim Halberstam of Sanz in 1876.

G14.5. R. David Moses Friedman, 1828-1904, Admur of Chartkov, and founder of the Chartkover Dynasty. His first center was in Potek, and in 1859 he moved to Chartkov. He was the author of *Divrei David*. He married 1) Feige (died in 1880), daughter of R. Aaron Twersky of Chernobyl and 2) his niece Rachel Leah, daughter of R. Shalom Joseph Friedman of

Sadagora, his eldest brother. He was considered one of the greatest *Zaddikim* of his generation.

G15.1. R. Nahum Mordecai Friedman of Chartkov, died in 1870, married his first cousin Bathsheba, daughter of R. Shalom Joseph Friedman of Sadagora.

G16. Wife of R. Haim Aaron Friedman, her first cousin.

G15.2. R. Israel Friedman, 1854-1934, succeeded his father as Admur Chartkov in 1904. He was the author of *Ateret Yisrael* and *Tiferet Yisrael*. He married his first cousin Ruchama, daughter of R. Abraham Jacob Friedman of Sadagora. After World War I he settled in Vienna, where he later died. He was an outstanding leader of the Agudat Israel Movement.

G16.1. R. Haim Aaron Friedman of Chartkov, 1878-1926, buried in Vienna. He married his first cousin, daughter of R. Nahum Mordecai, Admur Chartkov.

G17. Wife of R. Judah Zvi, son of R. Israel Friedman of Sadagora.

G16.2. R. Nahum Mordecai Friedman, 1874-1946, succeeded his father as Admur Chartkov in 1934. He settled in Israel in 1939 (Tel Aviv), became a member of the *Mo'etzet Gedolei HaTorah* of the Agudat Israel and was the author of *Doresh Tov*. He was buried in Jerusalem on the Mt. of Olives. He married Chaya Leah, daughter of R. Solomon Friedman of Sadagora.

G17.1. R. Solomon Friedman, 1894-1959, succeeded his father as Admur Chartkov in 1946, buried in Nachalat Yaakov. He married Rachel, daughter of R. Israel Friedman of Sadagora, and was the author of *Divrei Shlomo*.

G18. Zipporah, married Nehorai, and have a daughter Ruth.

G17.2. Sarah, married R. Jacob, son of R. Moses Heschel of Novominsk. (See Heschel Dynasty.)

G17.3. Gitel, married Moses Morgenstern (maternal grandson of R. Joseph Engel of Vienna).

G16.3. R. Dovber Friedman, died in Vienna in 1936, married Miriam, daughter of R. Isaac Friedman of Boyan.

G17.1. David Moses Friedman of London, married and has issue.
G17.2. Channah Feige.

G16.4. Miriam, married R. Manachem Nahum of Itcani, son of R. Abraham Joshua Heschel Friedman of Adjud.
G16.5. Chavah (died in 1943), married R. Zvi Aryey (of Zlatopoli-Chartkov), son of R. Mordecai Joseph Twersky, 1890-1968. They settled in Tel Aviv in 1939. He was the author of *HaTov veHatechlet*.

G17. Malka, married Phineas Biberfeld, and had a son, Michael.

G14.6. R. Mordecai Shraga Friedman, 1834-1894, Admur of Husyatin and founder of the Husyatin Dynasty. He married his first cousin, daughter of R. David Zvi Kabliski (son-in-law of R. Moses halevi Ephrati).

G15.1. R. Israel Friedman, 1858-1949, succeeded his father as Admur Husyatin in 1894. He was one of the first members of the *Chovevei Zion* Movement. After World War I he moved to Vienna and Lvov, and in 1937 settled in Israel, and was buried in Tiberias. He married Gitel, daughter of R. Aviezer Zelig Shapiro. (See Shapiro Chassidic Dynasty.)

G16.1. Chavah, married her first cousin, R. Menachem Nahum Friedman of Husyatin.
G16.2. Chaya Sarah, married R. Jacob, son of R. Isaac Friedman of the Buhusi Dynasty. He succeeded his father-in-law as Admur.

G15.2. R. Shalom Joseph Friedman of Husyatin, 1860-1883. He married the daughter of R. Ephraim Zalman Margolioth of Mazev. (See Chapter VII — Margolioth Family.)

G16.1. R. Menachem Nahum Friedman of Husyatin, 1880-1943. He married his first cousin, daughter of R. Israel Friedman (above) and succeeded his father-in-law in Lvov in 1937. He and his family perished in the Holocaust.

G16.2. R. Moses Friedman of Boyan-Cracow, 1881-1943. He married the daughter of R. Menachem Nahum of Boyan-Chernovitz, son of R. Isaac Friedman. He became Admur of Cracow in 1925, and was the author of *Darkei Moshe*. The family perished in the Holocaust.

G16.3. Sarah Sheindel, married R. Aaron Friedman of Sadagora. (See above G14.2/15.3.)

G15.3. Gitel, married R. Isaac Meir, son of R. Abraham Joshua Heschel Heschel of the Apt. Dynasty.

G15.4. Wife of R. Menachem Nahum of Chernovitz, son of R. Isaac Friedman of Boyan.

G14.7. Leah, married R. David Heilprin (Hailperin, Halppern and other spellings), 1821-84, son of R. Jacob Joseph of Berdichev, descendants of the author of *Sefer Seder HaDorot*, R. Jehiel Heilprin.

G15.1. R. Shalom Joseph Heilprin, 1856-1940, Admur Vaslui (Rumania). He married Leah, daughter of R. Isaac Friedman of Buhusi.

G16. R. Haim Dov Heilprin, 1877-1957, Admur Vaslui-Bucharest. He settled in Israel in 1950. He married the daughter of R. David, son of R. Simeon Solomon of Savaran.

G17.1. R. Jacob Joseph Solomon Heilprin, born in 1902, the last Admur of the Vaslui Dynasty. He married the daughter of R. Jacob Samson Kaner of Chechoyv (son-in-law of R. Moses Halberstam of the A Branch). They also settled in Israel in 1950, and had two daughters, married.

G17.2. Wife of R. Isaac Weiss of Jerusalem.

G17.3. Wife of R. Israel Lieb, son of R. Moses Judah Lieb Friedman of Pascani-Tel Aviv.

G17.4. Wife of Saul Edelstein of Tel Aviv.

G15.2. R. Mordecai Heilprin, married the daughter of Shabbatai Polnauer of Keshanov.

G15.3. Feige, married R. Solomon, son of R. Abraham Jacob Friedman of Sadagora, her cousin.

G14.8. Gitel Toyba, married R. Joseph, son of R. David Manzon of Berdichev.

G15.1. R. Levi Isaac Manzon, 1847-1917, of Vienna. He married the daughter of R. Michael of Ozipoli, and was the author of *Becha Yevorach Yisrael.* He had issue, and a grandson adopted the surname Graham.

G15.2. R. Haim David Manzon, 1850-1932, Admur Brody, married the daughter of R. Benjamin Zeev of Oziran.

G16.1. R. Dovber Manzon of Brody succeeded his father as Admur, and perished with his family in the Holocaust.

G16.2. R. Israel Manzon, 1879-1961, of Kalicz, settled in New York in 1939.

G17.1. David Manzon.

G17.2. Wife of Griffel. Their son, David Griff.

G16.3. Wife of R. Moses Weinstock, 1881-1964, died in Jerusalem.

G17. R. Israel Weinstock, Ph.D., Head of the Institute for Kaballah and Chassidism in Jerusalem.

VIZHNIZ CHASSIDIC DYNASTY

G14.9. Miriam (daughter of R. Israel Friedman of Ruzhin), married R. Menachem Mendel (1830-85) of Vizhniz, son of R. Haim Hager of Kossov. His wife died in Sokol in 1882. R. Mendel became the leader of the Vizhniz community and later their A.B.D. He became famous as a miracle worker and distributor of amulets. He also headed the *Kollel* Vizhniz and Maramuresh, a fund for the poor in Israel. When the Sanz-Sadagora conflict erupted, he attempted to settle the dispute between R. Haim Halberstam and the sons of the Ruzhiner, his father-in-law. He was the author of *Zemach Zedek* (1885).

G15.1. R. Baruch Hager, 1845-93, succeeded his father as Admur Vizhniz, and remained the leader of a large Chassidic following for
eight years. He married Zipporah, daughter of R. Aryey Lieb
Shapiro of Koretz. Seven of their nine sons were Chassidic Rabbis
as were three of their sons-in-law, thus resulting in the division
and split among the Chassidic followers. He wrote *Imrei Baruch*
(1912).

G16.1. R. Israel Hager, 1860-1937, Admur of Vizhniz, and later moved
to Grosswarden in Hungary. He founded the Yeshiva *Beit
Israel* and wrote *Ahavat Yisrael* (1943) and *Or Yisrael* (1938).
He married Hinde, daughter of R. Meir Horowitz of Dzikov.
(See Chapter XVI — Ropshitz Dynasty.)

G17.1. R. Menachem Mendel Hager of Vishva, 1885-1941. He married his first cousin, the daughter of R. Mordecai Hadrov
of Kolomya. They settled in Vishva in 1921, and he established the Yeshiva *Beit Israel* there.

G18.1. R. Baruch Hager of Vishva, 1908-45, married the daughter of R. Zvi Hirsch of Mishlonitz, son of R. Isaac Tuvia
Rubin. (See Chapter XVI — Branch VII.)

G19.1. Naftali Hager (New York).
G19.2. Zipporah, married Professor David Weiss of the Jewish Theological Seminary (New York).

G18.2. R. Haim Judah Meir Hager, 1912-69, married in 1935 to
Reize, the daughter of Eliezer Rinman. They settled in
Tel Aviv in 1960.

G17.2. R. Haim Meir Hager, 1888-1971, succeeded his father as
Admur of the Vizhniz in 1937. He married the daughter of
R. Zeev, son of R. Johanan Twersky of Rotmistrovke. They
settled in Bnei Brak in 1947. His teachings were published
in *Kuntras HaLikutim* (1949).

G18.1. R. Moses Joshua Hager, born in 1916, Admur Vizhniz-
Bnei Brak, married Leah, daughter of R. Menachem
Mendel of Desh (son-in-law of R. Jacob Samson Kaner—
see Chapter XIV — Branch A). Three of his daughters
married into three leading Chassidic Dynasties.

G19.1. Wife of the present Belz Rebbe, R. Issachar Dov Rokeah.

G19.2. Wife of the present Skvira-Monsey Rebbe, R. David Twersky.

G19.3. Sosha, married R. Aaron, son of R. Moses Teitelbaum of Sighet-New York.

G19.4. Wife of her first cousin, R. Menachem Ernster.

G19.5. R. Israel Hager, married the daughter of R. Meshullam Zusia Twersky, present Admur Loyev.

G19.6. Menachem Mendel Hager.

G18.2. R. Mordecai Hager, born in 1922, present Admur Vizhniz-Monsey (New York), married the daughter of R. Jacob Joseph Twersky of Skvira. They have fourteen children.

G19.1. R. Phineas Shalom Hager, married the daughter of R. Zvi, son of R. Abraham Abbish Horowitz of Kraly, son of R. Naftali Horowitz (of Malitsch — see Chapter XVI — Branch VII).

G19.2. R. Israel Hager, married the daughter of R. Eleazar Meisels of Ihel-Chicago. (See Chapter XVII — Teitelbaum Dynasty.)

G19.3. R. Menachem Mendel Hager, married the daughter of R. Isaac, son of R. Johanan Twersky of Rotmistrovke.

G19.4. R. Isaac Johanan Hager, married the daughter of R. Moses, son of R. David Halberstam. (See Chapter XIV — Branch C — G15.2/16.1/17.5/18.2.)

G19.5. R. Eliezer Hager, married the daughter of R. David Twersky of Skvira-Boro Park.

G18.3. Wife of R. Judah, son of R. Alter Horowitz of Dzikov. (See Chapter XVI — Branch VII.)

G18.4. Wife of R. Naftali Haim Adler of Netanya. (See Chapter XVI — Branch I.)

G18.5. Wife of R. Moses Ernster (Bnei Brak).

G19. R. Menachem, married his first cousin, daughter of R. Moses Hager.

G18.6. Zipporah, married R. Israel, son of R. Isaac, son of R. Moses Judah Lieb Friedman of Pascani. (See Chapter XV above.)

G17.3. R. Eliezer Hager, 1891-1946, of Vizhniz. He married Chavah, daughter of R. Isaac Meir Heschel of Kopzynce. He established the Yeshiva of *Damesek Eliezer* in Vizhniz. He was the author of *Damesek Eliezer* (1949), and settled in Israel in 1944. He is buried on the Mt. of Olives in Jerusalem.

G17.4. R. Baruch Hager, 1895-1964, of Vizhniz-Seret-Bnei Brak. He married 1) the daughter of R. Issachar Dov Rokeah, the Belzer Rebbe and 2) the daughter of R. Eliezer Nissan of Zinkov. He settled in Israel in 1947, and established the Yeshiva *Yacheh Yisrael* in Haifa.

> G18.1. Michael Hager (Haifa), married the daughter of Haim David Auerbach.
>
> G18.2. Eliezer Hager, married the daughter of Jacob Mordecai Broxan.
>
> G18.3. Moses Hager of Haifa.
>
> G18.4. Miriam married R. Eliyahu Sterenbuch (Antwerp).

G17.5. R. Samuel Abba Hager of Vizhniz, died in 1937, married the daughter of R. Moses Hager of Shatz, his first cousin.

G17.6. Wife of R. Shalom Rokeah of Sokol. (See Chapter XVII.)

G17.7. Wife of R. Alter Ezekiel Horowitz of Dzikov. (See Chapter XVI — Branch VII.)

G17.8. Wife of R. Zvi Haim Horowitz of Rymanov-Cracow. (See Chapter XVI — Branch VII.)

G17.9. Wife of R. Moses Haim Low.

G17.10. Wife of R. Abraham Joshua Heschel Heschel of Zinkov.

G17.11. Wife of R. Mordecai Shraga Friedman of Boyan-Chernovitz.

G16.2. R. Haim Hager, 1863-1932, Admur Ottinya (Itinia), died in Cracow. He married 1) daughter of R. Isaac Friedman of Buhusi and 2) daughter of R. Shraga Jair of Biala-Berzig. He settled in Stanislav after World War I, and wrote *Tal Chayim*.

> G17.1. R. Israel Shalom Joseph Hager of Ottinya, married his first cousin, daughter of R. Samuel Abba Hager of Horodenka.
>
> G17.2. R. Menachem Mendel Hager of Ottinya, married the daughter of R. Isaac of Tysmenitsa.
>
> G17.3. Wife of R. Aaron, son of R. Menachem Nahum Friedman of Boyan-Chernovitz.
>
> G17.4. Wife of R. Israel, son of R. Mordecai Shraga Friedman of Husyatin.
>
> G17.5. Wife of R. Jehiel Michael Hager, her uncle.

G16.3. R. Moses Hager, 1864-1926, Admur Shatz. He married the daughter of R. Abraham Heschel Heschel of the Apt Dynasty.

G17. Wife of her cousin, R. Samuel Abba Hager (above).

G16.4. R. Samuel Abba Hager of Kolomya-Horodenka, 1865-1895. Author of *Sefatei Tzadik*. He married the daughter of R. Moses Mordecai Twersky of Makarov. (See Chapter VII — Branch A.)

G17. Wife of R. Israel Shalom Joseph Hager, her first cousin.

G16.5. R. Jacob Isaac David Hager of Sterzinz, married the daughter of R. Issachar Dov Eichenstein of Dolina. (See Chapter XVII.)

G16.6. R. Phineas Hager of Borsa, died in 1941, married the daughter of R. Samuel Rokeah of Sokol, his first cousin (see G15.3 below). His daughter married David Mordecai Geschel of the Apt Dynasty.

G16.7. R. Shalom Hager of Damotch.

G16.8. Chavah, married R. Samuel Dov, son of R. Joshua Eliezer Chorodov, died in 1928.

G16.9. Rachel, married R. Mordecai, son of R. Haim Meir Chorodov.

G16.10. Sheindel, married R. Shalom Joseph of Chernovitz, son of R. Israel Friedman of Sadagora.

G16.11. R. Jehiel Michael Hager of Horodenka, married his niece, daughter of R. Haim Hager of Ottinya.

G15.2. R. Jacob Isaac David Hager, married the daughter of R. Meshullam Zusia of Talomatch.

G15.3. Sarah, married R. Samuel Rokeah of Sokol, son of R. Joshua, the Belzer Rebbe. She died in 1911.

BRANCH B

HESCHEL CHASSIDIC DYNASTY

G10.1. R. Abraham Joshua Heschel[3] (1749-1825) A.B.D. of Kolbuszov, Apt, Jassy and Medzibeh, one of the outstanding Chassidic leaders of his generation and a disciple of R. Elimelech of Lyzhansk. He married Sarah, daughter of R. Jacob of Turstein, and was the author of *Ohev Yisrael, Torat Emet* and his writings can be found in the *S'fatei Tzaddikim*. He was called the "Apter Rabbi."

As a young man R. Heschel heard the future in the rustle of growing things and in the footsteps of men. Then when he was alone in his room, he heard the future in his own limbs and became fearful, being unsure whether he could keep to the true way, knowing now where his feet were taking him. So he prayed that this knowledge be taken away from him, and his prayer was answered.

Once a great multitude gathered closely around the Apter Rabbi to hear his teachings. "That will not help," he cried to them. "Those who came to hear will hear even at a distance, and those who are not to hear, will not hear no matter how close they come." He taught: "A man should not choose the form in which he wishes to serve to Lord, but should be like a vessel that can willingly have anything poured into it—water, wine or milk."

He once explained how in his day one who chose not to sin and to adhere to his religion was worthier than the law-abiding Jew of previous generations. "Formerly the leaders of the Jewish community had the authority to punish transgressors, but now one may commit any offense against Judaism. Therefore this period is the best to achieve the complete redemption."

The beadle who summoned worshippers to pray in the morning at the synagogue once awakened the Apter Rabbi with three knocks on his window. R. Heschel felt unusually enthusiastic, dressed rapidly and hastened to the synagogue. When he reached there, he asked the beadle if he had thoughts of great holiness when he knocked on his window.

"No," he answered, "as I am not versed in concepts of holiness. But our family tradition is to recite the names of the Patriarchs, Abraham, Isaac and Jacob when we knock three times." It was this simple sincerity that had aroused the Rabbi to hasten so to serve his Master in prayer.

G11.1. R. Isaac Meir Heschel, 1770-1855, Admur of Zinkov, married Mirl, daughter of R. Haim Strauss, A.B.D. Dukla.

G12.1. R. Meshullam Zusia Heschel, Admur of Zinkov, died in 1866, married Sima, daughter of R. Moses Zvi of Savaran.

G13.1. R. Samuel Heschel of Zinkov, died in 1862, married Mintza, daughter of R. Abraham Twersky of Trisk.

G14.1. R. Isaac Meir Heschel, married his first cousin Feige, Mintza, daughter of R. Ephraim Zalman Margolioth of Mazev. (See Margolioth Family Pedigree — Chapter VII.)

G15.1. Nahum, surnamed Geschel.

G15.2. David Mordecai Geschel, married the daughter of R. Phineas Hager of Borsa.

G13.2. R. Haim Menachem Heschel of Zinkov, married 1) the daughter of R. David Twersky of Talnoye and 2) the daughters of R. Michal of Kashivke. He died in 1894.

G14.1. R. Phineas Heschel of Zinkov, died in 1916, married Malka, daughter of R. Isaac Friedman of Buhusi.

G14.2. R. Moses Heschel of Zinkov, died in 1923, married Feige
        Rikel, daughter of R. Mordecai, son of R. Moses Twersky
        of Korostyshev.

G14.3. Chaya Sarah, married R. Isaiah, son of R. Isaac Jacob
        Twersky of Makarov. (See Chapter VII — Branch A.)

G14.4. Deborah, married R. Feiwish of Zalischick.

G13.3. R. Abraham Joshua Heschel Heschel of Medzibeh, 1832-
        1887. He died in Kamenka, having succeeded his father as
        Admur Zinkov in 1866. He married Rachel, daughter of R.
        Shalom Joseph Friedman of Sadagora. Her mother and his
        father were first cousins.

G14.1. R. Israel Shalom Joseph Heschel, 1852-1911, named after
        his maternal grandfather, succeeded his father as Admur
        Zinkov in 1887. He married 1) Sarah, daughter of R.
        Abraham Jacob Friedman of Sadagora, but had no issue
        and 2) Batsheva Treina, daughter of R. Jacob Samson
        Shapiro of Bohopoli (son-in-law of R. Gedaliah Aaron
        Rabinowitz of Linitz, see below). She perished in the
        Holocaust in 1941.

G15.1. R. Abraham Joshua Heschel Heschel, 1892-1943, Admur
        of Tarnopol, married his first cousin, Miriam, daughter
        of R. Isaac Meir Heschel of Kopzynce. He succeeded
        his father as Admur Tarnopol, and perished there in the
        Holocaust with his family.

G15.2. Chava Sarah, married R. Mordecai Solomon Friedman
        of Boyan.

G15.3. Mirl, born in 1898, married in 1913 to R. Mordecai
        Shalom Joseph Friedman of Sadagora-Vienna-Tel Aviv.

G15.4. R. Isaac Meir Heschel of Medzibeh-Haifa, born in 1901.
        After his father's death in 1911, he succeeded him as
        Admur in Odessa, and later settled in New York. In
        1968 he settled in Haifa. He married Sarah (died in
        1972), daughter of R. Nahum Joel Rabinowitz of Kan-
        tikoziba-Haifa. They have three daughters, married
        with issue in Israel.

G15.5. R. Moses Heschel of Tarnopol, perished.

G14.2. R. Isaac Meir Heschel, 1861-1931, Admur Kopzynce. He
        married Gitel, daughter of R. Mordecai Shraga, son of
        R. Israel Friedman of Husyatin.

G15.1. R. Abraham Joshua Heschel Heschel, born in 1889, and
         succeeded his father as Admur in Vienna in 1931. He
         later settled in New York, where he died in 1967, and
         was buried in Tiberias. He married his first cousin,
         Sarah Bracha, daughter of R. Moses Mordecai Heschel
         of Novominsk.

G16.1. Israel Heschel, eldest, New York, married Chaya
         Freiberg. They have no issue.

G16.2. R. Moses Mordecai Heschel,[4] 1929-1975, Admur Kop-
         zynce-New York (Boro Park), married Channah,
         daughter of Hirsch Brandler. Their children, Isaac
         Meir, Zusia, Sarah Bracha and Abraham Joshua
         Heschel.

G16.3. Zusia Heschel, born in 1930, married Rochel Lustig
         (New York), and have issue, Shoshana, Esther, Sarah
         Bracha, Miriam and Dinah.

G16.4. Sheva, married R. Aaron David Flintenstein. Their
         children, Isaac Meir married with children in Jeru-
         salem, and Gitel, married to Shlomo Klein with issue
         in Boro Park.

G16.5. Malka (died in 1972), married Aaron, son of Mendel
         Lemberger (died in 1967). They settled in Israel, and
         had four married daughters, Leah, Miriam, Shoshana
         and Gita.

G16.6. Leah Rachel (perished in the Holocaust), married
         Jeruchem Fischel, son of R. David Horowitz, A.B.D.
         Stanislav. (See Horowitz Family — Chapter XVI —
         Stanislav Branch — G13.1/14.3/15.5/16.1.)

G16.7. Chava, married Zalman Gurari (Brooklyn, Crown
         Heights). Their children, Isaac Meir (married, Mon-
         treal), Esther (married Nahum Steinberg, Crown
         Heights) and Nathan (married, Buffalo).

G16.8. Myra, married R. Aaron Lieb Gartenhouse (died in
         1970). Their sons, Isaac Meir and Haim.

G16.9. Pearl, married R. Jacob, son of R. Mordecai Israel, son
         of R. Baruch Meir (of Azranitz), son of R. Nahum,
         son of R. Aaron Twersky of Chernobyl. (See below
         G11.4/12/13.2/14.2/15.2/16.3.)

G15.2. R. Moses Heschel, perished in the Holocaust in Austria,
         and was married twice.

G16.1. Eliezer Heschel, served in the Jewish Brigade in World War II, and settled in Antwerp. He has a married daughter.

G16.2. Rachel, married Gurari (Jerusalem), and have issue.

G15.3. R. Shalom Joseph Heschel (Bat Yam, Israel), married the daughter of R. Baruch David, son of R. Mordecai Dov Twersky of Hornistopol-Kolenkovitz. Their daughter Raya, married Mordecai S. Balminger (Tel Aviv), son of Jacob Joshua Balminger (son-in-law of R. Jacob Friedman of Husyatin).

G15.4. R. Mordecai Shraga Heschel, married the daughter of R. Israel Friedman of Leipzig-Boyan, having no issue.

G15.5. Blume Reizel, married R. Abraham Jacob Friedman of Sadagora.

G15.6. Miriam, married her first cousin, R. Abraham Joshua Heschel of Tarnopol.

G15.7. Chavah, married Eliezer, son of R. Israel Hager of Vizhniz. They had no issue.

G14.3. R. Moses Mordecai Heschel, Admur Novominsk, died in 1918. He married Reizel, the daughter of R. Jacob Perlow of Novominsk.

G15.1. Sarah Bracha, married her first cousin, R. Abraham Joshua Heschel (above).

G15.2. Esther Sima, perished in the Holocaust.

G15.3. Gitel, perished in the Holocaust.

G15.4. Deborah Miriam, married Aryey Lieb Dermer, perished in the Holocaust.

G15.5. R. Jacob Heschel, 1903-69, lived in London. He married Sarah, the daughter of R. Nahum Mordecai Friedman, and had issue, Te'eina married Dr. Michael Kendel, Ph.D.

G15.6. Professor Abraham Joshua Heschel, 1907-72.[5] He was one of the most outstanding Jewish thinkers and philosophers. He obtained his Ph.D. in Berlin at the University's *Hochschule fur die Wissenschaft des Judentums.* In 1937 he was appointed by Martin Buber as his successor at the central organization for Jewish adult education in Frankfurt-on-Main. After being deported to Poland by the Nazis in 1938, he taught at the Warsaw

Institute for Jewish Studies, and then immigrated to England. In London he established the Institute for Jewish Learning, and then settled in the U.S.A. In 1940 he became an Associate Professor at the Hebrew Union College in Cincinnati in Philosophy and Rabbinics, and five years later became the Professor of Jewish Ethics and Mysticism at the Jewish Theological Seminary in New York. He became known through his writings, and was one of the most influential of modern philosophers, being recognized by Jewish and Christian scholars alike. He translated early Jewish writings into contemporary thought, works on Maimonides, Kabbalah and Chassidism, and others in German, Hebrew and English. His concepts on religion and philosophy found expression in his most popular works in English, *Man Is Not Alone* (1951), and *God in Search of Man* (1956). At the time of his death he was writing a book on one of the masters of Chassidic thought, the Kotzker Rebbe.

He married in 1946 to Sylvia Strauss, and had a daughter, Chava Shoshana, born in 1952.

G14.4. R. Zusia Heschel of Medzibeh.

G14.5. Gitel, married R. Solomon Zalmina Zuckerman of Roshkov, died in 1915, son of R. Jehiel Joseph.

G15.1. R. Isaac Meir Zuckerman of Roshkov, married 1) the daughter of R. Mordecai Biederman of Lelov and 2) the daughter of R. Mordecai Twersky, Admur Loyev.

G15.2. R. Mordecai Zuckerman of Rezina, married Chaya, daughter of R. Moses Dan, son of Abraham Joshua Heschel Twersky of Skvira.

G15.3. R. Shalom Zuckerman of Roshkov, married the daughter of R. Isaac of Breszna. (See below — G11.4/12/13.2/14.1/15.4.)

G15.4. R. Jacob Zuckerman.

G15.5. Chaya Sarah, married R. Baruch Dov Twersky of Kalinkovitz. She died in 1942 and he in 1925. (See Twersky Family — Chapter VII — Branch B.)

G15.6. Blume Reizel, married R. Jacob Israel Rabinowitz of Charsan, author of *She'erit Yaakov*.

G15.7. Chava, married R. David Mordecai, born about 1889, son of R. Menachem Nahum Twersky of Talnoye. He settled in New York about 1920, where he died in 1956, the eldest of his father's three sons.

G16.1. R. Johanan Twersky, the present Admur Talnoye-Jerusalem. He was ordained at Yeshiva University, and later settled in Israel where he was active in the Ministry of Religion. He married Pearl, daughter of the Admur Strettin. Their daughter Gitel, married Jehiel Weinberg.

G16.2. Leika, married Harvey Schwam, died in an airplane crash. They had issue.

G16.3. Sylvia.

G16.4. Deborah.

G16.5. Edith, died in 1972.

G16.6. Nathan (Menachem Nahum) Twersky, New York.

G15.8. Wife of R. Haim Hager of Shatz.

G14.6. Wife of R. Moses Hager of Shatz.

G14.7. Wife of R. David Friedman of Buhusi.

G13.4. R. Jehiel Heschel, 1843-1917, Admur Krolevets, married Mirl, daughter of R. Joshua Rokeah, the Belzer Rebbe.

G14.1. Malka Deborah, married R. Zvi Aryey of Berdichev, son of R. Mordecai Twersky of Makarov. He died in 1935.

G14.2. Chaya Sarah, married R. Moses, son of R. Mordecai Twersky of Rotmistrovke.

G14.3. Frieda, first wife of R. Isaac Isaiah Halberstam of Chechoyv-Cracow. (See Chapter XIV.)

G14.4. Frumet, married R. Asher Isaiah of Pruchnik, son of R. Dovber Eichenstein of Dolina. (See Chapter XVII — Eichenstein Dynasty.)

G14.5. Leah, married R. Menashe Mariles, the last Admur of Ropshitz. (See Chapter XVI.)

G14.6. Rebecca, married R. Moses Zvi, born about 1891, son of R. Menachem Nahum Twersky of Talnoye, the second son. (See above G13.3/14.5/15.7.) He came to the U.S.A. about 1922, and settled in Philadelphia where he was the Admur Talnoye, as opposed to his brothers in New York and Boston.

G15.1. Meshullam Zusia (Sigmund), born in 1910, married in New York in 1934 to Leah, daughter of R. Menachem

Mendel Halberstam, Admur Gorlice-New York (See Chapter XIV — Branch E.) They settled in Philadelphia, and have issue.

G15.2. Feige (Francis), married 1) Taragon (Baltimore) and 2) Baruch Trachtman. Their children, Dr. Mendel Trachtman and Feige Zucker.

G15.3. Meir Twersky, married Riva Kurtzer (Seattle). Their children, David and Judith.

G15.4. Hinde (Anne or Ayalah), married R. Joseph Bornstein (son of R. Hanoch, Admur Sochotchov). They live in Jerusalem, and have issue.

G15.5. Menachem Nahum Twersky, married, and has issue. (Philadelphia.)

G15.6. David Twersky, married, and has issue. (Philadelphia.)

G15.7. Sheindel (Jean), married Gordon, and has issue. (Philadelphia.)

G15.8. Mordecai Twersky, married, and has issue. (Philadelphia.)

G13.5. Chaya Sarah, married R. Isaac Joel Rabinowitz of Kantikoziba. She died in 1905. He was the son of R. Gedaliah Aaron of Linitz, founder of the Chassidic Dynasty — see below.

G13.6. Zipporah, married R. Joseph of Shitova.

G13.7. Wife of R. Moses, son of R. Phineas Shapiro of Slovita.

G14. R. Isaac Meir Shapiro of Oman.

G12.2. Rachel, married R. Samuel, son of R. Zalman Ashkenazi (descendants of the Chacham Zvi — see Chapter XIII).

G11.2. Jochebed, married R. Dan, son of R. Isaac Yungerlieb of Radwill.

G12.1. R. Samuel Jehiel Yungerlieb, died 1862, married Blume, the daughter of R. Joseph of Ostilla. Their marriage became a famous occasion among the Chassidim and was known as "the Great wedding."

G12.2. R. Levi Yungerlieb of Radwill-Ozipoli.

G13. Wife of her first cousin, R. Abraham Joshua Heschel of Litshenitz.

G12.3. Blume Reizel, married R. Shalom Joseph Friedman of Sadagora.

G12.4. Wife of R. Isaac Twersky of Skvira. He died in 1885, and was the Admur and founder of the Skvira dynasty, son of R. Mordecai of Chernobyl. Their descendants still continue as leaders of the Skvira Chassidim. (See below.)

G11.3. R. Joseph Moses Heschel of Medzibeh.
G11.4. Dinah, married R. Israel of Litshenitz.[6]

G12. R. Abraham Joshua Heschel of Litshenitz, married his first cousin.

G13.1. R. Israel, father of R. Joseph of Tiverov.
G13.2. Wife of R. Menachem Nahum, died in 1871, son of R. Aaron Twersky of Chernobyl. He was Admur of Loyev.

G14.1. R. Mordecai Twersky died in 1909, married the daughter of R. Samuel Ashkenazi[7] (G11.1/12.2 above), Admur Loyev.

G15.1. R. Abraham Joshua Heschel Twersky of Chudnov, died in 1914, married the daughter of R. Jacob of Deliatyn.

G16.1. R. Haim Isaac Twersky of Loyev-Kiev, 1886-1943, married the daughter of R. Isaiah Halberstam of Chechoyv.

G17.1. Frieda, died young.
G17.2. Jacob Twersky, settled in Israel from the U.S.S.R., married and has issue.
G17.3. Mordecai Twersky, killed on the Russian Front in World War II. His wife perished at Babi Yar.
G17.4. R. Meshullam Zusia Twersky, present Admur Loyev-Chernobyl-Bnei Brak. He settled in Israel in 1934, and established a Yeshiva in Bnei Brak in 1959. He married the daughter of R. Jacob Mordecai Brandwein.

G18.1. Nahum Twersky, married Nechama, daughter of R. Elhanan Halpern (Bnei Brak).
G18.2. Channah, married R. Israel, son of R. Moses Hager (Admur Vizhniz).
G18.3. Isaiah Twersky, married the daughter of R. Shalom Michaelowitz (the Broder Rov).
G18.4. Feiger, married Leifer.
G18.5. Haim Isaac Twersky (Brooklyn) married.

G18.6. Joshua Heschel Twersky, married Miriam Channah, daughter of R. Aaron Mordecai Rutner.

G17.5. Rebecca Miriam Twersky, M.D. (U.S.S.R.).
G17.6. Jochebed.
G17.7. David Jehiel Twersky, married Shoshana Margulies, and have issue.
G17.8. Mirl, married Uri Shapiro of Kiev, and have issue.

G16.2. Wife of R. Jacob Perlow of Stolin.
G16.3. First wife of R. Isaac Admur Skvira-Tel Aviv, son of R. Moses Dan Twersky. (See Skvira Chassidim below.)

G15.2. R. Baruch Benzion Twersky of Uman, married the daughter of R. Eliezer of Ostilla.
G15.3. R. Shalom of White Field, married Nechamah, the daughter of R. Moses of Odessa.
G15.4. Wife of R. Isaac Pechenik of Brezna.
G15.5. Bracha, married R. Jerachemeel Moses of Kozenitz, son of R. Jehiel Jacob Hopstein. (See Chapter XVII — Shapiro Dynasty — G2.5/3.4/4.6/5.2.)
G15.6. Mira, married R. Israel Samuel Solomon Niehaus of Tomashov. He was the son of R. Meir Jehiel (1851-1935, Admur Tomashov-Chelm), succeeded his father in Tomashov-Chelm, and perished in the Holocaust.
G15.7. Wife of R. Isaac Meir Zuckerman of Roshkov. (See above — G11.1/12.1/13.3/14.5/15.1.)
G15.8. Pearl, married R. Aaron Twersky of Azranitz, her first cousin.
G15.9. Batyah, married R. Abraham Sefarad.
G15.10. Channah, married R. Abraham Jacob Friedman of Boyan. (See Friedman Chassidic Dynasty.)

G14.2. R. Baruch Meir Twersky, Admur Azranitz, died in 1911, married Miriam Reizel, the daughter of R. Abraham Joshua Heschel of Litshenitz.

G15.1. R. Aaron Twersky of Kishinov-Azranitz, married his first cousin, daughter of R. Mordecai Twersky of Loyev. All perished except one daughter.

G16. Bathsheva, wife of R. David of Ploesti, son of R. Shalom Joseph Friedman of Spikov. (See Friedman Chassidic Dynasty.)

G15.2. Mordecai Israel Twersky of Kotin, married his first cousin, daughter of R. Mordecai Twersky. They perished in the Holocaust.

G16.1. R. Aaron, perished with family. He married his first cousin, Gitel Leah Twersky.

G16.2. Abraham Joshua Heschel, died young.

G16.3. R. Jacob Twersky, Rabbi of the Bronx Park East Jewish Center, married Pearl, daughter of R. Abraham Joshua Heschel of Vienna-New York. (See above—G11.1/12.1/13.3/14.2/15.1.) Their children, Mordecai, Bathsheva and Isaac Meir.

G16.4. Malka, married her first cousin, R. Aaron, son of R. Alter Israel Simeon Perlow of Novominsk-New York, and have issue. (See below.)

G16.5. Chaya Sarah, married Velvel Roitman of Jerusalem, and have issue.

G16.6. Bracha Sheindel, married Aaron March (Washington Heights), and have issue.

G16.7. Reizel Miriam, married Eliyahu Lipkis (New York), and have issue.

G16.8. Feige Dinah, married Moshe Aaron Rindenow, and have issue.

G15.3. R. Isaac Twersky of Alesk.

G15.4. Feige, married R. Alter Israel Simeon Perlow of Novominsk. They had a number of children.[7a]

G16.1. R. Aaron Perlow, married his first cousin, Malka, daughter of R. Mordecai Twersky.

G16.2. Wife of R. Abraham Isaac Twersky, her cousin.

G15.5. Malka, married R. Moses Mordecai of Lublin, perished in 1943, son of R. Jacob Aryey Lieb (Admur Trisk, died in 1918), son of R. Abraham Twersky, founder of the Trisk Dynasty. He was the author of *Ohel Moshe*.

G16.1. R. Abraham Isaac Twersky of London, married the daughter of R. Israel Simeon Perlow of Novominsk-New York. They were first cousins.

G16.2. R. Aaron David Twersky of Grosskov, perished.

G16.3. R. Johanan Twersky, married the daughter of R. Issachar Dov Rokeah of Belz. They perished.

G16.4. Rikel, married R. Menachem Zvi Eichenstein of Chicago.

G16.5. Gitel Leah, married R. Aaron Twersky of Kotin. They were first cousins.

G15.6. Pearl, married R. Gedaliah Aaron Rabinowitz of Manisterich. (See below — Rabinowitz Chassidic Dynasty — G13.5/14.2/15.1.)

G14.3. Malka, married R. Aryey Lieb of Magrov, son of R. Joshua Rokeah, the second Rebbe of Belz.

G14.4. Batyah, married R. Joseph Meir Twersky of Makhnovka. (See Skvira Chassidic Dynasty — G13.1/14.1.)

G11.5. Wife of R. Mordecai.

G12. R. Jacob Joel; his son, R. Israel Shalom; his son, R. Moses Eliakim.

JERUCHEM FAMILY PEDIGREE

Ancestry

G10.2. R. Meir Jeruchem (brother of R. Abraham Joshua Heschel of Apt).

G11. R. Jeremiah of Bornov, a pupil of R. Menachem Mendel of Rymanov.

G12. R. Naftali.

G13. R. Ephraim Aryey, married Blume.

G14. R. Shraga Zeev Jeruchem, born in 1829, married Sarah, daughter of R. Isaac. He died in 1891 and she in 1898.

G15. R. Haim Isaac Jeruchem, 1864-1942,[8] born in Malitsch, Galicia, after his mother had had numerous miscarriages. During her pregnancy she was advised to stay in bed until the delivery, and her father, R. Isaac, prophesied the birth of a son, to be called Isaac recalling the Biblical verse in Genesis XXI 1-3: "And the Lord remembered Sarah. . . ." He married Rachel Dinah, who was born one month later than he, in 1864, and was the daughter of the *Gaon* (Genius) of Limanov, R. Nathan Halevi, son of R. Haim Goldberg (descendants of R. Nathan Shapiro, author of *Megalleh Amukot*). They had seven daughters and two sons. R. Haim Isaac became the A.B.D. of Limanov and Altstadt. He was the author of *Birkat Yitz-*

chak, published in Vienna in 1923, and *Birkat Chayim,* Responsa, published in New York in 1956 (which contains the family history and genealogy in the introduction).

G16.1. R. Aaron Jeruchem, born in Limanov (Poland) May 26, 1904, and died in Boston in 1970. He attended the Vienna Yeshiva from 1921-5, and married in 1933 to Dora (Miriam Deborah), daughter of R. David Halberstam of Sokolov. (See Chapter XIV — Branch A — G14.1/15.2/16.5/17.2.) They came to the U.S.A. in 1940, and the following year he became the Rabbi of Congregation Sinai, New York. He was the author of *HaAim Beyisrael* (1938), *Ohel Rachel* (1942), *Shuvah Yisrael* (1947) and *Loh Tishkach* (1949). Their sons, Moses and Haim Isaac David Jeruchem of New York.

G16.2. Chaya Jochebed, died in 1975, married 1) R. Phineas Joseph, son of R. Abraham Thumim (Chapter IV — Branch A), and had issue, and 2) R. Joseph, son of R. Nahum Zvi Thumim (Chapter IV — Branch F).

G16.3. Riva, married R. David Halberstam of Keshanov. (See Chapter XIV — Branch C.)

G16.4. R. Feiwel (Shraga Zeev) Jeruchem, married, and perished with his family.

G16.5. Blume Jached, 1885-1919, married in 1903 to R. Israel David, son of R. Isaiah Shalom Rokeah. The family perished.

G16.6. Channah Eidel, married R. Jacob Isaac, son of R. Abraham Abba Horowitz-Pentzer. (See Chapter XVI — Branch VII — G14.4/15.1 /16.3/17/18.)

G16.7. Leah, 1888-90.

G16.8. Bracha Frieda, married R. Joshua, son of R. Asher Isaiah Eichenstein (of Pruchnik). (See Chapter XVII — Eichenstein Dynasty.)

G16.9. Miriam Sarah (born in 1901), married in 1925 to R. Solomon Meir, son of R. Joseph Dov Kluger of Cracow. He died in 1934, and she perished with her family.

RABINOWITZ CHASSIDIC DYNASTY
OF LINITZ-MANISTERICH

Ancestry

G10.1. R. Abraham Joshua Heschel of Apt.

G11.1. R. Isaac Meir Heschel of Zinkov.

G12.1. R. Meshullam Zusia Heschel.

G13.5. Chaya Sarah, married R. Isaac Joel Rabinowitz of Kantikoziba.[9]

  G14.1. R. Phineas Rabinowitz, 1861-1922, Admur of Kantikoziba, author of *Ahavat Yisrael*. He married Sina Pearl, daughter of R. Mordecai Dov of Tomaspol.

    G15.1. R. Jacob Israel Rabinowitz, 1880-1941, author of *She'erit Yaakov*, married Blume Reizel, daughter of R. Solomon Zalmina Zuckerman of Roshkov. (See Heschel Dynasty above.)

    G15.2. R. Samuel Abba Rabinowitz of Zolkiev, born in 1883, married Channah Rachel, daughter of R. Naftali Rokeah of Noveria.

    G15.3. R. Menachem Nahum Rabinowitz, 1887-1959, Admur of Kantikoziba-Haifa, married Esther, daughter of R. Joseph Perlow of Koidanov.

      G16.1. Noah Isaac Joel.

      G16.2. Phineas.

      G16.3. Sarah Treina, married R. Isaac Meir Heschel of Medzibeh. (See Chapter XV — Heschel Family.) She died in 1972.

      G16.4. Shifra, married Gad Hakohen.

      G16.5. Channah.

    G15.4. R. Gedaliah Aaron Rabinowitz (Tel Aviv), married his first cousin, Sarah, daughter of R. Samuel Abba Rabinowitz.

    G15.5. Deborah, married R. Moses Perlow of Stolin. (See Perlow Family Chapter VII.)

    G15.6. Mirl Bracha, married R. Isaac, son of R. Mordecai Twersky of Skvira.

    G15.7. Sima Frieda, married her first cousin, R. Joseph Benzion Rabinowitz of Detroit.

    G15.8. Beila, married her first cousin, R. Jacob Rabinowitz of Philadelphia.

  G14.2. R. Joshua Heschel Rabinowitz, 1860-1937, Admur Manisterich-New York (where he died). He came to the U.S.A. in the 1920's and lived in the Brownsville section of Brooklyn. He wrote *Divrei Yehoshua, Yalkut Yehoshua, Torat Yehoshua, Nachalat Yehoshua* and *Torah Avot* (New York, 1926). This latter work contains a full biography and family genealogy, part of which he had copied from a manuscript written by his maternal grandfather, R. Heschel of Zinkov (Podolia). He married his first cousin, Margola Rachel, daughter of R. Phineas Rabinowitz.

G15.1. R. Gedaliah Aaron Rabinowitz, 1880-1919, killed in the Russian pogroms, married Pearl, daughter of R. Baruch Meir of Azranitz, son of R. Menachem Nahum Twersky of Chernobyl. (See Chapter XV — Heschel Family — G10.1/11.4/12/13.2/14.2.)

G16.1. R. Isaac Joel Rabinowitz, born in 1908, Admur Manisterich-New York (Brooklyn), married in 1939 to Leah, daughter of R. Joseph Thumim. (See Chapter IV — Branch F.)

G17.1. Gedaliah Aaron, born in 1940, married in 1963 to Miriam Wachtfogel (Chicago). Their children, Ayelet and Nahum Zvi.

G17.2. Breindel, born in 1943, married Ginsburg (divorced). Their son Simha.

G17.3. Rivke, born in 1947, married in 1966 Moshe Snow. Their children, Zipporah Feige and Joseph.

G16.2. Baruch Meir Rabinowitz, born in 1912, married Toyba Brandwein (Brooklyn).

G17.1. Pearl, married David Berger (Queens). Their children, Isaac and Miriam.

G17.2. Feige, married Israel Jacob Kaplan (Montreal). Their son Zvi.

G17.3. Channah, married David Katz (Washington Heights, N.Y.).

G17.4. Joshua Heschel.

G17.5. Margola Rachel.

G16.3. Feige, born in 1906, married Haim Wolkinson, lawyer (Washington, D.C.). Their children, Pearl, Miriam, Benzion and Gedaliah.

G15.2. R. Jacob Meshullam Zusia Rabinowitz, 1901-72, Admur Manisterich-Philadelphia. He settled in Ramat Gan (Israel).

G16.1. Dr. Phineas Rabinowitz (Rehovot, Weizmann Institute), married and has issue.

G16.2. Margola Rachel, married N. Perl (Jerusalem) and have issue.

G15.3. Sima Bracha, married R. Jacob Isaac, son of R. Isaiah Twersky of Makarov-Chicago. He died in 1945. (See Chapter VII — Branch A.)

G15.4. Elisheva, married and later divorced R. Jehiel.

G16. Beila, married in 1947, R. Zvi Hirsch, son of Dov Solomon Zakheim[10] of Razinai. He settled in New York in 1946.

G17.1. R. Dr. Dov Shlomo Zakheim (London), born in 1948, married Barbara Portnoy, and have issue.
G17.2. Joshua Heschel Zakheim, born in 1954 (New York).

G15.5. Others, died young.

G14.3. R. Meshullam Zusia Rabinowitz, 1869-1920, married Malka, daughter of R. Abraham Samuel of Brezna.

G15.1. Friedel, married R. Abraham Twersky (Tel Aviv).
G15.2. R. Joseph Benzion Rabinowitz (Detroit) died 1967/8, married his first cousin, Sima Frieda, daughter of R. Phineas Rabinowitz of Kantikoziba.

G14.4. Rachel, married R. Benzion Judah Lieb Twersky of Hornistopol. (See Chapter VII — Branch B.)

SKVIRA (TWERSKY) CHASSIDIC DYNASTY

ANCESTRY

G10.1. R. Abraham Joshua Heschel of Apt.
G11.2. Jochebed, married R. Dan Yungerlieb.
G12.4. Wife of R. Isaac Twersky of Skvira, 1812-1885, the first Admur of Skvira.[11] By this first wife he had two sons, Abraham Joshua Heschel and Menachem Nahum. His second wife was Chaya Malka, a daughter of R. Israel Friedman of Ruzhin, but they had no issue. His third wife, Channah Sima, daughter of R. Naftali Zvi of Skvira, bore him two additional sons, from whom are descended the present Skvira Chassidic leaders in New Square, New York. (See Chapter XVII — Rokeah Dynasty — G13.5/14.1/15.9/16.)

G13.1. R. Abraham Joshua Heschel Twersky, Admur Skvira, died in 1886. He married 1) the daughter of R. Samuel Ashkenazi (see Heschel Family Dynasty — G10.1/11.1/12.2 and Chapter XIII), and 2) daughter of R. Joseph Zilberprav.

G14.1. R. Joseph Meir Twersky, 1857-1917, Admur of Makhnovka, married Batyah, daughter of R. Menachem Nahum, son of R.

Aaron Twersky of Chernobyl. (Their fathers were first cousins.)

G15.1. R. Abraham Joshua Heschel Twersky, succeeded his father as Admur of Makhnovka, and married the daughter of R. David Aaron Twersky of Zorek. (See under Friedman Chassidic Dynasty.)

G15.2. Wife of her uncle, R. Dov Lieb Twersky (see below).

G15.3. Wife of her second cousin, R. Nahum, son of R. David Twersky of Skvira.

G15.4. Wife of R. Nahum, son of R. Mordecai Joseph Twersky of Zlatopol (see below).

G14.2. R. Moses Dan Twersky of Skvira, died in 1926, married the daughter of R. Haim Meir Chodrov of Berdichev. (His father and her mother were first cousins, she being a daughter of R. David Twersky of Talnoye.)

G15.1. R. David Twersky, married the daughter of R. Mordecai Twersky of Skvira. (Their fathers were first cousins.)

G15.2. R. Isaac Twersky, Admur Skvira-Tel Aviv, married 1) the daughter of R. Abraham Joshua Heschel Twersky of Chudnov (see Heschel Family Dynasty) and 2) the daughter of R. Mordecai of Constantin.

G15.3. R. Abraham Joshua Heschel Twersky, married the daughter of R. Aryey Lieb Braverman. He died in 1966.

G15.4. Chaya, married R. Mordecai of Rezina, son of R. Solomon Zalmina Zuckerman of Roshkov. (See below G13.2/14/15.2.)

G15.5. Deborah, married her first cousin, R. Isaac, son of R. Mordecai Joseph Twersky of Zlatopol.

G14.3. R. Jacob Judah Twersky of Skvira, died in 1920, married the daughter of R. Mordecai Twersky of Korostyshev. (Their fathers were first cousins.)

G14.4. Deborah, married her first cousin, R. Mordecai Twersky of Skvira (died in 1920).

G14.5. Malka, married R. Mordecai Joseph (died in 1929), son of R. David of Zlatopol, son of R. Johanan Twersky of Rotmistrovke.

G15.1. R. Isaac Twersky of Zlatopol, married his first cousin, Deborah, daughter of R. Moses Dan Twersky of Skvira.

G15.2. R. Zeev Twersky of Warsaw, married the daughter of R. Issachar Dov Rokeah, the Belzer Rebbe. (See Chapter XVII.)

G15.3. R. Nahum Twersky of Warsaw, married the daughter of R. Joseph Meir Twersky of Makhnovka (above).

G15.4. R. Zvi Aryey Twersky of Zlatopol — Israel, 1890-1968, married the daughter of R. Israel, son of R. David Moses Friedman of Chartkov. (See Friedman Dynasty — G14.5/15.2/16.5.)

G15.5. Chavah, married R. Abraham Elimelech Perlow, Admur Karlin. (See Chapter VII — Perlow Family — G14.2/15.3/16.5.)

G15.6. Goltze, married R. Shalom Joseph, son of R. Nahum Dov Friedman of Sadagora. (See Friedman Dynasty.)

G15.7. Miriam, married R. Israel Eliezer Kozenitz.

G14.6. (From second wife) R. Dov Lieb Twersky, married his niece, daughter of R. Joseph Meir Twersky of Makhnovka. He perished in 1920.

G14.7. Shifra, married R. David (died in 1941), son of R. Menachem Nahum Twersky of Rotmistrovke. (Their fathers were first cousins.)

G13.2. R. Menachem Nahum Twersky, Admur of Spikov, died in 1886, married his first cousin, daughter of R. David Twersky of Talnoye.

G14. R. Mordecai Twersky, Admur Spikov, died in 1914, married his second cousin, daughter of R. Johanan Twersky of Rotmistrovke.

G15.1. R. Isaac Nahum Twersky, died in 1943, of Rava-Rushka, married the daughter of R. Issachar Dov Rokeah, the Belzer Rebbe. (See Chapter XVII.)

G15.2. R. Moses David Twersky, married the daughter of R. Solomon Zalmina Zuckerman of Roshkov. (See Chapter XV — Heschel Dynasty.)

G15.3. Feige, married R. Shalom Joseph Friedman of Buhusi-Spikov. (See Chapter XIII — Friedman Dynasty.)

G15.4. Chavah, married R. Nahum of Warsaw, son of R. Jacob Aryey Twersky of Trisk. They perished in the Holocaust.

G15.5. Mirl, married R. Asher Perlow. (See Perlow Dynasty — Chapter VII — G14.2/15.3/16.1.)

NOTE—The present New Square Skvira Rebbe is R. David Twersky (married the daughter of the present Vizhniz Rebbe), son of R. Jacob Joseph (died in 1968), son of R. Israel, son of R. Isaac Twersky (G12.4 above) by his third wife.

CHAPTER XVI

HOROWITZ FAMILY PEDIGREE

INTRODUCTION

ANCESTRY

G3.3. R. Saul Wahl.

G4.6. R. Judah Katzenellenbogen.

G5.2. Dinah, married R. Naftali Hirsch Katz.

G6. R. Isaac Katz.

G7.3. R. Isaiah Katz.

G8. R. Menachem Meinish Katz.

G9. Wife of R. Meir Horowitz (*MaHaRaM* Tiktin).[1] He was Rabbi of Oheilev and Zlatchov, and in 1718 became A.B.D. Tiktin, where he wrote his approbation the same year to *Beit Yaakov*, published in Lvov 1786, and *Gaon Zvi* written in 1732, published in Prague 1737. He died in 1746, and was eulogized by R. Haim HaKohen Rappoport. His second wife was Matil, daughter of R. Ephraim Zalman Katzenellenbogen and they had a son from whom are descended the Ruzhin Chassidic Family.

In his old age, the Rabbi heard of a plan to pay him honor at a family celebration of his birthday. Those involved were twelve distinguished Rabbis, his grandsons, and he put a halt to these plans saying: "From the children whom the Lord has given me, I expect delight in the world-to-come and not in this world."

It was his custom to perform acts of mercy before he ate his meals and would refuse to break his fast until that opportunity arose.

Once before Yom Kippur a visiting preacher rebuked the congregation of Tiktin for being sinners. The Rabbi approached him and said, "You should

549

not have shamed me in public, but in private." "But I had no one particular in mind," came the reply. "Not so," said Rabbi Meir, "for my congregants are good people and only my sins could have been in your mind!"

G10.1. R. Aryey Lieb Horowitz, wrote an approbation to *Divrei Ha-Brit,* published in Zolkiev, 1729. His sons, R. Nathan, A.B.D. Horka, R. Saul of Tiktin.

G10.2. R. Isaiah Horowitz of Brody, married the daughter of R. Haim Landau, A.B.D. Podkamin. (See Landau Family Pedigree.)

G11. Wife of R. Simha, son of R. Moses Halberstam, grandfather of R. Haim, founder of the Halberstam-Sanz Chassidic Dynasty. (See Halberstam Family Pedigree.)

G10.3. R. Joshua Horowitz, A.B.D. Bisk, died in Zolkiev in 1767.

G11. Wife of R. Haim, son of R. David Halpern (A.B.D. Posen).

G10.4. R. Haim Horowitz, A.B.D. Shorigrad, wrote an approbation to *Tiferet Yisrael* published at Frankfurt-on-Oder, 1774.

G10.5. R. Nahum Horowitz.

G10.6. R. Naftali Horowitz, A.B.D. Tiktin from 1744 until his death.

G10.7. R. Menachem Meinish, A.B.D. Chovesk, also wrote an approbation to *Tiferet Yisrael.* (See G10.4 above.)

G10.8. R. Zvi Hirsch Horowitz, A.B.D. Chartkov from 1726 until his death in 1754. He married the daughter of R. Mordecai, son of R. Zvi Hirsch, son of R. Zechariah Mendel. They had eleven children. He wrote an approbation to *Bracha Avraham.*

He was greatly respected by the Besht, his master, who declared that he was one of three families in Israel who gave more respected sons to the rabbinical calling than any other: namely, Rabbi Samuel Shmelke of Nikolsburg and Rabbi Phineas of Frankfurt who were disciples of Dov Ber, the successor of the Besht.

Once when the two sons returned home from their studies under the Maggid, their father inquired of them what they had learned. "We have learned belief that the soul is the kernel and the body its shell," was their reply.

G11.1. R. Abraham Horowitz.

G11.2. R. Samuel Shmelke Horowitz, 1726-78. Together with his younger brother he studied in his youth under the Chassidic leader, Dovber the *Maggid* of Meseritz. He became Rabbi of Rychwal (1754), Sieniawa (1766) and from 1773 as A.B.D. of Nikolsburg (Mikulov) in Moravia, from where he became known as the Chassid Shmelke of Nikolsburg. He did much

HOROWITZ FAMILY

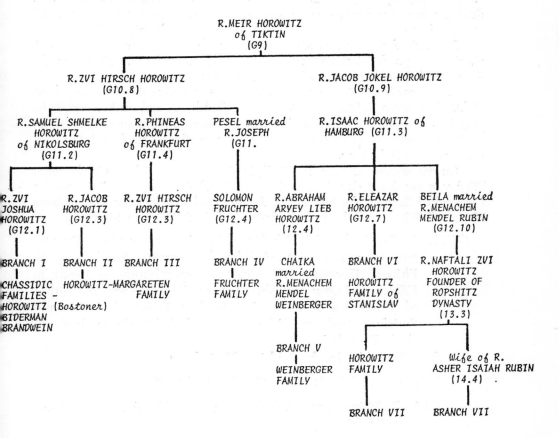

to spread the spirit of Chassidism throughout Poland and Galicia. Because of this, his last appointment led to bitter opposition but he was confirmed in office by the Empress Maria Theresa. Many stories and miraculous happenings were related about him. He had many disciples but kept much to himself leading an ascetic life. He was the author of *Divrei Shmuel*, published in 1862 and *Nezir Hashem*, published in 1869.

Upon his arrival in Nikolsburg to become the Rabbi there, R. Shmelke locked himself in a room and began to pace up and down, repeating over and over the various forms of welcome he anticipated. When the meeting was over, one man who had overheard him in the locked room asked him if he would explain his odd behavior. "By constant repetition I no longer felt any pride when these same phrases were addressed to me by the welcom-

ing committee. Thus their honors did not lead to self-pride. In this way I
interpret the saying (in Ethics of the Fathers) 'May another's honor be as
dear to you as your own—as you care not about the honor you pay yourself,
so should you not care about the honor payed to you by others.'"

He said: If one repents his transgressions because he fears punishment,
his sin is suspended but a record remains. If because he has displeased the
Almighty, his sin is erased and no trace remains.

It is recorded that he preached about seven different sciences on each
of his first seven Sabbaths as Rabbi of Nikolsburg, and on the eighth he
preached about the Torah. In this way he showed the community his ac-
quaintance with the sciences, but that he nevertheless preferred from ex-
periences the Holy Law.

On the second of Iyar (in 1778) Rabbi Shmelke said to his disciples:
"Today is my dying day. The soul of the Prophet Samuel is within me, for
I am called Samuel like him of the Levites, and like him my life has been
52 years." Whereupon he bade farewell and died sitting in his chair.

G12.1. R. Zvi Joshua Liebish Horowitz, A.B.D. Trevitch, Prusstiz
        and Jamnitz. He married his first cousin, daughter of R.
        Phineas Horowitz. He wrote an approbation at Brody in
        1792 to *Tal Orot* published Vienna, 1792. He was the author
        of *Chidushei HaRibaSH* published Przemysl, 1878, and
        Smichut Moshe published Lvov, 1869. His descendants in-
        clude Branch I.

G12.2. Wife of R. Jacob, Rabbi of Kostelberg.

  G13.1. R. Zvi Hirsch Horowitz, A.B.D. Viznik.

    G14. R. Phineas, married the daughter of R. Zvi Joshua Horo-
          witz, his second cousin.

      G15. R. Benjamin Horowitz, married his distant relative,
            Miriam, daughter of R. Eliezer Lipa Horowitz. (See
            Horowitz Family Pedigree — Branch V — Weinberger
            Family — G14.7/15.4.)

  G13.2. Second wife of R. Abraham Moses of Prezworsk (died
          1794).

G12.3. R. Jacob Horowitz. His descendants include Branch II —
        The Horowitz -Margareten Family.

G11.3. R. Nahum Horowitz, A.B.D. Presskov.
G11.4. R. Phineas Horowitz, 1730-1805.[2] He was born in Chartkov
        where his father officiated as Rabbi. He studied at first under
        his two brothers, R. Nahum and R. Samuel, and later under

Dovber the *Maggid* of Meseritz. He became the first Rabbi at Witkowo (Poland) and then at Lachowicze (1764). In 1771 he became A.B.D. of Frankfurt-on-Main where he remained until his death having served the community some thirty-four years. He held a private *Minyan* (Prayer Quorum) in his own home according to the Sephardic Rite, unlike the rest of the Frankfurt community. He was also friendly with the Rabbis Nathan Maas and Nathan Adler. He was a strong opponent of the *Haskalah* Movement and decried Mendelssohn's translation of the Bible into the German. His most prominent pupil was the author of the *Chatam Sofer,* R. Moses Sofer. He was the author of *Hafla'ah,* published in Offenbach, 1787. This was in three parts: 1) *Sefer Ketuvah,* Offenbach, 1787; 2) *Sefer HaMakneh,* Offenbach, 1801; 3) *Panim Yafot,* Ostrov, 1824, published by R. Ephraim Z. Margolioth. He also wrote *Shevet Achim* published, 1838. He married Reche Deborah, daughter of R. Joel Heilprin A.B.D. of Leshov. (See Chapter VI — Branch B — G6.4/7.1/8.6/9.2.)

Having resolved to remain in Meseritz under the tutelage of the Maggid, they found that the longer they stayed the less they found their master's conduct to their liking. He was concerned in excess with mundane matters, the house and his estate, and his livestock. Tasks were assigned to servants, and he acted at times in a strange manner conversing in the markets and streets with people of ill repute.

The Maggid taught the two scholarly brothers the Study of the Ethics, which they had given little attention to, and later convinced them of its importance. To them he said, "I found a house full of unkindled candles, and now that they are alight the house is filled with light."

Rabbi Phineas, on his arrival in Frankfurt-on-Main, where he had been elected Rabbi, received a great welcome. When he was questioned about how he felt at this time he replied that he felt as if he were a corpse being carried to the cemetery, and as if the multitudes were attending the funeral.

While at Frankfurt, his Chassidic followers once asked who should study the *Guide to the Perplexed* by Moses Maimonides. He replied, "The book is like a chemist's shop. He is skilled in the various remedies but to a layman it is dangerous to meddle. The smallest error may kill a man, inadequate precautions may lead to punishment and a mistake to loss of reputation."

Before Frankfurt, Rabbi Phineas was the Rov of a small town called Likhivitz. One cold winter night a traveller sought refuge in the Rabbi's house. Having been warmly received with food, drink and lodging, the man then inquired of the Rabbi, "As a poor, suffering laborer, am I assured of the world-to-come?" Rabbi Phineas replied, "More than you, your horse has more claim to the world-to-come. While you are now comfortable before the fire, your horse, a creature of God like yourself, stands out in the cold ready to move ahead without complaining."

G12.1. R. Meir Jacob Horowitz, 1759-1785, buried in Frankfurt-on-Main. He married the daughter of R. Saul, son of R. Aryey Lieb Lowenstamm. (See Lowenstamm Family Pedigree — Chapter XII.) Novellae of his appear in the *Hafla'ah* by his father.

G12.2. Wife of her first cousin, R. Zvi Joshua Horowitz.

G12.3. R. Zvi Hirsch Horowitz, author of *Machaneh Levi* and *Lachmei Todah*. His descendants include Branch III.

G12.4. Wife of R. Haim, son of R. Gedalliah.

G12.5. Wife of R. Abraham Haim, A.B.D. Zlatchov.

G11.5. R. Joshua Heschel Horowitz, A.B.D. Lublin and Ritshwal. He wrote an approbation in 1773 to *Tiferet Yisrael* (see G10.4. above).

G11.6. Eidel, married R. Moses Joshua, A.B.D. Starin.

G11.7. Leah.

G12. R. Simha, A.B.D. Lodmir.

G11.8. Wife of R. Jehiel Michael Halpern, A.B.D. Shrigrad.

G11.9. Miriam.

G11.10. Wife of R. Israel who succeeded his father-in-law, R. Zvi Horowitz, as A.B.D. of Chartkov in 1754 until 1766.

G11.11. Pesel, married R. Joseph.[3]

G12.1. R. Mordecai Stern.

G12.2. R. Abraham Adler.

G12.3. R. Samuel Shmelke Klein, author of *Tzur HaChayim*. He was A.B.D. Zülz, Hungary.

G12.4. R. Solomon Fruchter, head of the Fruchter Family — Branch IV.

G10.9. R. Jacob Jokel Horowitz, 1680-1755. He was first A.B.D. of Brody and later, about 1747, A.B.D. Glogau. He wrote numerous approbations in both towns. He married the daughter of R. Joshua Heschel, A.B.D. Tarla, son of R. Issachar Berish, son of R. Abraham Joshua Heschel of Cracow (see his Family Pedigree — Chapter IX). R. Jacob died on the 13th Elul and was eulogized by R. Abraham Meshullam, recorded in his *Divrei Meshullam.*

G11.1. R. Menachem Meinish Horowitz, A.B.D. Zmigrad, Galicia, and later A.B.D. of Lvov, where he died in 1765. In 1754 he wrote his defense in support of R. Jonathan Eybeschutz who had been accused by R. Jacob Emden, son of the Chacham Zvi Ashkenazi (see his Family Pedigree) of indulging in the art of magic. This letter appeared in the *Luchot HaEidut* written by R. Eybeschutz. He also wrote an approbation in 1757 on *Manah Eliyahu* by R. Elijah, published Zolkiev, 1758. He married Yita, daughter of R. Jacobke, A.B.D. of Glogau, father-in-law of R. Ezekiel Landau.

G12. R. Joshua Heschel Horowitz, A.B.D. Dombrovo. He wrote an approbation to *Asifat Yehudah,* published Frankfurt-on-Main 1763. He married Sheindel, daughter of R. Aryey Lieb, son of R. Abraham Reb Haim of Lublin. (See Chapter V — Branch B — G7.1/8.6/9.5.)

G13. Feigel, married R. Jacob Silverman.

G14. R. Samuel Shmelke Silverman, A.B.D. Bialystok.

G11.2. Wife of R. Benjamin Wolf Landau, A.B.D. Apt, son of R. Ezekiel, son of R. Zvi Hirsch Landau. (See Landau Family Pedigree — Chapter X — G8.4/9.)

G11.3. R. Isaac "Hamburger" Horowitz, 1715-1767.[4] As a young man he was A.B.D. of Horochov, and succeeded his father later at Glogau. In 1754, a year before his father died, he was elected A.B.D. of Brody where he wrote his approbation to *Ma'amar Kadishin,* published in 1764 at Prague, and also to the Amsterdam Talmud Edition in 1751, to *Tosfot Shabat* and *Ateret Rosh* in 1754 and to *Mishnat Chachamim* in 1765. In 1765, the Chief Rabbi (A.B.D.) of the large and famous Triple Community of Altona-Hamburg-Wandsbeck, the controversial R. Jonathan Eybeschutz died. The community now approached R. Isaac to accept their rabbinical seat and to become their leader. After accepting this position he served the community for only two years before his death in 1767, at the age of fifty-two. In Hamburg he wrote approbations in 1766 and 1767. His Responsa can be found in the works of his contemporaries, *Noda BiYehudah, Or Yisrael* and *Divrei Shaul.* He was also one of the Rabbis involved in the Cleves Get, and both he and R. Jacob Emden declared the divorce valid. (See story in Chapters III and XIII.) He was the author of *Matemei Yitzchak* (1904-5)

and *Matamei Yitzchak veLechem Matzah* (1911). He was
eulogized by R. Abraham Meshullam, as was his father before
him. R. Isaac was married three times, two being daughters of
the Babad Family. (See Babad Family Pedigree.) He had fifteen children.

While still Rabbi of Brody, the famous Hamburger Rov was strongly
opposed to the Besht (Baal Shem Tov). Said the Besht to his disciples, "Go
speak ill of me to Rabbi Isaac Horowitz. If this is done, this great man may
find satisfaction and his heart may rejoice," was his reply to the bewildered
and amazed looks of his disciples.

Rabbi Isaac Hamburger promised a dowry of six hundred golden eagles
for the marriage of his daughter to Rabbi Mendel, son of Rabbi Jacob of
Linsk. However the bridegroom's parents were disturbed by the bride's appearance. Nevertheless, they were persuaded by Rabbi Isaac Hamburger to
discuss it with their son, who wanted her for her nobility of character. By
agreement, the dowry was handed over before the betrothal, but again Rabbi Jacob of Linsk was against the marriage. However, Mendel persisted and
they were married. Said Rabbi Isaac Hamburger, "The Talmud teaches
that when a man takes a wife because of her beauty or wealth, their children will lack good character. But the groom did not wish for either looks
or money, therefore there is every hope they will have great children."

While Rabbi of Brody, Rabbi Isaac was approached by Rabbi Joshua,
a learned man, who requested him to write an approbation to his manuscript on Jewish Law. As Rabbi Isaac was leaving for Hamburg to become
their leader, he read the work and found it to be of great scholarship. "There
is a man greater than I," he told the community leaders on his arrival in
Hamburg, "and he should be your leader before me." However, this decision was not accepted and Rabbi Isaac became their Chief Rabbi, and Rabbi
Joshua was the Court Judge of Hamburg.

G12.1.   R. Mordecai Zvi Horowitz, died at Brody in 1810. He suc-
         ceeded his father as A.B.D. Horochov where he wrote an
         approbation in 1796 to *Tokef HaNes* published Lvov in 1797.
         He married twice: 1) the daughter of R. Moses A.B.D. Sata-
         nov, son of R. Naftali Hirsch, A.B.D. Dubno, son of R. Zvi
         Hirsch A.B.D. Halberstadt. (See Halberstam Family Pedi-
         gree); 2) Dinah, the daughter of R. Joseph, son of Ezekiel
         Landau (see Landau Family Pedigree). He was the author
         of Responsa *Lechem Matzah*, published in 1911.

G13.1.   Reizel, married R. Joel Nathan, son of R. Issachar Berish,
         son of R. Eleazar (A.B.D. Amsterdam).
G13.2.   Yota Deborah, married R. Meshullam Zalman of Vilna.

(See Gunzburg Family Pedigree — G6.2/7.1/8.3/9.2/10.2.)

G13.3. Brendel, married R. Mordecai Zadok Marshalkovitch of Dubno, son of R. David, son of R. Moses Parnas.

G14.1. R. Isaac, married the daughter of R. Moses Balaban of Lvov.

G14.2. Reitze, married R. Isaac Elijah Landau, author of *Me'aneh Eliyahu*. (See Chapter X — G8.1/9.2/10.2/11.2.)

G15. R. Samuel Landau of Dubno.

G14.3. Malka Mindel, married R. Jokel, son of R. Liebel son of Ber.

G14.4. Rachel, married R. Mordecai Zeev Ashkenazi. (See Chapter XII — Branch E.)

G14.5. Dinah Reizel, married R. Zvi Hirsch, son of R. Naftali Hirsch, son of R. Moses Pereles-Rappoport-Kohen. He was the author of *Ezrat Kohanim*. Their daughter, Frumet, was married to R. Abraham Teomim of Buczacz. (See Teomim Family Pedigree — Branch A and Chapter VIII — Branch A — G6.2/7.4/8.4/9.1/10.4/11/12.1.)

G14.6. Rikle, married R. Liebel, son of R. Abraham Parnas. (See Chapter V — Branch B — G7.1/8.1/9.2/10.3/11.1/12.1/13.2.)

G13.4. Hesa, married R. Jonah Joshua, son of R. Samuel of Levertov.

G13.5. Sarah, married her uncle, R. Isaac Naftali Hirsch, son of R. Moses (A.B.D. Satanov). (See above under R. Mordecai Zvi Horowitz.)

G12.2. R. Nathan, A.B.D. White Field and Dubno, where he approved in 1804 the publication of *Sha'ar Shamayim* published in Dubno in 1804. He married the daughter of R. Samuel A.B.D. Vilna.

G13.1. Wife of R. Moses Aaron, son of R. Abraham Abba Zvi Zussman. (See Chapter XIII — G8.10/9.14/10.1/11.3/12.1/13.3.)

G13.2. R. Joshua Horowitz.

G14. R. Zeev Wolf Horowitz.

G15. R. Jacob Jokel Horowitz.

G16. Pesel, married R. David Zvi Rubinstein of Zolkiev. (See Chapter VII — Branch B — Silberfeld-Rubenstein Family — G11.1/12.2/13.1 — page 315.)

G12.3. R. Jacob Joseph Horowitz, A.B.D. Alexnis, died in Brody in 1841. He married his cousin, daughter of R. Samuel, son of R. Jacob Babad. (See Babad Family Pedigree — G7.1/8.2/9.3/10.3.)

G13. R. Zvi Hirsch of Brody.

G14. R. Israel Solomon Horowitz, author of *Tehaluchot Olam*, published Lvov, 1900.

G12.4. R. Abraham Aryey Lieb Horowitz, died in Brody in 1803, married the daughter of R. Abraham Yekutiel (Zalman) Rappoport Pereles of Brody. (See Chapter VII.) Her brother was R. Moses, father of R. Naftali Hirsch Rappoport mentioned above — G12.1/13.3/14.5, and other brother, R. Jacob, was married to the daughter of R. Dovberish Rappoport. (See Rappoport Family Pedigree under descendants of Chacham Zvi Ashkenazi — G8.10/9.14/10.1.)

G13.1. R. Meshullam of Pietrokov.

G14.1. R. Meir of Pietrokov.

G15. Leah, married R. Jacob, son of R. Eliezer Lipa Horowitz, a distant relative. (See Horowitz Family Pedigree — Weinberger Family — Branch V — G14.7/15.2.)

G14.2. R. Motil of Pietrokov.
G14.3. R. Nathan of Pietrokov.
G14.4. Wife of R. Naftali, son of R. Menachem Mendel Weinberger (See below.)
G14.5. Wife of R. Joseph Asher Chajes of Warsaw.

G13.2. R. Isaac of Brody.

G14.1. R. Abraham Liebus.
G14.2. R. Mordecai Zvi Hirsch, married Rikel, daughter of R. Menachem Mendel Weinberger. (See Horowitz Family Pedigree — Branch V — G14.6.)
G14.3. Wife of R. Eliezer, son of R. Moses Shmelke Horowitz of Cracow.

G13.3. R. Menish of Rymanov.

    G14.1. R. Sander of Przemysl.
    G14.2. R. Phineas A.B.D. Voleh.

G13.4. R. Jokel of Cracow.

    G14.1. R. Liebel of Cracow.
    G14.2. Wife of R. Michael David Horowitz, Judge of Cracow.

G13.5. R. Naftali of Dukla.

    G14.1. R. Moses.
    G14.2. Wife of R. Moses, son of R. Menachem Mendel Weinberger, her first cousin.
    G14.3. Wife of R. Isaac, son of R. Meir Weinberger.
    G14.4. Wife of R. Aaron Gutwert.

G13.6. Chaika, married R. Menachem Mendel, son of R. Moses Weinberger of Dukla, head of the Weinberger Family. (See Branch V.)

G12.5. Rachel, married 1) R. Jacobke, son of R. Ezekiel Landau (see Landau Family Pedigree), and 2) R. Nahum Katzenellenpogen of Birz (see descendants of R. Joel Ashkenazi Katzenellenpogen — Chapter VIII.)

G12.6. Rebecca Esther, married R. Meshulam Igra (Egra) A.B.D. Tysmenitsa and Pressburg (from 1794-1801).

After Rabbi Isaac Charif of Sambor had not replied to the offer of the position of Rabbi of Pressburg, the Pressburg community then offered the position to Rabbi Meshulam Igra of Tysmenitsa. Hearing that Rabbi Isaac had been offered the position first, Rabbi Meshulam went to Sambor to investigate why he had not accepted it. Rabbi Isaac denied ever receiving the offer. Thereupon the president of the community admitted that he had received the letter from the community secretary, but they had decided not to inform their Rabbi. In this way they had hoped he would stay in Sambor in preference to the larger city of Pressburg. Even after this Rabbi Isaac declined to go, declaring, "The Divine will wanted Rabbi Meshulam at Pressburg and no human intervention should prevail against it." Thus it was that Rabbi Meshulam became the Pressburg Rov.

    G13. R. Isaac Elijah, married his first cousin. (See G12.11/13.2 below.)

G12.7. R. Eleazar Horowitz, A.B.D. Zalozhtsy, where he died in 1813. He married the daughter of R. Saul A.B.D. Amsterdam (son of R. Aryey Lieb Lowenstamm, a descendant of

R. Heschel of Cracow — see Lowenstamm Family Pedigree).
He is mentioned in the Responsa *Tiferet Zvi* and was the
progenitor of the Horowitz Family who occupied the Rabbinical seat of A.B.D. in the city of Stanislav for some four
generations. (See Horowitz Family Pedigree — Stanislav —
Branch VI.)

G12.8. Reizel, married R. Zvi Jacob, A.B.D. Podkamin, son of R.
Naftali Hirsch A.B.D. Dubno. (See Babad Family Pedigree
Introduction — G7.1/8.2/9.4.)

G12.9. Elke, married R. Naftali Hirsch, son of R. Haim (A.B.D. Podkamin) Landau. (See Landau Family Pedigree — G8.1/9.2
/10.5.)

G12.10. Beila, married R. Menachem Mendel, son of R. Jacob (died
in 1803) Rubin, A.B.D. Linsk.

    G13.1. R. Joshua Heschel, A.B.D. Janow, died in 1824.
    G13.2. R. Samuel Shmelke, A.B.D. Roman (Rumania), married
    the daughter of R. Haim A.B.D. Chernowitz, son of R. Sol-
    omon.

      G14. R. Mendel Horowitz.

        G15.1. Wife of R. Meir.
        G15.2. Ethel, married R. Hirsch Ehrlich.

          G16. Pearl, married R. Isaac, son of R. Haim Friedlander.[5]

            G17. Sarah, married R. David Shneebalg.

              G18.1. R. Haim, married and lives in Brooklyn, N.Y.
              G18.2. R. Shraga Feiwel, married and lives in London.
              G18.3. Others.

    G13.3. R. Naftali Zvi Rubin, adopted his mother's name Horo-
    witz and was the founder of the large Chassidic Dynasty
    of Ropshitz (Ropcycze). (See Horowitz Family Pedigree
    — Ropshitz — Branch VII.)

    G13.4. Wife of R. Ezekiel Halberstam. (See Chapter VII —
    Branch B — page 310 — G11.4.)

G12.11. Gitel, married R. Issachar Berish (Dovberish) Berenstein,
A.B.D. of Hannover.

    G13.1. R. Samuel, A.B.D. Amsterdam, married the daughter of

R. Jacob Moses Lowenstamm, A.B.D. Filehne. (See Chapter XII — Branch A — page 435.)

G13.2. Wife of R. Isaac Elijah, son of R. Meshullam Egra, her first cousin. (See above G12.6.)

G12.12. Hesa, married R. Jonah Joshua, son of R. Samuel of Lobatchov-Vilna.

G12.13. Sarah, married R. Haim A.B.D. Rozdol, son of R. Solomon (author of *Merkavat HaMishna*).

G12.14. Breindel, married R. Meir, son of R. Alexander Sender Landau.

G12.15. Toyba, married R. Saul of Brody.

G12.16. Pesel, married R. Moses A.B.D. Chartkov, son of R. Solomon Dovberish A.B.D. Glogau, son of R. Zvi Hirsch A.B.D. Halberstadt.

G12.17. Frumet, married R. Isaac Landau A.B.D. Vilna.

G10.10. Wife of R. Asher, A.B.D. Nadel-Alik, son of R. Jehiel Israel Eizes, A.B.D. Brest, son of R. Abraham (called Abba Mori).

G11.1. R. Hirsch, A.B.D. Novhardek.

G12. R. Haim, A.B.D. Zitel, married the daughter of R. Zvi Hirsch of Vilna.

G11.2. R. Solomon of Pinsk.

G12. Wife of R. Jehiel Michael, son of R. Mordecai Halevi Epstein.

G11.3. Wife of R. Abraham Horowitz, A.B.D. Lutzk.

G12. R. Avigdor Horowitz, A.B.D. Kamenka, married the daughter of R. Moses Zvi Meisels.

G13. R. Isaac Samson Horowitz, A.B.D. Chernowitz.

G11.4. R. Jehiel of Biala, Lithuania.

G12. R. Yekutiel Zalman of Biala.

G13. R. Shemariah Tannenbaum of Bornov.

G14. R. Jehiel Meir Tannenbaum of Bornov.

G15. Frumet, wife of R. Israel Menachem Mendel Wechsler of Tarnow. (See Chapter IV — Branch H — G11/12.4/13.1/14.2 — page 223.)

BRANCH I

DESCENDANTS OF

R. ZVI JOSHUA HOROWITZ
(INCLUDING HOROWITZ [BOSTONER], BIDERMAN
AND BRANDWEIN CHASSIDIC FAMILIES)

ANCESTRY

G3.3. Saul Wahl.
G4.6. R. Judah Katzenellenbogen.
G5.2. Dinah, married R. Naftali Hirsch Katz.
G6. R. Isaac Katz.
G7.3. R. Isaiah Katz.
G8. R. Menachem Katz.
G9. Wife of R. Meir Horowitz (*MaHaRaM* Tiktin) died in 1746.
G10.8. R. Zvi Hirsch Horowitz, died in 1754.
G11.2. R. Samuel Shmelke Horowitz of Nikolsburg, died in 1778.
G12.1. R. Zvi Joshua Liebish Horowitz.
G13.1. R. Abraham Joel Horowitz, mentioned in the *Chidushei HaRiBeS* by his father.

G14.1. R. Samuel Shmelke Horowitz of Sokolov, mentioned in the introduction of *Chosan Yeshuot,* published in Sokolov, 1811.
G14.2. R. Isaac Horowitz.
G14.3. Wife of R. Zvi Hirsch Berliner. (See Berliner Family — Chapter XII and Teomim Family — Chapter IV.)

G13.2. The second wife of R. Baruch Frankel-Teomim of Leipnik, author of the *Baruch Tam.* (See Chapter IV.)
G13.3. Wife of her second cousin, R. Phineas, son of R. Zvi Hirsch Horowitz.
G13.4. R. Samuel Shmelke Horowitz of Rzeszow.

G14.1. R. Meshullam Zalman Horowitz.

G15. R. Samuel Horowitz, author of *Nezir HaShem.*

G14.2. Wife of R. Moses, son of R. Zalman Pereles.

G13.5. R. Jacob David Horowitz.

G14.1. R. Noah Phineas Horowitz[6] of Brody, and later settled in Safed where he was known as the Rabbi of Magrov. He died there in

1875 and was buried in Tiberias. He married Achsah Riva, daughter of R. Joseph HaKohen of Magrov.

G15.1. R. Alexander Sander Isaac Horowitz of Sadagora, a follower of the Sadagora Chassidim. He married 1) the daughter of R. Abraham Jacob, having no issue, and 2) Toyba Chaya, and had issue, one son. He remarried and had further issue with descendants in Israel.

G16. R. Samuel Shmelke Horowitz (1860-1898), settled in Safed with his grandfather, R. Noah Phineas, when he was about three years old. He was buried in Jerusalem. He married in Jerusalem to Sheine Elke (died in 1942), daughter of R. Eleazar Mendel Biderman. (See below.)

G17.1. Toyba Chaya, married R. Naftali son of R. Abraham Brandwein.

G18.1. R. Samuel Shmelke Brandwein, died in Jerusalem in 1974, married his first cousin, Friedel, daughter of R. Phineas David Horowitz. (See below.)

G19.1. Naftali Jacob Isaac Brandwein (Jerusalem). His children, Shulamit (married Moses Goldzweig, Canada), Rivke (married Amir of Afula), Yafa, Phineas Jonah and Abraham.

G19.2. Rebecca Esther Rachel, married and has issue.

G19.3. Solomon Brandwein (Jerusalem). His children, Joshua, Ayal and Eitan.

G19.4. Moses (Jerusalem), married and has issue.

G19.5. Haim Brandwein (Bnei Brak). His children, Mattithiah and Orit.

G19.6. Eleazar Brandwein.

G18.2. Zusia Brandwein, married Nechamah Adler, of Jerusalem.

G19.1. Professor Haim Naftali Brandwein, married the daughter of R. Kossovsky.

G19.2. Meir, married the daughter of Professor Mirsky of Yeshiva University.

G19.3. Zipporah, married Moses Nob and have issue.

G18.3. David Moses Brandwein, married and had issue.

G17.2. Malka, died in 1971, married R. David Aryey, son of R. Abraham Brandwein of Jerusalem.

G18.1. R. Joseph Karmi (Canada), married and has a son, Aryey.

G18.2. Chaya, married Shabtai Ben-Dov (Jerusalem).

G17.3. Moses Aaron Horowitz, unmarried and the youngest child (Far Rockaway, New York).

G17.4. R. Joshua Horowitz of Jerusalem, 1894-1973, married Sheindel.

G18.1. David Horowitz of Bnei Brak, married and has issue.

G18.2. Rivke, married Menachem Mendel Friedman (New York). Their children, Rachel, Yafa, Nechama, Sarah, David (in Jerusalem) and Ezekiel, all married.

G17.5. R. Abraham Eleazar Menachem Horowitz of Jerusalem, died in 1918, married his first cousin, Sarah Leah, daughter of R. David Zvi Solomon Biderman. (See below.) They both died young.

G18. Wife of R. Joseph Kallach.

G17.6. R. Phineas David Horowitz, born in Jerusalem in 1877. In 1914 while visiting Austria, World War I broke out. He arrived in 1915 in the U.S.A., and settled in Boston, where he became known as the "Bostoner Rebbe." His wife and family came to the U.S.A. later on. His latter two years were spent in New York, where he died in 1941. He married 1) Rebecca, daughter of R. Aaron, son of R. Heschel Lieb Brandwein of Safed (she died in 1904, and her father was a brother of R. Abraham Brandwein mentioned above), and 2) Sarah Sacha, died in 1972, daughter of R. Jehiel Michael, son of R. Aaron Brandwein (a niece of his first wife). He had issue from both wives. His second wife joined him in the U.S.A. arriving on December 31, 1919, not having seen her husband for seven years.

G18.1. Friedel, born in Jerusalem in 1895 to his first wife, married in Boston to her first cousin, R. Samuel Shmelke Brandwein, in 1920.

G18.2. R. Moses Horowitz, born in Jerusalem in 1909, and arrived in New York in 1919, where he later became the New York-Bostoner Rebbe. He married in 1924 to Leah Friedel, daughter of R. Haim Abraham, son of R. Menachem Mendel Eichenstein of Zhidachov. (See Chapter XVII — G2.5/3/4.5.)

G19.1. R. Haim Abraham Horowitz, born in 1933, married 1) Miriam Adler and had a son, Jacob Isaac, and 2) Shoshana Ruchamah, daughter of R. Jonah Halevi Hass, in 1961, and had Rivke Riva, Israel Jonah, Malka Gitel, Esther Liebe and Judith Poria.

G19.2. R. Phineas David Horowitz, born in 1945, married Velke Esther Miriam, daughter of R. Meir Landau. (Descendants of the *Noda BiYehudah*, R. Ezekiel Landau — See Chapter X.) Their children, Mordecai Ziskind and Haim Abraham.

G18.3. R. Levi Isaac Horowitz, born in Boston in 1920, the present Bostoner Rebbe in Boston, succeeding his father there. He married Rachel, daughter of R. Naftali Leifer.

G19.1. R. Phineas David Horowitz, born in 1944, the Khust-New York Rabbi, married Sarah Beila, daughter of R. Joshua Grunwald of Khust. Their children, Moshe Shimon, Yisrael Aaron, Hentsche, Yehoshua and Jehiel Michal.

G19.2. Meir Horowitz, born in 1946, married to Sima Mosberg.

G19.3. Sheine Gitel, born in 1947, married R. Joseph Haim Frankel. Their children, Phineas David, Channah Hinde, Motil Feige and Shlomo Abraham Zvi.

G19.4. Naftali Horowitz, born in 1952.

G19.5. Taube Leah, married Moshe Haim Geltzahler (Monsey, New York). Their daughter, Sarah Sucha.

G18.4. Motil Feige, married R. Jacob Thumim of New York. (See Chapter IV — Branch A.)

G17.7. R. Reuben Nathan Nata Horowitz, married Nechamah Eisenbach.

G18.1. David Samuel Shmelke Horowitz.

G18.2. Matel, married Abraham Bledy.

G18.3. Sender Horowitz.

G18.4. Malka, married Mr. Shon.

G18.5. Rachel, married Jacob Zundel Kroizer.

G18.6. Abraham Horowitz.

G18.7. Phineas Horowitz.

G18.8. Reizel, married Nathaniel Goldberg.

G15.2. Dreize Horowitz, died in 1876, unmarried.

G15.3. Miriam Frume, 1841-1911, married R. David Zvi Solomon (1844-1918) the fourth Admur of the Lelov Chassidic Dynasty in Jerusalem, son of R. Eleazar Menachem Mendel (the third Admur, died in 1883), son of R. Moses (1775-1851, the second Admur Lelov and a son-in-law of the Holy *Yud* — see Chapter IV), son of R. David Biderman, the founder of the Lelov Dynasty.

G16.1. Malka Achsah, died in Jerusalem in 1963, married R. Mordecai David Weinstock, a professional scribe, 1876-1954, son of R. Alter Menachem Kalonymus Weinstock of Karlin, died in 1915.

G17.1. R. Moses Jair Weinstock. His sons, Joseph Menachem, Jacob Solomon, Isaac Samuel and Haim.

G17.2. R. Phineas Uri Weinstock. His children, Solomon, Simeon, Jacob Isaac, Ephraim, Moses, Baruch, wife of R. Abraham Adler and wife of R. Nachman Hirschbaum.

G17.3. R. Jacob Isaac Weinstock.

G17.4. R. Solomon Menachem Weinstock. His children, Meshullam Zusia, Zvi, and wife of R. Abraham Asaph.

G17.5. Channah, married R. Reuben Eisenbach. Their children, Solomon, Baruch, Menachem Shalom, wife of R. Isaac Moses Chen, wife of R. Abraham Aaron Sheinberger, wife of R. Phineas Poierstein, wife of R. Simeon Benjamin Streicher, wife of R. Eliezer Stipenski, and wife of R. Michael Himmelprav.

G17.6. Matil, married R. David Moses Spiegel. Their children, Reuben Issachar, Israel, Haim, wife of R. Haim Weinstock and wife of R. Baruch Brorman.

G17.7. Wife of R. Baruch Benjamin Zeev. Their daughters, Hadassah and Abital.

G17.8. Sarah Frieda Gitel, married R. Mordecai Kadner. Their children, Moses Nahum, Jacob Isaac, wife of R. Jacob Zuriel and wife of R. Isaac Strassburg.

G16.2. R. Jacob Joseph Biderman, 1861-1900. He married Toyba Leah, daughter of R. Abraham Dov Saraph of Safed.

G17. Tamar, the only child, married her uncle, R. Israel Saraph.

G16.3. R. Simeon Nathan Nata Biderman, 1870-1930, succeeded his father as the fifth Admur of Lelov in 1918, and was buried in Jerusalem on the Mt. of Olives. He married Channah Reize, daughter of R. Joseph Zanurt of Cracow.

G17.1. R. Phineas Haim Biderman, married his second cousin, Rivke, daughter of R. Jerachmeel Joseph Biderman. (See note 7 in Chapter IV.)

G18.1. Wife of R. Nahum Teitelbaum.
G18.2. Wife of R. Zvi Dor.

G17.2. R. Moses Mordecai Biderman, the sixth and present Admur of Lelov-Bnei Brak, born in 1903 and married the daughter of R. Abraham Schwarz of Przemysl. Their children, Abraham, Simeon, David, Phineas, Alter Eleazar Menachem, Issachar Dov, Shmelke, wife of R. Samuel Kopp, wife of R. Haim Eleazar Aronzik and wife of R. Samuel Rosenfeld.

G17.3. R. Jacob Isaac Biderman. His children, Simeon, David, Solomon, Israel Dov, wife of R. Joseph Weissberg, wife of R. Jacob Meisels and wife of R. Joseph Berenstein.

G17.4. Elisheva, married R. Menashe, son of R. Moses Joseph Lipschutz of Cracow.

G17.5. Rebecca Rachel, married 1) Abraham Joseph Brandwein and 2) R. Jacob, son of R. Samuel Ehrlich.

G16.4. R. Phineas Uri Biderman, died in 1937, married Gitel, daughter of R. Joseph David Biderman.

G16.5. Rebecca Rachel, married her first cousin, R. Abraham, died in 1927, son of R. Joshua Aaron, died in 1877, son of R. Nathan Judah Adler (descendants of the family of R. Nathan Adler of Frankfurt-on-Main mentioned in Chapter VI). R. Joshua Aaron was married to Deborah Golda, sister of Rebecca's father. (See Note 7 in Chapter IV.)

G17.1. R. Joseph Adler, 1887-1948.

G18.1. R. Jacob Isaac. G18.2. R. Moses.
G18.3. R. Eleazar Adler, Admur in Los Angeles.

G19. Miriam, first wife of R. Haim Abraham, son of R. Moses Horowitz of New York.

G18.4. R. David, 5. Wife of R. Zusia Brandwein, 6. Wife of R.

David Samat, 7. Wife of R. Ephraim Eizik, 8. Wife of R. Abraham Rosenblatt and 9. Wife of R. Bezalel Zawirt.

G17.2. R. Nathan Adler. His children, Moses, Aaron Joseph and Sarah, married Ashkenazi.
G17.3. R. Mordecai Adler.

G18. R. Naftali Haim, married the daughter of R. Haim Meir Hager of Vizhniz. (See Chapter XV.)

G17.4. R. Asher Adler. His daughter married R. Joshua Jacobson.
G17.5. Jochebed, married R. Jacob Rosenblatt. Their children, Moses, Abraham Solomon, wife of R. Phineas Barzel, wife of R. Mordecai Wispish and wife of R. Aaron Samuel Spiegel.

G16.6. Nechamah Rikel, married R. Aaron Joshua, son of R. Solomon Eliach.

G17.1. R. Jacob Isaac Eliach. His sons, Bezalel, David, Liebel, Haim and Zvi.
G17.2. R. Meir Eliach. His son, Aaron Joshua.
G17.3. Sarah, married R. Jacob Yisraeli. Their children, Haim, Meir, Moses and wife of R. Moses Frankel.
G17.4. Toyba, married R. Joseph Adler. Their son, Meir.

G16.7. Sarah Leah, married her first cousin, R. Abraham Eleazar Menachem, son of R. Samuel Shmelke Horowitz. R. Samuel married Sheine Elke, sister of Sarah's father.

BRANCH II

HOROWITZ — MARGARETEN FAMILY ORIGINS

ANCESTRY

G3.3. R. Saul Wahl.
G4.6. R. Judah Katzenellenbogen.
G5.2. Dinah, married R. Naftali Hirsch Katz.
G6.   R. Isaac Katz.
G7.3. R. Isaiah Katz.
G8.   R. Menachem Meinish.
G9.   Daughter, married R. Meir Horowitz, died in 1746.
G10.8. R. Zvi Hirsch, died in 1754.

G11.2. R. Samuel Shmelke, died in 1778.

G12.3. R. Jacob Horowitz, emigrated from Poland to Hungary about 1775.

G13. R. Isaac, about 1797-1845, married Blume Chaya (Julia), daughter of R. Israel Schwartz.

G14.1. R. Nathan Zvi (Ferenz) Horowitz, 1818-1869, married Miriam, daughter of R. Samuel Brunner of Dorogma.

G15.1. Julia, married R. Joel Margareten, who was born in 1837.
G15.2. Rebecca, married R. Edward Friedman.
G15.3. R. Joseph Horowitz, married Amelia Frank.
G15.4. R. Ignatz Horowitz, married Sarah Klein.
G15.5. Sarah, married R. Solomon Salomon-Scharff.
G15.6. Nachal, married R. Meyer Klein.
G15.7. Betty, married R. Joseph Ellenbogen.
G15.8. Rachel Leah, married R. Anton Glattstein.

G14.2. R. Jacob Horowitz, came to the United States in 1883. He married his sister-in-law, Mirl Chaya, daughter of R. Samuel Brunner, in 1848.

G15.1. Julia, married R. Adolph Prince.
G15.2. R. Joseph Horowitz, married Fannie Lichtman.
G15.3. Regina, married R. Ignatz Margareten.
G15.4. R. Leopold Horowitz, married 1) Esther Friedman and 2) Eva Kugelman.
G15.5. R. Moses Horowitz, married Julia Horowitz.
G15.6. R. Samuel Isaac Horowitz, married Ertha Ehrenfeld.

G14.3. R. Abraham Horowitz, married Kate Schulmeister.

G15.1. R. Ferencz Horowitz, married Pepi Gluck.
G15.2. Julia, married R. Samuel Friedman.
G15.3. R. Frank Horowitz, married Esther Friedman.
G15.4. Betty, married R. Adolf Grossman.
G15.5. R. Samuel Horowitz, married twice.
G15.6. Hannah, married 1) R. Bela Greenfeld and 2) R. Isidor Friedlander.

G14.4. Geha, married R. Chaim Klein.

G15. R. David, married Channah Klein.

G14.5. Hannah, married R. Akiva Baer.

NOTE: Full genealogical details of this large family can be found in *Dic-*

tionary and Genealogy of the Horowitz-Margareten Family, published in 1955.

BRANCH III

DESCENDANTS OF

R. ZVI HIRSCH HOROWITZ
author of MACHANEH LEVI

G9.   R. Meir Horowitz of Tiktin, died in 1746.

G10.8. R. Zvi Hirsch, died in 1754.

G11.4. R. Phineas Horowitz, died in 1805.

G12.3. R. Zvi Hirsch Horowitz,[7] died in 1817. He was born in Poland and succeeded his father as A.B.D. of Frankfurt-on-Main, where he wrote an approbation in 1777 to *Toldot Yosef,* published in Sedilkov in 1837. He was the author of *Machaneh Levi,* published in 1801 by his father. He published *Lachmei Todah* in Offenbach in 1816. He was married to 1) Sarah, daughter of R. Abraham Jekutiel Zalman Rappoport of Brody (see Margolioth Family Pedigree — Chapter VII — G8.4/9.1), and 2) Tova Landau in 1796.

G13.1. R. Joel Horowitz. His son, R. Isaac Horowitz, published *Givat Pinchas.*

G13.2. R. David Joshua Heschel Horowitz, born in 1760. He was Rabbi of Floss, and later became A.B.D. of Froienkriegen, where he remained until his death about 1825. He married the daughter of R. Eleazar Kallir, author of *Or Chadash.*

G14.   R. Lazar (Eleazar) Horowitz, 1803-1868, A.B.D. Vienna. He was the author of *Yad Eleazar.*

G13.3. R. Samuel Shmelke Horowitz, of Lvov, elected A.B.D. Brest, and died in 1841.

G14.1. R. Jerachmeel Horowitz, married the daughter of R. Joshua Zvi Meises. He died in Lvov in 1877.

G15. Wife of R. Saul Rokeah. (See Chapter XIII — G8.10/9.14/ 10.1/11.3/12.1/13.4.)

G14.2. R. Simha Horowitz of Plonsk.

G14.3. R. Meir Horowitz, A.B.D. Lvov, died in 1841.

G14.4. R. Isaiah Aryey Lieb Horowitz, 1812-1875, died in Lvov. He married Rebecca Ashkenazi, who was a descendant of the Chacham Zvi Ashkenazi.

G15. R. Samuel Alter Horowitz, 1841-1925. His son, Dr. Martin Horowitz.

G13.4. R. Jacob Joshua Horowitz, married the daughter of R. Ephraim Zalman Margolioth of Brody. He was A.B.D. of Zalozhtsy, and is mentioned in the Responsa of his father-in-law, *Beit Ephraim.* (See Chapter VII — G12.1 — page 293.)

G14.1. R. Zvi Hirsch Horowitz, died in 1873 in Brody, was the author of *Lekutei Zvi* and *Chemdat Zvi.* On his death, he was eulogized by R. Abraham Benjamin Kluger. This eulogy is found in his *Otot Lemoadim,* published in Pressburg.

G14.2. R. Phineas Horowitz, married the daughter of R. Anschel Stryer.

G15. R. Joseph Asher Horowitz of Dukla, married the daughter of R. Mordecai Zvi Weinberger. (See Horowitz Family Pedigree — Branch V — the Weinberger Family — page 573 — G15.4.)

G16. R. Jacob Joshua Horowitz of Stanislav.

G14.3. Dreizel, married R. Solomon Zalman HaKohen, son of R. Meir Zussman. (See Chapter XIII — G8.10/9.14/10.1/11.3/12.1.)

G14.4. Yaret, married R. Abraham Abba Zvi HaKohen, son of R. Meir Zussman. (See G14.3. above.)

BRANCH IV

FRUCHTER FAMILY

G10.8. R. Zvi Hirsch Horowitz.
G11.11. Pesel, married R. Joseph.
G12.4. R. Solomon, surnamed Fruchter.

G13.1. Elijah Fruchter.
G13.2. Eliezer Fruchter.
G13.3. Samuel Fruchter.

G14.1. Solomon Fruchter, of Zulz.

G15. Isaac Zvi Fruchter, of Zulz.

G16.1. Samuel Fruchter, of Sitshel, pupil of R. Yomtov Lipa Teitelbaum, married Chuntche, daughter of R. Ephraim Fischel, son of R. Menachem Rosenberg. They had eleven children, some of whom settled in New York and were the progenitors of a large family. Their children: Menachem Mendel (Brooklyn, N.Y.), Solomon (Jerusalem), Jacob Samson (New York), Zalman Lieb (New York), Israel (New York), Joseph Abraham (New York), Motil (Mordecai) (New York), Moses (New York), Haim (died in World War I), Eli (died in 1944) and Channah Beila (killed).

G16.2. Nathan Uri Fruchter of Zulz. His children also settled in New York and Israel. They are: Raphael (Tel Aviv), David (and his son, Samuel, in New York), Joseph Abraham (New York) and Alta, married Jacob Glazer.

G16.3. Solomon Fruchter of Sitshel.

G16.4. Jacob Samson Fruchter (New York). His children: Solomon Joseph, Menachem Israel and Helen (New York).

G16.5. Raphael Fruchter (New York). His children: Gitel, married Zvi Herring (New York), Isaac (New York), and Joseph (New York).

G16.6. Leah, married Nathan Uri Molk.

G16.7. Frumet, married Eli Dudovitz. Their children: Zalman Lieb (B'nei Brak), David (Haifa) and Rivke, married Moses Dudovitz.

G16.8. Dreza, married Joseph Ganz.

G16.9. Chentze, married Lazer Berkovitz.

G14.2. R. Abraham Uri Fruchter.

G14.3. R. Motte Fruchter.

G14.4. R. Jacob Fruchter.

G14.5. R. Israel Fruchter.

G15.1. Pesel, married R. Hirsch of Alik.

G15.2. Shprintza, married R. Fischel Gans, and had issue.

G15.3. R. Jacob Fruchter. His son, Solomon Zvi, father of David, father of Eliezer, father of Isaac, father of Alter Jeruchem Uri Fruchter of London.

NOTE: Full genealogical details of this family can be found in *Igeret Shlomo* (Hebrew), published privately in Jerusalem in 1960 by Solomon Fruchter.

BRANCH V

THE WEINBERGER FAMILY

G9.   R. Meir, A.B.D. Tiktin.

G10.9. R. Jacob Jokel, died in 1755.

G11.3. R. Isaac (Hamburger) Horowitz.

G12.4. R. Abraham Aryey Lieb.

G13.6.   Chaika, married R. Menachem Mendel Weinberger,[8] of Dukla, born in Plontsch and thus became known as Mendel Plontscher. He was the son of R. Moses (of Dukla, died 1845) and Hannah (died 1849), daughter of R. Zvi Hirsch Goldhammer of Dukla. R. Zvi Hirsch was also the father-in-law of R. Naftali Zvi Horowitz, founder of the Ropshitz Chassidic Dynasty. (See Ropshitz Horowitz-Rubin Family Pedigree.) R. Moses Weinberger was the son of R. Meir Weinberger. R. Menachem died in 1862 in Dukla.

    G14.1.   R. Moses Weinberger, married the daughter of R. Naftali, son of R. Abraham Aryey Lieb Horowitz, his cousin. (See Horowitz Family Pedigree Introduction — G10.9/11.3/12.4/13.5.) They had no children.

    G14.2.   R. Mordeccai Zvi Hirsch Weinberger, married the daughter of R. Wolf of Lvov.

        G15.1. Wife of R. Abraham Simha Horowitz. (See Chapter XVI — Branch VII — G14.1/15.4/16.1.)

        G15.2. Wife of R. Israel Abraham, son of R. Eliezer Lipa Horowitz. (See below G14.7.)

        G15.3. Wife of R. Samuel Zangwill, son of R. Kalman Kalonymus Kahan of Sighet. Another son of Kalman was married to another member of the Weinberger family. (See below G14.7/15.6.) The Kahan Family were descended from the renowned Talmudist, R. YomTov Lipman Heller (author of *Tosfot YomTov*).

        G15.4. Wife of R. Joseph Asher, son of R. Phineas, son of R. Jacob Joshua Horowitz. (See Horowitz Family Pedigree — Branch III — G13.4/14.2.)

        G15.5. R. Samuel, married Liebe, daughter of R. Eliezer Asher, son

of R. Isaac Landau A.B.D. Wladowa. (See Chapter VII —
Branch A — page 289 — G11.)

G14.3. R. Naftali Weinberger, married the daughter of R. Meshullam
of Pietrokov, son of R. Abraham Aryey Lieb Horowitz. (See
Horowitz Family Pedigree Introduction — G10.9/11.3/12.4/
13.1.)

G15.1. Leah, married R. Shalom, son of R. Jehiel Wagschal of Fristik. (See Chapter XVII — Shapiro Dynasty.) Five children
and their families perished in the Holocaust. One son survived.

G15.2. Phineas Weinberger.

G15.3. Judah Lieb Weinberger perished with his family.

G15.4. Other daughters.

G14.4. R. Meir Weinberger, married the daughter of R. Saul Landau,
Rabbi of Cracow.

G15.1. R. Shalom Shakna Weinberger, died in Paris in 1917. He
married the daughter of R. Hirsch Nathanson (uncle of R.
Saul Joseph, son of R. Liebus Nathanson of Lvov). (See
Ornstein-Ashkenazi Family Pedigree — Chapter XII.)

G16.1. Rachel, married R. Saul Eleazar Goldbaum (Judge, of
Dukla).

G17. Baruch Moses, perished with his family in the Holocaust.

G16.2. Chaika, born about 1867, died in 1941, married R. Solomon, son of R. Asher Korn (his second wife).

G17. R. Haim Zvi Weinberger, born in 1912, settled in New
York in 1946, the year he married Rosa, daughter of R.
Gedalliah, son of R. Aaron Zelig Lieberman (son-in-law
of R. Menachem Mendel of Linsk, son of R. Abraham Haim
Horowitz). (See Ropshitz Family Pedigree — G14.3/15.2
/16.2.)

G18.1. Gedalliah Ezekiel, born in 1947, married in 1968 to
Rachel, daughter of Ezekiel Zvi Schwartbaum. Their
sons are Isaac Joseph and Jacob Samuel Weinberger.

G18.2. Solomon Abraham, born in 1950, married in 1972 to
Gitel, daughter of Benjamin Schakna (son-in-law of
R. Mendel Halberstam). (See Branch C.)

G18.3. Solomon Shakna Zaida.

G15.2. R. Isaac Weinberger, married the daughter of R. Naftali, son of R. Abraham Aryey Lieb Horowitz. (See Horowitz Family Pedigree Introduction — G10.9/11.3/12.4.)

G14.5. Reize, married R. Abraham of Shendeshov, son of R. Jacob Jokel Horowitz. (See Ropshitz Family Pedigree — G14.2/15.3.)

G14.6. Rikel, married R. Mordeccai Zvi Hirsch of Brody, son of R. Isaac (of Brody) Horowitz. (See Horowitz Family Pedigree Introduction — G10.9/11.3/12.4.)

G14.7. Beila, married R. Eliezer Lipa, son of R. Israel Abraham Horowitz, of Stanislav. This branch of the Horowitz family is descended from a different line to those descendants of R. Meir Horowitz of Tiktin, (who was a descendant of R. Saul Wahl Katzenellenbogen). Their families during the nineteenth century, however, did intermarry significantly.

G15.1. R. Israel Abraham Horowitz, married his first cousin, daughter of R. Mordecai Zvi Weinberger (See above — G14.2/15.2.)

G15.2. R. Jacob Horowitz of Stanislav, married Leah, daughter of R. Meir Horowitz (of Pietrokov), son of R. Meshullam, son of R. Abraham Aryey Lieb Horowitz. (See Horowitz Family Pedigree Introduction — G11.3/12.4/13.1/14.1.)

G15.3. R. Isaac Meir, married the daughter of R. Baruch Brodetsky.

G15.4. Miriam, married R. Benjamin Levi son of R. Phineas son of R. Zvi Hirsch Horowitz. See Horowitz Family Pedigree Introduction — G10.8/11.2/12.2/13.1/14.)

G15.5. Hinde, married R. Benjamin Levi Horowitz (see G15.4).

G15.6. Sheindel (died 1888), married R. Moses Simha (died 1893), son of R. Kalonymus Kalman Kahan. (See above — G14.2/15.3.)

G16. R. Samuel Zangwill Kahan of Cracow, author of *Anaf Etz Avoth,* published in Cracow in 1903. This contains full genealogical notes on the families "Horowitz, Heilpern, Rappaport, Margulies, Schorr, Katzenellenbogen" and others.

G15.7. Rosa, married R. Joel Hornstein of Rodymysl.

BRANCH VI

HOROWITZ FAMILY OF STANISLAV

G9.   R. Meir Horowitz.

G10.9. R. Jacob Horowitz (1680-1755).

G11.3. R. Isaac Horowitz of Hamburg (1715-1767).

G12.7. R. Eleazar Horowitz, died in 1813.

G13.1. R. Aryey Lieb Horowitz A.B.D. Stanislav from 1784-1843. He was born in 1758 and studied first under his father and later under his uncle, R. Moses Egra, who ordained him. R. Aryey Lieb and his uncle were those who were persuaded by R. Hirschel Levin not to ban the *Besamim Rosh* by his son, which appeared in 1793. In 1836 he wrote an approbation to the Slovita Edition of the Talmud. His responsa appear in the works of others: *Nata Sha'ashuim; Beit Ephraim,* by R. Ephraim Zalman Margolioth; and *Dvar Halacha.* He opposed Chassidism and was the author of *Pnei Aryey* on Biblical commentary (1876) and responsa (1909) which appeared in the *Bar Livai* by his son R. Meshullam. He died in Tysmenitsa in 1844.

G14.1. R. Zvi Horowitz.

G15.1. R. Eleazar Moses Horowitz, A.B.D. Pinsk, died there in 1890. His *Hagahot* appear in the Vilna edition of the Talmud.

G16.1. Wife of R. Meir Schwartz.

G16.2. Wife of R. Baruch Halevi Epstein (1860-1942), author of the *Torah Temimah,* first published in Vilna 1904. He also eulogized his father-in-law, which is recorded in the *Nachal Dimah,* his first book, published in Warsaw 1890. His other books were, *Safah Le'Ne'emanim,* published in Warsaw 1893; *Mekor Baruch,* published in Vilna 1928 and New York 1954, containing historical and biographical information; *Mekor Baruch,* published in Vilna 1928, a commentary on the Jerusalem Talmud; *Avodat HaLeviim* and *Gashmi Bracha,* published in Cracow 1930; *Tosefet Bracha,* published in Pinsk 1937 and Tel Aviv 1964-5; and his last work, *Baruch She'amar* which was published shortly before the war in Pinsk 1938.

R. Epstein was the son of R. Jehiel Michal Epstein (1829-1908), author of *Aruch HaShulchan,* an authoritative work giving the *halachic* rulings which had been promulgated by Rabbinical authorities after the period of R. Joseph Caro. R. Jehiel was married to the sister of the famous *Netziv,* R. Naftali Zvi Judah Berlin (1817-93), who later married the sister of R. Baruch Epstein.

G15.2. R. Joshua Horowitz.

G14.2. R. Jacob Jokel Horowitz, a Judge in Brody. His sons were, R. Abraham Issachar, A.B.D. Chechinov, R. Baruch, A.B.D. Shvershin and R. Eleazar, A.B.D. Zulz.

G14.3. R. Meshullam Issachar Horowitz, 1808-1888. He was successively A.B.D. of Zbariz (1827-1842), Tysmenitsa (1843-1845), during which period his father died, and finally at Stanislav (1845-1888). The family and his descendants were to hold this latter position for some four generations according to his will *"Al kisi loh yeshev Zar"* ("No outsider to our family shall occupy my seat"). He was the author of *Bar Livai*, published in 1909. *Ein Dimah* (Cracow 1888) contains three funeral orations on his death delivered by his son, R. Saul, grandson of R. Haim Aryey and R. Phineas, A.B.D. Sokol.

G15.1. R. Joseph Horowitz, A.B.D. Ujscie Zielone (Ozca), author of *Alon Bachut,* a biography about his father, published in Drogobitch 1888. He was elected A.B.D. there from 1882.

G15.2. R. Jacob Jokel Horowitz, 1834-1915, A.B.D. Deliatyn and Stanislav, died in Stry. He was the author of *Avnei HaShoham,* published Lvov 1849; *Shirot Dodim,* Tarnow 1884; and responsa, *RiBaM,* Munkacz 1908.

G15.3. R. Saul Horowitz, 1831-1912, A.B.D. Ujscie Zielone from 1853, and then A.B.D. Tysmenitsa from 1883. He was the author of *Besamim Rosh,* published in Lvov 1874. He married Rebecca, daughter of R. Jacob Herz London, whose wife, Hinde, was a granddaughter of R. Alexander Sender Margolioth of Satanov (mentioned in Chapter VII Branch B).

G16.1. R. Haim Aryey Horowitz, A.B.D. Cracow at the turn of the century. He was the author of *Chayei Ari* (Cracow 1890); *Tikun Eruvin; Zichron Moshe,* a funeral oration on the death of Sir Moses Montefiore (Cracow 1886); *Ezrat Nedachim* (Cracow 1923); *Ein Dimah,* one of three funeral orations on the death of his grandfather, R. Meshullam Issachar (Cracow 1888), and *Kol Nehi* (Cracow 1889). He married Zipporah, daughter of R. Michael Cypres of Cracow. (See Chapter VII — Branch B — G6.3/7.1/8.2/9.1/10.2/11/12.)

G17.1. R. Michael Horowitz, the oldest son, a beer and wine merchant, died in Cracow in 1940. He married twice, firstly to Toyba Chaya Grushkevitz. He had one son from his second wife. He was the author of *Avodat HaLevi'im.* From his first wife:

G18.1. Meshullam Issachar (Salo) Horowitz, born in Cracow in 1891, a diamond merchant, married Mina Geldzahler. After her death, in 1964, he settled in Israel, where he died in 1968.

  G19.1. David Horowitz, born in Antwerp, Belgium in 1914. He settled in London, where he married Irene Welch.

    G20.1. Michael Horowitz, born in 1944, a lawyer.
    G20.2. Vivienne, born in 1945, married Maurice Wohl.

  G19.2. Thea (Toyba), born in Antwerp, Belgium in 1921, married in Havana in 1945 to Shulim Krauthammer born in 1904).

    G20.1. Dr Marcel Krauthammer, M.D., born in Rio de Janeiro in 1946, married in 1974 to Joy Melton.
    G20.2. Dr. Charles Krauthammer, M.D., born in New York in 1950, married in 1974 to Ruth Robyn.

G18.2. Helen (Hinde), born about 1900 in Cracow, and died in 1957 in Switzerland. She married Abraham Isaac Ungar of Jolin.

  G19.1. Henrich (Haim Joshua) Ungar, 1926-66, died unmarried.
  G19.2. Saly (Saul) Ungar, born in 1928, married Flora Levy. Their children, Yitzchak and David.
  G19.3. Thea, born in 1931, married Bernard Tepfer. They came to the U.S.A. in 1959, the year of their marriage. Their children, Abraham Isaac, Naftali Herz and Helen (Sarel Hinde).

G17.2. R. Eleazar Moses Horowitz, married Helena Yaner, author of *Tov Ayin*, published in Cracow 1935. He and his family (a son and three daughters) perished. One son survived, Hershel Horowitz of London, married and had issue.

G17.3. Reala, married Kalman Bergglass of Bochnia (near Cracow). They perished with their son Aryey Liebish (Leo).

G17.4. R. Zvi Hirsch Horowitz, born in Cracow in 1872 and died in Nice, France in 1945. He was the third son. When he was eighteen his novellae were printed in the *Chayei Ari* by his father. At the outbreak of World War I the family fled to Moravia and settled in Bruenn where he was A.B.D. of the

Machzikei HaDat Congregation. In 1916 he moved to Scheveningen and in 1919 to Dresden where he was A.B.D. of the *Shomrei HaDat* Congregation, and Chief Rabbi of the city from 1920. He later became Chief Rabbi of Antwerp, and in 1940 settled in Nice, where he died five years later.

He was a great scholar and was also interested in the history of the Jewish communities and their Rabbis. He collected manuscripts which he published in some of his works. Some of these were obtained from Holland on the death of R. Issachar Berish Berenstein who died in the Hague in 1893. He was the author of *Kitvei HaGeonim*, Pietrokov 1928, which was published by Hanoch Heinich Follman (mentioned in Chapter III); *Kitvei Yeshanim*, a collection of nine letters by R. Saul Levin (Berlin) to his brother-in-law, R. Jacob Moses Lowenstamm of Amsterdam during the period that R. Saul was forced to leave Germany because of his controversial *Besamim Rosh*, published in Budapest 1930; *LeKorot HaKehillot BePolanya*, 1969; a family genealogy appended to the *Tov Ayin* by his brother; and *Die Familie Lwow* in *Monatsschrift für Geschichte und Wissenschaft des Judentums* in 1928. This last article contains a detailed genealogy of the Lwow, Karl Marx and Hochgelehrter families in German.

He married Feige, daughter of Isaac Berel Wetchner of Dukla. She died in 1943. Two sons, Abraham (Adolph) and Haim Aryey (Leo), died unmarried.

G18.1. Rosa, 1897-1972, married Julius (Judah Aryey) Neumarkt of New York. He has a number of his father-in-law's manuscripts including the *Lekorot HaKehillot BePolanya*.

G19. Sarah Ruth, married Mordecai Ben-Joseph of Charlotte, North Carolina. They have no issue.

G18.2. Meshullam Zalman (Salo Peter) Horowitz of Ashville, North Carolina, born in 1898 and came to the U.S.A. in 1944.

He attended Yeshiva in Dukla until 1914, when the family moved to Bruenn in Czechoslovakia, and finally settled in Holland in 1916. Here he became employed in a Rotterdam coffee and tea importing house and later operated his own company in partnership in Danzig. He married in 1936 to Karoline Charlotte Strauss in The Hague (civil ceremony) and their religious wedding was conducted later in Berlin with his father and brother-in-law officiating. In the U.S.A. he settled in Murphy, North Carolina in the lumber business until retirement in 1968.

G19. Robert Horowitz, born in Danzig in 1937 and came with his parents to the U.S.A. in 1944. He schooled in Murphy, N.C., and received his Bachelor of Law from Yale University in 1964. From 1964-68 he worked for the Wall Street law firm of Cravath, Swaine and Moore, and thereafter, for a short time, as special assistant to the Director of Urban Technology and Research in the U.S. Department of Housing and Urban Development in Washington, D.C. Since 1969 he has specialized in tax law with a firm in New Haven, Conn.

He married in 1974 to Janice Brunig, and lives in Branford, Conn.

G18.3. Erna, married R. Dr. Ephraim Sonneschein, perished with three children.

G16.2. R. Phineas Horowitz, born in 1865 and died in Cracow in 1920. He was the A.B.D. of Bohorodezany, near Stanislav in East Galicia.

G17.1. Mirl, married Zalman Goldstoff of Cracow. (See Chapter IV — Branch J — G12.1/13.1/14.6.) They perished in the Holocaust.

G17.2. Reizel, married Freilich of Cracow, perished.
G17.3. Esther, married 1) Tamir and had issue, and 2) Dr. Landau (Tel Aviv).

G18. Phineas Tamir, agriculturist for the Israeli Ministry.

G17.4. Miriam, married 1) Engelhard, and had issue, and 2) Josef Folger.

G16.3. Esther, 1863-1907, died in Cracow. She married and later divorced Nathan Isaac Michelson, who settled in Cape Town, South Africa. (See Chapter XII — Michelson Family.) Her tombstone thus reads: "Esther Horowitz, daughter of Rabbi Saul halevi Horowitz, A.B.D. Tysmenitsa and sister of Rabbi Haim Aryey halevi Horowitz, A.B.D. here, Cracow, died in the prime of her life, aged forty-four years, after a serious protracted illness she passed away leaving her [two] sons behind." —no mention is made of her marriage.

G16.4. Sarah, died in 1934, married 1) Samuel Goldberg, and had six children G17.1 - G17.6, and 2) Berish Weinberg of Jaroslav and had a daughter, G17.7.

G17.1. Deborah Leah (Lora), married Moses Michael Eisenstein.

G18.1. Golda (Genia), married Fritz (Fred) Bauer (Brookline, Mass.). They had no issue.

G18.2. Rosa, married Max Weidenfeld (died in 1968).

G19. Sir (Arthur) George Weidenfeld, born in Vienna in 1919. He emigrated to England in 1938 and joined the B.B.C. where he worked in overseas intelligence and as a commentator of European affairs. He was also a lecturer at Chatham House and founded *Contact*, a journal of contemporary affairs and the arts, in 1945. Three years later he and Nigel Nicolson established the large publishing company of Weidenfeld-Nicolson. A subsidiary was established in Jerusalem in 1969, the same year he was knighted by Queen Elizabeth II.

From 1949-50, he was political advisor to Chaim Weizmann and later a member of the Board of Governors of the Weizmann Institute of Science. He was the author of *The Goebbels Experiment*, 1943.

He married 1) in 1952 to Jane Sieff, and had a daughter, 2) in 1956 to Barbara Connolly (nee Skelton) and 3) in 1966 to Sandra Payson Meyer.

G18.3. Regina, married and later divorced, died in Switzerland.

G17.2. Herz Goldberg, killed in World War I, having no issue.

G17.3. Miriam Judith, married Moses Freilich, and had a son who died young.

G17.4. Esther, married Herman (Hirsch) Scharf of Seret in Bukovina. They perished with two sons and a daughter. One survived,

G18. Rose, married Moritz Toprover, having no issue (New York).

G17.5. Aryey Lieb Goldberg of Cracow. One daughter perished.

G18.1. Esther (Erna), married Willie Greenbaum of Buenos Aires.

G18.2. Hela, married Simeon Haber of Ashdod.

G17.6. Helen, born in 1888, came to the U.S.A. in 1947 where she was reunited with her husband Joseph Kleinman of Vienna. They had no issue.

G17.7. Rebecca (Regina), married Emil Langsam (died in 1975) of Przemysl. They settled in Manchester. Their sons, Bruno and Alexander of Manchester.

G15.4. R. Isaac Horowitz (1828-1899), A.B.D. Stanislav, suceeding his father in 1888. From 1852 he was A.B.D. of Ottynia, and later of Zurawno. He was the author of *Toldot Yitzchak*, published in 1866, and *Meah Shearim*, published in 1887. He married Toyba, the daughter of R. Ephraim Thumim. (See Chapter IV — Branch A — G12.1/13.5.)

G16. R. Aryey Lieb Horowitz (1847-1909). He was ordained by Rabbi Joseph Saul Nathanson and Rabbi Haim Halberstam of Sanz. In 1871 he became A.B.D. Zalozhtsy, and later Seret in Bukovina. In 1879 he became A.B.D. Stry and was thereafter called the *Stryzer Rov*. He succeeded his father at Stanislav in 1904, and was the author of *Hegeh Aryey*, published in 1902, and *Harei Besamim*, the first volume published in 1882, second volume in 1897, and third and fourth volumes in 1958. He was decorated by Emperor Francis Joseph I in 1908.

G15.5. R. Eleazar Horowitz (1831-1912), A.B.D. Mariampol in Galicia from 1851-1856, and then A.B.D. Rohatyn from 1866-1912. Unlike his father, he was inclined toward Chassidism and was the author of *Dvar Halachah*, published in 1863, and *Ateret Zekeinim*, as an appendix to the *Pnei Aryey* by his grandfather, published in 1876.

G16.1. R. David Horowitz, A.B.D. Koslov from 1909 and later A.B.D. Stanislav. He was the author of *Imrei David*, published in 1934. He married the daughter of R. Haim Babad, A.B.D. Mikulonitz (See Babad Family Pedigree — Branch D).

G17.1. R. Jeruchem Fischel Horowitz, married the daughter of R. Abraham Joshua Heschel of Kopzynce (See Heschel-Apt Family Pedigree).

G17.2. R. Moses Horowitz, A.B.D. Stanislav.

G17.3. R. Eli Horowitz and Leah Horowitz, (17.4).

G17.5. Daughter, married and lived in New York.

G17.6. R. Nachman Horowitz, A.B.D. Koslov and Helitsch. He married his first cousin, Raatze, daughter of R. Joshua Heschel Babad, A.B.D. Podwoloczyska. They perished in the Holocaust. (See Chapter XI — Branch D — G13.2.)

G16.2. Beila Horowitz, married R. Joshua Heschel Frankel-Teomim. (See Teomim Family Pedigree — Chapter IV — Branch H — G11.1/12.1/13.1.)

G15.6. Dinah Horowitz, married R. Isaac Joshua Kliger, A.B.D. Greiding in Poland.

G16.1. R. Meir, A.B.D. Kracowitz. His son was the A.B.D. of Teschin, and he in turn had issue, living in London.

G16.2. R. Joseph, succeeded his father in Greiding and married Rachel, the daughter of R. Moses, son of R. Haim Babad, A.B.D. Mikulonitz. (See above and Chapter XI — Branch D — G12/13.1/14.3.)

G17.1. R. Meshulam Isaachar Kliger, perished in 1943. He was Rabbi of Mizrachi in Cracow, and married Gitel, the daughter of R. Eliezer Fesser of Gorlice.

G18.1. R. Isaac Joshua, perished with family.

G18.2. R. Eliezer, perished with family.

G18.3. R. Jerachmeel, perished with family.

G18.4. Esther, married Isaac, son of R. Abraham Jacob Liebes, himself a descendant of the Stanislav Horowitz family (See below G13.2). They live in New York.

G17.2. R. Haim perished, G17.3. R. Isaac Joshua perished.

G17.4. R. Moses, married Blume, the daughter of R. Isaac, son of R. Joshua Heschel Babad (See Babad Family Pedigree — Branch D — G13.2/14.5). They also perished.

G17.5. Eidel, married secondly R. Heschel Glazer of Przemysl.

G17.6. Dinah, married R. Mordecai Beryl.

G16.3. Chaya Sarah, married R. Zvi Hirsch Ashkenazi of Stanislav. (See Chapter IV — Branch A — G12.5/13.4/14.4.)

G16.4. Deborah, married R. Aaron, son of R. Joseph Zeev Halber-
        stam, as his second wife, and had issue as well. (See Halber-
        stam Dynasty — Keshanow Branch C.)

G13.2. Wife of R. Joshua Liebes.

  G14. R. Haim Aryey Liebes, A.B.D. Josefow, married the daughter of R.
        Elijah Horoshovsky, A.B.D. Drogobitch.
   G15. R. Joshua Liebes, A.B.D. Zlatchov.
     G16. R. Mordecai Dov Liebes of Yaritchov, died in 1921, married
           Miriam, daughter of R. Meir.

        G17.1. R. Abraham Jacob Liebes, A.B.D. Bilkamin, perished in
                1942. He married Bonah, daughter of R. Moses Joseph.
           G18.1. R. Isaac Eizik Liebes, born in Greiding and settled in
                   the Bronx, New York, member of the New York Beth
                   Din, married Esther, daughter of R. Meshullam Issachar
                   Kliger. (See above G15.6/16.2/17.1.) He was the author
                   of Responsa: *Beit Avi*, published in New York in 1971.
              G19.1. Eidel Binah (Adina), married Haim, son of R. Eze-
                      kiel David Halberstam (of Bobov). (See Halberstam
                      — Branch B.)
              G19.2. Bathsheva Rachel, married Moses, son of Eliezer
                      Sorotskin. They live in Israel and have issue: Jacob
                      and Eliyahu Meir.
              G19.3. Aviva Miriam.
              G19.4. Uri Liebus, perished in 1942.

           G18.2. Bathsheba, perished in 1943.

        G17.2. Frieda, married R. Elijah Zvi, son of R. Isaac Zeev, per-
                ished with family.

BRANCH VII

ROPSHITZ (ROPCZYCE) DYNASTY — HOROWITZ FAMILY

ANCESTRY

G9.   R. Meir Horowitz, died in 1746.
G10.9.   R. Jacob Jokel Horowitz, died in 1755.
G11.3.   R. Isaac "Hamburger" Horowitz, died in 1767.
G12.10. Beila, married R. Menachem Mendel, died in 1803, A.B.D. Linsk,
         son of R. Jacob Rubin.

G13.3. R. Naftali Zvi, 1760-1827, founder of the Dynasty of Ropshitz.[15]
He was first the A.B.D. there and later became the first Admur of
Ropshitz. He was taught by R. Elimelech of Lyzhansk and was
one of the main leaders of Galician Chassidism. He was the author
of *Zerah Kodesh*, sermons on the Torah and for the Festivals (published in 1868); *Ayalah Shelucha*, a commentary on Genesis and
Exodus (published in 1862); and *Ohel Naftali*, a collection of his
talks and tales about him (published in 1910.) He married a daughter of R. Zvi Hirsch Goldhammer of Dukla. (Another daughter was
married to R. Moses Weinberger of Dukla. See this Chapter —
Branch V.) His children and descendants adopted the surname of
Horowitz, and a son-in-law was the founder of the Rubin Chassidic Dynasty.

The Ropshitzer was against asceticism. Once when an old Chassid came
and showed how he wore sackcloth and mortified himself, he exclaimed:
"How mighty is Satan that he has succeeded in ensnaring an old man like
yourself."

His wife once commented to him: "For such lengthy prayer today, have
you improved the generosity of the rich in their gifts to the poor?" The
Rabbi replied: "I have accomplished half my prayer, for the poor are willing
to accept them!"

R. Zvi Elimelech of Dynow once offended the Ropshitzer. On visiting
him in order to placate him, the Ropshitzer said: "Indeed it is within my
power to punish you for your disrespect. But I shall refrain from using this
power, for the Lord said to Moses: 'Put off thy shoes from off thy feet' (Exodus 3.5). The word shoe (*Na'al* in Hebrew) contains the initials of the
words Bite, Sting and Hiss. In the *Ethics of the Fathers* (Chapter 2:15) it is
related that by these three methods the Sages inflicted punishment for disrespect. But Moses, the first Sage, was instructed not to use these if the sinner
repents."

He used to say: "I used to loath acceptance of a Rabbinical post, be-
lieving I would be forced into flattery, which I so despise. But when I observed that everyone, tailor, shoemaker or storekeeper must practice it, I
said to myself: 'Since flattery is unavoidable and universal, I may as well
be a Rabbi.'"

Once he came to a wealthy but miserly Jew for a donation. When the
miser heard of his arrival, he hid himself in the barn. The Ropshitzer, notic-
ing the miser steal away, summoned the man and said: "The Talmud says
that it is greater to welcome guests than the *Shechinah*. You have acted
properly, for when the Lord appeared to Moses, he hid his face, but when
we appeared, you hid your entire body in the barn."

On the occasion of his first sermon, he preached: "I am a worm and not a man, as the Book of Psalms recalls. But you, Chassidim, being afraid of worms, I expect thus your fitting obedience!"

The Ropshitzer took great care in concealing his piety. Once, when praying, lying with outstretched hands and feet on the ground at midnight, someone entered unexpectedly. The Rabbi turned and said: "If the people only knew how great is their Rabbi, they would respect him even more." As the Rabbi intended, the man left and related how the Rabbi was a vain boaster.

G14.1.   R. Eliezer Horowitz, studied under his father and succeeded him. He became Admur of Dzikov in 1848 and died in 1860.

As a young boy, Eliezer once became unruly and was rebuked by his father, the Ropshitzer. "Father, it is not my fault for I succumbed to the temptation of the Evil Impulse," answered the child. "Learn from the Evil Impulse how to perform your duty," said his father. "But father," replied Eliezer, "the Evil Impulse has no Satan to tempt him away from performing his duty!"

In his last will and testament he wrote, "My sermons should not be printed, for if my disciples will eat and drink excessively on the Sabbath, they will take my book, rest, open the book, and immediately fall asleep. I do not care to be their slumbering partner!"

G15.1.   Wife of her first cousin, R. Hanina, son of R. Jacob Horowitz.
G15.2.   Beila, married R. Meir Nathan, son of R. Haim Halberstam of Sanz. (See Chapter XIV — Branch B.)
G15.3.   R. Meir Horowitz, 1819-1877, Admur Dzikov, married the daughter of R. Kalman Pizeles. They had ten children. He studied under his uncle, R. Asher Isaiah Rubin, and R. Zvi of Rymanow, and was the author of *Imrei Noam.*

   G16.1.   R. Naftali Haim Horowitz, married the daughter of R. Moses Unger of Dombrovo (see Chapter XVII). He was the author of *Nechmad Chidushei HaShas* and *Mincha Chadasha.* He settled in Jerusalem, and died in 1895.

      G17.1.   R. Elijah Horowitz, A.B.D. Jolin.

         G18.   R. Menashe Horowitz, A.B.D. Jolin.

           G19.   Frieda, married R. Abraham son of R. Elijah Frankel-Teomim. (Chapter IV — Branch H.)

      G17.2.   R. Eleazar Horowitz.

         G18. Wife of R. Raphael Horowitz. (See below — G14.1/15.4/ 16.1/17.2/18.2.)

   G16.2.   R. Tuvia Horowitz, Admur Maden, died in 1886.

G17. R. Benzion Horowitz, Admur Maden, born in 1865, married Golda Leah, daughter of R. Phineas of Kinsk, son of R. Nathan David Rabinowitz. (See Chapter IV — G6.4/7/8/9.2/10.4.) They perished.

G18. Deborah Pearl, married R. Judah Joshua Spira. (See Chapter XVII.)

G16.3. R. Joshua Horowitz, succeeded his father as Admur Dzikov, died in 1913. He was the author of *Ateret Yehoshua* (Responsa published by his grandson, R. Haim), *Emek Halacha, Tosefet Mitzvah, Derech Malachim* and *Kedusha Meshuleshet.*
G17.1. R. Alter Ezekiel Horowitz,[16] born in 1879, succeeded his father as Admur Dzikov in 1913. He married the daughter of R. Israel Hager of Vizhniz. They perished in 1943.

G18.1. R. Haim Menachem David Horowitz, Admur Dzikov.
G18.2. R. Judah Horowitz, survived the Holocaust, the Admur Dzikov Jerusalem.

G17.2. Wife of R. David Spira of Bukovisk. (See Chapter XVII.)
G17.3. Wife of R. Menashe, son of R. Berish Eichenstein of Veretski. (See Chapter XVII.)
G17.4. Wife of R. Emanuel Weltfried, Admur Pavianitz-Lodz. He died in 1939.
G17.5. Wife of R. Phineas Nathan of Ridnik, son of R. Eliezer Zvi Safrin of Komarno. (See Chapter XVII — Eichenstein-Safrin Dynasty.)

G16.4. R. Jehiel Horowitz, 1850-1928, Admur Pokshavnitz-Tarnow, married the daughter of R. David of Keshanov, son of R. Haim Halberstam. (See Chapter XIV — Branch C.)

G17.1. Wife of R. Ezekiel David, son of R. Benzion Halberstam of Bobov. (See Chapter XIV — Branch B.)
G17.2. R. Naftali Horowitz, Admur Tarnow, died in 1931.
G17.3. R. Alter Horowitz, Admur Pokshavnitz, perished.

G16.5. R. Aaron Horowitz, died in 1919, Admur Biyetch, married Tilly, 1862-92, daughter of R. Haim Halberstam, founder of the Sanz Dynasty. (See Chapter XIV.)

G17.1. Rechel, married R. Weinberger of Sardahly. They had no issue.

G17.2. R. Alter Eliezer Horowitz, Admur Biyetch, married 1) Ita, daughter of R. Moses Judah Lieb, son of R. Solomon Spira (see Chapter XVII). They had one son and after their divorce, he remarried 2) Leah Horowitz, and had three daughters.

G18.1. R. Haim Solomon Horowitz of Stryzow-New York, married the daughter of R. Raphael Gross. He was the author of *Darkei Noam*.

G19.1. Raphael, killed in a plane crash. His son, Jacob Hirsch.

G19.2. Moses Lieb (Brooklyn, N.Y.), married twice and has issue from both.

G19.3. Zvi Hirsch (Hershel), married Rechel, daughter of R. Aryey Lieb, son of R. Isaac Tuvia Rubin. (See below — G14.4/15.3/16.2/17.3.) They have nine children, of whom Nechama Frieda married her first cousin, Haim Jacob Meir, son of R. Ezekiel Shraga Rubin-Halberstam.

G19.4. Jacob Jokel Horowitz (Brooklyn, N.Y.), married and has issue.

G19.5. Rivke, married Eli, son of R. Zalman Lieb, son of R. Moses Teitelbaum. (See Chapter XVII — G11.1/12.1/ 13.4/15/16.)

G19.6. Blume, married R. Moses (her first cousin), son of R. Naftali (Kristirer Rov-New York) son of R. Raphael Gross.

G19.7. Beila, married R. Menachem Adler (Toronto).

G18.2. Chaya, married R. David Kleinberger of Sanz. They perished with their two children.

G18.3. Rebecca, married R. Simha, son of R. Meir Gross.

G18.4. Beila Reizel, perished, unmarried.

G17.3. Tirzah, married R. Haim Segal Lieberman, Admur of Biyetch. The post was taken over by his younger brother-in-law, and he remained the Rabbi of Dobre.

G18.1. Rechel Deborah, perished, married R. Samuel son of R. Aaron Teitelbaum of Krinitz.

G18.2. Abraham Joshua Heschel Lieberman, married and has two sons (Israel).

G18.3. Sheindel, married Abraham England of the Radomsk Family. (See Chapter IV.)

G18.4. Miriam, married Hirsch Feldman, and have issue.

G18.5. Alter Lieberman (Brooklyn, N.Y.), married and has issue.

G19.1. Tirzah, married R. Judah Lieb Shapiro (Miami, Florida) and have issue.

G19.2. Aaron Isaac Lieberman.

G19.3. Haim Isaac, married and has issue.

G19.4. Jacob Lieberman.

G18.6. R. Isaac Lieberman, A.B.D. Ropshitz, perished.

G17.4. Deborah, married R. Issachar Dov, 1889-1969, son of R. Haim Jonah, A.B.D. Jeshov, son of R. Alexander Samuel Halpern of Lvov. He succeeded his father-in-law as Admur Biyetch-New York.

G18.1. Chaya Tilla, married Joel, son of R. Jonah Thumim of Vilktasch. They reside in London. (See Teomim Family — Chapter IV — Branch A.)

G18.2. Eleazar Halpern (Boro Park), born in 1917, married Rose, daughter of R. Aryey Lieb, son of R. Jehiel Teitelbaum of Kolbuszov. (See Chapter XVII.)

G19.1. Leah, married Isaac Meir Klahr (Pittsburgh, Pa.). Their children, Deborah and Haim Jonah.

G19.2. Jehiel Leibish Halpern, married Rivke Reizel, daughter of Jacob HaKohen Gesang.

G19.3. Sarah Rivke Rachel.

G18.3. Ezekiel Shraga Halpern (Brooklyn, N.Y.), born in 1915, married Chaya Frieda, daughter of R. Haim Dov, son of R. Samuel, son of R. Moses Halberstam of Bardiyov. (See Chapter XIV — Branch E.)

G19.1. Samuel Joseph Halpern, born in 1948, married Esther, daughter of Jacob Ferster. Their son is Issachar Menachem.

G19.2. Aaron Jonah Halpern, married Feigel, daughter of Solomon Laufer.

G18.4. Leibish, died in infancy.

G18.5. Alexander Samuel Halpern, born in 1923, married Mirl, daughter of Hirsch Sock. Their children, Deborah (married Joseph Leshkowitz), Hirschel Eliezer Lipa and Chaya Rosa.

G18.6. Miriam Beila, married Abraham, son of R. David Zusia
        Sheinfeld. Their children, David, Aaron Jonah and De-
        borah Dinah.

G18.7. Naftali Halpern, 1925-45.

G18.8. Mendel Halpern, born in 1926.

G18.9. Aaron Haim Halpern.

G18.10. Nahum Reuben Halpern.

G17.5. R. Abraham Zvi Hirsch Horowitz, Admur Biyetch-New
       York, born in 1887 and died in the U.S.A. He married Beila,
       daughter of R. Aryey Lieb Rokeah.

G18.1. R. Moses Horowitz, married the daughter of R. Aaron
        Horowitz (the Probiczner Rov, unrelated to the Ropshitz
        family). They perished with their family.

G18.2. Haim Joseph Horowitz, married and perished.

G18.3. R. Shalom Horowitz of Biyetch-New York, married Toyba,
        daughter of R. Ezekiel, son of R. Haim Jacob, son of R.
        Shalom Rosenfeld. (See Chapter XIV — Branch H.) They
        have five children.

G17.6. Zipporah, married R. Moses, son of R. Joseph Horowitz of
       Krasna, perished with their children.

G16.6. R. Asher Isaiah Horowitz, Admur Rymanov, married the
       daughter of R. Joseph of Rymanov. He was the author of
       Me'adeni Melech, and died in Cracow in 1934.

G17.1. Sarah Deborah, married R. Isaac of Rymanov, son of R.
       Israel Friedman of Sadagora. (See Chapter XV — Friedman
       Dynasty.)

G17.2. R. Zvi Haim Horowitz, Admur Rymanov, died in 1939, mar-
       ried the daughter of R. Israel Hager of Vizhniz. Their son,
       R. Moses Eliezer, perished in the Holocaust, was the last
       Admur of Rymanov. R. Zvi and his wife were first cousins.
       (See below.)

G16.7. Wife of R. Jacob Isaac, son of R. Israel Elimelech Unger of
       Jabna. (See Chapter XVII.)

G16.8. Wife of R. Shalom, son of R. Aaron Halberstam of Sanz. (See
       Chapter XIV — Branch D.)

G16.9. Wife of R. Israel Hager of Vizhniz (died in 1936).

G16.10. Wife of R. Israel Horowitz of Malitsch. Their fathers were
        first cousins. (See G14.2/15.1 below.)

G15.4. R. Israel Horowitz, born in 1814, became Admur of Bernov, and married 1) Jochebed, daughter of R. David Hager of Zablodov (and had issue), and 2) Beila, daughter of R. Abraham Haim Horowitz of Linsk (first cousins).

G16.1. R. Abraham Simha Horowitz, died in 1916, succeeded his father as Admur Bernov, and settled in Israel in 1909. He married the daughter of R. Mordecai Zvi Hirsch Weinberger. (See Horowitz Family — Chapter XVI — Branch V.)

G17.1. R. Isaac Jacob, born in 1864, married 1) the daughter of R. Reuben Horowitz of Dembitz, his second cousin (see below G14.1/15.5), and 2) the daughter of R. Zvi Hirsch, son of R. Moses Horowitz. (See below — G14.1/15.6/16.1.)

G18.1. R. Avigdor Horowitz, married Channah, daughter of R. Meir Horowitz of Linsk. (See below — G14.3/15.2/16.1 /17.3/18.4 — page 600.)

G18.2. Wife of R. Reuben, son of R. Mordecai David Horowitz. (See below — G14.2/15.2/16.1/17.1.)

G17.2. R. Alter Horowitz, Admur Stachev, married Miriam, daughter of R. Moses, son of R. Kalonymus Kalman of Neustadt. R. Kalman was the son of R. Joseph Baruch Epstein.

G18.1. R. Israel Joseph Horowitz of Riglitz, married Rebecca, daughter of R. Isaac Horowitz. (See below — G15.6/16.3.)

G19.1. R. Naftali Horowitz (New York), married and had issue, Isaac, Eliezer and Raatza.

G19.2. Esther, married R. Moses, son of R. Samuel Horowitz and had issue; a daughter married Nussbaum and a daughter married Gelma, and a son.

G19.3. Abraham Simha Horowitz (New York), married and had issue. His son, Alter Eliezer, married Rachel Leah, daughter of R. Menashe, son of R. Jacob Isaac Horowitz-Pentzer. (See below — G14.4/15.1/16.3/17/18/ 19.2.)

G18.2. R. Raphael Horowitz of Kolomya, married the daughter of R. Eleazar, son of R. Naftali Haim Horowitz. (See above — G14.1/15.3/16.1/17.2.)

G18.3. Four daughters perished.

G17.3. Bracha, married R. Mordecai, son of R. Zvi Elimelech Spira of Birch. (See Chapter XVII.)

G15.5. R. Reuben Horowitz, Admur Dembitz, known for his dancing the whole of the Sabbath from the age of thirteen years old.

G16.1. Alter, died young.

G16.2. R. Samuel Horowitz of Dembitz, 1865-1921, married the daughter of R. Jehiel, son of R. Isaac Lieb Wagschal of Fristik. (See Chapter XVII — Shapiro Dynasty.)

  G17.1. Wife of R. Isaac, son of R. Naftali Horowitz of Malitsch-New York. (See below — G14.2/15.1/16.1.)

  G17.2. R. Zvi Elimelech Horowitz, the last Admur of Dembitz, perished with his family.

  G17.3. R. Haim Jacob Horowitz, perished with his family.

G16.3. R. Naftali Horowitz, Admur Dembitz, perished with his family.

  G17. R. Reuben Horowitz, married Reizel, daughter of R. Simha, son of R. Simeon Alter Frankel-Teomim. (See Chapter IV — Branch H.)

    G18. Sarah, married Hirsch Meilich Kornreich (Brooklyn, N.Y.) Their children, Naftali Reuben, Judah Wolf, Simha Abraham, Reizel and Miriam.

G16.4. Wife of R. Bezalel, Admur Pilzano.

G16.5. Wife of R. Israel Joseph, son of R. Jacob Isaac (of Dombrovo) Unger. (See Chapter XVII — Unger Dynasty.)

G16.6. Wife of R. Isaac Jacob Horowitz.

G15.6. R. Moses Horowitz, Admur Rozvadov, died in 1894, married the daughter of R. Jekutiel Zalman Lieb Teitelbaum. (See Chapter XVII — Teitelbaum Dynasty — G11.1/12.1/13.6.)

G16.1. R. Zvi Hirsch Horowitz, succeeded his father as Admur Rozvadov, and died in 1918. After World War I he lived in Vienna and later in Rzeszow, where he died.

  G17.1. R. Ephraim Horowitz, married his first cousin, daughter of R. Abraham Haim Horowitz.

    G18.1. R. Moses Horowitz of Rozvadov, perished in the Holocaust.

    G18.2. Wife of R. Eliezer son of R. Joshua Spira of Rivochich. Their fathers were first cousins.

G18.3. R. Naftali Horowitz, the last Admur of Rozvadov, perished.

G17.2. Second wife of R. Isaac, son of R. Abraham Simha Horowitz. (See above G15.4/16.1/17.1.)

G17.3. Genendel, married R. Jacob Epstein. (See Chapter XIV — Branch E.)

G17.4. Menashe Horowitz, perished in Lvov with his family.

G17.5. R. Simha Haim Horowitz, married the daughter of R. Jacob Moses, son of R. Eliezer Zvi Safrin of Komarno. Their family perished. (See Chapter XVII — Eichenstein — Safrin Dynasty.)

G17.6. Wife of R. Elimelech, son of R. Naftali, son of R. Judah Horowitz of Malitsch. (See G14.2 below.)

G16.2. R. Abraham Haim Horowitz, 1850-1915, Admur Plontsch from 1894.

G17.1. R. David Horowitz, A.B.D. Pshezlov, and later Admur of Rzeszow, married Ruchamah, daughter of R. Simeon Alter Frankel-Teomim of Padgorze. (See Chapter IV — Branch H.)

G18.1. Miriam, married R. Alexander of Kolbuszov-New York, son of R. Aryey Lieb Teitelbaum. (See Chapter XVII.)

G18.2. Wife of R. Joseph David Epstein (See Chapter XVII — Eichenstein Dynasty.)

G17.2. R. Eliezer Horowitz, 1881-1942, married the daughter of R. Meir Judah Spira of Bukovisk. (See Chapter XVII.) He was Rabbi in Grodzisk and Tarnow.

G17.3. Wife of R. Ephraim, her first cousin, son of R. Zvi Horowitz.

G17.4. Wife of R. Elimelech, son of R. Zvi Joseph Rubin of Jasla. (See below — G14.4/15.4/16.2.)

G17.5. Wife of R. Joelish Teitelbaum of Satmar-New York.

G16.3. R. Isaac Horowitz, 1862-1940, Admur Stachin, married Esther daugther of R. Menachem Mendel Eichenstein of Zhidachov. (See Chapter XVII.)

G17.1. Rebecca, married R. Israel Joseph, son of R. Alter Horowitz. (See above — G15.4/16.1/17.2.)

G17.2. R. Judah Horowitz, Admur Stachin-New York, married his second cousin, daughter of R. Joshua of Rivochich, son of R. Zvi Elimelech Spira of Blozov. (See Chapter XVII.)

G18. Channah, married Obadiah Yudkovsky, and have issue.

G16.4. Wife of R. Zvi Elimelech Spira, Admur Blozov.

G16.5. Rosel, married R. Aaron Shnieur Zalman, son of R. Mordecai Dov Twersky. (See Chapter VII — Branch B — G7.4/8.2/9.6/ 10.4/11.2/12/13/14/15.)

G16.6. Channah Blume, married R. Shalom David, son of R. Jacob Isaac Unger of Jabna. (See Chapter XVII.)

G14.2. R. Jacob Horowitz, Admur Kolbuszov and Malitsch, died in 1839. On the death of his father he became a *Zadik* and because of the miracles ascribed to him, he was called the "Little Baal Shem Tov."

G15.1. R. Judah Horowitz, 1820-79, married Reizel Sarah, daughter of R. Haim Meir Jehiel Shapiro of Mogielnica. (See Chapter XVII — Shapiro Dynasty.) In his youth he studied under R. Eliezer Horowitz, Admur Dzikov and R. Haim Halberstam of Sanz, and became Admur Malitsch in 1837.

G16.1. R. Naftali Horowitz, 1845-1915, Admur of Malitsch from 1879, author of *Kedushat Naftali*. He married 1) the daughter of R. Meir Nathan, son of R. Haim Halberstam of Sanz (see Chapter XIV — Branch B), and 2) the daughter of R. Abraham Abbish Kaner.
From his first wife:

G17.1. Shprintze, married R. Haim Eliezer of Radlov, son of R. Jacob Isaac Unger of Dombrovo. (See Chapter XVII.)

G17.2. Rochma, married R. Sinai, son of R. Baruch Halberstam. (Chapter XIV — Branch E.)

G17.3. Tirzah, married 1) R. Benzion Halberstam of Bobov and 2) R. Jehiel of Kretchinev. The daughter from the second marriage was Rosa Blume of Warsaw, married.
From his second wife:

G17.4. R. Elimelech Horowitz, born in 1881, married the daughter of R. Zvi Horowitz of Rozvadov. He was the Rabbi in Malitsch, and perished.

G17.5. R. Eleazar Horowitz, A.B.D. Borowa (Galicia), perished.

G17.6. R. Menachem Mendel Horowitz, succeeded his father as Admur Malitsch, and married Frume Beila, daughter of R. Samuel, son of R. Phineas Frankel-Teomim. (See Chapter IV — Branch H.)

G17.7. R. David Horowitz, married the daughter of the R. of Jasla.

G17.8. R. Abraham Abbish Horowitz[17] of Kraly, married the daughter of R. Isaac Weiss of Spinka.

G18.1. Pearl, married R. Jacob Joseph Weiss, grandson of R. Isaac Weiss mentioned above. He is the Admur Spinka-New York-Bnei Brak. (See below — G14.4/15.3/16.1/17.1/18.2 /19.1.)

G18.2. R. Samuel Zvi Horowitz, Admur Kraly-Spinka-Williamsburg. One daughter Miriam, married Jehiel, son of Ezekiel Wagschal. (See Chapter XVII — Shapiro Dynasty.) Another daughter married R. Phineas Shalom, son of R. Mordecai Hager (Admur Vizhniz-Monsey).

G18.3. Miriam, married R. Schmidman (Queens, N.Y.).

G17.9. R. Isaac Horowitz, Admur Malitsch-New York, author and musical composer, married his relative, Chavah Pearl, daughter of R. Samuel, son of R. Reuben Horowitz of Dembitz. (See above G14.1/15.5/16.2.)

G18.1. R. Samuel Aaron Horowitz, born in 1923, married Channah Hecht. Their children, Chaya Gitel, Rechel, Menashe, Naftali and Reuben.

G18.2. Beila, married R. Simha, son of R. Abraham David Rubin, the Lancut Rebbe (Queens, N.Y.), and have issue.

G18.3. Rechel. G18.4. Ethel.

G18.5. Reizel Sarah, married R. Haim Israel Framowitz. She and a child were killed in 1966 and he remarried.

G17.10. R. Baruch Horowitz, died in New York in 1954, married the daughter of R. Eleazar, son of R. Elimelech Weissblum of Lyzhansk. (See Chapter XVII.)

G18.1. R. Abraham Abbish Horowitz, Malitsch-Lyzhansk Rebbe (New York), married and has issue.

G18.2. R. Jacob Horowitz, married and has issue.

G17.11. Beila Mirl, married R. Ezekiel, only son of R. Meir Jehiel Halstok of Ostrowce (Poland). Their family perished.

G17.12. Frieda, married R. Asher Lemel, son of R. Tuvia, son of R. Abraham Horowitz of Shendeshov. (See below.)

G17.13. Bracha, married R. David Teitelbaum of Przemysl.

G17.14. Zipporah, married R. Phineas Shemariah, son of R. Aryey Lieb Halberstam. (See Chapter XIV — Branch D.)

G17.15. Sosha, married R. Joseph David, Admur Sassov-Lvov-New

York, son of R. Eleazar Rubin of Glogov. (See Chapter XVI — Branch VII.)

G16.2.　R. Israel Horowitz, married the daughter of R. Meir Horowitz of Dzikov. (See G15.3 above.)

G17.1.　R. Haim Jehiel Horowitz, A.B.D. Reinzow, perished in 1942. He married the daughter of R. Hananiah YomTov Lipa Teitelbaum of Sighet.

G17.2.　R. Abraham Simha Horowitz, Admur Malitsch-Jerusalem. His family perished.

G15.2.　R. Hanina Horowitz, Admur Ulanov, died in 1881, married his first cousin, daughter of R. Eliezer Horowitz.

G16.1.　R. Haim Jacob Horowitz, born in 1851, succeeded his father as Admur Ulanov, married his second cousin, daughter of R. Moses Eliakim Unger of Dombrovo. (See Chapter XVII.)

G17.1.　R. Mordecai David Horowitz, married the daughter of R. Nahum Zvi Teitelbaum of Drogobitch. They perished. (R. Mordecai's sister married his wife's brother.)

G18.　R. Reuben Horowitz, married the daughter of R. Abraham Simha, son of R. Israel Horowitz of Bernov. (See above — G14.1/15.4/16.1.)

G17.2.　Shifra, married R. Phineas Rokeah. (See Chapter XVII.)

G17.3.　Wife of R. Mordecai David, son of R. Nahum Zvi Teitelbaum.

G16.2.　Esther, married R. Zvi Hirsch Spira, Admur Munkacs, author of *Darkei Teshuva*. (See Chapter XVII.)

G16.3.　R. Asher Horowitz, married Channah Golda, daughter of R. Eleazar Rosenfeld. (See Chapter XIV — Branch H.)

G17.　Sheindel, married R. Aryey Lieb Halberstam. They perished with their son, Haim Asher.

G15.3.　R. Abraham Horowitz, Admur Shendeshov, died in 1905, married Reize, daughter of R. Menachem Mendel Weinberger of Dukla. (See Chapter XVI — Branch V — G13.6/14.5.)

G16.1.　R. Tuvia Horowitz, 1878-1923, Rabbi of Shendeshov, married Charne, daughter of Asher Moses Lemel Dim.

G17.1. R. Abraham Horowitz, married Jochebed, daughter of R. Elimelech Frankel-Teomim. (See Chapter IV — Branch H.) They perished.

G17.2. R. Israel David Horowitz, born in 1899, settled in the U.S.A. in 1932. He married Jentel, daughter of R. Meir Moskovitz, Admur Shatz, and succeeded him as the Admur Shatz-New York. He died in the U.S.A. in 1966.

G18.1. R. Meir Horowitz, born in 1927, Admur Shatz-New York, married Sima, daughter of R. Asher Jonah, son of R. Eleazar Weinberger and have six children.

G18.2. Abraham Horowitz, born in 1932, married Blume, daughter of Samuel Schachter and have five children.

G18.3. Sarah (New York), married and divorced.

G18.4. Rachel, married R. Solomon, son of R. Moses Samuel Rotenberg. (See Chapter XVII — Eichenstein Dynasty — G2.1/3.3/4.3/5/6/7/8.)

G17.3. R. Naftali Horowitz, married the daughter of R. Isaac Horowitz of Stachin. They perished.

G17.4. R. Asher Lemel Horowitz, married Frieda, daughter of R. Naftali Horowitz of Malitsch. They perished.

G17.5. R. Benzion Horowitz, married the daughter of R. Eleazar of Sassov, son of R. Jacob Joseph Rubin of Glogov. (See below G14.4/15.3/16.1/17.1/18.3.) They perished.

G17.6. R. Haim Jacob Horowitz, married the daughter of R. Haim Pinter. They perished.

G17.7. Channah, married R. Zeida, son of R. Isaac Menachem Eichenstein. (See Chapter VII — Eichenstein Dynasty — G2.5/3.1/4.2/5.1/6.)

G17.8. Zipporah (perished in Cracow), first wife of R. Meilich Reinman. He had issue (See Chapter XVI — Branch VII — G14.4/15.4/16.1/17.1/18/19/20/21.1.)

G17.9. Beila, married and divorced, having no issue.

G17.10. Rachel, unmarried, perished.

G16.2. R. Alter Dov Horowitz, A.B.D. Stryzow, and succeeded his father as Admur Shendeshov in 1905. He died in 1930.

G16.3. R. Asher Horowitz, Admur Shendeshov-New York.

G16.4. Wife of R. Naftali, son of R. Zvi, son of R. Lieb Ehrlich.

G16.5. Wife of R. Shalom, son of R. Joshua Rosenfeld. He succeeded his father as Admur Kamenka.

G17.1. R. Naftali Zvi Rosenfeld, succeeded his father as Admur Kamenka.

  G18. Wife of her uncle, R. Isaac Rosenfeld.

G17.2. R. Menachem Mendel Rosenfeld, perished in 1944, married the daughter of R. Shalom Eliezer Halberstam of Rotsfurt. (See Chapter XIV — Branch F.) He was Admur Bistrich (Rumania).

G17.3. R. Haim Jacob Rosenfeld Admur Lvov-Keshanov, perished.

  G18.1. R. Joshua Rosenfeld, Admur Kamenka-Lvov, married the daughter of R. Shalom Rokeah of Lobatchov. (See Chapter XVII.)

  G18.2. Hannah, married R. Naftali, son of R. Haim Alexander Rosenfeld. (See Chapter XIV — Branch H.)

G17.4. R. Isaac Rosenfeld, Admur Rzeszow.

  G18. R. Abraham Joshua, married Sheindel, daughter of R. Haim Alexander Rosenfeld.

G17.5. R. Aaron David Rosenfeld of Yaritchov, married his first cousin, daughter of R. Alter of Yaritchov whom he succeeded as Admur.

G17.6. R. Reuben Rosenfeld, married his niece. He was A.B.D. Kamenka.

  G18. R. Shalom of Kamenka, perished. He married the daughter of R. Aaron Rokeah of Belz.

G17.7. Hannah Golda, married her first cousin, R. Shalom, son of R. Eleazar Rosenfeld.

 G16.6. Wife of R. Moses Eliakim Unger of Dombrovo. (See Chapter XVII.)

G15.4. Wife of R. Abbish Frankel.

 G16. R. Reuben Frankel.

  G17. R. Abraham Frankel. He had a number of children including,

   G18.1. R. Baruch Frankel.

    G19. R. Naftali Frankel, married Sarah, daughter of R. Aaron, son of R. Elisha Halberstam of Gorlice. (See Chapter XIV — Branch E.)

G18.2. R. Saul Frankel.

G19. R. Naftali Frankel.

G15.5. Wife of R. Heschel, A.B.D. Alpin.

G15.6. Wife of R. Naftali Unger of Jabna. (See Chapter XVII.)

G15.7. Wife of R. Jehiel, son of R. Isaac Lieb Wagschal. (See Chapter XVII — Shapiro Dynasty.)

G15.8. Wife of R. Eleazar, son of R. Moses, son of R. Isaac of Kozenitz.

G14.3. R. Abraham Haim Horowitz, Admur Linsk, died in 1831.

G15.1. Beila, second wife of her first cousin, R. Israel, son of R. Eliezer Horowitz.

G15.2. R. Menachem Mendel Horowitz, died in 1868, succeeded his father as Admur Linsk, married the daughter of R. Nathan Rabinowitz of Parziveh. (See Chapter IV.)

G16.1. R. Abraham Haim Horowitz, died in 1904, Admur Linsk, married the daughter of R. Issachar Berish of Istrik, son of R. Zangwill of Litovsk.

G17.1. Rechel Breindel, married R. Baruch, son of R. Moses Halberstam of Keshanov. (Chapter XIV — Branch C.)

G17.2. R. Simeon Horowitz.

G18. Wife of R. Issachar Dov, son of R. Menachem Mendel Rokeah of Dynow. (See Chapter XVII.)

G17.3. R. Meir Horowitz, 1843-1923, Admur Linsk, married Hinde, daughter of R. Naftali Zvi Parnes.

G18.1. R. Jacob Horowitz, married Eidel, daughter of R. Elimelech, son of R. Isaac, son of R. Elimelech Rubin. They perished with their five children.

G19. R. Elimelech Horowitz, born in 1911, married Rebecca, daughter of R. Aaron David, son of R. Shalom Rosenfeld. (See above G14.2/15.3/16.5/17.5). They came to the U.S.A. in 1947.

G20.1. Jacob, married Leah, daughter of Abraham Weinfeld, and have issue.

G20.2. Beila, married R. Simeon Zisholtz, head of a Yeshiva, and have issue.

G18.2. R. Menachem Mendel Horowitz, the last Admur of Linsk, married Chava, daughter of R. Abraham Shalom of Stropkov, son of R. Ezekiel Shraga Halberstam. (See Chapter XIV — Branch A.) The family perished.

G18.3. Rebecca, married R. Ezekiel Shraga Frankel-Teomim, son of R. Samuel Shmelke of Klasni. (See Chapter IV — Branch H.) They perished.

G18.4. Channah, married R. Avigdor, son of R. Isaac of Bernov, son of R. Israel Horowitz. (See above — G14.1/15.4/16.1/ 17.1/18.1.) They perished.

G18.5. Frieda, married R. Zvi Hirsch, son of R. Aryey Lieb Halberstam of Tarnow. (See Chapter XIV — Branch A.) They perished.

G18.6. Hentche, married her first cousin, R. Naftali, son of R. Koppel, son of R. Naftali Zvi Parnes. They perished.

G18.7. Beila, married R. Elimelech, son of R. Isaac Michael son of R. Ezekiel Paneth.

G17.4. R. Naftali Zvi Horowitz of Sanz.

G18. Rachel, married R. Jacob Avigdor mentioned below (G15.7 /16).

G17.5. R. Israel Horowitz. His son, Karmish.

G17.6. Wife of R. Phineas Haim Taub of Rozdol. (See Chapter XVII — Eichenstein Dynasty.)

G16.2. Toyba, married R. Aaron Zelig Lieberman. (See Chapter XVII — Rokeah Dynasty.)

G15.3. Wife of R. Avigdor Halberstam, Admur Dukla, brother of R. Haim of Sanz. (See Chapter VII — Branch B.)

G15.4. Wife of R. Meshullam Zalman, son of R. Aryey Lieb Lipschutz, A.B.D. Vizhniz. (See Chapter XVII — Teitelbaum Dynasty — G11.2/12.1.)

G15.5. Wife of R. Moses Haim Ephraim, A.B.D. Boligrad.

G15.6. Wife of R. Mendel Weinfeld of Gorlice.

G15.7. Chaya, married R. Abraham Issachar Avigdor. A number of children perished.

G16. R. Jacob Avigdor, Chief Rabbi of Mexico, died in 1967. He married his relative, Rachel, daughter of R. Naftali Zvi Horowitz (G15.2/16.1/17.4 above). Two daughters perished in the Holocaust.

G17.1. R. Isaac Chaim Avigdor, born in 1920, Rabbi of the United
Synagogue, Hartford, Connecticut, and past president of the
Connecticut Orthodox Rabbinical Council. He is married and
has four sons.

G17.2. R. Abraham Issachar Avigdor, born in 1929, Rabbi in Mexico, married and has three children.

ROPSHITZ DYNASTY — RUBIN, MARILES
and HALPERN FAMILIES

G14.4. Raatza, married R. Asher Isaiah, son of R. Eliezer Lipman Rubin.
He was the successor of his father-in-law, R. Naftali Zvi of Ropshitz, in 1827 as the second Admur of Ropshitz where he died in
1845. From him are descended the Chassidic Dynasty of Rubin-
Ropshitz as opposed to the Horowitz dynasty mentioned under
the children of R. Naftali Zvi, G14.1 through G14.3.

R. Asher Isaiah studied under the Seer (*Chozeh*) of Lublin, the
Maggid of Kozenitz, R. Mendel of Rymanov and R. Heschel of Apt.
He was the teacher of R. Ezekiel Shraga Halberstam, later Admur
Sieniawa, son of the Sanzer Rebbe. He was the author of *Or Yisah*.

G15.1. R. Menashe Rubin, the third Admur of Ropshitz, died in 1861,
author of *Lechem Sh'meinah*.

G16.1. Wife of R. Reuben Horowitz, Admur Dembitz, her first cousin.
They had no issue.

G16.2. Sarah, married R. Isaac Mariles, the fourth Admur of Ropshitz. He was the son of R. Simeon Mariles, Rabbi of Jaroslav,
author of *Torat Shimon*, son of R. Israel of Josefow. R. Simeon's
cousin was R. Jacob Isaac Horowitz, the *Chozeh* (Seer) of
Lublin.

G17.1. R. Menachem Mendel Mariles, Rabbi of Dubetsk, and suc-
ceeded his father as fifth Admur of Ropshitz. He married
Deborah Yita, daughter of R. Meir Judah, grandson of R.
Zvi Elimelech Spira. (See Chapter XVI — Branch VII.)

G18.1. R. Menashe Mariles, 1864-1933, sixth Admur Ropshitz,
married 1) Leah, daughter of R. Jehiel, died in 1917, son
of R. Meshullam Zusia Heschel (see Chapter XV), and
had four children (listed in order below), 2) Tamar, daughter of R. Asher, son of R. Naftali Rubin and had three chil-

dren (G19.5, 6, and 7), and 3) Esther, daughter of R. Samuel Aaron Flamm of Kortchin, but had no issue.

G19.1. Mirl, born in 1882, married in 1899 to R. Haim, son of R. Isaac Isaiah Halberstam of Chechoyv. (See Chapter XIV.) She currently lives in New York.

G19.2. Sarah, married R. Isaac, son of R. Elimelech Rubin. (See Chapter XVI — Branch VII — below.)

G19.3. Channah Mindel, born in 1887, married R. Elisha Halberstam of Gorlice. (See Chapter XIV — Branch E.)

G19.4. Rebecca, married R. Samuel Aaron, son of R. Isaac son of R. Samuel Aaron Flamm (mentioned above).

G19.5. R. Isaiah Mariles, 1885-1920, married twice and died in Berlin. His second wife was Margola Rost of Lobatchov, and had issue.

G20.1. Leah, married Samuel Rosenkrantz of Kolomya in 1932. They settled in Vienna, and had an only son.

G21. Professor Herbert S. Rosenkrantz,[18] born in Vienna in 1933. In 1959 he obtained his Ph.D. from Cornell University, and married the same year to Diana Green. In 1961 he joined the staff of the Department of Microbiology of Columbia University as Assistant Professor until 1965, when he became Associate Professor, and in 1969 Professor. In 1971-2, he was the visiting professor of Microbiology at the Hebrew University-Hadassah Medical School in Jerusalem. He has also received a number of awards and is the author of over 150 scientific papers.

Their children are Penina, Eliezer, Margalit, Dara and Joshua Amiel, and reside in Paramus, New Jersey.

G20.2. Rebecca Miriam, married (thirdly) Charles Strauhs of Vienna, currently of New York. She had no issue.

G19.6. Eidel, married R. Moses Safrin. (See Chapter XVII — Eichenstein-Safrin Dynasty.)

G19.7. Beila, married R. Isaac Lieberman, the seventh and last Admur of Ropshitz, and perished with their family in the Holocaust.

G18.2. Miriam, married R. Joshua, son of R. Zvi Elimelech Spira (grandson of the *Bnei Yisaschar* — see Chapter XVII — Spira Dynasty).

G17.2. Raatza, died young.

G16.3. Wife of R. Jacob Isaac, son of R. Israel Horowitz of Yevoinitch.

G17. Rachel Leah, married R. Abraham Abba, son of R. Nahum Hirsch Pentzer, A.B.D. of Riglitz. R. Abba died about 1923/4, and had an only son.

G18. R. Jacob Isaac Horowitz (-Pentzer), died in 1940 and was buried in Jerusalem. He was also A.B.D. of Riglitz and married Channah Eidel, daughter of R. Haim Isaac Jeruchem. (See Chapter XV — Jeruchem Family.)

G19.1. R. Nathan Horowitz (Monsey, New York), born in 1915, married Rachel Feige, daughter of R. Issachar Berish Rubin of Dolina-New York, and has issue. A son, R. Haim Jacob, married in 1964 to Nechama, daughter of R. Shalom Ezekiel Shraga Rubin-Halberstam. (See Chapter XVI — Branch VII.)

G19.2. R. Menashe Horowitz, married and has issue.

G19.3. R. Feiwel Horowitz, married and has issue. A daughter, Sarah, married R. David, son of R. Meir, son of R. Issachar Ber Rubin of Dombrovo. (See Chapter XVI — Branch VII.)

G19.4. R. Nahum Zvi Horowitz, married and has issue.

G19.5. Rebecca Malka, eldest, born in 1911, married R. Abraham Mordecai Engelstein of Cracow. The family perished.

G15.2. R. Aaron Rubin, Admur of Rymanov, died in 1847.

G16.1. Frume, married R. Naftali, son of R. Ezekiel Shraga Halberstam. (See Chapter XIV — Branch A — G15.1).

G16.2. R. Samuel Rubin, Admur Kortchin, died in Cracow in 1904, married Jochebed, daughter of R. Eleazar of Lyzhansk, son of R. Naftali Weissblum. (See Chapter XVII — Shapiro Dynasty.)

G17.1. R. Naftali Rubin, 1851-1938, Rabbi of Vizhniz, married twice. His first wife was Miriam Malka, daughter of R. Ezekiel Shraga Halberstam, Admur Sieniawa. (See Chapter XIV — Branch A.) They had nine children. His second wife bore two children, Chaya Sarah and Samuel.

G18.1. Rebecca, married R. Haim son of R. Nachman Steinitz. They perished.

G19.1. R. Asher Steinitz, perished.

  G20. Rachel, married R. Israel Newman (Williamsburg), and have four children, Asher, Channah Malka, Moses and Abraham Joshua.

G19.2. Leah Malka, married R. Elijah son of R. Asher Rubin. (See G17.2/18.1 below.)

G19.3. Rachel Feige, perished.

G19.4. Raatza, married R. Samuel, son of R. Naftali Rubin, perished.

G19.5. Nechama, married R. Joseph Haim Gevertzman, perished. (He was a descendant of R. Zvi Elimelech of Lyzhansk — Chapter XVII.)

G19.6. R. Nachman Steinitz, married, and perished with his family.

G18.2. R. Haim Baruch Rubin, Admur Vizhniz-Bochnia, married Dinah. They perished with some of their ten children.

G19.1. R. Abraham Joshua Heschel Rubin (Los Angeles, Calif.), married Chaya, daughter of R. Moses Fish. Their children, Haim Baruch, Dinah, Jacob and Ezekiel Shraga.

G19.2. R. Samuel Rubin, married Sheindel, daughter of R. Jonah Baron. (See Chapter XIV — Branch H.) They perished with their children.

G18.3. Mindel, married R. Isaac, son of R. Abraham Joshua Heschel, son of R. Elimelech Rubin of Sokolov. (See below — G14.4/15.4/16.2.)

G18.4. Raatza, married her first cousin, R. Nahum Ephraim, son of R. Aryey Lieb Halberstam. (See Chapter XIV — Branch A.) They perished in the Holocaust.

G18.5. R. Chunah Zvi Rubin, Admur Sambor-Sanz, married Achsah, daughter of R. Jehiel Nathan Halberstam. They perished without issue. (See Chapter XIV.)

G18.6. R. Jonah Rubin, married his first cousin, Beila, daughter of R. Asher Rubin.

G18.7. Feige Nechama, married R. Baruch Freund, perished with their family.

G18.8. Mirl, married and perished.

G18.9. Chaya Sarah, married R. Ezekiel Shraga, son of R. Mena-

chem Mendel Halberstam. (See Chapter XIV — Branch
C — page 497.)

G18.10. R. Eleazar Rubin, married and perished.

G18.11. Channah Rachel, married her first cousin, R. Avigdor, son
of R. Menachem Mendel Halberstam (Branch C — page
497).

G17.2. R. Asher Rubin, succeeded his father as Admur of Kortchin
in 1904. He married Jochebed Zipporah, daughter of R.
Elijah, son of R. Isaac, son of R. Issachar Berish Eichenstein,
Admur Zhidachov. (See Chapter XVII — Eichenstein Dynasty.) He died in 1932.

G18.1. R. Eli Rubin, married Leah Malka, daughter of R. Haim
Rubin.

G18.2. Beila, married R. Jonah, son of R. Naftali Rubin.

G18.3. Liebe Raatza, married (secondly) R. Isaac Meir Rappoport, the New York-Prager Rabbi. (See Chapter XI —
Babad Family Branch C — G12.1/13.7/14.1/15.2.)

G18.4. R. Mordecai Eleazar Rubin, married Channah, daughter
of Haim Reuben Wagschal. (See Chapter XVII — Shapiro
Dynasty.)

G17.3. R. Aaron Rubin, died about 1901, and had issue, including,

G18.1. R. Eleazar Rubin, father of R. Samuel Aaron Rubin (Israel).

G18.2. R. Mendel Rubin, died in 1957. His daughter Jochebed
Frumet, married Facete.

G17.4. Zipporah, married R. Joseph Liebus, son of R. Joshua Frisherman.

G18. Moses Frisherman, born in 1903, married (secondly) Malka,
daughter of Moses Greensweig. His first wife and children
perished.

G15.3. R. Menachem Mendel Rubin, 1806-75, Admur of Glogov, married Chavah Esther, daughter of R. Meir, son of R. Samuel halevi
Rotenberg of Apt.

G16.1. R. Jacob Joseph Rubin, died in 1874, married, 1) the daughter
of R. Liebish Nyhaus, (Rabbi of Tomashov, and son-in-law of
R. Meir Rotenberg), and 2) the daughter of R. Eleazar of Kozenitz.

G17.1. R. Eleazar Rubin of Glogov, 1862-1932, died in New York,
        married the daughter of R. Solomon Mayer[18a] of Sassov, and
        succeeded his father-in-law as head of the Sassov Chas-
        sidim. He was the author of *Zichron Eleazar*.

G18.1. R. Joseph David Rubin, Admur Sassov-New York, born
        in 1898, and came to the U.S.A. in 1933. He married 1)
        the daughter of R. Naftali Horowitz, Admur Malitsch, and
        2) Frieda, daughter of R. Shalom Rosenfeld. (See Chap-
        ter XIV — Branch H.) They had issue.

G18.2. Wife of R. Israel Haim, son of R. Isaac Weiss, Admur
        Spinka.

G19.1. R. Jacob Joseph Weiss, born in 1916, Admur Spinka-
        New York-Bnei Brak, married his first cousin, Pearl,
        daughter of R. Abraham Abbish Horowitz of Kraly, son
        of R. Naftali Horowitz of Malitsch. (See above — G14.2
        /15.1/16.1/17.8/18.1.)

G20.   R. Naftali Weiss, married Dinah Frumet, daughter of
        R. Haim Simha Issachar Dov Rubin. (See below —
        G16.2/17.3/18.4/19.6/20.1.) They have issue (New
        York).

G17.2. R. Alter Moses Haim Rubin.

G16.2. R. Meir Rubin, A.B.D. Glogov, 1830-1917, married Mirl,
        daughter of R. Joseph, son of R. Mordecai Unger of Dom-
        brovo. He succeeded his father-in-law as Admur Dombrovo
        and his sayings are collected in *Mevaser Tzedek*. (See Chap-
        ter XVII — Unger Dynasty.)

G17.1. R. Haim Jehiel Rubin, succeeded his father as Admur Dom-
        brovo, died in 1918 in Berlin. He married Deborah, daugh-
        ter of R. Alexander Sender Lipa, son of R. Isaac Eichenstein,
        Admur Zhidachov. (See Chapter XVII.)

G18.1. R. Issachar Berish Rubin, 1893-1962, Admur Dombrovo-
        New York. During World War I he escaped to Holland
        and later returned to Berlin where, in 1919, he married
        Chaya, daughter of R. Naftali, son of R. Azriel Bindiger.
        He came to the U.S.A. in 1939.

G19.1. R. Hyman (Haim Jehiel) Rubin, born in Berlin in 1921,
        and came to the U.S.A. in 1939. He married Dinah,
        daughter of R. Moses Joshua Cohen.

G20.1. Asher Isaiah Rubin, married Rachel Heuman, and have issue.

G20.2. Chaya, married Shlomo Teichman, and have issue.

G19.2. R. Azriel Rubin, born in Berlin in 1923, married Channah Sarah, daughter of R. Issachar Dov Shapiro.

G20.1. Chaya, married Shalom Ginzburg, and have issue.

G20.2. Shlamtzion, married Joseph Reinman, and have issue.

G20.3. Naftali Zvi Rubin, married Hodel Rosenbaum.

G19.3. R. Meir Rubin, born in Berlin in 1924, married Chaya, daughter of R. David Leifer.

G20.1. David Rubin, married Miriam Sarah, daughter of R. Feiwel, son of R. Jacob Isaac Horowitz-Pentzer. (See Chapter XVI — Branch VII.) Their son, Jacob Isaac.

G19.4. R. Naftali Zvi Rubin, born in Berlin in 1928, married Gitel, daughter of R. Haim Jacob Safrin (Admur Komarno-New York-Jerusalem). (See Chapter XVII — Eichenstein Dynasty.) They have issue, Chaya (married Judah Klein), Berish, Esther and Abraham Mordecai.

G18.2. R. Isaac Eizik Rubin, married, perished with three children. Others survived.

G19.1. R. Issachar Berish, Admur Dolina-New York.

G20.1. R. Haim Jehiel Rubin (New York).

G20.2. Rachel Feige, married R. Nathan, son of R. Jacob Isaac Horowitz-Pentzer. (See Chapter XVI — Branch VII — G14.4/15.1/16.3/17/18/19.1.)

G19.2. R. Alexander Sender Lipa Rubin.

G18.3. R. Eleazar Rubin, Admur Drogobitch, perished.

G19. Miriam, married Shalom Moskovitz (California).

G18.4. R. Alexander Sender Lipa Rubin, Admur Romain, died in 1963.

G19.1. Meir Rubin, District Judge in Tel Aviv.

G19.2. Haim Jehiel Rubin of Tel Aviv, Assistant Attorney General.

G19.3. Wife of Dr. Sternhelm of Tel Aviv.

G19.4. Wife of Bornstein.

G18.5. Chava, married R. Menachem Mendel, son of R. Alexander Sender Lipa Eichenstein. (See Chapter XVII — Eichenstein Dynasty.)

G18.6. Esther Gitel, married R. Menashe Mariles. Their sons, Sender Lipa of Haifa and Mendel of Belgium.

G18.7. Rachel, married Eleazar Mariles, and have issue.

G18.8. Tilla, married into the Rubin family.

G17.2. R. Shalom Rubin, succeeded his father as Admur Rzeszow, died in 1924, married Channah Mindel, daughter of R. Simha, son of R. Eleazar Spira. (See Chapter XVII — Spira Dynasty.)

G18.1. Toyba Chavah, died in 1970, married R. Abraham David, 1886-1963, son of R. Eliezer, son of R. Menachem Mendel Rubin (a descendant of the brother of the first Admur Ropshitz, R. Naftali Zvi Rubin).

G19.1. Mirl Geula, eldest, married R. Haim Moses son of R. Isaac Halberstam of Bardiyov. (See Chapter XIV.) They had no issue.

G19.2. Feige Rachel, married R. Moses, son of Benjamin Zeev Kornitzer. Their children, Benjamin Zeev (New York) and Shalom Akiva (Lakewood, N.J.).

G19.3. Rivke Hentsche. G19.4. Channah Mindel.

G19.5. R. Simha Eliezer Rubin, born in 1922, married Beila, daughter of R. Isaac, son of R. Naftali Horowitz of Malitsch. (See above — G14.2/15.1/16.1.) Their children, Naftali Samuel, Meir, Rechel and Abraham David.

G19.6. R. Shalom Rubin, born in 1926, Rabbi of the Bronx Young Israel Congregation, married 1) Channah Bunim, and had issue, and 2) Helen Silber. Their children, Mindy, Adina, Moses and Eliezer.

G18.2. R. Menachem Mendel Rubin, died before the Holocaust. His wife and family perished.

G18.3. R. Eleazar Rubin, married and perished.

G19. R. Simha Rubin of New York.

G17.3. R. Isaac Tuvia Rubin, 1859-1927, Rabbi of New Sanz, married Nechama, daughter of R. Haim Halberstam of Sanz. (See Chapter XIV.)

G18.1. R. Zvi Hirsch Rubin, A.B.D. Mishlonitz, married the daughter of R. Naftali, son of R. David Halberstam of Keshanov. (See Chapter XIV — Branch C.)

> G19.1. R. Solomon Rubin, perished, married Bracha, daughter of R. Benzion Halberstam of Bobov. (See Chapter XIV — Branch B.)
>
> > G20. R. Zvi Hirsch Rubin-Halberstam (New York).
>
> G19.2. R. Aaron Samuel Rubin, perished.
> G19.3. R. Haim David, Admur in Antwerp, died in 1938. His family perished.
> G19.4. Mirl married R. Sinai Dechner, A.B.D. Yevoinitch, perished with his family.
> G19.5. Sheindel married R. Baruch son of R. Mendel Hager. (See Chapter XV.)
> G19.6. Hena, married.

G18.2. R. Asher Isaiah Rubin, married the daughter of R. Mordecai David Unger of Zmigrad. (See Chapter XVII — Unger Dynasty.) He succeeded his father-in-law as A.B.D. of Zmigrad and later lived in Sanz. The family perished.
G18.3. R. Joseph Menachem Rubin, Admur Sanz, perished.
G18.4. R. Aryey Lieb Rubin,[19] 1891-1942, A.B.D. Chechinov-Tomashov, married Channah Rachel, daughter of R. Simha Issachar Berish, son of R. Ezekiel Shraga Halberstam of Sieniawa. (See Branch A.)

> G19.1. Hena, married R. Joseph Baruch, son of R. Isaiah Beer. He was A.B.D. of Widama (Pshedborz). The family perished. R. Isaiah was the son of R. Kalonymus Kalman who was a cousin of R. Haim Meir Epstein (mentioned in Chapter XVII — Eichenstein Dynasty).
> G19.2. R. Meir Rubin, unmarried, died in Russia.
> G19.3. R. Shalom Ezekiel Shraga Rubin-Halberstam, born in 1913 in Chechinov, and came to the U.S.A. in 1947. He married in 1945 to Sarah, daughter of Israel Jacob Topola. He is Admur Chechinov-New York.
>
> > G20.1. Hena Nechama, married in 1964 to R. Haim Jacob, son of R. Nathan Horowitz-Pentzer. (See Chapter XVI — Branch VII.) Their children, Abraham Baruch and Shifra.

G20.2. Chaya Malka, married (secondly) Moses Aaron Eisenbach.

G20.3. R. Aryey Lieb Israel Benzion, born in 1948, married in 1969 to Yente, daughter of R. Samuel, son of R. Joshua Haim Teitelbaum. Their children, Joshua Haim and Frieda Esther.

G20.4. R. Haim Jacob Meir, born in 1954, married his first cousin, daughter of Heschel Horowitz.

G20.5. Isaac Tovia Rubin, born in 1957.

G19.4. Malka, married R. Moses Nathaniel Jechlinska, where he was Admur, perished with two children.

G19.5. Frieda, married (his second wife) in 1948 to R. Solomon son of R. Benzion Halberstam of Bobov. (See Chapter XIV — Branch B.)

G19.6. R. Haim Simha Issachar Dov Rubin, born in 1923, married in 1950 to Riva, daughter of R. Joshua, son of R. Asher Isaiah Eichenstein of Pruchnik. He is Admur Tomashov-New York.

G20.1. Dinah Frumet, married R. Naftali, son of R. Jacob Joseph Weiss (Admur Spinka).

G20.2. R. Aryey Lieb Rubin, married Nechama Malka, daughter of R. Shabbtai, son of R. Haim Meisels. (See Chapter XVII — Teitelbaum Dynasty.)

G20.3. Joshua Jehiel, 4. Ezekiel Meir, 5. Mirl, 6. Asher Isaiah.

G19.7. R. Elimelech Rubin, born in 1926, married Friedel, daughter of R. Elijah Rappoport.

G20.1. Aryey Lieb, 2. Maasha, 3. Eliyahu.

G19.8. Rechel, married in 1952 to Heschel, son of R. Haim Solomon Horowitz of Stryzov. (See above — G14.1/15.3/16.5/17.2.)

G18.5. R. Moses Rubin, married Ita, daughter of R. Mendel, son of R. Eliezer Jeruchem Baron.

G19. R. Eliezer Jeruchem Rubin-Halberstam (Brooklyn).

G18.6. Chaya, married R. Haim, son of R. Eleazar Rosenfeld, perished. (See Chapter XIV — Branch H.)

G18.7. Miriam, married R. Michael, son of R. Jacob Shapiro (A.B.D. Luben). His mother was the sister of R. Morde-

cai Dov Twersky, Admur Hornistopol. (See Chapter VII
— Branch B.)

G17.4. R. Baruch Rubin, 1864-1936, A.B.D. Rizdoviz and Admur of
Kolomya, married Sarah, daughter of R. Menachem Mendel
Eichenstein of Zhidachov, (See Chapter XVII — Eichen-
stein Dynasty.) He was the author of *She'erit Baruch*.

G18.1. R. Jacob Israel Jeshurun Rubin, 1885-1944, of Sosregen,
married 1) the daughter of R. Moses of Solitza and 2) the
daughter of R. Haim Dechner of Seret. He became A.B.D.
of Seret in 1907, and was the author of *Zerah Kodesh Mitz-
vatah*.

G19.1. R. Menachem Mendel Rubin, Admur Muzhaya-New
York, married the daughter of R. Haim Meir Jehiel
(A.B.D. Ronzivo). He was born in 1922 and came to
the U.S.A. in 1948. He wrote *Minchat Yeshurun*.

G20. Wife of R. Benzion Halberstam, married in 1974 (New
York). (See Chapter XIV — Branch B.)

G19.2. R. Samuel Shmelke Rubin, Admur Solitza-New York
(Far Rockaway, N.Y.), born in 1925. He published
Raziel HaMalach, and was the author of *Tiferet Avot*.
He also established the Yeshiva *Tiferet Kehilat Yaakov*
in Jerusalem.

G19.3. R. Mordecai David Rubin, married the daughter of R.
Joshua Eichenstein. (See Chapter XVII — Eichenstein
Dynasty.) He is Admur Sosregen-New York.

G19.4. R. Joseph Meir Rubin, perished in 1945, and reinterred
in Tiberias in 1965.

G19.5. Mirl, married R. Shabbtai, son of R. Haim Meisels of
Sochotchov-New York. (See Chapter XVII — Teitelbaum Dynasty.)

G18.2. R. Meir Joseph Rubin.

G19.1. R. Menachem Mendel Rubin.

G19.2. R. Issachar Berish Rubin, Admur Kristier-New York.

G18.3. Wife of R. Haim of Rotsfurt, son of R. Shalom Eliezer Halberstam. (See Chapter XIV — Branch F.)

G16.3. Zipporah, married R. Joseph Zeev, son of R. David Halberstam
of Keshanov. (See Chapter XIV.)

G16.4. R. Joshua Rubin.

G17. R. Abraham Isaac Rubin, Admur Chirov, perished.

G16.5. R. Asher Rubin, Admur Stachev, died in 1936.

G15.4. R. Elimelech Rubin A.B.D. Sokolov, died in 1862.

G16.1. R. Isaac Bezalel Rubin of Brody, died in 1874, married Eidel, daughter of R. Shalom Rokeah of Belz. (See Chapter XVII — Rokeah Dynasty.)

G17.1. R. Elimelech Rubin of Jaworow, married Pesha.

G18.1. R. Isaac Rubin, married Sarah Mariles.

G19. R. Asher Isaiah Rubin, married Sheindel Rebecca, daughter of R. Isaac Rubin of Radechov.

G20. Channah Pesha, married R. Moses Halevi Moster.

G21.1. Jacob Asher, married Sarah Rachel, daughter of R. Meilich Reinman. (See Chapter XIV — Branch F — G14.6/15.2/16.3 and Chapter XVI — Branch VII — G14.2/15.3/16.1/17.8.)

G21.2. Wife of R. David Thumim. (See Chapter IV — Branch A.)

G18.2. R. Shraga Feiwel Rubin, A.B.D. Radechov and later Jaworow.

G17.2. R. Samuel Shmelke Rubin of Seret, died in 1905, married the daughter of R. Joseph Alter of Radovitz.

G18.1. R. Menachem Mendel Rubin of Seret.

G18.2. Wife of R. Haim Dechner, A.B.D. Seret. His daughter married R. Jacob Israel Jeshurun Rubin. (See above.)

G18.3. Wife of R. Moses of Kolomya.

G18.4. Wife of R. Eleazar of Borstein.

G18.5. Wife of R. Issachar Dov Alter of Altstadt.

G17.3. Elly, married R. Haim Meir Jehiel Shapiro of Radechov. (See Chapter XVII — Shapiro Dynasty.)

G17.4. R. Naftali Rubin, A.B.D. Radechov, married Tamar, daughter of R. Aryey Leib Nyhaus of Tomashov.

G18. R. Asher Rubin of Jolkeva, married Malka Frieda, daughter of R. Haim Eli Lieberman. (See Rokeah Dynasty — Chapter XVII.)

G19.1. R. Isaac Rubin, surnamed Glikman.

    G20.1. R. Joshua Glikman, married Deborah Pearl, daughter of R. Joshua Heschel, son of R. Haim Samuel Horowitz. (See Chapter IV — Branch H.)

        G21.1. R. Meir David Glikman, born in 1928, married Leah Metz. Their children, Dvora Pearl, Joshua Heschel and Sarah Malka.

        G21.2. R. Baruch Joseph Glikman, born in 1923. His children, Joshua Heschel, Hannah Dvora Pearl and Isaac Abraham.

    G20.2. Feigel Jochebed, married in 1922 to R. David Baruch, son of R. Haim son of R. Isaac Isaiah Halberstam of Chechoyv. (See Chapter XIV.)

G19.2. Tamar, second wife of R. Menashe, son of R. Menachem Mendel Rubin of Ropshitz.

G19.3. R. Haim Elijah Rubin, A.B.D. of Tarnopol, perished.

G19.4. R. Hanoch Heinich Rubin of Keshnov, perished.

G16.2. R. Abraham Joshua Heschel Rubin, Admur Jasla (Yaslo), died in Safed.

    G17.1. R. Zvi Joseph Rubin, 1855-1918, succeeded his father as Admur Jasla.

        G18.1. R. Elimelech Rubin, married the daughter of R. Abraham Haim, son of R. Moses Horowitz. (See above.)

        G18.2. R. Aaron Rubin of Preshov.

        G18.3. R. Menachem Mendel Rubin of Lvov, later Admur Jasla-New York, married the daughter of R. Tuvia Michal Halpern of Borjan. (See below.)

    G17.2. R. Isaac Rubin, married Mindel, daughter of R. Naftali, son of R. Samuel Rubin. (See above — G14.4/15.2/16.2/17.1 /18.3.)

G16.3. R. Alter Rubin of Sokolov.

G15.5. R. Jehiel Rubin of Kolbuszov. His daughter married R. Abraham Aaron, son of R. Jekutiel Judah Lieb Teitelbaum. (See Chapter XVII — Teitelbaum Dynasty.)

G16. R. Asher Isaiah Rubin, married the daughter of R. Alexander Sender, son of R. Isaac Judah Jehiel Safrin of Komarno. (See Chapter XVII — Eichenstein Dynasty.)

G15.6. Wife of Meshullam Feiwish Halpern, Admur Borjan (died in 1876), son of R. Naftali Herz Halpern, author of *Sefat Emet*.

G16. R. Abraham Zerach Judah Uri Halpern, author of *Amarei Yehudah*, succeeded his father as Admur Borjan. He married the daughter of R. Joel Moskovitz of Shatz, and had issue. From his second wife he had no issue.

G17.1. R. Mattithiah Haim Halpern, A.B.D. Dobshitz, and died in Padgorze.

G18.1. R. David Halpern, succeeded his father in Dobshitz, died in 1945, married Mindel, daughter of R. Samuel Engel.

G19.1. R. Elchanan Halpern of London, married and has eight children of whom six are married. A daughter, Rivke, married R. Joseph Moses Shneerson, and a son, Samuel David, married the daughter of R. Zvi Hirsch Meisels. (See Chapter XVII — Teitelbaum Dynasty.)

G19.2. R. Samuel Haim Halpern, perished in 1944.

G18.2. R. Asher Isaiah Halpern, born in 1905, A.B.D. of Cracow-Dembnik, married his first cousin, Channah, daughter of R. Jacob Frankel-Teomim. (See Chapter IV — Branch H.) He now lives in New York. His sons, Ezekiel, Professor of Bacteriology, and Jacob.

G18.3. R. Joel Halpern, Admur Jasla (Yaslo)-New York.

G18.4. Shlomtze, married R. Moses Judah, son of R. Joseph Haim Kirschbaum, perished.

G18.5. Miriam, married Seltenreich, perished.

G17.2. R. Feiwish Halpern, born in 1875, and perished in the Holocaust, married the daughter of R. Phineas Chodrov. He succeeded the *MaHaRaShaM* Schwadron as A.B.D. of Borjan.

G18.1. Rivke, married Bernard (Dov) Ort (Brooklyn, N.Y.), and have issue.

G18.2. R. Meir Halpern, perished. His sons, Aaron Halpern (Long Island, N.Y.) and Jacob Halpern (Israel).

G18.3. R. Naftali Halpern, died in New York in 1972, and had issue.

G18.4. Shlamtze, 5. Yente, 6. Meir, 7. Haim. All perished.

G17.3. R. Joel Halpern, born in 1887, Admur of Borjan, and settled in the U.S.A. in 1930. He died in 1955/6.

G18.1. Shlamtze, married Isaac Klang (Brooklyn, N.Y.), and have issue.

G18.2. Jochebed, married Moses Englander (Brooklyn, N.Y.), and have issue.

G17.4. R. Jehiel Michal Halpern, married the daughter of R. Solomon of Sassov, and became Admur of Sassov. He had a daughter, Shlamtze, and a son, R. Zvi Hirsch Halpern (1890-1971), who became Admur Sassov-Lvov-New York. R. Zvi's family perished in the Holocaust.

G17.5. R. Aaron Halpern, married Sarah, daughter of R. Meir Moskovitz of Shatz-London, and had issue. They were first cousins.

G15.7. Wife of R. Isaac Reich (see also page 436).

G16. Wife of R. Abraham Mattithiah Friedman (page 522).

CHAPTER XVII

THIS chapter contains the genealogy of some of the most prominent Chassidic Dynasties.[1] Its members, with those of the other dynasties mentioned elsewhere in this book, led the Chassidic movement to its greatest heights in the eighteenth to the twentieth centuries. Some of the dynasties presented here are not directly descended from the Katzenellenbogen family at their origin, but the amount of intermarriage within these few but famous families, defies the capabilities of any genealogist to establish the cousinhood relationships. Within each generation, until today, there was a multitude of close cousin marriages, thus bringing the world of Chassidic leadership under the control of the Rebbes and Admurim of these families. Indeed it seemed to be a family affair more intricate that the aristocratic intermarriages of the royalty and gentry.

Even today, despite the losses of Chassidic influences that once existed, the consciousness of family heritage is so ingrained that any descendant can trace his ancestry back to the Chassidic founding fathers in Hungary, Rumania, Poland, Galicia, Czechoslovakia and elsewhere, and his spouse can boast the same.

The present Admur and leader of the Vizhniz Chassidim in Israel, R. Moses Hager, as an example, is the father-in-law of the present Admur and leader of the Belz Chassidim, R. Issachar Dov Rokeah, of the present Admur and leader of the Skvira Chassidim in the U.S.A., R. David Twersky, and of a son (R. Aaron) of the present Admur and leader of the Sighet Chassidim, R. Moses Teitelbaum. His son is married to a daughter of the present Admur Loyev, R. Meshullam Zusia Twersky and his brother, R. Mordecai Hager, is the son-in-law of the late American Admur and leader of the Skvira Chassidim, R. Jacob Joseph Twersky (father of R. David Twersky above).

It is for this reason that these dynasties are given in some detail so as to facilitate identification of who is who in each generation of each dynasty. As mentioned in the beginning of the book, the order of names does not imply order of birth and seniority, unless stated.

EICHENSTEIN AND SAFRIN CHASSIDIC DYNASTIES OF ZHIDACHOV AND KOMARNO

G1. R. Isaac Eichenstein of Safrin in Hungary, a descendant of R. Yom-Tov Lipman Heller (*Tosfot YomTov*), died in 1800.

 G2.1. R. Zvi Hirsch Eichenstein of Zhidachov, died in 1831, a pupil of R. Elimelech of Lyzhansk and the *Chozeh* (Seer) of Lublin. He was the author of *Ateret Zvi, Sur Merah, Beit Yisrael* and others. He had five children, four of whom were daughters.

   G3.1. Sarah, married the Rabbi of Razla, R. Judah Zvi (See G2.2/3.1. below.)

   G3.2. Chavah, married R. Naftali Herzl of Sambor.

   G3.3. Reizel, married 1) Moses Haim Taub and had issue, 2) R. Joseph Rotenberg of Rozvo, and had issue, and 3) R. Dov Shapiro A.B.D. Talust.

    G4.1. Isaac Liebus Taub, married the daughter of R. Isaiah Shor (A.B.D. Jassy).

    G4.2. R. Solomon Taub, A.B.D. Razla, married Rebecca, daughter of R. Judah Zvi Eichenstein. (Below.)

    G4.3. R. Zvi Hirsch Rotenberg, married the daughter of R. Samuel of Helitsch.

     G5. R. Joseph Rotenberg, A.B.D. Klasni.

      G6. R. Haim Solomon Rotenberg.

       G7. R. Moses Samuel Rotenberg.

        G8. R. Solomon Rotenberg, married Rachel, daughter of R. Israel David Horowitz, Admur Shatz. (See Chapter XVI — Branch VII — G14.2/15.3/16.1/17.2/18.4.)

   G3.4. Rebecca, married R. Judah Lieb Ehrlich.

 G2.2. R. Moses Eichenstein of Sambor, became Admur of Zhidachov on the death of his brother in 1831. He married the daughter of R. Judah Judel, son of R. Moses and died in 1840.

G3.1. R. Judah Zvi Eichenstein, A.B.D. Razla, died in 1847. He married his first cousin Sarah, daughter of R. Zvi Hirsch Eichenstein of Zhidachov. He succeeded his father as Admur Zhidachov in 1840 and was the author of *Da'at Kedoshim, Amud HaTorah* and *Talumot Chochmah.* He had only daughters.

G4.1. Hinde, married R. Jacob son of R. David Hager of Zablodov.

G4.2. Miriam, (died in 1882), married R. Jacob son of R. Aaron Moses Taubes (A.B.D. Jassy).

G4.3. Breindel, married R. Ezekiel Shraga Halberstam of Sieniawa. (See Chapter XIV — Branch A.)

G4.4. Rebecca, married R. Solomon Taub of Razla. His mother and her father were first cousins.

G5.1. R. Judah Zvi Taub, died in 1886, married Hinde Chipa, daughter of R. Eliezer Zvi Safrin. (See below — G2.3/ 3.1/4.1/5.5.)

G6.1. R. Phineas Haim Taub, 1866-1935, married the daughter of R. Abraham Haim, son of R. Menachem Mendel Horowitz of Linsk. (See Chapter XVI — Branch VII.) He was first A.B.D. and later Admur of Rozdol, and the author of *Torat Chesed* and *Ohel Moed.*

G7.1. R. Jehiel Judah Taub, Admur Margareten in Transsylvania, and later in Rozdol, died in 1936. He was the author of *Lev Sameach HeChadash* and married the daughter of R. Moses David Ashkenazi.

His son is R. Menachem Mendel Taub, Admur Kalov-Israel, author of *Divrei Menachem.*

G7.2. R. Moses Ezra Taub, married the daughter of R. Baruch Rubin, perished.

G7.3. R. Jehiel Michal Zuckerberg, Admur Stry, perished with his family.

G6.2. R. Moses Taub of Kalov, died in Budapest in 1936, author of *Eit Ratzon.*

G7. R. Menachem Solomon, born in 1903, Admur Kalov-New York, author of *Chekel Tapuchin,* married Reizel, daughter of R. Issachar Dov Rokeah of Linsk. (See Chapter XVII — Rokeah Dynasty — G9.2/10.3/11.2/12/13.1/14.2/ 15/16.2/17.6.)

G6.3. R. Abraham Mordecai Shalom Taub, A.B.D. Pomarin, died in 1937, married the daughter of R. Solomon Mayer of Sassov, and succeeded him as A.B.D. of Sassov. (See Chapter XVII — Rokeah Dynasty.)

    G7.1. R. Judah Taub, perished in Zlatchov in the Holocaust.
    G7.2. R. Hanoch Heinich Taub, succeeded his father as A.B.D. Sassov, and also perished in Zlatchov.

G3.2. R. Koppel Eichenstein, A.B.D. Ridnik.
G3.3. R. Isaiah Eichenstein, died in Sniatyn.
G3.4. R. Jehiel Michal Eichenstein, succeeded his father in Sambor and died in Zhidachov. He was the author of *Ateret Zekeinim*.

G2.3. R. Alexander Sender (adopted the surname of Safrin), died in Ihel in 1818. He was the author of *Zichron Devarim*.

G3.1. R. Isaac Judah Jehiel Safrin, 1806-1874. He became the Admur and founder of the Komarno Chassidic Dynasty where he was called "Reb Itzikel Komarner." He married Gitel, daughter of R. Abraham Mordecai of Pinczow, and was the author of *Heichal HaBeracha, Otzar Chachamim* and others.

    G4.1. R. Eliezer Zvi Safrin, 1830-1898, succeeded his father as Admur of Komarno in 1874. He was the author of *Damesek Eliezer* and other works. He married the daughter of R. Joseph Sheiner of Turke.

        G5.1. R. Jacob Moses Safrin, 1861-1929, Admur Komarno. He married the daughter of R. Joseph Meir Weiss, the first Admur of Spinka.

            G6.1. Hinde, married R. Naftali Zvi Zilberstein.
            G6.2. Frumet, married R. Eleazar Epstein. He was the son of R. Haim Meir of Neustadt, where he became Admur in 1914 on his father's death, and later perished in the Holocaust.

                G7.1. R. Joseph David Epstein of Sokolov, married the daughter of R. David of Pshezlov, son of R. Abraham Haim Horowitz of Plontsch. (See Chapter XVI — Branch VII.) They perished.

                G7.2. Wife of her first cousin, R. Samuel, Admur Bendin, son of R. Elijah Bombach, perished in the Holocaust.

G6.3. Gitel, married 1) R. Haim Nahum Halberstam A.B.D. Mozhisk, and 2) R. Aaron Mendel Guterman of Radzymin.

G6.4. Rebecca, married R. Elijah Bombach A.B.D. Ozpinzi.

G6.5. Rachel, married R. Haim Eleazar Spira of Munkacs. (See Chapter XVII — Spira Dynasty — G3.2/4.1/5.1/6.)

G6.6. Hannah, married R. Simha Haim son of R. Zvi Horowitz of Rozvadov-Sander-Vishne. (See Chapter XVI — Branch VII.)

G6.7. R. Shalom Safrin, 1893-1937, Admur Komarno from 1929, married the daughter of R. Israel Perlow of Stolin. (See page 299.) A daughter, Feige Ness, survived the Holocaust.

    G7. R. Baruch Safrin, born in 1914, the last leader and Admur of the Komarno Chassidim, perished in 1943 in Sambor.

G5.2. R. Menachem Meinish Safrin, A.B.D. Plestin and Dobromil, died in 1913.

G5.3. R. Phineas Nathan Safrin, 1855-1933, A.B.D. Ridnik, married 1) the daughter of R. Naftali Haim of Zilin (no issue) and 2) the daughter of R. Joshua Horowitz of Dzikov. (See Chapter XVI — Branch VII — G14.1/15.3/16.3/17.5.)

G5.4. R. Abraham Mordecai Safrin, died in 1941.

He was Admur of Borisov, Galicia from 1898 and married the daughter of R. Haim Jacob Dominitz of Neustadt in Galicia.

G6.1. R. Haim Jacob Safrin, 1892-1969, came to the U.S.A. in 1932 and later settled in Jerusalem.

He was known as the Komarno Rov-New York, and married two daughters of R. Isaac Flamm, A.B.D. Krotoschin (a descendant of the Belz Dynasty).

From his first wife:

G7.1. R. Eleazar, married the daughter of R. Alter Safrin of Altstadt, perished.

G7.2. R. Shalom Safrin, Admur Komarno-Jerusalem, married the daughter of R. Israel Isaac Reizman, and have issue.

G7.3. R. Menachem Meinish Safrin, Jerusalem-Bnei Brak, married with issue.

From his second wife, Rebecca Hena:

G7.4. Channah Rachel, married R. Jerachmeel, son of R. Mordecai David Unger of Dombrovo. (See Chapter XVII — G2.2/3/4.3.) They have ten children (Brooklyn, New York).

G7.5. Hinde, married R. Akiva Moses Gottlieb, secretary to the Chief Rabbinate, Jerusalem, and have issue.

G7.6. R. Alter Isaac Elimelech Safrin, married Shoshana, daughter of R. Brandwein, Admur Turka, with issue.

G7.7. Gitel, married R. Naftali Zvi, son of R. Issachar Ber Rubin of Dombrovo. (See Chapter XVI — Branch VII.)

G7.8. R. Issachar Dov, married without issue.

G7.9. R. Joshua, born in 1934, married Thea Goldstoff, and have issue. (See Chapter IV — Branch J — G12.2/13.1 /14.2/15.2/16.1.)

G6.2. R. Eliezer Zvi Safrin, born in 1900, perished in the Holocaust.

G6.3. R. Alter Safrin of Sambor, perished.

G5.5. Wife of R. Judah Zvi, A.B.D. Razla. (See Taub Family above.)

G4.2. R. Alexander Sender Safrin of Komarno, married the daughter of R. Haim Moses of Stefan.

G5.1. R. Moses Haim Safrin, married the daughter of R. Yom-Tov Lipa Eichenstein (of Zhidachov).

G6.1. R. Alter Issachar Safrin, married the daughter of R. Samuel Shmelke of Seret. They perished.

G6.2. R. Zeida Safrin of Przemysl, perished.

G5.2. Wife of R. Asher Isaiah, son of R. Jehiel Rubin of Kolbuszov (See Chapter XVI — Branch VII.)

G4.3. Wife of R. Menashe Jacob Klingberg.

G5. R. Abraham Mordecai Klingberg, died in 1916, author of *Alfei Menashe* and *Alei Zayit*.

G6.1. R. Shem Klingberg, 1872-1943, author of *Ohalei Shem*.

G6.2. R. Zeida Moses Haim, perished.

G2.4. R. Lipa Eichenstein of Sambor.

G3. R. Tuvia Eichenstein.

G2.5. R. Issachar Berish Eichenstein of Zhidachov, where he became
Admur in 1831, and died the following year.

G3. R. Isaac Eichenstein, 1805-73, succeeded his father as Admur in
1832 and was the author of *Peirush MaHaRO*.

G4.1. R. Alexander YomTov Lipa Eichenstein, Admur of Zhidachov,
died in 1883. He married the daughter of R. Liebish Yolles.

G5.1. R. Issachar Berish Eichenstein, A.B.D. Veretski and Zhidachov, died in 1924.

G6.1. R. Menashe Eichenstein of Rzeszow, married the daughter of R. Joshua Horowitz of Dzikov. (See Chapter XVI
— Branch VII — G14.1/15.3/16.3/17.3.) He was the
author of *Alfei Menashe* and *Torat HaAsham*.

G7. R. Mattithiah Eichenstein, born in 1886 and died in the
U.S.A. where he settled in 1924. He was known as the
Dzikover Rov, after the town where his maternal grand-
father was Admur.

G6.2. R. Moses Eichenstein, died in 1935. He succeeded his father as Admur Veretski and Munkacs.

G7. R. Elijah Eichenstein, Admur Veretski and Munkacs.

G6.3. R. Asher Isaiah Eichenstein of Pruchnik, married Frumet,
daughter of R. Jehiel.

G7.1. R. Joshua Eichenstein of Grosswarden, 1896-1945,
married Bracha Frieda, daughter of R. Haim Jeruchem
of Altstadt. (See Chapter XV — Jeruchem Family.)

G8.1. R. Nathan Eichenstein, Admur Zhidachov-Tel Aviv,
born in 1928.

G8.2. R. Issachar Berish Eichenstein, succeeded his uncle,
R. Menashe Eichenstein, as Admur Klausenberg-
Petah Tikvah.

G8.3. Riva, married R. Haim Simha Issachar Dov, son of
R. Aryey Lieb Rubin of Chechinov-Tomashov. (See
Chapter XVI — Branch VII.)

G8.4. Blume, married her first cousin, Feiwel, son of R.
Jacob Isaac Horowitz-Pentzer (see Chapter XVI —
Branch VII.)

G7.2. R. Menashe Isaac Meir Eichenstein, died in 1971, Admur Klausenberg-Petah Tikvah, married the daughter of R. Simeon Schiff, Admur Lyzhansk.

G7.3. R. Shalom Eichenstein, Admur Zhidachov-Safed, married the daughter of R. Haim Sofer of Munkacs.

G5.2. R. Aaron Menachem Mendel Eichenstein, 1860-1920, died in Lvov. He was A.B.D. of Alesk. He married 1) the daughter of R. Hanoch Mayer, founder of the Alesk Dynasty (Chapter XVII — Rokeah Dynasty) and 2) Chavah, daughter of R. Haim Jehiel son of R. Meir Rubin of Glogov. (Chapter XVI — Branch VII.)

G6. R. Haim Eichenstein, married the daughter of R. Haim Abraham Eichenstein of Zhidachov. (See below.)

G5.3. R. Joshua Heschel Eichenstein, A.B.D. Chodrov.

G6. R. Issachar Dov Eichenstein, A.B.D. Dolina-Chodrov.

G7. R. Joshua Heschel Eichenstein, the first of the Chassidic leaders and Admurim to come to the U.S.A. in 1922. He married the daughter of R. Alter Zeev of Stryzow.

G8. R. Abraham Eichenstein, Admur Zhidachov-Chicago, married the daughter of R. Phineas Shalom Rotenberg (G4.2/5.5/6/7 below).

G9. R. Abraham Joshua Heschel Eichenstein, Admur Zhidachov-Chicago.

G5.4. Wife of R. Haim Moses, son of R. Alexander Sender Safrin of Komarno.

G5.5. Devorah, married R. Haim Jehiel, son of R. Meir Rubin of Glogov. Their daughter married her uncle R. Aaron Menachem Mendel Eichenstein (G5.2. above).

G5.6. R. Phineas Eichenstein, Admur Stry, married the daughter of R. Elimelech of Yaritch.

G6. R. Alexander Sender Lipa Eichenstein, Admur Stry, married the daughter of R. Shalom Rokeah of Lobatchov. (See Chapter XVII — Rokeah Dynasty.)

G5.7. R. Joseph Eichenstein of Tarnopol.

G6. Bathsheba, married R. Eleazar son of R. Mordecai Spira.

G5.8. Esther, married twice. Her second husband was R. Simeon Bezalel Neiman. Their grandchildren include members in Toronto.

G4.2. R. Shalom Jacob Eichenstein, died in 1885, Admur of Zhidachov from 1873.

G5.1. R. Isaac Menachem Eichenstein, 1879-1943, Admur Podhajce, married the daughter of R. Nahum of Borstein.

G6. R. Zeida Eichenstein, married and has issue (New York). His wife Channah, daughter of R. Tuvia Horowitz of Shendeshov. (See Chapter XVI — Branch VII — G14.2/15.3 /16.1/17.7.)

G5.2. R. Elijah Eichenstein, A.B.D. of Zakapone.

G5.3. R. Alter Eichenstein of Yaritchov, married the daughter of R. Joshua Rosenfeld of Kamenka.

G6. R. Gedaliah Eichenstein. His grandchildren include members in Petah Tikvah.

G5.4. R. Alexander Sender Lipa Eichenstein.

G6. Jacob Eichenstein (Munich, Germany).

G5.5. Wife of R. Naftali Ehrlich of Deliatyn.

G6. Sarah Channah, married R. Phineas Shalom Rotenberg.

G7. Wife of R. Abraham son of Joshua Heschel Eichenstein of Chicago. (See above G4.1/5.3/6/7/8.)

G4.3. R. Issachar Dov Eichenstein, Admur Dolina from 1873, died in 1886. He married the daughter of R. Abraham Brandwein of Strettin.

G5.1. R. Judah Zvi Eichenstein of Dolina, died in 1910.

G6. Wife of R. Joshua son of R. Moses Halberstam of Bardiyov (Branch E).

G5.2. Wife of R. Phineas, son of R. Moses Rokeah of Korev.

G5.3. Wife of R. Jacob Isaac David Hager. (See Chapter XV.)

G4.4. R. Elijah Eichenstein, 1834-75, author of *Zichron Eliyahu*, married the daughter of R. Liebus, A.B.D. of Razla.

G5.1. Wife of R. Moses Eichenstein of Zhidachov.

G5.2. Jochebed Zipporah, married R. Asher (A.B.D. Kortchin) son of R. Samuel Rubin (See Chapter XVI — Branch VII.)

G4.5. R. Menachem Mendel Eichenstein, 1840-1901, married the daughter of R. Haim Abraham Redlich of Mikoloyev.

G5.1. Esther, married R. Isaac (of Stachin) son of R. Moses Horowitz of Rozvadov.

G5.2. Rebecca, married R. David Mariles of Jaroslav.

G5.3. Mendel, married, perished in the Holocaust.

G5.4. Menachem Eichenstein.

G5.5. Sarah, married R. Baruch son of R. Meir (of Dombrovo) Rubin. (See Chapter XVI — Branch VII.)

G5.6. Hannah, married R. Meir, son of R. Haim son of R. Aaron Friedlander (who were descendants of the Katzenellenbogen family). He adopted his wife's surname of Eichenstein. They perished with six of their eight children in the Holocaust.

G6.1. R. Isaac Eizik Eichenstein (Forest Hills, N.Y.), married and has issue, Aaron Meir (married with issue), Joseph Mordecai (married with issue), Leibish (married with issue), Pearl and Chaya.

G6.2. Abraham Eichenstein, married and has issue.

G5.7. R. Haim Abraham Eichenstein, died about 1909 in Lvov, Admur Zhidachov. He married Riva, daughter of R. Ezekiel Goldschlak.

G6.1. Isaac, died young.

G6.2. Wife of R. Haim, son of R. Aaron Menachem Mendel Eichenstein of Alesk. (See above G2.5/3/4.1/5.2.)

G6.3. R. Menachem Mendel Eichenstein, Admur Zhidachov, married the daughter of R. Ephraim Horowitz of Rozvadov. They and their family perished.

G6.4. Friedel, married R. Moses son of R. Phineas David Horowitz (called the Bostoner Rebbe — See Chapter XVI — Branch I).

ROKEAH FAMILY AND CHASSIDIC DYNASTY OF BELZ

INCLUDING THE LEWIN-EPSTEIN, LOURIA, KLATZCO, ROBINSON AND RELATED FAMILIES
AND ALESK (MAYER FAMILY) DYNASTY

The founder of the Rokeah family was R. Eleazar, son of R. Samuel Shmelke (A.B.D. Olkusz), who came from Cracow and became A.B.D. of

Brody, where he wrote approbations in 1714, 1721 and 1731. He then became the leader of the Ashkenazi community of Amsterdam. For the occasion a golden ring was made with the inscription: R. Eliezer, son of R. Samuel, A.B.D. of Brody; and on the obverse side: appointed here on Wednesday, the 27th of Elul 5495 (1735). He did not remain here for long and left in 1740 to settle in Jerusalem. In Amsterdam he wrote approbations to *Zerah Yisrael* by R. Jacob, son of R. Joseph (Amsterdam, 1736); *Reishit Chochmah* (Amsterdam 1737); *Ohel Yaakov*, and others until he left. He arrived in Safed in 1741, and died there later that year. He was the author of *Ma'aseh Rokeach*, published in Amsterdam in 1700 by his sons, R. Moses and R. Shalom. (Through his first wife, Chavah, daughter of R. Samuel Shmelke Horowitz, he became the brother-in-law of R. Meir Horowitz (*MaHaRaM* Tiktin — Chapter XVI — G9), and his second wife was the daughter of R. Naftali Katz of Frankfurt (see Chapter V — Branch B — G8.10). He had two sons.

G9.1. R. Shalom Rokeah, A.B.D. Tiktin, married his first cousin, daughter of R. Moses Joshua Horowitz, A.B.D. Grodno (son of R. Samuel Shmelke Horowitz). He wrote approbations to *Sha'arei Binyamin* in 1752, *Ateret Paz* in 1757, *Siddur HaTeffilah* in 1759 and *Ateret Rosh* in 1766. He died in 1767, and his funeral oration can be found in the Responsa of R. Meshullam by R. Abraham Meshullam Zalman, son of the Chacham Zvi Ashkenazi.

G10.1. R. Joshua Rokeah, A.B.D. Pinsk.

G11.1. R. Haim, wrote an approbation to *Urim VeTumim*, published in 1826.

G11.2. R. Shalom Rokeah.

G12. R. Isaac Rokeah, married Bathsheba, daughter of R. Phineas, A.B.D. Shershov (author of *Nachalat Azriel*).

G13. R. Phineas Michael Rokeah, A.B.D. Shershov and Annipoli, died in 1891.

G11.3. R. Gad Asher Rokeah, married Chaya, daughter of R. Saul Levine of Pinsk. (See page 229.)

G12.1. R. Joshua Heschel Rokeah of Pinsk, son-in-law of R. Solomon, son of R. Akiva Eger.

G12.2. R. Gad Asher Rokeah of Pinsk.

G11.4. Sarah of Meseritz, died in Jerusalem.

G12. Deborah, married R. Michael Horowitz.

G10.2. R. Isaac Rokeah of Tiktin.

G10.3. R. Eliezer Rokeah of Tiktin.

G10.4. Feige, married R. Judah Lieb, A.B.D. Zbariz.

G10.5. Wife of R. Joshua, son of R. Judah Lieb Mirkes of Sokolov. (See Chapter V — Branch A — G6.2/7/8/9.3.)

G9.2. R. Moses Rokeah, A.B.D. of Zlatchov, died in 1753/4. He wrote approbations to *Birkat Yosef* and *Eliyahu Rabba* in 1742. He married 1) the daughter of R. Bezalel son of R. Naftali Katz and 2) the daughter of Chacham Zvi Ashkenazi. (See Chapters V and XIII.)

G10.1. R. Judah Lieb Rokeah, A.B.D. Zbariz. His novellae can be found in *ARba'ah Turei Even.*

G11. Eidel, married R. David, son of R. Levi (author of *Ateret Rosh*). He died in Vilna in 1794. Progenitors of the Rokeach Family and Lewin-Epstein Family.[2] See below.

G10.2. R. Naftali Rokeah of Brody, who published the *ARba'ah Turei Even* of his brother, married his first cousin, the daughter of R. Abraham Meshullam Zalman, son of the Chacham Zvi Ashkenazi.

G11. R. Shalom Zvi Rokeah, A.B.D. Kremnitz, died in 1801.

G12. R. Ephraim Rokeah, A.B.D. Rodwill and then Venice.

G10.3. R. Samuel Shmelkle (died in 1793), married Veitel, daughter of R. Israel Babad, son of R. Mordecai Yollis (of Brody — See Chapter XI — G7.1/8.1/9.1/10.2.)

G11.1. R. Sander Rokeah.

G12. Rachel Rebecca, maternal grandmother of R. Sander Haim, who published *Michtam LeDavid.*

G11.2. R. Eleazar Rokeah of Brody, married Rebecca Henna, daughter of R. Judah Zondel Ramraz, son of R. Moses, son of R. Todros. He died young, at the age of thirty-two in Warsaw, leaving three sons and two daughters. One was R. Liebish of Berdichev. Another was the founder of the Chassidic Dynasty of Belz, R. Shalom.

G12. R. Shalom Rokeah, the first Belzer Rebbe, 1779-1855, married his first cousin, Malka, daughter of R. Issachar Ber (A.B.D. Sokol) son of R. Judah Zondel Ramraz. This small town in

Poland was to become the center of one of the most important Chassidic dynasties of Galicia. Because he was orphaned as a child he studied under his uncle, R. Issachar Ber. In Sokol he was introduced to the Chassidic teachings of R. Solomon of Lutsk and he later studied under the *Chozeh* (Seer) of Lublin, the Apter Rov, Rabbi Abraham Joshua Heschel, the Maggid of Kozenitz and R. Uri Strelisker. The *Chozeh*, R. Jacob Isaac Horowitz, had him appointed the Rabbi of Belz and on his death in 1815, R. Shalom, now thirty-seven, became recognized as a *Zaddik*, revered in his splendid Beit Midrash in Belz by thousands of Chassidim. He was considered a Talmudic authority, was active in public affairs and an opponent of the Haskalah movement. His oft-quoted teachings and legends and tales about his miracles and activities are collected in *Dover Shalom*, published in 1910. He had five sons who continued the Belzer Dynasty, and two daughters. One of his sons-in-law founded the Dynasty of Alesk (Olesko).

Once R. Shalom's older brother asked how he managed to attain such perfection. The Belzer Rabbi replied: "When I became Bar Mitzvah our ancestor, R. Eleazar of Amsterdam, of Blessed Memory, appeared to me one night in a vision and exchanged my soul for another. And since that time I am a different person!"

R. Haim Halberstam, founder of the Sanz Dynasty once visited R. Shalom with his son Baruch. They found the Belzer leader and his wife sitting in a barren room with plain walls. Only a table and chairs were present. On their departure home R. Haim enquired of his son what impression the couple had made on him, and how the room in which they were seated appeared. "As we entered," replied Baruch, "they seemed like Adam and Eve before they sinned and as if their room was paradise."

R. Shalom explained why circumcision is performed on the eighth day. When we pay a visit we should first greet the lady of the house and then direct attention to the master. The infant is given an opportunity first to welcome the Sabbath Bride before he is initiated into the company of the Master.

The Ethics of the Fathers states: "Upon three things the world rests: the Torah, prayer and performances of good deeds." R. Shalom taught that every good Jew should adopt one of these as his major obligation — the Rabbis should concentrate on Torah, the Rebbe to devotional service and the plain Jew to the performance of deeds of kindness.

G13.1. R. Eleazar Rokeah, first-born child, died in 1881. He married the daughter of R. Aviezer Zelig Shapiro of Kozenitz.

G14.1. R. Aaron Rokeah, Admur Lobitch-Karolovsky.

  G15. R. Judah Zondel Rokeah, succeeded his father at Lobitch-Karolovsky.

    G16. R. Baruch Abraham Rokeah, Admur Przemysl.

G14.2. R. Judah Rokeah, Admur Dynow.

  G15. R. Menachem Mendel Rokeah, Admur Dynow, married
Rachel, Daughter of R. Aviezer Zelig, son of R. Eleazar
(of Kaloshin) Unger. (See Chapter XVII — Unger Dynasty.) R. Aviezer's wife was the daughter of R. Moses
Rokeah of Karov. (See G13.3 below.)

    G16.1. R. Zvi Elimelech Rokeah, Admur Przemysl, married
the daughter of R. Joshua of Przemysl.

      G17.1. Judah Frankel (adopting that surname), of Lon-
don.

      G17.2. Joshua Rokeah of London.

    G16.2. R. Issachar Dov Rokeah, Admur Linsk, died in Is-
rael in 1965. He succeeded his father-in-law, R.
Simeon Horowitz of Linsk. (See Chapter XVI —
Branch VII). He came to the U.S.A. in 1938.

      G17.1. R. Eliezer Rokeah, married Malke Feige daughter
of R. Haim Issachar Dov son of R. Moses Lifschutz. (See below G13.4/14.2.) They perished.

      G17.2. R. Abraham Haim Rokeah married Miriam De-
borah, daughter of R. Aaron son of R. Abraham
Landman. They perished.

      G17.3. R. Judah Rokeah, married Eidel, daughter of R.
Samuel Zvi Ramraz. They perished.

      G17.4. R. David Rokeah, perished.

      G17.5. Esther Rebecca, married R. Naftali son of R.
Phineas son of R. Naftali Rokeah — (See below
G13.5/14.5/15.1/16.) They perished.

      G17.6. Reizel, alone survived the Holocaust, married R.
Menachem Solomon son of R. Moses Taub of
Kalov-New York, (born in 1903). He wrote
Chekel Tapuchim. Their daughter, Chavah, mar-
ried R. Isaac Ashkenazi. (See Chapter IV and be-
low — G13.7/14.3.)

G16.3. Dinah, married R. Abraham Abba Wagner of Dynow.

G16.4. Malka, married R. Shalom, son of R. Todros son of R. Moses Rokeah. (See below — G13.3/14.4/15.3.)

G16.5. Tilla Toyba, married R. Jacob Isaac son of R. Joseph Shapiro. (See below — G13.3/14.2/15.1.)

G16.6. Gitel, married R. Naftali son of R. Zalman son of R. Zondel Rokeah, (See below — G13.4/14.1/15.5.)

G14.3. Wife of R. David Flamm.

G15. R. Shalom Flamm.

G16. Channa Sima, married R. David Rokeah (see below) of Lobatchov-New York.

G13.2. R. Samuel Shmelke, died young without issue.

G13.3. R. Moses Rokeah, Admur Karov, died in 1883, married Sheindel, daughter of R. Phineas of Jassy, son of R. Joseph (Yoske) Horowitz.

G14.1. R. Issachar Dov Rokeah, Admur Lobatchov, married Channah Asenath, daughter of R. Joseph.

G15.1. R. Shalom Rokeah, succeeded his father as Admur Lobatchov. He and his family perished. One daughter, Channah Asenath, was married to R. Simeon, son of R. Haim Halberstam of Chechoyv, and a son, R. Elimelech, married Golda, daughter of his father's first cousin, R. Isaac Mendel Rotenberg (see below).

G15.2. R. David Rokeah, 1872-1956, Admur Lobatchov-New York, married twice. He had two children from his first wife, Sarah and R. Jacob Isaac, and five from his second wife, Channah Sima, daughter of R. Shalom, son of R. David Flamm. (See above G13.1 /14.3.)

G16.1. Sarah, married in Buenos Aires.

G16.2. R. Jacob Isaac, married and perished.

G16.3. Malka, married R. Abish Goldman, perished.

G16.4. Beila, married, and died in Israel in 1943.

G16.5. R. Issachar Dov Rokeah, died in 1955, married Julia Schandor. Their sons, Amos and Shalom.

G16.6. R. Shalom, married Raatza Gottesman.

G16.7. R. Moses, married Rachel, daughter of R. Jacob Zvi Unger of Safed. She was also a granddaughter of R. Nahum Essrog of Safed. Their sons, Nahum Eleazar, Shalom and Issachar Dov.

G15.3. R. Joseph Judah Rokeah, married his first cousin, Rebecca Rachel, daughter of R. Menachem Phineas, son of R. Eleazar Spira of Lancut. They perished.

G16.1. Sarah, married and perished with family.
G16.2. Moses, married and perished with family.
G16.3. R. Zvi Elimelech Rokeah, 1896-1964, married Chaya Hinde, daughter of R. Mordecai, son of R. Zvi Elimelech Spira of Birch. He succeeded his father-in-law as Admur Birch-New York.

G17.1. R. Phineas Menachem Rokeah, born in 1926 (Jamaica, New York), married Leah Yolles, granddaughter of R. Jacob Kaner. (See Chapter XIV Halberstam — Branch A — G15.2/16.7/17.7.) Their children, Zvi Elimelech, Channah Sprintze and Rivke Esther.

G17.2. Abraham Simha Rokeah, born in 1920, married Zipporah Essrog (granddaughter of R. Nahum Essrog). Their son, Mordecai, and daughters, Bracha and Jochebed Malka.

G17.3. Channah Asenath, married Tuvia, son of Isaac Halberstam (Bardiyov). Their children, Rivke Rochel, Isaac Joshua and Miriam Bracha.

G17.4. Frieda, married Professor Samuel Sprecher (Israel). Their children, Joseph, Israel, Aaron, Bracha and Rachele.

G17.5. Mina Mindel, born in 1924, married R. Menachem Mendel, son of R. David Joshua Halberstam. (See Chapter XIV — Branch G — G15.1/16.1/17.)

G14.2. R. Samuel Shmelke Rokeah, died in 1915, Admur Kozenitz, but later settled in Radom after World War I. He married the daughter of R. Eleazer of Kozenitz.

G15.1. Wife of R. Joseph Shapiro. Their son, R. Jacob Isaac, married Tilla Rokeah.

G15.2. R. Eleazar Elimelech Rokeah, Admur Radom from
1915. He married the daughter of R. Meir Shalom
Rabinowitz of Kaloshin (son of R. Joshua Asher, son
of R. Jacob Isaac, the *Yud* — See Chapter IV — Introductory section).

G14.3. R. Abraham Joshua Heschel Rokeah of Przemysl.

G15.1. R. Zvi Hirsch Rokeah of Pomarin.

G15.2. R. Meir Rokeah of Kozlov, died in the United States
in 1942. He married Reina, daughter of R. Joseph
Alter Epstein of Magrov.

G16. R. Moses Rokeah, 1898-1970, Admur Kozlov-New
York, settled in the United States in 1931 and ac-
quired a large library of Hebraica. He married
Shlamtche, daughter of Aaron, son of R. Abraham
Judah Uri Halpern of Berjan. (See Chapter XVI —
Branch VII.)

G17.1. R. Meir Rokeah.

G17.2. Miriam Deborah, wife of R. Berish Schapiro
(Belz Yeshiva).

G17.3. R. Aaron Rokeah.

G17.4. Eidel, married R. Jehiel Michel Rotenberg of
Kosun.

G15.3. Zinah, married R. Judah son of R. Issachar Dov (of
Linsk) Rokeah.

G14.4. R. Todros Rokeah, Admur Nemirov.

G15.1. R. Zondel Rokeah, Admur Rzeszow.

G16. R. Israel of Ropko.

G15.2. R. Eleazar, Admur Drogobitch, perished.

G15.3. R. Shalom, Admur Rava, perished.

G14.5. R. Shalom Rokeah, Admur Greiding.

G15. R. Abraham Joshua Rokeah, Admur Greiding, perished.

G14.6. R. Phineas Rokeah, married daughter of R. Judah Zvi
Eichenstein Admur Dolina, and succeeded his father-
in-law as Admur Dolina on his death in 1910.

G14.7. Wife of R. Naftali Goldberg, Admur Zulz (died in
1907), author of *Kol Naftali.*

G15. R. Alter Goldberg, died about 1938. Known as the Admur Shebieck in Warsaw.

G14.8. Wife of R. Aviezer Zelig, son of R. Eleazar (of Kaloshin) Unger. (See Chapter XVII — Unger Dynasty.)

G14.9. Sarah, married R. Alter Meir David (1842-1911), son of R. Isaac Mendel (1822-74) Halevi Rotenberg (Admur Lelov, succeeding his father-in-law, R. Moses Biderman) Admur Walbrom.

G15.1. R. Joseph Nathan, became Admur Walbrom in 1911, and died without issue in 1914/5.

G15.2. R. Abraham Phineas Shalom, 1868-1930, Admur of Apt.

G16. R. Jacob Isaac Elchanan, Admur Chenzdechov Apt, married the daughter of R. Eliezer Finkler of Sosnowiec, perished in the Holocaust.

G17. R. Issachar Dov Rotenberg (Brooklyn, N.Y.), Admur of Vaidislav-New York. He married the daughter of R. Meir Moskovitz of Shatz-London and had issue.

G15.3. R. Isaac Menachem, died in 1939, became Admur Bendin in 1911. He married the daughter of R. Naftali Rokeah.

G16. R. Meir Rotenberg, married the daughter of R. Meir Shalom Rabinowitz of Kaloshin. He became Admur Bendin in 1939. He perished.

G15.4. Rebecca Rachel, married R. Aaron, son of R. Joseph Zeev, son of R. David Halberstam of Keshanov. She also married her first cousin, R. Joseph Judah, son of R. Issachar Dov Rokeah of Lobatchov.

G15.5. Shifra Channah Hena, married R. Isaac, son of R. Asher Isaiah Rubin. (See Chapter XVI — Branch VII.)

G15.6. R. Joseph Rokeah.

G13.4. R. Judah Zondel Rokeah, died in 1871, Admur of Ochan (near Lublin), married the daughter of R. Samuel Hirsch of Driscopoli.

G14.1. R. Ephraim Zalman, died 1895, succeeded his father as Admur Ochan in 1871, married the daughter of R. Zvi of Strelisk.

G15.1. R. Moses Rokeah, Admur Przemysl, perished in 1942, married the daughter of R. Shalom Landman. He became Admur in 1913.

G15.2. R. Isaiah Shalom Rokeah of Turka, Admur Vanivitch (near Sambor), perished in 1942. He was the author of *Yalkut Yosher*.

G15.3. R. Aryey Lieb Rokeah, Admur Horbitchov-U.S.A.

G15.4. R. Hananiah Rokeah, Admur Lutsk-Cleveland. He later settled in Israel where he died. His family perished.

G15.5. R. Naftali Rokeah, Admur Horbitchov, perished. He married Gitel, daughter of R. Menachem Mendel Rokeah, Admur Dynow. (See above — G13.1/14.2 /15.)

G15.6. R. Zondel Rokeah, Admur Horbitchov, perished.

G14.2. Wife of R. Moses Lifschutz.

G15. R. Haim Issachar Dov Lifschutz.

G16. Malka Feige, married R. Eliezer, son of R. Issachar Dov (of Linsk) Rokeah.

G13.5. R. Joshua Rokeah, the second (Middle or "Mittler") Rebbe of Belz, 1825-94, married Rebecca Miriam, daughter of R. Samuel Ashkenazi (son-in-law of the Heschel-Apt Dynasty, and himself a descendant of Chacham Zvi Ashkenazi — see Chapter XV — Heschel Family G10.1/11.1/ 12.2 and Chapter XIII). They had five sons and four daughters. R. Joshua provided his Chassidim with a framework of organization which maintained the following and which he ruled strictly. Like his father, he opposed the Haskalah, was one of the foremost Galician Orthodox leaders and established the *Machzikei Ha-Dat* organization. His teachings were published in *Ohel Yehoshua* (as part of his father's *Dover Shalom*, 1910).

He used to say: When you are overtaken by tribulation, know that you are being tested by the Almighty to see how you will accept it. If you endure and adhere to the teaching of Nahum Ish-Gamzu that "this too is for my good" your distress will vanish. You will not have to try further and you will then see how the misfortune was indeed for your good.

Although the first Belzer Rebbe commenced building his own synagogue with the help of his own closest Chassidic followers, the synagogue was not completed by him nor his son, Rabbi Joshua, or their descendants.

There is a legend that declares it will remain unfinished until the advent of the Messiah, who will then convey it to Israel.

G14.1. R. Issachar Dov Rokeah, the third Belzer Rebbe, 1854-1927, married 1) Bathsheba Nechama, daughter of R. Isaiah Meshullam Zusia, son of R. Aaron Twersky of Chernobyl and had issue, and 2) the daughter of R. Abraham Samuel, son of R. Joseph of Brezna. He succeeded his father in 1894 when he was forty. During World War I he was forced to wander from town to town, Rotsfurt, Munkacs (1918), and Holshitz (1921), and he finally returned to Belz in 1925. He was also a Galician teacher and headed the *Machzikei Ha-Dat,* established by his father. Unlike leaders of other Chassidic Dynasties, he opposed the Agudat Israel movement and any form of Zionism.

G15.1. R. Aaron Rokeah, the fourth Belzer Rebbe, 1880-1957, married 1) his first cousin, the daughter of R. Samuel Rokeah, Admur of Sokol, 2) Gitel, daughter of R. Baruch Goldstoff (later divorced — see Chapter IV — Branch J) and 3) the daughter of R. Jehiel Labin (descendant of the Eichenstein Dynasty). During World War II he was forced to flee to Sokol under the protective aid of his closest Chassidic followers and companions, and then to Przemysl, where he lost his wife and six children. After being confined in the ghettos of Vizhniz, Cracow and Bochnia, he finally reached Hungary in 1942 and managed to settle in Israel in 1944, where he reestablished the Belz Chassidim buildings and yeshivas, and *Battei Midrash.* He lived during his latter years in Tel Aviv, where he was active in supporting the Agudat Israel movement, which his father had so strongly opposed. He differed from his father in other ways as well, by leading a more ascetic life and instituting lengthy orders of prayer. Because he lost his family, his successor in 1957 was his nephew, then only a child of nine years of age.

G15.2. R. Mordeccai Rokeah, Admur of Bilgoray, born in 1882 and died in Tel Aviv in 1949. He settled in Israel with his brother in 1944 and was his closest associate.

G16. R. Issachar Dov Rokeah, the fifth Belzer Rebbe, born in Israel in 1948 and married the daughter of R. Moses Hager, leader of the Vizhniz Chassidim.

G15.3. R. Joshua Rokeah, Admur Jaroslav. Has issue in Israel.

G15.4. R. Shalom Rokeah, Admur Apt, the youngest son.

G15.5. Hena, married 1) R. Baruch, son of R. Israel Hager, and 2) R. Naftali Zvi Perlow (of Koidanov). Their sons, Michael Hager and Michael Perlow.

G15.6. Sarah, married Zeev Twersky, perished.

G15.7. Yente, married R. Johanan Twersky (of Horivshov), perished.

G15.8. Sheva, married R. Isaac Nahum (of Rava Ruska), son of R. Mordecai Twersky of Spikov. (See Chapter XV.)

G15.9. Chava Rachel, eldest daughter, married R. Phineas (perished in 1943), son of R. Mordecai (Velvel), of Ostilla, son of R. Mordeccai Twersky of Rotmistrovka.

G16. Treina, married R. Jacob (died March 31, 1968), son of R. David Twersky, Admur Skvira — New York.

G17.1. R. David Twersky, Admur of Skvira-New York, married the daughter of R. Moses Hager, Admur Vizhniz.

G17.2. Wife of R. Mordecai, son of R. Haim Meir Hager, Admur Vizhniz.

G14.2. R. Aryey Liebish Rokeah, R. of Magrov and Admur Rava-Ruska. He married Malka, daughter of R. Menachem Nahum, son of R. Aaron Twersky of Chernobyl. (See Heschel Dynasty — Chapter XV.)

G15.1. R. Joshua Heschel Rokeah, successor as Admur of Rava-Ruska.

G15.2. R. Isaac Eli Rokeah.

G15.3. R. Nahum Aaron Rokeah, Admur Magrov-Lvov, married the daughter of R. Moses Mordeccai Twersky of Makarov.

G16. Wife of R. Isaac Weiss of Spinka.

G15.4. Feige, married 1) R. Solomon, son of R. David Twersky of Skvira, and 2) R. Isaac Meir Kanal of Warsaw. No issue.

G14.3. R. Isaac Meir Rokeah, Admur Redin. His family perished.

G14.4. R. Samuel Rokeah, Admur Sokol, 1851-1911, married the daughter of R. Menachem Mendel Hager of Vizhniz. He became R. of Sokol in 1887 and Admur in 1894.

    G15.1. Wife of R. Aaron Rokeah, the fourth Belzer Rebbe, her first cousin.

    G15.2. Wife of R. Phineas Hager, of Borsa.

    G15.3. Wife of R. Aryey Lieb (of Mushina), son of R. Moses Halberstam of Bardiyov (see Chapter XIV — Branch E — G15.1/16.2).

    G15.4. R. Shalom Rokeah, Admur Sokol — Israel, died in 1963 and buried in Tiberias. He married the daughter of R. Israel Hager of Vizhniz.

        G16. R. Baruch Rokeah, Admur Sokol — New York, married and has issue (Brooklyn, N.Y.).

G14.5. R. Naftali Rokeah, Admur Noveria, died in 1905.

    G15.1. R. Phineas Rokeah, born in 1900, perished in the Holocaust. Admur in Lvov, he married the daughter of R. Jehiel Michal of Zovhil.

        G16. R. Naftali Rokeah, married Esther Rebecca, daughter of R. Issachar Dov Rokeah of Linsk. They perished.

    G15.2. Channah Rachel, married R. Samuel Rabinowitz, A.B.D. Zlukov.

    G15.3. Wife of R. Isaac Menachem, son of R. Alter Meir David Rotenberg. (See above — G13.3/14.9/15.3.)

G14.6. Chava, married R. Moses Mordecai Twersky of Makarov.

C14.7. Mirl, married R. Jehiel Heschel of Krolevets (see Heschel Dynasty).

G14.8. Reizel, married R. Zeev (of Warsaw), son of R. Mordeccai Joseph (of Zlatopoli), son of R. David, son of R. Johanan (of Rotmistrovka) Twersky.

G14.9. Frieda, married R. Simha I. D. Halberstam (page 488).

G13.6. Eidel, married R. Isaac Bezalel, son of R. Elimelech, son of R. Asher Isaiah Rubin (see Chapter XVI — page 612).

G13.7. Frieda, married R. Hanoch (Heinich) Dov, surnamed Mayer, son of R. Samuel, son of R. Meir. He was born in 1820 and studied under the *Chozeh* (Seer) of Lublin, R. Uri of Strelisk, R. Naftali Zvi of Ropshitz and his father-in-law. He became Rabbi in Satanow and Alesk (Olesko). From 1855, on the death of his father-in-law he became Admur and founder of the Alesk Chassidic Dynasty. He was the author of various works entitled *Lev Sameach*, and died in 1884.

G14.1. R. Isaac Mayer, 1829-1904, Admur Alesk, married the daughter of R. Yoske of Lashkovitz.

G14.2. R. Solomon Mayer, 1835-1919, Admur Sassov, died in Lvov where he settled five years before his death.

G15.1. R. Jehiel Michal Mayer, Admur Lvov.

G15.2. R. Joseph David Mayer, married Rachel.

G16. R. Hanoch, Mayer of Sassov — Kretzki, married the daughter of R. Hananiah Yomtov Lipa Teitelbaum. They perished. He was the author of *Ein Chanoch*.

G17.1. R. Hananiah (Leopold) Yomtov Lipa (died 1966), married his first cousin, daughter of R. Joel Teitelbaum of Satmar and succeeded his father-in-law as A.B.D. there. He settled in New York, later in Israel where he established *Kiriat Yismach Moshe*.

G18. R. Joseph David Mayer, succeeded him.

G17.2. R. Joel (Mayer) Teitelbaum, Admur Kirolhaz — Brooklyn, married the daughter of R. Haim Isaac Halberstam.

G15.3. R. Shalom Mayer of Pomarin.

G15.4. Wife of R. Abraham Mordecai Shalom Taub (See Chapter XVII — Eichenstein Dynasty.)

G14.3. Wife of R. Asher Anschel (died in 1896), Admur Stanislav-Alesk, son of R. Joel Ashkenazi (A.B.D. Zlatchov, see Chapter IV — Branch A — page 191.)

G14.4. Wife of R. Moses Zilberprav.

G15. R. Meshullam Zalman Joseph Zilberprav of Toprov

(1870-1944), married the daughter of R. Aaron of Koidanov (descendant of R. Aaron Perlow, Admur Stolin).

G16. R. Hanoch Dov Zilberprav, born in 1891, Admur Botosani-Koidanov-Tel Aviv, married the daughter of R. Mordecai Joseph Moses of Solitza, son of R. Joel Moskovitz of Shatz.

G14.5. Wife of R. Aaron Menachem Mendel, son of R. Alexander YomTov Lipa Eichenstein (Admur Zhidachov), and succeeded his father-in-law as Admur Alesk in 1884. (See Chapter XVII — Eichenstein Dynasty.)

G14.6. Rosa, married R. Haim Eli Lieberman (Halevi).

G15.1. R. Aaron Zelig Lieberman, married Toyba, daughter of R. Menachem Mendel (Admur Linsk) son of R. Abraham Haim Horowitz, Admur Linsk. (See Chapter XVI — Branch VII — G14.3/15.2/16.2.)

G16.1. R. Gedalliah Lieberman, died in 1920, married Channah (perished), daughter of R. Nahum Zvi Thumim (Chapter IV — Branch F).

G17.1. Abraham, perished.
G17.2. Feige Nisel, perished.
G17.3. Rosa (born in 1920), married R. Haim Zvi Weinberger. (See Chapter XVI — Branch V — G14.4 /15.1/16.2/17.)

G16.2. R. Hanoch Lieberman, married, and perished with his family.
G16.3. R. Shalom Lieberman. His daughter, Shevach Avigdor, in Israel.
G16.4. Sarah, married R. Zalman Lieb Reinman.

G17.1. Frieda, married R. Moses Rapps (New York), and have issue.
G17.2. Harry Reinman, married and has issue. (Brooklyn, N.Y.).
G17.3. Rosa, married R. Ezekiel son of R. Elisha Halberstam of Gorlice. (See Chapter XV — Branch E.)

G15.2. Malka Frieda, married R. Asher (of Jolkova), son of R. Naftali Rubin of Radechev. (See Chapter XVI — Branch VII.)

ROKEACH, LEWIN-EPSTEIN, LOURIA, KLATZCO, ROBINSON
AND RELATED FAMILIES

ANCESTRY

G8.   R. Eleazar Rokeah, author of *Ma'aseh Rokeach*.
G9.2. R. Moses Rokeah of Zlatchov, died in 1753/4.
G10.   R. Judah Lieb Rokeah of Zbariz.
G11.   Eidel, married R. David, who died in Vilna in 1794.
G12.   R. Levi, surnamed Rokeach, of Vilna, where he died in 1818, married
       Rachel, daughter of R. Noah son of R. Uri Shraga Feiwish Bloch of
       Vilna. (See Chapter VII — Bloch Family.)

G13.1. R. David Rokeach of Kossov.
G13.2. Feigel, died in Bialystok in 1864/5, second wife of R. Joseph son
        of R. Tuvia Zakheim of Vilna. From his first wife he had issue,
        R. Abraham Zakheim.

G14.1. R. Isaac Levi Zakheim, died in Rostov in 1878, married Perel
        (died in Vilna in 1880), daughter of R. Haim Nachman Parnas.
        (See Chapter V — Branch B — G7.1/8.1/9.2/10.3/11.1/12.3.)
G14.2. Keila, died in Vilna in 1821, married R. Aryey Lieb Gunzberg
        of Vilna.

G15. R. Gershon Gunzberg of Vilna, married the daughter of R.
      Jacob Pollak.

G16. Channah Keila, married R. Moses Aryey Lieb, son of R.
      Meshullam Feiwel Friedland of St. Petersburg. She died in
      St. Petersburg in 1888. R. Moses was a prominent Russian
      philanthropist born in 1826, and died in St. Petersburg on
      November 21, 1899. He was general army-contractor for the
      Russian Government for over thirty years, was an honorary
      citizen of St. Petersburg, and received several medals from
      the Government. He established an orphan asylum in St.
      Petersburg and a home for the aged in Jerusalem; however,
      his name is chiefly connected with the *Bibliotheca Fried-
      landiana,* a large library of Hebrew books which he presented
      in 1890 to the Asiatic Museum of the Imperial Academy of
      Sciences. A catalogue of this collection of manuscripts, in-
      cunabula and other books was compiled by Samuel Wiener
      under the title of *Kehillat Moshe.* Part of this material was
      utilized by Israel Tuvia Eisenstadt in the publishing of the

genealogical work *Da'at Kedoshim* (St. Petersburg, 1897-8), which forms the basis of many parts of this present book. They had six children.

G17.1. R. Joseph Meshullam Friedland, married his first cousin, daughter of R. Mordecai Friedland.

G17.2. R. Jacob Zangwill Friedland, married Eidel, daughter of R. Aaron Luria of Pinsk.

G17.3. Eila, married R. Joseph, son of R. Abraham, son of R. Joseph Zakheim of Vilna (mentioned above under G13.2).

G17.4. Deborah, married R. Moses Weinstein of Odessa.

G17.5. Gita, married R. Moritz Moscat.

G17.6. Anna, married R. David Socker.

G13.3. R. Aryey Lieb Rokeach of Walkavisk, where he died in 1871, married Mirl Ritevsky.

G14.1. Eidel, married Moses Klatzco (also Klatzko, Klatchko) of Vilna.

G15.1. Dr. Levy Klatzco, M.D. of Leningrad. His children Konstantin, Vladimir, Kathrin and Zetlin.

G15.2. Luba, born in Vilna in 1864 and died in New York in 1926. She married Dr. Leon Louria (1863-1923), in 1886. He graduated from the University of Moscow in 1888 and came to the U.S.A. in 1891, settling in the Williamsburg district of Brooklyn, New York. He was the Dean of the Jewish physicians of Brooklyn and one of the best known surgeons there. Besides being an attending physician of the Brooklyn Jewish Hospital since its foundation, he was a consultant to the East New York, Rockaway Beach and United Israel Zion Hospitals. He was also director of the old Broadway Bank of Brooklyn and the Manufacturers Trust Company, and an active worker in Jewish Communal affairs. He died in the Jewish Hospital of pneumonia as a result of an operation. On October 26, 1923 a rare tribute was paid to him at a memorial meeting at which over a thousand people, including six hundred physicians of Greater New York, gathered to honor his memory. The meeting was held under the auspices of the American Jewish Physicians' Committee of which he had been vice-president and governor.

Dr. Louria had an especially wide following. He was born in Russia, wore a Russian-type beard and was a brilliant diagnostician. . . .

I must say more about this rare man, Dr. Louria. As I said to the mourners at his equally remarkable funeral (attended by thousands, most of them poor, some of whom fainted from their grief), Dr. Louria "was more than just a physician; he was an angel of God upon earth, lover of his fellow men; his soul his work." Not only did his patients love him, but the doctors and nurses as well. . . .

It was a policeman who recalled to us that Dr. Louria had commenced his practice in a little basement office in Williamsburgh, treating visitors for fees as small as 25 cents. Just before his death his large calling list included many poor people who could still pay no more than the original 25 cents. They got the same professional care as his millionaire patients. . .

There is now a Dr. Leon Louria Memorial Hall at the Hospital.

> Nathan S. Jonas in his autobiography,
> *Through The Years,* New York, 1940
> Pages 147-8, Organization of The Jewish
> Hospital.

G16.1. Dr. Alexander Leon Louria, 1890-1949, was born in Moscow and came to the U.S.A. at the age of one year. He received his B.S. from Columbia University in 1910 and his M.D. in 1913. In 1923 he joined the staff of the Jewish Hospital in Brooklyn as chief attending physician, and in 1926 became Clinical Professor at the Long Island College of Medicine with a special interest in pulmonary diseases.

He remained on the staff at the Jewish Hospital for over a quarter century. On his death, he was described as "a brilliant physician, scholar, teacher, friend and a leader in his profession and amongst men" by his hospital associates. He was a director of the American Jewish Physicians' Committtee of the Federation of Jewish Charities; a member of the American Medical Association, Kings County Medical Society, Williamsburg Medical Society and the Society of International Medicine.

He was married to Ruth Meruk.

G17.1. Elaine, born in 1914, married Cornelius Ross. Their children, Jill (married Stephen Mottus, and have issue) and Neil.

G17.2. Ann, married 1) Harry Robbins, and had issue, Erica Brooks, and 2) Frank Geiffert of New York, and have Karen (married), Ingrid and Christina.

G16.2. Dr. Henry Walter Louria, born in 1896. He received his

M.D. from Columbia University in 1919 and trained in surgery at Peter Bent Brigham Hospital in Boston. He was a consultant at a number of hospitals including the Jewish Hospital in Brooklyn. He married in 1925 to Felice Jarecky.

G17.1. Dr. Ellen Lieberman, M.D. of Los Angeles, married 1) and had issue, Debbie, born in 1957, and 2) Harry Lieberman, and had William, born in 1965 and Susan, born in 1961.

G17.2. Dr. Henry Walter Louria, Jr., born in 1926, trained as a general surgeon at Columbia University, and married twice. His children, Kenneth, born in 1952 and Mark, born in 1953.

G17.3. Margo, born in 1928, unmarried.

G16.3. Dr. Milton Roland Louria, born in New York in 1898. He received his M.D. from Columbia University in 1928 and interned at John Hopkins. He was an attending physician at Sea View Hospital, Staten Island and the Brooklyn Thoracic Hospital, and associate attending at Kings County Hospital in Brooklyn. He married Lucy Littauer in 1924.

G17.1. Lee Louria, born in 1926, a lawyer in Darien, Conn., married in 1960 to Barbara Morris. Their children, Christopher, Leigh, Susan, Tyler, Amanda, Reed and Myles.

G17.2. Dr. Donald Bruce Louria, born in New York in 1928. He received his M.D. from Harvard in 1953. From 1960-64, he was Assistant Professor of Medicine at Cornell University, and Associate Professor there from 1964-69. Since 1969 he has been Professor and Chairman of the Department of Preventative Medicine and Community Health at the College of Medicine and Dentistry of New Jersey.

He married Barbara Watson in 1955 and has issue, Dana, Charles and Anne.

G17.3. Dana, born in 1930, married in 1952 to Dr. Gordon H. Cless (born in 1928) who received his M.D. from Tufts and specialized in anesthesiology. Their children, Holly, Bradley S. and Tracy.

G16.4. May born in 1891, married in 1913 to Dr. William Linder (1873-1945), Dean of Surgery at the Jewish Hospital in Brooklyn and the Israel Zion Hospital. He was born in Hungary and received his M.D. in 1896 from Bellevue Medical College. He was also a former Clinical Professor of Surgery at the Long Island College Hospital and a member of a number of medical societies. In 1935 he was appointed by Governor Herbert H. Lehman to the State Industrial Council. He had three children from his first marriage.

G16.5. Eleanore Grace, born in 1893, married Richard Blum.

G17.1. Richard Blum, Jr., born in 1917, married Joan Harris. Their children, Richard III and Eleanore.

G17.2. Howard Blum, born in 1919, married and has issue, Howard Jr. (married), Thomas and William.

G15.3. Simeon Klatzco, a pharmacist, married and had a daughter.

G15.4. Rachel, married Dr. Karkovsky (Krakowsky) of St. Petersburg. They had two daughters.

G15.5. David Klatzco, married and had issue. He died in the U.S.A.

G16.1. Louis Klatzco, 1890-1956, a Captain of the Chicago Police. His sons, Edward and Richard.

G16.2. Paul, unmarried.

G16.3. Harry, unmarried.

G15.6. Solomon Klatzco of St. Petersburg. He had two daughters.

G15.7. Leon (Leibel) Klatzco, a journalist, married and had issue.

G14.2. Necha, married Kalman Rabinowitch.

G15.1. Leibel Rabinowitch. His sons, Max, Abraham and Joseph (surnamed Lavie, father of Meir Lavie).

G15.2. Mendel (Max), surnamed Robinson, born in Kovno in 1863 and died in New York in 1948. He came to the U.S.A. via London, where he changed his name from Rabinowitch to Robinson, and settled in Birmingham, Alabama. He was a traveling salesman and married Fanny Wolowitz.

G16.1. Nora, born in 1907, married Sidney Goldman.

G16.2. Alfred, born in 1908, married Kate Feierstein. They have no issue. He was a Hearing Representative for the New York State Insurance Fund (New York).

G16.3. Helen, born in 1910, married Abraham Amchin (Florida).

G16.4. Florence Robinson, born in Birmingham, Alabama in 1911. From the age of sixteen she performed in major roles on the Broadway stage, became well known in radio to audiences from coast to coast, and was equally successful in the field of television.

Florence started her theatrical apprenticeship at Eva Le Gallienne's famous Civic Repertory Theatre in New York City along with Burgess Meredith, Howard DeSylva, Robert Lewis (the director) Richard Waring and others who attained prominence in the theatrical world. Her debut was as "Liza" in *Peter Pan,* and then appeared in *Cradle Song, The Inheritors,* and *Redemption* among other productions.

An article she wrote in the Sunday Drama Section of the New York Times brought her to the attention of Elmer Rice, who gave her the female understudy assignment in *We, The People,* which played at the famous Empire Theatre in New York, in *The Milky Way,* and finally an important role in the 1934-5 Broadway comedy, *Personal Appearance.* The play was directed by Antoinette Perry, for whom the famous "Tony" awards are named. Her role of "Gladys Kelcey" won her critical plaudits and awards, playing her part for over eight hundred performances.

Florence then turned to radio and was to perform on four to five thousand shows on all of the major networks, including many popular soap operas such as *Helen Trent, Just Plain Bill, Stella Dallas, Front Page Farrell, Big Sister, Aunt Jenny's Real Life* and other shows such as *Mr. District Attorney, Under Arrest, Big Story, Official Detective, City Hospital, Studio One, Norman Corwin Presents, The Molle Mystery Theatre* and many others.

In the field of television, she made her debut on *The Silver Theatre,* the first performance bringing her the first acting award ever given in television, to be followed by, *The Kraft Theatre, I Spy, Philco Playhouse, City Hospital, The United States Steel Hour, Red Buttons Show, The Edge of Night, Search for Tomorrow, Trial by Jury,* and others. These were interspersed with appearances on Broadway shows such as, *Steps Leading Up* and *The Assassin.*

In 1963 she became an Administrative Assistant in the Broadway Department of the Actors' Equity Association, the legitimate theatre union, and has since been active in speech teaching, specializing in diction and voice placement, in dramatic coaching and in auditioning talent for Studio '68 of Theatre Arts in London. In 1972 she settled in Abingdon, Virginia.

She married Francis C. Hayes (his second wife).

G16.5. Mildred, born in 1918, married Jack Sherman. Their daughter, Beth, born in 1961.

G16.6. Carl Robinson, unmarried (New York).

G15.3. Israel Robinson, 1874-1967, came to the U.S.A. about 1905 and married in 1909 to Eva Rabinowitch (died in 1962).

G16.1. Necha (Nora), died in 1972, married Sam Knauer. No issue.

G16.2. Charlotte, born in 1911, married Ben Jenkins. No issue.

G16.3. Helen, born in 1915, married in 1939 to Marvin Bloom (Jericho, Long Island).

G17.1. Dr. Peter Stephen Bloom, psychologist, born in 1943, married Sonia Olsen (Alexandria, Virginia). Their son, Eric, born in 1975.

G17.2. Nancy, born in 1946.

G17.3. Julie, born in 1954.

G16.4. Ernestine, born in 1918, married Herman Gruger (Chicago).

G17.1. Frederick Joel Gruber, settled in Israel and changed his name to Yechiel Bar Chaim. He is married and lives in Jerusalem.

G17.2. Daniel Charles, married in 1975 to Susan Green.

G17.3. Judith Esther.

G15.4. Isaac Rabinowitch, 1876-1940, married his first cousin, Hinde Kochkovsky, daughter of Fischel Rokeach (see G14.5/15.7 below). She lives in London.

G16. Fanya, married her first cousin, Israel Berz (see G14.5/15.8 below). They live in London. No issue.

G15.5. Alta (Mira) Kotok.

G16.1. Noe Kotok.

G16.2. Sarah Rivkin (Leningrad). Their daughters, Natasha and Marsha.

G14.3. Zlata, died in Israel about 1926, married Nissan Shapiro of Bialystok.

G15.1. Luba, married Abraham Pachter.

G16.1. Pinchas (Tel Aviv), married and has issue.

G16.2. Moshe (Yavneh, Israel).

G16.3. Jacob (Haifa).

G15.2. Sarah, 1880-1948, died in New York, married Kalman Friedman of Bialystok. He came to New York in 1912, and his wife and family reached there after World War I, in 1922.

G16.1. Dr. Louis H. Friedman, a dentist, born about 1903. His sons, George and Joseph.

G16.2. Rachel, married Isidore Greenberg. Their son, Peter (California).

G16.3. Miriam, died in New York in 1974, married and later divorced Mr. Tobias. Their children, Kalman and Susan (married Professor Norman Wiener).

G15.3. Miriam (Mary), married Max Wacks. Their children, Laurence and Beatrice (married Mr. Brown).

G15.4. Liebel Shapiro. His son, Benjamin, who was killed in the Israeli War of Independence in 1948, and left two children (Kibbutz Gennosaur, Israel).

G15.5. Faychke, married, had no issue.

G14.4. Ethel, married Moses Aaronson of Kovno.

G15.1. Jacob of Kovno. His sons, Max (Misha), married and had issue, Raphael, married and had issue and David, married and had issue.

G15.2. Dr. Mary Lewin, M.D., married Dr. David Lewin, M.D.

G16.1. Joseph Lewin, married Fanny Zlatkin. Their daughter, Ellen.

G16.2. Nina, married Fred Meyer (New York). Their children, Louis and Aviva.

G15.3. Liebel, a pharmacist in Leningrad. His son, Misha (Michael), killed in action in 1941.

G14.5. Ephraim Fischel Rokeach, the youngest son, married Esther Rachel Penina Kochkovsky.

G15.1. Luba, married Elia Levinthal. Their children, Talya and Felix (died young).

G15.2. Abba Itzig Rokeach-Kochkovsky.

G15.3. Maria, married Phineas Sperling. Their children Fischel and Hester.

G15.4. Leibish, named after his grandfather, perished with two children Jose and Alex. Another son, Dr. Boris Kochkovsky survived and lived in the U.S.S.R.

G15.5. Haim Israel (Charles) Rokeach, 1880-1970, married Sarah Schwartz in 1911. He came to the U.S. about 1898 and settled in Brooklyn.

>G16.1. Felice, born in 1912, married Warren Horace Thurman.

>>G17. Paul Robert Thurman, born in 1947, married Susan Charpentier.

>G16.2. Richard Rokeach, born in 1919, married Paula Rudolph. Their sons, Mark and Peter.

G15.6. Channah, married Mr. Segal. They had no issue and perished in the Holocaust.

G15.7. Hinde, born in 1886, married her first cousin, Isaac, son of Kalman Rabinowitch (see G14.2/15.4 above).

G15.8. Breina, born in Walkavisk in 1889 and died in New Jersey in 1973. She married Zalman Berz of Distinetz.

>G16.1. Fischel (Phillip) Berz, born in 1911, named after his maternal grandfather, unmarried. He lived in Paris, London and currently in New Jersey (Teaneck).

>G16.2. Dr. Israel Berz, Ph.D., Director of the Research Department of the London Electricity Board, married his first cousin, Fanya, daughter of Hinde and Isaac Rabinowitch (G14.2/15.4/16 and G14.5/15.7 above). They live in Croyden, near London, and have no issue.

>G16.3. Samuel Berz (Paris), married Betty Sagal. Their children, Charles, Miriam and Boris.

>G16.4. Rochelle, born in 1923, President of the local Hadassah Chapter, married in 1954 to Morris Rapoport (Teaneck, New Jersey). Their children, Saul, Jonathan, Daniel and Elaine.

G15.9. Samuel Rokeach-Kochkovsky, died young.

G15.10. Zlata, died unmarried.

G15.11. Eiga, born in 1896, married in 1920 to Michael Charmatz (Hollywood, Florida).

G16.1. Dr. Isabel Zackson, M.D., born in 1925, married Dr. Ephraim King Zackson, M.D. (New York). Their children, Channah, Saul and Ruth.

G16.2. Rita, born in 1928, married David S. Davidson (Chevy Chase, Maryland). They are both U.S. judges. Their children, Mina and Leo.

G14.6. Hinde, married Mr. Fineberg of Memel.

G15.1. Judith, married her first cousin, Eli Zeev Lewin-Epstein. (See below.)

G15.2. Emma Fink. G15.3. Rosalia Lekus.

G15.4. Maier Fineberg. His son, Dago (David) Fineberg of Switzerland.

G15.5. Salo Fineberg, having descendants in Israel.

G14.7. Israel Rokeach, born in Walkavisk in 1841. As a young man he settled in Kovno, thus settling in Lithuania from his native Poland, where he became associated with R. Isaac Elchanan Spektor (1817-96), the most important Talmudist of the latter nineteenth century, who was at that time the A.B.D. of Kovno. From him, Israel obtained his authoritative permission to establish a factory for the production of kosher soaps and perfumes in 1870, in partnership with his uncle, Isaac Ritevsky. By 1883, the business had expanded to include an additional store in Warsaw (Russia), where his nephew, Eli Zeev Lewin-Epstein managed the trade. His market expansion brought him into contact with R. Asher Anschel Stern of Hamburg who corresponded with R. Spektor about the Rabbinical Supervision of the factory. In 1890, having spent a while in Amsterdam, Israel arrived in the U.S.A., thus leaving the pogroms and hardships of Europe behind. Now fifty years old, he started anew by opening a kosher soap factory in New York. By 1913 his firm included land in Brooklyn under the title of I. Rokeach and Sons, Inc. Here he obtained the Certificates of Rabbinical supervision from R. Jacob Joseph, R. Hillel Cohen and then R. Dr. Phillip Klein. In 1924 he first produced a non-dairy, nonmeat soap made from coconut oil. From 1930 onwards, the supervisor was R. Jacob Levinson, who later wrote his biography entitled *Toldot Israel Rokeach* (New York, 1935). In

1933, when he was ninety-one years old, his son Levi, who was then the manager, died suddenly.

Israel Rokeach was both philanthropic and religious. He supported no less than fifty-one Yeshivas, twenty-six hospitals, fifteen orphanages and thirty-three other establishments of diffferent types. In his hometown of Walkavisk, he established the *Cheder Israel Rokeach,* and in Kovno he supported their hospital, orphanage and the *Kollel* founded there by R. Spektor. In 1929 he donated money for the building of the Yeshiva *Etz Chayim* in Jerusalem and helped establish the village of *Kerem Rokeach* in Israel, the trustees being himself; his nephew, Eli Zeev Lewin-Epstein; his sons, Dr. Aaron and Levi Rokeach; Dr. Samuel Lewin-Epstein (son of Eli Zeev); Elijah Aaron Kahana; Ephraim Sachor and Joseph Samuel Shapiro. In 1930 he established *Givat Rokeach* in Bnei Brak. He died some months after his son, in 1933, and was buried in the Mt. Lebanon Cemetery (New York). He married in Kovno to Channah Breindel, daughter of R. Aaron Cohen. She died in 1907. Their children were all born in Kovno. According to his will, he and his wife were reinterred in Israel on the Mt. of Olives.

G15.1.   Zeena (Selma), married Leon Kamaiky.

   G16.   Miriam, married Irving Lurie (Great Neck, Long Island). Their children, Barbara, Alfred and David, all married.

G15.2.   Fanny (Feigel), a dentist, married and later divorced Abraham Samuel. They had no issue.

G15.3.   Luba, 1872-1957, married Dr. Emil Gamson, M.D. One son, Arnold, died young.

   G16.   Henry Gamson, born in 1912, President of I. Rokeach and Sons from 1947-59. He married 1) Rhoda Fine, and had issue, Elliot (born in 1950), and 2) Rose Nathan. They reside in Tarrytown, New York.

G15.4.   Dr. Aaron Rokeach, M.D., died in 1946. He was President of I. Rokeach and Sons from 1933 until his death. He married Clara Sobel, but had no issue.

G15.5.   Dr. Louis Rokeach, dentist, died about 1956 unmarried.

G15.6.   Levi Rokeach, married Esther Rothschild. He was Vice-President and General Manager of I. Rokeach and Sons until his death in 1933.

   G16.1.   William Rokeach, born in 1911, married Beulah Mayer and

had issue, Abbie May, Lee and David. He lives in Deal,
New Jersey.

G16.2. Leo Rokeach, born in 1913, married, and had issue, Dr.
Michael Rokeach, Linda and Steven. They live in Florida.

G16.3. Hannah, married Dr. Maurice Bakunin, M.D., and had issue, Lee, Freddy and Mary.

G15.7. Miriam, married Morris Robinson. Their son, Albert, born in
1915, married Rosalind Michael, and had issue.

G14.8. Rachel, married Samuel Levinson.

G15.1. Lieb (Levi), married and had issue.

G15.2. Chaya Fineberg; having issue, Ethel (married Rosenhaltz),
Fanya (married Kailson), Isaac and Liebel.

G14.9. Eiga Rokeach, 1833-92, married Samuel Lewin-Epstein, 1838-
85, son of Eli Zeev Lewin of Vilna (who married Hena Necha
Epstein). The family were descendants of R. Samuel Edels,
known as the *MaHaRaSHa*. Samuel was a properous bookseller
in Warsaw.

G15.1. Eli Zeev (Wolf) Lewin-Epstein, 1863-1932, born in Walkavisk and died in Bad Nauheim, Germany. As a young man
he was the director of his father's bookstore and of the soap
and perfume firm established by his uncle, Israel Rokeach.
He joined the *Chovevei Zion* Movement after the 1881 po-
grom in Warsaw, and together with Zeev Gluskin (1859-
1949), he helped establish a society with the aim of establishing an agricultural settlement in Israel. He was also
founder of the Warsaw *Bnei Moshe* and *Menucha VeNa-
chalah* settlement societies. In 1890 he purchased land and
helped to found the settlement of Rehovot in Palestine and
was the spiritual leader of its settlers and head of the settlement committee. In 1900 he helped found the Carmel
Wine Company and settled in New York where he could
represent the company. During the following years he travelled to Europe on behalf of Jewry and played an active
role in politics. He frequently visited the U.S.A., serving as
director of the United HIAS Society and treasurer of both
the Federation of American Zionists and the Provisional
Zionist Committee. About 1918, he settled permanently in
Palestine and served as a member of the Zionist Commission

in 1919. He died while on one of his many trips to Europe, where he always promoted the Jewish interests of Palestine. He was buried in Rehovot. His memoirs were published as *Zichronotai* (1932).

He married his first cousin, Judith, daughter of his aunt, Hinde Fineberg. She was also buried in Rehovot.

G16.1. Miriam, 1886-1955, married R. Abraham Moses Hershman, D.D., D.H.L., 1880-1959, Rabbi Emeritus and leader of the *Shaarey Zedek* Congregation in Detroit. He was the author of *Rabbi Isaac Ben Sheshet Perfet and his Times* (1943); *Israel's Fate and Faith* (1952); *Religion of the Age and of the Ages* (1953). He also translated from the Hebrew, *The Code of Maimonides* (Book 14) as part of the Yale University Press Series in 1949.

G17.1. Zvia Ruth, born in 1910, currently of New York.

G17.2. Eiga Shulamit, born in 1913, currently of New York.

G17.3. Shalom David Hershman, born in 1918, married 1) Edith Miller and 2) Lillian Lewko. He lives in Detroit. From his first marriage:

G18.1. Susan, born in 1945, married Dr. Burton Ellis (Boston).

G18.2. Judith, born in 1946, married David Hinds (Chicago). Their children, Melissa (Miriam) and Adam Todd.

G18.3. Deborah Ann, born in 1948, married Jacob Schoenbaum (Virginia Beach). Their daughter, Rachael.

G18.4. Joel, born in 1951 (Ann Arbor).

From his second marriage:

G18.5. Miriam, born in 1962. G18.6. Joelle, born in 1970.

G16.2. Dr. Samuel Lewin-Epstein, 1889-1965, married Madeline Epstein. He was a dentist.

G17.1. Noah, 1928-44.

G17.2. Professor Jacob Lewin-Epstein, born in 1920, former Dean of the Dentistry Chair in Jerusalem. He married Marian Stormwind. Their children, Noah (born in 1950), Elijah Zeev (born in 1951) and Naomi (born in 1958).

G16.3. Rechaviah Lewin-Epstein, born in New York in 1892, but spent most of his childhood in Palestine. He established

the American Economic Committee for Palestine and remained its head until 1938. He also helped settle thousands
of refugees in Palestine where they could work in agriculture, industry and trade. In 1939 he returned to New
York to continue his economic work. He died in Cairo in
1942, while on his way to Palestine on a special mission.
This event has remained a shrouded mystery until today.
At the time of his death, he was in charge of the economic
work of the American Emergency Committee for Zionist
Affairs. In New York, the memorial service on the occasion of his death was conducted by R. Dr. Stephen S. Wise.
Rechaviah was buried in Rehovot, the settlement after
which he was named.

G16.4. Hyman   Lewin-Epstein,   1894-1964,   married   Florence
Steuer.

G17. Max (Mordecai Samuel) Lewin-Epstein, born in 1923
(New York), married Joan Mandel. Their children, Rich-
ard (Rechaviah, born in 1950), David, (born in 1954) and
Ann (Channah, born in 1960).

G15.2. Levi Lewin-Epstein, 1865-1938, married Reizel Licht.

G16.1. Samuel Lewin-Epstein, 1889-1964, married Penina Rappoport.

G17. Esther (Ata), born in 1919, married Isaiah Specktor.

G18.1. Chaya, born in 1944.
G18.2. Levi Specktor, born in 1946, married Yafa Zandman.
Their son, Shai Isaiah, born in 1972.
G18.3. Jacob Specktor.

G16.2. Eliezer Lewin-Epstein, 1898-1968, married Yuli Glazer.
He was a prominent Israeli industrialist and head of the
ORT (Organization for Rehabilitation through Training)
in Israel. He was also the head of Israel's largest printing
and publishing houses, who were the original printers of
Israeli postage stamps. His company also founded the
American-Israel Book Company, based in New York, in
partnership with the America Israel Paper Mills.

G15.3. Hena Necha, 1868-1929, married Noah Shapiro.

G16.1. Zvi Phineas Shapiro, 1893-1971.

G16.2. Eiga, 1894-1970.

G16.3. Joseph Samuel Shapiro, 1896-1964. He was Director of the Palestine Electric Corporation and one-time President of ORT.

G16.4. Jacob Shapiro, 1909-1953, married Raia Chabibi.

G17.1. Necha, born in 1936, married Mordecai Anaf. They have two children.

G17.2. Eiga, born in 1944, married Joan Chaik. They have three children.

G15.4. Leah Lewin-Epstein, 1870-1945, married Haim Prushansky.

G16.1. Samuel Prushansky (Tel Aviv), born in 1898, married Rachel Freund.

G17.1. Haim David, surnamed Albashan, born in 1937, married Shulamit Kozlovsky. They have three children.

G17.2. Leah, born in 1944, married Simeon Hoberman. They have two children.

G16.2. Joshua Prushansky, born in 1899, married Tamara Levi, and secondly, Miriam Kogan.

G17.1. Shoshana Necha, born in 1929, married Shlomo Lintzinberg. They have two children.

G17.2. Haim Prushansky, born in 1934, married Miriam Kaplan. They have three children.

SHAPIRO CHASSIDIC DYNASTY OF LYZHANSK-MOGIELNICA-GRODZISK

Rabbi Elimelech, known as the Lyzhansker, after the town of Lyzhansk where he was Admur, was the author of the well-known Chassidic work *Noam Elimelech* and also *Lekutei Shoshana*. His brother was the Chassidic leader R. Meshullam Zusia of Annipol (who died in 1800). R. Elimelech was a pupil of the Maggid of Meseritz and died in Lyzhansk in 1786. His wife, Shprintze, was the daughter of R. Aaron Rokeah, brother of R. Eleazar Rokeah of Brody (from whom are descended the Rokeah Chassidic Dynasty of Belz). Through this marriage, his family trace their lineage back to the Katzenellenbogen family. Through the marriage of his son, R. Naftali's daughter, Feige, to R. Haim Meir Jehiel Shapiro, the family became intermarried with the family of the famous R. Israel, the Maggid of Kozenitz.

G2.1. R. Lipa Eliezer, author of *Orach LeChayim,* Admur of Chemielnik, married the daughter of R. Fischel of Zizilnik.

G3.1. R. Aryey Lieb of Chemielnik.

G4. Wife of R. Samuel Abba Shapiro of Slovita.

G3.2. R. Elimelech, married his cousin, daughter of R. Eleazar.

G4. R. Abraham Gevertzman.

G5. R. Moses Isaac Gevertzman, Admur in Antwerp.

G2.2. R. Jacob of Mogielnica.

G2.3. Mirosh, married R. Elijah (of White Field), son of R. Jacob Jokel of Lancut.

G2.4. Wife of R. Israel.

G3. Wife of R. Isaac Lieb Wagschal.

G4. R. Jehiel Wagschal, A.B.D. Fristik, married the daughter of R. Jacob Horowitz of Malitsch. (See Chapter XVI — Branch VII.) He died about 1882/3.

G5.1. Wife of R. Samuel, son of R. Reuben Horowitz of Dembitz. (See Chapter XVI — Branch VII.)

G5.2. R. Jacob Isaac Wagschal.

G6. Haim Reuben Wagschal, only child.

G7.1. Channah, married R. Mordecai Eleazar, son of R. Asher Rubin (of Kortchin — Chapter XVI — Branch VII — G14.4/15.2/16.2/17.2/18.4).

G7.2. R. Alter Jacob Isaac Wagschal, married Dinah, daughter of R. Isaac son of R. Abraham Joshua Heschel (of Yasla) son of R. Elimelech Rubin (of Sokolov — Chapter XVI — Branch VII).

G8.1. R. Samuel Haim Reuben Wagschal, married and has issue (Monsey, N.Y.).

G8.2. Ezekiel Wagschal, married Channah Malka, daughter of R. Jehiel Greensweig, his first cousin, and have issue (Brooklyn, N.Y.).

G9.1. Rachel Miriam, married Lieb Klein and have issue.

G9.2. R. Jehiel Wagschal, married Miriam, daughter of R. Samuel Zvi Horowitz (Admur Spinka), and have issue. (See Chapter XVI — Branch VII — G14.2/15.1 16.1/17.8/18.2.)

G9.3. Asher Zelig Wagschal.

G9.4. Jochebed Mindel.

G9.5. Rivke Nechama.

G9.6. Naftali Haim Wagschal.

G8.3. R. Menachem Mendel Wagschal, Admur Sieniawa-BoroPark, married Shifra, daughter of R. Issachar Dov Rotenberg, and have issue.

G8.4. R. Joshua Wagschal (Williamsburg), married Chaya, daughter of R. Jacob (of Chakov) son of R. Sinai (of Zmigrad) Halberstam (Chapter XIV — Branch E). They have nine children.

G9.1. Eidel, married R. Moshe son of R. Naftali Zvi Labin. (Descendants of the Eichenstein Dynasty.)

G9.2. Mindy, married R. Haim Isaac son of R. Menachem Mendel Kahana (Admur Spinka-Bnei Brak).

G8.5. Malka Mindel, (died in 1975), married R. Aryey Lieb Lazer (Brooklyn, N.Y.).

G5.3. R. Shalom Wagschal, 1870-1938, married Leah, daughter of R. Naftali Weinberger.

G6. R. Asher Wagschal, born about 1907/8, settled in New York. He survived the Holocaust, but some of his children perished.

G7. Aryey Samuel Wagschal, born in 1947, lives in Monsey, New York.

G2.5. R. Eleazar, died in 1806, published his father's book and that of R. Zechariah Mendel of Jaroslav.

G3.1. R. Naftali, died in 1838.

G4.1. R. Isaac, married the daughter of R. Hirsch Eichenstein of Zhidachov.

G4.2. R. Jacob Lieb Weissblum.

G5. R. Elimelech Weissblum[5] of Ridnik and Sokolov, died in 1841.

G6. R. Eleazar Weissblum of Rzeszow, (1839-1910), author of *Mishneh LeMelech* (1902), married the daughter of R. David Halberstam of Keshanov (Chapter XIV — Branch C).

G4.3. Wife of R. Zvi Joseph of Ridnik.

G3.2. Wife of R. Moses Eliakim, son of R. Israel (the Maggid) of Ko-
zeniz.

G3.3. Wife of R. Samuel Zanwill Bindiger of Bardiyov.

G3.4. Feige, married R. Haim Meir (1789-1849), son of R. Aviezer Zelig
Shapiro (son-in-law of the Maggid of Kozenitz). His mother,
Pearl, was the sister of R. Moses Eliakim mentioned above (G2.5/
3.2). R. Aviezer Zelig died in 1814. R. Haim Meir was the founder
of the Chassidic Dynasty of Mogielnica.

G4.1. R. Jacob Isaac Shapiro of Blenov, died in 1882, author of *Emet
LeYaakov*.

G4.2. R. Abraham Joshua Heschel Shapiro of Mogielnica.

G4.3. R. Moses Joseph Shapiro of Grovitz, died in 1888.

G4.4. R. Aviezer Zelig Shapiro, Admur of Mogielnica, died in 1885,
married Feige, daughter of R. Abraham Jacob Friedman of Sadagora. (See Friedman Chassidic Dynasty — page 518.)

G5.1. R. Haim Meir Jehiel Shapiro, 1862-1924, Admur of Drogobitch, married Sheba, daughter of R. Isaac Friedman, founder
of the Buhusi Dynasty (See page 517). They settled in Jerusalem in 1922 together with some thirty families.

G6.1. R. Abraham Jacob Shapiro of Drogobitch, died in 1962,
married Esther, daughter of R. Nathan David Rabinowitz
of Parziveh. (See Chapter IV — G7.1/8.1/9.2/10.4/11/12.1
13.4/14.1.)

G7. Shalom Joseph Shapiro, known as Shin Shalom, born in
1904, author and poet. His *Yoman HaGalil* was published
in 1932.

G6.2. R. Aviezer Zelig Shapiro of Drogobitch, died in 1967, married his first cousin, daughter of R. Moses Lieb Friedman
of Pascani. (See Friedman Dynasty — page 516.)

G6.3. Wife of her first cousin, R. Aviezer Zelig, son of R. Isaac
Mordecai Shapiro (below).

G5.2. R. Isaac Mordecai Shapiro, died in 1930, married Zipporah,
daughter of R. Israel Friedman of Sadagora (page 521).

G6.1. R. Aviezer Zelig Shapiro of Gvodiz, died in 1943.

G6.2. R. Abraham Jacob Shapiro of Gvodiz, married the daughter of R. Israel son of R. Asher Perlow of Stolin. (See Chapter VII — page 299.)

G6.3. R. David Moses Shapiro (Brooklyn, N.Y.), Admur Gvodiz-Sadagora, married 1) daughter of R. Solomon of Bolichov, and 2) daughter of R. Zvi Feiwish of Zlitchik.

G6.4. R. Shalom Joseph Shapiro, married the daughter of R. Jerachmeel Moses of Kozenitz.

G5.3. Gitel, married R. Israel Friedman of Husyatin (See Chapter XV — page 524.)

G4.5. Wife of R. Abraham Elchanan Unger of Kaloshin. (See Unger Dynasty — Chapter XVII.)

G4.6. R. Elimelech Shapiro, Admur Grodzisk, died in 1892, author of *Imrei Elimelech* and *Divrei Elimelech,* married firstly the daughter of R. Jerachmeel Moses Rabinowitz of Parsischa, son of R. Jacob Isaac (the Holy *Yud*). (See Chapter IV — G7.1/8.1 9.2/10.4/11/12.4.) His second wife was the daughter of R. Haim Samuel Horowitz of Chentshin (See Chapter IV — Branch H.)

G5.1. R. Haim Meir Jehiel Shapiro, 1856-1873, (from the first marriage) married the daughter of R. Isaac Friedman of Buhusi (G16.7 — page 517).

G6. R. Israel Shapiro, born in 1873, succeeded his father as Admur Grodzisk. Because he was orphaned as an infant, he was raised by his grandfather, and married his first cousin, the daughter of R. Asher Perlow of Stolin (Perlow Dynasty — Chapter VII). He perished in the Holocaust in Treblinka.

G7. R. Abraham Elimelech Shapiro, 1897-1967, Admur Grodzisk-Jerusalem, married Malka, daughter of R. Jerachmeel Moses of Kozenitz. He published *Emunat Yisrael*, the sayings of his father, published in Jerusalem, where he had settled in 1922.

G5.2. Sarah Deborah (from the second marriage) married 1) R. Jehiel Jacob of Kozenitz, and 2) R. Asher Perlow of Stolin. R. Jehiel Jacob (surnamed Hopstein) died in 1866 and had an only son.

G6. R. Jerachmeel Moses Hopstein (1860-1909), lost his father when he was six years old. He married the daughter of R. Mordecai Twersky of Loyev (see Chapter XV).

G7.1. R. Aaron Jehiel, 1889-1942, Admur Kozenitz from 1909, and later in Lodz and Warsaw. He had no sons.

G7.2. R. Asher Elimelech, died as a result of an operation in Paris in 1936. He was Admur Kozenitz. His wife and family perished.

G7.3. R. Israel Eliezer, died in 1966, married the daughter of R. Mordecai Joseph Twersky of Zlatopol. He reached the U.S.A. after the Holocaust in 1948, and in Israel he established his court in 1966, but died shortly thereafter.

G5.3. R. Isaiah Shapiro (from the second marriage), died in Tel Aviv in 1945, married 1) Chaya Sarah, the daughter of R. Nathan Nahum Rabinowitz of Radomsk (Radomsk Dynasty — Chapter IV), and 2) the daughter of R. Israel Friedman of Boyan-Leipzig (G17.1 — page 519).

G6.1. R. Elimelech Shapiro, Admur Grodzisk-Tel Aviv since 1967.

G6.2. Esther, married Joshua Huberland (New York), son of R. Elijah Haim, son-in-law of R. Jacob Joshua Frankel. (See Teomim Family Branch H — G12.3/13.2.)

G5.4. R. Kalonymus Shapiro (from the second marriage) of Piatzne, author of *Chovat HaTalmidim*, perished in 1943. His son, Elimelech, also perished.

SPIRA CHASSIDIC DYNASTY OF MUNKACS-DYNOW

G1. R. Pesach Spira.

G2. R. Zvi Elimelech Spira, 1783-1841, author of *Bnei Yisaschar*.

G3.1. R. David Spira 1804-74, of Dynow, author of *Tzemach David* (Przemysl, 1879).

G4.1. R. Isaiah Naftali Herz Spira, died in 1885, Admur of Dynow from 1874, succeeding his father, author of *Hanotein Imrei Shefer*.

G5.1. Wife of her second cousin, R. Joseph, son of R. Zvi Elimelech Spira of Dynow.

G5.2. Wife of her relative, R. Nehemiah, son of R. Moses Lieb Spira.

G4.2. R. Zvi Elimelech Spira of Yovarnik-Blozov, 1841-1924, married the daughter of R. Moses Horowitz of Rozvadov (Chapter XVI — Branch VII). He was the author of *Tzvi leTzadik* (Cracow, 1925).

G5.1. R. Joshua Spira of Rivochich, 1862-1932, author of *Keren Yeshua*, married firstly, the daughter of R. Jacob of Deliatyn, and secondly, Miriam, daughter of the fifth Rabbi of Ropshitz, R. Menachem Mendel Mariles.

G6.1. R. Meir Spira, married his first cousin, daughter of R. Joseph Spira. He became Admur of Blozov. His son Joseph and the family perished.

G6.2. R. Israel Spira, Admur Blozov-New York, formerly of Pruchnik. He alone survived the Holocaust losing his entire family. He married 1) Pearl, daughter of R. Shalom David Unger of Jabna and 2) Breindel, previously married with two children who adopted the surname Spira.

G6.3. R. Eliezer, married the daughter of R. Ephraim Horowitz of Rozvadov. The family perished.

G6.4. Wife of R. Judah, son of R. Isaac Horowitz of Stachin. (See Chapter XVI — Branch VII.)

G5.2. R. Joseph Spira.

G6. Wife of R. Meir Spira, her cousin (above).

G5.3. Wife of R. Berachiah, son of R. Moses Joseph Teitelbaum.

G4.3. R. Meir Judah Spira, Admur Bukovisk, died in 1908, married the daughter of R. Israel (son-in-law of R. Haim of Kossov). He was the author of *Or LeMeir* (Przemysl 1913, Tel Aviv 1955).

G5.1. R. David Spira, succeeded his father as Admur Bukovisk, 1878-1924. He married 1) the daughter of R. Joshua Horowitz of Dzikov, and 2) the daughter of R. Hananiah YomTov Lipa Teitelbaum of Sighet.

G6. R. Alter Reuben Spira, 1905-1942, married his cousin the daughter of R. Phineas Joseph Kaner A.B.D. Zagorze.

G5.2. Wife of R. Phineas Joseph Kaner, A.B.D. Zagorze.

G6. Wife of her cousin, R. Alter Reuben Spira.

G5.3. Wife of R. David son of R. Joseph Spira of Dynow. (See above G4.1. and below G3.2/4.2/5.2.)

G5.4. Wife of R. Eliezer, son of R. Abraham Haim Horowitz of Plontsch.

G5.5. Deborah Yita, married R. Menachem Mendel, the fifth Rabbi of Ropshitz.

G3.2. R. Eleazar Spira, Admur Lancut, died in 1865, author of *Yodei Binah*, married the daughter of R. Joshua Heschel of Dukla.

G4.1. R. Solomon Spira, 1831-1893, A.B.D. Munkacs, author of *Shem Shalom,* married the daughter of R. Samuel Shmelke of Sassov.

G5.1. R. Zvi Hirsch Spira A.B.D. Munkacs, succeeding his father in 1893. He was born in 1845 and married Esther, daughter of R. Hananiah Horowitz of Ulanov. (See Chapter XVI — Branch VII.) He was the author of *Darkei Teshuva, Tzvi Tiferet, Be'er Lachai Roi, Tiferet Banim* and *Darkei Emunah.* He died in 1913.

G6. R. Haim Eleazar Spira, 1871-1936, A.B.D. Munkacs, succeeded his father in 1913. He was the author of *Minchat Eleazar* (1902-30, Responsa), *Divrei Kodesh* (1933, Sermons), *Chamisha Ma' amarot* (1922) and *Sefer Mash'mia Yeshua* (1919 and 1956). He married 1) the daughter of R. Shraga Yair of Bilberzig, and 2) daughter of R. Jacob Moses Safrin of Komarno. (See Eichenstein-Safrin Dynasty.)

G7. Wife of R. Jerachmeel Rabinowitz of Parziveh-Munkacs-Holon (son of R. Nathan David Rabinowitz — See Chapter IV — Rabinowitz Chassidic Dynasty). He succeeded his father-in-law.

G5.2. R. Moses Lieb Spira of Byetch-Sassov-Stryzow, 1850-1916, married the daughter of R. Baruch Halberstam of Gorlice, (Halberstam Chassidic Dynasty).

G6.1. R. Nehemiah Spira, 1874 — W.W.II., Rabbi of Sassov, Vienna and Stryzow, married the daughter of R. Isaiah Naftali Herz Spira of Dynow (G3.1/4.1 above).

G6.2. Ita, married R. Alter Eliezer, son of R. Aaron Horowitz of Byetch. (See Chapter XVI — Branch VII.)

G6.3. Mindele, married R. Haim Israel, son of R. Mordecai Spira. (See G4.2/5.1).

G4.2. R. Zvi Elimelech Spira, Admur Birch born in 1841. He married Frieda, daughter of R. Judah son of R. Jacob Horowitz of Malitsch.

G5.1. R. Mordecai Spira, 1870 — W.W.II, married Bracha, daughter of R. Abraham Simha son of R. Israel Horowitz of Bernov. (See Chapter XVI — Branch VII.)

G6.1. R. Eleazar Spira, born in 1887, Admur Kyvyashd-New York, married 1) Leah Hager of Radovitz and 2) Bathsheba, daughter of R. Joseph of Tarnopol, son of R. Alexander Yom-Tov Lipa Eichenstein (of Zhidachov). From his first marriage there was a daughter, Esther.

G7.1. Rikel, married R. Isaac Eizik, son of R. Meir Eichenstein of Zhidachov-New York and have issue (Queens, N.Y.).

G7.2. Hinde, married R. Moses son of R. David Halberstam (of Keshanov-Vienna) and have issue (Brooklyn, N.Y.).

G7.3. Mindel, first wife of R. Isaac Eizik Eichenstein, perished.

G7.4. Zvi Elimelech Spira, perished.

G7.5. Frieda, perished unmarried.

G6.2. R. Haim Israel Spira, married his second cousin, Mindele, daughter of R. Moses Lieb Hirsch Spira of Munkacs. They perished with their two children, Solomon and Beila.

G6.3. R. Moses Spira, married Shifra, daughter of R. Haim Meir Jehiel son of R. Israel Horowitz of Malitsch. Their daughter, Malka, perished in 1942.

G6.4. R. Solomon Spira, married secondly Liebe Kleinman. They have no issue.

G6.5. Toybe Chavah, married R. Jacob Avigdor, Rabbi of Drogobitch (his second wife), later divorced. They had no issue.

G6.6. Frieda, married R. Jacob Isaac Brandwein.

G6.7. Judah Joshua, born in 1890, married Deborah Pearl, daughter of R. Benzion son of R. Tuvia son of R. Meir Horowitz. (See Chapter XVI — Branch VII.)

G7.1. Raatza Zelda, died in New York, married Jacob HaKohen Spira of Boston, Mass.

G8.1. Bracha Leora, married Richard Orbach. Their son, Glen Stewart.

G8.2. Judah Amir (Boston, Mass.).

G7.2. Zvi Elimelech (Herman) Spira, came to the U.S.A. in 1946. He married Deborah, daughter of R. Jacob Zvi son of R. Isaac Isaiah Halberstam of Chechoyv. (See Chapter XIV — Branch G.)

G8.1. Chaya Sarah, born in 1953, married Menashe Karmel and have issue.

G8.2. Haim Judah Joshua, born in 1956.

G6.8. Chaya Hinde, married R. Zvi Elimelech son of R. Joseph Judah Rokeah. (See Chapter XVII — Rokeah Chassidic Dynasty.)

G5.2. R. Joseph Spira, died in 1933, married his father's first cousin, daughter of R. Isaiah Naftali Herz Spira (G3.1/4.1 above). He succeeded his father-in-law as Admur Dynow on the latter's death in 1885.

G6.1. R. David Spira, died in 1932, married the daughter of R. Meir Judah Spira (G3.1/4.3 above). His sons Eliezer, Menachem and Israel perished in the Holocaust. A daughter, Hena, married Baruch son of R. Isaac Halberstam of Gorlice.

G6.2. Sarah, married R. Haim Dov (of Bardiyov), son of R. Samuel Halberstam.

G6.3. Beila, married R. David Moses (of Dynow), son of R. Elisha Halberstam of Gorlice.

G4.3. R. Simha Spira, married the daughter of R. Zeev Wolf (Velvel) of Oziran.

G5.1. R. Eleazar Spira, 1865-1938, Admur Lancut.

G5.2. R. Zvi Elimelech Spira, married Deborah Rachel, daughter of R. Isaac Kuten of Tysmenitsa.

G6. R. Isaac Spira-Kuten (Brooklyn, N.Y.), married Feige, daughter of R. Elisha Halberstam of Gorlice. They have issue.

G5.3. Channah Mindel, married R. Shalom, son of R. Meir son of R. Menachem Mendel Rubin (of Glogov).

G4.4. R. Menachem Phineas Spira.

G5. Rebecca Rachel, married R. Joseph Judah, son of R. Issachar Dov son of R. Moses Rokeah (of Korev). He became Admur Lancut after his wife's grandfather. They perished in the Holocaust.

TEITELBAUM CHASSIDIC DYNASTY

The Teitelbaum family are not direct descendants of the MaHaRaM of Padua, but trace their lineage from the *ReMa*, R. Moses Isserles, the sixteenth century codifier. They are interrelated however by numerous intermarriages with other dynasties, such as Horowitz, Halberstam, Teomim and Babad. Their origins are given to keep the genealogy complete arbitrarily taking the dynastic progenitor, R. Moses of Ihel (Ujhely) as the tenth generation from R. Isserles (died in 1572) who was a relative of R. Meir Katzenellenbogen of Padua (died in 1565).

G10. R. Moses, son of R. Zvi Schiff, 1759-1841, founder of the Teitelbaum Dynasty and the author of *Yismach Moshe, Heishiv Moshe* and *Tefillah leMoshe*. He was Rabbi of Ihel and Sieniawa.

G11.1. Eleazar Nissan Teitelbaum of Drogobitch, 1787-1855, Rabbi of Sighet (in Marmarosh, Galicia).

G12.1. R. Jekutiel Judah (Zalman Lieb) Teitelbaum, 1808-83, Admur Ihel-Sighet and Rabbi of Stropkov, Gorlice and Drogobitch. He wrote *Yitav Lev, Yitav Panim*, Responsa *Avnei Tzedek* and *Rav Tov*. He married Rachel, daughter of R. Moses David Ashkenazi (author of *Toldot Adam*), A.B.D. Safed.

G13.1. R. Hananiah YomTov Lipa Teitelbaum, 1836-1904, author of *Kedushat YomTov*, married his first cousin, daughter of R. Joel Ashkenazi (A.B.D. Zlatchov) author of the Responsa *MaHaRI Ashkenazi*. (See Chapter IV — Branch A.) He was Admur of Sighet (Rumania), and their descendants are descendants of the Katzenellenbogen family.

G14.1. R. Moses Joseph Teitelbaum, succeeded his father as Admur Sighet.

G15. R. Jekutiel Judah Teitelbaum, A.B.D. Sighet.

G14.2. R. Joel Teitelbaum, Admur Satmar-New York, born in 1888. He married 1) the daughter of R. Abraham Haim Horowitz of Plontsch (See Chapter XVI — Branch VII — G14.1/15.6/16.2), and 2) the daughter of R. Avigdor Shapiro. His first wife and family perished in the Holocaust.

G15.1. Wife of her first cousin, R. Jekutiel Zalman Lieb Teitelbaum (died in 1944), son of R. Haim Zvi.

G15.2. Wife of her first cousin, R. Leopold Mayer.

G14.3. Second wife of R. David son of R. Meir Judah Spira of Bukovisk.

G14.4. Hesia, married Henoch son of R. Joseph David Mayer (of Sassov-Alesk). (See Rokeah Dynasty G9.2/10.3/11.2/12/13.7/14.2/15.2.)

G14.5. Sarah, married R. Shalom, son of Naftali Zvi son of R. Joseph Halberstam of Sanz.

G14.6. Wife of R. Ezekiel Shraga, son of R. Simha Issachar Dov Halberstam of Sieniawa. (See Chapter XIV — Branch A.)

G14.7. R. Haim Zvi Teitelbaum, 1880-1926, of Sighet, author of *Atzei Chayim*, married the daughter of R. Shalom Eliezer Halberstam of Rotsfurt. (See Chapter XIV — Branch F.)

G15.1. Hannah, married R. Judah Issacsohn (Los Angeles, Calif.), and have issue.

G15.2. R. Moses Teitelbaum, born in 1917, the only surviving son after the Holocaust, leader of the Sighet Chassidim in New York. He married Leah, daughter of R. Aaron Teitelbaum (G12.2/13.1/14.4 below).

G16.1. R. Aaron, born in 1947, married in 1966 to Sosha, daughter of R. Moses Hager the Vizhnitz-Bnei Brak Chassidic leader. (See Hager Chassidic Dynasty.) Their children, Mendel, Chaya and Sarah.

G16.2. Lipa (Leopold), born in 1948.

G16.3. Zalman Lieb, born in 1951, married in 1971 to Sarah, daughter of R. Morris Spitz and have issue, Haim Zvi.

G16.4. Shalom Eliezer, born in 1953, married.

G16.5. Chaya, married David Dov, son of R. Eleazar Meisels. (See below G13.3/14.1/15.4.)

G16.6. Wife of David, son of R. Zvi Hirsch Meisels. (See below G13.3/14.1/15.3.)

G15.3. R. Jekutiel (Zalman Lieb) Teitelbaum of Sighet, born in 1912 and perished in Auschwitz in 1944. He married 1) his first cousin, the daughter of R. Joel Teitelbaum of Satmar and 2) the daughter of R. Zusia Halberstam of Rotsfurt. He became Admur of Sighet when only fourteen years old.

G14.8. Wife of R. Haim Meir Jehiel, son of R. Israel son of R. Judah Horowitz of Malitsch.

G13.2. R. Abraham Aaron Teitelbaum, died in 1910, A.B.D. Kolbuszov, married the daughter of R. Jehiel, son of R. Asher Isaiah Rubin of Ropshitz. (See Chapter XVI — Branch VII — G14.4/15.5.)

G14.1. R. David Teitelbaum, A.B.D. Etshed.

G14.2. R. Jehiel Teitelbaum, Admur Kolbuszov, succeeding his father. He married the daughter of R. Aryey Lieb Rosenfeld of Moshizk.

G15.1. R. Aryey Lieb Teitelbaum, 1888-1941, Admur Kolbuszov, married the daughter of R. Haim Jonah Heilprin, A.B.D. Rzeszow. He lived in the U.S.A. from 1921 on.

G16.1. R. Alexander Samuel Teitelbaum, succeeded his father as leader of the Kolbuszov Chassidim in New York. He received his education at the Isaac Elchanan Seminary New York and married the daughter of R. David, son of R. Abraham Haim Horowitz of Pshezlov (Chapter XVI — Branch VII).

G16.2. Rose, married R. Eleazar, son of R. Issachar Dov son of R. Haim Jonah Halpern. (See Chapter XVI — Branch VII — G14.1/15.3/16.5/17.4/18.2.)

G16.3. Esther Beila, married R. Aaron son of R. Joshua Haim Teitelbaum.

G15.2. R. Moses Teitelbaum, perished.

G15.3. R. Haim Teitelbaum, perished.

G14.3. Wife of R. Moses David, son of R. Asher Anschel Ashkenazi. (See Chapter IV — Branch A.)

G13.3. R. Moses Joseph Teitelbaum, A.B.D. Zavrov, Stropkov and Ihel, married Hinde, daughter of R. David Halberstam of Keshanov. (See Chapter XIV — Branch C.)

G14.1. Reize Blume, married R. David Meisels, Rabbi in Ihel, born in 1865, author of *Binyan David* published in Warsaw in 1913.

G15.1. R. Haim Meisels, married Jached, daughter of R. Phineas Meilich Weissman. He was Rabbi in Szarvash (Hungary).

G16.1. Achsah (Violet), married R. Baruch David, son of R. Haim Joshua Halberstam of Bobov. (See Chapter XIV — Branch B.)

G16.2. Shabtai Meisels, married Mirl, daughter of R. Jacob Israel Jeshurun Rubin. (See Chapter XVI — Branch VII.)

G16.3. Chaya Yente, married Issachar Berish, son of R. Meir Joseph son of R. Baruch Rubin of Rizdoviz. (See Chapter XVI — Branch VII.)

G16.4. Joshua Zeev Meisels, married Chaya Mindel Levine.

G16.5. Zvi Hirsch Meisels, married Miriam, daughter of R. Simeon Israel Posen.

G15.2. R. Joseph Moses Meisels, eldest child, Rabbi in Oyvahr (Hungary), married the daughter of R. Ezekiel Paneth (author of *Kenesset Yechezkiel*). A number of children perished.

G16. Hinde, married R. Ezekiel Ruttner of Shamkut-New York.

G15.3. R. Zvi Hirsch Meisels, died in 1974, married 1) his first cousin, daughter of R. Haim Jacob, son of R. Moses Joseph Teitelbaum, and 2) the daughter of R. Joseph Paneth.

From his first wife:

G16.1. Hinde, married R. Abraham Leitner (Montevideo Rov), head of the Yeshiva *Binyan David* in New York. They have twelve children.
G16.2. R. Joseph Moses Meisels, married and has eight children.
G16.3. R. Jekutiel Judah (Zalman Lieb) Meisels, married and has eleven children.

From his second wife:

G16.4. Rebecca, married R. Aaron son of R. Leopold Teitelbaum of Nierbatur, and have issue. (See Chapter XVII.)
G16.5. Rosa Sarah, married R. Samuel David son of R. Elchanan Halpern. (See Halpern Family — Chapter XVI — Branch VII.)
G16.6. Chaya, married R. Israel Menachem Grunwald and have three daughters.
G16.7. David Meisels, married the daughter of R. Moses Teitelbaum of Sighet-New York.

G15.4. R. Eleazar Meisels of Ihel-Chicago, married the daughter of R. Joseph Paneth. They have issue including a son, David Dov, married to Chaya, daughter of R. Moses Teitelbaum of Sighet-New York, and a daughter, married to R. Israel, son of R. Mordecai Hager. (See Chapter XV.)

G14.2. Chatche, married R. Eliezer, son of R. Samuel Haim Horowitz of Chentchin.
G14.3. Bracha, married R. Naftali, son of R. Israel Jacob Teitelbaum of Walowa.
G14.4. Leah Zissel, married R. Liebish son of R. Ehrlich of Deliatyn.
G14.5. R. Berachiah Teitelbaum, died in 1917, married Altsche, daughter of R. Zvi Elimelech Spira of Blozov.
G14.6. R. Haim Jacob Teitelbaum of Limanov, died in 1935, married the daughter of R. Solomon son of R. Meir Nathan Halberstam (Branch B).

G15.1. R. Ezekiel, surnamed Halberstam, Admur Limanov-Jerusalem. His wife and family perished.

G15.2. Shalom, surnamed Halberstam, married and has issue, (Queens, N.Y.).

G14.7. R. Aryey Lieb Teitelbaum.

G14.8. R. Jerachmeel Teitelbaum, married the granddaughter of R. Joshua Rokeah, the second Belzer Rebbe.

G14.9. R. Nissan Teitelbaum, married his first cousin, daughter of R. Hananiah YomTov Lipa Teitelbaum.

G13.4. R. Elijah Bezalel Teitelbaum, died in 1918, A.B.D. Tyachevo.

G14.1. R. Moses Teitelbaum, Admur Tyachevo (Taish).

G15. R. Zalman Lieb Teitelbaum.

G16. Eli Teitelbaum, married Rivke, daughter of R. Haim Solomon son of R. Alter Eliezer Horowitz. (See Chapter XVI — Branch VII.)

G14.2. R. Haim Teitelbaum.

G15. R. Mendel Teitelbaum, one of ten Jews who escaped in 1944 from Tyachevo, and survived out of some five hundred Jewish families who perished there.

G13.5. Wife of her first cousin, R. Israel Jacob Teitelbaum of Walowa. (See below G12.2/13.1.)

G13.6. Wife of R. Moses Horowitz of Rozvadov. (See Chapter XVI — Branch VII — G13/14.1/15.6.)

G13.7. Wife of R. Baruch Halberstam of Gorlice. (See Chapter XIV — Branch E.)

G12.2. R. Samuel Teitelbaum of Gorlice, died in Cracow in 1888.

G13.1. R. Israel Jacob Teitelbaum, 1838-1924, A.B.D. Walowa, married 1) his first cousin, daughter of R. Jekutiel Judah Teitelbaum of Sighet, and 2) the daughter of R. Aaron Halberstam of Sanz (see Chapter XIV — Branch D). He wrote *Heitiv Eitiv* (1971).

G14.1. R. Moses David Teitelbaum, died in 1935, studied as did his father under R. Haim Halberstam of Sanz, and became A.B.D. Lapish. He married the daughter of R. Avigdor Halberstam of Dukla and published the *Yismach Moshe* as a new edition.

G15.1. R. Abraham Haim Teitelbaum, married the daughter of R. Aryeh Liebish Halberstam (Chapter XIV — Branch D), who was a brother of the second wife of his grandfather, R. Israel Jacob Teitelbaum.

G15.2. R. Jekutiel Judah (Zalman Lieb) Teitelbaum, Admur of Ihel-Sanz-New York, married Yita, daughter of R. Naftali Halberstam of Keshanov.

G16. Aaron Teitelbaum.

G17.1. Hilda, married Mordecai Friedman.
G17.2. Israel Jacob Teitelbaum (Queens, N.Y.).

G15.3. R. Isaac Samuel.

G14.2. R. Naftali Teitelbaum (died in 1975) of Nierbatur, married 1) the daughter of R. Moses Joseph Teitelbaum of Ihel (their fathers were first cousins).

G15.1. R. Tuvia Teitelbaum, married Raatza, daughter of R. Naftali Haim Halberstam (Chapter XIV — Branch E). Their children, Haim Elisha, Menashe, Pesel and Channah.

G14.3. Roza Blume, married R. Raphael Gross.

G15.1. R. Jekutiel Judah (Zalman Lieb) Gross, married and perished.
G15.2. R. Samuel Gross, perished.

G16.1. R. Moses Gross (Brooklyn, N.Y.), married and has issue.
G16.2. R. Bezalel Gross (Israel), married and has issue.

G15.3. R. Moses Gross, married and perished.
G15.4. R. Michael Gross, married and perished. His son, Jacob Jokel Gross (New York).
G15.5. R. Hananiah YomTov Lipa Gross, married and perished. His son, Elia Gross (New York).
G15.6. R. Aaron Gross, married and perished.
G15.7. R. Naftali Gross, born in 1901, married Malka, daughter of R. Abraham Steinitz, the Kristirer Rov. His sons are in the printing business.

G16.1. R. Isaiah Gross (Brooklyn, N.Y.), married and has issue.
G16.2. R. Raphael Gross, married and has issue (Monsey, N.Y.).
G16.3. R. Israel Jacob Jokel Gross, married and has issue. (Monsey, N.Y.).

G16.4. Sarah, married Eleazar Feferkorn (Monsey, N.Y.), and have issue.

G16.5. R. Michael Gross, married and has issue (Monsey, N.Y.).

G16.6. R. Moses Gross, married Blume, daughter of R. Haim Solomon Horowitz of Stryzow-New York. (See Chapter XVI — Branch VII.) They have issue.

G16.7. R. Samuel Gross, married and has issue (Monsey, N.Y.).

G16.8. Reize Hindel, married Moses Wozner (Monsey, N.Y.) and have issue.

G15.8. Malka, married R. Haim Solomon Horowitz of Stryzow-New York. (See Chapter XVI — Branch VII).

G15.9. Rikel, married R. Haim Eleazar, son of R. Samuel Teitelbaum of Gorlice.

G14.4. R. Aaron Teitelbaum, Admur Walowa-Nierbatur, married the daughter of R. Samuel Babad of Sander-Vishne. Thus his descendants were descended from the Katzenellenbogen Family. (See Chapter XI — Branch D.)

G15.1. Rachel, married R. Alexander Asher Babad. (Chapter XI — Branch D.)

G15.2. R. Hananiah YomTov Lipa (Leopold) Teitelbaum, originally A.B.D. of Nierbatur, settled in New York as the leader of the Walowa Chassidim. He married 1) the daughter of R. Israel Zvi of Kosoni, and 2) Feige, daughter of R. Nahum Ephraim son of R. Aryey Lieb Halberstam.

G16.1. R. Nahum Ephraim, married the daughter of R. Samuel Shmelke Rubin.

G16.2. R. Aaron Teitelbaum, married the daughter of R. Hirsch Meisels.

G15.3. Leah, married R. Moses Teitelbaum of Sighet-New York. (See above G12.1/13.1/14.7/15.2.)

G14.5. R. Solomon Teitelbaum, married the daughter of R. Moses Lieb Spira of Stryzow. He was Admur of Gorlice.

G15. R. Haim Eleazar Teitelbaum, married Rikel, daughter of R. Raphael Gross.

G16. Raphael Teitelbaum (Queens, N.Y.) married and has issue.

G13.2. R. Joseph Teitelbaum.

G13.3. R. Naftali Teitelbaum, married Bracha, daughter of R. Moses Joseph Teitelbaum of Zavrov-Stropkov-Ihel.

G13.4. R. Aryey Liebish Teitelbaum, married successively two daughters of R. Chunah Preiss of Ihel. He had three daughters from the first marriage.

G14.1., 2. and 3. Daughters.

G14.4. R. David Teitelbaum.

G14.5. R. Mordecai Teitelbaum.

G14.6. R. Meir Teitelbaum.

G14.7. Raatza, married R. Joseph Freund (Israel) and have eight children.

G14.8. Aaron Teitelbaum, married the daughter of R. Jeremiah Korn (who was a Dayan). He was born in 1903.

G15.1. Liebish Teitelbaum, married Golda Oestreicher and have nine children.

G15.2. Golda, married Israel Haim Menashe Friedman, Dayan of the Satmar Congregation in Brooklyn, N.Y. They have six sons.

G15.3. Raatza, married Isaac Moskovitz and have four children.

G15.4. Sheindel, twin of Raatza, married R. Joseph Hirsch Iliovitz and have four children.

G15.5. Jeremiah Teitelbaum, married Zirl Low and have five daughters.

G15.6. Sarah, married Jacob Joseph son of R. Haim Joshua Halberstam of Bobov. (See Chapter XIV — Branch B.)

G15.7. Samuel Teitelbaum, married Zirl Siegelbaum, and have six children.

G15.8. Lipa Teitelbaum, married Breindel, daughter of R. Moses son of R. David Halberstam of Keshanov. (See Chapter XIV — Branch C — G15.2/16.1/17.5/18.2.)

G14.9. Miriam, married Eli Goldberg (New York) and have five children.

G13.5. R. Aaron Teitelbaum.

G14. R. Menachem Teitelbaum, Admur Gorlice, married Jochebed, daughter of R. Abraham Horowitz of Shendeshov. (See Chapter XVI — Branch VII.)

G15. R. Joshua Haim Teitelbaum, 1883-1962, Admur Chenskovitz.

He married Rachel, daughter of R. Aaron, son of R. Nahum Zvi son of R. Eleazar Nissan Teitelbaum. (See below.)

G16.1. R. Aaron Teitelbaum, Admur Chenskovitz-New York, born in 1913, married Esther Beila, daughter of R. Aryey Lieb son of R. Jehiel Teitelbaum of Kolbuszov.

G17. Yente, married Jehiel, son of R. Ezekiel David son of R. Benzion Halberstam of Bobov. (See Chapter XIV — Branch B.)

G16.2. R. Samuel Teitelbaum, born in 1920, married the daughter of R. Naftali Haim, son of R. Elisha Halberstam of Gorlice. They have three married daughters and a son, Menachem Mendel Naftali. R. Samuel, is the principal of the Bobover Yeshiva.

G12.3. R. Nahum Zvi Teitelbaum, Admur Drogobitch, married the daughter of R. Mordecai David Unger of Dombrovo.

G13.1. R. Mordecai David Teitelbaum married the daughter of R. Haim Jacob Horowitz of Ulanov. (See Chapter XVI — Branch VII — G14.2/15.2.) He became R. of Stachin.

G13.2. R. Aaron Teitelbaum, Admur Drogobitch-Moshzisk, died in 1911. He had no sons.

G14.1. Chaya, married R. Haim Waks.
G14.2. Blume, married R. Simeon Lamm.
G14.3. Rachel, youngest, married R. Joshua Haim, son of R. Menachem Teitelbaum. (See above G12.2/13.5/14.)

G13.3. R. Menashe Teitelbaum, Rabbi in Brigel. (See below G11.2/12.1/13.2/14.1.)

G14.1. R. Naftali, married his cousin, Pesel, daughter of R. Aryey Lieb Teitelbaum of Ridnik.
G14.2. R. Haim. G14.3. Wife of R. Haim Dachner.

G13.4. R. Isaac Teitelbaum 1869-1944, A.B.D. Huskov.

G14. R. Ephraim Dov Teitelbaum, A.B.D. Huskov.

G15. R. Mordecai David Teitelbaum of Huskov, survived the Holocaust and settled in Beersheva in 1957 as Admur. He married the daughter of R. Joseph Meir Kahana of Spinka.

G13.5. Wife of R. Mordecai David, son of R. Haim Jacob Horowitz of Ulanov. (See G12.3/13.1 above.)

G12.4. Wife of R. Israel Rappoport, A.B.D. Tarnow, author of the Responsa *MaHaRI HaKohen*.

G11.2. Frieda, married R. Aryey Lieb, son of R. Haim Asher Lipschutz. He was born in 1767 and became one of the leading Chassidic scholars of his generation. He was the author of *Aryey Dobi Ilai*, Responsa *Ari Shebechaburah* and *Ateret Zekeinim*. He died in 1846. He was Rabbi of Kreshov, Sieniawa, Vizhniz and Brigel.

G12.1. R. Meshullam Zalman Jonathan Lipschutz, Rabbi of Brigel, married the daughter of R. Abraham Haim Horowitz of Linsk.

G13.1. R. Jeruchem Lipschutz of Tarnow, settled in Jerusalem about 1870 where he later died. He married Rachel, daughter of R. Moses David Gertner of Tarnov. He adopted the name of Teitelbaum. His daughters, Beila, married R. Bezalel Isaiah Berenstein of Jerusalem and Channah, married R. Raphael Gutwied.

G14. R. Aryey Lieb Teitelbaum, Rabbi of Kreshov-Ridnik, died in Berlin in 1921. He married Jochebed Rebecca, eldest daughter of R. Baruch Halberstam of Gorlice. (See Chapter XIV — Branch E — G14.5/15.6.)

G13.2. R. Tuvia Lipschutz, Admur of Brigel, died in 1912.
He married Mindel, daughter of R. Israel Isaac of Radoshitz.

G14.1. Channah, married R. Menashe, son of R. Nahum Zvi Teitelbaum, and had issue. (See G11.1/12.3/13.3 above.)

G14.2. Esther, married R. Mendel, son of R. Phineas Joseph Shapiro, A.B.D. Berhomet. Their son, R. Phineas Joseph Shapiro (his children adopted the surname Dachner), succeeded his father as A.B.D. (See Chapter XIV — Branch E — G15.6/16.3.)

G14.3. Zirl, married R. Noah son of R. Joseph Schiff of Tarna.

G13.3. R. Meir Lipschutz of Cracow.
His children, Moses, Eliezer and Channah, married Joseph Gertner.

G13.4. Rebecca, married R. Moses Spitz; their son, Jacob.

G13.5. Chaya Sarah, married her first cousin, R. Israel Meir Lipschutz of Janow.

G13.6. Mirl, married R. Abraham Zhinorer.

G12.2. R. Haim Dov Lipschutz of Janow, married the daughter of R. Joseph A.B.D. of Janow.

G13.1. R. Israel Meir Lipschutz of Janow.

      He married his first cousin, Chaya Sarah, daughter of R. Meshullam Zalman Lipschutz. Their daughter Pesel, married R. Samuel son of R. Moses Halberstam of Bardiyov. (See Chapter XIV — Branch E.)

G13.2. R. Joseph Zechariah Menachem Lipschutz of Slifya, where he became Admur on the death of his father-in-law, R. Jacob of Apt.

    G14.1. R. Aryey Lieb Lipschutz, Admur in Apt, died in Jerusalem in 1929. He married the daughter of R. Haim Meir of Pinczow, and was the author of *Yismach Tzadik* and *Yesod Likrah*. His three sons, R. Jacob, R. Moses and,

        G15. R. Issachar Ber Lipschutz, born in 1888, Admur Ungvar, and perished in the Holocaust. He married the daughter of R. Abraham Shalom Halberstam of Stropkov. (See Chapter XIV — Branch A.)

           G16.1. R. Baruch Abraham Lipschutz, married the daughter of R. Eliezer Lipa of Rotsfurt where he became Admur. They perished in the Holocaust.

           G16.2. R. Ezekiel Shraga Lipschutz-Halberstam, born in 1908, settled in Israel in 1948. He was Rabbi of Ramle until 1954, when he succeeded his mother's brother, R. Mendel Halberstam, as Admur Stropkov-Jerusalem.

           G16.3. R. Joseph Zechariah Lipschutz of Stropkov.

G13.3. R. Moses Lipschutz of Janow.

    G14.2. R. Jacob Lipschutz, Admur Rava-Ruska, perished.

    G14.3. R. Moses Solomon Lipschutz, Admur Tarnow.

G12.3. R. Aaron Zelig Lipschutz, Rabbi of Vishnitza, died in 1878, married Hinde, daughter of the Rabbi of Tarnograd.

    G13.1. R. Joseph Samuel Lipschutz. His sons, Moses, Aaron Zvi of Cracow, and Haim Liebus of Tarnow.

    G13.2. R. Nathan Nata Dov Lipschutz, died in 1916, married 1) Sarah, daughter of R. Solomon Zalman Viyellepola and 2) Alta Chaya, daughter of R. Isaac Hirsch Schiff.

      G14.1. R. Isaac Lipschutz. G14.2. R. Aaron Lipschutz.
      G14.3. R. Jacob Lipschutz. G14.4. Nechama.

G14.5. Feigel, married R. David Aryey Brisel. Their descendants live in Israel and New York.

G15.1. R. Moshe Lipschitz, born in Galicia in 1888 and went to study in Jerusalem at the age of twelve. After returning to Europe for a time, he settled in the U.S.A. first in St. Louis, where he was rabbi, and then in Philadelphia, where his father's followers, the Viyellepola Chassidim, established the *Machzikei HaDas* Congregation about 1930. He became known as the Grand Rabbi of Viyellepola-Philadelphia, and served the community until 1954, when he settled again in Jerusalem. He was greatly respected and honored by world leaders for his services to his people in religious and philanthropic activities, which he continued until his last days, passing away on July 8, 1975. He married Chaye Lichtman.

G16.1. Asher Zelig, born in 1910, of Philadelphia.

G16.2. R. Dr. Chaim Uri Lipschitz, born in 1912, of New York, ordained in 1938 in Jerusalem. In 1950 he became Rabbi of Congregation *Ohev Sholom,* Brooklyn, and Executive Director, Community Service Bureau of Yeshiva *Torah Vodaath and Mesivta,* Brooklyn, New York. In 1959 he received the honorary degree of "Doctor of Divinity" from St. Andrews College, London, and also from Philaethea College, Windsor, Canada, in 1965. In 1960 he became the Managing Editor of *The Jewish Press.* He was invited three times to open a session of the U.S. Senate with a prayer, and delivered an opening prayer in the U.S. House of Representatives in 1971. He has had many other affiliations and honorary appointments. He conducted programs in the field of radio and television, contributed many articles to various publications and encyclopedias, and authored a number of books, including *The Shield of Israel* (1940) and *Franco and the Jews* (unpublished).

He married Rivke Rachel Bernstein, and has issue: Beatrice, married Beer; Bina Esther, married Seitler; Sarah, married Stefansky and Ziona, married Katzman.

G16.3. Alta Frieda, born in 1920, married Shlomo Rosenberg of Philadelphia.

G16.4. Zvi Jacob, born in 1922, of Bnei Brak.

G16.5. Nathan Judah, born in 1924, of Jerusalem.
G16.6. Sarah, born in 1929, married Abraham Mordecai Kaufman.

G15.2. R. Haim, perished with his family in the Holocaust. Three children survived.

G16.1. Liebe, married Simha Orgel (Brooklyn).
G16.2. Sarah, married Mordecai Yaakov (Brooklyn).
G16.3. Jacob Isaac, married Sarah Yungreis (Brooklyn).

G15.3. Sarah, married Jacob Freund. She died in 1964 and he in 1974.

G16.1. Rivke, married R. David Horowitz (Jerusalem).
G16.2. Chaya Yita, married Fischel Gruber (Jerusalem).
G16.3. Nathan Nata, married Rachel Schlesinger (Jerusalem).
G16.4. Hadassah, married Mordecai Zvi Scheinberger.
G16.5. Alexander Sender, married Malka Schlesinger.
G16.6. Leah, married Simeon Eli Kreshevsky.
G16.7. Chaim Uri, married Hadassah Roth.

G15.4. Bracha, married Joshua Zeinwirth (Jerusalem).

G16.1. Chava, married Samuel Haim Shor.
G16.2. Nathan Nata, married Sarah Feigel Zaltzman.
G16.3. Joseph, married Liebe Schlesinger.
G16.4. Zvi Jacob, married Liebe Manderer.
G16.5. Mordecai, married Esther Schlesinger.
G16.6. Leah, married David Biderman.

G15.5. Channah, married Meir Lichtenstein.

G16.1. Chaya, married Moshe Krauss.
G16.2. Esther, married Samuel Zvi Weiner.
G16.3. Moshe Nahum, died in 1973, married.
G16.4. Rivke, married Judah Eizenstein.
G16.5. Beila, married Isaac Shavdran.

G15.6. R. Aaron, married Chaya Minzberg. Their children, Golda, Zvi Jacob, Beila, Rivke (married Eliezer Rotenberg), Abraham, Mattithiah and Nathan Nata.
G15.7. R. Zalman, married Eidel Roth.

G16.1. Chaya Sarah, married R. Zvi Niehaus.
G16.2. Rivke, married Samuel Zvi Weiss.

G16.3. Hinde, married R. Jacob Hanig.
G16.4. Binah, married, Israel Meir Halpern.
G16.5. Hadassah, married Berish Weinberger.
G16.6. Nathan Nata, married Nechama Hershkovitz.

G15.8. R. Eliezer, married Rebecca Weingarten.

G16.1. Aaron Joseph, married Rachel Rattman.
G16.2. Zvi Jacob.   G16.3. Chaim Uri.   G16.4. Moshe.
G16.5. Alta, married Menachem Manderer.
G16.6. Wife of Nathan Gruber.
G16.7. Leah, married Zvi Segal.   G16.8. Nahum Akiva.

G15.9. R. Phineas Lipschitz, youngest, married his niece, Channah
        Yita, daughter of his brother R. Haim.

G16.1. Alta Chaya, married Channaniah Rabinowitz.
G16.2. Zvi Jacob Lipschitz, married Rachel.
G16.3. Hinde, married Moses Klaphaltz.
G16.4. Nathan Nata, married Mirl Schlesinger.
G16.5. Michael, married.
G16.6. Hadassah, married Joseph Deutsch.
G16.7. Malka, married Schlesinger.   G16.8. Aaron.

G14.6. R. Alter Solomon Zalman, 1858-1892.

G13.3. R. Zvi Jonah Lipschutz of Vishnitza. His children, Moses Jo-
        seph, Isaac Reuben, Aaron and Channah (married Moses
        Landau).
G13.4. Chaya Leah, married 1) R. Feiwish Halpern of Berjan, and
        had issue, and 2) R. Simha son of R. Moses Bochner of Krosh-
        nov. Their daughter, Lifshe Bochner, married R. Aaron Nathan
        Wolf of Tarna.
G13.5. Rachel, married R. Ephraim of Radoshitz.
G13.6. Sarah Toyba, married R. Moses Krakover.
G13.7. Rochma, married R. David Weber, and had issue.
G13.8. Keila, married R. Judah of Dembitz.

G12.4. First wife of R. Ezekiel Shraga Halberstam, Admur Sieniawa.
        Their children were Naftali and Dreizel .(See Chapter XIV —
        Branch A.)
G12.5. Wife of R. Mordecai Zilberstein, A.B.D. Holeshitz.
G12.6. Wife of R. Zvi Hirsch Glanz.

G13.1. R. Mordecai Isaac Katz, A.B.D. Komarno.
G13.2. R. Mendel Katz.   G13.3. R. Joseph Haim Katz.

UNGER CHASSIDIC DYNASTY

G1. R. Mordecai David Unger, died in 1843, Admur of Dombrovo and founder of the dynasty.

G2.1. R. Jehiel Zvi Unger, Admur of Tarnow, married the daughter of R. Samson of Vohlin.

G3.1. Wife of R. Haim Halberstam, founder of the Sanz Dynasty.

G3.2. R. Mordecai David Unger, married the daughter of R. Benjamin Zeev A.B.D. of Zmigrad. He succeeded his father-in-law as Admur Zmigrad.

G4. Wife of R. Asher Isaiah, son of R. Isaac Tuvia Rubin. (See Chapter XVI — Branch VII.)

G2.2. R. Joseph Unger, Admur of Dombrovo, died in 1876. He succeeded his father, and married the daughter of R. Moses Eliakim of Kozenitz.

G3. R. Israel Elimelech Unger, Admur of Jabna, and later succeeded his father at Dombrovo.

G4.1. R. Jacob Isaac Unger, Admur Dombrovo, married the daughter of R. Meir Horowitz, Admur Dzikov. (See Chapter XVI — Branch VII.)

G5.1. R. Shalom David Unger, 1860-1923, Admur Jabna, died in Vienna. He married the daughter of R. Moses Horowitz of Rozvadov. (Chapter XVI — Branch VII.) He was the author of *Yad Shalom.*

G6.1. R. Israel Unger, Admur Jabna-New York. He died in New York in 1936. He was marrried to the daughter of R. Aryey Lieb Halberstam of Sanz. His wife and children perished in the Holocaust. Two daughters survived (unmarried).

G6.2. R. Eliezer Unger, 1890-1943, married 1) the daughter of R. Naftali Rokeah of Noveria. He was Admur Jabna-Tarnow, and 2) Udel, his first cousin, daughter of R. Aaron Twersky. Their children, Malka, Leah, Gitel and David Mordecai.

G6.3. Menashe Unger, journalist and writer of chassidism, married and had issue, Judy (married Carl Kaiserman, Manhattan).

G6.4. Pearl, married R. Israel, son of R. Joshua Spira, Admur
       Blozov as his first wife. She perished.

G6.5. Menucha, unmarried.

G5.2. R. Israel Joseph Unger, 1868-1942, married the daughter
       of R. Reuben Horowitz of Dembitz. He studied under his
       uncle, R. Joshua Horowitz of Dzikov, and was Admur Tar-
       now from 1913. He perished with his sons, Meir Elijah and
       Reuben.

G5.3. R. Judah Unger of Rzeszow, perished in the Holocaust.

G5.4. R. Haim Eliezer Unger of Radlov, perished with his sons
       Meir and Joseph. He married the daughter of R. Meir
       Nathan Halberstam, and also the daughter of R. Naftali
       Horowitz of Malitsch. (See Chapter XVI — Branch VII.)

G4.2. R. Moses Eliakim Unger, succeeded his father as Admur Dom-
       brovo. He married the daughter of R. Abraham Horowitz of
       Shendeshov. (See Chapter XVI — Branch VII.)

G5.1. R. Isaac Eleazar Unger, Admur Dombrovo.

G5.2. R. Meir Unger, Admur Cracow.

G5.3. Wife of R. Haim Jacob, son of R. Hanina Horowitz of
       Ulanov.

G5.4. Wife of R. Naftali Haim Horowitz. (See Chapter XVI —
       Branch VII.)

G5.5. R. Naftali Hirsch Unger of Dombrovo, married Sarah,
       daughter of R. Moses Halberstam of Bardiyov (Branch E.)

G6.1. R. Haim Joseph Unger, died in 1974, married Hannah
       Miller.

G6.2. R. Isaac Unger, married Rivke Gitel, daughter of R. Is-
       rael Parnas. They perished.

G6.3. Chaya Rivke, married R. Joseph Samuel Shmelke of
       Riglitz.

G6.4. R. Israel Aaron, surnamed Halberstam, known as the
       Kashauer Dayan in Montreal, married the daughter of
       R. Haim of Teitch.

G6.5. R. Baruch Abraham, surnamed Halberstam, married
       Malka Waldman.

G6.6. R. Jacob Elimelech, surnamed Halberstam.

G6.7. R. Solomon Zalman Lieb Unger, married Ethel Abromo-
       witz. (Brooklyn, N.Y.)

G4.3. R. Mordecai David Unger, married the daughter of R. Moses Unger of Sanz.

G5.1. R. Benzion Unger, Admur Sanz, married the daughter of R. Shalom Reinbach. The family perished.

G6. R. Jacob Isaac Unger, Admur in New York of the *Beit Yosef* Congregation in Brooklyn, N.Y.

G5.2. Wife of R. Nahum Zvi Teitelbaum of Drogobitch. (See Teitelbaum Family.)

G2.3. R. Menachem Mendel Unger, died in 1882, married the daughter of R. Meir Heschel (of Apt) A.B.D. Stovnitz.

G2.4. R. Abraham Elchanan Unger, died in 1883, married 1) the daughter of R. Joseph Horowitz of Turstein, son of the *Chozeh* (Seer) of Lublin, and 2) the daughter of R. Haim Meir Jehiel Shapiro of Mogielnica. (See Shapiro Chassidic Dynasty.) He was Admur of Kaloshin.

G3.1. R. Aviezer Zelig Unger, named after his maternal grandfather (the second marriage), and succeeded his father as Admur Kaloshin.

G4. Wife of R. Naftali Shapiro of Kaloshin. They perished.

G3.2. R. Joshua Heschel Unger of Grodzisk, died in 1892.
G3.3. R. Jacob Isaac Unger, Admur Kaloshin.

G4. Wife of R. Naftali Aryey Spiegel (1869-1949), son of R. Moses. He was the Rabbi of Chechoyv (near Lublin), and settled in the U.S.A. (See Chapter VIII — G7.1/8.1/9.1/10.7/11/12/13.3 /14.)

G2.5. R. Moses Unger, married Miriam, daughter of R. Haim Halberstam of Sanz. (See Chapter XIV — page 483 and note 1 to that chapter.)

GLOSSARY

A.B.D. — Av Beit Din (Head of the Rabbinical Court of the town).

Admur (plural-Admurim) — Term used for the leader of various Chassidic groups and dynastic masters. Meaning is "our master and teacher." Example: Admur Manisterich-New York, meaning "currently of New York, formerly of Manisterich (by birth or ancestry)." See also under Rebbe and Zadik.

Beit HaMidrash — House of Study.

Chacham — Sephardic title for Rabbi.

Chassidism — Religious faction established during the eighteenth century.

Chevra Kaddisha — Jewish religious burial society (of a particular town).

Darshan — Preacher or expounder of the Law.

Dayan — Religious Judge (of a particular town).

G — Generation. Thus G1 is the first generation, G2 the second, etc. Except for Chapter XVII all the generations are traced back to R. Meir Katzenellenbogen of Padua (G1). Example: G10.2/11.3/12.1 means the first child of the twelfth generation is from the third child of the eleventh generation, who is the second child of the tenth generation in that particular section or chapter.

If only one child is recorded in any particular generation, there may have been others, but these are unknown to the present author, thus the .1. is left in most of these cases.

The order of children does not imply order of birth, unless so stated. Mostly the order has been established to simplify the layout of subsequent generations.

Gabbai — Elected head of a synagogue or community.

Gaon — Rabbinical genius.

HaKadosh — The Holy (or Sainted); name give to martyrs.

Hesped — Eulogy or funeral oration. These were often printed in Rabbinical books.

Kehillah — The Jewish community of a town, or affiliated to a synagogue.

Klaus — Study-house or school, which also served as a synagogue.

683

Kollel   — A group of scholars in different towns in Israel who
                                were supported with funds from specific towns in
                                Europe and Russia, composed of either Chassidic or
                                Mitnagdic men devoted entirely religious study.

Malach   — Title given to Chassidic leaders, meaning "Angel."

Mitnagdim   — Opponents of the Chassidic movement.

Nasi   — Prince or President. The ancient meaning applied to
                                a Rabbi of higher standing than the A.B.D.

Ne'eman   — Trustee, second to the President, who also acted as
                                treasurer and chief secretary of the community.

Parnas   — President of a council or assembly. Also used for Ad-
                                ministrator or Head of a synagogue. See also Gabbai.

Pinkas   — The minute-book of the Jewish community of a town,
                                or of the various councils e.g. the Council of the Four
                                Lands.

R.   — See Rabbi.

Rabbi (also Rav/Rov)   — Master or teacher. A religious title also used for the
                                leader of the community. See A.B.D.

Rebbe   — Title for Chassidic leaders. Example: New York-
                                Bostoner Rebbe, meaning currently of New York,
                                formerly of Boston where he or his father was a
                                Rebbe. See also Admur.

Shechinah   — The Divine Presence.

Tallit   — Prayer Shawl.

Tefillin   — Phylacteries.

Yeshiva   — Academy for religious learning and teachings.

Zadik (Zaddik)   — Chassidic title meaning Saint. See Rebbe and Admur.

Pedigree Graphs and Charts   — = means married.
                                an arrow means — there were descendants.

Town names   — Tremendous difficulties arise in the names of the
                                smaller European towns as the Jewish version dif-
                                fered from the official name e.g. Satmar for Satu-
                                mare, Ostraha for Ostrow, Ospinzi for Oswiecim,
                                Shvershin for Szczecin. At different times the bigger
                                cities changed names under new rulers e.g. St. Peters-
                                burg became Petrograd from 1914-1924, and then
                                Leningrad. Kolozsvar was known as Klausenburg to
                                the German population and became Cluj after 1918,
                                as did Komarom become Komarno. Lemberg became
                                Lvov, Oswiecim Auschwitz, and Pressburg was known
                                in Hungarian as Pozsony and in Slovakian as Bratis-
                                lava. An even more complex change occurred with
                                Biala Cherckva (meaning white church) which Jew-
                                ish sources changed to Schwartztima and then to
                                White Field, so as to be unobjectionable.

Personal Names

Every attempt has been made to keep spellings consistent, the alternatives being given at times to make the location of the town or city accurate.

— Wherever possible an attempt has been made to standardize the surnames, but one branch of a family might adopt a different spelling e.g. Teomim and Thumim; Biderman and Biederman; Halpern and Heilprin; Rabinowitz and Rabinowicz and many others. Thus both versions are included.

Hebrew first names may seem different when they are really the same person. This is due to abbreviations or the inclusion of Yiddish additions. Thus Elijah is also Eli; Lieb is Leibish, Liebel or Liebus; Judah Lieb is Aryey Lieb and Naftali Zvi is Naftali Hirsch. At other times old sources might be uncertain e.g. Eliezer for Eleazar.

NOTES

A.A.L.   *Sefer Avot Atarah LeBonim* by R. Aryey Lieb Lipschutz, Warsaw 1928.

A.E.A.   *Anaf Etz Avot* by Samuel Z. Kahan, Cracow 1903.

A.T.Y.   *Ateret Tiferet Yisrael* by Ephraim Dorf, Tel Aviv 1968-9.

B.A.   *Beit Avi* by R.Y.I. Liebes, New York 1971.

B.L.L.   *Bnei Landau LeMishpechoteihem* by B. Friedberg, Padgorze 1905.

B.Y.   *Beit Yisrael* (Pietrokov 1913), reprinted in New York 1959, with a family genealogy, *Kerem Yisrael.*

D.K.   *Daat Kedoshim* by E. T. Eisenstadt, St. Petersburg 1898-9.

E.E.   *Eleh Ezkerah* (These Will I Remember), New York 1965, edited by Dr. I. Lewin.

E.J.   *Encyclopedia Judaica,* 1971.

G.S.   *Gedullat Shaul* by Zvi Hirsch Edelman, London 1854.

I.L.M.   *Iweh LeMoshav* by R. Eduard Duckesz, Cracow 1903.

I.V.   *Ir Vilna* by Hillel Maggid-Steinschneider, Vilna 1900.

J.E.   *Jewish Encyclopedia,* 1902-5.

K.F.   *Records of the Kacenellenbogen Family* by Meyer Ellenbogen, New York 1937.

K.N.   *Kiryah Ne'emanah* by Samuel J. Fuenn, Vilna 1915.

K.Nis.   *Kiryah Nisgavah* by Solomon Buber, Cracow 1903.

K.Z.   *Kur Zahav* by Moritz Frankel, New York 1928.

L.K.P.   *Lekorot HaKehillot BePolanya* by R. Zvi Hirsch Horowitz, New York 1969.

M.D.D.   *MiDor El Dor* by Nahum Twersky, Tel Aviv 1967.

M.H.D.   *Mofat HaDor* by Jekutiel Kamelhar, Munkacz 1903 (reprinted New York 1966, appended to *Shivat Tzion* by R. Samuel Landau).

M.L.G.O. *Mizkeret LeGedolei Ostraha* by Menachem M. Biber, Berdichev 1907.

N.N.   *Nitei Ne'emanah* by R. Mordecai Rubinstein, Jerusalem 1910.

S.H.C.   *Sefer HaChassidut* by Isaac Alfasi, Maariv Press, 1974.

S.V.S.   *Shem VeShe'erit* by R. Levi Grossman, Tel Aviv 1943.

T.B.D.   *Tiferet Beit David* by Meir Weinstock, 1969.

T.M.G.   *Toldot Mishpachat Ginzberg* by David Maggid, St. Petersburg 1899.

T.M.H.   *Toldot Mishpachat Horowitz* by B. Friedberg, Antwerp 1928.

CHAPTER I

1. R. Jehiel Luria (died in 1470), son of R. Aaron, son of R. Nathaniel, son of R. Jehiel, son of R. Samson Luria. See *Ma'alot HaYochasin* by R. Ephraim Zalman Margolioth, Lvov 1900 and *Mishpachat Luria* by A. Epstein, Vienna 1901.

    R. Samson was the son-in-law of R. Solomon son of R. Samuel Spira. R. Samuel was the son-in-law of R. Mattithiah Treves of Provence (born about 1325, and died in Paris about 1387). R. Mattithiah was appointed Chief Rabbi of Paris by Charles V and was the son of R. Joseph Treves, Rabbi of Marseilles about 1343.

    The Treves family claimed descent from the most prominent of all Jewish biblical commentators, *Rashi* (R. Solomon son of Isaac) through the latter's descendant, Judah Sir Leon of Paris (son of R. Isaac, son of R. Judah, son of the *Tosafist* R. Yomtov, son of R. Judah, the son-in-law of *Rashi*).

Rashi was said to have been descended from Hillel the Elder, and thus from the Royal Davidic family.

2. In 1550-1 he published the *Mishneh Torah* by R. Moses Maimonides with his own glosses and novellae, printed by Bragadin. Shortly afterwards the rival printer M. Justinian printed the *Mishneh Torah* with R. Meir's commentaries abridged. R. Meir solicited and obtained help in this matter from his second cousin, R. Moses Isserles (known as the *ReMa*), but the quarrel and recriminations finally led to the burning of the Talmud in 1554 by order of the Pope.

3. This was witnessed by the present writer on a visit to Padua in 1968. The old cemetery has been the subject of historical reminiscences. Many of those buried here can be found in *Notizie Sulle Famiglie Ebree Esistite a Padova* by Edgardo D. Morpurgo (1909) which includes a genealogical chart of the Katzenellenbogen family and states that the family emblem is a crouching cat.

4. G.S. contains these details from the manuscript by R. Phineas Katzenellenbogen kept in the Bodleian Library, Oxford.

5. The main source is D.K. See also G.S. and A.A.L. Regarding his children, D.K. omits G5.8, Saul and his son-in-law Naftali (G5.7). These are mentioned in A.A.L. which also states that Deborah married R. Jacob, A.B.D. of Lublin (see Chapter VIII), and the wife of Naftali is not mentioned by name. G.S. omits both sons-in-law, R. Jacob of Lublin and R. Naftali Hirsch, and makes Deborah the wife of R. Nahum of Slutzk. See also Chapter III, note 13.

6. In *Montasschrift* xiii/xiv.

7. See K.Z.

8. His descendants constitute Chapter IV.

CHAPTER II

1. See G.S.
2. Ibid. For the Maggid family see I.V.
3. For the Rubinrot family see A.A.L.
4. Ibid. for the Padua family. See also D.K. and J.E.
5. See Chapter VIII for R. Aryey Katzenellenbogen of Brest and his ancestry.
6. See Chapter V — Branch B and Chapter VII — Branch A (Margolioth).
7. See D.K. and New York Public Library Manuscript *PWO (Samuel) by Sanford A. Moss (1939). See also *Records of the Samuel Family* by Joseph Bunford Samuel (Philadelphia, 1912).
8. See *Genealogical Notes Upon the Family of Baron Henry de Worms, Sometime Member of Parliament for East Toxteth* by Bertram B. Benas (1940).
9. Ibid.
9a. Henrietta was a daughter of Horatio Joseph Montefiore of London (died in 1867 — see *The Jews Who's Who—Israelite Finance*, 1920, under Samuel, Harry), a brother of Sir Moses Montefiore (See Burke's *Landed Gentry*, under Montefiore). Thus Sir Harry Samuel was to become a partner in the banking firm established by his two uncles, Sir Moses and Abraham. Horatio married his

first cousin, Sarah daughter of Daniel Mocatta. Among their other Mocatta cousins was Frederick David mentioned on page 70.

Horatio Samuel was born in 1827 and died in 1870.

Descendants of Sir Harry Simon Samuel:

G16.1. Cecil Samuel, married in 1921 to Enid van den Bergh.

G17.1. Carol Cecil, born 1923, married in 1947 to Alan Patrick Simpson (Dublin). Their children, Maureen, born 1951, Grainne, born 1953 and Deidre, born 1954.

G17.2. Harry Cecil Samuel, born 1927, an orchestral conductor and composer, married in 1957 to Margaret Kathleen Creer (London). Their son, Malcolm, born in 1958.

G16.2. Geoffrey Beddington Samuel, married and had issue, one son, Harry. His children, Julia, Brian and Patsy (Canada).

10. See *The Adler Family* by Marcus N. Adler (London, 1909) and J. E. (De Worms). Nora was born in 1879 and died in Cape Town, South Africa in 1948.

11. See *Jewish Chronicle* (London), Oct. 18, 1889 and *The Jews of Britain* by Paul H. Emden (1943) for his descendants. The descendants of Samuel Henry Faudel-Phillips were traced by personal correspondence (including notes on the Thai Royalty from *The Siam Directory*). For Faudel-Phillips see also Burke's *Peerage and Baronetage*.

12. See note 10 and page 51.

13. See *Jewish Chronicle*, Feb. 6, 1914. For his son Bertram (died in 1968) see *Who Was Who* (1968). A picture of Baron Louis Benas can be found in *History of Hope Place in Liverpool Jewry* by Philip Ettinger (1930) page 12.

13a. Baron Levi was the son of the first Baron, Angelo Adolfo Levi, who settled in Florence, Italy in 1861 and was ennobled in 1864. Baron Georgo had four children.

1. Baron Anthony Levi, 1881-1944, married in 1912 to Margherita, daughter of Eduardo Philipson of Florence (and a son-in-law of the French financier and economist, Isaac Pereire). His obituary appeared in the New York Times, May 1, 1944. They had two children, Baron Roberto Enrico Levi, born in 1913 and settled in New York in 1944, who married in 1946 to Elisa Bianca Salvini del Leon Nero (and have issue, Anthony, born in 1948) and Giovanna, born in 1917, married in 1945 to Achille Foa of Turin (and have issue, Sandra, born in 1948 and Emma Stella, born in 1950).

2. Lina, married George Landau, formerly of Warsaw, having no issue.

3. Emmy, married the French senator and banker, Louis Louis Dreyfus (who died in 1940 — see his obituary in the New York Times, November 12, 1940). They had three children, Lina, married Jean Rheims of Paris, and have issue; Jean Louis Dreyfus, married and has issue; and Francois, married and has issue.

4. Baron Giacomo (Jack) Levi, died in 1969, married in 1927 to Maud Rosenbaum. They had a daughter, Nina, married Charles Sweeney of Philadelphia.

14. For Lord Pirbright see J.E. and note 8 above.

15. See obituary in *The Times* (London), Sept. 6, 1974. Prince Leopold was first married to Countess Bianca Treuberg, a cousin of King Manoel II of Portugal. She was the only daughter of Count Ernst von Treuberg of Bavaria, great-grand-son of Dom Pedro, first Emperor of Brazil.

16. *Who's Who in Germany* (5th edition).

17. See *David Salomons* by A. Hyamson (1939). Details of their grandchildren from

Who Was Who (for the Waley family), personal correspondence (Bruell, Raphael and Polack families), Burke's *Landed Gentry* (Sassoon family) and *The Cousinhood* by Chaim Bermant (London, 1971).

18. See note 8 above. Later descendants from personal correspondence. For descendants of his brother Phineas Moses (G13.4) see *The Cousinhood*, E.J. and Burke's *Peerage and Baronetage*.

19. For Sir David see *Jews of Britain* (Emden), *David Salomons* (Hyamson) J.E. and E.J. For the Wagg family see *Jews of Britain* and *Changing Faces* by Hannah F. Cohen (1937).

19a. Henry John's obituary appeared in The Times (London), Sept. 7, 1949 and his sister Elsie's June 27, 1949. Alfred Ralph is mentioned in *Who Was Who*. For the firm of Helbert, Wagg and Company see *Jews of Britain* (page 499). Only Henry John had issue. His son Kenneth Arthur married firstly to Rachel Katherine, daughter of Sir James Nockells Horlick, 4th Baronet, and had four sons, of whom Jeremy James Wagg married in 1964 (divorced in 1969) Susan Verney, only daughter of Lord John Henry Willoughby, 20th Baron de Broke.
Descendants of the Joseph family are recorded in *Americans of Jewish Descent* by Rabbi Malcolm H. Stern. Later details from personal correspondence with descendants (Mrs. Ashehoug, who still possesses the family Bible). For members of the Merton family see *Changing Faces* and *Who's Who* (re Sir Walter Merton). Other details from personal correspondence.

20. For the Goldsmid family see J.E., Burke's *Peerage and Baronetage* and *Pedigree of the Family Goldsmit-Cassel of Amsterdam* by Joseph Prijs (1937). The family of Avigdor-Goldsmid traces back to Rachel, daughter of Sir Isaac Lyon Goldsmid and not to Frederick David, as is recorded in some sources.

21. See Burke's *Peerage and Baronetage* (Agnew and Jessel families). Also personal correspondence.

21a. See Burke's *Landed Gentry* (1939) under Lucas of Oakash. Robert was born in 1898, Archibald in 1902 and Elizabeth in 1909. Her husband was the son of the first Baronet of Ardkinglas, Argyll. They have issue.

22. See New York Public Library Manuscript *PWO (Samuel) and *Records of the Samuel Family* for his descendants; Encyclopedia of Pennsylvania Biography, Volume 4, 1915 (Frank Samuel); obituary of Joseph Bunford Samuel in *The Philadelphia Inquirer*, January 3, 1929 and *History of the Jews of Philadelphia* by Henry Morais.

23. Robinson family details from personal communications.

24. *Who's Who in Philadelphia*, Vol. III, 1927 (Snowden Samuel).

25. See *Genealogische Übersicht über einige zweige der nachkommenschaft des Rabbi Meir Katzenellenbogen von Padua* by Max Wollsteiner (Berlin, 1930, second edition).

26. *Who's Who in America*. Other details from personal communications and correspondence.

27. *Tilla Durieux: Meine ersten neunzig Jahre* by Joachim Werner Preuss (Munich-Berlin, 1971).

28. *Die Grabinschriften des alten Judenfriedhofes in Eisenstadt* by Bernhard Wachstein (re Lackenbach) and D.K., J.E., and note 25 above (re Riesser family).

29. *Geschichte der Juden in der Kurpfalz* by Dr. Leopold Löwenstein (1895).

30. The original manuscript is in the possession of the present writer.

31. See note 25 above and Tama, *Transactions of the Parisian Sanhedrin*, London, 1807.
32. Foerder-Offenberg families mentioned in note 25 above, and from personal communications.
33. Details of his descendants were researched in great detail, primarily by Mrs. Thomas F.A. Plaut of Chevy Chase.
34. Details of Mannheimer and Seligmann families — see note 36 below.
35. For his descendants see K.F. Other details from personal communications.
36. Details from a pedigree chart compiled by Dr. Caesar Seligmann (a photocopy of which is in the possession of the present writer). He also wrote a comprehensive biography of the family (as yet an unpublished manuscript), a copy of which can be found in the Leo Baeck Institute, New York.
37. Details from personal correspondence with his son, Dr. Leo J. Selwyn.
38. Seligmann family details from personal communications.

CHAPTER III

1. Main source is D.K. See the family chronology at the end section.
1a. A daughter of Tuvia married Zvi Hirsch son of Judah (Yudel) Apatoff (Opatov, 1797-1868). See I.V. page 238. A great-grandson of Judah is mentioned on page 366.
2. I.V. mentions (page 208) that she was the wife of R. Uri Ber Gunzberg(not her sister Channah). This appears to be in error. Her niece Channah (G12.9/13.6) had three husbands (sic I.V.) and another is mentioned in D.K. (page 85 — end).
3. See K.F. Later descendants from personal correspondence and interviews.
4. Mentioned in *New York State Red Book*, 1955.
5. A.A.L. at the end section.
6. Details of these interrelationships can be found in the Ms. AR-A.42 114 (Itzig) (Leo Baeck Institue, New York) and *The Mendelssohns* by Alexander Altmann (University of Alabama Press, 1973). For the Mendelssohn lineage, see also the periodical *Genealogie*, Volume 8,16. Jahrgang, Heft 3, March 1967, pps. 644-55. Max Freudenthal in his *Aus der Heimat Moses Mendelssohns*, Berlin, 1900, mentions that in the Dessau Jewish Cemetery, he found the grave of Saul Wahl, Moses' grandfather, which states that he was a descendant of Saul Wahl the king. A picture of this tombstone can be found in the Jewish Encyclopedia (New York, 1903), Volume iv, p. 535.
7. *The Mendelssohn Family* by S. Hensel (New York, 1881), chapter one.
8. Ibid.
9. See note 6 above.
10. For full genealogical details of the Mendelssohn family until shortly before World War II, see Ms. AR-C. A.40 106 (Mendelssohn) (Leo Baeck Institute, New York). Other details are from the Mendelsohn-Archiv, Staatbibliothek, Berlin. Some of the later descendants are discussed in *The Mendelssohns: Three Generations of Genius* by Herbert Kupferberg, New York, 1972.
11. *The Mendelssohn Family* by S. Hensel (New York, 1881), chapter two.
12. Ibid. page 203.
13. A variant genealogy is given in T.M.G. He states that Dinah married R. Naftali Hirsch and that she was the daughter of R. Judah son of Pesia (G4.12, daughter

of R. Saul Wahl). This seems to be due to a confusion between R. Naftali Hirsch Katz (husband of Dinah, daughter of R. Judah Wahl, G4.6) and R. Naftali Hirsch Ginzburg, son-in-law of R. Meir Wahl, G4.1. See Chapter I, note 5.

14. See note 5 above for family details here.

14a. Both Saul Wahl and his son Meir Wahl had sons-in-law called Moses Katz. Also their sons included an Ari Lieb Katz and a Judah Lieb Katz respectively (which names are interchangeable). Understandably confusion regarding the correct line-age could exist. Here Zeev Wolf of Lomaz is included under Judah Lieb's children, whereas D.K. makes him a son of Ari Lieb Katz.

15. The Lwow and Marx families are discussed at length in *Die Familie Lwow* by R. Zvi Hirsch Horowitz of Dresden in *Monatsschrift für Geschichte und Wissenschaft des Judentums*, 1928, JHG 72, pp. 487-99, and in *Die Abstammung von Karl Marx* by B. Wachstein in *Festskrift I — Anledning af Prof. David Simonsens 70-aarige Fodseldag*, Copenhagen, 1923, pp. 276-89.

16. Juta family details from personal correspondence and interviews. See also *Southern African Dictionary of National Biography* by Eric Rosenthal (1966), page 192.

CHAPTER IV

1. Main sources of the Teomim family are D.K. and K.Z.

2. He records his wife's ancestry in his work *Nechmat Yosef*, New York (1949). See the introduction.

3. See S.V.S. under *Berdichev*.

4. See end section of A.A.L.

5. See S.V.S. under *Kamad*.

6. See M.D.D.

6a. The surname of this branch became Rabinowicz. In London he was known as the Biala Rabbi, and he married at the age of eighteen to Sheindel Bracha Perlow. Her father was the Admur of Novominsk, R. Alter Israel Simeon Perlow mentioned on page 540. His sister Pearl, married the Admur of Koidanov, perished in the Holocaust. His ethical will was published in London (1947) by his only son, R. Dr. Mordecai Jerachmeel Zvi Rabinowicz. Dr. Rabinowicz has been the Rabbi of the Dollis Hill Synagogue, London since 1951, was awarded the Jews' College Rabbinical Diploma by the Chief Rabbi, Sir Israel Brodie, Dr. S. Gaon, and others in 1955, is a lecturer in Chassidism, Jewish History and Judaism, and is the author of a number of books and booklets. His is also a frequent contributor to the *Jewish Chronicle* (London) and articles have also appeared in *The Journal of Jewish Studies, The Times Literary Supplement, The Jewish Quarterly Review, Historia Judaica* and others. He contributed seventeen articles to the *Encyclopedia Judaica* (Jerusalem, 1972) and its the editor of the *Encyclopedia of Hasidism* (to be published by the Hebrew Publishing Company, New York, in 1976-7). He married Bella Zimmels and they have three children, Nathan David, Jacob Isaac and Hannah.

7. See *Der Judische Polenkönig Saul Wahl und seine Nachfahren* by Arthur Czellitzer. See also T.B.D. for details on the Rappoport and Biederman families. For clarity, the Lelov Chassidic Dynasty (Biederman Family) is included here.

   G1. R. David Biederman.

      G2. R. Moses Biederman, 1775-1851.

  G3.1. R. Eleazar Menachem Mendel Biederman, died 1883.
    G4.1. R. Abraham Bezalel Alter Biederman, Admur Sossnowiec.
      G5. Wife of her first cousin, R. Mordecai son of R. Jerach-
      meel Joseph Biederman.
    G4.2. Jerachmeel Joseph Biederman.
      G5.1. R. Mordecai, married his first cousin.
      G5.2. Rebecca, married her second cousin, R. Phineas son
      of R. Simeon Nathan Nata Biederman. (See Chapter XVI
      — Branch I.)
    G4.3. R. David Zvi Biederman, 1844-1918, Admur Lelov, mar-
      ried Miriam Frume, daughter of R. Noah Phineas Horo-
      witz. (See Chapter XVI — Branch I.)
    G4.4. Deborah Golda, married R. Joshua Aaron Adler.
  G3.2. R. Solomon Jehiel Biederman.
    G4. R. Joseph David Biederman. (See Chapter IV following after
    note 7.)

8. See S.V.S. and A.A.L. D.K. states that the son-in-law of R. Solomon of Pinczow
  was R. Ari Liebus HaKohen of Neustadt and Pinczow, the son of R. Eleazar
  HaKohen of Vaidislav, and omits R. Ari Liebus of Zamocz. However S.V.S. states
  that R. Dov Zvi, son of R. Ari Liebus HaKohen of Neustadt was the son-in-law
  of R. Solomon of Pinczow (which appears to be incorrect). The sequence here
  follows A.A.L.
9. See S.V.S. under *Parsischa*.
10. Members of this family today call themselves Thumim (and not Teomim, as appears in most books).
11. This story was related by descendants to the present author.
12. See *Who's Who in America*.
13. Their descendants were traced from a manuscript in possession of R. Naftali Wein
  of New York, given to him by his grandfather, R. Samuel Ephraim Frankel
  (G12.3). The family dropped the Teomim and call themselves Frankel. Information obtained from personal interviews.
14. K.Z. and personal interviews.
15. See *N.Y. Times* obituary July 1, 1972.
16. Ibid. December 8, 1945.
17. Ibid. June 17, 1965.
18. See Chapter VIII under the section dealing with R. Abraham Katzenellenbogen
  of Brest.
19. See A.A.L. at the end section.
20. See Chapter XV, the first son of R. Israel Friedman of Ruzhin (1813-51).
21. Ibid.
22. See Chapter XVII, R. Joshua Rokeah of Belz.
23. Note again the spelling Thumim and not Teomim. The story is from the introduction of *Nechmat Yosef*, New York, 1949.
24. See E.E. volume III.
25. Ibid.
26. See Babad family pedigree, Chapter XI.
27. E.E. volume III.

28. See Chapter VIII.
29. Descendants traced from personal interview with Moses Wechsler of Jerusalem, director of Lewin-Epstein publishers.
30. See S.V.S. under *Ger*.
31. Family details from personal interview.
32. See Eichenstein Dynasty, Chapter XVII.
33. S.V.S. under *Radomsk*.
34. Brother of R. Joseph Kalish mentioned in Chapter VII — Branch B, the son-in-law of R. Eleazar Haim Waks.

CHAPTER V

1. See J.E. volume viii (1904) under Meisel. Also see the family pedigree chart in Chapter III (Wulff-Wahl-Itzig-Mendelssohn). R. Simha Bonem of Mohilev was a first cousin of R. Simeon Wulff of Vilna-Hamburg.
2. D.K. page 202, 204 and 206 and A.A.L. (end section).
3. See J.E. volume viii, page 609.
4. D.K. (page 192 et seq.) omits other sons mentioned in I.V. (page 294 and 297):
   G10.4. R. Eiser of Sokolov. G10.5. R. Meir of Orisvar. G10.6. R. Gershom of Slonim. G10.7. R. Abraham Eisenstadt of Mir.
   > G11. R. Michael Eisenstadt of Mir, author of *Shir Tehillah* (Sokolov, 1814), commemorating Czar Alexander I of Russia's victory over the French. In 1815 he was one of three elected deputies ordered by the Czar to reside at St. Petersburg where they were to bring all Jewish affairs before the government (see J.E. volume i, page 345). He married Eidel, daughter of R. Elijah Slutzki of Mir.
   > G12. R. Samuel of Mir.
   >> G13. R. Abraham Bezalel, died in Vilna in 1866, married Blume, daughter of Israel Rattner. Their son, Michael Jeremiah Eisenstadt, 1843-1889, died in Vilna.
5. See A.A.L. (end section) and M.L.G.O. for his descendants.
6. Ibid.
7. See K.N. and E.J. His grandson Jacob Parnas (G13.3) married Gitel, daughter of Judah (Yudel) Apatoff (see note 1a, chapter III).
8. These relationships are given in the chart below.

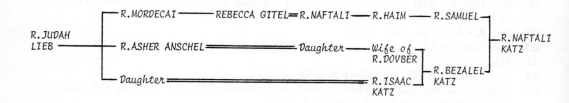

9. Also written Mirels. See I.L.M. (page 10) where it records he had a printing house in Berlin. Here he printed in the years 1702-3, 1712, 1716-17 (see J.E. volume xii, page 321).

CHAPTER VI

1. Later members of the family with the same surname (although the lineage is uncertain) included Chassidic leaders starting with R. Uri son of R. Phineas of Strelisk, who died in 1826.
2. See M.L.G.O. for the Heilprin family.
3. R. Jacob halevi Shor of Karoz was the son-in-law of R. Ezekiel Katzenellenpogen of Altona (Chapter VIII).
4. R. Ezekiel Landau mentioned in I.V. pps. 32-35.
5. Ibid, p. 247-8 for R. David Epstein.
6. i.e. Katzenellenpogen family.
7. See Lowenstein, *History of the Jews of Hanau* in *Judische Literalische Gesellschaft, JHB B14*, pps. 1-84. Page 24 mentions the relationship of the Adlers to R. Jacob Shor.
8. See J.E., E.J., and *The Adler Family* by Marcus N. Adler (Jewish Chronicle reprint, 1909).
9. Ibid.
10. *Our Crowd* by Stephen Birmingham (New York, 1967).
11. See J.E. for his biography and the article by M. Friedländer, *The Late Chief Rabbi, Dr. N. M. Adler* in *The Jewish Quarterly Review*, Vol. II, 1890, pps. 369-385.
12. See *Jewish Chronicle* (London), Jan. 24, 1890.
13. His descendants were traced from the monograph (see note 8) and personal correspondence with family members.
14. Personal communications.
15. *Universal Jewish Encyclopedia*, Vol. III, page 250 for Louis S. Cohen.
16. Ibid., Vol. VII, pps. 25-7 for Lewisohn family members.
17. Personal communications.
18. *Universal Jewish Encyclopedia*, Vol. IX, page 640 for Harold J. Solomon.
19. Personal communication and Burke's *Peerage and Baronetage*.
20. *Universal Jewish Encyclopedia*, Vol. VIII, page 108 for Lord Harry L. Nathan, and Vol. IX, page 613 for his photograph.
21. See I.L.M.
22. Family details from personal communications.
23. *The History of the Jews in Fulda* by P. Horn and N.H. Sonn (Jerusalem, 1971) page 79 et seq. Later Cahn descendants from personal communication.
24. Details about Nathan and Berthold Israel from personal communication.
25. See E.J. Vol. IX, page 1048.
26. See J.E. and E.J. Later descendants from personal communication.
27. Ibid.
28. Ibid.
29. See *History of Hope Place in Liverpool Jewry* by Philip Ettinger (1930) page 75, for Rev. Adler.
30. Family details from communication with H. Eccles.
31. Family details from communication with N. Sharp.
32. Family details from communication with Mrs. O. N. Heilbut.
33. Cleves Divorce Case (Get) is discussed in Chapters III and VI.
34. See D.K. re Rebecca as wife of R. Israel Lipschutz (page 117).
35. J.E. volume viii, page 100.

CHAPTER VII

1. See D.K.
2. For his descendants see also M.L.G.O. page 178.
3. For his descendants see also J.E., volume viii.
    Mordecai was known as the *Chasid,* and died as a young man in Brody, leaving behind two orphan children. They were raised by R. Zvi Hirsch of Brody, son of R. Samuel, their mother's brother.
4. A.T.Y. and S.V.S.
5. Ibid and S.H.C.
6. Ibid under Perlow Dynasty of Stolin-Karlin.
7. See A.A.L. at the end section.
8. See K.N. pps. 223-4 and D.K. p. 186 R. David Rokeach was the son-in-law of R. Judah Lieb Rokeah (see Chapter XVII). See also *Vilna* by Israel Cohen, 1943.
9. *Bialystok Photo Album* by D. Sohn, New York, 1951, page 21.
10. Most likely the son of Ari Lieb Pines mentioned on the bottom of page 270 of I.V.
11. Details of his descendants obtained from personal communications with Felix Bloch. His father Tewel Bloch is mentioned in the *Bialystok Photo Album,* page 350, with his photograph.
12. For his descendants see N.N. and A.E.A. (which gives several other children).
13. *Die Familie Lwow,* 1928. See note 15, Chapter III. For his mother see D.K. page 67.
14. See *Nefesh Chayah* with family history details printed in Israel by his grandsons, Joshua Eybeschutz (who corresponded with the present author) and Eleazar Alter.
15. See note 5 above.
16. Details of this branch are based on a letter written in 1898 by R. Eliakim Halberstam of Zbariz (G13.1) addressed to his niece, Gitel Rottenstreich in the U.S.A. in response to her request for the family genealogy prior to the marriage of her daughter. The remainder of the family details were supplied by David son of Eugene Halberstam.
    The contents of the letter —
    ". . . I was happy to hear that, with thanks to the Lord, you have a daughter whose time had come for marriage, may He soon send her a mate. Now I will relate the genealogy. My paternal grandfather was R. Ezekiel Halberstam. My father was the erudite R. Zvi Hirsch, A.B.D. of Kosiatyn. His (i.e. R. Ezekiel's) brother was the father of the righteous and erudite R. Haim Halberstam, A.B.D. of Sanz, whose name is known to many. My father on his mother's side, was a grandson of the righteous R. Mendel of Linsk, who was the son-in-law of the erudite R. Isaac, A.B.D. Hamburg.
    "My mother was the daughter of R. Haim David Margolioth, son of the erudite R. Getzel Margolioth, brother of the erudite R. Zalman Margolioth. Her mother was the daughter of the erudite R. Haim Mordecai Margolioth, the author of the book *Sha'arei Teshuva,* who was also a brother of R. Zalman Margolioth, and further up the holy genealogy one need not check further."
17. N.N.
18. Details from personal correspondence with R. Baruch Yosher, and from his book *Beit Komarno.*

19. See note 17. Details from personal communication with R. Judah Rubinstein, son of the author of N.N., and other family members.
20. See N.Y. Times obituary, March 25, 1969. Her brother-in-law was Francis Biddle.
21. Details from Helena Rubinstein Corporation, *Madame,* by Patrick O'Higgins, 1971, N.Y. Times obituary, April 2, 1965 and personal communications and interviews.
22. From Helena Rubinstein Corporation bulletin by Joseph Mann.
23. Ibid.
24. Details from personal interviews and correspondence. See also note 12.
25. Mentioned in *Ohalei Shem* by Samuel Noah Gotlieb, Pinsk, 1912.
26. Personal communications.
27. See above, note 12.
28. See J. E. (1902), volume iii and *Dor VeChachmav* by Moses Reines, Cracow, 1890. Both books contain his picture.
29. See N.Y. Times obituary June 14, 1965.

TWERSKY CHASSIDIC DYNASTY

CHILDREN OF R.MORDECAI
OF CHERNOBYL :-

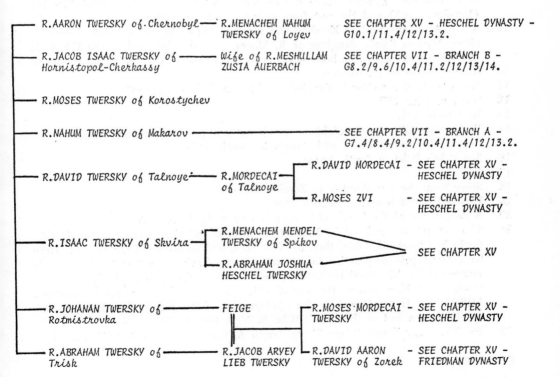

R.AARON TWERSKY of Chernobyl —— R.MENACHEM NAHUM   SEE CHAPTER XV - HESCHEL DYNASTY -
TWERSKY of Loyev   G10.1/11.4/12/13.2.

R.JACOB ISAAC TWERSKY of —— Wife of R.MESHULLAM   SEE CHAPTER VII - BRANCH B -
Hornistopol-Cherkassy   ZUSIA AUERBACH   G8.2/9.6/10.4/11.2/12/13/14.

R.MOSES TWERSKY of Korostychev

R.NAHUM TWERSKY of Makarov ——————————————— SEE CHAPTER VII - BRANCH A -
G7.4/8.4/9.2/10.4/11.4/12/13.2.

R.DAVID TWERSKY of Talnoye —— R.MORDECAI of Talnoye
— R.DAVID MORDECAI - SEE CHAPTER XV - HESCHEL DYNASTY
— R.MOSES ZVI - SEE CHAPTER XV - HESCHEL DYNASTY

R.ISAAC TWERSKY of Skvira —— R.MENACHEM MENDEL TWERSKY of Spikov
— R.ABRAHAM JOSHUA HESCHEL TWERSKY
SEE CHAPTER XV

R.JOHANAN TWERSKY of Rotmistrovka —— FEIGE —— R.MOSES MORDECAI - SEE CHAPTER XV - TWERSKY HESCHEL DYNASTY

R.ABRAHAM TWERSKY of Trisk —— R.JACOB ARVEY LIEB TWERSKY — R.DAVID AARON TWERSKY of Zorek - SEE CHAPTER XV - FRIEDMAN DYNASTY

CHAPTER VIII

1. See *Anshei Shem* by Buber (Cracow, 1895) No. 5.
2. Ibid. No. 242.
3. In his *Masa'ot Binyamin* (No. 98) he mentions R. Ashkenazi as his daughter's father-in-law (mechuten). However, some sources and manuscripts (possibly incorrectly) state that R. Benjamin Aaron's son, R. Bezalel was the father-in-law of R. Abraham, the grandson of R. Ashkenazi. If both are correct, then it is clear that R. Abraham married his first cousin.
4. See I.L.M. page 21-29 which includes a picture of his tombstone, and records all of his children (only three being mentioned in D.K. on page 111, viz. David, Jacob and the wife of R. Jacob Shor).
5. These descendants are recorded in *Galgulay Neshamot* (1907, Lublin edition, at the end of the book). For the Chassidic lineage see S.V.S.
6. Personal communication.
7. From a manuscript belonging to a member of the family Branch A in South Africa.
8. Dates obtained from a manuscript belonging to L. Ran, New York. For his wife's family, see I.V., page 183-4.
9. Mentioned on the title page of *Kol Omer Kerah*.
10. None of the usual records (which were written by the Mitnaggdim i.e. opposers of Chassidism) mention these descendants. Part is recorded in *Pnei Yitzchak* (Jaroslav, 1905) and the rest from personal communications.
10a. A son Abraham Saul of Kreshov was married twice, his second wife being his niece, Miriam Sarah, daughter of R. Moses Spiegel, who died in the U.S.A. in 1940. He had issue from both wives who live in the U.S.A. and have shortened their surname to Ellenbogen.
11. See introduction to *Zerah Yitzchak* by his son (Warsaw, 1898).
12. See I.V. page 259.
13. Ibid. page 301.
14. Ibid. page 235. Details of his descendants from personal communications.
15. Personal communications with family in South Africa.
16. See *Who's Who in South Africa*.
17. Ibid.
18. Story from the introduction to *Zerah Yitzchak*.
19. Personal research and communications.
20. A descendant of the family of leading Rabbis of the famous Volozhin Yeshiva.
21. The present writer lived in Israel from 1968-9 and then settled in the U.S.A., firstly in Cleveland, Ohio, then in New York, and finally in Elizabeth, N.J. Here he entered private practice in general surgery, having received his training in surgery at the Mt. Sinai Hospital of New York and the College of Medicine and Dentistry of New Jersey. He was also the author of *These are the Generations* (1969). He is mentioned in the bibliography of the E.J. under the title *Katzenellenbogen* and in the *Who's Who in New Jersey* (1975).
22. See *The Cape Times* (Cape Town, South Africa), December 2, 1974, page 1.

CHAPTER IX

1. See D.K. page 93 et seq., and A.E.A.

2. D.K. page 156 et seq.
3. See N.N.

CHAPTER X

1. He appears to have married firstly, Yarit, daughter of R. Ezekiel Landau, and on her death in 1733, he remarried her sister. See M.H.D. For their descendants (lacking in D.K.) see M.L.G.O. pps. 233, 293 and 330.
2. See I.V. pps. 92 and 159, and K.N. pps. 230 and 253.
3. Called R. Benjamin Brodie in D.K.
4. G11.4, G11.5 and G11.6 are found in D.K. and A.E.A., but lacking in *Bnei Landau LeMishpechoteihem*.
5. Not in D.K. See T.M.H.
6. Not in D.K. See J. E. (1905) under Landau and M.H.D.
7. Not in D.K. See *Beit Avi* by R.I. Liebes.
8. Not in D.K. See *Bnei Landau LeMishpechoteihem* and I.L.M.
9. Not in D.K. See I.L.M. page 17.
10. G9.3, G9.4, G9.7, G9.8 and G9.9 are not found in D.K. For R. Zvi Hirsch Landau See K. Nis. page 34. For R. Baruch Parnas see M.D.D. and L.K.P.
11. Only his son R. Ezekiel Landau is mentioned in D.K., but other children are recorded in B.L.L. and M.H.D.
12. He was the son of R. Jacob Ornstein who was so disliked by his wife's father, R. Eleazar Landau. See M.H.D. for his generation.
13. See J.E. (1905) under Landau.
14. See S.V.S. and S.H.C. for their descendants.
15. Not in D.K. These four sisters are mentioned in M.H.D. Kamelhar discusses as well the possible mistake of Yarit being married to R. Haim Landau and her sister Mirl to R. Jacob his son.
16. See note 1.

CHAPTER XI

1. See D.K., A.E.A. and A.A.L.
2. See *Toldot Mishpachat Shor*, by H.D. Friedberg, 1901. Note the two versions — Deborah, daughter of R. Alexander Sender Shor married R. Israel Levitzer and their daughter Veitel married R. Samuel Rokeah (sic. Friedberg) compared with R. Samuel Rokeah marrying the daughter of R. Alexander Sender directly (sic. D.K.).
3. See E.J. Other details of descendants are from the introduction of the reprinted *Minchat Chinuch* and personal communications. See also E.E. volume III page 146.
4. See E.J. under *Jerusalimski*.
5. See M.H.D.
6. See J.E. (1903), volume v. Later descendants were researched by Hans Jager (Vienna). See also Ms. AR — C.64.8-1773 (Leo Baeck Institute).
7. See Bernhard Wachstein, *Inschriften des alten Judenfriedhofes in Wien*, volume 2 (1917).
8. Ibid.
9. See E.J. under *Babad*.
10. Personal communications.

11. See E.E. volume IV page 108.
12. Personal communications.
13. See E.J. under *Babad*.
14. See E.E. volume III page 146.
15. Ibid. See also *Dos Yiddishe Vort*, volume XII, no. 109, April 1966. Other details from personal communications.
16. Personal communications.
17. See *R. Zvi H. Chajes* by Israel David Bet-Halevi, Tel Aviv 1956, J.E. (1902) volume iii, E.J. (under Chajes) and K. Nis. Other descendants traced through personal communications, including Julius Chajes. See also *H. P. Chajes: The Tribute of a Friend* by George Alexander Kohut, New York in *Adhandlungen zur Erinnerung an H. P. Chajes* (The A. Kohut Memorial Foundation, Wien, 1933, which also contains a childhood poem by Chajes).
18. See *Toldot Mishpachat Shor* and J.E. (1902) volume iii.

CHAPTER XII

1. For his descendants see D.K. and A.E.A.
2. See J.E. (1902) volume ii under Aryey Loeb ben Saul.
3. See J. E. (1904) volume iii.
4. See A.A.L. at the end section.
5. See J.E. (1902) volume ii.
6. See J.E. (1902) volume iii. See also the introduction to Chapter XVI — G10.9/11.3/12.11.
7. See J.E. (1904) volume viii under Levin, Hirschel.
8. See J.E. (1902) volume iii under Berlin, Saul.
9. Head of the Berliner family. The descendants are completely recorded in A.A.L. at the end section and in L.K.P. (page 197 et seq.). See also *MiYerushalayim ad Yerushalyim* by Jacob Kirschbaum, 1966.
10. *Beit Eked Seforim* by B. Friedberg and E.E. volume V.
11. *MiYerushalayim ad Yerushalayim* and personal communications.
12. See also S.H.C. page 185. For his son Israel Zelig, see E.E. volume I.
    The Morgenstern family is recorded in a booklet by A. Asher Ziv on the descendants of the ReMa (page 100). The genealogy of the Kalisch (Kalish) dynasty of Varka-Amshinov mentioned in this book is:
    G1. R. Isaac Kalish of Varka, 1779-1848.
        G2.1. R. Jacob David Kalish of Amshinov, 1814-1877.
            G3. R. Menachem, Admur Amshinov, died in 1917. He had three sons.
                G4. R. Joseph Kalish, Admur Amshinov, 1878-1936, married the daughter of R. Haim Eleazar Waks (see Chapter VII — page 308).
                    G5.1. R. Jacob David, died in 1942 and his family perished.
                    G5.2. R. Isaac Kalish, Admur Amshinov-New York.
                    G5.3. Wife of R. Benjamin son of R. Isaac Zelig Morgenstern (see text).
        G2.2. R. Menachem Mendel Kalish, 1819-1868, succeeded his father as Admur in Varka.
            G3. R. Simha Bonem Kalish, died in Tiberias, Israel, 1907, having succeeded his father as Admur in 1868. He had three sons.

G4. R. Abraham Moses Kalish, died in 1938.

    G5. R. Jacob David Baruch Kalish, Admur Varka-New York, married the daughter of R. Menachem Mendel Morgenstern of Wengrau (see text).

13. *Toldot Chochmei Yerushalayim* by Frumkin, page 256-7.

14. See note 9, E.J. under Michaelson, and E.E. volume II. Other details are from *Tirosh VeYitzhar* (Responsa) and personal communications with family members.

15. Details from correspondence with his son, Victor David Michelson. He was also the author of a pamphlet *The War Guilt of German Doctors*, published Cape Town, 1945.

16. Personal communication and *Who's who in World Jewry* (1965). His sister Judith Posek was married in Israel to a noted Irgun leader and one-time chief sanitary engineer of Ramat Gan, Israel.

17. *Who's who in World Jewry* (1965).

18. See D.K., J.E. (1902) volume ii, A.E.A. and E.J.

19. See E.J., J.E., *Anshei Shem* by S. Buber and *Shalshelet HaYachas Shel Mishpachat Ornstein-Broda* (a copy can be found in the Leo Baeck Institute, New York). *Anshei Shem* lists two sons and two daughters (page 150 and again page 169 — the two sons). From L.K.P., page 67, it would appear that R. Mordecai Zeev had two wives; first — the mother of Jacob Meshullam and two daughters; second — the daughter of R. Eliakim Getzel of Levertov (see Chapter VII — page 292), mother of Moses J. Heschel and a third son, Eliakim Aryey Lieb.

20. See E.J. and the *Encyclopedia of Zionism and Israel* (New York 1971). His memoirs were entitled *Zichronot*.

21. That he was a son-in-law appears to be correct, as is found in *Anshei Shem*. In A.E.A. he is mentioned as a son.

22. For these descendants see also J.E. (1903) volume v, *Anshei Shem* and E.J.

23. See *Universal Jewish Encyclopedia* (1941) volume IV. Other details from personal communications with his close associate S. Hurwitz of Switzerland.

24. A.A.L. (end section).

CHAPTER XIII

1. See D.K., I.L.M., A.A.L. and J.E. (1902) volume ii.

2. See M.D.D., S.V.S. and other Chassidic sources.

3. J.E. (1904) volume vii. Concerning R. Getzel his grandfather, see L.K.P., page 67.

4. See note 1, J.E. (1903) volume v and *Chachamei A.H.W.* by E. Duckesz, 1905.

5. Personal communications.

CHAPTER XIV

1. Dynastic details from S.V.S., M.D.D. and S.H.C. (with pictures). Later descendants and current members were traced by direct family interviews and correspondence. See Chapter VII — Branch B for his father's lineage.

    His children:

    Sons from his first wife:

    G14.1. R. Ezekiel Shraga, died in 1896 — BRANCH A (Sieniawa).

    G14.2. R. Meir Nathan, died in 1866 — BRANCH B (Bobov).

    G14.3. R. David, died in 1894 — BRANCH C (Keshanov).

G14.4. R. Aaron, died in 1904 — BRANCH D (Sanz).

G14.5. R. Baruch, died in 1906 — BRANCH E (Gorlice).

Sons from his third wife:

G14.6. R. Shalom Eliezer, died in 1944 — BRANCH F (Rotsfurt).

G14.7. R. Isaac Isaiah, died in 1943 — BRANCH G (Chechoyv).

Daughters from his first wife:

G14.8. Reitze, married R. Mordecai Dov Twersky of Hornistopol (page 309). They had five daughters: Sterna Feige, married R. Nahum Zalman (of Cherkassi) son of R. Aaron Moses Schneerson (son of R. Joseph Isaac son of R. Menachem Mendel of Lubavitch); Sarah Miriam, married her uncle, R. Shalom Eliezer Halberstam of Rotsfurt (page 504); Chaya Malka, married R. Moses son of R. David Gitterman; Esther Hindel, married R. Haim Isaiah son of R. Shalom DovBer Schneerson (son of R. Judah Lieb son of R. Menachem Mendel of Lubavitch); and Jochebed Rebecca, married R. Elisha Halberstam of Gorlice (page 500).

G14.9. Miriam, married R. Moses son of R. Mordecai David Unger of Dombrovo (page 681).

G14.10. Ita, married R. Eliezer Jeruchem Baruch son of R. Israel Isaac Baron.

G15.1. R. Menachem Mendel Baron, married his first cousin, Miriam Rechel Rosenfeld (See Branch H).

G15.2. Daughter, married.

Daughters from third wife:

G14.11. Nechama, married R. Isaac Tuvia, son of R. Meir Rubin (see G17.3 — page 608).

G14.12. Tilly, married R. Aaron, son of R. Meir (of Dzikov) Horowitz (see G16.5 — page 587).

G14.13. Friedel, married R. Eleazar Rosenfeld of Ospinzi (Auschwitz) — BRANCH H, Rosenfeld Family, page 506.

G14.14. Gutsche, married R. Joshua Bezalel Moskovitz (died in 1910). Their two married daughters perished in the Holocaust.

2. For the genealogy of the Ropshitz Dynasty, see Chapter XVI — Branch VII; for Eichenstein (Zhidachov) and Rokeah (Belz) Dynasties, see Chapter XVII; and for the Ruzhin (Friedman) Dynasty, see Chapter XV.

3. See Chapter IV.

4. See his biography in E.E. volume VI. Also see *Beit Komarno* by R. Baruch Yosher, 1965.

5. See E.E. volume I.

6. Ibid. volume VI.

7. Ibid. volume VI.

8. Ibid. volume V.

9. Ibid. volume V.

10. Ibid. volume IV.

11. Ibid. volume VI.

CHAPTER XV

1. This lineage is given in B.Y.

2. See S.V.S., E.J., A.T.Y. and S.H.C. Later and current descendants traced by correspondence and personal communications.

3. For his descendants, see books mentioned in note 2. He appears to have had a second brother, R. Kalman. For his ancestry see page 30.
4. See obituary in the *Algemeiner Journal* (New York) in Yiddish, April 4, 1975 and the *Jewish Observer*.
5. See E.J.
6. Some discrepancies exist regarding the lineage of his descendants.
7. S.V.S. appears to be in error by stating that R. Mordecai Twersky married the daughter of R. Isaac Meir Heschel instead of his granddaughter.
7a. Some of the family perished in the Holocaust. R. Alter himself died in 1933. One son, R. Joseph succeeded his father as Admur in Warsaw at the age of seventeen and died in 1945. Another brother is the present Novominsk-New York Rebbe, R. Nachum Mordecai Perlow mentioned on page 448 (see there for their family). Three sisters are Sarah, married R. Moses Eichenstein, brother of Menachem Zvi (page 541); Deborah, married R. Eleazar Eichenstein and Sheindel Bracha, married the Biala Rabbi of London, R. Nathan David Rabinowicz (page 179 — G14.4/15.2 and note 6a to chapter IV).
8. See introduction to *Birkat Chayim*, New York, 1956.
9. See sources of note 2. Also see the introduction to *Torah Avot*, New York, 1926 by R. Joshua Heschel Rabinowitz for biographical details.
10. See D.K. for the ancestors of the Zakheim family. The relationship of those recorded in this book are given below for clarity.
    R. Israel had three sons:
    1) R. Simeon, father of R. Zvi Hirsch, father of Beila (married R. Abraham son of R. Ari Lieb), mother of R. Aryey Lieb Zak (died in 1788), father of R. Tuvia and R. Jacob Zakheim. R. Tuvia was the father of R. Joseph (mentioned on pages 438 and 641), who was the father of R. Isaac Levi Zakheim (page 258) and R. Abraham Zakheim (page 438). R. Jacob (died in 1806) was the father of R. Gershon (died in 1835), father of R. Aryey Lieb Zakheim of Razinai (D.K. page 26). The later descendants were traced by personal communication, R. Aryey being the father of R. Samuel, father of R. Zvi Hirsch, father of R. Dov Solomon Zakheim (mentioned on page 545).
    2) R. Menachem Nahum whose daughter married her cousin, R. Haim.
    3) R. Shalom of Birz, father-in-law of R. David Katzenellenpogen (mentioned on page 339) and father of R. Haim who married his cousin. R. Haim was the father of R. Meshullam Zalman Zak (mentioned on page 148).
11. See note 2.

CHAPTER XVI

1. For his descendants, see the comprehensive genealogical work T.M.H. Also see A.E.A. particularly for the Stanislav branch, and D.K.
2. See E.J. for a comprehensive biography, and T.B.D.
3. See *Igeret Shlomo*, Jerusalem, 1960.
4. See I.L.M. and E.J. For all his children see *Igeret Yochasin* appended to B.A. For his wives see page 393 (G9.2/10), page 405 (G10.3) and page 407 (G9.6).
5. Personal communications.
6. See T.B.D. Also personal communications with R. David Thumim and S.V.S. on the details of the Lelov Dynasty. See also note 7 chapter IV.
7. See note 1.

8.   See A.E.A. for the descendants. Later descendants from personal communications.
9.   Ibid. See also E.J. for him and his descendants.
10. See his biography in E.E. volume I and *R. Baruch halevi Epstein* by E.Z. Tarshish Jerusalem, 1967 (Mosad HaRav Kook).
11. See *Beit Eked Seforim* and *Die Familie Lwow* (see note 15, Chapter III).
12. E.E. volume V.
13. B.A. and personal communications.
14. Ibid.
15. S.H.C., A.E.A., S.V.S. and personal communications.
16. See his biography in E.E. volume III.
17. Ibid. volume VI.
18. Personal communications.
18a. See G14.2 page 639.
19. See his biography in E.E. volume VI.

CHAPTER XVII

1.   Chief sources: A.A.L., A.T.Y., D.K., E.J., S.H.C., S.V.S. and T.B.D. A number of reprinted Rabbinical books contain much introductory genealogical details, and other details were obtained from many personal interviews and communications.
2.   Lineage recorded in A.A.L.
3.   See *Toldot Israel Rokeach* by R. Jacob Levinson (New York, 1935) for Israel Rokeach. Note the spelling difference between Rokeah and Rokeach which distinguishes the Chassidic Dynasty from the non-Chassidic family.

   A number of discrepancies exist in the Zakheim-Gunzberg family. D.K. states that Feigel died in 1864 (page 27), but I.V. 1865 (page 165). Similarly for Perel. A mistake in I.V. (page 165, note 8) makes Channah Keila a sister to Gershon Gunzberg, whereas she was his daughter (see her epitaph in D.K. *Yitron Daat,* page 24, and page 243 for her children). See J.E. Vol. V (1903) for Moses Friedland.

   Later descendants of Israel Rokeach were traced from personal interviews and communication.
4.   The family genealogy including current generations was researched by Samuel Prushansky. For a biography of E.Z. Lewin-Epstein, see the E.J. and *Encyclopedia of Zionism and Israel* (New York, 1971). Obituaries for Rechaviah and Eliezer Lewin-Epstein appeared in the *N.Y. Times.* For earlier generations, see D.K. page 186 and A.A.L. page 26 at the end.
5.   Some sources state that he was the son, and not the grandson of R. Naftali. S.H.C. states that he was the son of R. Menachem Dov.

INDEX

(Bold numbers contain the family genealogy)

P.82
MEZERITEZER